ABOUT THE AUTHORS

Thomas N. Garavan is a lecturer in human resource development at the University of Limerick.

Pat Costine is a Training and Development Consultant.

Noreen Heraty is a lecturer in human resource management at the University of Limerick.

TRAINING AND DEVELOPMENT IN IRELAND

Context, Policy and Practice

Thomas N. Garavan
Pat Costine
Noreen Heraty

Oak Tree Press

Dublin
in association with
Irish Institute of Training and Development

Oak Tree Press
Merrion Building
Lower Merrion Street
Dublin 2, Ireland

© 1995 Thomas N. Garavan, Pat Costine and Noreen Heraty
Reprinted 1997

A catalogue record of this book is
available from the British Library

ISBN 1-872853-92-7 (pbk.)
ISBN 1-872853-88-9 (hbk.)

Printed in Ireland by Colour Books Ltd.

CONTENTS

ACKNOWLEDGEMENTS

This book represents the culmination of extensive research and analysis in the field of training and development over a number of years and the authors owe a debt of gratitude to all of those who were involved in its completion, in one form or another. We are especially appreciative of the comments from those people who reviewed the material in the book and must acknowledge the numerous academics and training practitioners whose ideas about training and development have helped form the core of this text. A number of individuals deserve special thanks:

Colleagues at the University of Limerick were particularly supportive. We particularly acknowledge the support and encouragement of Professor Noel Whelan, Professor Donal Dineen, Paddy Gunnigle, Head, Department of Personnel & Employment Relations, Michael Morley, Thomas Turner, Joseph Wallace, Sarah Moore, Daryl D'Art, Gerard Fitzgerald, Noreen Clifford and Patrick Flood. A special word of thanks also to Eoin Devereaux for his valuable assistance with the data on employment training schemes.

A number of external sources are also acknowledged. In particular we would like to mention Christy Cooney, FÁS Cork; Michael Barry, FÁS Waterford; Carol Hogan of Carol Hogan & Associates; Con Egan, Kostal Ireland; Aidan Lawrence, Stratus Ireland; Judy Halford, Superquinn; Jean O'Keeffe, Avonmore Foods; Michael Ostinelli of Michael Ostinelli & Associates; Marie Connolly, Shannon Development Company; Chris Taylor of Chris Taylor & Associates; Dolores Carr, Unify; Austin Vaughan, Department of Education; Pat Campbell, FÁS Athlone; Cathy Edwards and Rita Johnson, Sheffield University; Mary Carroll, Irish Trade Board; Breda McNally, Department of Enterprise and Employment; Joan O'Riordan, Plassey Management and Technology Centre; Mary Coolihan, Institute of Public Administration; and Anna Cunningham, Shannon International College of Hotel Management. The Irish Institute of Training and Development is also thanked for its support.

Finally, we must single out five individuals in particular who made a significant contribution to the completion of this text: Kevin Brew, Bridie Barnacle and Mary Garavan for their valuable editorial skills, and Kim O'Neill and Deirdre O'Dwyer for their excellent data processing skills.

LIST OF TABLES

LIST OF FIGURES

ABBREVIATIONS

ACAS	Advisory, Consultation and Arbitration Service
ACE	Adult and Continuing Education
AnCO	An Chomhairle Oiliuna
AONTAS	National Association of Adult Education
ASTD	American Society for Training and Development
BIM	Bord Iascaigh Mhara
BTS	Technical Baccalaureate
BPR	Business Process Re-Engineering
CAD	Computer Aided Design
CAM	Computer Aided Manufacturing
CERT	Council for Education Recruitment and Training in Hotels, Catering and Tourism
CD	Continuous Development
CBF	Coran Beasloe agus Feola
CNC	Computer Numerically Controlled (Machine Tools)
CIF	Confederation of Irish Industry
CEDEFOP	Centre European pour le Development de la Formation Professionnelle (European Centre for the Development of Vocational Training)
COMETT	Community Programme in Education and Training for Technology
CBI	Confederation of British Industry
CEP	Community Enterprise Programme
CBT	Computer Based Training
EC	European Commission/European Community
EDO	Enterprise Development Officer
EEC	European Economic Community
EFTA	European Free Trade Association
ESB	Electricity Supply Board
ESF	European Social Fund
EU	European Union
FÁS	Foras Aiseana Saothair, Training and Employment Authority

FIE	Federation of Irish Employers
FUE	Federated Union of Employers
FWUI	Federated Workers' Union of Ireland
GDP	Gross Domestic Product
GATT	General Agreement for Tariffs and Trade
HR	Human Resources
HRD	Human Resource Development
HRM	Human Resource Management
HRP	Human Resource Planning
HTEP	High Technology Enterprise Programme
IBEC	Irish Business and Employers' Confederation
IDA	Industrial Development Authority
ICTU	Irish Congress of Trade Unions
ILO	International Labour Organisation
IITD	Irish Institute of Training and Development
IMI	Irish Management Institute
IMS	Institute of Manpower Studies
IPA	Institute of Public Administration
ITB	Industrial Training Board
IMF	International Monetary Fund
ILM	Internal Labour Market
IPM	Institute of Personnel Management
ISO 9000	An International Quality System
ILO	International Labour Organisation
JIT	Just In Time (System)
LCVP	Leaving Certificate Vocational Programme
LCVT	Leaving Certificate Vocational Training Certificate
MBO	Management By Objectives
MBA	Masters of Business Administration
MCI	Management Charter Initiative
MNC	Multinational Company
MRP	Materials Requirement Planning
MHAI	Mental Health Association of Ireland
MSC	Manpower Services Commission

NESC	National Economic and Social Council
NCEA	National Council for Educational Awards
NIHE	National Institute for Higher Education
NFMED	National Forum for Management Education and Development
NDC	National Dairy Council
NSVQ	National Council for Vocational Qualifications
NATC	National Association of Training Centres
NMS	National Manpower Service
NA	Needs Analysis
NVET	National Strategy for Vocational Education and Training
NCAV	National Council for Vocational Awards
OECD	Organisation for Economic Cooperation and Development
OLM	Occupational Labour Market
PMTC	Plassey Management and Technology Centre
PNR	Programme for National Recovery
QC	Quality Circle
QWL	Quality of Working Life
RMC	Regional Management Centre
SVQ	Standard Vocational Qualifications
SEA	Single European Act
SFADCo	Shannon Free Airport Development Company
SEM	Single European Market
TQC	Total Quality Control
TQM	Total Quality Management
TDLB	Training and Development Lead Body
TAGS	Technical Assistance Grants Scheme
TVEI	Technical and Vocational Education Initiative
VET	Vocational Education and Training
VEC	Vocational Education Committee
VP TP	Vocational Preparation and Training Programme
WCM	World Class Manufacturing
YEA	Youth Employment Agency

FOREWORD

I would like to compliment the authors of this book for producing a text on training and development that has been long awaited and anticipated by training professionals in Ireland.

With one broad sweep of the pen, the three authors take us down the labyrinthine road of training and development in Ireland, showing us a variety of training technologies and methods, as well as the diversity of issues, resources, and agencies which characterise the subject area. The breadth of vision and the scope of the material covered by the authors will be a revelation to practitioners and academics alike, who should find in this book a ready source of theory and practice, helping them to deepen their understanding of the purpose and role of training and development at individual, organisational and national levels.

Training and development in Ireland is in a state of flux, with the role of the Training Specialist undergoing major change, both in the depth of skills required and status within the organisation. The Training Specialist must become an agent of change, with an understanding of, and an expertise in the skills of Organisation Development and the Management of Change. Not only must they be able to analyse training and development needs accurately and ensure the delivery of the intervention, but they must be aware of the best theory and practice available to meet demands for customer satisfaction, for innovation, and for new work structures and organisational redesign. These initiatives aim at bringing out the best in our people by drawing on their personal motivation through involvement in continuous quality improvement. All the strains and stresses associated with the introduction of change must be faced by the Training Specialist, who is now asked to exert influence and authority on the direction the organisation will take. This book provides Training Specialists with an insight into the knowledge and skills needed to contribute to the changing world of business and enterprise.

The role of a training institute in Ireland has always been to develop its members professionally. The IITD, in providing for a variety of trainers from many walks of life, endeavours to illustrate and explain through its conferences and professional journal the many themes and methods of training that are of interest to its members. The Institute has been to the forefront in pointing the way of future trends in training and development, as well as providing a forum for discussion and debate on the pros and cons of new methods and practices. This book will provide Institute members with a common language and vocabulary for the discussion of new trends, as well as a critical analysis of existing theories and practices.

This book will also be a vital resource to students of our diploma certificate and other professional programmes, in that it provides a comprehensive view of training and development in Ireland. To a practitioner who has been engaged in tutoring students of the IITD diploma for the past six years, the book is a godsend. For the first time, we are provided with material and research that is suitable to an Irish audience. The logical, sequential nature of the chapters with well-illustrated text, theory and research data will save time in the preparation of classes, as well as provide material for discussion, interpretation, analysis, application and thesis writing.

I think this book should find its way on to the shelf of every practitioner and theoretician who is interested in the present state of training and development in Ireland, and I congratulate the authors for their painstaking work in producing it.

Chris Taylor
National President
Irish Institute for Training
and Development
Galway, April 1995

1

TRAINING AND DEVELOPMENT: CONCEPTS, ATTITUDES AND ISSUES

INTRODUCTION AND LEARNING OBJECTIVES

This introductory chapter will look at the scope of training and development, examples of training and development activities and its contribution to the organisation and the economy in general. After reading this chapter you will understand:

- the differences and the interrelationships between the concepts of learning, training, development and education;

- key terms such as strategy, policy, vision and mission as they apply to training and development;

- the alternative purposes of training and development in an organisational setting;

- the barriers to training and attitudes to training at organisational and national level;

- the contribution that a well trained, developed and educated workforce can make to the organisation and the economy;

- the costs and benefits of training and development.

KEY TERMS 1: LEARNING, TRAINING, DEVELOPMENT AND EDUCATION

First, let us begin with some pertinent definitions. The terms *training, development, education* and *learning* are synonymous to some. To others, such as those writing from the human resource development perspective, the activities are seen as being mutually inclusive. It is better to understand them as linked, where training is seen as both a part of, and a precondition for, development and education. The traditional reason for regarding training, development and education as distinct practices stems from the hierarchical divisions within organisations. Training in Ireland has evolved as something that is provided for non-management workers, whereas development and education have been treated as the preserve of those in management and the professions.

Such a divide presents a number of difficulties within a human resource development (HRD) perspective. Firstly, it undermines the assumption that all employees are a significant resource to be developed to their maximum potential; it follows that development and education cannot be restricted to management and professional grades. Secondly, it tends to obscure the fact that managers and other professional categories need training; management and professional work demands specific skills and competencies for which some form of training activity is required. From a HRD perspective, the connection between learning, training, development and education must be regarded as significantly interactive, each facilitating the other. HRD is defined as a strategically focused perspective on training and development. However, despite this close relationship, in theory training and development texts tend to treat them as separate. For expository purposes we will define each one separately.

Learning

Learning is generally defined as a process by which individuals gain new knowledge and insights to change their behaviour and actions. It is traditionally divided into the cognitive (intellectual), affective (emotional) and psychomotor (physical) domains. Schein (1992) points out that learning is not a unitary concept; there are distinct kinds of learning that have very different time horizons associated with them, and they may be applicable at different stages of a learning or change process.

Training

Training can be defined as a planned and systematic effort to modify or develop knowledge, skills, and attitudes, through learning experiences, to achieve effective performance in an activity or range of activities. There is no standard definition of training, however. Virtually every source uses its own definition. As an activity, it spans many boundaries, including the distinction between education and training, on-the-job and off-the-job training, training for young workers and adult training and formal and informal training through work experience. These diverse aspects of training are dealt with in later chapters.

Development

Development has been defined as the general enhancement and growth of an individual's skills and abilities, through conscious and unconscious learning, with a view to enabling them to take up a future role in an organisation.

Education

Education may be defined as a process or a series of activities which aims at enabling an individual to assimilate and develop knowledge, skills, values, and understanding that are not simply related to a narrow field of activity, but which allows a broad range of problems to be defined, analysed and solved. It may be understood in informal or formal terms.

In order to distinguish between learning, training, development and education, it is also necessary to consider the factors common to all four. To begin with, all four activities are essentially concerned with learning. Furthermore, development appears to be the primary process to which training and education contribute. In turn, this contribution facilitates the individual and the organisation, leading to the growth and realisation of the full potential of both. Meanwhile, educational qualifications are often seen as a prerequisite for a job, because they certify the individual's ability and suitability. This suitability may then be enhanced through training. Therefore, all four should be seen as complimentary components of the same process, i.e. the development of human potential or talent.

However, there are important distinguishing features of learning, training, development and education. These features are presented in Table 1.1.

In a training context, behavioural objectives are specific and are related to the present job. Education generally focuses on the individual and its objectives are less quantifiable as each individual's learning priorities differ. As development focuses on a future job or role, behavioural objectives also tend to be less precise.

The nature of the learning process is also different. Training involves learning in a mechanistic manner, i.e. learning is achieved as a result of stimuli and responses. On the other hand, organic learning emphasises a change in the individual, rather than in what they can do. The learning context of each also varies. Training, for instance, can be associated with "learning by doing", whereas education is more synonymous with "learning by thinking". In turn, development involves learning by "thinking, doing and feeling".

Table 1.1: Distinctions between Learning, Training, Development and Education

COMPARISON FACTOR	LEARNING	TRAINING	DEVELOPMENT	EDUCATION INFORMAL	EDUCATION FORMAL
Focus of Activity	On values, attitudes, innovation and outcome accomplishment	On knowledge, skills, ability and job performance	On individual potential and future role in workplace	On personal development and the experiences of life	On structured development of individual to specified outcomes
Clarity of Objectives	May be vague and difficult to identify	Can be specified clearly	Objectives stated in general terms	Objectives are unique to individual and may not be clearly articulated	Objectives stated in general terms
Time Scale	Continuous	Short Term	Long Term	Life Long	Specified period e.g. 10 years
Values which Underpin Activity	Assumes continuous change Emphasises break-through	Assumes relative stability Emphasises improvement	Assumes continuous change Emphasises maximising potential	Assumes incremental change Emphasises improvement	Often assumes stability Emphasis on breakthrough
Nature of Learning Process	Instructional or organic	Structured or mechanistic	Instructional or organic	Instructional or organic	Structured or mechanistic
Content of Activity	Learning how to learn, values, attitudes relevant to work	Knowledge, skills and attitudes relevant to specific job, basic competencies	Interpersonal, intra-personal and life skills	Life experience provides basis for education	Imposed and specified curricula
Methods Used	Informal learning methods, learner-initiated methods	Demonstration, practice, feedback	Coaching, counselling, guidance, mentoring, peer learning	Experience, observation, experimentation and reflection	Lectures, guided reading, debate, self-managed learning
Outcomes of Process	Individuals learn how to learn and create own solutions	Skilled performance of tasks which make up job	Improved problem-solving decision-making, intrapersonal/ interpersonal competence	Personal outcomes, internal to individual	External specified outcomes

COMPARISON FACTOR	LEARNING	TRAINING	DEVELOPMENT	EDUCATION	
				INFORMAL	FORMAL
Learning Strategy Used	Inductive strategies	Didactic tutor-centred	Skill-building and inductive strategies	Inductive strategies	Combination of didactic, skill-building and inductive strategies
Nature of Process	Inside out, seeks to do for self	Outside in, done by others	Combination of outside in and inside out	Inside out, seeks to do for self	Largely outside in, done by others
Role of Professional Trainer	To facilitate and guide	To instruct, demonstrate and guide	Guide, instruct, coach, counsel and mentor	Minimal, largely individual-directed	Act as an expert, instruct, facilitate and guide to learning resources
Document Trainer Philosophy	Existentialism: self-managed process	Instrumentalism: Transferring knowledge using formal methods and measuring results	Existentialism: one-to-one learning, self-managed learning	Existentialism: totally self-managed	Combination of instrumentalism and existentialism
Type of Need Emphasised	Individual and organisational needs	Organisational needs	Organisational and individual needs	Individual needs	Institutional and individual needs
Process of Evaluation	Continuous evaluation	Evaluation against specific job performance standards	Evaluation of skills and effectiveness	Evaluation against life goals and personal development	Evaluation in terms of pass/fail levels
Link with Organisational Mission and Strategies	Directly aligned with organisation's vision and requirements for success	Not necessarily linked to organisation's mission and goals	Directly aligned with organisation's vision and requirements for future, but depends on type of development	No link to organisation's mission and goals	Not necessarily linked to organisation's mission and goals
Payback to Organisation	Immediate and ongoing	Almost immediately in terms of skilled performance	Medium to long-term payback	No direct payback	Long term at most

The distinction between education and training is at times a function of their use, a typical example of which is the study of employment law. This may be part of an educational programme in business studies, but may equally comprise an element of a management training programme. A possible explanation for this phenomenon is that the term "education" has become unpopular in the industrial environment. Evidence of this may be gleaned from the change in titles from "training and education manager" to "training manager" over the last 20 years or so. Thus, education is perceived only in the context of the external training system, while training is seen as an activity which occurs within the organisation or in management centres.

In recent times, a considerable shift in emphasis has been witnessed in the content of education programmes. For example, MBA programmes, which were traditionally knowledge-based, are now undergoing a "conceptual and practical shift towards the skills of implementation and effectiveness" (Mumford, 1989). In addition, continuous development forges a further link between training and development, as it concerns the development of core transferable skills, in conjunction with task-specific skills (Harrison, 1993). Such core transferable skills incorporate problem-solving and decision-making skills, which are derived principally from the integration of learning and work. This has become more evident in the wider application of vocational education. However, some opinions reflect the view that the move away from academia would result in a weakening of ethical and cultural values.

It is suggested that the extent to which training would impart certain values is very much contingent upon its use. For example, consider equal opportunities training within an organisation that attempts to break down discriminatory barriers. If this training is solely prescriptive in nature, it may not result in attitudinal change. On the other hand, if the approach to its delivery facilitates the changing of attitudes, then a strengthening of ethical and cultural values may result. Moreover, the extent to which attitudinal transfer takes place is contingent upon the trainee's confidence. This raises another question about knowledge-based education programmes: to what extent will the knowledge and values imparted be transferred without accompanying training in skills such as communication, presentation, negotiation, and so forth?

Therefore, although certain distinctions may be drawn between learning, training, development and education, it is helpful to view them as complementary parts of the same process. As Truelove (1995) observes: "education, training and development and learning are interlinked and interdependent, rather than sequential and hierarchical". The adoption of this viewpoint clarifies the fact that each has something to lend to the other in developing human resources to their fullest potential. Indeed, their integration may be perceived as a fundamental characteristic of human resource development, which will be considered in a later chapter.

KEY TERMS 2: VISION, MISSION, POLICY, STRATEGY AND IMPLEMENTATION

We will use a number of strategic terms with considerable frequency throughout the text. These terms are subject to wide variation in meaning.

Vision

This is basically top management's view about what the organisation should be. This vision may be defined in very general terms but, nevertheless, will influence policies and practices in the training and development area. Various mechanisms will be used to communicate this vision. The role of top management is to have the determination, leadership, credibility and skills to drive the organisation towards achieving this vision.

Mission

Johnson and Scholes (1992) define mission as the organisation's *raison d'être*. It is the most general of objectives and is best understood as a statement rather than as a concept. It provides an articulation of general goals and has a long-term focus. Its primary value is perhaps as a vehicle for facilitating consensus, and it forms the foundation for strategy and plans as well as the functional activities that support them.

Strategy

Wickens (1987) describes strategy as getting the organisation from "here to here". Strategy identifies the approach used to accomplish the goals and objectives of the organisation. It answers questions relating to what business the organisation is in and how it will compete, and is concerned with evaluating alternative ways in which the mission can be achieved.

Policy

This is a specific statement and is usually an elaboration of the mission. It can be defined as a statement of intent on the part of the organisation vis-à-vis some set of activities or issues. Policy provides guidelines to managers to help them in devising plans and procedures. It sets limits. It also fulfils publicity and culture reinforcement functions for which training and development strategies must be formulated.

Implementation

This can be defined as the framework of plans, resources, responsibilities and evaluation criteria used to determine the efficiency and effectiveness of an activity. It may also include micro policies which specify the targets that must be established to achieve wider strategic objectives.

POSSIBLE PURPOSES OF TRAINING AND DEVELOPMENT

There is much discussion on the contribution, purpose and outcomes of training and development to the individual and organisation. Although many organisations now explicitly state that the training and development of human resources is amongst their strategic goals, it can generally be stated that it is an intermediate goal in the Irish context, which is intended to contribute to an organisation's goals of survival and growth. The organisational purposes of training and development can be said to be that of acquiring, developing and retaining human resources. It is through these goals that efficiency and maximum productivity are accomplished. In the most general sense, training and development, if properly carried out, should lead to greater work performance for individuals in an organisation. It is reasonable to assume that individuals are going to perform better if they know how to perform tasks correctly. However, there is a wide range of individual and organisational outcomes which training and development may produce.

Selection and Certification

This has both an individual and an organisational purpose. An important task of training and development is to ensure that an individual has the knowledge and skills needed to meet organisational job requirements. The possession of the correct profile of competencies should considerably enhance the individual's chances of selection for a job and furthermore enhance the organisation's promotion, career planning and succession processes.

Certification is another important outcome. If a job within an organisation requires certain skills or education then this may be looked for by means of some form of certification. The possession of such a certificate will lead the organisation to assume that the individual in question has certain fundamental competencies required for the position. Certification also allows the organisation to function more effectively and economically, as it cuts out the need to test the skills and competencies of the individual. Arrow (1962) suggests that the certification of training may be used as a time and money saving device as well as a filter. Williamson (1985) points out that the use of certification can be extended further and be used in the promotion of employees within the organisation.

It can therefore reduce the transaction costs of recruitment and promotion.

Dineen and Lenihan (1994) illustrate the link between certification and access to a job. In the case of CERT, the recruitment and training agency for the tourism industry, recruits are placed in colleges and training centres where they follow a set curriculum. The industry plays a major role through the provision of work experience and participation in the design of programmes. The provision of the necessary certification enhances the employment prospects of CERT graduates.

There is also a company example of an organisation involved in aircraft maintenance in the Mid-West region where trainers/recruits are taken in initially to follow a training programme leading to a certificate in aircraft maintenance. Employment opportunities flow directly from successful completion of the programme.

Metcalf et al (1994) suggest that while certification is seen as an important motivator for employees to train, employers may be less interested in training leading to qualifications. The IEF study (1992) found that engineering companies were more interested in training employees to company standards than certifying these skills externally. Callender et al (1993) also found that employers were not interested in qualifications. They found that only 6 per cent of employers were using NVQs or SVQs and 72 per cent were not interested in using them. Employers who were interested saw them as helping to improve staff development and performance.

Socialisation and Social Integration

It is initially impossible for an employer to specify in detail what an employee is expected to do during 100 per cent of their working day. Nordhaug (1990) points out that this has to be supplemented with a psychological contract which is often implicit. In general this means that as well as training in operational issues, the training and development given, in order to achieve efficiency, must also project the values, norms and attitudes of the organisation. The socialisation dimension of training and development is significant. It is generally accepted that an individual must understand the norms, values, attitudes and expectations of the organisation, both so that they know how to react and what to expect from the organisation, as well as what is expected from themselves. Van Naanen (1976) points out that individuals must learn the appropriate norms if they are to participate as members of the organisation. Some commentators, however, disagree with the notion of making employees' behaviour more predictable in order to reduce uncertainty and the need for direct supervision. They see it as a form of brainwashing and manipulation. However, it is generally accepted that training and development does perform this socialisation role.

Social integration is often cited as a further outcome of training. Nordhaug (1990) defines this purpose as one of integrating the total organisation. Such integration is nowadays often referred to as teamwork and is a natural follow-on from organisation socialisation in that the latter focuses on the single individual and the former focuses on everyone within the organisation. Training and development activities can facilitate social integration by allowing the exchange of ideas, a better understanding of working procedures in different parts of the organisation and through increased communication.

Legitimisation and Reducing Internal Vulnerability

Training and development can perform a legitimisation purpose in that it can set standards for employees to work towards. It can also be used to legitimise pay structures, compensation systems and career development activities. Pfeffer (1981) refers to this legitimisation function of training when he states that training and development is important in order to maintain the legitimacy of an organisation's internal labour market and in particular its promotion criteria.

Reducing internal vulnerability can stem from the division of labour within an organisation. According to Nordhaug (1990), it is generally assumed that the greater the interdependence among different departments of an organisation the more vulnerable the organisation or department is to potential hostile individual or group behaviour. If departments have specialised knowledge or knowledge that other groups within the organisation or department do not possess, it gives that department significant power. There are a number of studies which demonstrate the behaviour of groups within an organisation who possess knowledge or skills exclusive to themselves. Craig (1991) and Hinnings (1990) demonstrate that if training and development activities, whether knowingly or not, instigate the formulation of such skill groups, it will lead to inefficiency within the organisation through lack of task completion and non-achievement of targets and goals due to concentration of power in small groups. Training and development initiatives can, however, prevent this from happening by dispersing the knowledge over a wider radius. The most common of these strategies is that of despecialisation or cross-training. This should lead to reduced interdependencies and fewer power bases. Multi-skilling is a useful strategy for an organisation to use for a broad, highly skilled workforce.

Motivation and Retention

Training may be directed specifically at motivating and retaining employees. Gallie and White (1993) found in their study that employees ranked training fourth in a list of 15 possible features essential to do a good job, and availability of training was found to increase their commitment to their current employer. They also found that one-fifth of employees wanted training but thought it was unlikely they would get it.

There is also evidence to suggest that employers may feel pushed by employees' expectations of training, particularly where training is necessary for retention. Schuller and Bostym (1992) and Ross (1993) found that companies were likely to look favourably on an employee's request for specific training at least indirectly related to their job though not non-vocational. The reasons for doing so were many but included reward for commitment to the company, the perception that working life must be more than simply earning a wage, the need to retain good staff and the general perception that investment in human resources is a good thing.

Dysfunctional Training Outcomes

Training and development can be dysfunctional if there is a minimum of integration between the achievement of qualifications and the organisation's need for qualifications to fit current work activities. Nordhaug (1990) points out that this can take two forms, that of over-education and misplaced training. Both of these can cause inefficiency and hinder individual and team performance.

Over-education is a term normally used when referring to academic qualifications. However, it can be equally applied to an organisational training and development context. Over-education in this context refers to a situation where employees receive education and training which results in them being overqualified for a job they are carrying out. Collins (1979) and Borris (1983) highlight that over-education can result in employees who feel frustrated, have little or no job satisfaction and are left wondering why they bothered training in the first place. This dissatisfaction is likely to manifest itself in poor work performance and high turnover.

Misplaced training can often be caused by lack of understanding of the needs of the organisation. The wrong type of training may be carried out. There are many manifestations of this misplaced training outcome. This often occurs with employees who are sent on external programmes which have participants from many organisations. It is very difficult to gear external courses to a single organisation's requirements. This form of misplaced training can lead to a waste of resources in terms of time and money as well as demotivating individual employees. A more common form of misplaced training occurs where training activities are carried out without a proper training needs analysis. This is quite a common scenario and will again lead to a waste of resources and demotivation of the individual.

FACILITATORS AND IMPEDIMENTS TO TRAINING PROVISION

There is a growing volume of research on factors which facilitate and impede the provision of training within the organisation. Felstead and Green (1993) examined employers' growth and commitment to training. They found a clear recession effect. Companies that had experienced falling employment and contracting markets were more likely to decrease their training effort. Companies experiencing difficulties had a strong interest in cost-cutting and this might include cutting out a central training department or leaving training to more ad hoc action by supervisors and line managers.

Felstead and Green did, however, find that contracting markets and employment reductions did not lead inevitably to reduced training. Forty per cent of companies in their survey who reported an increased training effort had contracting markets or felt the need to reduce employment. Three reasons were suggested for this trend:

1. Competition: This involved a competitive strategy based on the production of quality products or the delivery of a quality service as a result of pressures from customers. Companies increasing training were likely to be registered for the BS5750 quality standard and gave a new priority for training of key groups in the company.

2. In some cases "floors" existed which prevented a reduction in training. These floors related to hazards which might make the use of untrained workers risky and costly and the existence of external registration, legal and voluntary. The need to pay attention to training floors also arose from competition since certain work in some markets was open only to firms with qualified staff.

3. Among those companies that decreased their training effort were short-term planners. Those who increased were more likely to take positive steps in their strategies such as implementing a long-term competitive strategy and seeking BS5705.

Felstead and Green concluded that no simple pattern of objective conditions was decisive in employers' choice whether to increase or decrease their training effort or the type of training policy which they adopted. This finding is supported by Rolfe et al (1993) who found that companies in broadly similar circumstances may develop very different patterns of training provision.

Dench (1993) found that companies coming to grips with competition and change in a dynamic and external environment train more. High training companies were:

- more likely to emphasise the quality of their product or service and less likely to emphasise price;

- more likely to be responding to a perception of rising customer expectations and to provide a range of products/services to many market niches;

- more likely to produce a distinctive product or service and to engage in new product development;

- more likely to have set out to improve productivity and quality and to do so by means other than cutting costs or contracting out; and

- more likely to have introduced changes in their work organisation like multi-skilling, new management structures and technology. They were also more likely to have taken initiatives to improve teamwork and customer service.

Dench found that the increase in training in unfavourable circumstances reflected moves towards greater overall dynamism. She also found that falling employment in the workplace made little difference to the organisation's willingness to train. However, size and ownership were significant. Small single-site companies were less likely than those that were part of a larger organisation to have increased their training efforts. Sectoral differences emerged. There was a relatively low propensity to increase training in manufacturing, construction, transport and communication, compared with the high priority in the service, distribution and energy sector. The IFF study (1989) found that competitiveness was a leading motive for training in the private sector, whereas in the public and voluntary sector, the maintenance of cultural and ideology were significant factors. The study also noted the relatively high proportion of non-trainers in construction, transport, wholesale and manufacturing, and in smaller firms and in companies competing in a local market.

According to De Vries and Warmerden (1992), impediments to training exist at three levels: the level of employee, the level of training supply and the level of the organisation.

Level of the Employee

While the traditional attitude to training has been that its initiation and organisation are the responsibility of individual organisations or state training institutions, a new line of thinking appears to place some of this responsibility on the shoulder of the individuals themselves (Bentley, 1991). This idea does not seem so unreasonable when one considers the degree of "mutuality" in training, i.e. that employees as well as the organisation will benefit (Taylor, 1991). They must be encouraged to seek opportunities for themselves, including initiating training. This may involve some cost on their part, but this cost must be seen as an investment — where better to invest than in oneself? This new form of thinking will only progress if the right attitude or frame of mind is created within the individual.

Individuals may be further encouraged to continuously update their skills and knowledge if the new type of career envisaged by Handy (1987) becomes a reality. He suggests that individuals will no longer have a single job or career, but rather a series, or "portfolio" of career paths, for which continuing training and education will be essential. This change, he argues, must be seen as an opportunity rather than a threat.

Robinson (1988) states that motivation is one of the major factors which influences a learner's response to training, and that it is important for employers to understand what motivates their employers. Nobody can force a person to learn. Therefore, for the training to be beneficial to the employee, and consequently the company, it is important for managers to understand and attempt to remove, any barriers to trainee motivation.

Metcalf et al (1994) asked employers to identify factors capable of motivating employees to train. Career progression and promotion were the most commonly cited, followed by money, job satisfaction, self-esteem, employer encouragement and support. No employer in the survey mentioned qualification as a motivator. The lack of these factors would reduce motivation to train. Employers also identified a number of other factors they believed acted as demotivators. Time demands on employees was the most important factor, followed by the cost of the training, a lack of perceived benefits, lack of confidence and a lack of information on the training available.

Level of the Training Supply

Training supply may not match training demand, especially in Ireland where provision is comparatively low or inappropriate.

The expected results will not accrue from the training unless the training provided is that which is actually needed to meet organisational goals, i.e. that organisations do not simply pick the training that is available at the time or whatever is "flavour of the month" (Long, 1992). The onus for a clear link between training demand and supply rests with those demanding and supplying the training. Management must be able to identify correctly the type of training that they require, e.g. through a training needs analysis, or a management and skills audit (Long, 1992). Training suppliers must provide information on what training is currently available. The suppliers should also aim to provide training requested by the employers, and which is currently not available.

One method of improving the supply-demand link may be for industry to work more closely with education establishments to develop more relevant courses suited to the needs and demands of business. In the US, it has been estimated that of the 2.4 million students who graduate each year 25 per cent are "functionally illiterate" (Yeomans, 1989), and that it is then up to industry to rectify the situation through training. In Ireland, attempts have been made to establish better links between third-level institutions and industry. This has been done through the creation of industrial liaison officers/committees in colleges and universities, and also by the work of the five UETPs (University Enterprise Training Partnerships).

Level of the Organisation

De Vries and Warmerden (1992) argue that person-related factors are far less of an impediment than those at an organisational level. Issues which may act as impediments to training at this level include the cost of training, lack of motivation or awareness, time constraints, the status of the training function and lack of top management commitment to HRD and training.

Cost of Training

An assumption of the systematic training model (Taylor, 1991), which views training as an investment rather than a cost, must be applied in organisations today. Like any investment, it will incur costs in the short term, but provide benefits or returns in the long term — in the context of training, this of course will depend on whether the training activities are related to organisational goals and needs. The reality of this theory, however, is that the payback from training is often difficult to measure, and managers often fail to see its link with profitability. In a study cited by Buckley and Caple (1992), only 33 per cent of respondents felt that there was a direct link between training and the achievement of corporate objectives. For many, training and development is seen as either "a necessary evil", an "employee benefit" or "nice to do" (Hall, 1984; Robinson, 1988). What they often fail to realise is that a more flexible and prepared workforce (through training) will be better able to cope with crises and help in regaining competitiveness.

According to FÁS, traditional Irish companies have an "aversion to paying for training"; rather, they tend to focus on profits and have little problem in investing in other areas, such as capital and new equipment. This is the crux of the problem for many organisations; they "invest" in other areas but "spend" on training. The difficulty in convincing organisations that spending on training is indeed an investment rests with the fact that the returns or benefits from training are often intangible, or at the very least difficult to measure.

Motivation/Awareness

While an employee must have the motivation to learn or train, it is perhaps equally important that the employer has the necessary motivation to make provision for training (Reid, Barrington and Kenney, 1992). The recent practice of downsizing the workforce, or demassing the ranks of management, has particular implications for training and motivation. Management must pay special attention to those that are left behind and who often have a greater degree of responsibility or simply more work to do (Sinclair and Collins, 1992). While this may mean that they need practical training, they are often not motivated, as many of their colleagues have left and they may feel insecure about the future.

One factor which may act as a demotivator for organisations in training their employees is that after spending money on their training and development, an organisation has no guarantee that the employees will stay and use their new knowledge and skills for the benefit of the company. It may very well be one of their competitors that reaps the rewards of this training. Certain incentives may encourage participation in training, such as the National Training Awards organised by FÁS and presented to organisations which have achieved a level of excellence in training.

Status/Commitment to the Training Function from Senior Management

A common complaint from training and development professionals is that the training department has a low status within the organisation and/or suffers from "bad press" (Sinclair and Collins, 1992) and that it often occupies a location peripheral to that of the other operational functions (Buckley and Caple, 1992). According to Sinclair and Collins, the root of the problem lies with training specialists themselves and senior management. It is suggested that the training function is unable to promote or develop the strategic aims of the organisation. More often than not, this is due to a low level of provision in terms of (a) financial resources — the training department is usually an area of low investment; (b) low quality staff — the qualifications and professionalism of training personnel is often questioned, as well as the amount of training they themselves receive; and (c) time and commitment. Senior management in particular are criticised for failing to give commitment to this area. Robinson (1988) adds that the opinion of many managers is that they did not have to be trained to get where they are today, and thus cannot see the need for training of employees.

Time Constraints

A final impediment at an organisational level, and one which so far has received little attention (De Vries and Warmerden, 1992) is that of time constraints on training. They argue that if the level of training does increase, management will have to develop a means of accommodating those who wish to participate in training, and of coping with substantial absences from work. Research by Pettigrew, Hendry and Sparrow (1988) has indicated that the weak link in the implementation of training plans is line management, and the main problem that they report is that of releasing staff. They term this the "hidden time-cost".

COMPETITIVE ADVANTAGE THROUGH HUMAN RESOURCES

People as a Critical Organisation Resource

In viewing people as a critical resource in the organisation, several factors must be taken into account. To begin with, the human resource is neither an homogeneous nor an interchangeable resource. As Stainer (1971) and Hussey (1988) point out, people are different from each other, in terms of education, personality, aptitudes, and so forth. Therefore, for an organisation to function effectively, specific employees must occupy particular positions.

On the other hand, the human resource can be perceived as a decision-making resource. This becomes an increasingly significant factor as the influence of more sophisticated technology is leading to a reduced demand for manual employees and an increase in demand for decision-making employees. The human resource can also be viewed as an income generating resource in that it has the potential to be productive and produce outputs. Of course, people are also a social resource and must be managed accordingly (Stainer, 1971). Indeed, this is clarified by Torrington and Hall (1991) who point out that the people resource is a dynamic one, having a will of its own.

The core beliefs, values and attitudes of employees form the culture of an organisation. Major implications for organisational success can ensue from this, as the culture of an organisation is often the key to such success. This is especially true in the case of a service industry, such as Aer Lingus, where its culture is projected out into the consumer world. An effective consumer culture can give the company a significant competitive edge. Indeed, it is now widely held among those in Aer Lingus that it is the culture of the organisation that attracts customers. The importance of the social aspect of the human resource is thus emphasised.

Management of Human Resources

Planning

As we have seen, employees are an income generating resource, and as such should be considered an invaluable organisational asset. However, in modern accounting conventions, the human resource is frequently viewed as an expense, and this perception has serious implications with respect to the planning for, and investment in, human capital. If an unplanned approach to human resources is adopted, a surplus of human resources may result. In turn, this is seen as an accounting expense and a drain on profits. Treating employees as a commodity triggers a self-fulfilling prophesy. If employees are viewed as a commodity little planning takes place. People are a necessity for any enterprise, but, unlike financial and material resources, they have been subjected to little planning attention.

Development

The prevalent commodity and cost approach tends to equate human resources with physical and economic resources, which has adverse implications for the development of employees. While it may seem superfluous to state that employees are capable of development, it is crucial that this is recognised within organisations and that employee potential is developed to the full. In this vein, Bennett (1988) indicates that, although many employees may not possess exceptional natural abilities, there are extraordinary levels of individual performance in many successful companies. Such achievements may be realised through training and development interventions.

Similarly, the development of managers is critical for the development of the organisation as a whole, as it is managers who take decisions concerning training. Consequently, if they have not followed a developmental process themselves they may not recognise the importance of training and, furthermore, are unlikely to support or endorse the training and development process. This view is supported by Harrison (1993) who states that "inadequately skilled and poorly educated managers are unlikely to see the need for anything but a similarly low and narrow level of skills for all other employees".

This characteristic of the human resource differentiates it from other resources, because people as a resource must take decisions about their own management.

Investment

In summarising the importance of training and development within organisations, Reid and Barrington (1994) observe that the UK is increasingly viewing education and training as potentially able to make a contribution towards solving economic problems. At a personal level, people now have expectations of increased responsibility, status, and remuneration in organisations. Frequently, training and development are the key to the realisation of these expectations, but, for this to occur, investment is required.

It can be argued that the amount of training and development provided has to be a major litmus test of whether HRM is making significant inroads within an organisation. Sisson (1989) has argued that training and development is crucial for a number of reasons. An organisation which fails to train will find itself dependent upon the external labour market. Furthermore, it is more likely to regard its workforce as little more than a cost to be incurred. An organisation which does train is more likely to engage in complementary HRM activities and it has the potential to draw symbolic value from its actions. The key message is that it values its employees and they are to be viewed as an important resource.

Thurley (1990) points out that a HRM model tends to focus on skill development. Even in its "hard" manifestations short-term market forces may lead rational employers to train for immediate job requirements in the apparent absence of alternative sources of labour. There is some evidence in the Irish context that limited training opportunities are being offered by employers for this reason.

In the Irish context, the report of the Advisory Committee on Management Training (1988) highlighted some alarming statistics:

- Twenty per cent of the top 1,000 companies in Ireland spent nothing on management training in 1987.

- More than 50 per cent of companies spent less than £5,000 on management training in 1987.

- Foreign-owned companies spent on average 50 per cent more on training and development than Irish-owned companies.

Perceptions of what is necessary for business survival differ significantly between the Advisory Committee and top managers of major Irish companies. Therefore, not only is there a danger that employees will not be developed to their fullest potential, but also an inherent danger that employees will become demotivated in their present roles if their expectations are not realised. Additionally, it is likely that underdeveloped managers will be blind to the training and developmental needs of employees. Such a situation has major implications for the success of any company.

It must further be stressed that the development of the human resource will only be effective if it is intertwined with the strategic objectives of the organisation. Only in this manner will all the resources of the organisation be used together in the best possible conjunction (Zenger and Blitzer, 1981; McEwen and Young, 1988).

Training as an Economic Instrument

As we move towards the 21st century, the world economy is experiencing increased globalisation. Major advances in technology, especially in the area of telecommunications, are making international trade easier and faster. In what has become a globally competitive marketplace, industrial success is achieved through implementing higher standards of product and service excellence.

This search for excellence has initiated a revival of interest in human capital — skills and productive knowledge embodied in people — as a primary source of economic activity. The notion of human capital was first espoused by Adam Smith (1776), when he pointed to the "stock of capital embodied in men through training, study and education". This is echoed in Porter's (1985) belief that human resources are one of the key means of achieving competitive advantage. The foundation for this belief has its basis in the multiple changes in industry and services sectors, which highlight the importance of labour quality and productivity as key competitive factors.

Increased global competitiveness has simplified the imitation of marketing, financial and manufacturing techniques, thereby reducing the competitive advantage of organisations. Opinion has thus shifted from labour being viewed as an undifferentiated factor input, as recognition is increasingly given to the value of enterprise training and learning. In a competitive and rapidly changing business environment, the role of learning within organisations is becoming increasingly important. This was particularly highlighted by projections in *Fortune* magazine (1992), which forecasted that product and service lead times will shrink in the 1990s, increasing the relevance of learning as it becomes a critical element in maintaining a competitive base. Indeed, the view has been expressed that, in this sort of world, the ability of an organisation to learn faster than its competitors may be the only sustainable advantage.

It is now accepted that labour quality and productivity can be significantly improved through prior education, and enterprise training and learning, to deliver sustainable competitive advantage. Therefore, only those organisations that comprise people who are responsive to change, and which embrace an ethos of continuous development and learning, will prove successful. We will examine the economic arguments for training in the next chapter.

THE SIGNIFICANCE OF TRAINING AND DEVELOPMENT: NATIONAL AND ORGANISATIONAL PERSPECTIVES

The importance of training and development is highlighted by the difference between improved productivity and declining competitiveness in the international marketplace. Despite all the technological advances of our time, organisations are still managed and operated by people, and it is their knowledge and skills which is vital to sustained success. Training and development of human resources is now accepted as a prerequisite for survival and success in today's global economy, where the relationship between productivity and competitive performance in international trade has become an established feature.

The international importance of training and development, in this context, is reflected in a comparison of economic productivity performance. Since 1972, the EU has experienced a gradual decline in its share of world markets, due to low levels of productivity. Over this period, US and Japanese productivity rates have been running level, but Europe has only achieved 65 per cent of the US and Japanese rates. If the high growth sectors, such as electrical and electronic goods, are scrutinised, the contrast is even greater. Here, European productivity is only half that of the US, while the Japanese rate, at 236 per cent, is double that of the US level.

It was in response to this state of affairs that the Culliton Report (1992) indicated that education and training are a more critical element of policy, affecting not just industrial but overall economic welfare.

National Importance

The importance of education and training at national level, not just in Ireland, but in every industrialised country worldwide, is recognised as one of the principal forces in achieving economic growth. This was clearly emphasised in the Culliton Report (1992), which indicates that "in an increasingly integrated and competitive world, skills and knowledge constitute one of the few areas where an economy can command differential competitive advantage."

This perspective is supported by two decades of accumulated evidence by the OECD (1989). Here the "association between schooling and labour productivity" is affirmed, and the link with a "positive impact on macroeconomic performance and individual well-being" is also highlighted. Hence, it is clearly evident that a highly skilled workforce, appropriate to industrial activity in any economy, will result in high levels of productivity. In order to attain these required high levels of skill, investment in training and learning is essential. Moreover, the responsibility for such investment must be embraced, not just by the State, but also by individual organisations.

In their submission to the Culliton Report on Industrial Training in Ireland, Roche and Tansey (1992) suggest that

> effective economic training enhances the range and depth of the productive skills possessed by the national workforce. The resulting gains in productivity raise output, exports and incomes throughout the economy.

They further outline a "Chain of Causation" (Figure 1.1) to illustrate the linkage between investment in training and education and indicators of economic performance. Training and development will only become a crucial determinant of the pace and shape of a nation's economic development if it is pursued efficiently, economically and with a market-led approach. As Roche and Tansey (1992) comment: "an insufficiency of such training, or its inefficient provision, can force the economy onto a permanently lower growth path future".

The reality of the importance of training and education on a national scale can be observed by the increase in nationwide funding for training and education in the US, from $60 billion in 1970 to $136 billion in 1990. According to a 1990 survey by *Training* magazine, 39.5 million employees received 1.3 billion hours of formal employer-sponsored training, at a total cost of $29 billion. The enormous increase in training investment emanated from an analysis of comparable international statistics which revealed that the US was losing competitive advantage as a result of poor productivity. This low level of productivity was attributed to the US spending less on training than its main competitor nations. Between 1960 and 1985, US productivity grew at an annual rate of 2.7 per cent, compared to a 5.4 per cent average in each of its major foreign competitors. Over the same period, productivity rose by 8.5 per cent in Japan, 6.2 per cent in the Netherlands, 6.5 per cent in Belgium, 5.4 per cent in Italy and by 4.8 per cent in Germany.

The importance of training in Ireland, from a national perspective, was further highlighted by Roche and Tansey (1992) who found that up to 45 per cent of employees are in need of further training, and skill deficiencies are resulting in lower levels of productivity and competitiveness. Given the widely recognised difficulty in establishing accurate countrywide data, the actual situation may be even less encouraging. The upgrading of skills is thus an issue of national priority. Indeed, the government expressed concern at the fact that 20 per cent of the top 1,000 companies in Ireland spend nothing at all on management devel-

opment, coupled with the fact that craft workers, supervisors and operatives receive less training than their counterparts in competitor nations.

The issue of training as a vital contributor to national economic welfare and growth is further apparent when a perspective of industry and
company skills analysis is taken.

Figure 1.1: Chain of Causation

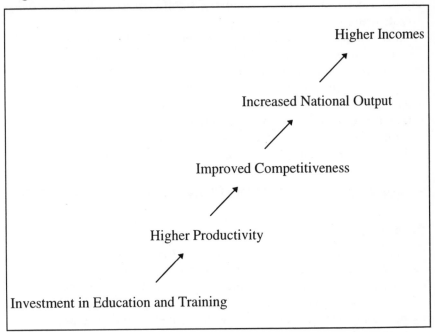

Source: Roche and Tansey, 1992.

Industry Significance

The importance of training and development is evident in today's global
economy. Industry-specific circumstances, choices and outcomes emphasise national advantages in relation to particular market dominance
of some countries' industries. Prime examples include: Italy, in footwear, textiles and jewellery; Korea, in apparel and electronics; Sweden,
in precision engineering; and Japan, in shipbuilding and semi-
conductors. The major reason for this dominance is that, within each
country, a particular industry or sub-sector of an industry has acquired,
through a combination of training and experience, a significant pool of
skilled employees. Consequently, a quality workforce of this nature has
proved capable of producing goods at a decidedly competitive advantage
in the international marketplace.

The rapid inroads made by the Japanese car industry in world markets provides an outstanding demonstration of this point, with Honda and Toyota, for instance, surpassing Chrysler in the US domestic market. An integral component of such achievement has been extensive training and the building up of a highly skilled workforce. In 1963, Honda started its car production facility, setting out to become the biggest and best car manufacturer in the world. Since then, it has grown faster than any other car manufacturer, achieving significant gains in productivity over its major competitors.

Interestingly, Honda attributes its success to huge investments in training and its resulting highly skilled workforce. Industrial training, then, improves industrial productivity, not only on the shop floor but also in supervisory management of industrial processes and executive management of industrial enterprises. Furthermore, the training process within a specific industry contributes to the collective good of a national economy, developing a strong national competitive advantage through a wider and more advanced skills base in that industry.

TRAINING AND DEVELOPMENT AND BUSINESS STRATEGY

Corporate Strategy

Let us look first at the nature of business strategy and planning. An organisation's corporate strategic plan is a comprehensive plan or action orientation, which sets critical direction and guides the allocation of resources. As with any strategy, the corporate planning process is initiated by decision-makers, to establish the objectives of the business and the route through which these will be progressed and achieved. Corporate strategy has been defined as the process of determining the major objectives of an organisation and defining the strategies that will govern the acquisition and utilisation of resources to achieve those objectives. Sharplin (1985) outlines it as the choice made by an organisation's decision-makers that specifies the plans formulated to match strengths and weaknesses with problems or opportunities in the external environment.

The corporate strategic plan is therefore comprehensive in scope and reflects the overall direction of the total organisation, and represents a more systematic approach to planning. Through this approach, it assesses the current position vis-à-vis organisational objectives, selects a strategy, and implements it through action plans. Since a prime organisational objective is to sustain long-term profitability through high levels of productivity and competitiveness, the training and development of human resources must receive due recognition and status as a critical strategic activity. It is the strategic management concept which accepts the profound uncertainty of the processes involved, and which demonstrates most accurately how aspects of human resource management are inextricably linked to competitiveness.

Strategic Role of Training and Development

We have already seen how this link has been established, and that the strategic training plan must form a fundamental element within corporate strategic planning. A strategic training and development plan, then, is a core necessity, if the goals set by management with regard to human resources are to be fully realised, and to ensure that the right people, with the requisite skills, are in the appropriate positions within the organisation.

Of course, in the maelstrom of today's globally competitive environment, organisations are faced with a number of alternative strategies in an effort to overcome uncertainty and risk effectively. Because of the existence and promotion of alternative strategies within organisations, the involvement and influence of the training and development function is strongly advocated. To date, however, this has not been the case in many organisations, and very often training and development specialists are excluded from vital strategic decision-making. Indeed, their function is often perceived as one of relatively low influence in the running of the organisation.

To counteract this perception, a strategic role for the training and development function must be supported at the highest level of an organisation. It must be emphasised that support in this context means active commitment to the principle that the training and development function is an integral part of an organisation's activities. Furthermore, the basis for this commitment must be the acknowledgement of training and development as a major factor in establishing and maintaining level of effectiveness and a central component of an organisation's operating system — its human resources. Failure to acknowledge this fact, at the highest level, means that the effectiveness of an organisation will inevitably be curtailed, thereby casting a shadow over its levels of productivity and competitiveness, and consequently over its future success.

Contribution to Corporate Strategic Planning

The research indicates that effective training and development functions are riveted to the organisation's mission and goals, and display a constant awareness of ongoing organisational needs (Zenger, 1988). Adopting this approach situates the training and development function in the vanguard of business operations, focusing on providing relevant training solutions and making a continuous contribution to effectiveness and excellence. Thus, by identifying and fulfilling immediate training needs, the development and implementation of training plans interlock with the corporate master plan.

Hussey (1988) identifies six specific areas where the training and development function can make a major contribution to corporate strategy:

1. *Strategy Formulation.* Relevant training and development interventions can be designed and utilised to challenge the assumptions on which current corporate plans are based, or to examine strategic options.

2. *Strategy Implementation.* Appropriate initiatives can facilitate broad understanding of strategic plans and their impact on individuals and jobs, on a company-wide basis. Initiatives such as these can help to build employee commitment by increasing the transparency of plans and the rationale behind them. Additionally, implications can be explored in a positive context and responded to by the formulation of personal action plans. In this vein, training activities may also be devised to complement the implementation process itself.

3. *Policy Implementation.* As with strategic plans, new policies or changes to existing ones can be effectively implemented with the aid of appropriate training and development activities.

4. *Corporate Culture.* Training and development must be viewed as an essential vehicle in the culture creation or change process, ensuring that corporate strategies and culture are entirely compatible.

5. *Environmental Change.* Changes in the business environment continuously pose threats which may judiciously be transformed into opportunities through pertinent training and development activities. The training and development function can play a vital role in the organisation by assisting in the identification of changes, as well as easing the path to successful transition.

6. *Solving Problems.* The training and development function can play a proactive role in identifying problems and appropriate training activities and by making a significant contribution to their solution.

These six areas provide a vivid and practical illustration of ways through which training and development can become a core contributor to the development and implementation of corporate strategic plans. Nonetheless, as we have previously seen, the training and development function is quite often excluded from this level of operations — a situation which, in effect, precludes it from having the type of contribution outlined. The common incidence of this state of affairs can be attributed, to a large degree, to the prevailing philosophies and attitudes towards training, development and education.

ATTITUDES TO TRAINING AND DEVELOPMENT

Given the important role that the development of people can play in facilitating the achievement of business goals, why is it that support for the activity is so variable from one organisation to another in Ireland? Why do many other EU companies invest more heavily in training and development and generally have a more business-like approach? We will examine attitudes at both organisational and national level.

Organisational Attitudes

Harrison (1993) identifies six possible attitudes which are equally applicable to the Irish context:

1. *"We're doing it already" or "We don't need it here"*. This set of attitudes arise from a combination of ignorance and complacency amongst key managers within the organisation, as well as amongst training and development practitioners who should be adopting a more systematic and collaborative approach to their role. The Galvin Report (1988) points out that training and development practitioners should demonstrate greater political sensitivity in obtaining agreement to training and development priorities, promote learning opportunities and evaluate the results of training. Poor practices on the part of training and development practitioners breeds complacency, which is manifested in terms of little investment in training and development because of the doubts about the payback. A further outcome may be the assumption that what is done is OK.

2. *"There's no point in training people for our competitors"*. The poaching argument is commonly used in Ireland to explain why employers do not train staff or develop their employees. We will deal with the poaching argument in more detail in Chapter 2. However, for the moment, the key point is that the poaching argument can perpetuate a vicious circle. Harrison (1993) suggests that some organisations poach skills, while others over-invest and retain their skilled employees by means of long-term internal development and progressive reward policies. Other companies over-invest but do little else with the result that they lose many skilled employees to "poachers". The poachers invest no money in training and development unless poaching fails. In the final analysis, few individuals have incentives to invest for themselves.

3. *"Training and Development is a good thing"*. Many commentators such as Burgoyne, Stuart and Pedlar (1984) put forward the view that development is of itself a worthy thing for an organisation to invest in. It is implicit in many motivation theories that individuals will seek

to realise their potential, will react positively to opportunities for development and will become more committed to the organisation.
Burgoyne (1988), however, warns that it tends to focus too much on
the individual and the systems necessary to implement individual
training, and not enough on the development of the organisation as a
whole. Pedlar and Boutall (1988) also support this view. They believe that while development is a good thing it often results in a
fragmented approach to the development of people — coherent
training and development is done on a whim and little consideration
is made of the return to the organisation.

4. *"Development is a necessary business investment"*. This view suggests that investment in human resource development will automatically lead to improved business performance. Much of the literature
on excellence identifies training and development as a component of
successful organisations. Peters and Waterman's (1987) contribution
did place human resources on the agenda, though the relationship
between individual and organisational performance remains a vague
one.

5. *"Employee development should be a strategic activity"*. This attitude
reflects the emergence of strategic-led human resource development,
which we will consider later in this text. Essentially, this attitude
views training and development as arising downstream from business
strategy formulation. Training and development interventions are
linked to the achievement of specific targets at all levels within the
organisation. Training and development will facilitate the implementation of business strategy.

6. *"Training and development should achieve a learning organisation"*.
This is the most current attitude. Training and development is viewed
as an organisational learning process that permeates the organisation
and influences decision-makers at all levels. This is a proactive
stance for training and development to adopt and has a major role to
play in sharpening and reinforcing culture.

National Attitudes

There are a number of attitudes which characterise many Irish organisations and which influence policy decision-makers at state level. Some of
these attitudes have been highlighted in a number of research studies.
These studies illustrate a relatively consistent picture.

Figure 1.2: Training and Development Attitude Continuum

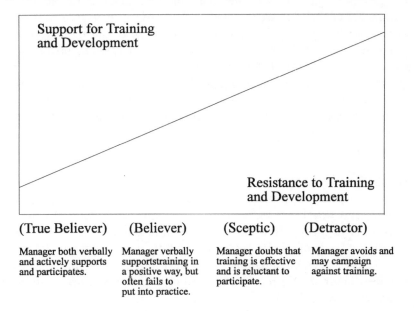

Support for Training
and Development

Resistance to Training
and Development

(True Believer)	(Believer)	(Sceptic)	(Detractor)
Manager both verbally and actively supports and participates.	Manager verbally supportstraining in a positive way, but often fails to put into practice.	Manager doubts that training is effective and is reluctant to participate.	Manager avoids and may campaign against training.

Source: McDonald, G. (1989) "Manager Attitudes to Training", *Asia Pacific HRM,* Vol. 27, No. 4, p. 65.

AnCO Report

The first official statistics for training of the employed were made available in the 1985 Labour Force Survey. AnCO (1987) stated that the figures represented a serious lack of continuing training and re-training. Six and one-half per cent of all employed persons (7 per cent of those employed in the 15-49 age category) had received education or training, including on-the-job training, during the four weeks prior to the survey. This figure compares with 10.4 per cent in Britain.

The category receiving the most training was the 15-19 age group (30 per cent — the same as the UK figure). This percentage fell dramatically in the older age groups: down to 4.9 per cent for the 25-34 cohort (10.9 per cent in the UK) and 2.5 per cent for the 35-49 category (7.2 per cent in the UK). AnCO concluded that this is not simply a reflection of a smaller need for initial vocational training among older persons. The purpose of the training was as follows:

- further training for present job — 71 per cent;

- first vocational training — 17 per cent;

- re-training for other job — 6.5 per cent;

- other (presumably general education) — 5 per cent.

The Galvin Report

The Galvin Report (1988) stated that while Ireland's international competitors demonstrate a strong belief in the value of management training, Irish expenditure is significantly lower than that of our more successful competitors. In 1987, over 20 per cent of the top 1,000 companies spent nothing on management development or did not know how much they spent; over one half spent less than £5,000. This situation was particularly serious in small, new or Irish-owned companies (foreign companies spent on average 50 per cent more than indigenous ones). In all, an average of 1.4 per cent of total payroll was spent on management training and development.

The Culliton Report

The Culliton Report (1992) outlined a number of recommendations for training and development. *Industrial Training in Ireland* (Roche and Tansey, 1992), a report which presented a negative picture of training, formed the basis of the key recommendations made in the Culliton Report. The two recommendations (see Garavan, 1992, and the FÁS Commercial Report, 1993) relating to training and development within the organisation were:

1. Training for the employed is inadequate in quality and quantity considering the present skill deficiencies. It must become a priority.

2. There should be no subsidies or grants for firm-specific training (i.e. training that is unique to one firm only), but rather general training which is valuable to many organisations.

The Price Waterhouse Cranfield Study

This study illustrates that there is a considerable gap to be bridged before these aspirations become reality. On training expenditure, the Price Waterhouse Cranfield Study (Gunnigle,1992) shows that 37 per cent of Irish organisations spent 2 per cent or less on training, with another 39 per cent not aware of how much they spent. Irish-owned companies spent significantly less on training than American/Japanese or European companies. A large proportion of grant support (48 per cent in Irish companies) was spent on manual skills training, which falls into the specific training category. However, expenditure levels have increased over recent years and there does appear to be an intention to make further increases in the coming years (Garavan, 1992).

The National Development Plan

The general insight into training, provided by these reports, has not changed significantly in recent years, and the overall outlook has been a decidedly negative one. At Government level, an important emphasis is currently being placed on the area of human resources. The Irish National Development Plan (1994-1999) allocated £3,108 million to this area, out of an approximate total of £20,000 million. The education, training and development programmes to be co-financed by the State, public bodies and EU aid will be focused on the following areas:

- initial education and training;
- continuing training for the employed and unemployed;
- training for the disadvantaged.

According to FÁS, however, the vast amount of this money will go towards training and educating the unemployed and the young. The reason for this is that the State (through FÁS) ultimately sees training of the employed as the responsibility of industry itself. Giving money to industry for training, is a "transfer of resources of profit takers (i.e. industry)". The Government, it is argued, cannot justify such an exchequer transfer, but can justify training the young and unemployed.

The ESF Survey

The most recent survey that provides an insight into training activity and attitudes in Irish business, was carried out under the ESF Programme Evaluation Unit in 1993, and surveyed over 200 companies. It paints a slightly more positive picture of training in Ireland. The main theme to emerge from this survey is that, while there is a substantial and commendable amount of training going on in Irish industry, there are limited systems in place to maximise the benefits of investment in training. The evidence for this is the significant lack of basic procedures, e.g. training needs analysis, planning, employee appraisal or budgeting. This is reinforced by the apparent lack of certification of employee training and the low rate of employer contact with local educational establishments.

The following are some of the main results of the survey: Concerning current training practice, 86 per cent of companies provided training for their employees; however, 73 per cent did not have a training budget. This would reinforce the view that, while employers claim to train their employees, there is a significant lack of planning or structure to the training being provided. Of the companies that did not provide training, the reasons given were that their company was too small, some admitted to "not having considered training", and other reasons given were specific to the companies involved. Overall, the results of the survey indicated a lack of a strategic approach to training.

The key factors that motivate employers to train are to improve quality, improve production and achieve recognised production standards. It follows, therefore, that the most common types of training carried out are quality training, safety training, training for new technology, "sitting by Nellie" (i.e. learning by observing a more experienced colleague at work), and specific training.

Companies were asked to identify the single most important challenge for the next five years. For the majority, it was the area of growth/expansion, while other important areas were survival, foreign competition, domestic competition and quality. It is interesting to note that of those who identified survival as the single most important challenge 80 per cent claim that they provide employee training, yet 57 per cent had no training plan, while 83 per cent had no training budget.

Concerning contact with training agencies, the majority of the contact was with FÁS and the IDA (84 per cent and 48 per cent respectively). There appears to be limited awareness of the activites and services of other agencies. Thirty per cent of those who have contact with FÁS are simply talking to a FÁS representative or seeking advice. Fifty-seven per cent of the respondents had used a private training agency in the last year — for 37 per cent the agency actually designed and delivered the training event. One may conclude from this group of surveys that attitudes to training are less than positive at industrial level.

COSTS AND BENEFITS OF TRAINING AND DEVELOPMENT

The espousal of particular philosophical positions may be influenced by varying perceptions of the costs and benefits associated with training and development. Here an overview of the costs and benefits of training and development is outlined both from the organisational and the individual perspective.

Initially, we shall concentrate on costs, bearing in mind that these have a double-edged connotation; that is, while training and development inevitably involves financial outlay, it is spurious to consider this without also taking into account the costs associated with too little, or indeed, no training or opportunity cost of releasing workers for training.

Costs of Training/Development

Training costs have been defined as those deliberately incurred by an organisation to facilitate learning, with the expressed intention of reducing learning costs (Reid et al, 1992). They may be segregated into two specific types:

1. Fixed costs — those that remain constant despite the amount of training and development that is provided, such as the maintenance of a training centre, salaries of permanent training staff, etc.

2. Variable costs — those that vary in accordance with the amount of training and development provided, such as consumable materials, course fees and expenses and the loss of production.

Costs of Inadequate/No Training

Providing inadequate training and development, or indeed none at all, can carry severe consequences for any organisation. Prais (1991) adopts this approach when considering national training strategies. He enumerates the costs of a lack of investment in training and development in the following terms:

- Lack of adequately trained personnel, in particular intermediate skilled staff responsible for the running and administration of a wide range of activities. Prais examined similar plants in a number of industries. In each one, because of a lack of training at the intermediate levels, senior personnel had to spend much longer on basic chores, to the detriment of strategic development and other more relevant tasks.

- Lack of skilled personnel on production lines. His research showed that when machines broke down the employees manning the line were usually unable to rectify mistakes and had to wait for skilled maintenance to arrive — so increasing downtime.

- Lack of people with technological education and skills. Without people who possess technological education and skills, manufacturing flexibility cannot be achieved. In a survey of European companies, De Meyer and Ferdows (1991) demonstrates that only four European companies had any kind of integrated computer-aided design (CAD) and computer-aided manufacturing (CAM) equipment.

- Lack of an educated workforce: Two-thirds of companies in the survey reported that only top and middle management understood the strategies, goals and objectives of their companies.

Other costs of not training include the following:

- poor productivity and under-utilisation of equipment and machinery;

- increases in rejects, losses, material wastage, and damage to equipment and machinery;

- reduced capability for timely filling of orders, leading to adverse effects on customer service, increased customer complaints and ultimately to lower sales;

- lack of awareness of health and safety procedures, possibly resulting in injuries, fatalities and expensive compensatory claims;

- poorly developed problem-solving and decision-making skills perpetuating "management by crisis" and "firefighting";

- employees inadequately prepared for jobs, resulting in job dissatisfaction and low morale; and

- new staff experiencing induction crises, increasing the propensity towards high absenteeism and staff turnover.

Reid et al (1992) bracket many of these as "learning costs" attributed, in the absence of training and development, to a process of unplanned learning experiences.

In any case, it is not difficult to imagine how consequences such as these, with their obvious bottom-line financial repercussions, can place a critically severe strain on the viability and survival of any organisation.

Benefits of Training and Development

Although an unambiguous and direct causal link between training and development and improved organisational performance has yet to be conclusively demonstrated, there is widespread agreement about the perceived benefits of high levels of training and development activity. It should be pointed out, however, that these perceived benefits will depend on the purpose for which training and development is undertaken. McEvoy and Butler (1990) suggests four sets of dualisms.

1. *Substantive versus Symbolic*. Is training and development intended to meet an objective skill gap or does it constitute a cultural symbol?

2. *External versus Internal*. Is training and development intended to address external behaviour such as physical motor skills or is it focused on internal psychological processes such as attitudes and values?

3. *Change versus Results*. Is the purpose of training and development to be perceived in terms of behaviour/attitude change or does it relate to observable results?

4. *Work versus People*. Is the training and development given to those who need it to improve their performance in a given area, or is it given as a reward to those who have already demonstrated good performance?

The benefits of training and development, having regard to its explicit or implicit purposes, can be considered at both individual and organisational levels.

Individual Benefits

Benefits at an individual level may be considered under two main categories: intrinsic and extrinsic.

Intrinsic benefits are classed as "non-tangible" and may be associated with the achievement of personal satisfaction. As such, the provision of training to an individual can give rise to intrinsic benefits in a variety of ways, including:

- enhanced status in the workplace;

- opportunities to fully develop talents and abilities;

- greater confidence in the performance of work;

- feeling of increased usefulness and "belonging" in the organisation;

- sensing personal achievement, growth and advancement;

- perceived recognition.

Extrinsic benefits may be seen in terms of their contribution towards the attainment of more tangible rewards, such as:

- increased earning capabilities (from the acquisition of additional skills, improved productivity performance, etc.);

- improved internal/external job mobility and labour market value;

- greater security of employment;

- enhanced promotion prospects.

Organisational Benefits

The previous individual benefits, both intrinsic and extrinsic, are probably catalysts for improving workforce morale and motivation, thus providing benefits for the organisation into the bargain. A significant reduction in the costs of insufficient or no training, as previously outlined, may also be reasonably put forward as a benefit of training in this context.

Additionally, a range of further benefits can be identified, among the most important being:

- improved ability to tackle the challenges imposed by ongoing and rapid changes in technology, work organisation and the external environment;

- improved capacity to cope with the intensity of national and international competitive conditions;

- critical support available for the successful implementation of a series of broad human resource management strategies, policies and
activities;

- increased prospects of organisational synergy and coalescence producing positive outcomes above those anticipated;

- greater workforce flexibility, particularly where multi-skilling
strategies are pursued.

In essence, the benefits of training and development may be summarised
by the unique opportunity presented for harmonising the development of
individuals and the organisation itself. Unfortunately, the key to this opportunity has remained unturned in far too many cases.

PLAN OF THE BOOK

This book revolves around five overall themes: (a) concepts and issues
related to training and development as a discipline; (b) the contribution
of training and development at national and organisational levels and the
factors determining the shape and nature of training and development in
the future; (c) the management and organisation of the training and development function; (d) the operation of training at national level; and
finally, (e) design and delivery of learning events.

In Part 1 we examine key concepts and issues in training and development, the economics of training and development, the historical evolution of training and development in Ireland and contemporary trends in
management and organisations affecting training.

In Part 2 we focus on the issues involved in establishing and managing a training and development function within the organisation. This
includes an examination of the role of key stakeholders within and external to the organisation, the formulation of training and development
policies and plans and strategic-led training and development.

In Part 3 we focus on the design and delivery of learning events. We
consider developments in learning theory and its implications for learning design, delivery and evaluation. Contemporary issues such as accelerated learning, the learning organisation and the learning community
are considered.

The book recognises that training and development can be understood in at least two different ways. First of all, it can be viewed as an
operational systematic activity concentrating on the design, delivery and
evaluation of training and development. The second perspective is much
broader, focusing on the management of training and development in an
organisational and national context with the consideration of learning in
a more holistic fashion. We adopt the broader perspective in this book.

2

THE ECONOMIC DIMENSIONS
OF TRAINING AND DEVELOPMENT

INTRODUCTION AND LEARNING OBJECTIVES

This chapter aims to introduce training and development in an economic context and specifically within the labour market. The policies associated with training and development can be seen as a specific set of responses to the way labour markets operate. This important relationship has been underplayed in many training and development texts, yet it is of significance. This chapter aims to address that gap. After reading this chapter you will understand:

♦ the link between education, training and development and economic performance;

♦ the present state of training and development in Ireland;

♦ the usefulness of an economic analysis of training and development;

♦ the contribution of the institutional perspective as an explanation of the role of education, training and development;

♦ alternative theoretical economic models of training and development.

TRAINING AND DEVELOPMENT IN IRELAND: SOME GENERAL TRENDS

In order to put our discussion of economic issues in context a summary of the Irish training and development situation is necessary. A number of general statements can be made.

There is a common view that Ireland lags behind other countries in the provision of vocational and educational training (VET). This finding is well documented in many publications, for example, the Roche and Tansey Report (1992), reports from international organisations such as the OECD (1990) and in many smaller research reports. Figure 2.1 shows the estimated share of young people aged 14-24 in education in member states of the EU and Figure 2.2 shows the participation of 16-18 year olds in education or training. These figures point to wide discrep-

ancies in educational attainment levels between countries, even where
they are offset, to some extent, by part-time training received in employment. However the data show that Ireland does indeed lag behind
many of her European neighbours with the exception perhaps of the UK.

**Figure 2.1: 16–18-Year-Olds Participating in Education or
Training in the Member States 1985–86**

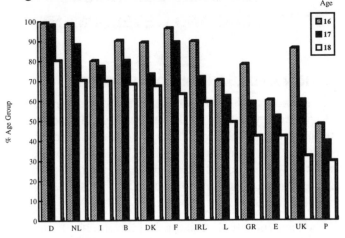

UK = 1986–87; Italy, Portugal = 1987–88
Source: Commission of the EC, *Employment in Europe,* Brussels, 1990, p. 113.

**Figure 2.2: Share of Young People in Education in the
Member States, 1988**

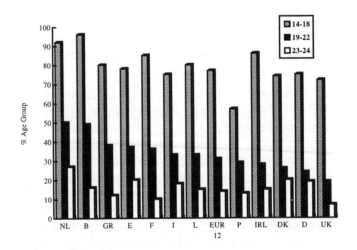

Source: Commission of the EC, *Employment in Europe,* Brussels, 1990, p. 113.

The VET system in Ireland has led to a significant increase in some forms of training activity. Labour force surveys indicate that there has been some improvement in the proportion of employees receiving job-related training.

Ireland, like the UK, has a bias towards academic achievement rather than towards more broadly based vocational and educational training. Enrolments in third-level institutions have increased significantly during the 1980s and early 1990s. This suggests that the bias towards education rather than training remains a strong feature of the Irish VET system. Figure 2.3 shows that in Ireland the number of full time third-level student numbers has increased steadily between 1984 and 1990.

Figure 2.3: Full-Time Third-Level Student Numbers 1984/85 to 1989/90

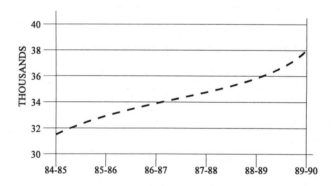

Source: Higher Education Authority Report (1990), Accounts and Student Statistics 1989/1990.

Ireland has a relatively large number of workers receiving no training or training of very low quality leading to no qualifications or at best poor qualifications. The evidence suggests that as much as 45 per cent of the workforce receive no training at all. There is evidence to suggest that Ireland has, in some cases, encouraged low minimum training standards rather than higher quality training. This is evident at the highest levels in the organisation. In a survey by Roche and Tansey (1992) the chief executives of the 1,000 largest private sector companies ranked technical (14 per cent) and production management (6 per cent) training needs of top managers relatively low in terms of overall priority. The study concluded that such results were indicative of a complacency about technological matters and, moreover, that many Irish managers were deemed to be poor judges of their own training requirements. McIver (1992) demonstrates that critical skill deficiencies exist in the Irish economy at all levels.

The level of company investment in training has not increased significantly. Stokes, Kennedy and Crowley (1993) found the number of companies planning to increase their spending on staff training had decreased marginally (-1 per cent). They did, however, find that a considerable number of employers planned to maintain their level of spending on training. This suggests a situation of relative stability, but the trend was clearly out of line with the optimistic views expressed by employers about the future.

THEORIES OF THE LABOUR MARKET

There are many theoretical perspectives on the operation of the labour market. However, for our purposes we will focus on three: the competitive labour market, institutional and radical perspectives.

The Competitive Labour Market Perspective

The basis of this model is neo-classical economics. Its starting point is that our resources are scarce in relation to our wants, and therefore we have to make choices about their allocation. In making these choices we act in a rational way. The process of rational individual maximisation works this way:

- Individuals have an ordered set of preferences.

- Individuals act to maximise economic well-being in the light of their preference schedule.

- Individual's preference schedules are independent of those of other individuals. This means that A is not influenced by the preference schedules of B when ordering preferences.

The model basically predicts that wage rates are determined by the marginal productivity of labour, and the number of workers employed will vary universally with the wage rate. The marginal revenue productivity of labour is the increase in total revenue which occurs when one extra unit of labour is employed. From a training and development perspective, the model argues that cost-minimising organisations face a number of decisions: the amount of search to be undertaken in the labour market to acquire staff, how to acquire and retain skills in the workforce and how to obtain and maintain desired effort levels. It also postulates that training and development will only be adopted by rational organisations where the ratio of benefits to costs exceeds that of other approaches. This implies that there may be considerable variety in organisations since the costs and benefits of different policy options are contingent on features of the organisation and the labour market.

The model may operate best in a loose, unskilled external labour market where search costs are low due to the plentiful supply of unskilled labour relative to that of skilled workers. Employees are therefore more likely to accept high labour turnover in preference to high levels of training. In the case of skilled employees the model predicts that structured internal labour markets will exist. Employers are more likely to contribute to the costs of training of skilled employees. Generally the perception is that training and development policies must result in net cost reductions to the organisation.

The Institutional Perspective

There have been many refinements of the competitive model with the result that there are considerable overlaps with institutional theories. However, the main point of departure is the rejection of individual maximising behaviour by the institutional perspective. The institutional argument is that preferences are not independent but interdependent. Organisations make decisions by taking into account the actions of others. Organisations also have to consider how others will respond to specific strategies and tactics. The institutional perspective accepts that employers need to retain skills, etc., but it places more emphasis on the role of group norms, customs and collective power. An institutional perspective on training and development would see it as a means of co-opting workers into the culture and norms of the organisation. This may include programmes of multi-skilling and management development. Training and development is viewed as an efficiency-oriented response to the conflict that exists between external demands for organisational flexibility and the inefficiencies within the internal labour market. It does not assume, however, that those training and development policies will be successfully implemented because the institutional perspective stresses the role of different stakeholders in the implementation process.

The Radical Perspective

This perspective takes as its starting point class differences. Capitalists have a class interest in weakening workers' capacity to resist exploitation. This perspective postulates that capitalists will reduce the skill content of jobs with the result that employees are easily replaced and it transfers knowledge and control of the production process. Braverman (1974) is a key exponent of this perspective. Braverman argues that the development of scientific management has deskilled jobs and thereby reduced the amount of control over effort levels that workers and trade unions can exert. Edwards (1975), on the other hand, argues that organisations set up internal labour markets based on job ladders, narrow task specialisation and differentiation. There is also a distinction between primary and secondary labour markets. Workers in the primary labour market enjoy relatively good pay, benefits and working conditions and receive considerable amounts of training. Workers in the secondary labour market are paid low wages, receive few fringe benefits, have little job security and receive little or no training.

The radical perspective views training and development as a strategy for extending managerial control over employees. However, the need to divide workers in order for this to happen means that some must gain at the expense of others. The primary workers are most likely to be the beneficiaries. Beardwell and Holden (1994) argue that these benefits may be transitory because the attempt to divide into primary and secondary markets may be a precursor to the redesign and regrading of primary sector jobs. Workers in the secondary sector are less likely to receive training and development and are therefore the main losers.

EDUCATION, TRAINING, DEVELOPMENT AND ECONOMIC PERFORMANCE

The human capital perspective, which we will consider later, treats education, training and development as an investment and emphasises the direct impact of skill creation on productivity. Mojset (1991) identifies the role of education and training systems in the context of a national system of innovation.

Research evidence (Arrow, 1962; Denison, 1967) supports the view that economic success depends on the ability of firms to develop more advanced production processes. The argument is made that this can only occur if accompanied by a corresponding development of workforce and management skills. Research suggests that improvements in the quality of labour, due mainly to education and training initiatives, contribute up to one-quarter of the rate of growth of national income with an average contribution of just under one-tenth. Barro (1991), reporting on a 98-country study, found that low-income countries tend to catch up with high income countries if they have high human capital investment per person in relation to their per capita GDP.

At the level of the individual there is also strong evidence of the influence of high education and training attainment. NESC Report No. 95 (1993) points out that there is a much higher likelihood of long term unemployment for those holding no qualification. The core of the long-term unemployed in Ireland have no formal school qualifications. Research by the OECD (1990) demonstrates that those in the labour force with incomplete upper secondary education and no formal training are more likely to be unemployed.

The recognition of this potential link between investment in education and training initiatives and economic development has prompted many EU countries to be concerned with policy reform in this area. Examples of such policy initiatives include putting greater emphasis on curriculum assessment and certification, an intensive promotion of increased private sector training both on and off the job, as well as many school-to-work transition initiatives.

These initiatives have in some cases produced negative outcomes. Specifically, increased spending on training and development does not yield any significant changes in work practices and management. Employers in some cases still demonstrate a preference for firm-specific training and an unwillingness to share the cost of training and development initiatives. In many cases within the EU the state is generally perceived as having a co-ordinating function in setting up sector-specific training initiatives and in taking an active role in ensuring that skill requirements beyond those relevant to the workplace are met.

It is argued that effective economic training produces many significant benefits. Training can be defined as economic where it is undertaken with the sole purpose of achieving an economic return. Such economic training can be differentiated from training provided to meet objectives such as socialisation, cultural and holistic objectives. Training at a national level may be provided to deal with unemployment or social problems.

Roche and Tansey (1992) identify six benefits of a high level of investment in economic training:

1. It promotes national economic development by ensuring that the potential for national economic growth is optimised. Insufficient training or a poor level of training can lead to skill shortages which in turn inhibit the growth of the economy.

2. Economic training improves individual productivity. This relationship may apply not only to shop-floor employees but also to supervisory and executive management grades.

3. Economic training has the potential to improve an industry's adaptability and its capacity to absorb changes in product and process technologies. It is generally accepted that industrial capability will be significantly enhanced by the range and depth of skills proposed as each level of operations is expanded.

4. Extensive economic training facilitates the introduction of more advanced physical capital. Many commentators view the introduction of

advanced manufacturing technology as labour-displacing. However, the evidence signifies that the relationship is not that simple. Economists now argue that the potential for factor substitution within modern industry is significantly limited. Labour and physical capital tend therefore to be complementary rather than substitutive.

5. The existence of a pool of highly skilled labour at all levels is used as a mechanism to attract foreign industry to Ireland. It is often cited by foreign investors as a reason for locating in Ireland.

6. A skilled labour force will become a significant differentiation factor within a Single Market.

THE TRAINING/ECONOMIC GROWTH LINK — SOME RELATIONSHIPS

Let us start with a general statement. The economic analysis of training and development, and the theoretical underpinning of training policies at national level, have received little attention from economists (see Schultz, 1963; Becker, 1962; and Mincer, 1974). Conventional economic analysis of the contribution of training and development used (a) economic concepts such as the market failure arising from firms that fail to train because of other firms poaching or threatening to poach trained workers; and (b) economic growth theories to trace the link between education and training and output, growth and productivity. This approach is still popular and one we will deal with later. Denison (1967) suggested that education and training made only a comparatively small contribution to post-war European economic growth. Subsequent research by Romer (1986) and Lucas (1988) suggests that the cumulative impact of investment in human capital may be more significant.

In the 1950s it was generally accepted that economic growth was proportional to the size of the physical capital stock, so that increments in the stock of capital would automatically result in higher growth rates. These early models resulted in two policy prescriptions: (a) increase the flow of national savings; and (b) use these funds to increase the economy's physical capital stock. They paid little attention to the role of labour quality or training. Labour was generally characterised as an undifferentiated quantity, a simple factor input.

The 1960s witnessed a revival of interest in human capital as a primary source of economic growth. Labour ceased to be viewed as an undifferentiated factor input. Instead it was accepted that labour quality and productivity could be increased by investment in education and training initiatives. Some of the research is worthy of consideration.

Arrow (1962), focusing on technological change, viewed new machinery as a vehicle of progress, through the embodiment of learning from experience. The experience derived in production means that successive vintages of machinery have lower manning requirements. The argument goes, then, that there are increasing returns to output. Within Arrow's model, education and training has a major role to play. Technical training is the means whereby past and present production experience is mediated to the present and future workforce. If successive vintages of machinery are more technically advanced this assumes a labour force which is capable of utilising such machinery. Kadlor and Mirlees (1981) advocate that a continuous upgrading of the labour force is likely to be required to absorb the new investment.

Romer (1986) has attempted to conceptualise the role of knowledge, and therefore, by implication, the contribution of training and development to economic growth. In Romer's model profit-seeking, forward-looking organisations and individuals invest in knowledge which is a factor of production. Because private investment in knowledge is likely to have external effects, i.e. it becomes a public good, the production of knowledge can lead to an increasing return on physical capital and an increasing role of economic growth. Romer (1986) views education and training as the means which facilitate individual investment in knowledge production.

Lucas (1988) also emphasises the external effects of investment in human capital. He argues that human capital investment in aggregate has an effect on productivity, but individuals, in making their own personal decision as to how much human capital to accumulate, do not take this into account, since their own decision will have only a minimal impact on the aggregate. Lucas further postulates that if there are such external effects then employees at the same level of human capital will have higher marginal productivity in an environment characterised by generally high levels of human capital. He also states that an economy could maintain a growth rate advantage relative to another economy to the extent that it had a greater investment in training and learning-by-doing.

This analysis suggests a significant positive relationship between the initial stock of education and training input and subsequent growth performance in an economy.

THE MATCHING PLANT FINDINGS

Many of the general economic growth theories on the link between training and development and productivity are considered conceptually weak. An alternative methodology is the matching plant technique. This involves a series of matched plant comparisons across different countries. While this is a little-used methodology in the Irish context, one significant study by Hitchins and Birnie (1993) involved a three-plant comparison between Ireland, Denmark and the Netherlands. A number of findings were highlighted:

- There was a significant shortfall in terms of comparative physical productivity, i.e. the volume or number of units of output per employee.

- All three Irish plants had lower value added per head than their continental counterparts.

- The products of the Irish firms were generally of a lower quality than those of the Danish/Dutch counterparts. This finding is consistent with other studies of small firms in Ireland.

- The Irish sample was characterised by a weaker capacity to innovate.

- The level of formal skills was similar to the continental comparisons. However the findings demonstrated that Danish in-company training was superior to that of the Irish counterparts.

- There were also constraints on the supply of certain specialised and higher skills in the Irish firms. Irish managers were as well-qualified as their counterparts but there was an undue reliance on out-of-date product and company strategies.

Hitchins and Birnie (1993) concluded that certain types of specialised skills seemed to be missing especially in areas such as R&D, design and marketing. They also pointed out that it is difficult to discern the particular effect of education and training on economic performance. The quality of the labour force and of management are linked to particular cultural, institutional and political factors. Investment in research and development, business investment in education and innovation are related to the state of the economy, industrial policy, education policy and many other factors.

The matching plant studies do however demonstrate that lower quality skills, less attention to detail, inadequate supervision and quality control procedures, and less skilled management with poorer marketing and financial skills all affect the quality of the Irish product.

EDUCATION AND TRAINING: AN INSTITUTIONAL APPROACH

Finegold and Soskice (1988) can be credited with an institutional critique of the role of education and training in an economy. Their seminal article, "The Failure of Training in Britain", argues that there is a two-way relationship between education and training and the economy. They argue that:

> Britain's failure to educate and train its workforce to the same level as its international competitors has been both a product and a cause of the nation's poor relative economic performance. . . . The best way to visualise this argument is to see Britain as trapped in a low-skills equilibrium in which the majority of enterprises staffed by poorly trained managers and workers produce low quality goods and services. The term equilibrium is used to denote a self-reinforcing network of societal and state institutions which interact to stifle the demand for improvements in skill levels.

Finegold and Soskice (1988) explain this low skills equilibrium in terms of four variables:

1. A post-war political consensus in favour of a gradual expansion of general and academic education and the delegation of training largely to employers.

2. An inappropriate policy-making structure characterised by a weak central bureaucracy and decentralisation of power throughout the education and training system.

3. An attenuated role for the vocational element in the education and training system as a whole due to the lower status accorded to non-academic education. The domination of central bureaucracies by those with no background in, or empathy with, vocational education, and the equation of training with apprenticeships has led to rigidities in overall training provision.

4. A range of interrelated aspects of the UK's industrial and economic structure, which in combination diminish both the demand for and supply of education and training. They identified these as:

   • comparatively weak management, with an underemphasis on technical skills and production and an overemphasis on accounting;

   • a lack of cohesion and central control in both the employer and employee organisations, which leaves them with effective incentives or sanctions in relation to education/training;

   • a strong concentration of British industry on standardised price-elastic products and a limited presence in, and poorer than average trade performance in, skill- and innovation-intensive products — these features being recently exacerbated by a trend towards subcontracting of skilled maintenance work and the deskilling of work by new technologies;

- patterns of authority, work organisation, recruitment and career structure which are critical to an emphasis on long-term development.

The fundamental point of the Finegold and Soskice analysis is the two-way nature of the causation characterised by a vicious circle of low productivity and weak education and training systems. Low productivity is underpinned and reinforced by an inter-locking series of institutions and practices. Finegold (1991) has expanded the analysis to include the possible impact of corporate organisation sources of finance and competitive position.

The question arises whether this institutional critique has relevance to Ireland. NESC Report No. 95 (1993) suggests that many of its elements have application to the education and training system in Ireland. They suggest that an analysis of the industrial and sectoral structure of the Irish economy would lead to the conclusion that this structure interacts with Irish institutions to produce a variant of the low-skills equilibrium. The report concludes that Finegold and Soskice's analysis has major implications for future education and training policies. The key theme identified is the need for a strategic focus; this means policies related to particular sectors and sub-sectors, and to the specific role of training as one element in long-term development.

The institutional perspective is not without its limitations. One argument suggests that an analysis of education and training in this fashion is productionist in orientation, implying an instrumental and vocational view of the purpose of training and development. This argument is generally rejected. Countries with superior vocational training systems have education systems which provide a good general foundation. Furthermore, they have broad vocational training with a significant general educational requirement.

The institutional approach has also been criticised on the basis that it neglects the issue of access to education and equality of opportunity in favour of a narrower focus on improving skill levels. This criticism is rejected by commentators on the basis that the institutional perspective critically analyses the adequacy of education and training systems.

Heyes and Stuart (1994) have criticised the explanation on a number of points. Essentially they argue that Finegold and Soskice fail to examine the impact of workplace industrial relations on training issues. They also argue that analysis of the workplace fails to move beyond a stated belief in the efficiency of co-operative industrial relations in facilitating the adoption by firms of a high-skills strategy.

They also attack the theory on the basis that developments in production remain unexplained. The supply and the demand for skilled labour and the role that skill, characterised as a factor input, may play in the production of high quality goods has received too much focus. Heyes and Stuart argue that skill, unlike qualifications, is not a quantifiable variable. The underlying dynamic by which employees become skilled is difficult to explain using aggregate training data. Skill is better understood as the outcome of a social process rather than a factor input. Finegold and Soskice (1988) imply that management action is determined by a set of institutional constraints operating at the level of the national economy and within organisations. Heyes and Stuart (1994) argue that management strategy is better understood as encompassing a broad agenda related to the organisation of production and labour utilisation. Training is not simply a means of giving employees technical capabilities; it also is the means by which management seek to elicit the active co-operation of workers. There is much evidence that companies provide training designed to inculcate values and behaviour characteristics consistent with the corporate culture (Hendry, 1991; Sewell and Wilkinson, 1992).

THE MARKET FAILURE EXPLANATION

Within the context of the wider economy, company training possesses the characteristics of a collective rather than a private good. Trained workers are generally free to move from job to job; therefore, firms investing in their training cannot be certain of recouping their investment. Trained employees may leave the firm before the return of the training investment accrues. Similarly, it is argued that competitor firms may wish to gain advantage over those firms that provide enterprise training by poaching this skilled labour. It follows, therefore, that the personnel trained by one firm effectively become available to other firms through poaching. Since the economic benefits of enterprise training cannot be achieved with certainty by the firm providing the training, all firms will seek to poach the skilled workers they need rather than bearing the costs of training employees.

This greater incentive to poach rather than train can result in a generalised underprovision of investment in enterprise training, leading to subsequent skill shortages. Therefore, enterprise training may be subject to market failure. Three forms of failure can be identified.

First, individuals may be deterred from training and development because the capital market is imperfect. Put simply, it means that, because of existing costs, individuals cannot finance the training which they would be willing to undertake.

Second, there is the poaching explanation. This argument takes the line that firms fail to train because they fear that non-training firms will "poach" trained employees.

Third, employment contracts may restrict employers and employees from achieving an efficient outcome. There is a line of argument which suggests that an efficient outcome cannot be achieved without continual re-contracting. This is necessary in order to reflect unanticipated changes in the value of human capital.

Chapman (1993) suggests that firms will be divided into three groups:

1. Training firms that are willing to train their own workers. These will typically be high-wage firms and as a result are able to restrict poaching through an effective internal labour market.

2. Non-training firms that are discouraged from training because of the possibility of poaching. These firms will generally employ unskilled workers and are likely to recruit trained workers from the training firms.

3. Non-training firms that choose a low-skill labour force because they would never train their own employees even if no threat of poaching existed. These firms may be unavailable to provide training for a variety of reasons, i.e. small size, poor performance and insufficient internal staff to provide training. They are most likely to recruit their skilled worker requirements at a premium from other firms.

A recent study by the OECD (1990) reinforces the view that the market failure explanation still has application. It argued that private market-based decisions on the part of firms and individuals will lead to less than socially-optimum training. Furthermore, as the social benefit of a managerial increase in training investment would exceed the benefits to the firm, there will be considerable under-investment.

Roche and Tansey (1992) identify four other causes of market failure in the training context:

1. Trainees cannot afford to pay for general training; since organisations will refuse to bear general training costs for fear of poaching they transfer the costs to the trainee. These training costs can manifest themselves in several ways: rates of pay for business that are below the prevailing rate of the job when held by a skilled worker, and specific payments to employers for the training services provided. It is generally accepted, however, that young employees may become unwilling to subsist on the low pay given during the training period, especially if alternative employment opportunities exist.

2. Institutional barriers to the provision of general training. Where rates of pay for labour market entrants are high relative to the pay of existing experienced workers, firms will economise on the provision of

training. Roche and Tansey identify rigid pay relativities and minimum wage legislation as institutional factors inducing this outcome.

3. Industry structure research by Walsh (1994) demonstrates that large firms tend to spend a higher proportion of their total wage bill on training than smaller firms. Larger companies are more likely to train a greater proportion of their staff. Many explanations have been put forward for this higher incidence of training amongst larger companies. Among these are lower rates of employee turnover, extensive internal labour markets, better initial screening and selection procedures. Small firms on the other hand significantly under-train. There are approximately 6,500 small firms in Ireland accounting for 80 per cent of Irish industrial employees. This structure significantly handicaps the level of enterprise training in Ireland.

4. Geographical externalities: There is significant labour mobility between Ireland and Britain, to the extent that they effectively form a joint labour market. For highly trained and skilled workers there are many motives to emigrate, with the result that Ireland has experienced a significant brain drain, particularly in the graduate area.

The belief that market failure was extensive, and that such market failure led to skills shortages, significantly influenced the introduction of the levy/grant scheme under the Industrial Training Act 1967. Other countries introduced similar schemes. The objective of these schemes has been to correct the presumed market failure in enterprise training. Training grants were to be used to reward the providers of training, while non-recoverable levies would punish those firms that refused to train. The schemes hoped to eliminate skills shortages and enhance economic growth.

In Ireland the levy/grant scheme operated on the following terms: industrial firms typically paid training levies of 1 per cent to 1.5 per cent of total salary/wages annually. Firms could claim back up to 90 per cent of the nominal levy contributions if their training performance was deemed adequate as assessed by FÁS. The remaining 10 per cent of the levy was absorbed by FÁS. Overall, the levy/grant scheme became largely a paper transaction. Where training performance is deemed satisfactory, firms pay the net levy due. There have been a number of modifications in the scheme, with the result that participating firms now pay a net levy of approximately 0.11 per cent of annual payroll to FÁS. Two million pounds is raised annually from the net levy. The cumulative result of these modifications is that the levy/grant scheme has been largely dismantled.

The market failure explanation poses the question of what is the best solution. Even if it is taken as establishing that market failure occurs, and that this results in insufficient training provision, there is the fundamental question as to which types of training should be encouraged. The alternatives are many. Should it be specific or general training? On- or off-the-job training? Supervisory or operative training rather than vocational training? There is also much choice in the way in which market failure should be addressed. Many policy options have been suggested, e.g. encouraging labour mobility, reducing state intervention, establishing an appropriate institutional framework.

The market failure explanation has many followers, largely because it puts forward a good reason why the market might under-provide for training and development. Its primary implication is that some form of market intervention might solve the under-provision problem. The exact nature of this intervention is open to question with many possible policy prerequisites.

Recent studies by Elias and Healey (1994) and Metcalf et al (1994) cast doubt on the market failure explanation and in particular the poaching hypothesis. Elias and Healey found that a significant proportion of employer-provided training is firm-specific. This means that employer-provided training should be associated with lower levels of outward mobility for the organisation providing it. Indeed, they found that formal training leads to a substantial reduction in outward mobility from the employer providing the training. The lack of investment in general training, however, may be because of its potential to increase the mobility of employees.

Metcalf et al (1994) found that whilst the possibility of poaching was acknowledged by many employers, most saw it as a necessary risk and that training their employees was more important. However, this fear appeared to reduce support for training, particularly for less skilled employees. Small employers seemed more prone to linking training and increased staff turnover.

SPECIFIC ECONOMIC THEORIES OF TRAINING

There are many economic theories which are useful to our understanding of how individuals choose whether to train, or how they choose a job with a particular training context, and how firms decide on labour skills and recruitment methods. We will explore some of these theories next.

Human Capital Theory

Human capital theory is generally regarded as the main basis for the modern economic analysis of training and development. It has a long history and can be traced back to the writings of Adam Smith (1776). The main elements of this theory are as follows:

- Individuals are wealth maximisers who will calculate a discounted net present value for different training and development options and base their choice on the maximum from these calculations.

- Training is distinguished by its portability between firms. Becker (1962) makes a distinction between general and specific training. General training is distinguished by its applicability to many employers. Economic theory would in general suggest that employers will not pay for general training because they cannot hope to reap a return on their investment. Therefore the cost of general training will be borne by employees. Specific training is defined as acquisition of a skill valuable to one employer. Economic theory, in general, argues that the employer will have to pay for this training, since the employee is acquiring a skill with no external value or reward.

- Wages will be determined by individual human capital which depends on education, training and job experience.

Becker argues, in contrast to the market failure explanation, that the incidence of training costs will be determined by the type of training undertaken by the firm. He postulates that rational employers will only invest in training where the net present value of the exchanged productivity, resulting from training at minimum, equals discounted training costs, both direct and indirect. Direct training costs arise from the provision of formal, in-house and off-the-job training activities whereas indirect costs are related to output foregone in the process of training. The incidence of these training costs depends on whether it is general or specific training.

Specific training is unique to the firm and of little use to competitors. There is no external market for this training so the possibility of poaching does not arise. Specific training can therefore be characterised as a private good. In contrast, the enhanced productivity of general training is of value to other firms. Generally-trained employees are likely to be poached by competitors who are able to offer them higher wages. It follows, then, that firms will seek to avoid the costs of general training since they can not be sure of reaping the benefits. General training is therefore said to be a collective good. Becker argues that it is the trainees who pay for training because of the low wages they receive. Apprenticeship schemes are a good example of this principle in operation.

There have been a number of modifications of the basic model. One model basically advocates that labour market entrants face a two-period time horizon. In the first period they make a decision whether or not to train. The model assumes full employment in all labour markets and that all trained workers take up skilled employment. It also assumes that all labour market entrants are homogeneous in all relevant respects but one. They differ in terms of their subjective rates of discount, i.e. individuals with a low discount rate will train, and those with a high discount rate will job search, all things being equal.

Another variation of the human capital theory allows for the possibility that all types of workers may become unemployed because of job rationing. This variation has three essential elements. First, workers who enter training are not allowed to job search. Second, the training opportunities are subsidised in the form of an allowance to the trainee. Third, at the end of the training period, the opportunity for employment is enhanced for those who participated.

Human capital theory is not without its critics. The segmentation of training costs into general and specific is considered rigid. Roche and Tansey (1992) see them best treated as polar opposites, with real-world enterprise training lying on a continuum between the two. Most organisational training interventions include elements of both general and specific training. It follows, then, that the costs of training could be shared between employers and employees in proportion to their expected relative shares on the final return.

Another major issue relates to the variation in skills that might be acquired. The skills could be technical with specific job requirements or they could be supervisory and management skills which are partly technical but may also be acquired through job experience which cannot be acquired off the job. There is little explanation in human capital theory of the different forms of job training that can take place and why some of it is characterised as specific and some as general. Access to training and development in the form of segmented labour markets has largely been ignored. Indeed, there are considerable doubts about the application of human capital theory to segmented labour market situations.

A further criticism of human capital theory concerns its lack of any institutional content. In particular, trade unions have been largely ignored in the analysis of human capital while the firm is simplistically treated as an input-output mechanism. Given these criticisms it is now generally accepted that human capital theory on its own is not a sufficient explanation.

Roche and Tansey (1992) characterise Becker's formulation as excessively schematic, but agree that it casts significant doubt both on the extent and focus of market failure in enterprise training. They suggest two reasons.

First, if firms are prepared to finance the full costs of specific training in anticipation of capturing the full rate of return on such investments, then there can be no significant under-investment in specific training. Second, if the costs of specific training are imposed on trainees themselves, then it is impossible for firms to under-invest in general training, since they will refuse to bear general training costs in any set of circumstances. They conclude that the market failure explanation may overstate the extent to which firms will under-train, hence the need to consider failure reasons beyond the parameters of the individual firms.

Transaction Cost Models and Contracts

Hashimoto (1981) has made a significant contribution here. He uses the concept of transaction costs to explain the sharing of training costs and benefits between employees and firms. The basic hypothesis is that we should expect the division of costs and benefits of training to be shared by firms and employees. The actual sharing of costs and benefits will depend on the type of training provided by the firm. This model suggests three possible mechanisms for the sharing of costs and benefits:

1. Firms may fix wages to achieve an agreed share of costs and benefits.

2. Firms and employees may rely on some kind of observable prediction of productivity to base the sharing; or

3. Firms may formulate contracts which put restrictions on employees leaving the firm once trained.

Labour contract theory, which is a variant of the transaction costs models, suggests that information of many sorts will influence the wage–employment outcome. This outcome in turn will indirectly influence training and development decisions. Implicit labour contract theory is based on four key assumptions: (a) employees are risk-averse, (b) employers are risk-neutral, (c) the price of labour varies over time, and (d) employees have a reservation wage. The effects of this implicit contract may be illustrated as follows: If employees and firms have an implicit contract which in some way reduces labour turnover, with employees more reluctant to leave the firm and the firm more reluctant to fire because of hiring costs and the possibility of litigation, then the firm and employees may be inclined towards training which increases productivity within the firm even if such training also has a degree of portability.

Information, Signalling and Screening Models

Spence's work (1973; 1974) is considered the seminal approach on the concept of signalling. He describes the job hiring process as a lottery for both employee and employer. The employee will normally be able to acquire many details about the employer based on reputation, size, pub-

lished documents, etc. On the other hand the employer is more restricted. He will be able to observe fixed attributes such as age, sex, etc.
and other variable attributes which employers can control. These are
referred to as signals. The Spence model is based on five assumptions:
(a) workers can be categorised into those with high productivities and
those with low productivities; (b) education, training and development
signals can be acquired at different costs for both categories of workers;
(c) firms cannot distinguish high- from low-productivity employees before hiring takes place; (d) there is no discounting; and finally, (e) employees and employers are risk-neutral. Where training or education is a
signalling device workers will have an incentive to undertake training
and education even where no actual productivity gains occur.

Structural Models

These represent some of the less well developed theoretical aspects of
training. There are a number of developments worth noting under this
heading. The first relates to the distinction between an occupational labour market (OLM) and an internal labour market (ILM). OLMs depend
on certifiable knowledge and a market for portable labour skills. ILMs
are based on a structured job grouping in which employers recruit at
certain points of entry with a preference for internal promotions. There
are several arguments that favour OLMs as an appropriate labour market
structure for the procurement of training. The emphasis of ILMs on
specific rather than general skills may induce firms to reduce training
costs by limiting the range, depth and accessibility of the training which
they provide relative to the training for regulated apprenticeships and
industry-wide skill qualifications.

Further dimensions refer to the concept of labour market segmentation, i.e. the division of labour markets into primary and secondary. Jobs
in the primary labour market have high wage, good working conditions,
employment stability, job security, workplace rights and privileges, and
good chances of job progression. Secondary jobs lack these advantages.
There is strong empirical evidence to support the view that there is limited access to training opportunities in the secondary labour market.
Ashton, Maguire and Spilsbury (1990) demonstrate that, whereas higher
occupational orders or segments receive formal training over a long period of time, those in the lower segments receive little or no formal
training.

Chapman (1993) points out that labour market structures are partly
exogenous to the labour market but are also dependent on government
policy and legislation covering issues such as certification, equal opportunities and trade unions, etc. The labour market structure, being partially endogenous, develops in response to many external influences. He

warns that it is dangerous to see labour market structure from a single perspective, such as training. Policies based on such an assumption could lead to further anomalies and inefficiencies in the provision of training.

SUMMARY

This chapter has sought to highlight some of the economic dimensions of training and development. It will be apparent that there is a fundamental debate about the possible links between education and training and economic performance. It is clear that from a purely economic perspective supervisory or operative training is a complex issue. There are several agents to consider. First, individuals will undertake training decisions at several stages of the occupational life cycle. Second, a large part of training takes place within the firm as firms train workers for particular jobs. Third, training is an important area of policy intervention, and an entirely laissez-faire approach to education and training seems impracticable even in a highly market-oriented economy. In a mixed economy such as Ireland's, a government training policy of some sort is a necessary part of economic management. It is also difficult to imagine an entirely hands-off approach to training in the youth labour market in Ireland where there are many external factors in operation.

Economic theories of training cannot lay claim to an entirely integrated body of ideas. However, the contribution is significant, particularly ideas such as human capital, general and specific training, labour market structure and information.

3

THE FRAMEWORK OF NATIONAL VOCATIONAL EDUCATION AND TRAINING: ITS EVOLUTION AND STRUCTURE

INTRODUCTION AND LEARNING OBJECTIVES

This chapter aims to describe the evolution of the national system of training and vocational education in Ireland. The chapter provides a basic "map" of Ireland's training framework. Aspects of this framework will be explored in greater detail in Chapters Four and Five. After reading this chapter you will understand:

♦ the historical context within which the Irish national system of training and vocational education framework emerged

♦ the various legislative initiatives designed to establish such a framework

♦ the development of AnCO/FÁS as a national training agency

♦ the attitudes of Irish trade unions to the training and development of employees.

THE EVOLUTION OF NATIONAL TRAINING AND VOCATIONAL EDUCATION — POLICIES, STRATEGIES AND INSTITUTIONS

The Guild System

Historically, the major influence on Irish economic development was its isolated status within the British Empire. While Britain was benefiting from the industrial revolution in the latter part of the nineteenth century, Ireland was still trying to recover from the Great Famine. The death of almost 1.5 million people during the famine (1845-50), followed by mass emigration of at least another million, left the country desolate. Economic development was centred mainly in the northeast of the country, while the remainder of the island continued to carve out a meagre existence from agriculture. Despite these contrasts, the history of training in Ireland can, like Britain, be traced back as far as the *guild system*. The impact of the guild system in both countries explains the many similarities between their respective "training histories" (notably government attitudes, reform, etc.).

The Norman conquest of Britain in the eleventh century brought with it the guild system from mainland Europe, with merchants settling in Britain and using the guild system to control and regulate trades. This system was also to follow the invaders into Ireland and commence the British influence on trade and training in this country.

The guilds became self-contained and self-perpetuating through a process of controlled apprenticeships which provided each craft with a ready supply of trained craftsmen, but in numbers that left the power and control of each guild beyond question. Training became an integral feature of these apprenticeships. The apprentice was viewed as his master's property, bound by contract to serve his master faithfully for seven years, while simultaneously learning his trade. The origins of craft apprenticeships may be traced to this era.

The gradual decline of the guilds in mainland Europe and Great Britain was hastened by the rise of the factory system of production in the late eighteenth century. This system used the concept of the division of labour, combined with the mechanisation of the production process.

Industrialisation

The rapid growth of industrialisation, and its increased utilisation of the division of labour, gave rise to a form of work classification. Groups within the labour force became broadly categorised as managerial, clerical, technical, skilled, semi-skilled and unskilled employees. These categorisations also reflected the growing organisation of trade unions around particular groups of workers, for example, skilled/craft unions, semi-skilled and unskilled/general unions, clerical and technical/white collar unions. In overall terms, a recognisable training entity was most associated with craft apprenticeships, and this system was to become the central focus of the earliest initiatives in vocational education and training. In those dawning years, a combination of social background and solid education was held to bestow suitable leadership qualities on managerial staff while appropriate initial educational qualifications opened the door to other white collar positions. Formal training was largely considered superfluous for semi-skilled and unskilled employees.

Meanwhile, the changes taking place in the composition of the workforce and the nature of industry were soon to be reflected in governmental policy initiatives and in legislation. Ireland was still a predominantly agricultural country, a fact mirrored in the statutory reform which took place at the end of the nineteenth century.

In order to trace and fully understand the origins of vocational train-ing in Ireland, it is necessary to consider the beginnings of vocational education, since it was from initiatives in this area that vocational edu-cation and training, as we now know it in Ireland, gradually evolved.

Early Attempts at Reform

The City and Guilds of London was established in 1878 with the objec-tives of advancing technical and scientific education. Through an exami-nation system it initiated the development of courses and formulated recognised standards of attainment. Around this time, some significant developments had taken place in the large urban areas in Ireland such as Bolton Street College in Dublin and the Crawford Institute in Cork.

The British government responded to this change of emphasis by en-acting the Technical Instruction Act of 1891. This Act made provision for funding by local authorities for technical education in the schools, and was seen as a new departure towards satisfying the training needs of industry which heretofore had been largely privately funded. This was soon followed in Ireland by further legislation. The Agricultural and Technical Instruction (Irl) Act of 1898 introduced the first form of regu-lated apprenticeship in this country and specified that all training and instruction for apprentices should be given on the job.

However, the title of the Act reflected the structure of the Irish econ-omy at that time and it lacked detail on how to organise these apprentice-ships. It could be classified as aspirational in nature, rather than as di-rectly contributing to significant reforms, because overall it had little effect on apprenticeship training in technical or agricultural areas in Ire-land. Indeed, by the time of Irish independence in 1921, the training of apprentices was in a very poor state.

Irish independence set the development of the Irish economy in mo-tion, and a Government-appointed Commission on Technical Education in 1926 was heavily critical of the educational system, particularly con-cerning its inability to meet the development needs of trade, industry and agriculture.

Statutory Reforms

The Vocational Education Act (1930) introduced a new structure by es-tablishing 38 committees, called Vocational Education Committees (VECs), which were responsible for the provision of a suitable system of continuing education and technical education in its committee area. Op-erating on a regional basis, the membership of each committee was se-lected by the local authority and consisted of representatives from local educational, cultural, industrial and commercial interests. An emphasis was placed on "vocational training" which was defined in terms of full-time second level training in literacy and scientific subjects, augmented by some concentration on manual skills. Meanwhile, the attention of the continuing education side was focused on providing full or part-time courses, catering for craft skills, commerce and manufacturing skills. Significantly, the Act did not specify any compulsion on the employer to send apprentices on any of the courses organised by the VEC.

Arising from the recommendations of the 1926 Commission, the Apprenticeship Act (1931) attempted to achieve the reorganisation of the apprenticeship system. This represented the first systematic effort at regulating the Irish apprenticeship system, giving the Minister for Industry and Commerce power to institute apprenticeships on a statutory basis for certain designated trades or occupations. The main provisions of the Act centred around the formation of apprenticeship committees with responsibility for regulating apprenticeship training in the designated areas, for example, construction, electrical, and so forth. Committee membership was comprised of employer and employee representatives from each trade, and three others appointed by ministerial direction. The committee formulated rules governing (a) the length of apprenticeship and numbers employed; (b) apprentices' wage levels, overtime rates, and working hours; (c) age limits for entry and educational requirements; and (d) the regulation of training.

In relation to training, the committees were empowered to make representations to the Ministry for Education for the provision of appropriate courses. Employers were obliged by statute to release apprentices for these courses, providing such a course was held within three miles of the workplace and took place during normal working hours. The Act also compelled employers to maintain records of all wages paid and all hours worked by apprentices, to enable each committee to account for the numbers in their trade. In effect, the Act laid down rules governing the co-ordination of each trade. It also included an interesting feature, in the light of subsequent events, which stipulated that apprenticeships were open to male applicants only, thereby blatantly discriminating against female employees.

This Act is now perceived as being largely ineffective, as it merely laid down ground rules for the co-ordination of the apprenticeship system. Considerable abuse of apprentices ensued, paralleled by a variable standard of training programmes for the designated areas. To compound these difficulties, certain trades were in demand by industry; for example, engineering and construction, while others were in decline. The organisation of apprenticeship schemes was very much scattered amongst the thriving industries, for example, transport, steel, textiles, and footwear, leaving other sections lagging behind.

To tackle these problems a new Government Commission on Youth Employment (1943) recommended improvement and extension of the system. The Commission suggested establishing a National Apprenticeship Committee to control and co-ordinate apprenticeship training at national level, with responsibility for all trades, to replace the existing committee system. There was general recognition that the origination of apprentices on a committee basis was ineffective and led to quality problems and other inconsistencies.

Statutory reform continued in the form of the Apprenticeship Act (1959) which attempted to address the problems caused by the multiple responsibilities allocated under the 1931 Act. Under its terms, a national body, An Céard Comhairle, was set up, consisting of a chairman, five employers' representatives and five employees' representatives, on an eleven member council. This body was vested with the authority to examine the methods used by any trade for the recruitment and training of apprentices, and had a number of specific activities:

- undertaking reviews of the theoretical and practical aspects of training;

- setting down appropriate educational qualifications for entry into apprenticeships;

- designing and establishing suitable means for the recruitment of apprentices;

- ensuring the release of apprentices from work to attend technical college;

- overseeing the provision of on-the-job training to allow apprentices to reach the desired skill levels;

- establishing a system whereby the progress of apprentices was supervised, including a system of examination in the theory and practice of the trade.

The new Act applied to all trades and industries, except agriculture, professions, and clerical occupations. It was successful in its aims to a large degree, but it concentrated mainly on meeting the needs of industry in traditional areas like manual and skilled trades, for example, fitters, plumbers, electricians, etc. More importantly, outside of the apprenticeship system, Ireland was slow to recognise the need for training.

Economic Decline

In overall terms the Irish economy about this time was inward-focused, with the policies adopted by Eamonn de Valera and successive Fianna

Fáil governments concentrating on the imposition of trade barriers and the preservation of ownership of industry at national level. Manufacturing industry was still a very small employer when compared to agriculture and commerce, and merited little attention in national planning terms. Indeed, foreign ownership of industry was barred and there was inappreciable emphasis on export markets and foreign trade. Consequently, expansion of indigenous industry was stunted, and there was little scope or encouragement for the importing of new technologies and systems from abroad. With the exception of the statutory reform on the apprenticeship front, no coherent training policies were pursued at national level. The voluntarism system, which was also prevalent in Britain, was very much to the fore. The Irish industrial sector was left to its own devices to provide the skills necessary for its growth.

By the mid-1950s agriculture was no longer able to provide the sustained growth necessary for full employment, and a downward economic spiral was further exacerbated by the breakdown of Anglo-Irish relations. There followed a period of mass emigration during this time comparable to that of the 1840s, with many choosing to move to postwar Britain, which was in the process of rebuilding its infrastructure and economy after six years of destruction.

Unlike Ireland, Britain was attempting to retrain its workforce with particular emphasis on youth employment and the retraining of war veterans. Furthermore, the Carr Committee highlighted the need for greater emphasis on skill training in Britain industry. This resulted in the establishment of the Industrial Training Council and the enactment of the Industrial Training Act (1964) which had three ambitious objectives:

- to link the provision of training to the needs of economic and technological development;

- to establish and improve standards of industrial training;

- to apportion the burden of training costs more fairly.

Furthermore, a training levy/grant scheme was introduced. This development was to heavily influence Irish policy makers in this area in later years.

Rampant Voluntarism

The experience of the 1950s and 1960s encapsulates the traditional Irish ambivalence to training practice as an aspect of human resource management within the firm and the economy as a whole. In a context of relative British economic health, the complacency of industry and government hindered the progress of movements aimed at training reforms.

Nonetheless, while reformers like the British Association for Commercial and Industrial Education did at least exist, the Irish landscape was barren in this respect.

The period following the Second World War in Britain was a landmark for training policy, as it was indeed for many aspects of industrial and labour policy. This period witnessed a renewed interest in the position of young people in industry with government action in the field of training concentrated on this issue. State involvement in training provision itself was progressively run down.

Ireland experienced a shortage of skilled labour in the early 1950s, especially in the engineering field. However, this was not considered worthy of government action. Training — which mainly meant apprenticeships — was deemed the preserve of joint government negotiation between both sides of industry, and the governmental role was a purely advisory and facilitative one. While this voluntaristic stance did little to develop training in Ireland, movement in the direction of reform remained slow right up to the end of the decade. Suggested reforms included direct financial aid from government to companies in respect of apprenticeship training, and the introduction of some system of statutory training levy whereby companies which did not themselves train might contribute to the training costs of others.

A most significant factor in the lack of progress towards reform was the fact that neither side of industry was motivated to press for major change in the voluntarist structure of training provision. Employers, though pressed in some sectors by skill shortages, were prepared to pay the wages necessary to poach the skilled labour they required from their competitors. Trade unions concentrated on consolidating the apprenticeship system, following the logic that maintaining defensive control over conditions of entry led to skilled labour attracting a good price. The principle of voluntarism, and the maintenance of the status quo, therefore appeared to suit everybody.

In the meantime, inadequacies in the apprenticeship system began to show through. The national agreements dealt with issues such as specified age entry limits, ratios of apprentices to skilled workers, probation periods, remuneration, and demarcation between trades. However, the extent and form of regulation varied widely from industry to industry. For instance, from the limited information available, the scheme in the printing trade was detailed and uniform, whereas in engineering the guidelines were purely a framework within which actual practices differed considerably. One feature the schemes did share was not an impressive one — a concentration on the form of apprenticeship rather than on the content of the actual training given. The typical time period for apprenticeships was still five years, two years longer than most of our

European competitors, with the notable exception of Britain. While there was an increase in day-release for further education throughout the 1950s, this was still not obligatory. Additionally, no standard system of qualifications was attached to the obtaining of skilled status other than that of time served.

Winds of Change

As the 1960s dawned it seemed increasingly clear that the voluntarist approach to training was failing to meet national needs. The cumulative effects of skilled labour shortages, lack of training outside the apprenticeship systems, and the narrow content of apprenticeship training itself, had begun to take their toll. Ireland lagged behind its main European competitors in terms of the average skill levels and educational qualifications of its workforce. However, if the diagnosis of Ireland's training illness was fairly clear, agreement on a possible cure was altogether more contentious. The Department of Labour and the educational establishments were somewhat more advanced than industry in recognising the need for reform. Employers and trade unions remained unconvinced and, to a large degree, unconcerned that there was a major problem with a voluntarist system that allowed both sides to pursue their different interests in relative harmony, through the apprenticeship framework. Skilled labour could attract a good price. Employers were left to train or not to train according to their short-term cost criteria, while negotiation between both sides of industry and the government remained a purely facilitative one. Relative, if fragile, economic security allowed this complacency to flourish.

It was to take the perception of harsher economic conditions in the early 1960s, and a new determination on the part of the government led by Seán Lemass, to inspire attempts at major reform. There is considerable agreement that this government was responsible for dragging the Irish economy into the twentieth century. Ireland had joined the International Monetary Fund (IMF) in 1957, and shortly afterwards the World Bank. The Economic Development Report of 1958 added its impetus to the liberalisation of trade and commerce, and a more outward looking economic focus began to emerge. Controls on foreign ownership of Irish industry were removed in 1963, import tariffs were removed over the period 1962-64, and in 1965 the Anglo-Irish Agreement on Tariffs and Trade was signed. These initiatives reflected government policy aimed at creating a more open economy with the emphasis on attracting foreign investment to Ireland.

A cornerstone of this policy was the encouragement given to foreign companies to locate here, through tax incentives, capital investment grants, advance factories, and so forth. With the arrival of these companies, vocational and skills training took on a new impetus, although the skill base remained very weak. It is worth noting that the influx of these multinational companies, many of whom espouse the training and development of employees as a fundamental priority investment, represents a landmark influence on training in this country, which has persisted to the present day. Meanwhile, tourism and agriculture were also targeted for development with a view to reaching foreign markets. The Farm Apprenticeship Board was set up in 1963 to provide training for young farmers, and the Council for Education, Recruitment and Training (CERT) was established by the Tourist Board to handle education and training in the tourist and hospitality sector. This change in economic policy led to a considerable slowdown in emigration and actually resulted in many emigrants returning to Ireland to work or to establish their own business.

As a response to an International Labour Organisation (ILO) report on vocational education in 1962, a Dáil committee was set up in 1963. There was a general acceptance of the need to tackle the problem of retraining of the unemployed. The bulk of the unemployed were unskilled and in dire need of training so that the kind of workforce necessary for attracting foreign companies would be more readily available. The mid-1960s represents a watershed in national training policy, when the recognition of a number of significant issues was instrumental to the subsequent change of direction. The general conclusions reached were that:

- the voluntarist system facilitated the perpetuation and enhancement of familiar problems and allowed them to continue untackled;

- there was no effective national body to keep apprenticeship and other training activities under review;

- there was an insufficient number of skilled workers to meet the growing demands of the developing Irish economy;

- a small number of employers trained well, for example, Guinness and Bewleys, and their skilled workers were often poached by those who invested little in training;

- the State itself provided a poor example in this regard with inappreciable investment in training in the public sector;

- training methods were also poor, with few formal qualifications, and the training situation was in considerable need of improvement.

In response, the Government White Paper of 1965 adopted many of the recommendations of the ILO Report and set about establishing a national Industrial Training Authority.

The Industrial Training Act (1967)

The period from 1967 to 1980 is characterised by significant upheaval and reform of the training system at national and organisational level. The Industrial Training Act of 1967 repealed the 1959 Act and established An Comhairle Oiliúna — AnCO. This body was empowered by the Act to assume full responsibility for all industrial training, including apprenticeships, and its functions included the provision of training at all levels of industry and the provision, facilitation, encouragement, assistance, co-ordination and development of training initiatives.

A special Council was instituted to manage AnCO and was advised by seven training committees based on individual sectors of the economy. They were: textiles, clothing and footwear, construction, food, drink and tobacco, engineering, printing/paper and chemicals. The activities of AnCO were designated into three key areas:

1. *Training Advisory Service.* Through this service, trained advisors (including the IDA, SFADCo, and Údarás na Gaeltachta) acted as consultants to industry. Their activities incorporated the assessment of company training needs, the drawing up of training plans and programmes (covering operator to management levels) and the sanctioning of grants.

2. *Training for Individuals.* Training centres were established in conjunction with the provision of external training courses for individual trainees. Courses were aimed at unemployed or redundant workers, those otherwise seeking retraining for new skills, school leavers, and at assisting some community based initiatives.

3. *Apprenticeship Training.* AnCO was empowered to make detailed provisions for the training of apprentices and statutory designated areas in this regard included construction, engineering, metals, electrical, motor, furniture, printing and dental craft work. Three broad responsibilities were specified in relation to apprenticeship training:

   - ensuring apprentices complied with statutory entry requirements;

   - arrangements for off-the-job training on either day or block release courses;

   - monitoring training with employers through a log book, which apprentices also had a role in maintaining, and which was signed by

a supervisor or training advisor when an apprentice reached a
certain standard in a designated area.

Funding for AnCO was provided by the government, but the Act also
allowed for the imposition of a levy/grant scheme, similar to that introduced to Britain in 1964. The stated objectives of the scheme were (a) to
make firms aware of the benefits of systematic training, and of its contribution to the economic development of the enterprise; and (b) to dis-
tribute equally between employers the cost of relevant industrial training.

The scheme itself took several factors into consideration, including
company size, gross payroll levels, and the amount of training provided.
The levy amounted to between 1 per cent and 1.25 per cent of annual
gross payroll. Varying portions of the levy could be recovered, for example, companies with less than 50 employees could claim back 90 per
cent, while those employing between 51-500 could claim back between
50 per cent and 90 per cent. An upper limit of £50,000 was payable to
any one company, or £2,800 in respect of any one employee. The general
purpose of the scheme was to tax prime industry into accepting its responsibility for its own training, while simultaneously fostering a systematic approach to training and development.

The 1967 Act represented a significant change in government policy,
reflecting an interventionist strategy aimed at sweeping away the concept
of voluntarism. It also heralded an institutional role for a National
Training Agency.

Education Reform

There has been a long-standing ambivalence in education circles towards
the employment-related aspects of education. When coupled with the
rapid changes that were occurring in the 1960s, this contributed to a
situation where the qualifications of those leaving the education system
were significantly out of tune with changed employment structures.
Some attempts were made to deal with this issue between the late 1950s
and early 1960s, and indeed a comprehensive survey was undertaken by
the OECD between 1962 and 1965. The survey examined the present and
future requirements of scientific progress and economic growth, culminating in a report published by the National Economic and Social
Council (NESC) in 1966 called *Investment in Education*.

The report prompted many changes including the introduction of the
Free Education Scheme for all second-level students. Another target was
the heretofore streaming of students to either academic-oriented Chris-
tian Brothers-type colleges or manual-oriented vocational schools. On
this issue, the emergence of community and comprehensive schools
made it possible to integrate the curriculum of secondary and vocational

schools, thereby providing a practical option for all students. In a further innovation, technical subjects were introduced for the Leaving Certificate, sounding the death knell for the Group Certificate and making it possible for students to combine academic and technical subjects.

The role of third-level education was also considered, as the availability of an appropriate supply of highly skilled manpower, with innovative and entrepreneurial capabilities, was seen as a key factor in Ireland's future economic development. Specific emphasis was given to the supply of scientific, management, and marketing skills. A joint OECD/Department of Education Report, *The Training of Technicians in Ireland*, resulted in the appointment of the Steering Committee on Technical Education. This was to prove an influential innovation, directly contributing to a significant increase in the stock of highly skilled manpower during the 1970s. For instance, the total number of people with scientific and technical qualifications rose considerably, from 22,000 (or 73 per 10,000) in 1971 to 50,000 (or 144 per 10,000) in 1981. During this same period, the total number of scientists increased by 156 per cent while the number of those with degree level qualifications grew by more than 117 per cent. These figures demonstrate not only the significant increase in the numbers of those with scientific and technical qualifications, but also the impact of the restructuring of the higher education sector, which now placed increased emphasis on the provision of Diploma and Certificate awards.

PLACEMENT SERVICES IN IRELAND

In an historical context, the concept of a state placement service goes back a long time, but a formal system was not put in place until 1971. The primary function envisaged for the original labour exchanges, established under the Labour Exchange Act (1901), was to provide a means through which job seekers and employers could make contact with one another. However, a situation evolved where the placement function was reduced to a relatively minor and ancillary activity within the labour exchange framework.

Very little change occurred in this state of affairs until the 1960s, when attention was again focused on the question of re-organising the placement service. This arose out of a growing view that both training and placement merited greater consideration, and the Department of Labour organised a review of the placement service in 1967. Consequently, a paper was produced in 1968 entitled *The Placement and Guidance Service*, and its main thrust was consistent with the then prevailing economic philosophy. This visualised economic expansion being facilitated in the first instance, with the following expectation of conditions being created which would allow the alleviation of other economic and social problems.

The report recommended a very forceful role for the new service to the extent that it should involve itself in the general job-filling sphere, in competition with informal and personal means of finding employment.

In response, the National Manpower Service (NMS) was established in 1971 within the Department of Labour. The NMS had two key functions, namely, the provision of a placement and occupational guidance service and the administration of a number of employment schemes, for example, Work Experience Programmes, Employer Allowance Scheme, and the Social Employment Scheme. The organisation grew quickly and by 1986 it had established 44 permanent offices throughout the country. Staff employment was subject to some fluctuation, however, rising to nearly 200 by 1976 but suffering a decline in 1977 as a result of cutbacks provoked by the 1974-77 recession. Nonetheless, after 1978 the service again grew rapidly.

Its expenditure rose from £0.5 million in 1974 to £3.75 million in 1983, and its activity levels also increased. The number of vacancies notified to the service escalated from 22,000 in 1973 to over 50,000 in 1983, but fell substantially in subsequent years because of the recession. There was a significant increase in the number of job seekers registered each year, from 38,000 in 1973 to 135,000 in 1983.

THE INSTITUTIONAL ROLE — THE DEVELOPMENT OF A NATIONAL TRAINING AGENCY

Let us now turn our attention to the development of AnCO/FÁS as a national training agency.

AnCO (1967-75) — The Early Years

The setting up of AnCO, and the introduction of the levy/grant scheme, created a greater focus on industrial training than had existed previously. Companies were compelled to adopt a systematic approach to analyse training needs, draw up training plans, appoint training managers/officers, and to foster top management support for the whole training process. In addition, companies were expected to evaluate their training and provide specific documentation to AnCO. Subsequently, industrial training expanded under a number of different headings: the introduction of permanent training centres, the promotion of in-company training in the industry and building sectors by means of the employment scheme, measures to update and improve the apprenticeship system, and special initiatives to counter youth unemployment.

In tandem with these developments, the early 1970s heralded a considerable upsurge in economic activity. The influx of foreign multinationals created valuable employment for both skilled and non-skilled workers alike. In 1973, Ireland joined the EEC which was to open new frontiers for the economy, and the European Social Fund grants to Ireland were a boost to investment in education and training (for example, the grant in 1973 was £4.1 million). Total state outlay on all training in the non-agricultural sector between 1973 and 1983 rose from £8 million to £133 million, which represents an annual average rise of 17 per cent in real terms. This rate of increase far outstripped the real growth rate in domestic output which averaged some 3.3 per cent over the same period. The increase in AnCO activities can also be gauged by focusing on the numbers trained. In 1984 the number of persons who attended formal AnCO courses was 39,400 compared with just over 5,000 in 1974; the number of adult trainees (that is, non-apprentices) was 10,200 in 1989, compared with 800 in 1974. AnCO was the major recipient of European Social Fund grants from 1974 to 1981.

The recession brought about by the oil price shocks in the mid-1970s had a disastrous effect on the Irish economy. Indeed, from this time to the mid-1980s the Irish economy drifted into crisis, with consequential increases in unemployment figures and emigrant numbers. High levels of Government borrowing for current expenditure from 1977 onwards created a soaring foreign debt. In addition, the world recession resulted in a withdrawal of many foreign companies from Ireland. Instead of being attracted by tax incentives they found themselves burdened with high costs, particularly wages, which rocketed in the 1970s and 1980s due to rising inflation and interest rates.

The prominent adage of training budgets being the first target of cost-cutting measures rang true again in this instance. One of the major implications of the recession was that Government spending on education and training was significantly curtailed, and cut-backs in education put considerable strain on the system. Companies faced with rising costs and shrinking markets focused on what they considered to be non-essential spending, and many companies saw training and development expenditure as an unnecessary cost in time of recession.

AnCO in the Spotlight

The economic conditions of the late 1970s placed AnCO in an unwelcome spotlight. The multiplicity of agencies seeking resources, paralleled by the growing scarcity of funds, was now a major problem. The perception of widespread duplication of functions precipitated severe criticisms of AnCO, some of which are worthy of interest:

1. In its annual reports, AnCO based its effectiveness on the numbers trained in each of its divisions each year. These statistics illustrated that AnCO had its "fingers in a lot of pies", but considerable doubt was expressed about the quality of the training and the competency of AnCO to provide such a wide range of training activities.

2. There was considerable evidence to suggest an over-dependence on AnCO as a supporter of training. A White Paper on Manpower Policy, published in 1985, estimated that AnCO-sponsored training accounted for almost 40 per cent of all training activities for the period 1982-85. It also estimated that AnCO were responsible for over 60 per cent of training in the industrial sector, and for over 80 per cent in the engineering and metal sector. In the distribution and general services area, however, training was almost exclusively provided by means other than through AnCO.

3. AnCO emphasised its special relationship with private companies, especially the multinationals, arguing that it had developed a long record with particular companies which ensured its influence and control over their training systems. However, many companies were critical of the AnCO concept of training activities, highlighting its emphasis on systems that involved considerable paperwork. This was seen to create a situation where training specialists were ultimately judged on their ability to recover the levy paid, rather than the innovativeness or relevance of their training activities.

4. Considerable resentment was building up over AnCO's access to European Social Fund monies. Many organisations, such as the Irish Vocational Education Association, singled out AnCO as being too costly, with accusations being made concerning the duplication of courses that were already available in many of the technical colleges. Furthermore, the Institute of Guidance Counsellors criticised AnCO's move into the area of personal development/life skills, arguing that this area should come within the remit of schools. Their argument was fuelled by the lack of funding for the educational system which prohibited such an initiative, and they suggested that funds should be redirected from AnCO to the educational sector.

5. AnCO's involvement in youth employment, and the attendant use of external consultants, gave rise to special concerns. Many commentators estimated that between the period 1978-85, an average of £1 million per year was paid to consultants to run courses for AnCO. For its part, AnCO defended the use of such consultants, arguing that this was necessary in order to maintain a high degree of flexibility and to respond effectively to the changing needs of the unemployed. None-

theless, specific criticisms were made of AnCO's approach in this area, claiming that:

- criteria for the selection of external consultants were insufficiently clear, and consultants' activities were not closely monitored;

- analyses indicated that private consultants concentrated primarily on management and business skills, tending to avoid more re-source-intensive training programmes which entailed greater capital expenditure on machinery and equipment;

- many community groups were unhappy at having consultancy firms foisted on them, as this severely curtailed any opportunity to run the programmes themselves;

- the usefulness of externally-run programmes was seriously called into question; statistics later produced by FÁS and others illus-trated that placement rate results for such external training was very low — 32 per cent within one year of the programme.

The build-up of adverse comment concerning the activities of AnCO continued unabated. Agencies such as the Irish Management Institute (IMI) and the Institute of Public Administration (IPA), as well as educa-tion and training professionals, became very critical of the role of AnCO, while industry viewed it as being wasteful of resources and more con-cerned with paperwork than training effectiveness.

Technical Assistance Grant Scheme (TAGS)
TAGS represented AnCO's main mechanism for promoting management training within organisations, providing up to a 50 per cent refund of course costs. A Management Training Task Force, set up in 1982, se-verely criticised this scheme and recommended its replacement by a new management and supervisory support scheme. Its main proposals in-cluded the following:

- grants should only be given in respect of approved management and supervisory programmes run by trainers and training organisations requested by AnCO;

- specific criteria for trainer qualifications, experience, expertise, and facilities should be established and adhered to;

- there should be a variable rate of grant assistance that was more sensitive to the needs of sectors with greater training requirements;

- foreign language training should be eligible for support;

- AnCO should carry out a systematic evaluation of its support for management and supervisory training on an ongoing basis.

The Levy/Grant Scheme

Criticisms of the levy/grant scheme had been voiced in the late 1970s and early 1980s and had risen to severe proportions by 1985. There was a general consensus that the scheme had enhanced the overall training situation in Ireland. The number of training managers/officers and training instructors employed by firms had increased considerably, and there was general acceptance that the level and quality of training had been significantly improved. Notwithstanding this, it was becoming evident that the scheme had fulfilled its purpose and that reform was necessary.

In this vein, many training managers suggested that the scheme was now doing a disservice to the advancement of training in industry. The Irish Institute of Training and Development (IITD), which represents many trainers in Ireland, claimed that the amount of training undertaken by organisations was seriously curtailed by the extensive preliminary paperwork required to satisfy AnCO's increasingly bureaucratic requirements. Some of the many specific criticisms levelled at the levy/grant scheme were as follows:

- companies were obliged to use up large amounts of money just to administer the scheme;

- there was considerable evidence that small firms were unable to benefit from the grants, with the paperwork involved perceived as being too onerous;

- little impact on adult training was evident and retraining was largely ignored by many companies;

- the overall system lacked a strategic focus, and the industry-based nature of each scheme meant that there was still no economy-wide training strategy being developed;

- the scheme failed to differentiate between areas where there was considerable under-provision and those that enjoyed a good training record and therefore required less support.

Management Training

In response to an AnCO report on Management Training and Development, published in 1984, the IMI objected to a proposal that AnCO should assume a co-ordinating role in this area. Indeed, early in 1986 the Minister for Labour directly assailed AnCO's attempt to move from its craft/shop floor emphasis into the white-collar management training field. That same year the IMI produced a report which pointed to "competition, confusion and wasteful friction" in AnCO's relationship with others involved in the training of managers. It went on to suggest that "AnCO should take no new initiatives which would further extend its role to management training and development". This expression of grievance by the IMI was mainly centred around AnCO's funding at a time when there had been progressive withdrawal of government financial support for the IMI. The situation had therefore arisen where both a user-owned institute and a state agency were contesting to fulfil the same national role.

Industry Perceptions of the National Training System

In 1985, in the midst of a sea of criticism, the Confederation of Irish Industry (CII) carried out a comprehensive analysis of the Irish training system. They called for an extensive review of the levy/grant scheme and in so doing also set out their perceptions of important priorities and responsibilities of the key parties involved in the training system. Their main arguments are worth recording, and may be summarised as follows:

- in a period of rapid technological and market changes, education and training are crucial factors in the struggle to improve competitiveness and achieve further employment;

- the government is responsible for ensuring the provision of basic education and transferable skills which are necessary for entering employment;

- enterprises are responsible for the provision of relevant specialised training which is necessary for their economic development;

- Irish industry recognises the need to provide for retraining and the continuing education of its existing workforce, particularly in technical fields;

- both employers and employees have a mutual interest in availing of education and training;

- employees should be willing, in their own interest, to invest in further education and training, outside of working hours if necessary;

- recognition was given to the historical position of apprenticeship in Ireland in the sphere of education and training of craftspersons, and it was pointed out that the decreasing role of craftspersons within manufacturing industry must be recognised, together with an increasing demand for technicians and skilled operatives.

This statement of priorities by the CII was very important. It represented the first time in over 20 years that the issue of training and development had been addressed in such a comprehensive way by an organisation that represented a significant part of Irish industry. Indeed, the relevance of many of the main points outlined in their review has not waned in the intervening period.

White Paper on Manpower Policy (1986)

A White Paper on Manpower Policy, published in September 1986, examined the role of all actors involved in manpower policy. In relation to the role of Government and employers, it stressed the primary responsibility for training provision resided with employers, but also stated that Government intervention was necessary. Employers should accept their particular responsibility to maintain and develop the competence and productivity of their employees through training. Government intervention, on the other hand, was consistent with policy objectives, as well as making a positive contribution to economic growth and social progress.

In general terms, the White Paper called for a broader concept of training and development and made specific comments on a number of issues. Included among its key proposals were that:

- the National Manpower Service, AnCO, the Youth Employment Agency, and CERT be amalgamated under one body to be called the National Manpower Authority;

- training grants to industry be based on a more selective approach (that is, linked to approved company development plans and concentrated on key skill areas);

- the levy/grant scheme be retained but payment of grants to be examined to ensure more effective targeting;

- training for redundant workers over 25 be given a greater priority;

- the apprenticeship system be revised and modernised with a view to developing a system based on standards achieved to ensure a satisfactory balance between supply and demand and a reduced cost to the state while still maintaining quality;

- the Technical Assistance Grants Scheme be replaced by a more selective scheme;

- an Advisory Committee be established to ensure a clearer articulation of the management training needs of Irish business.

The White Paper provided the impetus to the Government to make significant institutional reform and to streamline the training system.

Labour Services Act 1987

The Government's response to the White Paper was the enactment of the Labour Services Act (1987), which represented the first attempt in 20 years, at state level, to reform the training system and bring it into alignment with economic objectives pursued by the government. This Act provided for the establishment of FÁS (Foras Áiseanna Saothair), thus amalgamating the National Manpower Service, AnCO and the Youth Employment Agency into one body. CERT was excluded largely because of the tourism lobby which argued that because of the skill shortages, and the importance of tourism as an employment growth sector, CERT should remain independent and provide a specialised service. The Act set out a number of key functions for FÁS, among the most important being as follows:

- to provide, or arrange for, encourage and foster the provision of training and retraining for employment;
- to manage, administer and co-ordinate employment schemes and to assist in the co-ordination of such schemes organised by other bodies;
- to provide advisory services in the following areas:
  - services whereby persons seeking and persons offering employment in the state are brought into contact with each other;
  - services consisting of the placing of persons in employment;
  - services consisting of guidance, advice and information in respect of choice of career and employment;
- to facilitate and assist local community groups, and co-operatives of workers or of members of local communities, in the provision of employment;
- to collect, prepare and publish information and forecasts in relation to services or activities provided or carried on by FÁS and to carry out research into training, employment and placement issues.

In the second stage reading of the Bill, the Minister for Labour outlined five challenges facing FÁS in the following five years. FÁS should:

- provide assistance for the unemployed, particularly those in the long term category;

- provide assistance, through special labour market and education interventions, for poorly qualified school leavers;

- encourage the development of the Irish workforce in terms of its competitiveness;

- encourage the development of small business and enterprises;

- provide pre-departure information and advice to persons contemplating employment abroad.

The Act envisaged a significantly expanded policy role for the Minister and Department of Labour, as signalled in the 1986 White Paper on Manpower Policy. FÁS would be required to seek the advance approval of the Minister for Labour and Finance for its future plans, and the Act also granted the Minister discretionary powers over the involvement of FÁS in specific activities. Nonetheless, the Minister did perceive that the act would provide the new body with a considerable degree of flexibility in conducting its day-to-day operations within the agreed framework.

The Board of FÁS was to consist of a Chairman, appointed by the Minister, four representatives nominated by ICTU and a further four from employer organisations, with one representative each serving the interests of education and social welfare, youth organisations, the Department of Finance, and the Department of Labour respectively. Two worker directors, selected from the employees of FÁS, concluded the make-up of the Board. The Act also set out arrangements for the transfer of staff from the three existing bodies to the new authority.

The Minister envisaged FÁS as a labour-intensive service, doing invaluable work for the economy and the community, and offering job satisfaction to its own employees. He did not, however, visualise any major dismantling of the existing services of the NMS, YEA or AnCO, but instead saw them being adapted over time to achieve a more regionally based and integrated service. His aspiration was for FÁS to move towards the provision of more effective services at local level. The period between 1987 and 1991 therefore represented a time of significant change for FÁS. In the immediate aftermath of the Act, a meaningful shift in its activities was evidenced, away from company-based facilitation activities towards an increase in community and youth employment type training programmes.

FÁS's Response to the 1987 Act

In the years since 1987, FÁS has introduced many significant changes. Some of these are worth noting.

- By 1990, FÁS was largely operating as an integrated localised service, as envisaged by the Minister. During the previous three-year period some 80,000 people had participated in training programmes (excluding those designated as job-search), while over 40,000 people had taken part in employment schemes. Total expenditure by FÁS on such activities amounted to £400 million, of which approximately £196 million was spent in 1990.

- In 1988 FÁS launched a review of the apprenticeship scheme, and in 1989 they produced a discussion document, "Apprenticeship – A New Approach", for the Minister for Labour. The broad outline of their proposed scheme was agreed by the social partners under the Programme for Economic and Social Progress (PESP) in 1991. The funding for the new system was to be discussed under the auspices of the Central Review Committee of this programme.

- A job training scheme was introduced early in 1990, aimed at people on the live unemployment register whose job prospects would be enhanced by a period of work experience and training, and who were referred to employers by FÁS. Under this scheme, participants are placed with employers for a period ranging between 13 and 20 weeks, with normal training allowances paid by FÁS and employers meeting the training costs.

- An Industrial Restructuring Programme was also initiated in 1990, with the stated objective of assisting small and medium-sized enterprises, with up to 500 employees, to improve their competitiveness through training. The training support scheme, set up in 1986, was utilised to achieve this purpose. Two levels of grant assistance were applied: 80 per cent for companies with 50 or fewer employees, and 50 per cent for those employing between 51 and 500. Furthermore, specific areas were targeted, such as total quality, languages, supervisory and management development and training for women.

- Some novel initiatives introduced by FÁS during the period served to illustrate the cultural change taking place within the organisation. For instance, a Manpower Forecasting Unit was established in 1990 as a joint venture between FÁS and the Economic and Social Research Institute (ESRI). Its aim is to identify occupational requirements and to anticipate potential imbalances in the demand for and supply of skilled labour. Also in 1990, a new FÁS TV service for job seekers was launched, providing home access to information on jobs (through the Aertel service). In the same year came the introduction of the Equal Opportunities Plan, which focused on promoting greater participation of women in the labour force, and breaking down traditional occupational patterns.

By 1991, FÁS had established 17 training centres and 46 employment service offices located in various parts of the country. Additionally, a facility was created for the holding of clinics in towns without permanent employment service offices.

While a considerable amount of FÁS's activities are directed towards reducing unemployment and fostering community-based initiatives, it still provides services to industry. This service now operates on a regional basis, using a network of training advisors. There are also industry experts at national level who oversee the development of FÁS's activities in relation to the various industrial sectors by liaising with the Industrial Training Committees which supervise the overall identification and planning of training in their respective sectors. The reformed levy system now provides another mechanism for encouraging training within the designated areas, as firms are required to pay a non-refundable levy of 0.1 per cent of gross payroll.

The Culliton Report

The Culliton Report (1992) made two specific recommendations about training and development at national level:

1. The provision for training at work is inadequate. New structures are needed to remedy the situation. An institutional reorganisation of FÁS should be adopted to reflect the sharp distinction between support activities for the unemployed and industry-relevant training. These two activities should at a minimum be separated into two distinct divisions. In the longer term a more radical approach may be necessary.

2. A greater proportion of FÁS resources and activities should be allocated to industry-relevant training directed towards those at work and preparing for work.

These recommendations clearly espoused an interventionist approach on the part of the State, while acknowledging the role of the Labour Services Act (1987) in shifting emphasis away from in-company training to the Social Employment Scheme and other youth employment initiatives. The Report pointed out that about 90 per cent of FÁS's budget was absorbed on activities that could not generally be described as training. Roche and Tansey (1992) argued that FÁS is a very complex organisation, with a set of multiple objectives both economic and social, coupled with a wide span of activities and programmes. They also suggested that

FÁS is deserving of closer analysis due to its position and the national resources it has responsibility for managing. Roche and Tansey identified five possible configurations for a reformed FÁS, which are shown in Figure 3.2 at the end of this chapter.

Research undertaken by Garavan (1992) suggests that there is some confusion about the role of FÁS amongst employing organisations. Table 3.1 presents the attitude of organisations towards the role of FÁS as a facilitator and supporter of training within organisations. The responses indicated that FÁS has an image problem and is to some extent out of touch with the training issues within organisations today.

The following summarises the strong perceptions:

• The perception that industrial training has a low priority in FÁS's policy-making strategy. This view is shared by Roche and Tansey (1992) who point out that a consequence of leaving FÁS in its present configuration is that industrial training will continue to receive a very low share of the total FÁS budget.

• Respondents believed that FÁS puts too much emphasis on systems and paperwork and not enough on the quality and delivery of training activities. This criticism was held by a very significant proportion of organisations.

• There was a strong perception that FÁS lacks the expertise to understand the training problems of the modern Irish company. This may be a consequence of FÁS's size and complexity.

• There was the view that FÁS lacks a clear focus in the way it carries out its activities and respondents are not too sure of the role it is playing in the Irish training scene. This perception also received support from Roche and Tansey in their commentary on industrial training in Ireland.

The Department of Enterprise and Employment (1993) has also surveyed employers' perceptions of FÁS. The most significant finding is perhaps the fact that almost 50 per cent of respondents perceived the agency as less than customer-focused, while almost 50 per cent perceived that it was not in touch with the needs of business.

Table 3.1: Perceptions of Organisations to the Role of FÁS as a Facilitator of Training within Organisations

Perception of FÁS	% Total Organisations N = 155	% Small Organisations N = 67	% Large Organisations N = 88
FÁS puts too much emphasis on systems and paperwork and not enough on the quality of training	82%	85%	80%
In-company training has too low a priority in FÁS's policy-making	77%	75%	80%
FÁS lacks the expertise to understand the training problems of the modern organisation.	61%	63%	59%
FÁS is not in tune with the special needs of small companies	58%	90%	34%
FÁS lacks a clear focus in the way it carries out its activities	57%	72%	47%
FÁS puts too much emphasis on individual training and not enough on strategic planned organisational training	54%	57%	52%
FÁS is not sufficiently responsive to the constraints within organisations	54%	75%	39%
FÁS is too much at the mercy of Government	37%	46%	30%
Industrial training advisors within FÁS are very committed to training	30%	37%	24%
FÁS is slow to adopt modern approaches to training and development	30%	16%	40%

Source: Garavan, T. N. (1992)

IBEC's Analysis of Industrial Training

The Irish Business and Employers' Confederation (IBEC) carried out a comprehensive review of industrial training in 1994. They identified a number of important weaknesses in our national system.

- National policy on training is primarily driven by the state with the result that employers have only a consultative role and are not directly represented in important bodies.

- There is insufficient state support for industrial training. The training support scheme is totally inadequate.

- Training provision is currently fragmented between state agencies, education institutions, consultancies, private training organisations and industrialists.

- Companies need to invest more in training but the real problem in many small firms may be less to do with increasing their investment in training and more to do with the need to get a better return from any investment made.

- There is a major imbalance of resources allocated between support for training for the unemployed and training for those in employment. The report cited an expenditure figure of £280 million for the unemployed and £1.8 million for those in employment.

The report concluded that employers wanted to make an important contribution in providing training and development. They made a range of recommendations (Figure 3.1). IBEC acknowledged the passive role played by employers to date and the consequent inadequate provision that resulted.

Figure 3.1: IBEC Recommendations for Industrial Training

- Leading and influencing the development of national training policy for the employed and the co-ordination of Government services to support industry.

- Researching industry training needs and clearly articulating the training needed in key business growth areas to support business development. Direct consultation and the development of pilot projects would be a key part of this function.

- Encouraging and promoting truly effective and cost-efficient training which supports organisation objectives and improved performance.

- Playing a leading role in the development of a national framework of vocational qualifications for off-the-job and in-company training.

- Influencing the training environment in firms by generating greater awareness of the contribution of well-structured training to business competitiveness.

- Developing appropriate initiatives to satisfy the training and development needs of small business.

- Securing direct financial support for training initiatives which meet specific criteria and standards, with the actual training carried out by approved trainers of whom FÁS would be one option. In this way, company-relevant training would receive a greater level of support.

- Improving the quality and design of training programmes for those in employment.

- Planning and setting performance and quality standards for training programmes.

- Setting priorities for the use of EC grants to support training.

- Evaluating the effectiveness of training supports and programmes.

- Promoting and establishing a quality training mark for companies with the objective of developing company accreditation as a requirement for the future availability of grant-aided training.

- Developing initiatives to meet gaps in training provisions particularly in the service sector.

- Ensuring that industry's interests are fully and powerfully represented on sectoral and educational bodies in the planning and organisation of education and training for industry.

FÁS FINANCIAL SUPPORT FOR INDUSTRIAL TRAINING

FÁS initiated a major review of its activities in 1988. Part of this review consisted of a major survey carried out by the Market Research Bureau of Ireland (MRBI). Significant findings of this survey included the following:

- In 37 per cent of the respondent companies no one had received any training in the past year.

- In over 65 per cent of the companies no one had received any off-the-job training in the past year.

- Companies saw training needs for a large number of their employees. Of the employees in industry, some 131,000 (45 per cent) were deemed to be in need of training. Of the employees in service companies, 228,000 (34 per cent) were deemed to be in need of training.

- Most firms do no expect any significant changes in the amount of training carried out in the future.

- Twenty-six per cent of industrial companies and 21 per cent of service companies had vacancies for positions which they could not fill.

These findings formed the context of FÁS's Development Plan 1989-1993. The Plan put forward a series of measures FÁS should take to create a more effective and equitable labour market, and to facilitate economic recovery. A Training Support Scheme was designed, taking into account the constraints which were evident within the industrial/services sector. Four particular constraints were identified:

1. The demand for employment in the Irish economy was expected to increase substantially over the period of the plan as a result of a combination of increased consumer expenditure, expansion of exports and greater levels of investment — assisted by European Structural Funds. The skills of the existing labour force were not considered to be sufficient to fill the vacancies which would arise.

2. Many firms — particularly in the indigenous sector — would have to improve their competitive capacity if they were to survive in the Single European Market. This would entail developing markets and specialised products and devoting greater resources to staff training.

3. A shortage of skilled workers to meet the requirements arising from the projected increase in economic activity over the period of the Plan would come about.

4. Certain firms — particularly indigenous ones — might not possess sufficient management/technical expertise and skills to survive the competition of the Single European Market.

The Training Support Scheme has a budget of £4 million annually. This budget is divided among the regions, in relation to the working population of the area, but a portion of the funding can be assigned for special projects/studies on a national basis. The Training Support Scheme is operational from January to December each year. The budget is allocated to each region at the beginning of each year, and is subdivided in proportional representation to the level of employment within the region. Table

3.2 shows the breakdown. The amount of grants paid in 1991 totalled £3,183,775 and £2,643,434 in 1992.

Table 3.2: Training Support Grant Allocations, 1991-93

Region	Grants Paid £ 1992	per cent	Grants Paid £ 1991	per cent
South East	360,032	13.6	353,908	11.1
Dublin North	419,748	15.9	453,362	14.2
North West	149,324	5.6	182,540	5.7
Midlands	222,359	8.4	216,679	6.8
Mid West	245,313	9.3	361,549	11.4
Dublin South	192,970	7.3	234,026	7.4
Western	196,613	7.4	184,758	5.8
North East	314,838	11.9	274,387	8.6
South West	95,430	3.6	451,911	14.2
Dublin West	446,807	16.9	470,655	14.8
Total 10 Regions	**2,643,434**	**100**	**3,183,775**	**100**

The scheme, while not addressing all of the shortcomings identified in the Culliton Report, did go some way towards encouraging companies to train and in the long run may achieve its overall objectives.

It is possible to calculate the overall commitment of industry to training taking the grants awarded to each region and calculating the level of grant paid versus the amount credited. In 1991 grants accounted for 67 per cent of total training expenditure whereas in 1992 it was 45 per cent. The increase in the total cost by industry and the decrease in the amount of grants between 1991 and 1992 was made possible by changing the level of grants awarded — from 80 per cent to 65 per cent for small firms, from 50 per cent for medium and large firms to 40 per cent for medium and 25 per cent for the large. The budget also changed: 50 per cent of the overall allocation of the budget went to small industries, 30 per cent for medium-sized industries and 20 per cent for the larger companies.

However, an examination of the type of training activity the training support grant is spent on shows that manual skills training constitutes the most significant proportion, followed by health and safety training. Management development and business strategy account for a very small percentage overall. Table 3.3 presents a breakdown of grant-supported training in 1991-92.

Table 3.3: Grant-Supported Training and Development by Companies in Ireland (N = 155)

Type of Training Development Activity	Per cent of Training and Development Grants Supported by Ownerships		
	Irish	US/ Japanese	European
Business Strategy	3%	16%	8%
People Management and Supervision	6%	11%	19%
Customer Service Quality	10%	15%	21%
Health & Safety	22%	6%	11%
Management Development	10%	20%	14%
Manual Skills Training	48%	32%	27%

Source: Garavan, T. N. and Heraty, N. (1992)

Roche and Tansey (1992) have a number of major concerns about the scheme as a mechanism of support for industrial training, notably the following:

- The lack of budget for the Training Support Scheme programme limits the potential that this programme has to improve competitiveness through supporting the training of people in employment.

- The lack of available budget to support training in industry reflects the political priorities of responding to the growing number of unemployed people.

- There is an urgent need to improve the competitiveness of industry and the lack of sufficient and well directed support for training may mean that many firms will not respond to the challenges posed by the single market.

- The fundamental problem facing FÁS in the industrial training sphere is that there is an urgent need to rapidly upgrade the skill base of Irish industry. But many firms do not recognise this need and FÁS does not have the necessary budget to build the skill base on its own.

This scheme is still in place, however, and its overall effectiveness has yet to be assessed.

TRADE UNIONS AND TRAINING

We will now examine the attitudes of Irish trade unions to training and development. In general, the priority granted to education and training of representatives and other members contrasts significantly with established trade union attitudes towards the training and development of members as employees. While research (Costine, 1994) points to training and development as historically being a low-priority issue for Irish trade unions, there are indications that attitudes in this respect may be undergoing significant change. We will examine trade union attitudes to training and development from traditional, current and futuristic time perspectives.

Traditional Attitudes

In the traditional sense, and in overall terms, Irish trade unions may be said to have adopted a passive or neutral stance towards the provision of training for their members. Furthermore, the nature, scope and extent of training activities were viewed as a managerial prerogative and decision-making control in relation to core training issues was not subject to trade union focus, attention or challenge. In this vein, the traditional priorities of trade unions have lain elsewhere, a fact manifested in their pre-occupation with maintaining or improving pay and working conditions (Hillery et al, 1975; Roche and Larragy, 1987). In a wider context this reflects the traditional trade union concentration on limiting or countering employer power, leaving the right of managerial prerogative itself unchallenged (Fox, 1966; Hyman, 1975; Storey, 1991; Gunnigle and Flood, 1990).

However, further down a variable scale of priorities, attention is drawn to the diversity of sectional interests in training between trade union categories.

• *General.* With regard to structures being linked to skill ranges, the majority of employees in this category found themselves on the bottom end of this scale, saw themselves as naturally unskilled. Training did not feature significantly on this agenda.

- *Craft.* Here, skilled craftsmen can be said to have nurtured the apprenticeship system and to have held a traditional interest in training as an integral part of the apprenticeship process.

- *White-collar.* In this category a major commitment to training and development was evident, but only within the technical sphere of activities.

In essence, however, training and development was not an entity impinging on the general mindset of trade unions, and few coherent policies in this area were evident. This was reflected in the passive acceptance, without trade union intervention, of the nature and extent of training and development activities received, or not received, by members in the workplace. Indeed, with the categorisation of work being dictated by management, and "Taylorist" lines being followed in the breakdown and nature of work, elaborate or lengthy training was not deemed a necessity. Little interest in pursuing training was visible from employers, who saw training as a cost rather than an investment, and such training as did take place was seen as informal and focused on a narrow range of skills.

Meanwhile, at national level, Irish trade unions have for many years been involved, as a social partner, in aspects of vocational education and training, as well as industrial training. The differing levels of trade union involvement between education and training, have been outlined by Murphy and Coldrick (1989). In effect, the involvement of the social partners in training has a statutory basis, while their role in education has not. In terms of vocational education, trade union representation is limited to possible selection of individuals, by local authorities, to serve on local Vocational Education Committees (VECs), On the other hand, in vocational and industrial training trade union representation is featured on many tripartite bodies and institutions.

This statutory based representation began with the enactment of the Apprenticeship Act (1931) and has continued through the Apprenticeship Act (1959), the Industrial Training Act (1967), and the Labour Services Act (1987). Thus trade union representation has existed on the board of AnCO and is a current feature on the board of FÁS, constituting a presence at the highest policy-making forum, in tandem with participation on lower level sectoral advisory committees, sub-committees, and working parties.

Furthermore, the Irish Congress of Trade Unions (ICTU) has played an integral role in successive national economic and social programmes, which have been viewed as a key component in achieving wide-ranging consensus on Government policy and direction in these areas. However, it seems fair to suggest that, in this respect, the main concern and priority of the ICTU has been the setting of pay increase guidelines for the private and public sectors.

Participation and involvement at national level has thus been well established. However, with respect to national training policy and direction, few dissenting trade union voices have been heard. This was certainly the case in 1985, when the Confederation of Irish Industry (CII) saw fit to carry out a comprehensive review of the Irish training system, while the trade union movement seemed content with the status quo. As far as the issue of training was concerned, trade unions and industry swapped roles, with the latter posing as agitator and the former playing the part of the change-weary establishment.

Current Attitudes

With the passage of time, Irish trade union attitudes to training and development have undergone significant change. This burgeoning interest may be attributable to the following influences:

- the pace of technological change has necessitated an adjustment in the type of craft maintenance skills required;

- technological advances are constantly threatening traditional work and jobs, linking training and retraining to security of employment;

- a growing commitment to training is arising from the example of multinational companies and through the encouragement of State agencies;

- the tendency of a better educated workforce to seek greater job satisfaction is raising general expectations of trade unions, which are being looked to by members for opportunities to utilise talents and abilities;

- the integral role of training and development in implementing new forms of work organisation initiatives (such as Total Quality Management, World Class Manufacturing, Human Resource Management, etc.) — initiatives which have brought issues such as workforce flexibility, employee commitment and involvement, team working, and job re-design, very much to the fore.

In response to these influences, Irish trade unions have adopted what might best be described as a defensive stance. This stance represents support for, or even promotion of, training activities directly associated with the defence of members' pay and conditions of employment, and with the upgrading of members' skills. Thus training has now become part of the Irish trade union negotiating agenda, and several particular considerations may be highlighted in this respect:

- elimination of discrimination in opportunities for training;

- provision of particular skills in training schemes, especially pertinent to craft workers and technological advances;

- protection against loss of earnings;

- increasing skill levels as a basis for higher pay;

- facilitating members' re-deployment or re-employment in redundancy or rationalisation situations;

- opportunities to improve the conditions of all employees, emanating from the blurring of established divisions within the work-force (manual/non-manual; staff/hourly paid; unskilled/semi-skilled/skilled);

- avoidance of situations where changing skill requirements might lead to polarisation of the workforce (that is, the existence of minority of skilled and highly paid employees in conjunction with a majority of de-skilled employees who would not enjoy similar pay conditions).

The orientation of these considerations suggest similarity with the trade union approach in a general British context, as described by Rainbird (1990) and reflecting a focus on defending existing patterns of training from employer-initiated changes.

Meanwhile, there are indications that a further broadening of the trade union view of training and development is afoot. For instance, the ICTU has highlighted the fact that in the area of raising the skill levels of existing employees, Irish firms lag well behind their European counterparts (Duffy, 1993). In outlining an argument for improving this situation, Duffy refers to several deficiencies in the Irish training scene, including:

- the need for companies to engage in greater consultation with trade unions in the area of training and development;

- the focus on very job-specific training without any element of personal development;

- the tendency of firms to design their training with a view to maximising grant recovery, rather than focusing on the needs of individuals being trained;

- the absence of formal training agreements.

He goes on to state that training requirements fall into two broad categories — the need to keep upgrading existing skills and the need to meet the challenges of a total change in work practices brought on by changes in technology. These general themes are also embraced in a report commissioned in 1993 by the ICTU, entitled *New Forms of Work Organisation — Options for Trade Unions*, in which the need to ensure adequate skills training, as well as providing opportunities for personal development, is associated with the introduction of new work organisation strategies. In addition, William A. Attley (Joint General President, SIPTU) has stated his belief that the success of the Irish economy depends in large measure on high levels of skills and knowledge, and that it is the intention of trade unions to press for its vision of a highly skilled and flexible workforce (Attley, 1994).

The signals emanating from the Irish trade union body, then, suggests a recognition of the following influences:

- the importance of training and development in contributing to improved organisational effectiveness and competitiveness (especially within new forms of work organisation);

- the national focus on training and development, as a factor in the country's future economic welfare, arising from the Culliton Report (1992) and the reverberations in the wake of its publication;

- the potential offered by training and development issues for involvement in joint trade union/management structures, thereby giving a greater foothold in the participative arena.

Driven by these influences, the trade union stance on training and development seems destined to enter a new phase, reflective of a more progressive approach than witnessed heretofore.

Future Commitment and Involvement

While some core elements of a defensive orientation may persist, it is probable that broader aspects of training and development will engage Irish trade union attention. This attention may well be fashioned into coherent training policies and proactive collective bargaining interventions, in search of training agreements and the establishment of joint trade union/management training structures. The blueprint for such endeavours already exist in the UK and the continent, as the examples below demonstrate.

Training Policies

Rainbird (1990) has outlined the statement of training policies made by TASS which include:

- unions have a major role to play in training policy and implementation at all levels;

- training should be a continuous process with no artificial barriers to progression;

- positive action is required to eliminate discrimination;

- trainees should not be used as a cheap labour substitute;

- training is needed in managerial, supervisory and commercial skills;

- the training system of other countries should be studied, with the priority of catching up with the resources devoted to industrial training elsewhere.

Training Committees

Ideas on establishing workplace training committees to stimulate training action have been expanded by Willis (1988), in tandem with the right to training for all employees along the following lines:

- a certain quality of training in every working year, with paid time-off, where appropriate, or allowances/grants;

- the absence of discrimination with regard to this right;

- full consultation about what training would be most effective;

- nationally and internationally recognised standards of training.

Willis sees these rights being backed up by legislation and implemented through workplace training committees operating on a joint consultative basis. Thus, a forum is created whereby individuals, represented by their union, and management can work out this entitlement to training in the best interests of both the individual and the company. This committee would also oversee training audits and draw up training plans for the enterprise (envisaged as part of a wider "Human Resource Development Plan" which would incorporate recruitment and promotion). The possible workload of a training committee is given to include:

- monitoring external best practice and new developments in the field of training and development;

- selection of target groups;

- knitting together training and enterprise career partners;

- design, organisation and assessment of training;

- determining the qualifications needed by the enterprise;

- monitoring and assessing process and initiating improvements.

Training Agreements

Among the logical provisions of training agreements, as outlined by Webb (1989) for instance, may be found:

- a contractual right to training for each employee for the duration of their employment, after a minimum period of service;

- jointly agreed methods of non-bias aptitude testing;

- setting up of a joint management/union training committee, to assess skill shortages and potential areas of redundancy due to technological change, and to issue guidance to all employees;

- trade union right of access to all manpower plans;

- individual career planning and counselling made available on an annual basis;

- equal opportunities given priority at all levels of staff planning;

- regular bulletins on manpower planning and technology made available to all employees.

If the apparent increase in Irish trade union awareness and interest in training and development is to be transferred into future active intervention, the mechanisms of training policies, agreements and committees will become important. It also seems logical to suggest that, following the devisal and adoption of policies, the pursuit of agreements and joint committees may be considerably strengthened if embodied within a legislative framework. The existence of such a framework in Germany, for example, grants consultation rights to trade unions in respect of a wide range of issues. This has led to the initiation of efforts by workers' representatives to improve opportunities for exerting influence in areas such as the structuring of the content of work, working systems, the extent of the division of labour, and employer's planning in respect of personnel and training issues (Mahnkopf, 1992).

We have thus examined the Irish trade union approach to training and development in traditional, current and futuristic terms, and noted that the traditional passive stance has been replaced by an interventionist strategy, albeit one with largely defensive and narrowly focused overtones. Furthermore, foundations for the espousal and pursuit of broader strategies have been laid.

Attley (1994) has put forward the notion that a new type of trade unionism is emerging which makes more social and economic sense in the realities of today's competitive environment. A core aspect of this progression is movement towards the concept of partnership building between management and employees, in which trade unions play a participate and active role. In this vein, the issue of training and development offers substantial scope for a consensual approach, as indeed indicated some time ago by Hillery et al (1975). If Irish trade unions were to decide on pushing forward with such an agenda, the following outcomes could ensue:

- more cordial employee relations, through agreement on the benefits of a training and development ethos for all organisational stakeholders;

- members' perceptions of trade unions becoming more congruent with their broadening expectations;

- opportunities opening up for trade unions to gain a more secure foothold on the participatory ladder, through involvement in joint training structures;

- trade unions having a more radical influence on national training policies, especially by their pursuit of legislative measures to support training and development opportunities for employees.

Of course, the stance taken by company management in response to this type of approach remains to be seen. Past experience reflects little meaningful progress on the participative front, but building common agreement on the importance of training and development must surely merit serious consideration. On this issue at least, and for both sides in the employee relations interface, "us" should represent all organisational stakeholders, with external competitive forces being cast in the role of "them". The resulting promotion of training and development into a more central and strategic role offers the potential prize of greater organisational effectiveness and competitiveness, and a consequent accumulation of wider economic and social benefits.

KEY MISTAKES MADE AND POSSIBLE REFORM

At national level Ireland has made a number of fundamental mistakes in the area of national training and development policy. These are worth summarising.

Setting a Poor Example

The state has handled its own training badly. It exhorts private enterprise to develop and implement corporate training plans, and yet the state itself does not operate such a process.

Wasteful Use of Training Resources

During the last ten years or so the Government has invested heavily in training, almost to the point where organisations have become dependent on such funding, with very uneven results. This raises a pertinent question: If private enterprise squandered its resources in this fashion, would it remain competitive or indeed stay in business?

Short-term Thinking

The Government and AnCO/FÁS have tended to look for measurable results from changes in national training strategy much more quickly than is reasonable to expect. This has resulted in cursory examinations of the training process, with changes in the direction of training policies following in rapid succession. Since the 1960s, diverse messages from different sources concerning training have been given to individual employers and this has given rise to much confusion. The current overall position is that the average employer seems to have learned very little about, and pays scant attention to, the economic benefits which can accrue from innovatively designed human resource development systems.

Focus on Occupational Training

Since the mid-1980s there has been a preoccupation in Ireland with training to reduce mass unemployment (particularly youth unemployment). This, in turn, has switched the emphasis of national training strategies away from the existing business enterprise and its needs, towards the creation of a network of non-business organisations. These have been established for the purpose of implementing youth training, which is not directly or immediately related to business needs. Because of this, the value of training for organisational improvement has been diminished in the eyes of many employers.

The provision of youth training, particularly through initiatives aimed at reducing unemployment in that category, is meritorious and warranted. However, if attendant strategies obscure instead of promote the value of training in organisations, the prospect of even higher unemployment becomes an increasingly likely consequence.

Too Many Training Administrators and Instructors

The particular approach adopted in relation to state intervention in training has led to the employment of a large number of people to administer training, an equally large number of those who instruct on a limited range of skills. However, there has not been a pro-rata increase in the number of training specialists operating at management level within enterprises. In effect, this reflects a debilitating shortage of strategically-placed specialists, who have both the credibility and skill to make training and development happen within a business environment and to produce measurable economic results by so doing.

Emphasis on the Idea that Training can be Contracted Out

The cumulative effect of all state intervention has served to represent training to employers as something which is essentially provided by external agencies. It also serves to reinforce the perception among individual managers within a business that training is something which other people (that is, trainers) can do for them. These features have manifested themselves in the existence of a large number of organisations providing services which the employer should be providing directly. Academic institutions and consultants are a typical example of this.

Studies carried out by FÁS have highlighted the prevalence of inadequate levels of training provision, a fact reinforced more recently by the "Industrial Training in Ireland" report prepared by Roche and Tansey (1992). Indeed, it is their contention that employers are reluctant to provide anything more than the basic minimum level of training for their employees.

It is hardly surprising therefore, that the Culliton Report (1992) should state boldly that training for those at work in Ireland is deficient, being constrained by "the capability and willingness of firms to invest in upgrading the skills of their employees". Government policy has resulted in a dependency relationship and Irish employers are not prepared to voluntarily bear the cost and effort involved in training to the extent evident in Germany and France, for example (Harrison, 1992). Furthermore, there have been insufficient efforts to adopt a collective approach, involving trade unions, employees, and employing organisations in devising training plans.

Government policy and the activities of FÁS have failed to develop a culture that values "overtraining", which in this context means a richness and diversity of competence that can be utilised with planned strategic change.

Indeed, many Irish employers regard overtraining as wasteful — an attitude which is partially caused by a short-term focus in our strategic planning, particularly due to FÁS and its emphasis on training the individual rather than the needs of the total organisation, and finally due to our attitudes to human resource utilisation in general.

The Need for Additional Reform

With regard to providing the critically required impetus to the concept of continuing training in this country, the Labour Services Act (1987) seems less than effective legislation. It does not make a significantly positive statement about the role of training within organisations and the need to allocate more resources and commitment in this vital area. Among the specific issues it fails to embrace are the following:

1. The stipulation that a minimum amount of total labour costs be allocated towards training. It is suggested that, in order to respond effectively to initiatives in other countries, an initial level of 2 per cent should be included, with tax relief applicable to additional expenditure over and above this statutory minimum.

2. The necessity for organisations to draw up an annual training plan, which would include details such as:

   - how it was intended to use training for technological and other major organisational changes;

   - the types of general training activities to be undertaken and the resources being committed to them;

   - the qualifications of the training specialist charged with implementing the training plan.

3. Such a planning process would encourage organisations to treat training as a strategic activity, rather than perceiving it as an operational activity with a limited contribution to make to business success.

4. The requirement for organisations to devise mechanisms which would incorporate the active involvement of key individuals and groups with an interest in training. Some of our continental partners have instituted training committee structures whereby employees/trade unions are involved in devising training plans and overseeing their implementation.

5. The stipulation that organisational training plans should be approved by the local FÁS office. There should be a regular monitoring system of the implementation process and an attempt to audit its effectiveness. FÁS has taken some of these ideas on board, but their emphasis has been on individual training plans rather than organisational ones,

and the related paperwork is considered laborious, especially for the small organisation.

6. The need for the Government itself, and its departments, to act as a positive role model in respect of commitment to the concept of training. A useful provision in the legislation would be one whereby eligibility to tender for Government business is contingent on the production of a feasible training plan.

7. The need to focus on the quality of training at national and organisational levels. Those responsible for the allocation of funds for training purposes should satisfy themselves as to the nature of the training requirements, the quality of the delivery mechanism, and in particular the qualifications and credibility of the trainers who provide it. This stipulation should be equally applicable both to in-house specialists and external consultants. Furthermore, multiple assessment criteria should be utilised — evaluation only in terms of numbers trained should not be considered sufficient. The IITD Code of Practice has useful and specific guidelines on these issues.

SUMMARY

In this chapter we have provided an overview of the evolution of a national vocational education and training system in Ireland. We have examined its history from the guild system to the considerable legislative and institutional reform which has taken place this century. The major concern of this chapter is with description and analysis in general terms. The evolution has been marked by periods of interventionism and voluntarism on the part of the State. The national training agency has evolved from a highly centralised bureaucracy to a more regionalised decentralised organisation in the late 1980s and early 1990s. Irish trade unions, an important agent within the total system, have traditionally demonstrated passivity towards the training and development of employees. This attitude has shifted somewhat in recent years and the future looks more promising for union commitment and involvement in company training decisions. This examination of the overall system allows us to examine individual elements in the next chapter.

Figure 3.2: Alternative Options for the Restructuring of FÁS

Options	Advantages	Disadvantages
Retain the status quo	• Little administrative disturbance. • Little danger of jeopardising existing ESF funding of FÁS schemes. • Keeps the unemployed to the forefront of labour market policy.	• Industry training will continue to receive a very low share of the total FÁS Budget. • The priority attached to industry training will continue to be swamped by FÁS's multiple objectives. • The perception of FÁS by industry as not playing a key role in the provision of industrial training. • There is no impetus to improve the skills base of Irish industry.
Retain economic training in FÁS and transfer non-economic schemes to the Department of Social Welfare	• This transforms FÁS into an industry training organisation. • There would be greater emphasis on industry training as a result. • The essential welfare nature of many existing FÁS schemes would be acknowledged. • There would be considerable scope for integrating and rationalisation of all non-economic programmes for the unemployed within Social Welfare.	• There would be political difficulties in accepting that many on existing FÁS schemes will not get jobs. • ESF funding could be jeopardised if no perceived training element was preset in such schemes when administered by Social Welfare. • Social Welfare would find itself encumbered with operating and administering activity-based schemes, which they have no experience in operating.

Options	Advantages	Disadvantages
Separate FÁS into two divisions • Industrial Training • Employment Support	• It would minimise administrative disruption while still effecting a real change in increasing the organisation's support for industrial training. • The Industrial Training Division would have a very clear economic focus. • There would no longer be a confusion of economic and social objectives within FÁS. • An industry training division specifically focused on industry's training needs would establish credibility with, and attract support from, industry. An industry training division within FÁS would thus become the principal state mechanism for influencing both the quantity and quality of training in Irish industry. • It would maintain contact for the unemployed with industry and with the labour market. • Existing ESF supports for FÁS schemes would not be jeopardised by organisational changes.	• Administrative change for the sake of change would not in itself lead to any policy improvements with regard to raising skills in industry. • Divisionalising FÁS activities could lead to dislocation at regional level. • FÁS would remain encumbered with a multiplicity of objectives. • A thoroughgoing divisionalisation of FÁS activities could involve the duplication of administrative systems at regional level. However, such a complete divisionalisation of FÁS operating structures is not being proposed. Instead the consultants envisage the appointment of a new Assistant Director General with responsibility for training in industry. Those activities currently servicing industry's training needs (TSS, the ITC's, Industry Advisory Schemes, Apprenticeship and Levy Grant) would be grouped within the new Industry Training Division, reporting to the new A.D.G. Responsibility for industry training would be vested in specific personnel in the existing FÁS Regional offices.

Options	Advantages	Disadvantages
Abolish FÁS and transfer its activities thus: • Schemes to Social Welfare • Industrial training supports to IDA • Remedial training to the education system • Training centres to Vocational Education Committees.	• If success, such a major rationalisation could yield significant cost savings. In particular as student numbers at second level decline through the latter years of the 1990s, spare capacity teaching plant will become available within the education system. • The reality of existing activities would be properly recognised and assigned to those responsible for them. • The advantages resulting from such transfers to the IDA and to Social Welfare enumerated in Options 2 and 3 above would apply. • There would be significant gains from integrating vocational education, at both second and third levels with training in training centres. • Such an integration of vocational education and training facilities would open the way to a more integrated approach to on- and off-the-job training, as in Germany.	• The role of the Department of Labour would be severely diminished. • It would involve very substantial organisational and functional changes in a wide range of areas. • Such a reorganisation would of its nature be long-term. • It is not clear that the system could accommodate change on such a scale. If the transfer of responsibilities failed, the consequences could be catastrophic. • The unemployed could be marginalised as a result. • ESF funding for schemes would be jeopardised if these were operated by Social Welfare. • Social Welfare would find itself operating activity-based schemes in which it has no experience.

Options	Advantages	Disadvantages
Retain FÁS as an agency for the unemployed and transfer all industrial training and training support to the IDA	• The IDA already have experience in making industry training grants. • It would allow the state, through the IDA, to develop a more integrated approach to the development of individual companies. • The IDA have a clearer view than FÁS of industry strategies, national and international. • It is envisaged here that the IDA would facilitate and support but not deliver training to industry. • Delivery would be contracted out to firms, state agencies and the relevant educational institutions.	• There is no guarantee that such a transfer would result in more support for training in industry. • Industry training could find itself lost as a subset of total IDA activities. • FÁS would become effectively the implementation arm of the Department of Social Welfare. • The unemployed would be further distanced from industry and from the labour market. • The co-ordinating role of both FÁS and the Department of Labour would be diminished.

Source: Roche, F. and Tansey, P. (1992), *Industrial Training in Ireland*

4

ELEMENTS OF THE IRISH SYSTEM: VOCATIONAL TRAINING, APPRENTICESHIPS AND CONTINUING EDUCATION

INTRODUCTION AND LEARNING OBJECTIVES

This chapter focuses on specific elements of the national training and vocational education system in Ireland. Chapter 3 described the system in general terms. Having completed this chapter you will understand:

♦ the state of vocational education and training in Ireland;

♦ the evolution and operation of the apprenticeship system and its reform;

♦ the development and operation of youth training schemes in Ireland and their contribution to reducing unemployment;

♦ the key elements of adult and continuing education in Ireland.

VOCATIONAL EDUCATION AND TRAINING IN IRELAND

General Education

In Ireland full-time education is compulsory for children aged between 6 and 15 years. Children are educated in primary schools up to the age of 12, after which they proceed to secondary level. Second-level education is provided in five types of schools: secondary, vocational, comprehensive, community schools and community colleges. Traditionally, in Ireland second-level education was classical-academic in orientation and generally intended to prepare students for third-level education and white collar occupations, while vocational schools provided technical education and practical training in preparation for the world of work.

At second level there are two state examinations, the Junior Certificate and the Leaving Certificate. Seventy-three percent of those entering second-level education complete the Senior Cycle and 85 per cent of these follow the Leaving Certificate programme. Other options (though not available in all schools) are a transition year, a Vocational Preparation and Training Programme (VPTP), a Leaving Certificate Vocational Training Certificate (LCVT) and a Senior Cycle Certificate.

The Leaving Certificate is the most important senior cycle option. At present it lasts two years and it is necessary to study subjects at higher level to progress to university. There are 31 approved subjects at Leaving Certificate level that are both technical and academic in emphasis. The research evidence, however, illustrates a low level of availability of technical subjects and their low take-up as examination subjects.

There has been a considerable increase in the number of students taking business and applied subjects since the late 1960s. However, certain subjects are still more popular than others. Engineering workshop, agricultural science, construction studies and technical drawing are still taken by small numbers. Gender stereotyping is still evident in the number studying vocational subjects. Less than 2 per cent of girls study technical drawing and less than 1 per cent study engineering or construction studies.

In 1991-92 some 12 per cent of Junior Certificate students opted for a transition year. Approximately 115 of the 828 second level schools offer this optional year. The evidence suggests that there is an almost total transfer to the Leaving Certificate programme the following year. The purpose of this year is to provide a broad educational experience including social education, media education, moral education, communication skills and experiential learning opportunities.

Vocational Programmes at Second Level

There are three programmes with a vocational orientation: the Leaving Certificate Vocational Programme (LCVP), the Senior Certificate Programme and the Vocational Preparation and Training Programme (VPTP). Established in 1989, the LCVP is an option within the traditional Leaving Certificate programme. Its general aim is to provide a more practical, vocational orientation. Students are required to take a minimum of two technical subjects as well as Irish, a modern continental language and one other subject. Students are also required to undertake a minimum of four weeks work experience. The statistical evidence available for 1991-93 illustrates that approximately 5 per cent of the Leaving Certificate cohort take this option. This is generally seen as disappointing considering that it was hoped that up to 30 per cent would be following this option by 1994. Participation on this programme is, however, limited to schools which provide the compulsory technical subjects. This partly explains the low participation rates by girls.

Since 1986, 15,000 students have followed an experimental Senior Certificate programme in approximately 60 selected schools, largely in the Munster area. This programme consists of a range of vocational subjects including work and communication skills, general technology, computer applications, social and cultural studies. The programme places an equal emphasis on the development of practical skills and on skills associated with traditional schooling. Unlike the Leaving Certificate, the Senior Certificate is not marked by grades. The programme to date has been very successful.

The third vocational-oriented programme is the Vocational Preparation and Training Programme (VPTP). This programme has been available since 1984 and its general aim is to bridge the gap between traditional education and the world of work. The content of VPT programmes can be broken down into three components (see Table 4.1).

Table 4.1: The Structure of VPT Programmes

Sector	Time Allocated	VPT2	Activities
Vocational Studies	40%	20-30%	Practical work in one of the following: Engineering, Construction, Agriculture, Services, Crafts and Design, Commerce, Electrics/Electronics and Science
Work Experience	25%	30-40%	Related to vocational sector chosen, although in some cases work simulation may be accepted as a substitute.
General Studies	35%	10-20%	Designed to promote personal development and generalisable knowledge, interpersonal skills, computer familiarisation, mathematical and literacy skills, along with a positive attitude to learning, adaptability and initiative.

Source: NESC Report No. 95. Education and Training Policies for Economic and Social Development. Dublin, October 1993.

VPT programmes are divided into two one-year self-contained programmes. VPT1 is a basic programme to provide students between 15 and 18 years, who have completed compulsory education, with basic skills. In VPT2 there is a greater emphasis on the development of vocational skills and work experience. In 1991/92 almost 6,000 students took VPT1 and 16,000 completed VPT2. Commentators have highlighted two particular difficulties:

1. The standard certification only records completion of the course. While some schools do encourage students to take external tests there is a lack of standardisation in assessment and certification procedures.

2. VPT programmes were not based on an analysis of labour market needs. They are largely funded by the European Social Fund and concern has often been expressed that they are driven more by funding than by the requirements of the labour market.

APPRENTICESHIP TRAINING IN IRELAND

Apprenticeship has traditionally been the path to employment in skilled occupations in Ireland. It primarily operates in a number of "designated trades" such as engineering, construction, motor, electrical, printing and furniture. Statistics available for 1992 illustrate that 3,000 apprentices are recruited each year and at present there are about 14,000 apprentices in 40 separate trades. Forty-seven percent of those who enter apprenticeships have a Leaving Certificate as a basic qualification, though it is not possible from existing data to say which trades are using this entry requirement most.

The training programmes employed in statutory apprenticeships are regulated by FÁS. Apprentices are normally recruited by employers, and undertake a four-year period of apprenticeship. The first year is normally spent in a FÁS training centre or VEC college of technology learning the theory and practice of the trade. The remainder is spent in employment, with further release to a technical college for theoretical instruction at various intervals. Apprentices who successfully complete the programme are issued with a Completion of Apprenticeship Certificate by FÁS and a Senior Trade Certificate by the Department of Education. Apprentices are also eligible for the award of the National Craft Certificate which is awarded jointly by the Department of Education and FÁS.

Reform of the Apprentice Training System

The apprenticeship system in Ireland has been the focus of ongoing statutory reform since the Agricultural and Technical Instruction (Irl) Act of 1899. However, over a prolonged period, attempts at reform were concentrated more on regulating the system itself than on the actual content of the training received by apprentices. Thus, while the provision and monitoring of training was catered for, eventual qualification as a craftsperson was considered mainly in terms of time served and not on demonstrable skills attained.

The impetus for changing this situation arose from the 1986 White Paper on Manpower Policy, which perceived the existing apprenticeship system as "costly, inflexible and inefficient". This prompted the then Minister for Labour to initiate a comprehensive review of the system by FÁS, drawing where necessary on the experience and achievements of other countries. Subsequently, a Discussion Document, entitled "Apprenticeship — A New Approach" was issued by FÁS (1989).

In acknowledging scope for improvement from the perspective of apprentices, employers, and providers, this document identified three different aspects of the need for change.

Government Concern

Government concern emanated from the criticisms contained in the 1986 White Paper, which set out objectives for a revised approach that would (a) be based on standards achieved rather than on time served; (b) ensure a satisfactory balance between supply of, and demand for, apprentices; and (c) reduce the financial cost to the State while maintaining quality.

Overcoming Weaknesses in the Current System

FÁS considered 30 submissions in formulating proposals for revision, and noted the key demands of a standards-based system, improved entry mechanisms, and cost effectiveness, in its deliberation. Taking these into account, four fundamental weaknesses of the current approach were identified for corrective action:

- the absence of compulsory competency-based standards which an apprentice should attain as a craft worker;

- the rigidity of the existing system, in terms of its failure to cope with requirements for updating skills in line with evolving technology;

- the inequity of the entry mechanism, where entry was not always based on the best candidate getting an apprenticeship place;

- direct intake by employers, resulting in the recruitment of 1,000 apprentices per year to jobs of disparate training potential in terms of the standard of training available and access to off-the-job training.

European Trends

With the onset of the Single European Market it was recognised that a high skill base would be required in order for Ireland to be competitive. Some of the issues for consideration in the light of this requirement included the following:

- most European countries were already operating standards-based apprenticeship systems;

- the prospect of mutual recognition of qualifications within the EU, leading to increased pressure for competency-based apprenticeship certification;

- job mobility for Irish workers in the EU would only come if their qualifications were internationally recognised;

- the advanced involvement of industry in apprenticeship training in other European countries compared to the situation in Ireland;

- the need in Ireland for one unified standards-based apprenticeship system which would afford equality to all.

Having put forward proposals, FÁS, in recognising the need for extensive consultation, invited submissions from all interested parties before embarking on changes to the existing system.

The consultative process was further advanced by the inclusion of proposals for a new apprenticeship system in discussions by the social partners on the PESP Agreement of 1991. Indeed, a summary of the intended provisions in this regard appeared in the PESP document itself, where it was also stated that Advisory Committees, representative of the ICTU and IBEC, should be established to oversee their implementation.

Subsequently, a comprehensive review procedure was carried out in relation to developing revised apprenticeship curricula. A survey of industry was undertaken to establish the scope of each trade, and to identify current and anticipated skills needs and their frequency. In addition, a detailed industry study was carried out in leading firms to identify the standards required in each trade, and to compose relevant occupational profiles. Finally, new curricula were written encompassing each trade, by a team of subject-matter experts nominated by employer bodies, trade unions, the Department of Education and FÁS.

A New Standards-Based Apprenticeship System

In conjunction with the new system, FÁS issued two explanatory documents, namely, "A Scheme that Measures Up to Your Needs" (for employers) and "A Scheme to Help You Measure Up" (for apprentice applicants). An overview of the new scheme has also been presented by Clancy (1994). Figure 4.1 presents an outline of the system.

Entry Requirements

Apprentices must be at least 16 years of age and must have attained a minimum Grade D in 5 subjects in the Junior Certificate or equivalent.

In addition, there are special provisions for mature entrants, education-ally disadvantaged persons, and individuals with disabilities. Recruit-ment is now seen as the responsibility of the employer, who may refer to a panel of persons wishing to become apprentices, drawn up by FÁS. In a significant change from the old system, a single method of entry will be operated and apprentices must be registered with FÁS at the com-mencement of the apprenticeship process.

Training Provisions
A modular structure has been applied which comprises seven phases, four on-the-job and three off-the-job (that is, Phases 1, 3, 5 and 7 are undertaken with an employer and are industry-based; Phases 2, 4 and 6 are pursued in FÁS, educational colleges or in other FÁS-approved cen-tres).

On-the-Job Training
The initial phase, intended as a minimum period of three months, is in-troductory in nature, covering the basic skills of the trade, safety aspects, and the world of work. This phase facilitates the apprentice's under-standing of the trade, and allows the employer to assess the suitability of the candidate. The remaining on-the-job phases are designed to enable the apprentice to practice and further develop skills and learning from off-the-job phases.

Off-the-Job Training
The maximum duration of off-the-job phases will generally be 40 weeks (that is, Phase 2 — 20 weeks; Phase 4 — 10 weeks; and Phase 6 — 10 weeks), during which time the apprentice learns the fundamentals of the trade in terms of skill and knowledge. The entire training content will be provided in a single institution, to enable integration of practical and theoretical learning. This innovation requires trainers to be competent in delivering both technical skills and relevant related knowledge.

In accordance with statutory provisions, release of apprentices by employers for off-the-job training is deemed compulsory.

Assessment and Certification
A comprehensive procedure has been devised through which apprentices will be assessed at a number of stages, during both on- and off-the-job phases. During the on-the-job phases, apprentices' competence will be assessed in terms of skill, knowledge and attitudes in the performance of specific tasks, to the required standards under working conditions. Each task must be successfully carried out on two occasions. During these phases, apprentices will be assessed on the basis of exercises and proj-ects, together with standardised practical and theoretical tests.

Figure 4.1: An Apprenticeship Training Model

Module 1	Broad-based Training Module in one of the following sectors (off-the-job training)				
	Construction	Engineering	Motor	Electrical	Printing
Module 2	Basic Skill Development Module in a specific trade (off-the-job training)				
	Bricklayer Cabinetmaker Carpenter/joiner Painter/ decorator Plasterer Plumber Stonecutter Wood machinist	Fitter Sheet metal worker Metal fabricator Toolmaker Turner	Heavy vehicle mech. Const. plant fitter Motor mech. Agricultural mech. Light vehicle body repairer	Electrician Instrument mechanic Refrigeration craftsman	Compositor Bookbinder Carton-maker Graphic repro. Litho/Plate maker
	In-house Test				
Module 3	Development of Skills Module A On-the-job development of basic, specified standards to be achieved (in-company training)				
	COMPETENCY TEST 1				
Module 4	Further Skills Development Module (off-the-job training in a specific trade)				
	In-house Test				
Module 5	Development of Skills Module B Specific standards to be achieved (in-company training)				
	COMPETENCY TEST 2				
Module 6	Specialist Skills Development Modules (off-the-job Training)				
	In-house Tests				
Qualification	National Craft Certificate				

In tandem with off-the-job tests, assessment points have been established for each trade in respect of on-the-job performance measures. Provision is made for a limited number of repeat attempts in all phases, but apprentices must pass a specified minimum number of assessment procedures at each phase. Results of all tests and assessments will be monitored for the purpose of issuing a National Craft Certificate.

The new system will also facilitate progression to further educational qualifications and allow the apprentice to continue to technician level at a recognised national and international standard.

Responsibilities and Roles

Specific responsibilities, duties and roles have been set for employers and apprentices. The employer's role and responsibilities include:

- registering the apprentice with FÁS within two weeks of recruitment;

- providing a safe place and system of work, with proper equipment and processes;

- training the apprentice in the skills, knowledge and techniques of the particular trade, in accordance with the apprenticeship rules;

- paying the apprentice an appropriate wage, as agreed by contract;

- allowing FÁS access to the apprentice in the place of employment, to monitor training and progress;

- giving prior notice to FÁS in the event of termination of apprenticeship due to redundancy, and taking all reasonable steps to have the employer's obligations under the apprenticeship contract transferred to anther employer.

Among the most important duties and responsibilities of apprentices are:

- to work for their employer with care and skill, obeying the reasonable and lawful instructions given;

- to be diligent and honest, to refrain from wilfully disrupting the employer's business or disclosing confidential information;

- to observe the duty of taking care of one's own and others' health and safety;

- to apply diligently to learning all aspects of the chosen occupation;

- to complete all required phases of training and assessment.

Financial Arrangements

Agreed financial arrangements encompass funding, wages and allowances. Training costs and apprentice wages during on-the-job phases are borne by the employer, while training costs associated with off-the-job phases are met from Exchequer or EU funds.

During off-the-job training, apprentices in four industrial sectors — Construction, Motor, Printing and Paper, and Engineering (excluding Electronics) are paid an allowance from an apprenticeship fund. This fund was created through the introduction of an Employers' Apprenticeship Levy (0.25 per cent of annual payroll), which replaces the existing levy grant scheme in these four sectors of industry.

In all other sectors, apprentice costs during off-the-job training are the responsibility of the individual employer, although travel and accommodation allowances, financed by Exchequer and EC funds, are contributed by FÁS.

Support Services

A range of support services is provided by FÁS, including Apprentice Training Packs, training and development for in-company supervisors and assessors, on-the-job monitoring, and advice and assistance on all aspects of apprenticeship.

These points constitute the main features of the new system. It was decided that its introduction would be on a phased basis and piloting in a number of trades is already under way. It was intended that the remaining trades would switch over to the new system in September 1994.

Benefits of the New System

The new system should confer a number of important benefits on employers and trainees:

- It is based on uniform, pre-specified and industry-agreed standards, and will ensure the highest levels of skill for individual firms and the Irish labour market generally.

- Structured ongoing assessment will give more comprehensive and valid evidence of attainment, to both employers and apprentices.

- The modular apprenticeship structure will facilitate cross-skilling, allow for flexibility as required, and ease updating for future technological developments.

- Craft certification will enhance the national and international status of craftspersons, as well as that of Irish firms employing them.

- Higher-level career opportunities will be opened up for craftspersons, through designated further education and training.

- Special arrangements have been devised to encourage special groups (for example, early school leavers, mature entrants, the disabled, and women) into apprenticeships.

The new standards-based apprenticeship scheme does represent a major step forward. However, it should be noted that the question of the overall duration of apprenticeships in each trade is not yet settled. This is to be determined by the training/education/developmental requirements of each trade and is the subject of a review which is expected to be completed in 1995. The new scheme itself has taken a considerable amount of time to get off the ground, bearing in mind that comprehensive changes were first proposed in the White Paper of 1986, and that the then Minister for Labour had, in 1989, expressed a hope that the new system would be in operation by 1990.

One of the weaknesses of the new system is the limitation of the areas or occupations designated for apprenticeships, with 40 such areas designated in Ireland compared to 450, for example, in Germany (Clancy, 1994). While additional occupations have been selected for possible development, no firm progress has been reported in this regard. It is also worth noting that the number of apprentices/craftspersons in manufacturing industry stands at approximately 55,000, out of a working population of more than 300,000, and that there are no designated apprenticeships in a services sector employing in excess of 600,000.

Future manpower demands, both in Ireland and abroad, are increasingly likely to centre around the requirements of an adaptable, flexible, and above all, skilled workforce. To enable the Irish workforce, particularly our young people, to grasp the opportunities presented in the labour market of the future, the foundation laid by the new apprenticeship scheme, must be continuously built on by expansion and review.

YOUTH TRAINING INITIATIVES

In common with most Western European countries, the issue of youth unemployment has been one of major concern and considerable debate in Ireland since the 1970s. Indeed, this problem is particularly acute in Ireland, which, by tradition, has had a relatively high birth rate, with almost 50 per cent of the population under the age of 25.

In conjunction with recent trends in unemployment (which have risen to record levels) and the high numbers exiting our education system, a considerable burden is being placed on our employment support systems. Furthermore, the link between employment opportunities and basic levels of educational attainment has been well established. For instance, in 1991 a Department of Labour survey of school-leavers showed that one year later 37 per cent were in employment, 36 per cent were engaged in full-time further education, 17 per cent were unemployed, 8 per cent had emigrated, and 2 per cent were not available for work. Unemployment among those who had attained their Leaving Certificate stood at 12 per cent, while the corresponding figure for successful Junior Certificate students rose to 32 per cent. Only fifty-three per cent of school leavers who failed to obtain a qualification were employed one year later. For this latter category, youth training initiatives represent the only real opportunity to secure employment and avoid becoming yet another long-term unemployment statistic.

During the 1970s and early 1980s, Ireland responded to the rise in youth unemployment by expanding the provision of training and temporary employment programmes for the unemployed. Growth in unemployment led initially to the introduction of a range of schemes, with a primary rationale of providing temporary jobs. The range of schemes which became available are now briefly reviewed.

Objectives of Training Schemes

The objectives of the many schemes introduced may be summarised collectively as increased employability, developing basic skills, and encouraging attitude changes towards employment among the participants. It was intended that all of the participants would be exposed to work discipline, good time-keeping and supervision. However, increased employability is also dependent on variables such as the value of the work experience gained, the nature of the skills acquired and the quality of the supervision.

With the exception of the Community Youth Training Programme and the Work Experience Programme, little emphasis was placed on the training objectives of the schemes, while the training content of the latter was considered to be very unsystematic. The kind of work available through the schemes usually involved a low skill content and value, which did not realistically enhance future employability. As a result, it was widely suggested that all schemes should have a more pronounced training element.

Because the schemes were developed at different times, their modes of operation and conditions of employment were variable. Three distinct features were evident, however:

- The duration of employment differed considerably from one scheme to another.

- Payment levels varied significantly despite the similarity of the project work involved.

- The schemes were heavily biased towards males, as illustrated by the participation figures (the nature of the projects and work experience activities provided through the schemes partly explains their inherent sex bias).

The programmes had a symbolic impact as they were evidence of a willingness on the part of the government to do something about youth unemployment. The schemes represented part of Irish macroeconomic policy, being viewed as a short-term response to the structural problems in the labour market and resulting rise in unemployment. There is evidence to suggest that the schemes did create a number of jobs that would otherwise not have existed (for example, in 1985 over 65,000 people participated in such programmes). Conversely, however, there was widespread evidence of a tendency for employees to view participants as cheap labour — research undertaken in 1982/3 estimated a cost of £9,000 per (temporary) job.

Specific Criticisms and Problems

A significant criticism, up to 1982, was that no single agency held responsibility for youth unemployment and that no single administrative unit considered how the schemes related to overall manpower policy objectives. Specific problems highlighted in this context included:

- A number of schemes were project-based, resulting in competition for recruits.

- The variable rates of pay made some schemes more attractive than others.

- Weak links between the NMS and the project schemes led to recruitment difficulties.

- There was significant overlap between the objectives of the various schemes.

- The level of control and monitoring differed considerably from scheme to scheme.

The schemes were also heavily criticised for their preoccupation with economic development, with many commentators believing that the individual development of participants should have been of paramount concern. A number of further criticisms were voiced and may be summarised as follows:

- The overall concentration of decision-making power in Dublin and the lack of input by local communities in this regard.

- The zealous application of rigid criteria meant that worthy projects were sometimes excluded.

- The multiplicity of actors involved (Government ministers, local authorities, AnCO, the NMS, voluntary organisations, etc.) hindered cohesion, focus and effective use of resources.

- The range of schemes was unable to cope with the rapidly changing age structure, with a high proportion of the population under 25.

- Considerable difficulties were encountered in targeting the range of schemes towards specific areas of youth unemployment, because the unemployment statistics were not desegregated on the basis of age (up to 1980) and because the live register under-represented youth and female unemployment.

- Some people managed to drift from one scheme to another, due to the lack of communication between the organisations concerned.

- The schemes failed to reach many disadvantaged young people who did not come into contact with the employment agencies.

As a response to these criticisms, the Youth Employment Agency was created in 1981.

The Youth Employment Agency (YEA)

The YEA was established through the Youth Employment Agency Act, and envisaged closer co-operation and co-ordination among the many actors involved in combating youth unemployment. Its manifesto included support for community and co-operative enterprise, specialist employment subsidies, and the promotion of individual enterprise. A Youth Employment Levy (1 per cent of gross earnings) was imposed to ensure that adequate funds were available for the YEA and to allow the promotion of schemes on a continuous basis without the usual budgetary constraints.

Unfortunately, the creation of the YEA was adjudged to have added to the problem of multiplicity, in terms of agencies and actors involved. Training continued to remain inadequate, and those most in need were still not being reached. In 1987, the YEA became part of the merger which saw the formation of FÁS, and at this stage an extensive review of existing schemes was undertaken. Many of these were subsequently abolished, but one of the most important new schemes introduced was called Youthreach.

Established by FÁS in 1989, Youthreach was a programme aimed specifically at the estimated 10 per cent of early school-leavers without any qualifications. This scheme encompasses periods of up to two years placement in companies, during which time participants attend education and training programmes and receive a weekly allowance. While this represented a significant response, with a range of more specialised schemes being introduced, it has had little overall impact on the youth employment problem in general.

Youth unemployment decreased somewhat during the mid-1980s but recent trends indicate that this category of unemployment is very much on the increase. At present, Ireland's unemployment rate is the highest in the EC, at approximately 16 per cent, and almost one quarter of those unemployed are under the age of 25. While various reasons have been cited for this high rate of youth unemployment, a couple of significant changes have occurred with respect to traditional youth employers:

- The employment embargo in the Public Service since 1982 has led to a decline in the recruitment of young people to a sector which had previously been regarded as a substantial employer in this context. In 1982 the Civil Service accounted for 10 per cent Leaving Certificate student take-up, whereas in 1988 it accounted for a mere 1.8 per cent.

- The banking sector, which absorbed 25 per cent of similar students in 1982, now accounts for less than 15 per cent.

It is unlikely that the problem of youth unemployment will be solved or eliminated in the short term or even in the foreseeable future. However, it is evident that Ireland cannot sustain such high levels of unemployment, especially in an environment where our very ability to remain competitive will depend to a large degree on our availability of a highly skilled and motivated workforce.

The Employment Impact of Youth Training and Unemployment Schemes

The most comprehensive analysis (Breen, 1991) of the impact of youth training schemes in Ireland produced a number of important conclusions, which are summarised as follows:

- By late 1987, virtually all of the 1981-82 school leavers who had not continued to third level were still in the labour market (91 per cent). Of this cohort, 73 per cent were in jobs, 18 per cent were unemployed, and 1 per cent were on a FÁS training programme or temporary employment scheme. Almost everyone who was in the labour market had obtained at least one job, and it was calculated that only about 2 per cent of the cohort were still seeking their first job. Over the entire five-and-a-half years for which the cohort was traced they had had, on average, two jobs each and one spell of unemployment. Hence, while the image of young people in labour market moving in and out of jobs with great frequency may be true in some cases, it is not typical of the overall picture.

- How young people fare in the labour market is very closely linked to the level of educational qualifications they possess. For those who left school before completing any examination, 50 per cent of their time was spent in work, 45 per cent in unemployment and the balance in training or temporary employment schemes. Those who left following the Group/Intermediate Certificate spent around 70 per cent of the period at work, and 28 per cent of the time unemployed. Meanwhile, for the best qualified — those who left school having completed the Senior Cycle — 81 per cent of the period was taken up in employment, with 16 per cent of the time spent in unemployment.

- Labour market differentials based on educational qualifications increased over the period of the study. However, virtually all of this increase occurred within the first 24 to 30 months out of school, and this initial growth of differentiation was followed by aggregate stability. A similar pattern has been noted in other countries, which points to this initial period being crucial to the formation of longer-lasting labour market differentials arising from differences in educational qualifications. The study concluded that differentials widen because of the cumulative, self-reinforcing processes at work in job acquisition and job loss. These results suggest that young people who have had a previous job are in a better position than those who have never worked, and the longer a job-seeker has been unemployed, the smaller are the individual's chances of employment. Furthermore, higher probabilities of job loss are linked to jobs with low pay (in manual and lower non-manual occupations), and apply to people who have poor employment or labour market records.

- Early labour market experiences are strongly shaped by educational qualifications. Hence, a cycle is entered in which poor qualifications lead to a poor labour market record, leading to longer periods of unemployment and/or employment in unstable jobs, which further damages the labour market record. It is by such processes that educational differences are turned into labour market differentials.

The study analysed the effectiveness of State programmes (training and temporary employment) in increasing the likelihood of unemployed young people securing jobs. The results were not particularly encouraging. For example, participating in a FÁS training programme improves the chances of obtaining a job immediately, by about 20 per cent. However, just one year afterwards, the probability of being in a job shows little or no difference between participants and similar unemployed non-participants. The findings present an important agenda for policy-makers.

TRAINING PROGRAMMES FOR THE UNEMPLOYED IN GENERAL

In addition to the many training schemes aimed at reducing youth un-employment, a number of training programmes are also available for the unemployed in general. These offer unemployed people the opportunity to participate in activities normally incorporating a mixture of theoretical training and practical on-the-job experience. Among the schemes implemented to date are the ones listed below.

Social Employment Scheme

The Social Employment Scheme (SES) was introduced by the Department of Labour in 1985 and is currently administered by FÁS. It is a temporary employment scheme targeted at the adult long-term unemployed. Devereux and Ronayne (1993) point out that the scheme has both social and labour market objectives, but it can generally be stated as enhancing the labour market prospects of participants by providing the long-term unemployed with access to periods of temporary employment. It was envisaged that the scheme would assist participants in a number of ways: remotivate them through contact with employment, help them re-acquire the discipline of work, facilitate the refinement of crucial skills and the development of new ones.

It has become the main labour market measure specifically dealing with adult long-term unemployed. At the end of 1988 there were about 18,000 participants. Devereux and Ronayne (1993) calculated that the SES accounts for almost three-quarters of all long-term unemployed training participants. The scheme operates by providing temporary part-time employment for persons aged over 25 years. It typically takes the form of 20 hours per week every week, or 40 hours per week on alternate weeks over one year. Eligibility for the scheme is based on social welfare status. The scheme, while funded by FÁS, is operationally dependent on a range of bodies, such as local authorities, communities, etc. for its implementation.

The training dimension of this programme has come in for significant criticism. Devereux and Ronayne (1993) have completed the most comprehensive analysis to date. Based on their survey of over 1,000 participants they found that over one-third reported that they were unsatisfied with the opportunities they were provided with to use their skills while on the programme. This resulted in highly demoralised and demotivated participants. The scheme concentrates on mainly semi- and unskilled manual occupations and allows participants to use their existing skill base. This, it is argued, does not enhance their position within the labour market. The scheme provides little or no opportunity to acquire new skills which are linked to employment opportunities. Almost half of the participants in the Devereux and Ronayne study had no opportunity to acquire new skills while on the SES.

The authors identified four conditions that must be met if an effective skills dimension is to be achieved:

1. There is a need to identify, support and develop quality work projects that have a capacity to provide a variety of work experiences.

2. Some mechanism of skills acquisition needs to be built into the programme. This might include job motivation, skill sampling, off-site training periods, and mixed-skill work teams.

3. Skills attained and developed must bear a relationship to patterns of skill demand in the local economy.

4. Formal training options need to be incorporated into the scheme, accompanied by the linking of participants to further education and training options on completion of the scheme.

Overall, the training element of the scheme is poor. However, it does facilitate the participant in that it provides a break with the experience of unemployment and all its negative aspects.

Vocational Training Opportunities Scheme

Introduced in 1989, this scheme was designed to provide training for long-term unemployed people over the age of 21. The scheme provides the opportunity to engage in second-chance education and training — participants may pursue Leaving Certificate or particular skills-based courses. Trainees receive the equivalent of unemployment assistance and follow courses at selected vocational training establishments.

Job Training Scheme

Introduced in 1990 as a pilot job training scheme for the unemployed, initial results from this scheme were very disappointing. Its main elements constituted the following:

- It originated from collaboration between FÁS, ICTU and FIE and CII (now IBEC).

- FÁS hoped to make 10,000 places available, giving special consideration to the long-term unemployed and early school-leavers.

- FÁS had to be assured by companies opting for the scheme that they intended to increase their employment levels.

- Trainees were to be placed with employers for periods ranging between 13 and 20 weeks.

- The cost of training would be borne by employers, with 75 per cent reimbursed by FÁS.

- The overall objective visualised definite job opportunities in the placement company for the trainee at the end of the training period.

FÁS itself is the major provider of training programmes for the unemployed, and almost 150 courses in specific skills are provided in its network of training centres. Duration varies, but courses are usually four to six months long. All training costs, including trainee allowances, are incurred by FÁS.

More general training programmes for the unemployed are also run by FÁS, such as the Alternance Programme, which provides a mixture of basic skills training and work experience for older persons.

ADULT AND CONTINUING EDUCATION

There is considerable interest in adult and continuing education (ACE) in Ireland and it is perceived as an area that could make a significant contribution to the level of knowledge and skill within the community. However, to assess ACE within the context of the national training scene, it is important to establish a clear definition of what is meant by the concept. Statements by many commentators, and by education bodies, have led to some confusion in this respect.

Adult education involves the implementation of practical strategies and policies that encourage and facilitate individuals whose education was interrupted, terminated, or prematurely ended in youth to return to the educational arena. It is normally associated with providing opportunities for study with a degree of formality for those who have completed some education, either at primary or post-primary level.

Continuing education provides facilities and opportunities for those in full-time employment whose full-time schooling has ceased. This context includes part-time evening courses, modular-based programmes and open learning activities.

These two areas are not to be confused with *recurrent education*, which bears a number of similarities. Recurrent education's basic premise is that opportunities for personal educational/intellectual development should be available as a right over every individual's lifetime. Facilities should be in place for those in the "first chance category", as well as for those entering for a "second chance". It therefore rejects the traditional "finite" idea of education undertaken and completed over a particular time in favour of ongoing "lifelong" education. Therefore, while it does encompass the idea and basics of ACE, it differs quite substantially in its concepts, philosophy, aims and aspirations.

Characteristics of Adult Continuing Education in Ireland

Before looking at specific issues in this area, it may be helpful if we outline some of the characteristics of ACE in Ireland. O'Sullivan (1989) sets out five categories of ACE provision (Figure 4.2) and also identifies a number of fundamental characteristics associated with ACE.

Participation

The dominant ethos of ACE is that of open access for all adults through a variety of modes of provision. Research, however, identifies patterns of participation which strongly suggest that this ethos is far from being achieved. A trend evident from many studies is that scientific and technical subjects are almost exclusively studied by males, while business and commercial subjects are taken equally by both sexes, and liberal and social subjects are pursued mainly by female students. In addition, younger adults are more likely to study vocational subjects, lower socio-economic groups lean more towards scientific and technical subjects, while higher socio-economic groups show greater participation in business, commercial and social subjects. In overall terms, those with the highest levels of participation in ACE have benefited most from their initial contact with the educational system.

Motivation

The motivation of students to attend adult classes is one of the most frequent discussion topics among adult education providers. Research supports the view that the typical basis for attendance is a wish to learn a specific skill or body of knowledge. This desire stems from either a perceived inadequacy in social or occupational spheres, or the need for self-improvement and self-evaluation.

Characteristics of the Adult Learner

A considerable body of research exists which shows that adult students in Ireland have particular common characteristics, among them being:

- difficulties in finding time to study;

- the necessity to undertake long journeys in order to attend classes;

- inhibitions, due to factors such as disposition, confidence and self-conception;

- high drop-out rate, especially on open learning programmes.

Figure 4.2: Fundamental Characteristics of Adult and Continuing Education

	Liberal	Social	Vocational	Certification	Inventionist
Content/Orientation	Active and conceptual courses of a self-development, hobby/recreational nature	Social, political and economic studies, community development, leadership, family life and parenting courses	Largely in-service courses, not generally leading to marketable qualifications	Re-entry to second- and third-level educational programmes on a full time or part time basis	Basic and social skills, sheltered training, consciousness-raising and remedial activities
Providers	• Vocational education committees (second-level schools and regional technical colleges) Institutions such as • The People's College, Dublin • Institute of Adult Education • RTE • Sporting and cultural organisations	• Macra na Feirme • Muintir na Tíre • Marriage advisory councils • University extra-murals • RTE Institutions such as • The People's College, Dublin and Institute of Adult Education	• FÁS • Irish Management Institute • Institute of Public Administration • Teagasc • Trade Unions • College of Industrial Relations • Third-level colleges	• Second- and third-level education institutions • Correspondence colleges • Professional bodies such as IITD, IPD and MII	• Literacy schemes • National Rehabilitation Institute • Prison service • Compensatory schemes • Advocacy and activist groups representing minorities and the disadvantaged

Source: Adapted from O'Sullivan, D. (1989) "Adult and Continuing Education in the Irish Republic: A Research Guide" *International Journal of Lifelong Education*, Vol. 8, No. 3, (July-Sept 1989) pp. 211 - 234.

While these highlight negative features, research has also shown that adult learners demonstrate a greater capacity to pass courses, and are better at maintaining class spirit and contributing to the overall learning experience.

Outcomes

A number of studies indicate that adults perceived themselves to have changed in significant ways through contact with formal courses or learning situations. Commonly cited outcomes include:

- gains in skills and knowledge appropriate to family, community, occupational and social positions;

- changes in the way such positions were related to or participated in ;

- increase in extroversion, empathy and liberalism;

- greater inclination to attend to media coverage of politics, economics, and current affairs;

- acquisition of knowledge, competencies, and dispositions necessary for business.

In this context, the type of outcome reported is very much contingent on the type of study programme pursued.

Structure and Organisation of Adult and Continuing Education

It may appear from the previous analysis that ACE is in a healthy state in Ireland. AONTAS (the National Association of Adult Education — the national co-ordinating body for adult and continuing education) pointed out, however, that it is generally unplanned and uncoordinated, with responsibility for its structure and organisation not allocated to any particular government department. Nonetheless, it does play a central role in our education and training scene, occupying in the process the minds of Government, industry and individuals. While there is undoubtedly much divergence in attitudes, central to the perspective of all parties is the notion that ACE should allow those who are no longer in full-time education the opportunity to participate. By extension, there exists the further view that such learning and education is not the sole prerogative of youth.

Our present system is the consequence of past practices. History has a significant part to play in the issue of what is presently available from the government, industry and voluntary organisations in Ireland. Up to the early 1960s, educational structures remained basically unchanged in

Europe. However, the entire fabric of living was altered by the impact of new technology, especially in the realm of computing with the advent of the microchip. These changes continue to the present time, but perhaps are viewed as less radical than in the period between the mid-1960s and 1980s. Nonetheless, the 1960s were the foundation years in terms of setting the agenda for the standards and structures of the future. Despite its physical separation, Ireland was not immune to the changes which were affecting mainland Europe.

The primary effect of the changes mentioned was acutely felt in education. The existing structures were considered insufficient to cope with the rapid pace of change. It was logical to assume that, since change was becoming a permanent facet of life for most individuals (for the foreseeable future), continual or lifelong learning would be perceived as the ideal antidote for the problem of coping with this "permanence of change". The extent to which this notion was taken on board by Government and other institutions is open to question.

Provision of Adult and Continuing Education

Course Providers

Data provided by AONTAS (1989) demonstrate that most adult education courses in Ireland are provided through State agencies and institutions. The main statutory providers are the Vocational Education Committees and a number of Community and Comprehensive Schools established since the 1970s. Voluntary secondary schools, universities, regional technical colleges and colleges of technology are also very much to the fore in this area. Other agencies provide more specific types of adult education courses, and among a long and varied list in this category are: FÁS; Teagasc; Rehabilitation Institute; RTE; Regional Health Boards; Health Promotion Unit; Dublin Institute of Adult Education; People's College; National College of Industrial Relations; Macra na Feirme; public libraries; museums; art galleries; various Irish language, youth, church and other organisations; and various associations and agencies. Finally, there are a number of other providers among non-formal voluntary groups involved in areas such as creative writing, travellers' education, women's interests, unemployment action, etc.

Course Organisation

Providers are mainly responsible for organising and advertising their own courses. Within the VEC system this is usually undertaken by Adult Education Organisers, 50 of whom were appointed in 1979. Courses are organised on an ad-hoc local basis and correspond with attempts to match the anticipated demand with the potential supply of learners and tutors. As with any product or service, these efforts invariably feature continual attempts at testing the marketplace, to see which courses will prove self-financing.

Following the Kenny Commission Report on "Lifelong Learning", Adult Education Boards, each comprising 12 members, were established in each VEC area in 1984. The recommended membership of the Board is two from the VEC; one each from Teagasc, FÁS and the library authority; and seven other organisations involved in adult education, while the Boards may also appoint three observers. The primary function of these Boards are to assess the educational needs of adults in the area, prepare a suitable programme of courses and activities, administer finances, and prepare an annual report for the VEC and the Minister for Education. They are also involved in the allocation of funds made available through the Adult Literacy and Community Education Budget for Disadvantaged Groups.

Types of Courses Offered

A wide variety of adult education courses are provided, ranging from those that are once-off and short-term to the long-term degree kind. Most short-term courses last approximately ten weeks, deal with a specific subject, are of the more traditional hobby, leisure or commercial type, and do not lead to any recognised qualification. Other courses frequently involve some kind of examination, either at second level or third level, and culminate in certificate, diploma or degree qualification.

An important element of adult education has been the provision of literacy and basic education courses. Adult education also entails varying the level of study and the frequency/length of attendance in accordance with the needs of the individual.

More recently, there has been a growth in social and personal development-type courses, through which participants gain a better understanding of themselves and the society within which they live.

Course Certification

Very few adult education courses are formally recognised, either by way of specific awards (that is, certificate/diploma) or by being linked into a system whereby units of credits may be gained towards a nationally recognised award. Indeed the most common certified study programme is the Leaving Certificate, which, it must be said, is specifically designed as an examination for school children finishing full-time second-level education. Certificate and diploma courses are, of course, provided (mainly in business disciplines), while universities and other third-level institutions have traditionally provided intensive degree programmes. Some universities have attempted to address the certification issue, with limited success to date.

Participation in Adult and Continuing Education

Numbers participating in adult and continuing education has grown steadily. AONTAS (1994) estimates that some 300,000 adults take part annually, a figure that is almost three times higher than the number of students involved in third level education.

A complete cross-section of the community participates — from the young to the elderly, from those living in rural areas to city-dwellers, from those who cannot read or write to those with university degrees. However, O'Sullivan (1989) demonstrates that there are higher levels of participation among certain sectors. For instance, women are more likely to participate than men, and participants are more likely to be in the 22-44 age group, from a city, full-time employed and of Leaving Certificate standard.

A cause for concern is the lower level of participation by men, especially those in the long-term unemployed category, and by those who have not completed full-time second level education. Despite the current existence of several schemes, greater action is required from the Government to support and encourage the unemployed to engage in education. There are more barriers to access than there are open welcoming doors and systems of support.

Funding of Adult and Continuing Education

Education is one of the government departments which has a very significant budget at its disposal. For example, its expenditure in 1993 was £1.166 billion. Out of this budget, adult education received approximately one-sixth of one percent (0.16 per cent), a fairly obvious indication that lifelong learning has not exactly been a Government priority.

Adult education is predominantly self-financing, which means that the core costs of provision, including tuition fees, materials, and publicity, must be covered from course fees. In effect, this means that the viability of courses is dependent on the numbers enrolling, and also dictates that, as costs of provision increase, so too do the fees paid by adult students.

In a fairly recent development, some courses are exempt from the strict self-financing rule, a move designed to make such courses accessible to those who missed out on educational opportunities first time around and can least afford to pay. Other activities, such as those associated with the Educational Opportunities Scheme and the Adult Literacy and Education Budget, are also exempt in similar manner. However, this latter budget has been grossly underfunded, in that it is expected to finance adult literacy and community projects for the entire country.

On this point, it is important to bear in mind that literacy and community education activities depend on a large pool of volunteer labour, and their continued survival is frequently subject to surpluses generated by other fee-paying courses. By having to rely in this way on the demand for other adult education courses, their very existence, not to mention the extent of their activities, is precarious from year to year.

The existing funding arrangements for adult education means that the vast majority of courses are run on a commercial basis, and are only provided if they attract sufficient numbers of people willing to pay the fees to cover the costs involved. Most participants, even those in the less well-off category, have to pay for themselves. Furthermore, this very valuable service to the community is forced to compete in the marketplace against highly-advertised consumer goods. There is no budget for publicity, and any financial outlay on advertising must be recouped through raising the cost of courses.

Another important aspect of the lack of funding is its negative effect on the promotion of adult education in general, despite the efforts of AONTAS (the National Association of Adult Education), NALA (the National Adult Literacy Agency) and IVEA (the Irish Vocational Education Association) and providers who generally promote their own courses. This fact has been highlighted by two important government commissions concerning the development of adult education in Ireland: "Adult Education in Ireland" (the Murphy Report, 1973) and "Lifelong Learning" (the Kenny Report, 1984).

This inadequacy of State funding is undoubtedly one of the main problems hindering the development of adult education in Ireland. ACE does not have a coherent structure, nor are there definite plans or policies for its future development. The participation of those who have most to gain (that is, the poor, the less well-educated, and the disadvantaged) is most inhibited by the strict self-financing approach. All of this is in stark contrast to the situation in many European countries, where the contribution of adult education to social and economic development is greatly recognised and a genuine commitment to the concept of lifelong learning is clearly demonstrated.

Tutors and Teaching

One of the significant characteristics of ACE in Ireland is its almost exclusive staffing by part-time teachers and volunteers. Course schedules tutors are appointed for a term, and employment is largely determined by student numbers.

Tutor recruitment is commonly an unplanned process, generally dependent on finding someone with knowledge or expertise in a particular area or topic. Many adult tutors are school teachers, while others are drawn from a range of business, social, cultural and religious organisations. Because of the low status of adult education, as reflected in its funding, there are no established career structures for tutors, nor are there promotional opportunities or salary scales available, which would attract people who may be interested in making a career in adult education.

The training of adult educators in Ireland is very poor. The lack of emphasis is based on two false assumptions: that people trained to teach children can automatically apply a similar expertise to the teaching of adults, and that people with a high level of knowledge or expertise in a particular subject or topic can naturally impart this to others. Apart from the literacy schemes and some other organisations, very few schemes exist, although a minority of adult tutors take personal steps to improve their skills by attending relevant courses, seminars or workshops.

Many tutors themselves do not realise the importance of training, leading to a perpetuation of traditional teaching methods based on lectures rather than more participative learning methods.

Adult Learning Needs

Restrictions imposed by the self-financing philosophy have led to a situation where adult education has largely become a middle-class pursuit, reflecting the interests of the more articulate and better-off. On the other hand, its lack of formal structure has allowed it the flexibility to adapt to a variety of needs, and in recent years it has become an important source of "second-chance" education. Developments in day-time education, basic education, and alternative methods of teaching and facilitation demonstrate that adult education has both the potential and the flexibility to become a positive initiative in the educational arena.

There is general acceptance that adult learning needs are undergoing a radical transformation which must be recognised and catered for by the system. Some pertinent issues already identified in this regard include:

- The most striking demographic factor to be faced is the gradual transformation from a predominantly young population to a large older population. This will have implications for the development of adult education which will include creative ways of using the skills and experience of older people.

- Swift technological advances have meant changes in job and career patterns, leading to the likelihood of people changing jobs and careers more frequently, thus necessitating retraining and more specific educational opportunities.

- The growing trends of job sharing, early retirement, and voluntary redundancy will mean that people have more time to follow a whole variety of educational pursuits.

- As changes in society impinge on traditional family structures, there is an ever-growing tendency for women to continue their careers and so increasingly seek opportunities to improve their skills and abilities. This has brought about a demand for day-time education which is mainly taken up by women.

- The influence of the media figures prominently in our culture, through television, radio, video and computer technology, while multi-channel access has broadened the variety of imported visual material. The resulting heightened awareness of global issues has highlighted the need for developmental education which aims to advance critical insight of local, national, and international issues, based on an understanding of world economic and political processes.

Some providers, organisers, and teachers have attempted to respond to emerging areas of interest in adult education. This is manifested in efforts to anticipate and meet the demand for social and personal development courses, and a style of provision through which adult education is seen as a process whereby mature people are facilitated to learn rather than subjected to traditional "classroom" teaching. However, the pattern of developments is generally sporadic and unplanned.

Reform of Adult and Continuing Education in Ireland

AONTAS (1989) and (1994) suggests five areas where reform is necessary. These represent a well thought out position on the existing problems in the area of adult education, and are summarised as follows:

1. There cannot be any real progress in the development of adult education in Ireland until the government provides the necessary funds and acts upon its responsibility to ensure a proper lifelong system of education for us all.

2. There have been two Government commissions which investigated the role of adult education in Irish society and made explicit recommendations as to how it could best be developed. The development of adult education depends not on further commissions or deliberation, but on adequate funding, without which it will remain out of date and out of place in a modern European-oriented Irish society.

3. AONTAS, NALA, IVEA, and some university departments are actively engaged in the development of adult education. However, the development of proper policies and teaching practices requires funds for carrying out the necessary research, as well as planning, developing and initiating pilot programmes. Unless these organisations have sufficient funds for curriculum development, training and the crea-

tion of innovative programmes, adult education in Ireland will only continue to stagger along, or stagnate.

4. For an emerging area of interest to grow, and for its growth to be sustained, it is necessary to plan for its development. This process would include discussions on issues with various interest groups, resulting in the initiation of pilot projects and courses, identification of people with skills and expertise, and evaluation of projects undertaken. AONTAS would like to see itself as a forum for new ideas and areas of interest in adult education. The continual development of new courses would lead to a demand for a more relevant system of adult education, which would help people to reflect on the issues which affect their lives. Teaching materials and methods which are stimulating, and lead to questioning and discussion, must be part and parcel of such education.

5. Developing new courses, and responding to new areas of interest, also inspires the need for research and the requirement for personnel and facilities. This will necessitate clear policy planning and commitment on the part of providers and the Department of Education, coupled with realistic funding to ensure growth.

MANAGEMENT EDUCATION AND TRAINING IN IRELAND

Development of Management Education and Training

The study of commerce and business in the Irish university system dates from the early part of this century. An examination of the subject content of business or commerce degrees in the 1950s would show a strong emphasis on accountancy, economics and law. In the late 1960s and early 1970s there was a rapid expansion in the area of business administration. This expansion followed the "American model" where the study of business remained an integral part of the traditional university structure. This allowed the university to bring about an immediate impact on business practice as the candidates were usually senior managers.

In addition to the expansion of undergraduate activity in the business area, specialised masters programmes in the functional areas of business came into evidence. The development of Regional Technical Colleges in the 1970s brought business education outside the main university cities. These colleges began to offer two-year certificate level and three-year diploma level programmes in a wide range of business and management subject areas.

Traditionally, the accounting profession has been a major contributor to management education in Ireland. The 1970s and early 1980s saw a significant expansion in part-time professional programmes. In addition to the accounting bodies, other professional associations such as the Institute of Marketing and the Institute of Personnel Management also expanded their educational activities. The Irish Management Institute, established in the 1960s and jointly funded by business and government, put a considerable effort into raising the level of management practice in Ireland. During the 1970s and 1980s it became one of the main providers of short courses for practising managers. Regional training organisations and consulting houses played a significant role in the in-company management development activities over this period.

Existing Provision of Management Education

Undergraduate Management Education

Basic education in business management is available through the certificate and diploma courses at the Regional Technical Colleges, and primary degree courses at the universities and institutions of higher education, as well as at some selected colleges. These courses provide a broad basis for the analysis of business information and problems, and some specialist expertise in practical managerial skills. Subjects studied usually include core foundation subjects such as accounting, economics, law, statistics, management information systems, and functional studies such as marketing, finance, personnel, production, and business strategy. Increasingly, project work forms a larger component of academic programmes.

The two-year certificate and three-year diploma programmes normally have lower entry and exit qualifications, but students who reach a sufficiently high grade may proceed to degree-level work at selected universities. In addition to the general business certificates and diplomas, there are also subject-specific ones in the areas of accounting, finance, personnel, marketing as well as industry or sectoral-specific ones such as tourism, agribusiness, etc.

Postgraduate Management Education

High honours students emerging from the primary degree programmes may proceed to higher-level qualifications, usually masters degrees. Given that the first MBA offered in Ireland in the mid-1960s was an executive part-time programme, most of the other MBA programmes which were subsequently launched followed this model, unlike many other European universities which initially adopted the immediate postgraduate MBA mode. This probably reflected the general availability of excellent undergraduate business degrees, and postgraduate specialist masters degrees. A review of the background of the majority of the ex-

ecutives attending MBA programmes indicated that their primary qualifications were in non-business areas. The research component of these
programmes is normally built around the participant's own work activity.

In the 1970s and early 1980s the Irish Management Institute, in association with Trinity College, Dublin, launched a series of degree level
executive programmes, modelled largely on an "action learning" approach.

The university business and commerce graduates form a major and
growing proportion of the intake of trainees for the professional accounting bodies. This trend has accelerated since the early 1980s when the
universities launched postgraduate professional diplomas in association
with the professional bodies.

The universities have also significantly increased the output of specialist graduate masters' programmes in such areas as management information systems, industrial relations, personnel management, international marketing, and banking and finance.

Lately, universities have moved into the company development mode,
and are operating a series of experiential programmes designed to increase the already well-developed links between the universities and the
business community.

Doctoral programmes in business are limited in numbers, and follow
the traditional research-driven mode. These are largely utilised to develop teaching and research faculty.

Post-Experience Management Education

Traditionally, this has been largely provided by the Irish Management
Institute in the form of a wide variety of short- and medium-term
courses. Of late, this has been paralleled by other educational institutions offering specific courses designed largely for specialist industry
and business needs. University business schools have begun to offer
company-specific management development programmes for major organisations, following the trend set by the consulting houses and the
Irish Management Institute. There is also a significant level of
"educational transfer" through individual consultations between organisation and business school faculty.

Professional Education

The role played by the professional institutes in specific areas of business practice is significant. Areas such as accountancy, marketing,
banking, public administration, personnel management, etc. are served
by recognised professional bodies which monitor examinations and only
admit candidates for membership on the basis of the results of such examinations and a sufficient exposure to professional practice. Members

are entitled to use the appropriate letters after their names to signify their status in the profession.

Evaluation of Existing Provision

There has generally been little attempt to comprehensively assess the training and development provisions for Irish managers, but two sources do provide relevant data. In 1984, AnCO surveyed 15 private learning organisations to identify the level of management training activity they supported. Four key findings emerged:

- Twenty-five per cent of the organisations were fully engaged in management training and development.

- Open courses were the most popular method of conducting management education and development.

- A considerable number of organisations were involved in providing in-company training.

- The most popular areas covered on management training and development programmes were general management, personal skills, finance, marketing, corporate planning, production, personnel/IR, law and languages.

The structure and extent of management training was examined in the Galvin Report (1988). It saw the provision of formal education and development as covering a broad range of activities and being widely dispersed across universities, colleges, professional institutes, and private providers. It identified three main routes to management:

- The specialist route — whereby an individual by virtue of specialist or functional expertise (which may or may not include a formal qualification) attains a management position.

- The business qualification route — whereby an individual acquires a business qualification and attempts to secure a management position on this basis.

- The generalist route — whereby an individual with a general third-level qualification, or without any specific qualification, progresses to a management position.

The structure and extent of management training in Ireland is seen to reflect these main routes to management both at pre-entry and post-experience levels.

This report reinforced the previous finding that formal courses were the most popular form of management training and development provision. Other aspects of this provision included the following:

- The IMI and IPA (Institute of Public Administration) were the main providers of management training and development programmes.

- In the private sector, the IMI has a significant impact among the top 1,000 companies, but less so at medium-sized business level. FÁS was the next most important training agency for industry, followed by the universities and overseas courses.

- In the public sector, the IPA, which caters specifically for the public service, and the universities were the main agencies employed.

- There was support for the notion that a greater degree of attendance exists at courses in the areas of functional and technical skills, rather than general management skills.

Generally universities and colleges are trying to bridge the gap between the academic science of management and the practical realities of industry. Mid-career programmes, involving considerable time commitment, are provided by the universities for individuals currently in management positions or those aspiring to such positions. These include MBAs, diplomas, and courses leading to professional qualifications. Some of the universities have made attempts to cater for the post-experience graduate who seeks to get into business, and for practising managers who want to become up-to-date with specific functions without taking a degree course.

With the notable exception of large multinationals, most companies place almost total reliance on the use of external training and development agencies to organise their training and development. This is not the most satisfactory strategy if one considers the potential problems of relevance and learning transfer. Some external trainers have recognised this and have adopted approaches such as action learning as a means of strengthening the link between course material and the work situation. However, this serves to highlight the uneven quality of existing provision, and little attention has been given by FÁS to the evaluation of providers or the formulation of proposals to deal with the considerable duplication of services which exist. It is accepted that there is a need for some form of co-ordination, to help users identify the most appropriate solutions to their management training and development problems, and consequently to make better use of scarce resources. However, there is no coherent policy informing the Government role, nor is there a policy or framework informing the educational sector on what they should provide.

The lack of guiding principles has left Ireland looking to the US and the UK in search of ideas, leading to the adoption and application of the MBA model. This, however, poses a number of major problems within the context of the training and development of Irish managers. Among these are:

- The education base necessary to develop MBA programmes is not present among many managers at all levels in Ireland.

- Many Irish programmes tend towards specialisation and fail to provide the generalist/strategic view which is required for effective management.

- Many of those pursuing MBA qualifications come from engineering backgrounds and are using this qualification as an entry mechanism into management. On the other hand, the MBA is not being undertaken by many of those already in management positions who are in need of management development.

- MBA programmes are very costly and consequently are not feasible option for many small companies.

- The Irish culture may not provide an appropriate backdrop for US-type MBA programmes, and no research has been undertaken to identify the applicability of American models in an Irish context.

It has been widely suggested that present provision of, and facilities for, management education and development do not have significant penetration. Only those companies with advanced training and development policies and systems are participating, and it can be strongly urged that these participate entirely of their own volition. Greater incentives are required to encourage more widespread participation, especially in relation to small firms (almost 90 per cent of these carry out little or no management training), and it is generally accepted that a reformed approach in this area is an urgent necessity.

REGIONAL MANAGEMENT EDUCATION AND TRAINING PROVIDERS

A further important development in the early 1980s was the formation of regional training organisations with state and industry support. The first such organisation, the Regional Management Centre (RMC), was set up in 1977 by AnCO, Shannon Development Company, and education and industry representatives. By the early 1980s the RMC was beginning to make a significant contribution to the training needs of industry and similar organisations were established in Galway and Cork. A study undertaken by the University of Limerick (then NIHE) in 1984 (Garavan, Jankowicz and Pattinson) examined the role of such organisations with survey participants (150) citing a number of important advantages. Some of these are listed below:

- They enabled a more even distribution of external training facilities. This was especially relevant to the West, Mid-West and Southern regions of the country, which had been poorly served in this regard until 1980.

- Having local training centres meant less travelling for participants and lower costs for client organisations. This factor proved particularly beneficial to small companies, who could not afford an expensive outlay on training services.

- Local training organisations had the potential to foster a better relationship with client organisations and were therefore in an advantageous position to provide training that was more job-related and relevant.

- Local training centres could be more innovative and better able to respond effectively to local conditions.

- Technical training had shown a considerable increase in the early 1980s and local training centres were seen to have made an important contribution here by having mechanical facilities/tutors close to the client base.

- Having long term evening/modular based courses in close proximity helped companies to overcome the difficulties imposed by participation of key personnel in courses of long duration.

- The 1980s has witnessed a phenomenal growth in adult education in Ireland. Local training centres, by providing facilities and tutors, gave access to such education for participants who otherwise would not have had the opportunity.

Nonetheless, industry respondents also indicated some limitations to the development of local training centres. For instance:

- Some organisations were more in favour of on-the-job training and did not attach any value to the local availability of external training resources.

- A proliferation of training and advisory bodies had been established by the early 1980s, leading to a duplication of services and a situation where training facilities were not being fully utilised. Respondents also questioned the quality of the courses provided by some private training organisations.

• Any new training organisation must adopt a professional approach if it is to be successful and it may prove difficult for a small regional organisation to establish and maintain such professionalism.

• Unhealthy competition, instead of co-operation, can develop between training organisations, especially at local level.

Despite these reservations, regional training organisations had carved out a significant role in the Irish training system.

PROPOSAL FOR REFORM OF MANAGEMENT EDUCATION

The Galvin Report identified five areas where reform was necessary:

1. *Commitment to management training.* The level of commitment to management training and development in Ireland is unacceptably low, and expenditure on initiatives in this area is insufficient in relation both to international practice and national needs. It was further noted that, while the situation is serious throughout the public and private sectors, it is especially serious in small, Irish-owned, and small, new, Irish-owned companies.

2. *Guidelines for management development.* There are no generally accepted guidelines for management development. While activities take place both on and off-the-job, it appears that organisations are insufficiently aware of the range of development opportunities available, or of the appropriateness of particular methods of development.

3. *Lack of standard business knowledge.* Managers tend to lack a common core of relevant business knowledge and skills. There is no clearly recognised route to management in Ireland, hence individuals are typically promoted to managerial positions as a result of their performance in a specialist function. In such situations, managers may not have acquired training in the particular skills of management, nor indeed have any strong business foundation. The report also indicated that where individuals enter the ranks of management via a business qualification, they may lack the most appropriate foundation for this later development as managers.

4. *Participation of small businesses.* Managers in small businesses tend to have lower rates of participation in formal development activities. It was indicated that managers in this category are less likely to avail of formal developmental opportunities because of the cost to the company of their absence, as well as the actual course costs incurred.

5. *Role of the State*. The State's role in funding post-experience management training is (a) unclear, (b) inconsistent, and (c) not geared towards the realisation of national objectives. State expenditure on management development is largely attributable to business education (£12 million in 1986) while direct spending on management development is considerably less (£3 million in 1986). Furthermore, State spending is mainly channelled through a subsidy to providers of management training and development, and not directly to the users. The report also suggests that State expenditure in this area does not follow funding principles, and that the State has little control over the effectiveness of the money expended.

In response to the weaknesses highlighted, the Committee put forward recommendations which were intended to provide the basis for redirecting future efforts in relation to management training and development in Ireland. These may be summarised as follows:

- The establishment of an action group that would spearhead a campaign for the promotion of management development, in an effort to raise the level of awareness in Irish industry and gain commitment from Irish companies.

- The drawing up of guidelines for management development, which would be promoted as a code of good practice for organisations and management and serve to eliminate ambiguity in this context.

- The drawing up of guidelines for business education, with the intention of encouraging providers in this area to offer a broadly common curriculum, thereby reducing disparity between similar qualifications. Entwined with this was the proposal that providers offering scientific or specialist courses would include at least one core business module, to assist functional specialists should they be appointed to managerial positions during their careers.

- State spending should be re-directed away from the present support of providers of management training, to the support of users.

- Incentives should be offered to assist small businesses in both drawing up and implementing management development programmes, thus ensuring that all sectors participate in such activities.

The Committee reiterated the point that responsibility for initiatives in management training and development rested firmly on the shoulders of those at executive and senior management levels. Furthermore, these initiatives should be strategic in focus, effective in aiding organisations to achieve their corporate goals, and carefully evaluated and modified as and when necessary. Adopting this approach should significantly enhance the prospect of Irish managers possessing the skills and capabilities required if their companies are to compete successfully in EU and world markets.

Little appears to have occurred by way of initiatives since the publication of the Galvin Report. While 1991 was designated the "Year of the Manager", the Government has not taken any significant steps to implement the recommendations made, in terms of resources or other supportive interventions.

SUMMARY

In this chapter we have examined four elements of the national training and vocational education system in Ireland: vocational education, apprenticeship training, youth training and adult and continuing education. We have examined the evolution of each of these areas, their present operation and the need for reform in each area. We have discussed some of the major problems faced by each area. Each area examined highlights a common set of problems: lack of resources, lack of co-ordination, needs of the sector not clearly identified. Chapter 5 will continue to examine other elements of the national system.

5

ELEMENTS OF THE IRISH SYSTEM: TRAINING FOR TOURISM, ENTERPRISE AND SPECIAL CATEGORIES

INTRODUCTION AND LEARNING OBJECTIVES

This chapter continues to explore elements of the national vocational training and education system in Ireland. Specifically, we examine training within the tourism sector, training for enterprise and entrepreneurship, training for people with disabilities and training issues within the travelling community. Finally, the issue of an integrated national system is considered. Having read this chapter you will understand:

♦ the extent of training within the tourism sector and the key weaknesses that need to be rectified;

♦ the various initiatives taken to encourage enterprise;

♦ the problems involved in providing training services for people with disabilities and the travelling community;

♦ the difficulties involved in achieving an integrated national system.

TRAINING FOR THE TOURISM INDUSTRY

The Key Providers of Training

The organisations providing training and development within the tourism sector include CERT, professional trainers and other professional bodies. While Bord Fáilte has overall responsibility for the tourist industry, training within the industry is the responsibility of the Council for Education, Recruitment and Training (CERT). This body recruits, co-ordinates and delivers training to individuals preparing for employment as well as those already employed within the industry. The central objectives of CERT are (a) to achieve high operational practices and standards within the tourism industry through a professionally trained workforce at every level, and (b) to assist in the provision of a higher-quality product which aids economic performance, job creation and the sustaining of employment. In order to achieve these broad objectives CERT makes use of educational establishments as well as organising in-house training. CERT has four training centres located in Dublin, Cork and Limerick and a series of courses are also organised in the College of Catering and the RTC network throughout the country. These centres, together with a number of leading hotels, are used to run specialised and short courses. CERT provides a wide range of courses in areas such as accommodation, bartending, hotel management, receptionist skills and so forth.

Groupings of people within the tourism sector avail of facilities provided by professional trainers. Large hotel groups such as the Great Southern Hotels, the Ryan Group, Jury's Group, Doyle Hotel Group and Fitzpatricks use the services of professional organisations to provide industry-tailored programmes.

Other professional organisations that provide training within the sector include the National Dairy Council (NDC), which provides training on the use of dairy products and on a wide range of topics related to their areas; Bord Iascaigh Mhara (BIM), which provides extensive programmes on the cooking and presentation of fish; and Córas Beostoicc agus Feola (CBF), which provides training on the preparation and presentation of meat products.

There are two bodies that set standards and issue nationally recognised certificates. The NCEA certifies management programmes within the Regional Technical Colleges, the College of Catering and Shannon College of Hotel Management, while the National Tourism Certification Board, through its committee system, undertakes research on educational needs, the design of training courses, assessment procedures, and awards certificates within the industry.

Quality of the Existing Provision

A number of criticisms can be made of training provision within the industry. CERT has traditionally built up its expertise for the more narrowly defined hotel and catering industry rather than the broader tourism industry. Commentators such as Deegan (1994) and King (1993) point out that while placement rates of trainees has been consistently high, the measures used to assess effectiveness are not very informative about the quality of trainees. Training outputs tend to be measured in quantitative rather than qualitative terms.

CERT programmes have been criticised for targeting a specialist market. Many of the programmes apply to sectors of the industry which can afford to hire specialists. However, a large sector of the industry, namely the Bed and Breakfast sector, can not afford specialists. The B&B sector requires employees with a broad range of skills. Staff employment within this sector is often recruited from within the family and the seasonal nature of the work makes the jobs ideally suited for school-going children. It is difficult for people in this sector to attend full-time programmes of a long-term duration.

CERT programmes have further been criticised for their lack of flexibility. The core subjects which are common to most CERT programmes include business administration, food preparation, reception techniques, beverages, etc. One could argue that greater multi-skilling should be encouraged to create a pool of skilled employees, whose presence could significantly improve the professionalisation of the business and the overall quality of the service provided.

Much of the training provided within the industry is classroom-based. This has many advantages in that it allows knowledge and skills to be developed in a controlled environment, but it ignores the fact that the tourism sector demands a wide range of interpersonal skills, which, it is often argued, can only be acquired in real-life situations.

There is a general lack of commitment to training within the tourism industry, despite the efforts of CERT. The general level of awareness of changing consumer patterns in international tourism is weak in Ireland. The average hotelier and heritage site manager rarely has a research function available to give guidance in crucial areas of emerging market trends. The net overall result has been a lack of investment in the training and retraining of staff to meet the needs of the modern-day tourist. The lack of emphasis within the industry on language skills at a time when Irish tourism is becoming increasingly reliant on continental European visitors bears testament to this viewpoint. The lack of attention to these matters is a reflection of the "voluntarist" nature of technical and vocational education in Ireland, where the choice remains with individual firms to decide how and what type of training they should undertake. This reflects an inadequate appreciation of the fact that much of the benefits of training are external to both the individual firm and the person being trained. This problem relates to tourism in much the same manner as the industrial sector. Under the German "dual" system of apprenticeships in industry, a mixture of compulsion, sense of social obligation and collective institutional arrangements act to prevent such market failure. For example, most German companies train beyond the level which might be justified within the narrow interests of their own company.

Low levels of demand for certain skills in Ireland might be indicative of a certain level of complacency about training needs. Low awareness of world class tourism standards may make Irish managers poor judges of their own training requirements. The emphasis placed on managerial training needs was given far less priority by Irish companies than by their competitors. In addition, the link between a lack of training and low level innovation is a mechanism whereby poor skills standards are translated into poor product quality.

There has been a great deal of emphasis within CERT on training for the unemployed. While such schemes are appropriate in an economy of endemic unemployment, these schemes should not be confused with the provision of higher standards of training. This point has been addressed by Roche and Tansey (1992) in relation to the industrial sector where they recommended that training should be institutionally separated from the organisation of job schemes for the unemployed. A similar approach should be adopted for the tourism sector.

There must be a serious attempt to follow "best practice" in tourism training. An analysis of matched plants in the industrial sector in Ireland with their counterparts abroad found that skill levels and product quality in Ireland were below that of our competitors. A study of "best practice" and skill needs in tourism should be undertaken as a matter of priority.

Management training should be given greater priority both in terms of fundamental business skills as well as those specifically related to the needs of the tourism industry. Greater emphasis must be placed on the "Europeanisation" of the training process. This requires a better knowledge of the European visitor and their culture; language training skills at all levels in the industry and training in all forms of new technology.

Finally, given the changing role of CERT, from a narrow hotel and catering focus to a broader remit, resources should be allocated to "training the trainers". There must be a movement away from the previous narrow focus towards the identification of tourism opportunities exclusively within the hotel sector. Developments in cultural tourism, environmental tourism and tourism for the aged and unemployed will require a host of skills which Ireland simply does not possess at present.

ENTREPRENEURSHIP AND ENTERPRISE TRAINING

Although there are many notable exceptions, Irish people in general have not been given to entrepreneurial tendencies. The pattern followed by the vast majority of individuals involves passage through the education system, with a subsequent quest for secure employment in an existing enterprise or perhaps the public service (Deegan, 1994). This traditional pattern was heavily reinforced by the education system itself, where curricula were designed to facilitate the acquisition of sufficient knowledge and learning to attain standardised educational qualifications. In turn, the extent of success and achievement evident in these terms largely determined the type of "job" or "work" a person entered into. In all of this, there was little to encourage the development of an entrepreneurial or a "risk-taking" approach.

In our fast changing society, traditional patterns are constantly being overturned and this fact is particularly evident in the concept of "secure employment". The scale of the unemployment problem has severely blighted this notion, and the traditional sources of work and jobs are constricting in a seemingly interminable cycle (for example, the public sector — the civil service, nursing, teaching, professional and banking sectors; and across a spectrum of industrial employments) (O'Connor and Lyons, 1982, 1983). Recent years, therefore, have witnessed a much greater focus on enterprise and entrepreneurship. Considerable efforts are being made to encourage a greater number of people to become involved in enterprise ventures. State agencies have been to the forefront in this promotional activity, and training is frequently a feature of the support systems available in this context.

State Agency Training Programmes

In 1992, a report on support policies for business start-ups and the role of training in Ireland was prepared by the European Centre for the Development of Vocational Training (CEDEFOP). This report outlines the main State agencies supporting enterprise development and training, and evaluates some of the training programmes provided. We will concentrate initially on the training provision within the main schemes available through these agencies.

FÁS — Enterprise Programme

This programme is aimed at unemployed people wishing to start their own business, but also caters for community groups and worker co-operatives who wish to become involved in enterprise development. Entry requirements stipulate that participants must be registered as unemployed for a certain period of time.

The programme itself consists of two phases. During the initial ten weeks, participants follow a business appraisal training programme, which facilitates assessment of the trainee's proposed project and the formulation of a business plan. The second phase is directed towards enabling trainees to successfully start their business — income support, enterprise workshops and access to business advice.

Trainees are entitled to an allowance during phase one, and to enterprise payments during phase two (normally for a 40-week period). All trainees are vetted by FÁS prior to entry, and admission to the programme is dependent on the potential viability of the proposed venture and its compliance with relevant legislative and other criteria. On the operational side, logistical problems, such as distances to be travelled by rural-based trainees, requirements for more specialised technical training, and cost factors associated with small intake numbers, have been an apparent feature of the programme. Currently, FÁS is considering the use of distance and open learning facilities to facilitate those with travel difficulties.

The Enterprise Programme has been evolving since its inception in 1983 (as a 26 week start-your-own-business programme) for employed persons interested in starting their own business. Part-time evening courses are provided in FÁS regional training centres to meet these needs. A part-time programme called "Women in Enterprise" is also available to women trainees within the enterprise programme.

The FÁS Enterprise Programme was the subject of two studies in 1988 — one was conducted by the ESRI and the other by a FÁS working party. Brief details of some of their findings are summarised here:

- 12 per cent of entrants dropped out before completing the scheme.

- Among those businesses which survived to the end of the Enterprise Programme year, 21 per cent failed over the following 13 weeks (when the weekly allowance ran out).

- At the time of the study, 60 per cent of businesses were still operating.

- It was estimated that the net effect of the programme was to remove 32 people, for every 100 entrants, from the live unemployment register for one year.

- A greater linkage was recommended between training and the programme, and it was advised that enterprise training should be available (though not obligatory), prior to the start-up, for all those accepted onto the programme.

- It was recommended that a more streamlined approach should be adopted and that a new single enterprise programme should be based on a modular approach, with one six-week core element, followed by a range of flexible options. A new, more integrated programme along these lines was subsequently established nationally.

FÁS Community Enterprise Programme

The FÁS Community Enterprise Programme (CEP) is an initiative designed to support the development of enterprises by community and co-operative groups. It is perceived as a complementary intervention to the programmes and assistance supplied by other statutory agencies in relation to business start-up. These include the IDA, County Development Teams, Shannon Free Area Development Company (SFADCO), Údarás na Gaeltachta, as well as agencies with specialist functions in areas such as marketing, exporting, product development, science and technology, etc. The programme promotes the forging of key connections with community-based sources, including trade unions, chambers of commerce, community and youth organisations, third level colleges, area partnership companies and professionals in existing businesses.

The concept of Community Enterprise Development grew in Ireland during the early 1980s as a response to the threat posed to "disadvantaged" communities, in particular, by exceptionally high levels of unemployment. The approach adopted was rooted in community development and is based on the premise that (a) a community without an adequate economic base that enables its people to earn a living is not a viable community; (b) the impetus to improve the quality of life within the community by generating economic activity must come first from within; and (c) it can only progress by marrying local energies with external sources of help.

It was perceived that enterprise activity could contribute to the economic well-being of the community by creating worthwhile and secure jobs, providing goods and services needed locally, training surpluses for community benefit, and creating a multiplier impact on the community through the circulation of increased income.

In addition to yielding specific economic benefits, it was seen that the direct involvement of communities enhances their self-confidence about their ability to decisively influence the course of local economic development, and that the success of any enterprise initiative within the community, however small, can act as a powerful catalyst for development.

The community enterprise programme was shaped by the experience, learning, and the successes and failures of existing ventures in the Republic, Northern Ireland, Britain and North America.

Operations of CEP

In its early years, CEP provided grant-aid and business advice to community businesses and workers' co-ops, but by 1986, it had become clear that the benefits of such interventions were limited, short term and ultimately dubious. Thereafter, a more integrated developmental approach was adopted. Financial support became contingent on applicants undertaking modular training with a view to progressing the dual development of the group and the enterprise.

While business advice and grant aid provision had hitherto been processed through the regional FÁS offices, the new approach generated activities that needed to be supported by additional structures, systems and resources.

An Enterprise Development Officer (EDO) was appointed in each region as an "outreach" worker promoting the concept of enterprise among community groups, processing applications for participation in the programme, tailoring training modules for participating groups, and co-ordinating the activities of a panel of local facilitators contracted to deliver the training.

At national level, EDOs reported to the Programme Manager and were responsible, as a central team, for (a) the ongoing development of training materials and resources; (b) the selection, recruitment and ongoing training of facilitators; and (c) the monitoring of reports to their External Training Manager who, as administrator of budgets, approved or rejected applications for training grants and other financial supports on the basis of finances currently available.

Programme objectives, then, were clearly set out, and consistency in training activities towards meeting those objectives was facilitated by strong central control — a small group of EDOs working closely together under the direction of the Programme Manager and liaising regularly with facilitators at local, regional and national briefing/training events. The frequency of such contact generated high levels of involvement and motivation, fuelled also by the ongoing development of relevant skills.

Training content and approach were crafted with a view to maximum practicality and flexibility, focusing on empowering and supporting enterprise groups to meet their own needs and objectives. Ready access to resources was ensured by the location of training materials and equipment at the regional office of each EDO. It was further planned to build up, in each region, a data bank and a panel of professionals willing to give inputs in areas of expertise such as finance, marketing, legal incorporation etc., at strategic times in a group's development when the facilitation process highlighted a need for such interventions.

Programme operations were innovatively designed to encourage in participating groups the proactive behaviours essential to fulfilling their own objectives as well as those of the programme.

Developments during the Period 1986-94

The CEP model has now been in operation for eight years, during which time it has been subjected to progressive changes, both internal and external. The implications of internal changes have not been monitored or evaluated, and external developments have gone unacknowledged.

Programme objectives are driven by an explicit socio-economic ideology that empirical evidence would suggest has been all but abandoned in favour of other, conflicting organisational exigencies. While the programme's mission is to stimulate economic activities in the areas of greatest need, such is the competition for programme funding in the community employment sector that programme officers have been forced to disregard this prime objective in order to build up a portfolio of success stories that will win support for subsequent projects.

The unspoken reality is that few, if any, of the CEP success stories to date can be traced back to targeted areas of need. Rather, they are the stories of entrepreneurs already armed with the resources, with the relevant education, skills and experience, and with the acumen to recognise and utilise the opportunities represented by participation in such a programme.

Towards ensuring CEP's survival, regional External Training Managers have increasingly been assessing applications for participation using the criterion of potential commercial success rather than urgency of need. Ironically, then, a programme established to serve groups in need of supportive interventions is supporting such groups less and less, because, to survive, it needs to associate with groups that will justify its existence — groups that would be likely to succeed without its intervention.

Tangible Training Outcomes
The experiences of EDOs and facilitators working within disadvantaged communities would indicate that programme objectives, while laudable, have remained to a great extent aspirational:

- In respect of the target group, unaddressed interpersonal/social needs and economic circumstances are an obstacle to the success of training interventions.

- In its implementation, the programme has failed to deliver on a number of key requirements.

- There has been no attempt to reshape the CEP model on the basis of experience, outcomes, and the internal and external factors impinging on these.

Facilitation of enterprise groups in disadvantaged communities can be both challenging and rewarding; it is invariably frustrating. A group may display the ability and commitment required to establish a commercially viable enterprise but, more often than not, it has no direct experience of what is involved. A group may be free from — or able to overcome — the interpersonal and social barriers associated with long-term unemployment, but more frequently it is disadvantaged in terms of essential skills such as literacy, communication, teamwork, and so on, as well as core values such as work ethic, accountability, time-keeping etc. The replacement of a dependency culture with an enterprise culture is a socio-political challenge requiring a response of a magnitude greater than any management training intervention can hope to supply.

Even if the requisite skills, experience and attitudes are in place, it is increasingly clear that the key to accessing resources is having resources (for example, matching funds) and groups endeavouring to stimulate enterprise activity in disadvantaged communities find themselves without the leverage to negotiate, operating as they do in an environment deficient in basic economic infrastructure and resources.

In this context, CEPs objectives appear altruistic, and the repeated failure of enterprises in target areas, supported up to a start-up point, to survive in the medium or long term, has gone unexamined. While both internal and external validation are consistently carried out during the training period, no efforts have been made to isolate the factors leading to failure in the post-training period, on withdrawal of supportive interventions.

Has the programme failed to promote its attitudinal aims towards empowerment in place of dependency, and/or is it failing to deliver on the knowledge and skills required in an increasingly competitive commercial environment? Are the module contents and training approach the best means of achieving these ends? Such questions have not been examined.

Have the intended integrated structures and linkages towards facilitating the application of acquired knowledge, skills and attitudes become a reality? The intention to offer CEP as a complement to other forms of assistance, and to forge links with both statutory and community sources of support, has not been followed through as a planned strategy. Were such systematic interconnections to be developed, they would go some way towards tackling the problem of access to resources besetting the target group. The will to pursue this approach is absent, however, since the bulk of groups currently participating in the programme are of a kind competent to build their own networks. Besides, inter-agency competition and territorialism are so endemic that any prospect of meaningful collaborative action seems naive.

Effects of Regionalisation on Operations
The CEP structure was regionalised within two years of its inception, with a view, primarily, to more efficient administration, but also to ensure its continued responsiveness to local needs and conditions. This has led to regional changes of emphasis, without any central monitoring of their sources, their consistency with objectives, or their interconnectedness.

The central team of EDOs has become a perfunctory mechanism; in practice, each operates independently in their region, accountable only to an External Training Manager for financial and administrative purposes. In consequence, EDO's priorities are now more inclined to be budget- rather than training-related — while they are responsible for interpreting training needs and devising strategies for meeting them, no regulatory criteria are imposed, outside of those applying to budget use.

With the dismantling of central control, facilitators are similarly cast adrift, operating as independent consultants rather than as part of a programme team. But, just as regionalisation has enhanced the CEP's ability to respond to local groups' needs, it has also rendered the CEP vulnerable to the individual agendas of EDOs and facilitators. This vulnerability is exacerbated by the informality of recruitment procedures: EDOs are now recruited through regional networks — their backgrounds (and corresponding world views) vary from the social sciences to the commercial business sector. Facilitators, in turn, are recruited by EDOs.

Indeed, the abandonment of facilitative practices, never discussed as a policy issue, is locally in evidence, linked with the cessation of facilitator briefing/training events since regionalisation. Recruits, since that time, have not benefited from the promotion or practice of the requisite skills, except in the odd instance when a year-end budget excess has been used by an EDO to mount a local training event. Facilitator involvement is low as a consequence, and their motives are more likely to be personal/social than programme-linked.

Differences in training emphasis are clearly linked with differences in training personnel's own views, skills and experiences, and may range from a community development to a commercial approach, from the ideological to the pragmatic. Trainer style may be located at any point of the spectrum, from trainer-centred to learner-centred; from pedagogical to interactive. Indeed, instances occur where group concerns dictate, to the extent that the training programme is used as an unplanned, reactive support, addressing each crisis or issue as it occurs, and losing sight of the overall process of development.

The specific emphasis obtaining in any training module, then, may derive from the agenda of the group, the facilitator or the EDO, depending on local circumstances and in the absence of regulatory mechanisms to ensure consistency of operations across the regions, or adherence to core programme objectives. CEP's flexibility, once seen as its key strength, appears — in changed circumstances — to be its greatest weakness.

Materials and Resources

With regionalisation also came a halt to the ongoing development of materials and resources. Materials originally developed for the needs of the target group are, in many instances, quite unsuited to groups now participating in the programme. The emphasis on product development in the training modules most commonly delivered is anachronistic in light of the significant growth, in recent years, of the service industry — indeed the enterprise activities of the overwhelming majority of CEP groups during the last eight years have been in the service sector, in response both to commercial trends and to capital cost considerations.

By now, there is a common understanding that module materials are, in many areas, irrelevant to actual needs, but it is left to the facilitator to adapt them, to redress the faults and fill the gaps. This is an entirely ad hoc strategy; many facilitators will edit or rewrite materials, some will replace them with materials from other sources, motivated by the desire to maintain their own credibility — and, in the process, go some way to protecting the credibility of the programme also! But variations in facilitators' skills and experience, as well as their ability to access appropriate materials, must inevitably be reflected in regional disparities in the quality of training provision.

Equally ad hoc is the availability of resources. Resources required by a facilitator for conducting a training session — for example, flipcharts, markers, overhead projectors, video recorders, photocopying facilities, and so on — once available at the EDO's office, have also fallen victim to changing budgetary priorities. Facilitators are now required to procure their own materials and equipment, submitting invoices up to a modest allocation for each training module. This is yet another measure that loosens the connection between the facilitator and the programme and, in terms of providing quality training, places the facilitator's personal motivation at a premium. The facilitation fee, payable on the basis of contact hours — with a token payment for preparation/administration time — has not increased in eight years, and is a disincentive to any commitment of time towards resource provision.

Early planning for the provision of data banks and panels of professional expertise for specialist consultation lost its impetus following regionalisation — left to the discretion of individual EDOs, it bore fruit in some regions while not in others. Some personnel, unmotivated to provide such a resource, would make the argument that encouraging groups to access information and expertise for themselves is an essential part of the empowerment process. Perhaps so, but regional inconsistencies in the provision of such resources point to manifest gaps in the understanding and interpretation of core programme values and objectives.

FÁS — Co-operative Development Unit

The establishment of a Co-operative Development Council and Unit, with its own development budget, was first announced in the Programme for National Recovery (PNR) (1987). The fundamental role of the Council, which consists of trade union, employer, Government and worker co-operative representatives, is to promote the co-operation concept as a vehicle for employment.

The Co-operative Development Unit, in turn, is responsible for implementing Council policy. It operates under the responsibility of FÁS, and its role encompasses four main functions: promotion, research, training and business advice. In this way, it assists individual worker co-operatives with general business training, as well as advice and other supports.

OTHER ENTERPRISE TRAINING INITIATIVES

Shannon Development/Limerick Innovation Centre — The Entrepreneurs Programme

Organised and administered by the Limerick Innovation Centre, this programme is designed to assist entrepreneurs in establishing their own businesses (it was formerly known as the High Technology Enterprise Programme (HTEP)). Rather than focusing on those who are unemployed, it seeks to help highly qualified professional and managerial individuals who wish to start a business venture. Participants are therefore required to possess a solid educational background combined with prior business knowledge and management skills. Having come through a selection process, 30 or so participants from a range of industrial sectors are selected for the programme each year.

The programme consists of tutorial and consultancy sessions, run over a six-month period. In addition, it incorporates a number of residential week-ends, designed to encourage team-building which is considered a vital outcome of the programme. Topics covered on the course include business planning, marketing, product identification, finance, legal aspects, and launching a new venture. The programme also includes contributions from successful entrepreneurs, case histories and analysis of entrepreneurial successes and failures in Ireland and abroad.

Through its intensive input, the programme is designed to represent the founding phase in a new enterprise venture, and its culmination visualises the formation of small management teams with the requisite skills for successfully launching and running of a high-technology company.

An external evaluation of the HTEP was carried out in 1989 which showed that participants found the programme interesting and focused, helping to clarify their desire to become an entrepreneur. A survey of all participants over the previous six years established that the programme had significant employment impact, with a considerable number of companies being formed and more than four hundred jobs being created.

Shannon Development/FÁS — Community Enterprise Programme

This programme is designed to assist community enterprise projects through all stages of development. It offers a range of supports, which include training models, advice on a range of business-related activities and grant incentives.

Under the auspices of FÁS, Community Enterprise Programmes have now spread throughout the country. Six training modules are provided, under the guidance of a FÁS-selected and -sponsored facilitator, and they focus on exploring community enterprise, business organisation, idea generation, business development, trading and business review and consolidation.

Shannon Development — START Programme

This initiative aims to enable budding entrepreneurs to learn the rudiments of new company formation and to encourage enterprise venture start-ups. It comprises four sessions, spread out over four evenings, at a number of locations in the Mid-West region, and focuses on key issues in the formation of a business. The programme targets professionals, experienced managers, and individuals or community groups with ideas and/or resources.

Forbairt — Management Development Programme

Forbairt, formerly the IDA, provides grant assistance for management development through a programme which is tailored to meet the specific needs of small companies. It is conducted in-house, using external consultants selected by FÁS (which administers the programme) and is aimed at developing key management skills. Four modules make up the programme content: records and management systems, business planning, strategic planning and strengthening the management team.

IMI — Business Development Programme

Aimed at owner-managers of small industrial businesses who have a strong commitment to expansion, this programme is sponsored by Forbairt and other State and private organisations. It has a duration of 18 months and its content includes modules on general management, business planning, marketing, financial planning, personnel management/industrial relations and information systems.

From the preceding examples it can be seen that considerable support, by way of training provision, is available through State agencies for those interested in starting, or in some cases expanding, a business. It must be said however, that reference to training and development itself are noticeably absent from all course contents.

EDUCATION FOR ENTERPRISE

Another aspect of promoting and encouraging entrepreneurship relates to the topic of enterprise within the education system. As already outlined, there has traditionally been little to encourage individual enterprise or entrepreneurship in the second-level education system. However, in more recent years the topic of enterprise and education is one which has been raised in Ireland, particularly in relation to third-level studies. Indeed, in 1986 a workshop devoted to this general theme was organised by the National Council for Education Awards, in which a number of interesting points of view were put forward (NCEA/IDA, 1986), including:

- The higher education system has a role to play in both helping to overcome cultural barriers to the development of enterprise in Ireland, and in providing a grounding in skills which facilitate the transformation of entrepreneurial drive into successful business ventures.

- Universities offer a degree of responsibility for the process of enterprise development which might otherwise not be possible. If the talented youth of Ireland are to be channelled into the development of enterprises, they must be approached and educated while they are in a university setting.

- Colleges must get closer to the world of business — improved linkages between colleges and industry are very important.

- The preparation and cultivation of "entrepreneurial attributes" should begin at primary and secondary level.

- Institutions of higher education must address methods of developing entrepreneurial studies in the formal curriculum, in extra-curricular activities and in leisure and vacation periods.

VOCATIONAL TRAINING OF PEOPLE WITH DISABILITIES

Definition of Disability

A major difficulty in focusing on the needs of people with disability in the Republic of Ireland arises from the fact that there is no accurate, comprehensive data available on the number of people with disability. This has very serious consequences for policy makers and training agencies who aim to address the vocational training needs of such individuals (Murphy, 1994).

Before an attempt can be made to estimate the number of people with disabilities, it is first necessary to agree on a definition of the term disability. No precise operational definition of disability has been established in Ireland and as a result there is confusion among policy makers and service providers as to the exact population being referred to by the term "people with disabilities".

We shall adapt the International Labour Organisation (ILO) definition. According to this:

> any person whose prospects of finding employment, keeping a job and advancing in his/her chosen occupation are diminished due to a recognised mental or physical handicap is to be considered disabled.

The National Rehabilitation Board definition of a disabled person, in the context of employment, also gives a valuable insight into the nature of disability. This definition states that:

> a disabled person is a person with a physical, sensory, or psychological impairment which may:
> - have a tangible impact on their functional capability to do a particular job, or
> - have an impact on their ability to function in a particular physical environment, or
> - lead to discrimination in obtaining or keeping employment of a kind for which they would otherwise be suited.

The population of people with disabilities is very diverse. Four broad categories of disability can be identified, namely (a) physical disability; (b) mental illness; (c) mental handicap; and (d) sensory disabilities. High levels of differences exist within and between each of these categories.

Within the mentally handicapped group there are four categories defined as mild, moderate, severe and profound. In the case of mental illnesses the range varies from "severe stress" conditions to "serious mental illnesses" which may be long term or chronic. The range of physical disabilities is even more complex and includes orthopaedic impairments, infectious diseases, genetic and congenital disorders, traumatic injuries, neurological injuries, heart disorders, arthritis and bronchitis. Sensory disabilities, such as deafness, range from conditions of being hard of hearing to being profoundly deaf.

The absence of accurate comprehensive data on the number of people with a disability in Ireland means that only estimates are available. This estimate will depend on whether a broad or narrow definition is taken of disability.

The International Labour Organisation estimates that "10 per cent of any population group are mentally or physically handicapped to such an extent that they require special help in making a satisfactory adjustment to community life". This estimate is broadly supported by the National Rehabilitation Board (NRB) which states that "at the most conservative estimate there are 300,000 people with disabilities in Ireland".

Many voluntary groups which represent people with disabilities have collected their own figures on the number of people with specific disabilities. The Mental Health Association of Ireland (MHAI) say that "one person in nine will be affected by mental illness at some point of their lives". They also state that "one per cent of the total population will suffer from schizophrenia at some stage in their lives". There are 5,000 people registered blind in Ireland and approximately 17 per cent of the population have a hearing impairment. Over 500,000 Irish people have some form of arthritis.

Calculations of the number of people with disabilities are restricted through not having a consistent definition of disability. Despite this limitation it is clear that people with disabilities represent a sizeable proportion of the population. Because many people have "hidden" disabilities, such as arthritis and learning disabilities, and many others are excluded from participation in employment and social activities, the size of the population with disability is perceived by many to be much smaller than its actual number.

Vocational Training — The Demands of People with Disabilities

As we have seen there is huge diversity among people with disabilities. They are not a homogenous group whose needs, be they vocational training or otherwise, can be assumed to be the same (Murphy, 1994).

Unfortunately, this is how the needs of disabled people were addressed in the past and elements of this simplistic view prevail today. Voluntary, charitable organisations have been very much to the fore in developing services for people with mental handicap. Exclusive services have also been developed for people with mental illness by the Department of Health, and these were largely centred around the psychiatric hospital. People with a physical disability or sensory disability have also been given services geared specifically towards people with one disability.

The provision of services on the basis of disability groupings is based on the assumption that these groups have homogenous needs and the medical model which pervaded these organisations meant that professional persons — be they psychiatrists, social workers, psychologists or other medical personnel — determined what the needs of their "patients" were, and the person with the disability was given no say in deciding their own actions. People with a disability were largely treated under an "eternal childhood" syndrome which promoted a protective, charity-oriented, lifelong support concept for people with disabilities.

Only in the past few years have the "medical" and "charity" models of addressing the needs of people with disabilities been challenged. The Forum of People with Disabilities was formed in 1990, with an agenda that:

- puts people with disabilities first;

- recognises that people with disabilities know best their own needs, desires, hopes, fears and expectations;

- promotes empowerment, choice, participation, action, consultation, working together, people with disabilities as consumers, and civil rights.

The 1970 Health Act obliges Health Boards to make available services for the training of people with disabilities. This Act gave responsibility for addressing the vocational needs of disabled people to the Department of Health rather than the Department of Labour (or Department of Enterprise and Employment at present), suggesting that this decision was influenced by the old medical view of disability rather than made on a vocational needs basis.

The National Rehabilitation Board (NRB), a statutory body, was established in 1957 under the Department of Health. It plays a central role in helping people with disabilities to identify and address their vocational training needs. Any person with a disability may go to the NRB free of charge for occupational guidance and training.

Vocational assessment is one of the key aspects of NRB's occupational guidance service. It is the process by which individual aspirations and aptitudes are discovered and evaluated. Many people with disabilities have a poor awareness of their aptitudes or aspirations, often as a result of a very sheltered upbringing that did not facilitate personal development through community activities. For these individuals, vocational assessment is of crucial importance in helping them to select and pursue the most suitable vocational options.

The vocational training needs of people with disabilities must be assessed on an individual basis as is the case for non-disabled people, since it is the same labour market that both groups hope to enter. Nevertheless, some factors will require greater consideration for people with disabilities. In the case of many people with mental illness, pre-vocational training may be essential in order to help them develop interpersonal skills before they can pursue specific courses or employment. Young people with a learning disability are more likely to require pre-vocational training than their non-disabled colleagues because of personal development deficiencies or because of uncertainty about what career they wish to pursue.

A person's disability can have a large influence on the vocational options open to them. No matter how great a disabled people's desire is for a certain occupation, their intellectual functioning or disability can rule it out as a possible career. In many cases the person with the disability may be capable of particular vocational training if adequate support facilities are available. Because of the low awareness by training agencies of the particular needs of people with disabilities (and because of a lack of willingness to address these), the range of vocational training options has been unduly restricted.

It is estimated that 79 per cent of people with disabilities are unemployed. According to Dr. Arthur O'Reilly, Chief Executive of NRB, "300,000 people with disabilities have become this country's most isolated, unemployed and welfare-dependent minority". While factors such as employers' prejudices, lack of adequate aids and appliances for disabled employees, and an inaccessible environment contribute to the low employment rate of people with disabilities, it is evident that the failure of vocational training services to address their specific needs contributes to further inhibiting factors.

REHABILITATION TRAINING

Vocational Training Provision for People with Disabilities

The vast bulk of training for people with disabilities in Ireland is provided in specialised rehabilitation settings. The history of rehabilitation services and the large part played by charitable, voluntary organisations has already been described. Rehabilitation is defined as "the restoration of the person with a disability to the fullest mental, physical, social, vocational and economic usefulness of which they are capable". Rehabilitation training refers to those rehabilitation activities aimed at improving participants employability and work skills.

Training for People with Mental Handicap

For the greater part of this century, people with mental handicap were provided with rehabilitation services by a number of religious organisations of which the largest were the Brothers of Charity, the Sisters of Charity and St. John of God Brothers. Up to the 1950s, services for people with mental handicap centred around the provision of "activation and sheltered work". The two aims of activation were "to condition the individual to the work habit and to develop social habits". Sheltered work aimed at maximising the productive potential of people with mental handicap, but without giving any remuneration to the worker. These early services provided to people with a mental handicap were located in large institutions away from towns, with women and men segregated. The emphasis was on custody not training.

The mid-1970s saw the beginning of a re-organisation of rehabilitation services for people with a mental handicap and a change in strategy for the development of vocational training for people with a disability. Large institutions that had developed for decades were disbanded in favour of new "community workshops". These workshops catered for much smaller numbers of people with disabilities focusing on open employment and the provision of long-term sheltered employment for those who could not make it to the level of open employment.

Rehabilitation training for people with a mental handicap, if measured from a criteria of preparing people for open employment, was a dismal failure. A survey of leavers in 1989 from ESF-funded rehabilitation training programmes found that only 15.1 per cent of leavers with a mental handicap were employed at the time of the survey.

A report in 1990 entitled "Needs and Abilities" by a review group on mental handicap set up by the Minister of Health made many valuable recommendations for the development of rehabilitation services. The report made a clear distinction between the needs of people with an "intellectual disability" and those with general learning difficulties. This latter category would include what in the past has been categorised as people with mild mental handicap and people bordering between low average intelligence and mild mental handicap. The report called on the Department of Education and Department of Labour to "take action to facilitate those with general learning difficulties in pursuing further education, vocational training and employment placement for school leavers". This recommendation has been taken up by many of the mental handicap rehabilitation services, as they no longer offer services to people with mild learning disabilities. Unfortunately, however, many of these people with mild learning disabilities are falling between two stools, as they do not have the academic qualifications to gain places on FÁS courses, yet are being turned away by specialised rehabilitation services.

Training for People with Mental Illness

Psychiatric services in Ireland developed from the old policy of institutionalisation. Mental illness was a highly feared and misunderstood illness by society with many people entering psychiatric hospitals to remain there for the rest of their lives.

Sadly, despite the advances in the understanding of mental illness, many of the old structures for caring for people with mental illness still remain. A study group on the development of psychiatric services in its report in 1982 stated:

> At present, the psychiatric hospital is the focal point of the patients' psychiatric service in most parts of the country. Large numbers of patients reside permanently in these hospitals — many of them have lived there for years in conditions which in many cases are less than adequate because of overcrowding and capital underfunding. In addition, staff and public attitudes have tended to concentrate effort on hospital care as a result of which community facilities are relatively underdeveloped. The hospitals were designed to isolate the mentally ill from society and this isolation still persists.

In the past ten years the Department of Health has made an effort to overhaul psychiatric services by developing "comprehensive community-orientated, sectoral and integrated service", where the varying needs of people with mental illness would be cared for in the community with a specific remit for rehabilitation and training. This was a big departure from what previously existed — training had not been an issue in the old days. A community-oriented strategy envisaged the provision of a locally-based community service where the big psychiatric hospital would be replaced by smaller, more intimate services. The lack of funding, however, has meant that many of the community services promised have not been delivered and as a result Ireland has nearly twice the rate of admissions to psychiatric hospitals per capita as France, Denmark or England.

The success of the new mental health strategy depends largely on the social and vocational skills training provided to cope with everyday life. However, Health Board personnel and the medical profession are not trained to assess training needs or to provide training services, yet they have been given the responsibility under the Health Act for providing these services. The Health Boards have greatly increased their training services over the past decade as sizeable European Social Fund grants were taken up. This training was vocational in nature, as required under funding regulations, but could be either pre-vocational or skill-specific. The standard of this training was often very low and was only a modification of the sheltered employment which had been set up to activate people with mental illness during an earlier period. A more rigorous monitoring system by NRB, and the insistence on accreditation and certification by all rehabilitation training centres, now means that the Health Boards/rehabilitation centres must raise their training standards to those of mainstream training agencies or else be removed from the ESF funding system.

Training for People with Physical and Sensory Disabilities

There is significantly less involvement by large influential agencies or the Department of Health agencies in the physical and sensory disability area. As a result, there are relatively few rehabilitation agencies solely for people with physical and sensory disability. This situation can be partly attributed to the high number of fragmented organisations serving different disability groups. The bigger representative groups include the Irish Wheelchair Association, the National Council for the Blind in Ireland, the National Association for the Deaf, Cerebral Palsy Ireland, the Arthritis Association and the Spina Bifida Association. None of these bodies have a significant involvement in vocational training.

The Rehabilitation Institute (Rehab) training centres are open to people of all disabilities and cater for the largest number of people with physical or sensory disability availing of rehabilitation training. Rehab runs pre-vocational and vocational skills training programmes from its 16 centres around the country.

People with a physical or sensory disability can also avail of training programmes run by training centres under the aegis of psychiatric services. Very often, however, this group of disabled people do not want to be associated with people who have a mental illness or a learning disability and are more likely to demand mainstream training. Indeed, many of them do not use the services of the NRB and pursue mainstream options. Accurate figures are not available for the numbers of people with a physical disability pursuing mainstream training at this time.

Levels of Rehabilitation Training

ESF-aided rehabilitation training is made up of three distinct categories, called level 1, level 2 and level 3.

Level 1 training is a pre-vocational modular training programme which gives trainees the opportunity to evaluate their vocational prospects by sampling a minimum of three different occupational areas. Personal effectiveness and social development of the trainees is a central aim of these programmes and 50 per cent of the training time must be devoted to this area. Trainees are enabled to build up generic work habits and become familiar with the pressure of working life. Level 1 programmes can have a maximum duration of three years.

Level 2 training programmes offer vocational training for specific occupations up to what might be termed "semi-skilled" level. Examples of these occupations would be a commis-chef, electronics operative, carpenter's mate and industrial sewing. Trainees are required at the end of the programme to perform at least to the minimum level recommended by industry, with some level of individual responsibility and with only limited supervision. Level 2 programmes also provides personal effectiveness training. The target trainee would be required to have functional literacy and numeracy, have the potential to do practical tasks and to transfer learning to a variety of settings. The training approach is mainly a mixture of trainee-centred and trainer-led methods and the duration of these programmes is a maximum of three years.

Level 3 training programmes provide skill-specific training to an intermediate level. The training is occupation-specific and trainees are brought to the level of a skilled worker, for example, programming, graphic design, quality control or carpenter level. Graduates should be able to perform tasks on their own and with little supervision. The trainee learns a broad range of technical skills, including many that are complex and non-routine. The training approach is primarily trainee-centred or self-directed learning.

Advantages and Disadvantages of Rehabilitation Training

The vocational rehabilitation training services in Ireland have been described, and many unfavourable comments made on them. This does not mean, however, that specialised rehabilitation is without merit, as many people with disabilities greatly benefit from the service. Additionally, there are many rehabilitation providers who meet the highest training standards and whose staff show the highest commitment to developing people with disabilities. The criticisms made are still valid, however, in the Irish context, and need to be addressed. Specific advantages include the following:

- Programmes are longer and allow more time for trainees with disabilities to learn. This is often essential for people with learning disabilities.

- Individualised programmes are allowed within the generic programme.

- Extra facilities and resources are available to meet specific needs of people with disabilities.

- Greater detail in design and delivery is permitted.

- Rehabilitation courses can address personal or social skill deficits.

- A trainee-centred approach exists, or is aimed at, in many programmes.

- Rehabilitation training places are often easier and quicker to access for people with disabilities.

- Trainers have a better understanding of disability.

The main disadvantages include the following:

- People with disabilities are segregated from non-disabled people.

- A stigma often applies to attending these centres.

- A dependency culture pervades many rehabilitation centres.

- Certification exists for only a small number of rehabilitation programmes at present.

- Rehabilitation instructors often see their roles as carers or supervisors rather than trainers.

- Production pressure can take precedence over training in the many rehabilitation training agencies which produce goods or services commercially.

FÁS and People with Disabilities

Government policy advocates the fact that FÁS programmes be open to disabled people capable of undertaking the training involved. The Assistant Director General of FÁS, Mr. Henry Murdoch, stated at the International Rehabilitation Conference in Dublin that "FÁS is not permitted to take any special measures on behalf of people with disabilities as it is Government Policy that special interventions for people with disabilities in the labour market are the responsibility of agencies operating under the umbrella of the Department of Health". This statement embodies the

FÁS "cop-out" vis-à-vis the vocational needs of disabled people. In fact, Murdoch saw FÁS having little significance for people with disabilities when (in the same speech) he said "It is likely that the number of persons with disabilities who will be able to participate in FÁS programmes will continue to be small and certainly insufficient to satisfy the demand for integration".

Ther are a number of reasons why FÁS may be reluctant to offer training opportunities to disabled persons. The authors' experiences indicate six possible explanations:

1. It is believed that disabled persons are often lacking in educational and social skills which would be necessary to enable them to complete training successfully.

2. There is a belief among certain FÁS personnel that disabled persons require much greater time and energy commitments on the part of instructors as compared with that required for non-disabled trainees.

3. Many disabled trainees are believed to require a much longer training period than others in FÁS centres.

4. FÁS staff simply do not have the expertise and the experience to deal with disabled trainees, except the least complicated cases.

5. Many FÁS staff hold the view that the job placement rates of disabled trainees are likely to be below average.

6. Many FÁS personnel believe that disabled people are a special group with special needs who already have available to them a vocational rehabilitation training system which can and does cater adequately for their needs. It follows that some FÁS staff do not see it as their responsibility to undertake training on behalf of disabled persons and at most provide training only for those who are minimally disabled.

These perceptions are often incorrect and result in significant training access problems for disabled trainees.

There is a general consensus that FÁS has catered very poorly for the needs of people with disabilities to date. While many individual FÁS staff have been sympathetic and helpful to people with disabilities, the overall policy has been one of ignoring their special needs and rights. People with disabilities are only acceptable if they meet with all the FÁS rules and regulations.

There are some signs that FÁS is becoming more inclusive to people with disabilities. The new apprenticeship scheme has 50 places allocated to disabled people. The recent National Programme promised more training opportunities for people with disabilities in FÁS.

TRAINING PROVISION FOR THE TRAVELLING COMMUNITY

The Development of Traveller Training Centres

The first Training Centre for Young Travellers opened in Ennis in April 1974. Funding to get the project underway was raised by public appeal and a building was provided by the Sisters of Mercy. In 1976 the National Association of Training Centres (NATC) for Travelling People was initiated in reply to a need felt that such centres be set up throughout the country. It was also felt that a united voice could gain more support from the Department of Education and Department of Labour. Relevant Government departments were forthcoming in their support and many training centres sprang up, offering a mix of activities developed from traditional skills.

Following ongoing discussions between NATC, the Department of Education (through the VECs), AnCO and the Youth Employment Agency (now FÁS) a "Code of Practice" was compiled (1984) which has become the blueprint for the operation of the training centres. Each centre is run by a local management committee who employ a Director, and funding is as follows:

The Department of Education, through the Vocational Education Committees, supply:

- 100 teaching hours per week for a 24-place centre

- funding to cover costs of heat, light and power

- funding to cover costs of materials required for educational purposes

- maintenance of premises.

FÁS supplies:

- allowances for trainees

- a per capita training grant

- a contribution towards the Director's salary

- an agreed rent.

Each centre is run by a community-based management committee composed of one chairperson plus eight members. The members include a representative from the VEC, FÁS, Local Committee of Travellers, a traveller, and other interested parties such as a social worker for travellers, Social Services or Community Council representative, or a Health Professional. The Code of Practice recommends that each management committee member should have a clear commitment to the welfare of the travelling people.

Objectives of Traveller Training Centres

The Code of Practice sets out the aim of training centres for travellers as follows:

> to help young travellers to develop their full potential, to break the cycle of illiteracy and social deprivation in which they are trapped and to enable them to become, as soon as possible, self-reliant and self-supporting members of society.

The Code sets out the following objectives to achieve these aims:

1. To compensate young travellers for their deprived social status by making educational/training facilities available to them.

2. To help them to discover and attain their own aspirations.

3. To give them the freedom to make a real choice about their future way of life.

4. To provide them with the tools of learning, literacy and numeracy, as well as with the practical skills of future trades.

5. To allay their fears of the settled community and help to give them self-confidence and self-respect.

6. To give them the social life-skills necessary for a full and contented living in today's world.

The Training Approach

The training course offered is mainly a skills-orientated course with heavy reliance on practical training coupled with related instruction. The following training strategies are recommended by FÁS to achieve training plan goals (Earley, 1993).

Trainee-Centred Learning

This means allowing trainee take responsibility for their own learning by placing them in the learning environment where they can equip themselves with such skills as planning, problem-solving, using own initiative etc. Such skills are applicable and essential to any work environment.

Experiential Learning

Experiential learning techniques are introduced to generate experience which trainees can examine and learn from individually or in small groups. They have been developed on the basis that people learn best from their own experiences, provided that this experience can be examined and conclusions tested.

Trainer-Centred Learning

Trainer-centred learning occurs where the trainer takes on the role of the expert in the subject and imparts the necessary skills, knowledge and guidance to an individual or small group by whatever means/techniques at their disposal.

Motivation and Guidance

Motivation and guidance is an important element of this programme especially for those who are unqualified. The methods of instruction are important in the learning strategy but one of the most important is the motivation of the trainees. Where trainees are properly motivated they possess confidence and belief in themselves which acts as a major incentive in learning.

Assessment of Training

On commencement of training a trainee assessment book is opened for each individual trainee. This assessment book is the standard FÁS introductory vocational skill logbook as used in other FÁS training courses. The assessment book records the weekly progress in each subject area undertaken by the trainee and also records their aptitude and attitude to work. These records are completed by the staff of the centre. Each trainee assessment book contains an individual training plan section which is completed by each individual trainee. In this section the trainee maps out their own work goals and standards to be achieved and this is reviewed regularly in consultation with the Director of the Centre.

If on completion of the 48 weeks training, the trainee is able to demonstrate an ability to the minimum standard for each module, they are eligible for certification with the City and Guilds of London Institute.

Quality of Training Provided

Training centres are filling a great void in the overall education of travellers as, in most cases, they prefer to attend the centre in place of attending school (Dwyer, 1988; O'Connell, 1992). Being in the more intimate smaller groupings with mostly their own peers, and removed from the academic pressure of mainstream education, it is both under-

standable and expected that their performance should improve. While
the overall aims and objectives for the centres set out in the Code of
Practice are admirable, some question whether they go far enough to
break down the barriers and hostilities that exist between the two communities. It is this area of social development and acceptance which
needs to be tackled. At present the main focus in training centres is on
skills training. However, were the training course to be spread out over a
longer period of time, more work could be done in areas of personal development, health education, and other topics pertaining to their own
future.

The Need for a Positive Image of Travellers

The perception of travellers by a large percentage of the settled community is negative; travellers know this through the hostilities they experience in relation to accommodation, access to work and admittance to
pubs, discos, and so on. Any change will depend on a degree of trust
being built up, but this depends on the two communities interacting. The
training centre curriculum could be broadened to include more organised
events that involve such interactions, through inter-school and inter-
community debating, public speaking, sports activities, exhibitions of
work, etc. While such activities are already underway, they lack specific
objectives and purpose.

Staff Training and Development

Commentators have indicated that there is a need to recognise that the
staff/trainers employed in training centres are working with a specific
group of people, and consequently require specialist training. Yet little
formal support and training assistance has been given in this area. For
training centres to show greater success in the future in helping staff,
training programmes must be put together to aid staff to fully develop
their own potential and recognise the contribution that they can make.

ACHIEVING AN INTEGRATED NATIONAL VOCATIONAL AND TRAINING SYSTEM

In looking at the national framework for training and vocational education, the extent of shared involvement and responsibility is patently obvious. In the overall picture, several Government departments, numerous
Government agencies, many State, semi-state and private bodies, institutions and organisations, not to mention voluntary organisations, combine and compete, argue and agree, over many aspects of training and
vocational education. Realistically, the basic trends underlying this

multi-faceted approach are unlikely to induce major structural changes in the foreseeable future. Nonetheless, it is feasible to outline (see Harrison, 1992, in a British context) a vision, mission, and strategy for future developments in this vital area, which may gain common acceptance in this country.

Vision

The vision encompasses education for children, consisting of foundation learning consistent with their abilities and aspirations, as well as being harmonised with the range of employment opportunities likely to be available to them on leaving school. It further envisages the active participation of all adults in a lifelong process of learning, culminating a greater capacity for self-development.

Mission

The mission is to achieve an integrated system of vocational education and training, whereby complementary academic and vocational learning serves to obfuscate traditional boundaries. It is also to provide a coherent framework within which (a) the school education process transmits relevant vocational preparation and qualifications; (b) opportunities are open to all young people who have left school to avail of relevant vocational training linked to qualifications; and (c) structures exist whereby all adults are encouraged and enabled to pursue the acquisition of usable and marketable skills, in a national and international context.

Strategy

The strategy focuses on:

- progressively introducing the national curriculum in schools and ultimately linking it to the National Vocational Qualification system;

- improving vocational education in schools in order to clarify the system and expand choice, and to promote parity of esteem between academic and vocational qualifications,

- creating a new post-16 vocational education and training sector.

National Council for Vocational Awards

A significant recent development in this country has been the establishment by the Minister for Education of the National Council for Vocational Awards (NCVA) in October 1991. Its brief is to develop a comprehensive assessment and certification system for a wide range of vocational educational and training programmes, and its terms of reference include, subject to approval of the Minister for Education, to:

- structure courses in vocational/technical education and training, as provided by the education system, on a modular basis;

- develop an appropriate framework of levels of qualifications for these courses;

- develop modular content for the core modules of such courses to be applied at national levels;

- review and approve regionally specific modules as proposed by regional co-ordinating groups;

- establish guidelines, criteria and standards for the assessment of participants' performance by individual course providers;

- monitor compliance with criteria and standards through an ongoing review of national returns on performance and the auditing of individual course providers on a targeted/sampling basis;

- certify participant's performance based on the outcome of assessment by course providers, subject to compliance with assessment criteria and standards;

- accredit the awards of a limited number of examining bodies of long standing in the field of vocational/professional education;

- act as a national agency for the recognition of relevant vocational qualifications obtained in other member states of the European Community and as an Information Centre for authorities in other member states in relation to NCVA qualifications.

Since its inception, the Council has undertaken a large programme of work, including a review of the programmes under its remit and an examination of international, especially European, trends in the certification of vocational qualifications. It has also proposed a framework of vocational qualifications for programmes within its remit, at three levels, within the context of a five-level framework for vocational qualifications.

National Framework for Vocational Qualifications

The proposed framework has been outlined in an NCVA document "Preparing for the New Europe — A National Framework for Vocational Qualification" published in 1992 and further explained by O'Dalaigh (1994). It is broadly in line with current international practice and allows access to vocational qualifications to anyone who can satisfy certain criteria.

A significant element of its structure is the modular basis of its programmes, which facilitates the accumulation of credits. This structure has been specifically designed to overcome the previous confusion and disquiet over the relative value of different qualifications obtainable in this country, through a disparate collection of examining and certifying bodies. It offers a coherent framework, and acts as a system of quality control which ensures high status and internationally recognised and marketable vocational qualifications. Among the features of the integrated system are the following:

- It allows for a diversity of provision and a flexible approach to curriculum design.

- It meets the needs of participants, allowing equal access to all who wish to attain vocational qualifications, through a variety of routes.

- It provides for integration of school-based and work-based learning.

- It offers pathways of progression to further education and training on the basis of credit accumulation.

- It is easily understood and implemented — programmes, courses, and modules can be located within the framework and the relationship between them is clear.

- It provides quality assurance through assessment of a range of specific learning outcomes.

Let us now look briefly at the various qualifications awards and their routes of entry.

National Foundation Certificate
This certificate is due for introduction on a pilot basis in 1995, and is aimed at those who have poor, or no, formal qualifications. Its modular structure will incorporate a small number of core areas and a wide range of elective modules, which may be combined to achieve the award. The proposed structure offers an opportunity for those who participate in full-time or part-time, formal or informal programmes, to attain this award over a period of time appropriate to their circumstances.

National Vocational Certificate Level 1
In the expanding range of options which will be made available within the senior education cycle, it is envisaged that Level 1 vocational modules will be accessible, in a variety of curricular areas, to participants in

Transition Year, Leaving Certificate, and Leaving Certificate Vocational and Applied Programmes.

It is also anticipated that modules will be available for those wishing to progress from the National Foundation Certificate stage, ensuring flexibility of access for the wide range of potential participants in this context.

National Vocational Certificate Level 2

The development of awards at this level was addressed as a priority to cater mainly for the large and growing number of students opting for continuing vocational education at post-Leaving Certificate level, and for adults involved in the Vocational Training Opportunities Scheme. Five Boards of Studies were established, and, following an extensive and development programme, around 46 awards at this level were launched for 1993-94.

Although conforming to a common structure, Level 2 awards are extremely varied in scope and content. The award is based on completion of a minimum of eight modules: five vocational, two general studies, and one preparation for work/work experience, with modules designated as core or elective.

National Vocational Certificate Level 3

The framework outlined provides for progression from Level 2 to Level 3 awards, but the structures for this, as well as the possible routes of progression from NCVA awards to higher level education and training, have not been finalised.

Although much development work still needs to be done, this proposed framework for vocational qualifications must be seen as a positive move on the overall integrationist front. It promises access to a previously uncharted route towards certifiable qualifications for a wide range of people, including:

- early school-leavers;

- those unemployed (75 per cent of whom have no qualification);

- those in employment who do not have formal qualifications;

- adults, especially women, wishing to return to education and employment;

- the disadvantaged and those with special needs;

- those retraining for new areas of employment.

Among further issues raised by O'Dalaigh (1994) in relation to certification which also merit consideration in the pursuit of greater integration of vocational education and training, are:

- the relationship and links between NCVA and other professional bodies and external agencies;

- the proposal to establish a National Education and Training Certification Board;

- the expansion of links between industry and the further education sector;

- the general trend in a number of European countries away from a narrow skills-based approach to initial vocational training, towards broader and more flexible education and training aimed at providing overlapping capabilities, combined with occupational skills and knowledge;

- the identification in an NESC Report of characteristics of an individual who has been prepared for work, as:

  - basic competence in literacy, numeracy, science and information technology

  - ability to apply knowledge and skills which have been acquired in school or training in the work situation

  - ability to work with others and a sense of responsibility

  - positive attitudes towards flexibility, innovation and entrepreneurial activity

  - general or specific knowledge and skills relating to a particular occupation, which are acquired in special training or apprenticeships

  - developing satisfactory methods for the accreditation of prior learning.

SUMMARY

In this chapter we have continued to examine elements of the national system of vocational training and education. The emphasis in this chapter has been on understanding the operation of elements given less priority within the overall framework, including training for the tourism sector, training for enterprise and enterpreneurship, training provision of people with disability and training provision for the travelling community. All of these sectors are marked by underprovision at national level and a lack of resources to eliminate deficiencies within their particular area. Finally, the chapter considered the issue of a national framework for vocational training and education with an emphasis on flexibility, access, coherence, progression and articulation.

6

TRAINING, DEVELOPMENT AND MANAGEMENT EDUCATION: INTERNATIONAL COMPARISONS

INTRODUCTION AND LEARNING OBJECTIVES

This chapter makes comparisons between training and development systems within and without the EU. Special attention is paid to training and development in Japan, the USA and low unemployment countries such as Norway, Sweden and Switzerland. We also focus on European management education. Having read this chapter you will understand:

♦ the key differences between countries in terms of training and development systems;

♦ the structures, systems and policies of specific countries;

♦ the significant role of learning in low unemployment countries;

♦ the evolution and pattern of management education in Europe;

♦ the significance of the single European Market in terms of its training and development implications.

KEY DIFFERENCES BETWEEN COUNTRIES

It is widely accepted that varying areas of emphasis, as well as difficulties in accessing appropriate information, preclude strict international comparison of training and development systems, especially in statistical terms. To facilitate the extraction of significant policy issues emerging from international comparison, it is necessary to conduct an international overview. Particular aspects of the key differences between various countries have been outlined in the Handy Report (1987), by Harrison (1992) and by Burgess (1993).

National Investment in Training and Development

There are a number of features which indicate the key differences in national investment in training and development. These are described below:

- Beginning with the education system itself, Denmark's public expenditure on education accounted for 6.8 per cent of GDP in 1988. Along with Finland this represents the highest proportion in OECD countries, and may be compared with a figure of 4.7 per cent in the UK. The compulsory school leaving age generally ranges between 14 and 16. However, attendance at a vocational training school is obligatory for all young German people aged between 16 and 18 who have not continued with full-time education. In other countries, such as Belgium and the Netherlands, similar categories of young people are obliged to attend part-time vocational training. Of these countries, the proportionate number of young people who continue in full time education until the age of 18 is far higher in France (70 per cent), Denmark (90 per cent), Japan (95 per cent) and the US (80 per cent), than in the UK (30 per cent) and in Ireland (all approximate figures).

- In 1989, 65 per cent of Germany's labour force possessed vocational qualifications. In France, the comparable figure stood at 40 per cent and in the UK at 33 per cent, while Ireland's figure was certainly lower still. This may be reflective of greater levels of integration of initial vocational training with the state education systems in Germany and France.

- The so called "dual system" in Germany features statutory initial vocational training, with on-the-job and off-the-job elements incorporated in an apprenticeship with a company. Initial vocational training is integrated with the education system in Belgium, France, and the Netherlands, amongst others, and the state bears the cost of this training.

- On the management development front, it is widely accepted that, in terms of qualifications possessed and levels of training received, Ireland and the UK lag significantly behind countries such as Germany, France, Japan and the US. For instance, approximately 85 per cent of top managers in the US and Japan are educated to degree level compared to an estimated 24 per cent in Britain.

Industrial Training Systems

Under the voluntarist principles espoused in Ireland and the UK, the cost of industrial training is mainly borne by employers. Although a similar situation exists in other countries such as Germany and Japan, a far greater commitment to industrial training is evident, driven by a well-developed training culture. In France, there is a legal requirement stipulating compulsory employer funding and the production of an annual training plan.

In Germany and France there is much greater participation by trade unions in the training process, with extensive statutory provisions for workforce consultation in the development and implementation of training plans. In Belgium, the Netherlands, and Denmark, for example, high levels of co-operation exist between the State, employers, and trade unions on training policies. Indeed, Ireland is one of the few European countries where legislation covering employees' right to paid time-off for training is not in place.

National Human Resource Planning Systems

There is a national emphasis in Japan on ensuring that all its young people receive a thorough broad-based education, and the acquisition of relevant vocational skills is largely retained for the employment situation. The national skills equilibrium resulting from this approach may be explained by the "job for life" employment philosophy, and the unique concentration on training and development within companies serves to provide the required specific skills.

Many European countries, such as France, Germany and Denmark, focus on building up a store of occupational skills through well-designed initial vocational training systems (in some cases integrated with higher secondary education).

Although efforts are being made in both Ireland and the UK to remedy the situation, it is an accepted fact that the labour force in both countries contains a very high level of individuals who possess no vocational qualifications whatever, many of whom are young unemployed.

Occupational Standards

The National Council for Vocational Awards has initiated the development of a national certification system for vocational education and training programmes in Ireland. In many other countries — for example, Germany, France and Japan — systems for the assessment and certification of occupational standards have been the norm for some time. In Germany the standards for the dual system of initial vocational training are agreed between the State, employers and employee representatives. A range of initial vocational and training qualification standards are applied through the education system in France. Meanwhile, in Japan, skills assessment and qualification operate through a nationally controlled system.

A COMPARISON OF COUNTRY-SPECIFIC SYSTEMS

Particular aspects of vocational education, training, and development in specific countries have been detailed in Handy (1987), Harrison (1992), NCVA (1992), and Burgess (1993), and the following accounts draw extensively from these sources.

Germany

The approach to education and training adopted by Germany has long been the envy of many of its competitor countries. Based on a school system which ranks among the best in the world, the dual system of initial vocational training, supplemented by devotion to management education and development and high levels of continuing training, has made a significant contribution to Germany's high-skill economy and standing as a major industrial power.

In a situation where the entire vocational education and training system is carried out and rigorously regulated by regionally-based state and employer partnerships, an inherent responsibility for training young people, in order to create a national reservoir of skills, is accepted by business organisations. The path to economic progress has also been strongly underpinned by a social partnership alliance of employers and trade unions, especially their joint co-operation on training which is regulated by statute. Although the cost of initial and continuing training is borne by employers, the promotion of vocational training is also the focus of financial and institutional support.

The success of the Germany system is significant. Mahnkopf (1992) points out that:

- Almost 80 per cent of the economically-active population possess either a school-leaving certificate or a certificate of vocational training.

- Over the last decade the percentage of unskilled employees has fallen almost continuously — this latter reduction is particularly applicable to female employees, whose level of qualification has risen significantly.

- The view has been expressed by some employers' representatives that the vocational training system, which has been associated with a policy of overtraining, has become a distinct competitive advantage in the global environment.

Let us examine the main elements of the German vocational education and training system in more detail.

Secondary and Higher Education

There are a number of different routes through the secondary education process and a decision on the path followed is based on examination results and teacher assessment, thereby embracing the concepts of streaming, selectivity and specialisation (Burgess, 1993; Mahnkopf, 1992).

The most academically gifted (around 33 per cent of pupils) attend a Gymnasium, a route geared towards eventual entry to university education. The remainder attend vocational or teacher schools, and flexibility allows access by suitably qualified students to a Gymnasium, or to higher education on the basis of vocational training and additional study. In conjunction with core and other subjects taken, pupils at a Gymnasium must study a foreign language and either maths or a physical science. While the syllabus of vocational school has a technical base, subjects such as economics, languages, and social studies are also included.

Higher education may be pursued in State-run universities and polytechnics (which offer more vocationally-oriented courses), or in private institutions (many of which offer technical and business education). In contrast to Ireland and the UK, students spend six years, on average, at university.

Initial Vocational Training

Although entry may derive from any of the educational streams outlined, there is a statutory requirement for the attendance of all young people who have not continued in the formal education system to participate in the dual system of initial vocational training. In what is essentially viewed as a form of apprenticeship, trainees in this system are engaged in a contract with a firm, receiving in the process extensive on-the-job and off-the-job training and theoretical instruction. The off-the-job element also includes subjects such as maths, science, social studies, economics, commerce, and physical education. The usual contract term runs for three years, during which time a nationally-negotiated wage rate is paid by the employer.

An outstanding feature of these apprenticeships is the huge variety of occupational classifications covered. In a further contrast with Ireland and the UK, almost 400 occupations are recognised for apprenticeship training, with some 125 of these being in craft trades. Curricula are mostly agreed by employers, employees, and relevant federal and regional ministries. As the aforementioned core classifications form the basis for more than 20,000 adult occupations, trainees acquire qualifications which can be put to general use, and the mobility of trained workers is greatly enhanced.

Minimum legal criteria are stipulated for companies providing apprenticeship training, among them being appropriate facilities and supervision by a suitably qualified instructor (typically a master craftsman). Where such criteria cannot be met, a situation generally pertinent to smaller companies, approved inter-company training centres may be utilised. These are usually funded through a combination of employer associations and public authorities.

The system is co-ordinated and managed by chambers of industry, commerce, crafts and agriculture, and membership of such a chamber is compulsory for all trading employers (this means in effect that all firms are obliged to pay a levy to the chambers, thereby creating a substantial financial resource). Their role incorporates the organisation of examinations and the certification of qualifications, as well as supervision and monitoring of training activities.

The dual system of vocational training has however been subjected to some criticism, most notably in regard to (a) the lengthy period required to attain the basic skills, (b) the excessive theoretical content, and (c) the general inflexibility and inconsistent standards arising from lack of co-ordination between examining bodies.

Despite these criticisms the success of the system is widely acknowledged and some of its major benefits include the following:

- The provision of knowledge and skills, which are linked to work experience, contributes to a sense of achievement, is motivational, and promotes independence and responsibility.

- The resulting skill level of employees, in tandem with an ample reservoir of qualified foremen, relieves highly-qualified technical and engineering staff from day-to-day shop floor responsibilities.

- A direct link is formed between training capacity and the demand for skilled labour.

- The creation of a workforce with skills and work attitudes strengthens their competitive capability in the delivery of goods and services.

A general breakdown of the numbers completing initial training sees some 50 per cent being employed in the specific occupation for which they were trained, 10 per cent undertaking their military or civic service, 13 per cent pursuing further education or training, 10 per cent entering unemployment, and the remainder working in some new area or entering into a fixed-term employment contract.

Further and Continuing Education

For those with a basic vocational training qualification, there are opportunities to proceed with further education or training activities. Many of these are aimed at attaining technician, foreman or, in the case of craft occupations, *meister* level. To cater for these aspirations, there are a variety of vocational education colleges and trade schools.

Considerable encouragement is given to those in employment to participate in continuing training activities, and there are wide-ranging opportunities available in this regard. There is an emphasis on the provision of continuing training by companies themselves. Company training of this sort is promoted by state-funded activities, and it is considered an issue of importance by trade unions.

Company training may comprise training given in-house, through a public training facility, or through private training providers (for whom criteria have been laid down to ensure quality standards). On an individual basis, databases and advice on training opportunities may be accessed, and there are a huge number of institutions where part-time or distance learning activities are pursued.

The Federal Labour Institute is the fulcrum for much of the state-encouraged training activities. Indeed, it has multiple responsibilities: (a) the administration of the federal employment service (job placement, careers advice, and job counselling); (b) the promotion of vocational training and retraining; (c) the provision of training opportunities for employers and employees; and (d) job creation/training schemes in East Germany. The Institute also administers the allocation of a range of funding schemes and facilities, by way of grants and loans to individuals, employers, and vocational training institutions.

Workforce consultation is consolidated by legislation whereby works councils and employers must cooperate on a range of training matters. Legislation also covers the right to a set amount of paid leave for education and training each year. German trade unions have traditionally maintained a strong voice on issues surrounding initial vocational training, as well as supporting greater skill orientation on the part of employers (Mahnkopf, 1992).

Management Education, Training and Development

The culture of education and training and the status attached to qualifications, which typifies the German experience, is even more pronounced in the field of management. This is reflected in the emphasis on appropriately educated and relevantly qualified people in the management recruitment and selection process, and has lead to a situation where almost two-thirds of top managers are educated to degree level.

Pre-entry education is then a significant factor in deciding if an individual is deemed suitable for a management position. Handy (1987) sees the recruitment criteria for front-line managers as including:

- direct relevance of studies for future jobs

- the grade received in final diploma examination

- fluency in at least one foreign language

- traditional apprenticeship highly regarded

- a doctorate, or a second course of studies, for certain positions

- periods of early practical experience in business

- the personality of the applicant.

Degrees in scientific and engineering subjects are considered much more appropriate for potential managers than those in the arts. Entry graduates are not judged on their performance. They are expected to successfully complete a "management apprenticeship", frequently incorporating on-the-job training and job rotation, before being recognised as true management material. As a result of these selection standards, many managers do not begin their careers within a company in earnest until their late twenties.

In an interesting similarity with many countries, including Ireland, the extent of post-entry management development activities is strongly dependent on company size — that is, the larger the firm the greater the concentration on such activities. Nonetheless, management development is a widespread activity and managers generally enjoy greater opportunities for training and development than other employees. It is common for large companies to provide extensive training and development programmes internally, most frequently for lower and middle management, with a job- and company-specific focus. Medium-sized and small companies tend to rely more on external expertise. Only a small number of universities provide relevant courses, but there are many sources of external training and development provision. Many courses are offered by private training organisations, and the chambers of commerce also organise a variety of management development programmes and seminars.

The United Kingdom

Vocational education and training, and training and development have, for some time, been the subject of much criticism, debate and reform in the UK.

The Industry Training Boards (ITBs), established through the Industrial Training Act (1964), were to fall victim to many of the criticisms levelled at AnCO in Ireland, especially that of excessive administration and bureaucracy. As a result, this industry-based system was effectively dismantled by the Employment and Training Act of 1973, and the subsequent creation of the Manpower Services Commission (MSC) led to a more centralised strategy (see Reid et al, 1992). In the late 1970s, the rising tide of unemployment, especially among young people, became the primary catalyst for linking training and employment initiatives. In the early 1980s, the MSC was abolished and replaced with the Training Agency (TA), and a new National Youth Training Scheme (YTS) was established.

Further developments followed: an adult-focused Employment Training Scheme; the establishment of Training and Enterprise Councils (TECs) and Local Enterprise Councils (LECs); and, in 1988, the creation of a National Training Task Force (NTTF). The TA was subsequently replaced by a Training, Education and Enterprise Division (TEED) within the Department of Employment.

This catalogue of events reflects the absence of a coherent strategy in this area, and among the weaknesses attributed to the system were:

- training being primarily viewed as the responsibility of government;

- centralised planning, leading to training being tackled at national rather than local level;

- the absence of statutory measures, either compelling employers to invest in training or penalising those who did not;

- the bureaucracy of the system and the inflexibility of its associated programmes;

- training being promoted and/or carried out for training's sake.

The early 1990s have seen a less centralised and more diverse approach being adopted in a major effort at further reform. However, there remains considerable scepticism concerning the current effectiveness and eventual success of the vocational education and training strategies being pursued.

Secondary and Higher Education

The education system in the UK is in a state of flux, being the focus of wide-ranging initiatives impinging on curricula, syllabi, and qualifications.

The official school-leaving age stands at 16 years. There is growing concern at two particular aspects of the education system: (a) the standards being achieved at primary level in basic skills (reading, writing and numeracy); and (b) the numbers leaving school at 16 without any vocational qualification. A two-pronged approach is being adopted to improve this situation, based on the introduction of a National Curriculum into schools with assessment targets set for attainment at specific ages (5, 7, 11, 14 and 16), and the application of a Technical and Vocational Education Initiative (TVEI) linked to a Certificate of Prevocational Education. Similar to the situation in Ireland, secondary education has been dominated by academically-based syllabi, and reforms in the examination system are aimed at increasing competence-based assessment and facilitating greater integration of vocational skills. A National Vocational Qualification (NVQ) system has also been introduced.

Higher education is provided by a wide array of institutions, including universities, polytechnics (granted the status and title of universities in 1992), technical colleges and colleges of further education. This sector has also been the subject of major reforms, reflecting an orientation towards governing bodies which are representative of industrial, business and professional interests.

Initial Vocational Training
In tandem with the greater integration of vocational training and education, Youth Training programmes are aimed at young people leaving school prior to higher education levels. These programmes are run by TECs and incorporate periods of on-the-job and off-the-job training. Trainees are encouraged to acquire NVQs.

Further and Continuing Education
A national strategy for vocational education and training (NVET) in the UK has been devised, encompassing six strategic objectives which may be summarised as follows:

- more effective investment by employers to develop requisite workforce skills;

- providing opportunities and encouragement for young people to achieve their full potential and to acquire skills in line with the needs of the economy;

- placing a greater emphasis on individual self-development;

- developing the abilities of the unemployed and disadvantaged, and enhancing their job opportunities;

- providing high quality and flexible education and training, attuned to individual and employer needs;

- promoting the growth of a national enterprise culture.

The aforementioned TECs have been given a central role in the implementation of these objectives. These councils are legally autonomous bodies, which operate on a local basis and are centrally funded. Although membership extends to representatives from local education, training and economic development activities, and trade unions, it is heavily biased towards employers, who fill two-thirds of the membership on each council. The responsibility for developing and implementing programmes aimed at achieving the strategic objectives outlined has been devolved to the TECs.

The net effect involves the development of business plans which incorporate (a) the provision of education and training opportunities for young people; (b) the planning and delivering of training for the unemployed; (c) the promotion and support of training for the employed; and (d) the promotion and support of enterprise and business growth.

Management Education, Training and Development
Deficiencies in the area of management education, training and development in the UK have been extensively highlighted in a succession of reports and studies, including Coopers and Lybrand (1985), Mangham and Silver (1986) and Handy (1987). These indicate a distinct lack of emphasis on this vital activity among companies in general, and identify a comparative low level of relevant qualifications among those occupying management positions. It has been widely suggested that prevailing attitudes reflect the traditional reliance on background and character as primary criteria for "management material" and the presumption that "leaders are born not made". Of course, this is a wide generalisation, and there is ample evidence that many organisations take a more professional view, demonstrated in their recruitment policies and their investment in management training and development.

In fact, business studies are significantly to the fore in the higher education sphere, with a variety of undergraduate and postgraduate degrees and diploma courses being provided in a wide range of institutions. However, there has been an imbalance of choice in favour of accountancy and related studies over those in scientific or technical fields. This in itself can be related to the traditional pre-eminence of qualifications in the former category as a criteria for top management positions in the UK.

Some initiatives have been attempted in recent years to advance the issue of management development, including the establishment of the National Forum for Management Education and Development (NFMED) as a policy-making body for setting and developing management and supervisory standards. In addition, there are indications that management development is perceived in increasingly important terms by organisations, and that greater investment is being committed to this activity. Nonetheless, the UK experience in this regard, as in the overall realm of training and development, remains far adrift of many of its main competitor countries.

France

The French system has been the subject of considerable reforms, introduced over a number of years, which have resulted in a higher level of integration of education and vocational training. Allied to this, companies have been required by statutory obligations, first enacted in 1971, to devote a certain percentage of their total wage bill to training. A further initiative to promote training has been the establishment, in 1988, of tax credits, apportioned to expenditure on training which is over and above the legally required amount. Similar to the German experience, employers are required to devise training plans, in consultation with employee representatives. Furthermore, there is a common commitment between the State, employers and trade unions to raising the profile of initial vocational training and continuing training within organisations. This emphasis has been reflected in the conclusion of a number of collective agreements which have incorporated agreed training arrangements.

The success of the French approach is illustrated by the fact that:

- in 1978, 25 per cent of school-leavers possessed no qualifications, while this figure had dropped to some 13 per cent by 1991;

- by 1986, more than 70 per cent of those in the 16-18 age group were continuing in full-time education;

- in 1990, companies spent an average of 3.1 per cent of their wage bill on training, compared to the statutory requirement of 1.4 per cent;

- in current terms, problems of skill shortage have largely been resolved.

Some particular problem areas have been identified, notably in the apprenticeship system and in the growing shortages of engineers, and these have been the focus of very recent initiatives.

Secondary and Higher Education

Full-time education is compulsory until the age of 16, at which stage lower secondary schooling, featuring a broad curriculum of general education is normally completed (some students opt to attend a technical school from the age of 14). Higher secondary schooling offers two basic choices — further general studies, leading to higher education; or initial vocational/technical training, leading to technical qualifications and possibly also to higher education.

A variety of higher education facilities exist. Technical universities, where entrance is based on school reports, offer two- and three-year qualification courses, some of which can lead to further studies at a university. Universities are State-run and entrance is open to those who have acquired a school leaving certificate — "the baccalaureate". Courses generally follow a four-stage route — two years to a diploma, another year for a bachelor degree, a further year for a masters degree, and two subsequent years of postgraduate studies for a specialised diploma or a doctorate. Finally, *grandes écoles* are elitist and highly selective, with entrance granted only on the basis of a specific examination which requires some two years of preparatory study. Some of these are run by the State, others by the Chamber of Commerce, and some are private institutions. Courses, which normally run for three years, lead to a highly-prized diploma qualification.

Initial Vocational Training

As already indicated, initial vocational training is part of the school education system, and may be integrated with general studies, usually in a "vocational training lycée" (LEP). Courses, which consist of general education and practical and theoretical training (including company-based activities) lead to a range of qualifications. The CAP three-year diploma is awarded on the basis of professional skill in a particular trade, while the less specialised two-year BEP diploma is awarded for skills which are required in a particular professional, industrial, commercial, administrative, or social sector. Both diplomas can provide a passage to further studies in pursuit of a "Technical Baccalaureate " (BTS) or a "Technical Diploma" (BT).

The French apprenticeship system covers some 300 trades, mainly associated with craft-based occupations. The provisions of the system were traditionally agreed between the State, employers and trade unions, but these were revamped by collective agreement and subsequent legislation in 1992. Apprenticeship training is modular in form and comprises both on-the-job (in-company) and off-the-job (at an apprenticeship centre). It has further similarities with the new scheme being introduced in Ireland in that all apprenticeships must be registered with the CFA. The system is partially financed by an apprenticeship tax, levied on all employers. Trainees' wage rates are based on the national minimum wage and were substantially increased in the latest legislative reform. An increase in female participation has been evidenced, with recent figures suggesting that more than 30 per cent of participants are female.

Further and Continuing Education

In France, the right of employees to continuing vocational training is enshrined in the legislative framework. Provision is made also for paid time-off for continuing vocational training within certain conditions. Furthermore, as already indicated, there is a statutory requirement on companies to apportion specific levels of expenditure to training, and to produce annual training plans, in consultation with employee representatives. These stipulations ensure that widespread opportunities exist for participating in further and continuing training activities. As in most other countries, however, specific imbalances in training provision may be noted, including:

- larger companies invest more in training than medium or small companies;

- men are more likely to receive training than women, although the gap in this instance is relatively narrow (approximately 82 women to every 100 men);

- the incidence of training provision decreases in scale from high-profile job (52 per cent) to blue collar employees (25 per cent).

Nonetheless, there is a considerable emphasis on continuing training and it is estimated that around a quarter of the workforce receive some formal training each year. Apart from training organised in-company, there are a multiplicity of public and private facilities for training provision. Private training organisations under the aegis of the Vocational Training Federation operate within an agreed code of conduct and to specified minimum quality standards.

Substantial funds are invested by the State in encouraging participation in, and the organisation of, training for the young and/or long-term unemployed, and for disadvantaged groups. The primary focus of training for the unemployed is centred on providing training in work situations to those who have failed to acquire basic qualifications, and thus might be perceived more in terms of initial vocational training. A variety of such schemes exist, with some initially devised for younger people but extended to embrace the long-term unemployed in general. The schemes mainly constitute contract periods in employment linked to a range of incentives offered to employers.

Management Education, Training and Development

Following a somewhat elitist tradition, French managers, certainly at the top level, are generally highly educated and usually graduates of a *grande école*, where they may have acquired an engineering degree, a higher business studies diploma, a doctorate, or a business qualification similar to an MBA.

In a system with few national counterparts, managerial ranks (known as *cadres*) enjoy legally-recognised status, arising from decrees issued in 1946. There are two routes to the rank of *cadre*: (a) recruitment of high-calibre technically qualified individuals who have applied this knowledge through job experience; and (b) internal promotion of less-qualified individuals who have gained extensive experience. The ranks of the former category are most likely to achieve subsequently top management positions, especially in larger companies. Indeed, individuals with engineering degrees predominate at top management level.

The notable emphasis on intellectual ability and pre-entry education has led to some discourse on the need for complementary management, leadership and interpersonal skills. In this regard, larger companies are more likely to invest in external management development programmes (normally of a relatively short duration), with medium-sized and small companies tending to concentrate on less formal in-company training. External provision is catered for by numerous management and business schools and centres, which offer a range of general and specific courses.

The United States

The achievement culture in the US, which places a high value on individual achievement and success, is very visible in the education and training sphere. In this context, the acquisition of qualifications may be equated with visible achievement, which helps to explain the high levels of participation in adult continuing education, especially in courses leading to recognised awards, such as degrees and diplomas. This individual focus is further carried over into organisation, where an emphasis on self-development is evident, and personal initiatives in this direction are often supported and encouraged. However, there is little apparent reference to formal vocational training systems, such as those operated in other countries.

Education

Commentary on the US education "system" is complicated by the independent and decentralised nature of the state "system" in administrative and legislative terms. Nonetheless, the following statistical information serves to highlight some aspects of education in the US.

- In most cases school attendance is compulsory up to the age of 16.

- High school diploma graduation rates exceed 70 per cent.

- Almost 50 per cent of high school graduates continue their education on either a full or part-time basis. In general, full-time relates to four-year undergraduate college courses, while part-time means a two-year community college associate degree course.

- Undergraduate degree programmes tend to comprise two years of general studies, followed by two years "majoring" in a specific discipline. In 1986, around 24 per cent of such majors were taken in business and management subjects.

Training

Apart from work placement schemes aimed at the unemployed and disadvantaged, which are sponsored at local government level, there is little official intervention in the training and development area. Whether or not companies wish to train their employees, and the extent and nature of training activities provided, are decisions left entirely to management discretion. The seemingly universal situation, whereby the scale of training provision increases with company size, is equally applicable in the US, although it is important to interpret this as a generalisation that has many exceptions.

The worldwide success of the Japanese industry has had a considerable effect on the US marketplace and highlighted the need for US organisations, especially in the industrial sector, to improve competitiveness. More recent developments, in the shape of market globalisation, have accentuated this focus, and there are indications that an increasing number of companies are investing more heavily in training and development as a catalyst for improvement. It is, of course, widely acknowledged that some of the larger US corporations, such as AT&T, IBM, Xerox, etc., have long adopted this view, committing vast resources to training and development in the process.

Management Development

In the US, being educated to degree level is almost a prerequisite for any individual seeking a career in management. Furthermore, with the US being widely recognised as the progenitor of the MBA, it is hardly surprising that this qualification is seen as the pre-eminent key to entry into the ranks of business management. While the academic source of such an acquisition may determine its relative value, and despite the often suggested variance of quality in the diversity of MBA programmes available, its popularity, in student choice terms, remains undiminished.

MBA programmes are also pursued on a part-time basis by those who have entered management positions on the basis of other degree qualifications, and also by others in employment who aspire to such positions. With some notable exceptions, the provision of management development courses by universities is not a usual feature. There has been some movement towards executive MBA programmes, with business schools providing courses geared towards meeting the needs of specific industries, and towards business schools providing expertise for management development-type programmes in partnership with specific companies. As indicated, many of the bigger corporations have extensive training facilities and resources, and management development is perceived as a core internal activity in these cases. There is also a growing realisation, again most particularly in bigger companies, that formal education must be reinforced by ongoing on-the-job learning opportunities.

Japan

Quality of product and service, founded on the competitiveness derived from continuous improvement in organisations' operating processes, has been one of the outstanding hallmarks of Japanese success in world markets. Indeed, the terms "quality" and "continuous improvement" have become synonymous with Japanese business culture. Training, development, and the process of learning have been absorbed into the very essence of this culture, and are considered fundamental elements of its sustenance and proliferation. This may also be reflective of the value and emphasis placed on study and learning in wider Japanese cultural traditions.

An outstanding feature of the Japanese approach is the initial concentration, through the education system, on inculcating a learning ethos. The academic process is geared towards building up a store of general and theoretical knowledge, allied to a capacity for problem-solving. In subsequent employment, the expectation is that this intellectual grounding will be adapted and applied, at all levels, to result in constant innovation and continuous improvements in operational effectiveness.

Secondary and Higher Education

The word "superb" is one commonly used to describe the Japanese education system, which is highly centralised and tightly controlled by the Ministry of Education. School attendance is compulsory up to the age of 15, a period entirely financed by the State, but the numbers continuing in full-time education are thought to be higher (some 96 per cent of young people) than anywhere else in the world.

There is little integration of vocational training and education; the education system focuses primarily on providing broad-based knowledge and learning. With educational standards set extremely high, and an immense value bestowed on attainment, the system is consistently referred to as being fiercely competitive. Teaching skills and standards are also set at an exceptional level, and teachers are highly committed to their work.

A high proportion of Japanese young people — around 40 per cent — continue on to third-level education, usually opting for either a two-year college or a four-year university course of studies. Higher education facilities include national, public and private institutions, and concentration on academic and theoretical learning is a common feature. More recently there has been substantial movement towards business-studies programmes, primarily at graduate level.

Training

The induction period is considered a very important training phase in Japanese companies, where, especially in bigger firms, the notion of a "job for life" persists. This initial contact therefore represents the formation stage of a lifelong relationship between the employee and the company, and every opportunity is utilised to indoctrinate the new trainee into the culture and ethos which will become an ongoing "way of life" in employment terms.

Following induction, it is usual to introduce the new employee to a wide range of work experience activities and on-the-job training. There follows an ongoing process of learning, through work experience and both on- and off-the-job training activities, as well as encouragement to pursue further general education outside of work. Thus, an endless cycle of formal and informal, natural and contrived, learning opportunities are embedded in a company environment conducive to consequent action in pursuit of improved operating effectiveness.

In Japan, training is perceived very much in investment terms, rather than as a cost, and this is reflected in the resources provided. Training departments are a company norm, as are training facilities. Indeed, many of the bigger corporations also have institutionalised education and training facilities of their own. Although training expenditure per employee does increase with company size, even in small and medium-sized companies, there is a contrast with most other countries in that training and development commands a central role in the organisation framework.

Management Education, Training and Development

The ranks of Japanese management are overwhelmingly dominated by university graduates, and almost exclusively so at top management levels in larger organisations. Nonetheless, it is possible for non-graduates to climb the management ladder, but this progress is slower and less certain.

Indeed, even for graduates, progression in the promotion stakes usually follows a slow but steady pattern, with a "home-grown" management development philosophy, where seniority and experience are significant features of this phenomenon. Managers therefore follow a similar introductory routine to all other employees, featuring an induction training period, on-the-job training and job rotation. On an ongoing basis, considerable emphasis is placed on mentoring, coaching and counselling as on-the-job training activities, embodying the widespread concept of passing on knowledge and experience. Off-the-job training and development activities include "company classroom sessions" and external courses and seminars. Embracing a continuous process of self-development is also actively encouraged and facilitated.

External management development provision is available through a range of training organisations, management academies and qualified training consultants. This entire framework is closely monitored by State agencies and ministries, which are variously responsible for approving and licensing the body of training providers.

EUROPEAN MANAGEMENT EDUCATION

In examining management education systems in Europe, it is necessary to distinguish between two broad types of management education.

The first consists of pre-experience, pre-career or initial business education, which takes place after the completion of secondary education, or in some cases after a period of higher education. It generally consists of a first degree or diploma or a masters-level programme which follows on directly from other education.

The second category consists of post-experience training or continuing education which is an integral part of the career development of managers. This category may take many forms, including executive MBAs, in-company training programmes, short courses and professional programmes which cover a wide range of general and specialist topics geared towards all managerial levels.

While it is commonly proposed that high priority should be given to post-experience management education, there are, however, varying degrees of emphasis across Europe.

Background

National education systems in Europe demonstrate considerable diversity, whereas most business schools throughout the United States share common origins and traditions. Business and management education in

Europe evolved through a complex variety of institutions, with the majority of European business schools emerging after the second world war. Significant expansion has, however, taken place during the 1960s and 1970s.

European business education has its roots in the scientific, industrial and commercial revolutions of the seventeenth to nineteenth centuries. This period led to a rapid expansion in the demand for skilled technical and professional personnel. Many commentators point out, however, that few European universities recognised business and management studies as a responsible academic discipline. Business administration was, in some cases, considered a sophisticated form of vocational training. However, a number of significant developments during the 1940s and 1950s brought management education centre-stage. A significant impetus to the development of professional management education was given by the scientific management movement in the United States in the 1930s. This led, in the United States at least, to a new emphasis on the industrial centres.

Pre-experience Business Education

There is a variety of higher education routes in Europe through which people prepare for a business career. Many courses in law, engineering, science, and economics provide some opportunity to study aspects of business or management, although these studies tend to be marginal to mainstream course requirements. Core business education is available as well. All countries in Europe have at least some programmes that provide an initial higher qualification in business studies or allied subjects such as accounting, marketing, business computing or human resources.

The demand for full-time pre-experience business education has been reflected in the massive expansion of higher education in Europe from the 1960s onwards. More recently, there has been a further shift in demand, deriving from employers' interest and a more vocational emphasis in education, that is reflected in an increase in enrolments in higher business and allied courses. There is room for improvement in Europe, especially if we consider that some 25 per cent of the 18-25 year old age group are enrolled in higher education — the corresponding figure in the US is about 50 per cent.

Courses in Europe are characterised by an important selection threshold at secondary or high school before undergraduate studies, in contrast with the American educational system where the main selection occurs between the bachelor and master level.

Given the substantial expansion of student numbers in business and management studies in recent years, competitive selection for entry to full-time, pre-career, higher business education is almost universal. The nature and stringency of selection requirements, however, varies. Some require rigorous preparatory examinations. Others require entrance tests and interviews. In almost all cases students must achieve high exam rates at second level but some exceptions are made, for example, for mature students. In some countries a second selection threshold occurs after the first year of studies from which only some 50 per cent may continue.

Pre-experience courses generally combine studies in basic disciplines such as economics, quantitative methods, behavioural science and computing with functional studies such as marketing, finance, human resource management, business organisation and law. Most include integrative studies in business policy and international business. Many require a period in a work placement or the preparation of a practical business project. Most of these courses include minor or major areas of specialisation to enable students to develop special interests and abilities and to prepare them for specialist professional roles on graduation. Work placement experience may vary from a few months to one year.

These initial business programmes lead to diplomas and degrees which naturally vary in level depending on selection requirements, the length of study (usually from two to five years), the nature of the curriculum and the intensity of the study regime. The types of qualification awarded range from a two-year "technician" diploma, to a three- or four-year first degree course or licence, to a one- to two-year postgraduate diploma or masters degree.

Post-experience Management Education

It is generally accepted that if Europe intends to maintain an important economic role in the global environment it needs to combine a united home market with a concentration on knowledge-intensive economic sectors. These sectors are subject to ever-reducing "life cycles" of knowledge. Both of these factors underline the importance of post-experience management education. Equally, human resources are inceasingly perceived within companies as a critical means of achieving business effectiveness. Human resource management is therefore increasingly linked with the "bottom line".

Buckley and Caple (1992) point out that education may contribute in three areas towards the development of a person: by providing knowledge, by creating skills and by changing attitudes. The input of educational institutions in the first area of knowledge is clear. But more and more the second and third areas are being addressed by educational institutions, often in close co-operation with on-the-job training, job rotation, etc. It must be recognised, however, that all post-experience training has limitations and can only play a complementary role to in-company experiences and activities.

As post-experience management education has increased in importance there has also been a substantial enlargement of the target groups of participants that this type of education caters for. While the private sector has experienced major expansion, a notable tendency has been an increase of training effort in the public sector. In the 1960s, executive development programmes were specifically directed at high potential mid-career managers, concentrating on despecialisation courses in general management. Nowadays, target audiences range from supervisory to management to corporate and senior managers.

The distribution of post-experience training efforts remains uneven. The statistical evidence shows that companies spend mostly somewhere between 1 and 6 per cent of their gross salary costs on in-company external training. Of this overall figure, a substantial amount is spent on the top 5-10 per cent of the organisation, in most industry sectors. It must be noted, however, that at the highest levels few attend training sessions (Harrison, 1992). Another broad category of managers to whom little training attention is given are older managers (above 40-45 years) as well as managers who have reached a plateau in their career. With the rapidly changing business world there is a need to make an optimal use of the experience available within companies. Efforts are often excessively concentrated on young high fliers.

Finally, the limited use of training by small business managers is significant. Gibb (1993) suggests that there is a low basis of trust of consultants and trainers, and many training programmes fail to meet the needs of small businesses. There is a pressing need to find the right way to address this audience, for research shows that next to a lack of financial resources, poorly-qualified management is the second reason for bankruptcy of small companies.

There exists a large number of providers of post-experience management education in Europe. Universities and colleges play some role but they cover only a minority of the offerings. The bulk of this type of education is provided by management centres which may be independent but often have links with other organisations such as chambers of commerce, employers' organisations, or some individual companies (for example, publishing houses). Consultancy firms, government agencies and local interest groups also provide a great deal of training especially for small businesses.

The general trend to which all providers have to respond is the growing relationship between training and organisational goals and performance improvement. This practical orientation has in the past decade led to an increase of "tailor-made" offerings. In order to avoid a "myopic" single company approach new forms have been found. Consortia of companies are in co-operation with educational institutions to design relevant courses.

Although the "corporate classroom" phenomenon is less developed in Europe than in the United States, European companies are now developing co-operative agreements with certain educational institutions to create forms of corporate classrooms in Europe. If European educational institutions are prepared to adapt to the specific needs of companies, a desirable movement in the direction of real partnership will occur. If higher education is unable to answer in such a way, the alternative may prove to be a parallel educational system of corporate classrooms alongside regular educational offerings.

The European management training arena has changed considerably since the 1960s in terms of length, content and educational approach. Originally, most post-experience executive development programmes were rather long, often 12 weeks or more. In line with the market demand for shorter but more frequent courses, management centres have adapted their products. Courses which last more than five weeks are the exception; while most fall within the one to three week's range, even shorter programmes (of only a few days duration) are also common for top managers. A number of modular-designed MBA programmes have also been developed.

Several trends in industry — such as the flattening of organisations, stronger integration of functions and an increase in project-oriented approaches — have led to a growing demand for training in organisational skills ranging from communication and negotiation to team building and leadership training. Experiential learning, combining a variety of teaching mechanisms, has become a particular feature of such programmes.

Delivery of Courses

The wide variety of national cultures and educational systems evident in Europe has led to considerable diversity and experimentation in didactic approaches which is a significant feature of European management education. Innovations may be found at every point in the business education spectrum ranging from the Chicago (quantitative) to the Harvard (case study) approach (Daft, 1995). But in many there will be a complex mix. Foundation disciplines such as quantitative methods, economics, law, and behavioural science may be found alongside a concern with functional studies such as finance, marketing or personnel and integrative studies such as business strategy or international operations. Theoretical and analytical studies may predominate over behavioural and activity-based ones, or vice versa. Curricula are influenced by many European factors: the national origins and development of schools, the diverse character of the way they are governed and the wide variety of systems of organisation.

Delivery of courses tends to vary as a result. While in many institutions training continues to be conducted on fairly traditional lines through lectures, discussion and tutorials, there is increased emphasis on group work and self-instruction. The increasing use of computers and advances in telecommunications are leading to more individualisation of learning and to learning methodologies that are more easily deployed. Many programmes are now available through combinations of full-time, part-time, home-based or workplace study.

Furthermore, there has been a recent and rapid increase in the development of modular course structures and national and international credit transfer systems. These developments have inevitably led to changes in modes of assessment, which in most European business programmes now include a mix of formal examination, continuous assessment, group project assignments, objective testing, and tutor, or group, feedback.

European management education is thus characterised by a range of offerings from residential courses, via courses combined with study tours, project-based teaching, computer-aided training, to distance learning. Distance learning has moved on from the traditional correspondence course. Today it operates through sophisticated multimedia pedagogical tools. The distance learner has abandoned text and lecture notes for the PC and interactive video disks. Finally, non-orthodox methods such as action-learning and outward-bound courses similarly appear to be increasingly in demand in some countries: the former because it meets the need for results-oriented training and the latter because it is seen as a powerful method for leadership training and team building.

At every level, business plays a significant role in management education, not only through its own in-house or on-the-job training, but also in co-operation with business schools. At the pre-career level, business provides industrial training and opportunities for project work. At postgraduate and post-experience level, the co-operation ranges from work with schools on the design of in-house training programmes and consultancy to the use of schools to provide specialist courses or experience for executives.

International Orientation

A significant characteristic of European management education is its strong international orientation both at pre-career and post-experience level. The internationalisation of business schools or management centres takes a variety of forms:

- internationalising courses in a wide range of disciplines

- adding international courses to the curriculum

- adding language courses to the curriculum

- offering work or study assignments abroad for students

- exchange faculty members

- exchange students

- setting up double-degree programmes

- setting up fully integrated joint programmes with foreign institutions

- undertaking joint research, consultancy and publication with colleagues abroad.

The pattern of international business education is highly diverse, but there is general agreement on the overall objective to expose students and faculty to an international climate, and in particular to involve them in the experience of studying and working outside a national culture.

Resources

In Europe, as elsewhere, the oil price crisis of the 1970s had far-reaching effects on business and on management education. Many business schools experienced a temporary dip in demand for post-experience courses as firms reviewed their personnel and training commitments. This resulted in tighter budgets and pressures for shorter, more relevant courses. Cuts in internal training departments contributed to an upsurge in demand for external assistance. By the 1980s business schools were experiencing "boom" market conditions. All major centres were adding facilities and making higher profits. This was supplemented by renewed interest, and increased investment, in the "human factor" of management, after decades in which management training had given priority to analytical and quantitative issues. Life cycles of programmes were shortened. In many cases a parallel move to a more practical, "in-company", emphasis was accompanied by increased demand for consultancy services from business schools.

A rather different situation prevailed in the universities and higher vocational schools in the public sector. Central and local government authorities, faced with severe cuts in public expenditure, passed these on. There were reductions in both capital and recurrent expenditure. Generally it was left to institutions to decide for themselves on the distribution of the economies they had to make. As faculty costs account for a large percentage of total budgets, there were cuts in faculty budgets resulting in higher student/staff ratios and reductions in research activity. There were also cuts in building, equipment and library allocations.

One outcome of this was that some European institutions that had previously regarded themselves as academic, and perhaps insulated from "real life", were required to confront the same problem as their colleagues in business. New initiatives were taken to enter into a more positive dialogue with business and industry.

The financial situation in Europe contrasts with that in the United States where business schools have closer relations with business and, consequently, better financial support. In Europe, sudden contraction of public funding could not be cushioned by a parallel increase in financial support from business and it will take time to build such support. This is not to say that many firms have not supported management education. They have funded research, provided facilities, sponsored students, financed faculty posts and endowed chairs. Through trusts and foundations, they provide much indirect support. But schools in the United States have maintained a closer and more co-operative relationship and have greater experience of fund-raising.

The key resource of business schools is their faculty and the intellectual capital they represent. They are wide variations in the approaches used to provide the manpower than is required to maintain the high-quality teaching and research expected of schools.

There are a number of sources of faculty. Schools may appoint faculty from a largely academic background where advanced qualifications and substantial publications in theoretical fields are prerequisites. Such staff may be required to keep in touch with business developments through consultancy and internships in firms. A second faculty source concerns former businessmen with some business qualifications who are employed largely for the nature of their practical experience. But as their knowledge can rapidly become out of date, they are also encouraged to undertake research and consultancy. In some cases a substantial input is made by practising businessmen who are able to transfer their experience in a classroom or seminar-workshop environment. Given the multiple tasks of business schools, most commentators would argue that some balancing among these types of experience is necessary.

Some schools comprise mainly permanent faculty, but many have developed with only a small core of permanent staff and rely on short-term inputs from managers or faculty from other academic institutions or departments. In a few centres, such as Management Centre Europe, the permanent core only comprise course directors and designers who co-ordinate the inputs of a variety of visiting teachers.

New Challenges in Management Development

The increasingly complex nature of business and changes in social attitudes have led to recognition that employees at all levels have the potential to make a more informed, intelligent and creative contribution to the life and work of an organisation. Hence a new emphasis on employees as a human resource has emerged. The careful development of manpower is seen as a key issue for progressive management, with human resource management regarded as a central aspect of overall business strategy.

In recognition of the increasing costs of skilled manpower and an awareness of the value of intellectual capital, more emphasis is placed on rigorous selection, attractive conditions of service, job satisfaction and career planning.

At the same time there has been renewed concern with productivity featuring the linking of managerial performance and results to innovative incentives schemes. Consequently there has been a trend towards increased line management responsibility and a parallel paring down of staff functions — allowing for less complex, more transparent organisation. Concomitantly, management education is now focusing on preparing managers for horizontal, rather than vertical, movements. More direct "pay-offs" are sought from education and training and there has been an increase in demand for tailor-made courses. The personnel function has gained increased status and its human resource management function has been emphasised.

The development of the qualities that are required to operate successfully in this environment is generally thought to involve three areas of management training, although there is debate concerning any precise classification.

1. The *acquisition of knowledge* involves a grasp of professional, technical, organisational and business environment information on which the manager's task is based.

2. The *acquisition of skills* refers to those characteristics such as problem-solving, communicating, motivating, negotiating, which are required to enable the manager to carry out his function.

3. The *development of aptitudes and attitudes* is required to enable the manager to achieve high performance; judgement, creativity, flexibility, mental agility, resilience, self-reliance, energy, initiative, courage, a willingness to take risks, combined with a respect for ethical standards. In particular for operations in an international context, the manager needs to be able to respond positively to widely different environments and cultures.

There is continuing debate about the place and emphasis of the above in management development programmes. It has always been acknowledged that some combination of studies in basic disciplines, functional areas and integrative subjects is a good foundation for management. But there is now less pressure for intensive qualitative methods and more for behavioural, environmental and public policy studies, reflecting the current concerns of business. The case method is under scrutiny in so far as it may reflect a static and historically-outdated view of a business situation rather than a live, dynamic view. There are pressures for more studies which have immediate practical applications.

A major current debate concerns the behavioural component of programmes. This has always been an aspect of management training, involving skills development and action learning, but the focus now has turned to such matters as developing entrepreneurial and leadership characteristics. While some argue that these can neither be taught nor measured, others organise outdoor "leadership" courses and refer to precedents in military training.

In responding to these needs, some companies are making specific provision in time and money for the personal development of their managers in order to remedy any deficiencies in areas such as sensitivity, committee working and communication.

There is widespread recognition of the need for more frequent, continuing education periods of training in response to rapid change in the business environment. The implications of the above have been to modify the traditional approach to management development through external courses by placing more emphasis on "on-the-job" management development, and on in-company training programmes. A major shift has taken place towards more work-based learning.

Business schools and centres are increasingly working with firms in designing systems of learning that involve less attendance at teaching institutions. In this sense one can anticipate the development of standardised learning modules that can easily be customised to match the general learning needs of the individual manager within the specific context of the firm's activities.

It is recognised that management development is a matter of concern for both the organisation and the individual (Mumford, 1994). The dynamic business environment has urged management to become more mobile. Some managers will continue to spend most of their career with one firm while many others will experience frequent job and career changes. In these circumstances, managers seek training that will equip them to work more effectively for their current employer but at the same time to be of interest to potential employers. While it is argued that many contemporary skills and aptitudes are transferable, it is also noted that it can take a considerable time for a manager to become fully effective in a new organisation.

The arrival of mobile management has had two consequences: (a) there has been an increase in demand for widely recognised and validated management training programmes that provide a qualification that is accepted beyond the confines of a particular firm or industry; and (b) there has also been a proliferation of specialist management training organisations and consultants who work with companies to undertake specialist forms of skill and attitude training to meet specific company needs.

There is a widespread view throughout Europe that the professionalisation of management will only be achieved by increased management education. A major challenge is to provide managerial training for the many managers in business, especially in small and medium-sized enterprises, that have neither qualifications nor training, and to maintain continuous updating for all managers. The evidence of escalating demand for, and investment in, management education of all types, and at all levels, suggests that whatever approach is adopted, management development will increasingly be seen to play a key role in business activity.

MBA Programmes

There has been intense discussion for some years about the role and value of full-time MBA programmes which have not established the same status among management qualifications in Europe that they have achieved in the United States (Heywood, 1989). This may be due to the fact that higher management qualifications in Europe have been obtained by such a diversity of routes. There have been pressures to enhance the standing of higher management qualifications and to increase the number of managers with MBAs. In this context the example of management education in the United States is often quoted with its production of 70,000 MBAs annually.

But there have been counter-arguments. In many European countries higher education in a specialist field such as law, engineering, economics or the humanities has been regarded as an extremely good foundation for the development of future managers. There is a quality control problem in such an environment as the European one, where accreditation procedures are extremely difficult, if not impossible, to apply due to differences in national educational systems. Some critics refer to the fact that only a very limited number of MBAs enter industry and that most of them become consultants or investment bankers. It is therefore argued that combining a higher education in foundation disciplines followed by part-time management qualifications or an MBA programme is preferable. But this should not obscure the fact that full-time postgraduate programmes in business and management have attracted some of the brightest students and have equipped many of them to play key roles in business.

It would appear, therefore, that, while not a universal preparation for top management roles, the full-time postgraduate programme has much to offer at certain stages of a manager's career and in certain companies (Kakabadese, 1990). The educational value of a lengthy period away from the pressures of day-to-day work in an academic environment in which very broad questions are discussed may make an important contribution to building creative management teams. It is notable in this context that the popularity of company/university MBA programmes is increasing. In the market we see a tendency towards one-year instead of two-year MBA studies and an increased number of part-time MBA offerings, mostly spread over two or three years.

Interdisciplinary Studies

A large proportion of business managers hold qualifications in disciplines other than business or management — for example, engineering, law, economics, or humanities. Management organisations have argued for many years that, because of this, some elements of management should be included in these curricula. In some cases this has happened. Few students entering these fields will be exempt from the exigencies of business and there is thus a case for incorporating some elements of management in their programmes. While such inputs may be more appropriately made in special studies after graduation, it would still be possible, for example, to include management subjects as major options for those students who proposed to practise in a business or a professional environment.

Within many European management schools, the links between business administration and other disciplines are discussed. An increased emphasis on creativity and innovation has, for instance, stimulated several schools to see whether combination with some (liberal) arts classes would be beneficial to the teaching of these topics in business curricula. The interest in business ethics has stimulated similar changes in the direction of philosophy and history.

The dramatic technological developments and their consequences for the business world have probably had the biggest impact in stimulating co-operation with other disciplines. Many schools are experimenting with combined business and engineering curricula, and it seems that this tendency might increase in the near future.

Finally, the closer interlinking of private and public sector activities in many European countries has raised again the issue of general schools which teach both public administration and business management. This is an issue because generic schools, and programmes, are a rare phenomenon in Europe.

There seems to be some agreement that more European PhD programmes in business administration would be desirable instead of having to depend on the recruitment of faculty members holding a PhD in another discipline (such as economics, sociology, mathematics) as is still widely the practice at present. Much of the multidisciplinary teaching which is required in management education has been difficult to promote due to the mono-disciplinary background of business faculty.

However, even when the initial qualifications of faculty members are sufficient, management centres are confronted, in a period of high technology and rapid change, with "burnout" and updating problems. In post-experience training activities faculty members are sometimes confronted with the fact that they are less up-to-date than operational managers. Keeping up with the recent developments in one's own field of specialisation, as well as with developments in business, requires high motivation of faculty members as well as excellent co-operation with the business world.

TRAINING AND DEVELOPMENT IN LOW UNEMPLOYMENT COUNTRIES

We will now give an overview of training and development in low unemployment countries, drawing extensively from the recent study in this area by Kerins (1993). In line with the objectives set out in this work, it is accepted that the approach to developing human resources in these countries cannot be verified as a decisive factor in their low level of unemployment. However, as these levels are undoubtedly low in comparative terms, an overview within this context is considered worthwhile in seeking to identify lessons which may be put forward as a basis, at least, for improvements in the Irish situation.

The countries featured in the aforementioned study were Norway, Sweden, Japan, Austria and Switzerland. The average rate of unemployment in Norway between 1960 and 1986 stood at 1.4 per cent, and while it subsequently showed an increase on this astoundingly low figure, it has remained low by international standards. Furthermore, current trends and projections indicate downward movement, in addition to a very high labour participation rate. The unemployment rate in Sweden varied between 2 per cent and 3.5 per cent during the 1970s and 1980s, and was anticipated to stabilise at around 4 per cent by 1993. In Japan, rates have been consistently below 3 per cent, and a figure of 2.3 per cent was forecast for 1993. Austria's performance in the battle against unemployment has for many years been counted as one of the most impressive in the OECD and this excellence is expected to continue, with a level of around 3 per cent expected for 1993. Finally, the rate in Switzerland was for many years below the 1 per cent mark, and projections for 1993 stood at 1.4 per cent (by previous standards, it actually stood at a relatively high 5 per cent in the third quarter of 1993). Compared to many EC countries these low levels of unemployment are notable indeed — consider the Irish experience of recent years where levels have been running close to 20 per cent.

As Kerins (1993) highlights, the five featured countries are extremely varied in many respects. There are readily identifiable differences in size and in density of population, as well as in culture, political, historical and demographic factors. Neither is there uniformity in the extent of centralisation, state involvement, or even reliance on foreign trade. It is also worth pointing out that, while the four European countries are OECD members, Sweden and Austria have only recently joined the EU.

There are striking similarities, however, in some significant areas — most notably in relation to the focus on the issue of unemployment and the attachment to the inherent value of learning.

Focus on Unemployment

In all five countries, the issue of unemployment commands a dominant position on the political and social agenda. The aim of full employment, driven by national consensus, is pursued with constant vigour, and this objective is widely held as the overriding economic priority. In the words of Kerins (1993): ". . . the goal of full employment permeates society and public concern is raised if the dole queues begin to rise."

While unity of purpose exists on this issue, each country has taken its own approach to maintaining low levels of unemployment. In some instances — such as in Norway, Sweden, and Austria — strong social partnership agreements underwrite national policies, whereas in Switzerland trade unions play a relatively minor role at national level. In Norway and Sweden active labour market policies for those unemployed or threatened with unemployment have been pursued, and selective government intervention by way of subsidies to the private sector is also a feature. The Ministry of Labour and Social Affairs holds responsibility for activities promoting full employment in Austria. Meanwhile, in Japan, a full-employment ethos springs from the constitutional right to work of all citizens, supported by legislation and the dominance of a "partnership" employee relations ideology at company level.

Many other reasons may be cited in particular cases and instances as contributing to low unemployment — various fiscal approaches, wage bargaining sensitivity to the related jobs cost factor, wage levels, oil revenues, immigration controls and laws, strong competitive output, etc. However, a sustained national focus on achieving full employment and an unswerving commitment to reducing unemployment levels reflect the major recurring collective theme.

Role of Learning

A strong learning ethos is evident across all five countries, with learning holding a high societal value. In Norway and Sweden, the theme of life-long learning is very much to the fore, and wide-ranging opportunities exist for adult participation in fundamental education (life-long learning) and in recurrent education (recurring periods of education).

We are already familiar with the emphasis on initial learning and education in Japan and the subsequent continuation of a positive attitude towards learning and knowledge at adult level. Education commands a high priority in Austria, where, to a large degree, qualifications dictate social standing and status. Meanwhile, a strong link has been forged between economic policy and vocational training in Switzerland, where much of their economic prosperity is attributed to education and training.

Again, however, there is wide divergence between the five countries in their various systems of, and approaches to, education and training. For instance, the Norwegian Ministry of Education and Research is responsible for all levels of education — primary, secondary, higher and adult education. Furthermore, adult education incorporates a wide range of activities — popular and second chance education, job-related training, and in some circumstances even in-company training. While adult education in Sweden is supported by well-developed structures, there is a marked absence of similar arrangements for adult education in Austria, Switzerland or Japan. In the area of apprenticeship, the system in Austria, Switzerland and, in more recent times, Norway bears close resemblance to the dual-system of upper-secondary education operated in Germany. In Japan and Sweden, on the other hand, upper-secondary education is almost exclusively "school"-oriented (although it must be borne in mind that, in Japan especially, the curriculum at this level comprises an extensive mix of vocational and general subjects) and there is far less priority attached to gaining skilled status through an apprenticeship system.

These are some general examples of the many different systems in operation, and the variety of approaches taken, in the various countries. However, it is the unity in relation to the perceived value of learning, and the priority attached to education and training, linked to a national emphasis on developing skill and knowledge levels, which represents an outstanding feature.

Special Characteristics of Low Unemployment Countries

We will now outline some specific points of interest, and, as we have already looked in some detail at the Japanese system, we will concentrate on the other four countries.

Norway

An interesting aspect of the apprenticeship system in Norway is the operation of training rings and training offices. Training rings enable the sharing of responsibility for training apprentices by two or more enterprises, although one enterprise, through a signed agreement with the trainee, accepts primary responsibility. Training offices, on the other hand, are co-operative bodies formed by a number of firms wishing to share the responsibility for apprenticeship, and feature a signed agreement between the trainee and the training office itself.

A voluntary organisation having adult education as one of its main activities may become an approved body and thus eligible for State funding. Extensive state grants are also available to support all adult education activities, including approved in-company courses.

The Labour Directorate operates a wide range of labour market schemes, of which skills training forms by far the largest element. These include vocational training courses, youth work training groups, work experience and training, and in-company training (for employees (a) working in firms with structural problems, (b) who need to be retrained for specific jobs, and (c) entering employment through the manpower authorities and need training).

Mention must be made of folk high schools. These offer residential school programmes (usually of six or twelve months duration) for young people, where courses normally follow a general, broad-based curriculum. Their emphasis is on fostering positive attitudes, personality development, and the learning process arising from informal pupil-teacher contact. Although privately run, folk schools receive 90 per cent of their funding from State grants.

Sweden

Study circles, whereby a number of people engage jointly in the study of one or more given subjects, have gained enormously in popularity. Study circle leaders perform a co-ordinating role, but learning organisation and processes are decided by consensus. A wide range of topics are studied but non-career related subjects, especially music, art and drama, are the most commonly pursued. Study circles fall within the remit of adult education, and by fulfilling certain basic requirements participants may avail of subsidies and municipal grants.

Folk high schools are also a feature in Sweden. Here, however, course provision, which ranges in length from two days to six months, is not aimed specifically at the younger age group. Schools are organised by adult education associations, as well as other groups (trade unions, religious groups, etc.) and there is active student participation in the planning and implementation process. State grants constitute the main source of finance.

A further interesting aspect of adult education is the concentration on provision of educational opportunities for intellectually handicapped adults and those with poor reading, writing or mathematical skills. With regard to the latter category, participants normally undertake some 20 hours of study each week and are eligible for an hourly payment (to compensate for loss of earnings, or as an incentive in the case of those unemployed).

Sweden's labour market structure is basically split into two divisions under the Ministry of Labour: the National Labour Market Board (AMS) and the Labour Training Group (AMU). Two particular aspects of their operations are singled out for special mention. Firstly, AMU, through its regional bodies, is a provider of vocational education and training, in competition with other providers. However, although State-owned, its activities are run on a strictly self-financing basis. Secondly, AMS, through its regional boards, is responsible for employment services and is allocated funds to purchase training in this context. This is approached on the basis of price and quality, and although AMU is the largest supplier, training is also purchased from other providers.

Through legislation enacted in 1984, in-company training, which has a primary aim of preserving and creating employment, is supported by State subsidies.

Austria

An interesting aspect of post-compulsory education in Austria is its vocational school system, which is attended by more than 80 per cent of pupils (the balance attend academic upper secondary schools). Within this system there are three types of school, each providing medium and higher level courses — each of which offers a range of specifications, and apprenticeship — which encompasses over 200 skilled occupations. Some additional features associated with this system may be highlighted, including:

- School specialisation, at both medium and high levels, is mainly industrial and business-oriented.

- The predominant apprenticeship sectors are crafts, commerce, industry and tourism.

- Apprenticeship options tend to follow traditional male/female categorisations (technical and trade-oriented for males, commercial and clerical for females).

- Responsibility for the apprenticeship system is split. The in-school portion, as part of the education system, comes under the jurisdiction of the Ministry for Education, Arts and Sports; in-firm training lies within the remit of the Ministry for Trade and Industry.

- The apprenticeship system is seen more in terms of an introduction to working life than as a road leading to narrow specialisation. As such it is flexible, facilitating both occupational interchange and the acquisition of double qualifications.

Switzerland

While many other forms of education are highly decentralised, post-compulsory vocational education in Switzerland is regulated on a federal basis. This extends to inter-cantonal uniformity in the administration of the apprenticeship system. There are several avenues through which vocational education may be pursued — State or State-approved business schools, arts or crafts schools and apprenticeship.

The apprenticeship system, featuring a dual system somewhat similar to that of Germany and Austria, is well-developed and renowned for its excellence. Some 80 per cent of vocational education and initial training is channelled through this system. An unusual aspect of vocational education in Switzerland is the significant role, defined in legislative terms, of professional associations. Of particular interest is the provision, mainly through these associations, of an experiential training period in the form of an introductory course. These are provided in each apprenticeship year and serve to bring trainees up to date with the latest relevant working techniques.

It is also worth noting that a special supplementary course is provided for weak apprenticeship trainees. Additionally, in the case of manual trades, those who are unable to complete the theoretical elements may follow a special elementary training course, with an official certificate awarded on completion.

Implications for Training and Development

Kerins (1993) concludes that a significant factor common to the five countries is the relative high quality of the education and training systems, and the consistent attention they command. It is suggested, therefore, that these countries fully merit the label "learning societies". Furthermore, it is only on this issue, along with the notably resolute focus on unemployment, that a collective comparison of major importance may be drawn.

On the basis, then, that the high priority attached to developing human resources in these countries is a potentially influential contributor to their low level of unemployment, some resultant implications for training and development may be put forward.

As indicated by Kerins (1993), a strong consequential link may exist between the education and training systems, labour force quality, overall productivity and economic performance of the five countries. Indeed, we can remind ourselves here of the chain of causation (Roche and Tansey, 1992) outlined in Chapter One, which, in a general sense, offers fundamental support to this standpoint. It could therefore be argued that the national learning ethos apparent in each of the five countries is a major contributor to economic performance.

A similar recognition cannot be claimed to exist on a national scale in the Irish situation. While pockets of such cognisance are undoubtedly in evidence, this perspective has not seeped into the national consciousness to anything like the same extent as in the five countries reviewed. In these circumstances, the potential influence and impact of training and development, as espoused in these examples of low unemployment countries, remains largely untested as a catalyst for reducing our critically high rate of unemployment. In suggesting a sea-change in this state of affairs, it can also be put forward that learning from the experience of other countries may be a judicious initial step on the journey toward the adoption, on a nationwide scale, of a more beneficial learning process. Elevating the priority, status and effectiveness of training and development, in our private and public sector organisations, must be regarded as a core element of such a process.

THE POLICY ISSUES ARISING FROM INTERNATIONAL COMPARISON

Having taken an extensive international overview of training and development systems and approaches, we will now consider the policy issues arising from such an exercise. In this regard, Kerins (1993) concludes his study with some interesting recommendations. Handy (1987) and Harrison (1992) provide further commentary from a UK viewpoint, much of which is seen to be equally applicable in an Irish context. In outlining the following issues, reference to these sources is acknowledged.

Commitment to Initial Vocational Education and Training, Continuing Education and Training, and the Concept of Lifelong Learning

In many countries, there is an outstanding commitment at State level to the overall vocational education and training process. This commitment extends to those in and out of employment, and across youth and adult categories.

Practices in Germany, France, Austria and Switzerland, for example, indicate that the distinctions between education and training, and between vocational and non-vocational education and training, are less marked. In Norway and Sweden, a far greater education/industry relationship has been developed, and manpower planning models reflect a more focused approach to providing needed skills for those unemployed or threatened with unemployment. While the Irish apprenticeship system is being overhauled, it remains to be seen if the wide range of designated occupations, flexibility, and special facilities for weaker trainees, evident in other countries, will be fully taken on board. The widespread priority and acceptance of the need for continuing training, to facilitate the creation of a flexible and adaptable workforce, stands in stark contrast to the situation in this country. A similar contrast may be drawn with the support for adult education in countries like Norway and Sweden. Furthermore, the concept of "overtraining" in the context of developing richness and heterogeneity of competence which can be utilised when planning strategic change is widely embraced in Germany, Japan and other countries, but considered wasteful by many Irish employers.

Perception of Training as an Investment

We have seen that in Germany, Japan and the US the cost of training is borne mainly by employers. In France, the legislative stipulation on the amount which must be expended on training is, typically, exceeded by employers, and in many countries where strong State support exists the responsibility for training remains with individual organisations. While the pro-rata investment in training is almost universally higher in larger companies, medium-sized and small enterprises in Japan, Germany, Norway and Sweden (amongst others) take training very seriously and accord it relatively high investment. In most of our competitor countries, training is perceived as an investment rather than as a cost, and is the focus of long-term strategic planning. Again, this may be contrasted with our own general situation where, in medium-sized and small firms in particular, government policy has resulted in a dependency relationship. Employers are reluctant to bear the cost of training or to take the primary responsibility for its implementation, and in many cases where training does occur, it is seen only in terms of providing a short-term solution to an immediate problem.

Pre-entry Qualifications and Post-entry Training and Development of Managers

Far higher levels of pre-entry qualifications of those entering the ranks of management have been noted. This is particularly so in Japan, Germany and France. Furthermore, in these cases, the qualifications acquired are considered more appropriate, having specific business orientation and featuring greater pro-rata levels from scientific, engineering and technical fields. Post-entry training and development, in Germany and Japan especially, is widespread, and there is considerable focus on firm-specific on-the-job activities. In general, graduates must also undergo a relatively lengthy settling-in period, with job rotation high on the training agenda during this time. A significant factor in this approach is the immediate exposure to training and development received by budding managers, thereby etching the importance of such activities in their mindset. In Ireland, by contrast, management qualifications and training and development lack similar emphasis. Apart from the negative resulting effects in terms of managerial expertise, this has led to a situation where many managers fail to attach priority to the training and development of their employees.

Social Partnership Approach to Training

There are many examples of a strong social partnership approach to the issues of training. While disagreements may arise over specific aspects of training, in many countries the State, employers and trade unions are unified on its importance in the context of economic competitiveness, at both individual company and national levels. Furthermore, in Germany and France training is the focus of legislative measures, which frame individual employees' rights to training and to collective representation through training agreements and structures at company level. Such measures serve to promote the concept of training amongst employees, and add impetus to companies' training provision. There have been insufficient efforts made to adopt a similarly collective approach in this country.

General Emphasis on Standards and Independent Control Systems

In the immediate post-compulsory education bracket, there is a far greater general emphasis on the attainment of vocational qualifications by young people who do not pursue full-time academic education. Indeed, participation in vocational training is obligatory on a full-time basis in this context in Germany, and on a part-time basis in other countries, while targets of vocational attainment are incorporated into the secondary education system in France. Meanwhile, in Japan the outstanding emphasis on in-firm training activity is supported by a national skill-testing and qualification system. Compared to Ireland, much greater numbers of young people attain vocational qualifications, especially in Germany and France, and this contributes to generally higher workforce skill levels.

The policy issues arising from international comparisons present considerable challenges to the way training and development has been approached in Ireland. The more committed and better co-ordinated efforts evident in many of the countries reviewed highlight inadequacies of our system. Due to our historical relationship with the UK, and indeed due to our physical closeness, we have tended, in many of our training system reforms, to take a lead mainly from that quarter. However, a number of commentators have identified a variety of changes needed in the UK approach, and their critical comments broadly echo the policy issues outlined here. In seeking examples of best practice, therefore, we need to learn from successful experiences in the wider international community.

In this vein, no country's systems are claimed to represent a perfect model, nor is the comprehensive adoption of another's approach, even if this were feasible, suggested as an unerring way forward of this country. However, in constantly seeking to improve the development of our own system, we should be willing to adapt core elements which have proved successful elsewhere. If necessary, these may be modified in line with our own requirements and situation. We can also learn from specific features of others' experiences. For instance, training rings and offices, as operated in Norway, may prove a beneficial vehicle for combinations of our medium-sized and small enterprises; study circles and greater utilisation of community based facilities, based on the Swedish experience, may provide opportunities for widening our participation in adult education. These are just two examples, but they illustrate the possibility which could flow from expanding our own learning processes to include the accumulation and assimilation of wider international practice and experience.

THE SINGLE EUROPEAN MARKET: IMPLICATIONS FOR TRAINING AND DEVELOPMENT

The dawning of the Single European Market in 1992, through which the 12 member states of the EU became further unified and plan to operate as a single economic unit, has effectively established a new marketplace in global terms. As a result of this unification process, the previous internal restrictions and barriers to the movement of goods and services, capital and people have largely been removed. Companies are now free to operate anywhere within this new market, signalling not only significant opportunities, but also unprecedented competition.

Indeed, much of the increased complexity of operating in a global environment also holds good in this context, and the role of training and development, as previously discussed, is seen as no less vital in importance. However, there are important implications for training and development, in terms of this new European Union, which merit further attention.

Legislation

It can be expected that ongoing enactment of new legislation will have a continuous impact on training and development, at both organisational and overall European levels.

Through a multiplicity of Directives, far-reaching changes in social legislation will impinge on organisational decision-making across a range of issues. While huge differences previously existed from country to country, a common legislative system will now strive to create unified standards throughout the EU. The EU Social Charter, for example (from which Britain alone has opted out), frames a common approach to conditions of employment and employment relations in general. Many employment-related topics come under the focus of EU social policy-making, including: employment law; working conditions; safety, health and welfare at work; equal opportunities and worker participation.

In addition, influential figures at EU-level have for some time supported the notion of ongoing training as a basic right for all employees. This apiration has now been enshrined in the Social Charter, which states that "every EC worker must be able to have access to vocational training throughout their working life". As outlined by Harrison (1992), all member states are to aim for continual training systems, in line with the objective of enabling all working people to improve existing skills or acquire new ones. There is also considerable movement towards the provision of standardised vocational programmes, which feature a flexible system of obtaining credits in pursuit of commonly recognised vocational qualifications.

Training implications of legislative initiatives will be centred around the need to understand new regulations and changes to old ones, and to be aware of all EU developments affecting the organisation. Many Directives will impinge on managers, employees, and different areas of operations, and the training function must play a primary role in planning appropriate methods for the acquisition of relevant knowledge and understanding by those affected. Overseeing the implementation of the proposed universal right to training will be considerable.

Language/Culture

Despite the integrative advances achieved in the ongoing movement toward European unity, there remains a tremendous tide of national identity within individual countries. This situation is likely to prevail, and indeed the aims of the EU have never incorporated its refutation, nor promoted the notion of a comprehensively harmonised European state. The emphasis has been on greater social and economic integration, not on a rather implausible merger of collective national cultural characteristics.

In business terms, the most important consequence of this is the fact that companies which respect and harness these cultural differences add to their competitive edge in the European marketplace. One obvious element of primary significance in this regard is language. Although studies have shown that English is the dominant language (to adult-speaking ability), there are a number of reasons why an increasing number of European companies are likely to require a range of language skills.

Recruitment of foreign language speakers may prove a useful approach in certain circumstances, but, as a general ongoing policy, language training for many existing staff is increasingly likely to become a necessity for companies. This places responsibility on the training function for identifying the relevant training requirements, and for devising the most appropriate methods for their fulfilment. In prioritising training needs, the emphasis may be placed on those in a particular function (for example, marketing/sales) or group (for example, the top management team), on various combinations of people, or on individuals. However, although it may seem an obvious comment, the priority should be dictated by operational circumstances and the question: "Who needs language training?" Too often employees are asked: "Who wants language training?", irrespective of the company's precise need.

The nature of the training need must also be ascertained, and the current level of skills should be compared to the level of skills required to ensure training efficiency. A wide variety of methods exist for language learning in group or individual situations, and an assessment of individual learning styles should be considered an integral part of the decision-making process in this regard. As it is widely acknowledged that language is best learned through total immersion in the relevant culture, the obvious cost of providing such a facility must be weighed against the specific nature and extent of the training needs.

It is important to stress the existence of similar diversity at EU level, a fact easily underestimated through the relative proximity of the member states. The training function must therefore be vigilant in promoting the understanding of this phenomenon — as applicable to a wide range and variety of market preferences and to local, as well as national, customs, traditions and other cultural characteristics.

Shifts in Training Approach and Structure

A European perspective on some important shifts in training approaches and structures may be summarised as follows:

1. In general terms, small and medium-sized firms, especially those involved in traditional occupations and industries, have been less inclined to embrace a training and development ethos. However, with the advent of the Single European Market, greater numbers of these companies are beginning to identify the need for training and are increasing their efforts in this area. Driven by the search for a competitive edge, the expansion of these activities puts further pressure on firms in this sector to move away from a non-training stance, contrary to the existing pretext that this stance reflects the sectoral norms.

2. Many organisations throughout Europe, regardless of size, are coming to the realisation that an ad hoc approach to training is far less effective in providing the required competitive advantage. Much more so than in the past, a rapidly growing number of organisations are preparing training plans and strategies which are linked to business goals, in tandem with forming long-term strategies to develop the skills and abilities needed for future success. For instance, Rajan (1992) reports that one in four German organisations adopt education and training plans; in Austria, the figure is one in three; and in Swit-

zerland, two in five. Again, as competitive pressures initiate the expansion of these activities, so also will the onus to move forward from an ad hoc approach become wider and more urgent.

3. While traditional learning methods and types of training programmes are still dominant, many new forms of learning are also being developed. Technological advances, in conjunction with the spread of open and distance learning facilities and programmes, considerably increase opportunities for a personal approach to learning. Through these developments, individuals are enabled to plan, structure, schedule, organise and control their own learning to a far greater degree than hitherto. As a result, training functions in organisations are afforded a more flexible approach when planning training activities.

4. The concept of self-directed learning must be supported by the appropriate organisational climate and cultures. Training specialists will need to assume a broader role, incorporating that of facilitator, tutor, advisor and consultant. Line managers, in adopting more of a team-leader role, will need to become involved in the identification of training needs and act as part-time trainers, coaches and mentors.

5. One of the major concerns of EU action programmes is the development and strengthening of networking, co-operation and collaboration of education and training services. Recent initiatives in this category have seen the formation of a number of European trainer networks, including the European Institute for Vocational Training, the European Network of Trainers Associations, and the Centre for the Development of Vocational Training. Further ongoing developments are focused on EU-wide open learning systems and networks of universities and other institutions involved in open learning. On a more domestic level, the COMETT programme encourages collaboration between universities and enterprises within the same region.

6. The topic of standardisation of competencies and qualifications throughout the EU is the focus of ongoing debate and consideration. Central elements concern the definition of competencies relevant to various categories of occupations, the establishment of qualifications which would gain widespread acceptance, and the accreditation of previous qualifications, learning and experience. This form of integration is likely to lead to an increase in the mobility of technical and professional staff, signalling greater competition for skilled people. Training functions must therefore devise strategies which offer long-term growth and developmental opportunities to help organisations retain key personnel.

7. Changes in work organisations and the introduction of new technologies are now commonplace events in many European organisations. Traditional skilled and semi-skilled occupations are coming under constant threat as they are frequently deemed surplus to emerging requirements, and the notion of a permanent, pensionable job is fast becoming a throwback to another era. However, this can only be achieved with the assistance of a highly skilled, flexible, adaptable and motivated workforce, supported and led by a team of managers who have been developed specifically to cope with the demands of international management. The vital importance of training and development in helping to create an ethos which promotes and supports these conditions cannot be overstated. Moreover, the training function itself must act positively and decisively, continuously focusing on providing the most relevant and effective service to an organisation undergoing radical and constant change. In so doing, it will repay with interest the resources, skills, and credibility which an organisation must invest in training and development in order to maximise its resources in the Europe of today and the future.

SUMMARY

This chapter has focused on the international dimension of training and development. We have drawn attention to key features of our competitor training systems and how they are responding to the challenges of a global market. We outlined key features of training and learning in low unemployment countries and their general characterisation as learning societies. The development of management education in Europe demonstrates considerable diversity in terms of institutions, systems and pedagogical approaches. Finally, we examined the training and development implications of the Single European Market, in particular the increasing emphasis on planned proactive approaches.

7

THE ENVIRONMENT, ORGANISATION AND WORKFORCE OF THE FUTURE

INTRODUCTION AND LEARNING OBJECTIVES

In this chapter we will consider the future of training and development. Having read this chapter you will understand:

♦ the important international and national practices which will influence training and development practices;

♦ the key changes in the business environment and how they may drive training and development activities;

♦ the range of emerging organisational responses to the business environment and their implications for training and development;

♦ the range of training and development responses which are likely to emerge in the future.

Figure 7.1 on the following page outlines the key trends. The chapter is structured around headings in this figure.

THE INTERNATIONAL AND NATIONAL CONTEXT OF TRAINING AND DEVELOPMENT

The business literature identifies a range of factors that have training and development implications, including competitive advantage, national cultural differences, business structures and institutional factors.

National Competitive Advantage

The competitive advantage of nations has traditionally been explained in terms of factors of production. Porter (1990) has identified four key determinants of a nation's competitive advantage: (a) factor conditions such as production; (b) factor demand conditions such as demand for products and services; (c) the presence of related and supporting industries and firm strategy; and (d) structure and rivalry. Differences in terms of these four features help explain differences in national performance. Factors such as highly skilled labour, advanced technology, engineering skills and level of investment in research and development, also serve to sharpen a country's competitive edge.

Figure 7.1: Key Trends in Training and Development

Contextual Factors Influencing Future Training and Development Practices	Business Environment Drivers of Training and Development	Emerging Organisational Responses	Specific Training and Development Responses
• Competitive advantage of nations • Natural cultural differences • Business structures • Institutional features	• Business restructuring • Technological advances • Economic pressures • Changing values and expectations of workers • Changing composition of the workforce	• Globalisation and transnationalisation of business • Mergers and acquisitions • Greater stakeholder involvement • New organisation structures • New forms of change strategies • Emerging styles of management	• Structural change in the training function • New models of learning • More use of technology in training • Greater emphasis on performance • More emphasis on diversity • Greater use of external training providers

Porter (1990) argues that many factors mitigate against training investment within the economy and by implication its contribution to competitive advantage. Some of these mitigating factors include the nature of business ownership, centralised decision-making processes within organisations, poor management and little interest in high worker productivity.

National Cultural Differences

Cultural differences are significant in terms of explaining differences in training and development across borders. There is some consensus that national cultural features may act as constraints to the use of managerial theories and training and development techniques (Hendry, 1991). Hofstede (1993) argues, for example, that the validity of many management theories stops at national borders. He identifies four key differences in terms of national culture:

1. *Power Distance*, which indicates the extent to which a society accepts and expects that power in institutions and organisations is distributed unequally. It is associated with the degree of centralisation of authority and the extent of autocratic leadership. Ireland is a low power distance country. Employees expect superiors to be accessible and will bypass their boss frequently in order to get things done.

2. *Masculinity,* which refers to the extent to which the dominant values of society are male, i.e. assertiveness, acquisition of money and not caring for others. Ireland is generally considered a masculine society.

3. *Individualism*, which describes the extent to which individuals are integrated into groups. Where individualism is high, people expect to take care only of themselves and their immediate family and the opposite applies when individualism is low. Ireland is reported as a moderately individualist society in Hofstede's study.

4. *Uncertainty Avoidance*, which measures the extent to which people in a society feel threatened by ambiguous situations and the extent to which they try to avoid unstructured situations. Ireland scores low on uncertainty avoidance.

These cultural differences have significant implications for training and development. They create assumptions about the role of training and development, the level of centralisation of training and development activities and the attitudes towards career development and job training.

Institutional Factors

Institutional factors affecting training and development include (a) the role of the State; (b) national business systems of education and training; (c) labour relations systems; and (d) employer/employee bias in terms of labour legislation.

Whitley (1992) identifies 16 characteristics of national business systems. Figure 7.2 presents this analysis. In terms of the features outlined, Ireland would be characterised as low in terms of decentralisation of economic policy-making and the use of intermediate organisations, and moderate in terms of the degree of management discretion from owners. Ireland would rank high in terms of task, skill and role specialisation, and in the differentiation of authority, roles and expertise, and moderate in areas such as decentralisation, levels of work groups authority and subordinate relations.

Figure 7.2: Comparative Characteristics of Business Systems

---

1. The Nature of the Firm
- The degree to which private managerial hierarchies co-ordinate economic activities
- The degree of managerial discretion from owners
- Specialisation of managerial capabilities and activities within authority hierarchies
- The degree to which growth is discontinuous and involves radical changes in skills and activities
- The extent to which risks are managed through mutual dependence with business patterns and employees

2. Market Organisation
- The extent of long-term co-operative relations between firms within and between sectors
- The significance of intermediaries in the co-ordination of market transactions
- Stability, integration and scope for business groups
- Dependence of co-operative relations on personal times and trust

3. Authoritative Co-ordination and Control Systems
- Integrative and interdependence of economic activities
- Impersonality of authority and subordination activities
- Task, skill and role specialisation and individualisation
- Differentiation of authority roles and expertise
- Decentralisation of operational control and level of work group autonomy
- Distance and superiority of managers
- Extent of employer-employee commitment and organisation-based employment's system

---

Source: Whitley, R. D. (ed.) (1992), *European Business Systems: Firms and Markets in their Natural Contexts.* London: Sage.

The social, legislative and welfare context influences many aspects of training and development, such as the formalisation of education and training qualifications, provisions for training in legislation on health and safety, equality and redundancy. Ireland has a significant range of employment legislation. This legislation prompts many organisations to carry out training initiatives, especially in the areas of health and safety and the application of disciplinary procedures.

Business Structures

Countries are characterised by differences in national business structures. Ireland has unique features in terms of the numbers employed in the public sector and the size of businesses. Public sector employment in Ireland is considerable compared with other European countries such as Germany and the Netherlands. There is also a significant demarcation between public and private sector organisations in terms of training practices. The public sector is more conservative in training practices and is more likely to support formal training courses than the private sector. The level of training investment is considerably lower in the public sector than it is in the private sector.

There is a large number of small enterprises in Ireland. The small size of Irish enterprises significantly fragments the training and development effort and may help explain our overall low investment.

BUSINESS ENVIRONMENT DRIVERS OF TRAINING AND DEVELOPMENT

The environment of Irish business is changing dramatically. The environment covers a range of domains including economic pressures, technological advances and social and demographic trends

To understand the significant change which has occurred, it is helpful to call to mind the "open systems" model of a business organisation. As outlined by Mullins (1989), organisations take inputs from the external environment (people, finance, raw materials, information, etc.), transform these through a series of activities (a process) into outputs (goods, services, etc.), in pursuit of specific objectives (turnover, profit, etc.). Organisations do not operate in isolation, but influence and are influenced by the environment, both internal and external, within which they operate. Thus, being in constant interaction with their external environment, organisation are subjected to forces in this domain which are a permanent influence on their capacity to successfully achieve their objectives. In recognising this fact, managers need to identify, evaluate, react to (or even pre-empt), the elements and forces in the external environment which may affect their organisation's performance (Koontz and Weihrick, 1988). Recent history suggests that technological, economic, political, legal, social and ethical factors must be placed at the forefront of such considerations.

1. *Political, Economic and Legal Developments*: While the disintegration of the former Soviet Union and its satellite nation states is considered by many to be the major political feature of the last decade, other global events — such as the Gulf War, the turmoil in the Balkans, the return of Hong Kong to Chinese sovereignty, the ending of

apartheid and the creation of a "new" South Africa — create threats and opportunities for firms in the international marketplace. Meanwhile, economic and legal aspects of the Maastricht and GATT agreements, together with further expansion of the European Union, particularly at its Eastern borders, not to mention the rising industrial capability in the Far East and in many of the less-developed countries, add further complexity to the business environment. Ireland, like many of its European neighbours, has productivity problems and in terms of our competitiveness, we rank 13th of the 22 OECD countries. Many changes have been introduced in Irish organisations to deal with economic pressures and at national level there have been attempts to control public expenditure, restructure the labour market and move towards privatisation.

2. *Technological Advances*: Advances in the field of telecommunications and information technology have resulted in ever faster, more sophisticated, and less costly access to information. Such facilities, which were previously the preserve of only the biggest of organisations, now allow the smallest companies to tap into global markets and conduct business anywhere in the world. Furthermore, by virtue of their wider accessibility, these facilities have a levelling effect on competitive advantage in relation to their utilisation. Indeed, this factor itself is a major reason for massive research and development inputs contributing to further growth in this area. Technological developments have contributed to improvements in modes of transport and in its supporting infrastructure, thereby extending the compass of distribution while also increasing its dependability. Further spin-offs of the technological revolution, such as increased participation in, and wider horizons of, travel, coupled with international media access, have led to trends reflecting the globalisation of consumer tastes.

3. *Social and Demographic Changes*: This area encompasses many significant issues for international business, such as trade with countries that contravene internationally-recognised basic human rights conventions; social and moral responsibilities in ecological and environmental matters; widely differing ethical, cultural, and social norms; social and moral responsibilities regarding employment standards in underdeveloped nations; ethical business dealings in general, and so forth. It also includes important demographic trends. Europe in general is facing an ageing workforce, though statistical evidence illustrates that, by 2010, Ireland will have the smallest proportion of people over 60 at approximately 12 per cent. Another significant demographic change is the increased participation of women in the

Irish labour market. According to EU statistics, two-thirds of new jobs between 1985 and 1990 were taken by women. Between 1979 and 1989 participation by women in the labour market increased from 13 per cent in 1979 to 17 per cent in 1990. However, their share in part-time employment decreased from 71 per cent to 68 per cent during that period. Generally, however, the number of part-time and temporary employees has increased.

4. *Changing Values and Expectations of the Workforce*: There is evidence to suggest that during the 1980s there was a significant change in employees' attitudes towards work, leadership style, career management, working hours, etc. Hammett (1994) suggests that there is a new generation of highly educated workers who want greater opportunity for employee development, flexibility, autonomy and more motivational work assignments. Research by McCarthy (1994) suggests that the ideal job in Ireland is one that offers flexibility, autonomy, responsibility, variety and opportunities for self-development.

Figure 7.3 presents a range of these environmental pressures that are driving innovation in training and development practices.

Figure 7.3: Social and Economic/Competitive Pressures on Training and Development

Economic/Competitive Pressures	Social/Demographic Pressures
• International competition	• Rising unemployment
• Productivity concerns	• Changing population structures
• Removal of trade barriers	• Increased participation of women in labour market
• Privatisation of public enterprises	• Increase in part-time and temporary employment
• Shorter product development times	• Increased levels of education
• Advances in technology	• Increased skill shortages
• Trade agreements and economic urbanisation	• Changing values and expectations of employees
• Restructuring and nationalisation of business	• Shift to non-manual jobs

EMERGING ORGANISATIONAL RESPONSES — THEIR IMPLICATIONS FOR TRAINING AND DEVELOPMENT

The new economic environment in Ireland, Europe and the rest of the world is creating a need for new forms of organisation and new business practices. A wide range of responses is emerging, including globalisation, changes in organisation design, new change strategies.

The environment within which organisations operate has been subjected to a radical transformation in recent years. Twenty years ago most companies tended to operate in a predominantly domestic environment. This was largely attributable to two sets of circumstances: firstly, the benchmark for achieving competitive advantage was set against domestic competition; and secondly, the effort, ability and cost of competing in a wider context was above the capability of all but the largest of organisations. These factors represented a particular mindset to which most companies were attuned, determining, in effect, the structure and scope of their operations. Many domestic enterprises, performing successfully in their own country, did eventually develop an export orientation. In effect, however, while marketing and selling their products abroad, these companies still largely operated from a national perspective. Despite having a more international outlook than "purely domestic" companies, they tended to rely, as before, on a domestic sense of competitiveness and advantage, unaware of, or not fully comprehending, the potential impact on their export trading activities of trends and events in foreign marketplaces.

The Global Organisation

Striving to take advantage of this new global market, then, is the *global organisation*. It has been defined as a company that has fully integrated operations — product and process design, manufacturing, and vendor management — in different parts of the world (ASTD, 1990). While successfully achieving globalisation may be a long and complex process, it is not just the preserve of large organisations. As soon as a company steps outside its own operational base, a move which has been greatly influenced (probably enforced) by the changing environment, it may well be on the road to globalisation.

A four-step evolution, representing stages in the journey to becoming a global organisation, is described by Adler (1991): Domestic, Exporter/ International, Multinational, and finally Global. In order to have the capability to survive in a constantly changing and complex environment, multinational companies must be prepared to shift from centrally-controlled and bureaucratic positions. Successful globalisation demands total comfort with demographic and cross-cultural business dimensions, and an adherence to a flexible, change-oriented, operational approach. Environmental scanning becomes a strategic priority, assisting in the perpetual search for potential products or business, culminating in cost-effective delivery to responsive markets.

Whatever tag is attached to organisations with international business operations, there is widespread agreement on the elements necessary for success in global competition. A commitment to flexibility is an absolute, as is a sense of customer focus in relation to local and regional conditions, customs and culture.

Adopting an "insider" stance is fundamental for penetrating market-places before local and international competitors are equipped to export rival products. It is also necessary for the globalising company to display a differentiated global strategic intent. Further prerequisites are the ability to manage diversity, and the importance of broad-based technology, resource and market allocation schemes (See Kirconnell, 1988; Rhine-smith et al., 1989; Ohmae, 1990; Rhinesmith, 1991).

The twin topics of globalisation and international management have attracted considerable commentary. Much of the attendant focus has been on marketing, resource allocation, technology transfer and organisational configuration, pertaining to strategy, information flow, and control requirements. However, the extent of success enjoyed by global organisations will depend upon the knowledge, skills and attitudes of their management and employees. Let us therefore turn our focus and attention to training and development considerations for the globally oriented organisation.

Training and Development in the Global Organisation

Globalisation and international management present new challenges to many training specialists, especially those who have been witness to the evolution from domestic to global orientation within an organisation. It has been stated that these developments represent a new, and not fully understood, concept for the training and development function, leading to inadequate methodologies to develop the "global gospel" in managers and in corporate culture.

One of the difficulties faced in determining the approach to training and development in the global arena, is the existence of what Hodgetts and Luthans (1991) suggest are the basic philosophical positions of multinational corporations. They identify four such positions that can influence training considerations:

1. *Ethnocentric* — people from the home base are given charge of key international positions, and the values and interests of the parent company guide strategic decisions. Hence, the headquarters team and

affiliated world-wide company managers share similar experiences, attitudes, and beliefs on operational management.

2. *Polycentric* — local nationals are placed in key management positions and strategic decisions are tailored to suit the culture of the host country. In this instance, local managers are responsible for appointing and developing their own people.

3. *Regiocentric* — local managers, from a particular geographic region, control operations, and the interests of the parent company are blended with those of its subsidiaries on a regional basis. This approach often relies on regional group co-operation of local managers.

4. *Geocentric* — a global approach is taken to decision-making in seeking to integrate diverse regions of the world. In this case, appointments are made on the basis of qualifications and all subsidiary managers are regarded as equal to those at headquarters.

The diverse nature of the training demands encapsulated within these examples is immediately obvious. If these demands, and those imposed by further considerations (for example, different cultural influences on learning styles and activities, management roles and approaches, etc.) are to be successfully met, a comprehensive training strategy must be adopted.

A number of critical competencies have been identified by Goldstein et al, (1989) as a guide to the training demands of a globalising firm. These are presented in Figure 7.4

In attempting to identify necessary approaches to the provision of such competencies, Hodgetts and Luthans (1991) report the prevalence of six major types of cross-cultural training programmes:

1. Environmental briefings, to provide information about geography, climate, housing, schools, etc.

2. Cultural orientation, designed to familiarise the individual with cultural institutions and value systems of the host country.

3. Cultural assimilators, using programmed learning techniques designed to provide the participant with cultural encounters.

4. Language training.

5. Sensitivity training, designed to develop attitudinal flexibility.

6. Field experience, which sends the participant to the country of assignment to undergo some of the related emotional stress involved.

As this latter list illustrates, developing the openness, adaptability and personal skills and versatility consistent with success in new and unpredictable conditions demands structured learning and training activities, as well as personal on-the-job learning experiences.

Figure 7.4: Key Competencies of the Global Company

Job Factor • Technical skills • Acquaintance with host country and headquarter operations • Managerial skills • Administrative competence	*Relational Dimension* • Tolerance of ambiguity • Behavioural flexibility • Non-judgementalism • Cultural empathy and low ethnocentrism Interpersonal skills
Motivational State • Belief in the mission • Congruence with career path • Interest in overseas experience • Interest in the specific host country culture	*Language Skills* • Host country language • Non-verbal communication

CHANGES IN ORGANISATION DESIGN AND STRUCTURE

A distinguishing traditional feature of many Irish organisations has been their attachment to hierarchical structures. We can readily relate to the traditional design of an organisation chart, where lines of control and authority flow downwards through a series of levels, in ever-increasing and -widening spans. To a large extent, the normality of such a structure has become ingrained in our collective consciousness because of its predominance over many centuries in religious, state, military, and many other bureaucratic institutions. However, in more recent times, hierarchical structures, in the context of business organisations at least, have been the focus of much critical analysis and commentary. These criticisms have been aimed, in particular, at large organisations, where the problems of excessive authority/bureaucracy have tended to be more pronounced. Figure 7.5 illustrates the shift from Fordist to post-Fordist production modes in terms of organisation technology, organisation structure and job design features.

Employee Relations/Management Styles

There is much discussion of changing management approaches to employee relations and emerging management styles. Some important issues here include the following:

- Although the extent of change is a matter of some debate (Gunnigle, 1991), there has been a general movement away from autocratic management styles and the dominance of a purely industrial relations approach in personnel management policies.

- We have already stated the increased willingness of trade unions and employees to consider new ways of working and to pursue a less adversarial approach to employee relations, a fact reiterated by Attley (1994).

- A better educated workforce is seeking to extend its contribution beyond just performing a narrow range of largely manual tasks.

- There is a growing awareness of the potential benefits wrought by developing a greater measure of control and responsibility to employees. Hence, the concept of "empowerment" is becoming more popular and widespread.

- Work organisation is being structured around the empowerment theme, with a focus on teamwork, autonomous work groups, and cellular manufacturing processes.

- Corporate cultures and organisational value systems, which emphasise the notion of reciprocal commitment and welfare (in relation to individual employees and the organisation) are very much in vogue.

Changes in the value systems of organisations are therefore part of the underlying trend in employee relations and management styles. The worth and value placed on the commitment and active involvement of the workforce, and the efforts made to solicit this, provides a key conceptual difference between a control and a commitment ethos (Mooney, 1989; Morley and Garavan, 1993).

These current trends, then, act as a signpost to underlying movements which are impinging on the shape and direction of future organisational systems and structures.

Cluster Structures

Quinn-Mills (1985) advocates that many organisations will adopt more organic structures until they eventually achieve what he terms the *cluster structure*. This term describes groups of people drawn from different disciplines and undifferentiated by job title, who work together on a semi-permanent basis. Its features are set out as follows:

- group size varies from 30 to 50, with sub-clusters of 5-7 people;

- residual or no hierarchy;

- no direct reporting relationships;

- decision-making delegated to lowest possible level (those who actually perform the work);

- leadership rotates with task competence;

- members of the group are responsible to the group as a whole for performance and quality, thus accountability is ensured;

- groups are linked by contacts among members, and interface with the company through the residual hierarchy.

There have been some arguments to the effect that an organisational move to pure clusters may be too radical and that theory in this instance is advancing faster than practice. However, this example does serve to illustrate the direction in which both theory and practice are likely to continue to move.

The Network Organisation

One particular criticism levelled at the traditional type of organisation is its perceived inability, because of its mechanistic nature, to adapt and respond to the changes in its environment. Its typical hierarchical structure is seen as a barrier to timely decision-making and effective communications, while its inherent bureaucracy is viewed as an obstruction to initiative, innovation and flexibility.

In proposing an organisational format which is attuned to current and future demands, Hastings (1993) proposes the concept of organisational networking as "the implementation of a range of processes that result in a devolution of power and responsibility, and the breaking down of organisational boundaries". The characteristics of the resulting organisation may be summarised as follows:

- *Radical decentralisation* of tasks, power and responsibility, thereby splitting the organisation into small, autonomous and accountable units.

- *Intense interdependence*, featuring widespread use of coalitions and project teams in a multi-disciplinary approach to tasks and common goals. Significantly, this co-operative orientation encompasses not just individuals within the organisation, but also the organisation it-self in its macro-environment.

- *Demanding expectations* are held by individuals of the organisation, by individuals of each other, and by the organisation of its people.

- *Transparent performance standards* are set and measured, and results are widely communicated. This process is designed to promote im-provement rather than competition.

- *Distributed leadership*, whereby widely exercised responsibility is accompanied by leadership which is task-oriented and expertise-based, rather than role-oriented and position-based.

- *Boundary busting*, as exemplified by the elimination of all barriers (physical, personal, hierarchical, functional, cultural, psychological and practical) to co-operation and communication.

- *Networking and reciprocity*, epitomised by open and direct relation-ships, spontaneous sharing of information, and an intuitive spirit of interchange.

These characteristics reflect many of the dimensions previously outlined as being pertinent in the context of the new organisation. In particular, they fully embrace the notion of employee participation and empower-ment, organic structures and systems, and a consistent organisation cul-ture.

Hastings (1993) sees organisational networking being implemented through four core processes: networking within the organisation, net-working between organisations, hard networks, and soft networking. Networking within the organisation is primarily aimed at inducing an open approach to communication and transcending its boundaries. How-ever, specific networks, comprising particular internal groupings, are also seen as a means of focusing activities and expertise on a variety of important issues. The need for networking between organisations is an ever-increasing one, as the competitive pressures of market globalisation become a stimulus for greater co-operation and collaboration between organisations and the forging of strategic alliances and partnerships. Hard networks relate to the effective utilisation of developments in the field of information technology, in order to maximise the quality and availability of information and enhance the communication process. Soft networking essentially refers to the development of informal contacts, connections, and relationships, internally and externally, which enable individuals to access and mobilise key resources.

The overriding theme of organisational networking, then, is one of co-operation, reciprocity and trust, leading to mutual gain. It envisages considerable individual autonomy, the encouragement of innovation, and the continuous exchange of information and learning.

The Virtual Organisation

The concept upon which the virtual organisation is based has already been touched upon, in the foregoing discussion of networking between organisations. However the term *virtual organisation* describes a newly emerging type of company that has advanced beyond the simple collaboration described above. It is defined as

> a temporary network of independent companies — suppliers, customers, even erstwhile rivals — linked by information technology to share skills, costs, and access to one another's markets. It will have neither central decision making nor organisational charts. It will have no hierarchy, no vertical integration. (*Business Week*, 1993)

There are a number of different perspectives on the virtual organisation. Hopland (1993) uses the term "virtual" to describe an enterprise that can marshal more resources that it has on its own by using both internal and external collaboration. Sparrow and Hiltrop (1993) point out that the virtual corporation is a temporary network of independent companies able to share costs, skills and access to global markets and contribute what they are best at by making the best of information.

The characteristics of this new organisational model may include:

- extensive utilisation of information technology to link up far-flung companies and entrepreneurs;

- less formal and less permanent partnerships and alliances, built on the basis of fulfilling mutual needs within specific marketing opportunities;

- each partner contributing their key capabilities, increasing the potential for excellence across functions and process;

- positions of mutual reliance and trust emanating from a strong sense of interdependence;

- traditional boundaries and borders becoming blurred by the overlap and co-operation between customers, suppliers and competitors.

The virtual organisation represents a possible vision of the future, where temporary organisations are created as a response to specific opportunities and demands. Indeed, its origins may be seen in the growing number of strategic alliances and partnerships being witnessed today, and in the high incidence of product and service "outsourcing". Such alliances, of course, are not strictly new, but the financial outlay and the mobilisation of resources required to operate successfully in a global environment are prompting collaboration between even the biggest operations. In this situation, the sharing of costs and resources can pave the way for mutual advantage instead of mutual disadvantage and, even for competing companies, this prospect is perceived as making sound business sense. Furthermore, advances in information technology are now easing previous difficulties, extending the range of possibilities and facilitating rapid growth in this area. For instance, teams of people from different organisations and operating in diverse locations can share and discuss ideas, information and knowledge on a real-time basis.

There are, however, obstacles on the path to progress towards the virtual organisation. Many of these are centred around the required changes in organisational vision sets and value systems. For instance, an organisation and its management have to relinquish total control over operations and be prepared to share information and expertise with competitors. Managers have to accede trust themselves, and gain the trust of others outside of their familiar territories. While success is easily shared, blame for even minor setbacks is more acceptably allocated to someone else, especially "outsiders". Training and development will have a key role in tackling these obstacles, with strategies in this area particularly focused on bringing about effective behavioural changes.

NEW CHANGE MANAGEMENT STRATEGIES

A number of change initiatives are being practiced by modern organisations.

The Total Quality Management Environment

It has been almost two decades since Japanese economic superiority was proclaimed. Their gradual domination of world markets, with a succession of manufactured products, was widely attributed to their focus on providing unequalled product and service quality. This economic tidal wave caused a reaction of seismic proportions in Western economies and subsequent reverberations were felt across a wide spectrum of manufacturing industry.

The situation prompted outpourings from a plethora of "gurus" who expounded their "quality" panacea for the ills of Western industry. The adoption of such a focus on quality has since been widely promoted through many variations on a similar theme. Additionally, many of these variations have been incorporated into "quality management" processes such as Statistical Process Control (SPC), Continuous Improvement Process (CIP), Total Quality Control (TQC), and Total Quality Management (TQM). Of these TQM has proven by far the most popular, certainly in Britain.

We will therefore take TQM as the standard-bearing example of current trends in quality management. TQM has been described as a process by which companies can identify, measure and seek to improve the way in which they conduct every facet of their business. Some of its essential features, according to Oakland (1989) and Atkinson (1989), include:

- top management leadership (by example)

- management-driven top-down approach

- active involvement of all employees

- changing organisational culture

- building teams and teamwork

- pivotal role for training and development.

According to Morley and Garavan (1993), TQM needs to be viewed as a two-part process, involving (a) the harnessing of all people's commitment in the organisation towards achieving the goal of complete customer satisfaction, and (b) the development of systems and procedures which allow for continuous improvement.

This distinction is vital. New technology, new systems, and new concepts may of themselves produce some improvements in effectiveness, but this may not be sustained unless sufficient attention is devoted to the harnessing of commitment. As many contributors emphasise, world standards of organisational effectiveness are not achievable without fully developed and committed people at all levels in the organisation.

The World Class Manufacturing Environment

The huge progression witnessed in computer technology capability has spawned numerous systems-based techniques of improving production control and effectiveness. These might be said to have advanced from Material Requirements Planning (MRP), through Manufacturing Resource Planning (MRP II) and Just-in-Time (JIT), to World Class Manufacturing (WCM). These advances have been largely charted in seminal works by Wright (1986) and Schonberger (1986). We have witnessed a progression, therefore, from techniques for improving control of production and inventory levels, to techniques for improving the overall effectiveness of all organisational functions, as represented by WCM.

WCM, according to Schonberger (1986), is a term which describes "the breadth and the essence of fundamental changes taking place in larger industrial enterprises". Among its driving forces, he sees:

- management of quality

- cellular or flow-line plant/work organisation

- flexible multi-skilled workforce

- employee involvement

- building improved customer and supplier relationships

- integrated information systems

- automation

- equipment maintenance

- extensive training and development.

In tandem with improved information technology and production processes, WCM places a distinct emphasis on greater employee involvement in problem-solving and decision-making at the point of production.

The Empowerment Environment

The increasing emphasis on employee involvement and participation has led to a particular focus on the concept of employee empowerment. The term "empowerment" has become something of a buzzword in many organisations, and although enjoying a growth in popularity it may not always be fully understood. Certain conditions are necessary to create and sustain an environment where empowerment can thrive. Dobbs (1993) identified four such conditions, which are summarised below:

1. *Participation* — an organisational climate must be fostered which encourages employees to become actively and willingly engaged in their jobs, and to care about improving their daily work processes and relationships.

2. *Innovation* — employees must have the freedom to exercise creativity, to explore new approaches, and to display entrepreneurial skills.

3. *Access to information* — in a devolved decision-making environment, there must be open and speedy access to relevant data.

4. *Accountability* — employees must be given responsibility over their decisions and subsequent actions, and made similarly accountable.

Empowerment signifies the expansion of an employee's role to ownership of a complete task, heralding a revised psychological contract at work, where fulfilment is exchanged for commitment. Furthermore, the notion of empowered (or self-directed) teams, as espoused by Wellins and George (1991), effectively merges the concept of empowerment with advances in the socio-technical and work structuring spheres.

The distinguishing characteristics of such teams, in the context of their work, include:

- sharing management and leadership functions;

- planning, controlling and improving work processes;

- setting goals, creating schedules, inspecting work and reviewing performance;

- preparing budgets, ordering materials, dealing with suppliers, controlling inventories;

- identifying training needs, recruiting new members, and administering internal discipline;

- assuming responsibility for product and service quality.

Job rotation and multi-skilling are core aspects of empowered teams, increasing their versatility and flexibility. Value and system changes are also combined, as employees are encouraged, not solely to take up new roles, but to become active participants in the transition process itself.

Business Process Re-engineering

A growing number of Irish organisations are beginning to adopt elements of *business process re-engineering* (BPR). BPR uses tools and techniques already developed as part of TQM and JIT initiatives, and applies them as part of a broader business procedure. Figure 7.6 presents similarities and differences between Total Quality and BPR.

Business process re-engineering has major implications for training and development practices. Johansson et al (1993) identify areas where training and development will make a contribution:

- higher levels of empowerment

- enhanced teamwork

- cross-functional business process knowledge

- technology-knowledgeable senior leaders

- operational leaders with enhanced coaching role

- small centres of functional experts acting as advisors to business process teams.

TRAINING AND DEVELOPMENT RESPONSES TO THE NEW ORGANISATION

The trends we have discussed in this chapter have major implications for training and development. A study of 80 Irish training and development specialists replicating the American training and development questionnaire illustrated a number of important perceptions. Figure 7.7 presents the results at the end of this chapter. Many Irish training and development specialists identified continued globalisation as a significant influence on how they will operate in the future. In terms of technology, respondents viewed the increased use of computer technology to create, store, use and share information as significant.

Irish training and development specialists anticipate a wide range of training trends in the next ten years. The five most significant ones are:

- structural change in the training function

- self-directed training and increased team learning

- greater use of technology in training

- an increased emphasis on high performance work

- delivery of training just-in-time.

These anticipated changes set a major agenda for the training and development functions. The main ones include the following:

1. Training specialists will need to learn how to learn in a cross-cultural context. They will need a deep knowledge of other cultures (and their history) and an appreciation of the international interdependence that characterises today's business world. This will be increasingly important with the opening up of Eastern Europe and the continuation of mergers/take-overs well into the 1990s.

2. Training specialists will need to become more multicultural in outlook and skills. Typically this may require an ability to define and handle the problems in adapting to different cultures, including the cultural shock often experienced when moving into a new job in a different country. They will also need to tackle the problems of multicultural working where, through satellite communication, buffers are removed which may then expose managers' cultural vulnerabilities, for example, in the cultural sensitivity of decision-making.

Figure 7.6: Comparing Total Quality (TQ) and Business Process Re-engineering (BPR)*

Possible Similarities	Possible Differences	Potential Common Problems
1. Cost reduction, quality improvement, performance improvement, and/or culture change are objectives 2. Top management support is advocated as necessary 3. Workflow focus 4. Empowerment advocated 5. Logical, data-based approach utilised 6. Continuous improvement advocated 7. Determining and meeting customer expectations advocated 8. Teams typically relied upon to produce significant improvements 9. Follow-up advocated	1. BPR takes a "zero-based" approach to processes (i.e. first asks if the process should be eliminated) 2. TQ may seek to improve existing processes. It typically emphasises and may begin with use of a specific set of tools (eg SPC, cause and effect diagrams); BPR uses any and all tools (including TQ tools) as a means for improvement 3. BPR advocates attacking "head-on" any cultural or systematic "sacred cows" (eg organisation reporting relationships, performance measures, rewards) that may block implementation: TQ usually operates within a function or department, hence some barriers to improvement are outside the function's or department's control 4. TQ may (initially) be focused on skill-building via classroom training; BPR is focused on designing and conducting forums where candid communication takes place, followed up with actions on the job; training may be used but not necessarily as a critical or initial activity 5. BPR has often begun in white-collar work; TQ has often begun in operations / manufacturing	1. Emphasis on process activity versus results. 2. Event-drive versus integrated into culture/fabric/daily operations of organisation 3. Staff- or conduct- versus user-driven 4. Initiative broad, versus obtaining early success to build credibility

* The lists are generalisations; both TQ and BPR may be conceived and implemented differently from the above in any given setting

Source: Reprinted from C. Schneier, D. Shaw and R. Beatty, "Companies attempts to improve performance while containing costs: Quick fix versus lasting change", *Human Resource Planning*, 15(3), 1-26, 1993, with kind permission of the Human Resource Planning Society.

3. Corporate visions will need to be owned, shared and matched by the skills to realise such visions. Also, organisations will need to create the world to fit these visions. A better fit is required also between management development and business strategies.

4. Change will become ever more rapid and complex, requiring organisations to be able to process and share information quickly and move it around in whatever permutations are required to meet needs. As a consequence, hierarchies will become flatter and give way, in part, to networks. This will require managers to manage more by expertise and example than by power and authority. Job boundaries will become more flexible, and an increased priority will be placed on the building of effective one-to-one relationships. Organisations will need to tune in more closely to people's motives and changes in values.

5. Training specialists will need a better understanding of the role of industry within the wider community. This may require changes in the way they manage, and additional skills to manage possible conflict in responsibilities. Social responsibility will become an integral part of business strategy. Partnerships between industry and management education are likely to increase as is the case already.

6. Organisations will, through demographic changes, come to terms with the need to accept even more women managers into their ranks. This will probably result in increased diversity in role-relationships between men and women. Since the vast majority of our organisations have been designed by men, such a development may lead to radical changes in organisation structure. This could result in an added richness, much to be welcomed.

7. Training specialists will still require a strong base of fundamental skills and techniques. Moreover, without them they will be increasingly vulnerable and exposed. As networking becomes more structurally established within organisations, different skills will be required for managing people at the core of the organisation compared with managing those closer to the periphery (for example, associates).

8. The effective management and use of information technology will become a distinguishing criterion of success for training functions. The acquisition and speedy transfer of information through the use of IT is already providing organisations with a keen competitive edge.

9. Managers will need to develop greater self-insights in respect of their values, motives and talents; how they feel about power, influence, manipulation and ethics. They will need to develop greater awareness of their own patterns of thinking, feeling and acting, and to be more in touch with their perceptual filters and biases. Organisations will need to give top priority to self-development, and thereby self-managed learning, to enable people to fulfil their potential. Individuals will need to create and use self-development opportunities as an integral element in their organisation's development. The organisation will need to value its people as its greatest asset and invest accordingly.

10. There will be increased recognition that many issues cannot be effectively dealt with using rational, logical and cognitive thinking approaches. Greater emphasis will therefore be placed on the feelings, emotions, intuition and beliefs and values which drive managers.

11. Learning within the organisation will need to be shared more effectively. The wise will need to share their wisdom more. The innovators will need to inculcate innovative skills and abilities in others. The concept of intrapreneurship will become integrated within an increasing number of organisations. Learning will need to become the key tradable asset of an organisation.

12. Training specialists will need increasingly to manage complex, live, critical, messy problems with no clear boundaries under real risks of failure. They will need to reinforce and celebrate success more, and to forgive failures and use mistakes as learning opportunities. If a mistake is punished the opportunity to learn is lost. If an organisation is going to take on learning as a major asset it will need to be in a state of syndic tension with its environment, i.e. to feel uncomfortable but not unmanageable. It should be constantly seeking to obtain the highest effectiveness of the interchange between learning and change.

13. Management trainers/tutors will need to develop a rich repertoire of training methods in recognition of the different preferences of learning styles of managers, so that the effectiveness of the learning process is maximised. In relation to techniques / methods, emphasis will need to be given to when and how to use them, and whether or not to use them from an ethical standpoint. The whole provision of management learning will need to become more integrated with the learning styles of individuals. Effective provision will be achieved by trainers who bridge the language (jargon) gap, and talk to managers in their own language.

SUMMARY

In this chapter we have examined a range of contextual and environmental factors that will impact on the training and development function in the future. These trends will require a new set of responses from training and development including structural changes in the training function, new models of learning, greater use of technology in delivering training, a greater use of external training providers and a greater emphasis on using training in performance management. A study of Irish training and development specialists highlights a significant level of awareness with these issues and the types of responses which they are expected to make.

Figure 7.7: Irish Training and Development Perceptions of Business and Training Trends

ISSUES	A Probability (1-7) 7 = most probable	B Effect on T&D (1-7) 7 = greatest effect	C Effect on Company (1-7) 7 = greatest effect
BUSINESS TRENDS	(n) = overall rank n = rank within trend category		
Global Competition			
The demands of the global economy will continue to change the way businesses are organised and operated. Performance will be measured in term of the speed, variety, convenience, timeliness and quality of products and services in the eyes of customers.	6.85 (1) 1	5.2 (8) 4	5.45 (2) 1
Partnerships will characterise the global business environment and dictate many of the new rules of doing business.	5.55 (11) 6	4.26 (21) 13	4.8 (11) 7
Communication and information networks will blur national and corporate boundaries even more than today.	5.75 (7) 4	5.05 (18) 11	4.85 (10 8
Universal performance standards, such as the IS0 9000 series, will increase in use and importance.	5.65 (19) 10	4.7 (22) 13	4.5 (16) 8
Radical Transformation of Organisations			
Organisations will take many new forms. The ability to design organisations and to manage their change will be more important than ever.	5.55 (11) 6	6.15 (2) 2	5.25 (5) 3
Interest in creating "high-performance work organisations" will increase. These are organisations in which work is re-organised, re-designed or re-engineered to improve performance.	5.9 (6) 2	6.6 (1) 1	5.3 (4) 2

ISSUES	A Probability (1-7) 7 = most probable	B Effect on T&D (1-7) 7 = greatest effect	C Effect on Company (1-7) 7 = greatest effect
Decades of breaking work into even smaller tasks are coming to an end. Instead, teams of employees will be responsible for key business processes from beginning to end.	5.6 (10) 5	5.75 (3) 3	5.3 (4) 2
Impatience with the rate of change will cause many companies to re-engineer (create from scratch) their key processes. Others will seek gradual and continuous improve-ment through quality and other efforts. Some will do both.	5.7 (8) 3	5.25 (14) 9	5.1 (7) 4
Organisations built on a few core competencies will begin to appear. In such companies all other work will be done by temporary and contract workers as needed. Some people call these "virtual corporations".	4.65 (24) 12	5.25 (14) 9	4.25 (20) 9
Large scale lay-offs will continue.	5.25 (17) 9	5.35 (12) 7	4.5 (16) 8
Self-directed careers will be the norm.	5.3 (16) 8	5.15 (16) 10	4.5 (16) 8
Employees will have to take more responsibility for changing their behaviours and for learning.	5.5 (6) 2	5.7 (6) 4	5.45 (2) 1
Employers will have to work hard to earn employees' trust.	5.9 (6) 2	5.7 (6) 4	5.45 (2) 1
New Styles of Leadership			
There will be less distinction be-tween employees and managers in terms of authority, status and role.	5.05 (20) 11	5.3 (13) 8	4.9 (9) 2

ISSUES	A Probability (1-7) 7 = most probable	B Effect on T&D (1-7) 7 = greatest effect	C Effect on Company (1-7) 7 = greatest effect
Leadership by teams will become more common. Key leadership issues will be designing organisations, managing chaos and change, and deciding who will make decisions.	5.5 (12) 7	5.5 (9) 5	5.3 (4) 2
TECHNOLOGICAL TRENDS			
Creation of the Information Superhighway to Stimulate Many New Applications of Technology			
Digital electronics, optical data storage, ever more powerful and portable computers, and distributing computer networks (such as internet) will change the way information is created, stored, used and shared.	6.0 (5) 3	5.4 (11) 1	5.1 (7) 3
Companies will extend their computing power to customers and suppliers. This is called "social computing"; some predict it will be a major source of learning.	5.3 (16) 4	4.35 (23) 4	4.6 (14) 4
Technology More Integrated with Work			
More work will be computer-mediated or done with the help of electronic devices. The technology to aid people at work will become more portable and more user-friendly.	6.15 (4) 2	5.35 (12) 2	5.55 (1) 1
Computer power will continue to migrate from the mainframe to the desktop to the briefcase to the user's hand.	6.25 (2) 1	5.2 (16) 3	5.45 (2) 2

ISSUES	A Probability (1-7) 7 = most probable	B Effect on T&D (1-7) 7 = greatest effect	C Effect on Company (1-7) 7 = greatest effect
TRAINING TRENDS			
Structural Change in the Training Function			
Companies will continue to experiment with centralisation and decentralisation, searching for the right mix of overall direction and local delivery of training.	6.2 (3) 1	5.85 (3) 1	5.0 (8) 7
Training delivery will continue to shift from professional trainers to non-trainers such as managers, team leaders and technical workers.	5.35 (15) 7	5.6 (8) 5	4.75 (12) 8
Companies with large numbers of temporary, contract or at-home workers will face the challenge of how to train, motivate and commu-nicate with an ad hoc workforce.	5.5 (9) 3	5.8 (4) 2	5.35 (4) 2
Emphasis on Performance			
The emphasis in business on high-performance work will shift training content away from isolated skill-building and information transfer to performance improvement and support.	5.65 (9) 3	5.8 (4) 2	5.3 (5) 3
More training will be delivered just-in-time and directly in the context of a job or a task.	5.75 (7) 2	5.75 (5) 3	5.35 (3) 1
Many New Models for Learning			
The transfer model of learning will face serious challenges from new models that account for the way people learn — in the context of work, by interacting with others, and through their experiences. Learning will be much more integrated into work itself.	5.45 (12) 4	5.6 (8) 5	5.15 (5) 5

ISSUES	A Probability (1-7) 7 = most probable	B Effect on HRD (1-7) 7 = greatest effect	C Effect on Company (1-7) 7 = greatest effect
Self-directed learning and team learning will increase.	5.05 (20) 10	5.65 (7) 4	5.25 (6) 4
Interest will grow in how organisations learn and how they evaluate learning.	5.0 (21) 11	5.15 (17) 8	4.5 (16) 12
Group training events will be used less to transfer information or teach skills and more to motivate, to bond groups, and to generate knowledge.	4.8 (23) 13	5.0 (19) 10	4.35 (18) 14
More Government Interest in and Support for Training			
The government will take a stronger role in technology transfer, school-to-work transition, dislocated work training and incentives for employers to train.	4.2 (25) 14	4.25 (24) 13	3.75 (21) 16
The amount of government-mandated training will increase — especially to ensure safety, to accommodate protected groups, and to help dislocated workers.	4.7 (22) 12	4.85 (20) 11	4.4 (17) 13
More Use of External Training Providers			
Large companies will increase their use of outside training providers for the design, delivery, and even administration of training. These include two-year and four-year colleges, training companies and consultants, and trade and labour organisations.	4.7 (22) 12	5.0 (19) 10	4.3 (19) 15
Small companies in need of training will increase their reliance on partnerships with other small companies, with community colleges and with government and civic organisations.	5.4 (13) 5	4.8 (22) 12	3.7 (22) 17

ISSUES	A **Probability** **(1-7)** **7 = most** **probable**	B **Effect on** **T&D** **(1-7) 7 =** **greatest** **effect**	C **Effect on** **Company** **(1-7) 7 =** **greatest** **effect**
Technologies that change how, when, and where people work will also change how, when and where they learn.	5.35 (15) 7	5.25 (14) 7	4.6 (14) 10
The digital technology developed for the information superhighway will influence the way training and performance support are designed and delivered.	5.25 (17) 8	5.1 (17) 8	4.55 (15) 11
The fields of instructional systems design and computer systems design will merge further.	5.2 (18) 9	5.05 (18) 9	4.3 (19) 15
More Emphasis on Diversity			
Monocultural workforces and homogeneous customer bases are disappearing. Companies will devote more effort to being aware of cultural differences and to incorporating diverse values into their practices, products and services.	4.2 (26) 15	3.4 (25) 14	3.2 (23) 18

Note: Column A shows how participants ranked the probability on a scale of one to seven that each trend will be significant in the next ten years. Column B ranks the effects the trends would have on the training and development professional if it did become significant. Column C ranks the effect the respondents think the trend would have on their companies.

8

THE ORGANISATIONAL CONTEXT OF TRAINING AND DEVELOPMENT

INTRODUCTION AND LEARNING OBJECTIVES

In this chapter we start to examine the organisational and management dimensions of the training and development function. We begin by exploring the contextual influences on the training and development function and how it may affect the way in which the function operates. Having read this chapter you will understand:

♦ the nature of the training and development function's stakeholders and their priorities and rules;

♦ the influence of the organisation's strategies and policies on the training and development function;

♦ the relationship between the size of the organisation and the level of training and development activity;

♦ the influence of technology and change on the activities of the function;

♦ the power position of the training and development function and how it can acquire and hold on to power.

KEY STAKEHOLDERS IN THE TRAINING AND DEVELOPMENT PROCESS

In setting the scene for the organisational context of training and development, it is important not only to identify the key stakeholders in the training and development process, but also to examine their philosophies, values, and expectations. There is general acceptance of a stakeholder theory of the modern organisation (see Evan and Freeman, 1993; Millstein and Katsch, 1981; Freeman and Reid, 1983) that defines stakeholders as those groups who have a stake in, or a claim on, the firm. Translated to the training and development context, the theory suggests that each stakeholder group has a right, not just to be treated as a means to some end, but as legitimate participants in determining the "ends" —

(the future direction of training and development activities within the organisation).

Who are the Key Stakeholders?

Stakeholders in the training and development process, then, include anyone whose actions can affect the management of associated activities within the organisation. Because of their mutual interactions, each stakeholder has a vested interest in what the training and development function does, and vice versa. Stakeholders may also be cast as claimants, to the extent that they depend on the training and development function for the realisation of some or all of their goals, while the function in turn depends on its key stakeholders for the full realisation of its mission. By virtue of this dependency relationship, each stakeholder is, in effect, an advocate that furthers the goals of the training and development function.

In attempting to segregate the key stakeholders from a training and development perspective, it is useful to draw on the two definitions of the term "stakeholder" outlined by Freeman and Reid (1983). The broad definition includes any group or individual who can affect, or is affected by, the business/function. In relation to the business itself and, as indicated by Darling (1993), this group might be seen to include shareholders/directors, top management, employees and the community/economy in general.

A narrow definition includes those groups who are vital to the survival and success of the business/function. In relation to the training and development function, the definition may be deemed to include internal and external stakeholder groupings. Thus, key internal stakeholders are proposed as the training specialist, the individual learner, the line manager, top management, and the human resource/personnel specialist; while the external category includes national training advisors, external training providers/consultants, trade unions, and educational establishments.

Philosophies, Values and Expectations of Key Stakeholders

At the outset, it is prudent to bear in mind the danger of concentrating too heavily on the formal structure of the organisation as a basis for stakeholder identification. The informal stakeholder must not be overlooked; groups in this category must be identified and their importance assessed. Key training and development stakeholders may also belong to more than one group, and may line up in different groupings depending on their perspective on particular issues. Indeed, it is often the activities of the training and development function itself which trigger the formation of stakeholder groups.

An interesting insight into the organisational mindset of key stakeholders may be elicited from Garavan's (1995) research, based on detailed analysis of 16 Irish companies, using training records, documentary analysis, and interviews with key stakeholders. Figure 8.1 at the end of this chapter presents an analysis of their dominant expectations and values vis-à-vis training and development function. Values, in this instance, may be defined as positions that key stakeholders have about how training and development strategies should happen or be in the future, and essentially represent a statement of their ideal position. These value positions are important because they influence how a key stakeholder acts, and will consequently determine their responses to specific actions of the training and development function.

Let us examine each of the stakeholder groups separately.

Internal Stakeholders

Top Management

Top management values concerning training and development are tied to the desire of top management to change attitudes and cultural values within the organisation. This applies particularly to areas such as disposition to change, team work and innovativeness. The top management stakeholders articulate moderate levels of commitment to training and development activities. They see these activities as making a contribution to improving performance, creating a committed workforce and facilitating change initiatives.

Many top managers point to the role of training and development as a strategic lever for the achievement of organisational objectives. They perceive it as a means of helping the organisation to implement its strategies and of assisting managers to think in a strategic way. Business needs drive training and development so little emphasis is often placed on individual needs. The prevalent view was that individual employees are responsible for their own development, although this was qualified in a number of cases by the statement that the organisation has a key role to play in giving the employee direction in this regard. The general consensus of top management is that training and development is an important line manager function; line managers should take greater ownership of training and development activities and participate in their delivery. The role of the training and development function itself is seen in terms of it providing advice and consultancy to line managers.

A wide range of quantitative and qualitative measures of training and development outcomes was reported, with a significant proportion of top managers identifying increased productivity and flexibility as key evaluative criteria. Other important criteria include the extent to which change is facilitated, performance is increased, and allocated resources are utilised.

Line Managers

The critical values which underpin line managers' perspective on training and development are that it should be skill-based and centred on the current job. This reflects a narrow focus and clearly eliminates, or at best diminishes, the role of career and management development initiatives in the organisation. Many of those interviewed in this group identify training and development as their responsibility and feel that they should be involved in the total process, including design and delivery. Time constraints, however, were highlighted in this regard. The line managers see the training specialist as best performing an advisory and consultancy role in the area of policy formulation. They place an emphasis on appropriate consultation mechanisms through which their views can be reflected in agreed training and development policies.

This group advocates training and development as a useful catalyst for breaking down categorisation barriers, with strategies such as multi-skilling contributing to the removal of demarcation lines and facilitating interchangeability. However, only a small proportion of those interviewed believe that training and development has a role in building effective teams or in encouraging teamwork throughout the organisation. This serves to highlight the predominantly individual focus of many line managers.

The evaluation criteria suggested by this group are generally consistent with their key values. Considerable concentration is evident on the attainment of skilled performance in the shortest possible time, the contribution to cost savings within the department, and the immediacy of payback. Criteria relating to line manager involvement in the training and development process was also reported. In an overall sense, line managers tended to have a short-term outlook, typified by their emphasis on job-related training. This clearly differs from the values held by top management, and indeed from those held by training specialists, as we will next see.

Training and Development Specialists

The research illustrates that specialists in this field see training and development primarily in terms of supporting the achievement of corporate goals. They further perceive it as a means of facilitating organisational and job change. However, a number of those interviewed in this group did cast training and development in a maintenance role within the organisation. The specific role of the training specialist was predominantly expressed as being in the service, advisory, or consultancy category. A general perception of training specialists was that line managers and individual learners should have a vested interest in the process, as they are the stakeholder groups in the best position to assess learning needs and evaluate the outcomes of training and development. In contrast to line managers, the training specialists' perspective of the process is broad and clearly embraces issues like self-development, career development, and management development.

Significantly, many training specialists registered comments concerning the importance of having credibility, the need to increase their power and influence within the organisation, and the necessity to operate in a professional manner. These comments reveal underlying doubts about their credibility, power and status within the organisation.

On the evaluation front, a combination of qualitative and quantitative criteria are used by training specialists. Key qualitative measures include the quality and relevance of training and development strategies, the integration of these with other activities, and the realisation of objectives set out in the planning process. A strong strategic focus is evident in these criteria, which are reinforced by the quantifiable measures adopted. These include statistics such as the number of training days undertaken, training course days, and the numbers and categories of employees trained. Other, less emphasised, quantifiable criteria include those with an individual focus, including examination pass rates, increased performance, and the enhancement of promotion prospects. Interestingly, training specialists indicate little evaluative attention to process issues such as their working relationship with line managers and the level of individual involvement in the training and development process.

Individual Employees

Individual employees tend to have a limited perception of the role of training and development. Nonetheless, they clearly desire involvement in the training and development process and seek significant financial support from the organisation for individual development. In advocating that training and development activities should meet their personal needs, they regard improved labour mobility, the avoidance of skill obsolescence, and opportunities to attain some form of certification as important issues in this respect. Of less concern are factors such as the use of training to enhance job security and the achievement of status and recognition.

In terms of evaluation, considerable consistency is noted between the types of values individual employees espouse and the criteria (Garavan, (1995) used to assess training and development activities. Criteria most often cited include the extent of their involvement in decisions about training and development and the level of financial support given by the organisation. The achievement of certification and the elimination of training gaps are also mentioned. Despite this desire to achieve certification, low priority is attached to measurement by way of examination pass rates. A similar projection emerges for the level of self-development as an evaluation criterion. Process-type criteria recorded include the amount of feedback received and the development of career paths as part of, or as a consequence of, training and development interventions.

A considerable gap is apparent between trainees and training specialists in relation to the extent of the former group's involvement in the training and development process. Training specialists give this a very low priority, perhaps due to the perception that they have ownership of the process, whereas individual learners view it as highly important.

Personnel/HR Specialists

In 10 of the 16 organisations studied, training and development activities were part of the personnel function and the training specialist reported directly to the personnel manager/director. This illustrates the importance of the personnel specialist stakeholder group.

Personnel specialists have a wide range of values and priorities which, for the most part, are consistent with those of the training specialist. They are concerned that training and development activities should have a strategic link and should integrate effectively with personnel management activities. In addition, they perceive training and development as a complementary rather than a superior activity within the overall sphere of the personnel/human resource management function. Like training specialists, they see training and development as a means of facilitating change within the organisation and as a long-term investment. Regarding the extent of involvement of other stakeholders, they envisage a key role for the line manager. However, personnel specialists do not embrace the notion of individual learner involvement, outside the realm of accepting responsibility for their own development.

They cite both qualitative and quantitative criteria for evaluation. Included in the quantifiable category are numbers of trainees/types of activities, level of state grant support (through FÁS), utilisation of budgeted allocation and, more idealistically, cost/benefit analysis of activities pursued. Process issues dominate the qualitative measures cited. Among these are the effectiveness of trainer performance, the level of co-operation between the training specialist and line managers, and the extent to which training and development activities support the strategic objectives of the organisation.

External Stakeholders

It is to be expected that external stakeholders would have broader-based philosophies and priorities, and that their evaluation criteria would be significantly different, from those of internal stakeholders. Let us now examine the extent to which this is so.

National Training Advisors

The following is based on interviews with the training advisors associated with the companies studied, as well as key managerial personnel within the National Training Agency (FÁS) itself. The type of values espoused reflect the broad brief of FÁS within the Irish training and development scene and the roles played by the company training advisors. Considerable emphasis was placed on the use of training and development to promote equality of opportunity and greater access, and to meet the needs of special categories of worker (i.e. long-term unemployed, recent redundant, and people with disabilities). The advisor group see the primary responsibility for training and development residing with the individual firm, but also recognises a need to provide special assistance to smaller firms. Like the top management stakeholder group, they view training and development as a long term investment strategy which enhances company performance and improves the competitiveness of Irish companies in an international context. However, unlike the internal stakeholders, the advisors align training and development with wider social objectives, perceiving it especially as an instrument for coping with high unemployment. For the advisors, the issue of certification assumes a low priority. This is in marked contrast to the priorities of individual learners who see certification as a means of increasing labour mobility and opportunities for promotion.

The evaluation criteria cited in this category are broad indeed, and would seem to pose significant problems in measurement terms. They include the level of private sector expenditure on training and development, the extent of reduction in the unemployment pool, the elimination of skill shortages, and the level of expenditure on general training. Further criteria cited were increased labour mobility, achieving a balance between technical and management training/development initiatives, and the level of return on State expenditure in the training and development arena.

Trade Unions

Trade unions merit inclusion as a key stakeholder group in many of the companies studied. By tradition, Irish trade unions have attributed little priority to training and development activities in the collective bargaining context. However, new initiatives in work organisation and workforce management, as well as participation in National Social and Economic Programmes, have moved training and development up the trade union agenda.

The types of values and priorities highlighted reflect the traditional concerns of trade unions: protection and enhancement of members' rights and the securing of benefits in return for concessions. A particular feature of all the trade union officials interviewed is the high level of consensus evident in the role of training and development. Values which are given a high priority include equality of opportunity in the selection and provision of training and development, and the need to secure a legal right to minimum levels of provision in any one year. There is specific concern that discrimination on the basis of age, sex, physical disability, sexual orientation, or job category in terms of training provision, should be eliminated. They wish to see training policies fitting in with existing agreements and a significant number espouse the notion of having a specific training and development agreement. The possibility that productivity claims could arise in cases where new skills or knowledge increase production output is also acknowledged. In overall terms, trade unions tend to view training and development as a means of equipping employees to take full advantage of job opportunities that arise, and are concerned that initiatives in this regard be matched in terms of increased potential for promotion, bonuses, etc. They also advocate the involvement of the individual in the identification of learning needs and in the design and planning of trade and development activities.

Trade union officials tend to favour a limited form of evaluation, with the focus of the criteria mentioned being on the individual learner or on wider social objectives. Particular emphasis is placed on the extent to which the organisation meets its legal requirements, the payback to employees for acquiring additional skills, and the amount of resources expended by the organisation on training and development activities.

External Training Providers
Available research indicates that external trainers are an important stakeholder in the Irish context, in that companies make significant use of external training providers, either on an external or in-house basis. They primarily perceive their role in terms of giving a professional service to clients (founded on a sound knowledge and expertise base), addressing the specific needs of clients, and being innovative in the delivery of their training and development activities. For this group, the ethical dimensions of their role are a major consideration. Consequently, values espoused include: avoiding conflicts of interest, upholding the confidentiality of information received in the consulting process, and refusing to participate in political manoeuvres or tactics within the client organisation. Other important priorities revolve around the need to keep

abreast of contemporary trends in their field, and the establishment of a long-term relationship with the client organisation.

Here, levels of client satisfaction dominate the evaluation landscape. This is reflected in the practice of immediate post-course evaluation, where methods tend to focus on participants' reactions and the general level of satisfaction with the service provided. Criteria relating to ethical dimensions are also given priority, as is the extent to which client needs are met. Less emphasised criteria include the degree to which knowledge is being updated, the long-term benefits of the intervention to the individual and the client organisation, and the return for the client organisation on its investment. The analysis suggests that the primary evaluation emphasis is placed on short-term criteria. Interestingly, this is in marked contrast to the priorities of top management and training specialists, who adopt a longer-term perspective.

Educational Establishments

Seven educational establishments, with a reputation for, and a history of, providing educational activities for the business sector, form the basis of the analysis for this category (Garavan, 1995). They also have existing relationships with the organisations studied.

An interesting range of priorities are identified in respect of the educational stakeholder group. The dominant priorities in this regard are to enhance the skill base of key decision-makers within industry, to educate managers and develop positive attitudes towards minorities and the environment, to foster relationships between educational establishments and industry, and to provide quality management educational activities. Values which receive a low priority include two particular needs: to provide ease of access to education and management development activities which result in certification, and to provide education activities that meet the requirements of industry. The latter are significant because Irish educational establishments are generally criticised for their apparent lack of priority in both of these areas.

Educational establishments emphasise evaluation criteria such as the number of education programmes provided, the number of industrial participants, the number of training course days, and the numbers and levels of certification achieved. The educational component of programmes is seen as very important, especially in relation to the breadth of content and the extent of attitude change induced. This stands in contrast to those internal stakeholders who have a more skills-oriented perspective. Finally, the degree to which the image of education is enhanced as a stakeholder is not viewed as a significant evaluation factor.

We can see from the value positions taken and the types of evaluation criteria expressed by each stakeholder group, that there are many areas of convergence and divergence in terms of their perceptions and expectations in relation to training and development. This represents a significant factor in setting the organisational context of training and development; one that must be given due recognition and consideration, especially by the training specialist. The extent of organisational success derived through the training and development function, and indeed its own status and influence within the organisation, is greatly affected by the effectiveness of stakeholder management.

ORGANISATIONAL STRATEGIES AND POLICIES

As we have already seen in Chapter 1, the overall effectiveness of training and development is very much affected by the extent of its linkage to the corporate mission or purpose, and hence to the strategic objectives of the organisation. Hussey (1985) discusses the role of training in relation to the formulation and implementation of strategies and policies.

We have already advocated the involvement of the training and development function in the formulation of organisational strategy and objectives. As Clutterbuck (1989) argues, many corporate strategies are conceptualised and formulated without reference to the training and development function and, as a consequence, "people" implications are not fully considered. This can lead to a multiplicity of problems in the implementation stages, as deficits in the knowledge, skills, and attitudes required to successfully achieve strategic objectives are revealed. Such an approach to strategy formulation impinges greatly on the effectiveness of training and development. It forces a reactive approach to problems as they arise, rather than proactive involvement in identifying potential difficulties and in proposing timely and appropriate solutions.

Hussey (1985) supports this notion. He suggests that the appropriate involvement and effective actions of the training and development function could prevent:

- unforeseen problems arising during the implementation stages;

- poor co-ordination of implementation activities;

- competing activities and crises from diluting the implementation priorities of management;

- the failure of employees to cope with change and new experiences;

- inadequate leadership skills hindering management's ability to direct the implementation process;

- untimely identification of critical skill gaps;

- imprecise definition of key implementation tasks and activities.

The essential message which emerges, therefore, is that in order to maximise effectiveness, the "people" variable, and the potential impact of training and development in effecting change in this variable, must be a primary consideration in the formulation of organisational strategies and policies. The reality is, however, that in many organisations this is not the case. As a result, training and development is often relegated to performing a perfunctory role, and its potential contribution is significantly reduced.

Ultimately, the organisation must rely on its people to formulate and implement strategies and policies. The manner in which training and development is utilised in these processes affects not only the knowledge and skill boundaries of those involved, but also the behavioural dimensions implicitly guiding their approach. Effective training and development can ensure the application of an appropriate range and mix of competencies that enable the organisation to secure its current competitive position. It can also provide a means of extending the range and mix of competencies to enable the organisation to maintain, or shift the emphasis of, this position in the future. In advocating that it should mirror, and be congruent with, the organisation's strategies and policies, it must be seen as imperative that training and development is itself an integral component of such strategies and policies. Figure 8.2 at the end of this chapter suggests relationships between organisation strategy and training and development activities.

The following is an outline of the training and development implications of alternative strategies.

Single Product

A single product strategy and a functional structure are usually associated with unsystematic, largely on-the-job training. The training function is perceived in maintenance terms and lacks a strategic orientation. There is a lack of clear standards and very little evaluation of results is undertaken.

Single Product (Vertically Integrated)

This describes a situation where the company produces a single product but controls all stages of the production process. In this situation a more systematic training approach is likely to be adopted. The role of the training function is more clearly defined, evidenced by a problem-centred orientation towards its activities. An "experienced worker standard" may be applied, and some attempts may be made to achieve cross-training and multi-skilling.

Growth by Acquisition

A structure based on strategic business units commonly results from a strategy of growth by acquisition. Here, training is a systematic activity and carries a greater strategic focus. The training specialist and function enjoy considerable status, and formal training policies and plans are a feature. Cross-training and multi-skilling are fully embraced, with an emphasis placed on measurement of resulting skill levels.

Concentric (Internal Product Diversification)

This describes a situation where the company moves into related product areas by means of new product development. In this situation, the training emphasis is on productivity and return on investment. Training policies and plans flow from an explicit mission, which is founded on the training function's strong strategic role. Multi-skilling and specialist technical training are core activities.

Conglomerate Diversification

Organisations pursuing a conglomerate diversification strategy, featuring multiple product lines and a multiple array of consumers, are structured along "global organisation" lines. The importance of the training function is reflected in its representation at corporate level, and its high involvement in strategy formulation and implementation. On-the-job training methods incorporate sophisticated technology, and advanced systems drive cross-training, multi-skilling, and technical training. Standards are evaluated on an ongoing basis.

ORGANISATION SIZE AND TRAINING AND DEVELOPMENT

There is significant support in the literature for the view that the size of the organisation impacts on the nature and extent of training and development. At a general level, smaller companies generally invest less heavily in training and development (even on a pro-rata basis) and are more likely to hold a short term perspective of its potential benefits. Hyman (1992), in his survey of training practices in Scottish firms, found that training and development responsibilities vary considerably between large and smaller organisations. His finding indicates that most organisations employing less than 50 employees did not have a specialist training function and training and development decisions were typically the responsibility of senior management. Training and development was largely instructional and a minor concern of those organisations.

In medium-sized organisations there was a greater tendency to elect someone to be responsible for training and development, but a training department was not likely to exist. Training and development expenditure was determined at board or senior management level and the training specialist was given an opportunity to become marginally involved in policy decisions. A training department was more likely to exist in larger companies with the training specialist reporting at senior management/director level. Training expenditure decisions were still made at senior level but the training manager had significantly more discretion over training strategies and activities.

Heraty (1992) found a significant relationship between organisation size and the training and development budget. Companies employing less than 50 employees spent less than £30,000 on training and development. Since smaller organisations tend to have lower resources than their larger counterparts, it would be expected that they would rely heavily on funds made available from the State. The research illustrated the majority of companies receiving grant assistance were small to medium concerns. Table 8.1 shows the relationships between training and development budget and organisation size.

THE NATURE OF THE EXTERNAL ENVIRONMENT AND ITS IMPACT ON TRAINING AND DEVELOPMENT

The external environment continuously triggers ongoing changes in organisations. The volatility of ongoing developments in the political, economic, social, demographic, scientific and technological spheres ensures that organisations, in seeking to maintain their competitiveness, cannot afford to seek solace in the status quo.

Table 8.1: Organisation Size and the Size of the Training/Development Budget

Training and Development Budget	Organisation Size				
(£ Thousands)	<50	50-200	201-500	501+	Total
Less than £60,000 p.a.	19%	9%	9%	7%	44%
£60,000 — £119,000	3%	5%	5%	3%	16%
£120,000 — £199,000	0%	3%	7%	0%	10%
£200,000+	0	3%	9%	18%	30%
TOTAL	22%	20%	30%	28%	100%

Source: Heraty, N. (1992) "Training and Development: A Study of Practices in Irish-owned Companies", mimeo, University of Limerick.

Darling (1993) comments on the ever increasing rate of change in the external environment, and provides a current snapshot of such changes:

- shorter product life cycles arising from more rapid development of new products;

- technological developments effecting changes on the nature of products and operational processes;

- domestic markets being exposed to competitors with "world class" ability and ambitions;

- fluctuations in financial exchange rates impinging on competitiveness;

- more intense and focused competition creating pressures in terms of adding value, raising productivity and cutting costs;

- the surge of political and social interest in environmental protection — again in the Irish situation, we have witnessed a rise in public concern over the possible environmental impact of certain industries.

These examples provide just a flavour of how trends and events in the external environment affect organisations, and the likely reality is that the extent and pace of change will increase and become even more unpredictable. In the face of this reality, more and more organisations are focusing on the "people" side of their business in an effort to develop effective coping mechanisms. The ensuing demand for a workforce with the abilities and attitudes to enable the organisation to successfully adapt to changes in its environment has major implications for training and development. Organisations will need to:

- take action to attract and retain the best people;

- ensure that the complete range of talent and potential available is assessed and that this resource is fully exploited and developed;

- bring training and development strategies onto the agenda at the most senior levels.

The precise nature of the influence of the external environment on the training and development function will depend upon the level of environmental uncertainty which characterises the external environment. Duncan (1972) characterised the external environment in terms of environmental complexity, measured in terms of a simplicity-complexity continuum and environmental change, measured in terms of a stable-dynamic continuum. This framework illustrates four possible scenarios:

1. *Low Uncertainty (Simple-Stable):* Organisations within this category typically operate in external environments that have a small number of elements. These elements remain the same over time or change at a very slow pace. This type of environment is experienced by food processing companies, soft drink manufacturers, and container manufacturers. Companies which operate in a simple environment are less likely to experience skill obsolescence. Once they have invested in initial training these skills and knowledge will have a long shelf life. Similarly, such organisations are less likely to engage in major change initiatives and are therefore less likely to invest heavily in management organisation development.

2. *Low-Moderate Uncertainty (Complex-Stable):* Organisations who experience this type of uncertainty have external environments that contain a large number of external elements and these elements are dissimilar. These elements do, however, remain the same or change at a slow pace. This type of environmental uncertainty is encountered by organisations such as universities, insurance companies, chemical companies and appliance manufacturers. Organisations with low-moderate uncertainty external environment have high initial training requirements but these skills are less likely to become obsolete over time. The dominant philosophy will prescribe the maintenance of the status quo and this will be reflected in the type of management training and development which is initiated.

3. *Moderate-High Uncertainty (Simple-Unstable):* Organisations who experience this type of environmental uncertainty have external environments that have a small number of similar elements. These elements are subject to frequent change and may be very unpredictable. This type of environmental uncertainty is experienced by organisations such as toy manufacturers, fashion houses, music companies and the manufacturers of personal computers. These organisations are likely to invest considerable money on training and development activities. They also require employees to have positive attitudes towards change.

4. *High Uncertainty (Unstable-Complex):* Organisations who experience this type of uncertainty have external environments that contain a large number of dissimilar elements. These elements are subject to frequent change and can be very unpredictable. This type of environmental uncertainty is encountered by organisations who operate in the electronics, aerospace, telecommunications and airline industry. These organisations are likely to use training and development as an important strategy for managing the external environment. Such organisations will require managers who have skills in planning and

forecasting and have the ability to cope with uncertainty. Training in teamwork is more likely to be a significant requirement in an organisation with this type of external environment.

THE INFLUENCE OF ORGANISATIONAL CULTURE ON TRAINING AND DEVELOPMENT

Organisation culture exerts a powerful influence on training and development activities. Culture assumes significance usually because the strategy of the organisation, the type of people who hold power, and its structure and systems reflect the dominant managerial ideology or culture. Furthermore, such managerial ideologies may be more important than environmental factors in guiding organisational response. There is a small amount of commentary on the influence of culture on training and development practices. Ogbanna and Wilkinson (1988) suggest that organisations which have clans, as opposed to hierarchies, have denser human relationships and networks and place more value in the individual and individual development. There are a number of ways in which the influence of culture on training and development may be examined.

Culture and Organisational Forms

Let us begin by looking at the relationship between culture and organisational forms, using Chandler's (1962) three organisational forms as a vehicle for this purpose.

The Single Function or Department Organisation

This category of organisation is dominated by a single activity such as marketing, research, or manufacturing, and the associated corporate culture may be described as unsophisticated. In this situation, culture change and training activities follow an ad-hoc pattern, and there may be little perceived need for training.

The Multi-Function Organisation

When a single function organisation grows through vertical integration, both backwards into sources of supply and forward into markets, this form of organisation tends to emerge. Competitors will have entered the picture and the concern for competitiveness will, according to Fombrun et al (1984), cause the organisation to pursue a growth strategy based on either (a) substantive or process innovation in the production of the company's output, thereby creating a unique market niche of quality or function, or (b) cost efficiency and the ability to minimise output prices, thereby increasing market share. The organisational culture is thus dominated by this striving for either cost control or innovation. In line with the drive towards establishing a competitive edge, training is geared towards ensuring that competency levels of employees meet or exceed those of competitors, especially in the quality and customer service areas.

The Multi-Divisional (or Conglomerate) Organisation

The multi-divisional form is typified by product and market diversification, and Rumelt (1974) classified such organisations along a continuum ranging from single product conglomerates to holding companies. Business-level cultures tend to dominate in the holding company variety. However, in the former the human resource systems of the different businesses are integrated to promote a binding corporate culture. Here the training emphasis relates to the need to reinforce and maintain clearly defined cultural values and beliefs.

Culture and Structure

An alternative way of examining the influence of culture on training and development may be approached by drawing on the work of Handy (1985), who identifies four main types of culture and links these with particular forms of structure. Indeed, an in-depth and informative analysis along these lines has been undertaken by Harrison (1992) and we will confine ourselves to a summary based on this work.

Power Culture and Web Structure

This culture is associated with organisations where power is centralised and control resides with one person or a small core group of people. This situation prevails at small owner-managed or "family" firms. The ensuing web structure is visualised through the strands of power and influence spreading out from a central source. Key decision-making is the natural preserve of those at the centre, outcomes are imposed with minimum consultation and success is dependent on results consistent with those desired by the power source.

In this type of culture, training requirements, and the nature and extent of training activities, are likely to be dictated by the central power block. Employees are seen as a means to an end, rather than as a vital resource, a factor mitigating against taking individual development needs into account.

Role Culture and Pyramid Structure

The bureaucratic nature of the role culture and pyramid structure is instantly recognisable in the "traditional" organisational model. Here, the chief executive sits at the top of the organisation chart, and descending levels of authority and control unfold beneath, normally divided on a functional basis. Rules and procedures are a pervasive feature, and the importance of decision-making is aligned with hierarchical levels. Communication is predominantly downward. Innovation and creativity are generally unrecorded and stifled.

In the role culture, the influence of the training function is a natural by-product of its hierarchical position, although a politically astute training specialist may succeed in raising the relative scale of its profile. In either case, training activities will most likely be dictated by specific operational needs at departmental levels.

Task Culture and Net Structure

The existence of a task culture may emerge in an organisation, or part of an organisation, where specific jobs or tasks are approached on a project basis. Formal and positional levels of authority give way to an informal dispersal of specialist expertise, and the resulting matrix-type structure is compared, in this instance, to a net. In this culture, the concept of teamwork is heavily promoted as a means of success, as is task-centred initiative.

Training in this situation is therefore focused on building teamwork and interpersonal skills. Individual needs must also be catered for, in terms of updating knowledge and expertise, and the facilitation of experiential learning and self-development is common.

Person Culture and Galaxy Structure

The basis of this culture is the unique contribution of one person in whom specialist skills and/or knowledge resides. The position of such a person in relation to their staff or department is likened to that of a bright star around which a galaxy of lesser stars revolve.

An individual around whom a person culture becomes established may strongly resist the suggestion of personal training needs. Additionally, with this individual's values permeating the cultural environs, efforts to determine or fulfil the training needs of those within the immediate firmament may be neglected or rebuffed. However, it has been suggested that co-operation may result from an appeal to the individual's expertise or ego.

Culture and Organisational Life Stages

Organisations have life-cycles that alter company culture at various stages. These cultural changes affect training and development. This chain reaction can be illustrated using Schein's (1986) identification of three distinct stages in an organisational life-cycle.

Early Stage

New companies, and those in their formative years, remain firmly under the influence of their founders. They need a focused and clearly defined culture as a means of gaining a sense of identity. Major implications for the training and development function arise from the need to assist the organisation to articulate and evolve that identity through culture management.

Mid-Life Stage

Companies in the mid-life stage have established their identity and have developed strong sub-cultures within the overall organisational culture. The training function has a front-line role to play in diagnosing these sub-cultures and in devising and implementing planned change programmes in an effort to re-assert the cultural influence desired by management.

Decline Stage

At this stage the company may have to re-evaluate the fundamental assumptions on which it was founded, due to lack of success in combating environmental changes and competition. Aligned with a re-vitalisation strategy, the training and development function's efforts are directed towards changing the existing culture, so that the company can avert the processes through which market share may be regained.

Figure 8.3 at the end of the chapter presents the relationships.

"World Class" Culture

In more recent times managerial ideology has focused on the core characteristics associated with "best run", "achievement-oriented", "excellent", "world class" organisations. These characteristics include (a) an action focus; (b) high customer awareness; (c) intrapreneurship; and (d) employee autonomy. It is suggested by implication that a model which assumes low employee commitment simply cannot match the standards of excellence set by world class manufacturers.

Cultural change may therefore be driven by business demands. This is clearly significant as business priorities and responses change at a rate much faster than heretofore, requiring that cultural realignment become the norm rather than the exception. The problems of conversion to a new mode of thinking and behaving are largely smoothed where the pre-existing culture of an organisation is one that is receptive to such ideas. Nonetheless, value shifts are never easily won and the concept of ongoing cultural realignment presents a formidable challenge to the training and development function.

It is clear, therefore, that there are a number of potential cultural influences which impact on training and development. Of course, in an overall sense, a critical factor in determining the success or otherwise of training and development is the existence of what Pettigrew et al (1989) describe as a positive training culture. The most potent expression of such a culture arises when top management are explicitly supportive of training and development.

ORGANISATIONAL TECHNOLOGY AND THE TRAINING AND DEVELOPMENT FUNCTION

Organisational technology has been described as the way in which work and work processes are organised, and the type of technology used. The changes wrought by technology are significant and ongoing, affecting workers at all levels. These technological changes require new and different skills (Fisher, 1986).

The impact of changing technology is already apparent in an ever-expanding range of areas. Radical developments have occurred in the field of information technology, and employees at all levels are increasingly required to manipulate information. Techniques such as computer-aided design (CAD) and computer-aided manufacturing (CAM) are becoming ever more sophisticated, and their use is becoming more and more widespread. Ongoing advances in production technology are proving a catalyst for the upgrading of existing skills, the adoption of new skills, and the re-skilling of displaced employees.

Developments in these and many other areas are therefore forcing a realignment of training strategies. These must now embrace the provision of appropriate learning for employees experiencing these changes, in tandem with facilitating maximum utilisation of the new technologies themselves. Walton (1985) identified a number of ways in which new technologies may influence the organisation's human resources:

- Applications of new technology sometimes narrow the scope of jobs and sometimes broadens them (deskilling and enskilling).

- It may emphasise the individual nature of task performance or promote the interdependent nature of the work of groups of employees.

- It may change the focus of decision-making towards centralisation or decentralisation with implications for the nature of the organisation's hierarchy.

- It may create performance measurement systems that emphasise learning and self-control or surveillance and hierarchical control.

- It can increase the flexibility of work schedules to accommodate human preferences or it can decrease flexibility and introduce shift work operations.

Type of Technology and Its Training and Development Implications

The literature makes a distinction between organisation-level technology and departmental technology. Organisational technologies are of two types — manufacturing and service. Manufacturing technologies include traditional manufacturing processes and computer-based manufacturing systems. Manufacturing technology is usually classified in terms of its technical complexity:

- *Small Batch and Unit Production*: These firms tend to be job shop operations that manufacture and assemble small orders to meet specific needs of customers. Small batch production relies heavily on the human operator. It requires a high level of individual skill.

- *Large-Batch and Mass Production*: This is a manufacturing process characterised by long production runs of standardised parts. Output often goes into inventory from which orders are filled. Mass production has a low skill requirement due to its repetitive nature.

- *Continuous Process Production*: Here the entire process is mechanised, where automated machines control the continuous process and outcomes are highly predictable. The worker's skill requirement is high and largely of a technical nature.

Computer-integrated manufacturing is made up of three components:

- *Computer-Aided Design (CAD)*: Computers are used to assist in the drafting, design and engineering of new parts. Designers guide their computers to draw specified configurations on the screen including dimensions and component details.

- *Computer-Aided Manufacturing (CAM)*: CAM controls fabrication, production, materials handling and assembly. It also permits a production line to shift rapidly from producing one product to any variety of other products.

- *Administrative automation*: This involves the computerisation of accounting, billing, inventory control and shop floor trading.

The combination of these three components represents the highest level of computer-integrated manufacturing. CAM has major implications for the skill base of the organisation and by implication the nature of training and development activities. Employees need the skills to participate in teams. Training is broad (so workers are not overly specialised) and frequent, so employees are up-to-date. Expertise tends to be cognitive so employees can solve problems. A CIM environment tends to require low specialisation, decentralisation and self-regulation.

Service technologies are characterised by five dimensions: simultaneous production and consumption, customised output, customer participation in the production process, intangible output and a high labour component. These technologies have major implications for skills and training. For one thing, the skills of core employees need to be higher. Employees require knowledge and awareness to handle customer problems rather than just enough to perform a single mechanical task. Hence service employees need social and interpersonal skills as well as technical skills. Northcraft and Chase (1985) argue that because of higher skills and structural dispersion, decision-making often tends to be decentralised in service firms and normalisation tends to be lower. This requires employees who are multi-skilled and highly flexible.

Each department of an organisation has a distinct technology. Perrow (1987) has characterised departmental technologies as follows: craft, routine, non-routine and engineering technologies. Each has distinct skill requirements. Routine technologies are characterised by little task variety and the use of objective procedures. The tasks are formalised and standardised. The training and development requirements are minimum and the skills acquired will remain useful for a significant period of time. Craft technologies are characterised by a fairly stable stream of activities. Tasks require extensive training and experience because employees respond to intangible factors on the basis of wisdom, intuition and experience. Engineering technologies tend to be complex because of the substantial variety in the tasks performed. Employees normally refer to a well-developed body of knowledge to handle problems. Engineering and accounting tasks fall into this category. Non-routine technologies have high task variety and the conversion process is not well understood. Experience and a high level of technical knowledge is required to solve problems and perform the work.

Bridging the Skills Gap

One of the primary concerns of the training and development function is that of bridging the skills gap that emerges between the existing skills of the workforce and the skills required to enable the most effective utilisation of new technology. Clancy (1988) outlines a ten-step approach to achieving this purpose. It consists of the following:

1. Develop a proactive stance and attempt to anticipate the changes resulting from the introduction of new technology, rather than reacting to problems as they occur.

2. Adopt a business perspective, by examining issues such as economic adaptability, labour market trends, and investment in human resources, in analysing and determining training priorities.

3. Elicit the active support and commitment of top management, thus elevating the status of training within the organisation.

4. Seek to obtain the support and involvement of employees in the early stages of the process, especially those affected by short-term displacement (for whom retraining is necessary).

5. Divide the workload and involve people from all areas of the organisation, drawing particularly on the experience of those who have previously acquired the skills necessary to cope successfully in similar situations.

6. Set down early successes by concentrating initially on relatively simple training solutions.

7. Use proven solutions which are known to have succeeded in similar situations.

8. Ensure familiarity with the technologies of the organisation, putting training and development in the position of relating to management and employees alike.

9. Establish realistic time-frames, seeking to balance time pressures with practical considerations.

10. Set realistic expectation levels, stressing the need to refrain from immediate judgements and to look beyond initial results.

Changing technologies can therefore prove a catalyst for the training and development function to review its approach, forcing it to adopt a more proactive stance.

The Work Organisation Factor

Changes in technology very often affect the way work itself is organised. Decisions concerning how work is organised in this context will determine how tasks are allocated between the technology and the people interfacing with it, and the nature of this relationship may have a significant effect on performance (Buchanan and Boddy, 1982). Two distinct forms have been associated with this people-technology relationship: the decisions concerning work organisation can result in distancing employees from the task, limiting the contribution they can make; or, work may be organised in a manner which promotes a high degree of convergence between the employees and the task. In suggesting that the training and development function should expedite a complementary rather than a mediating relationship, Buchanan and Boddy (1982) identify several areas in which it can influence decisions, including:

- The manner in which current tasks and skills, and the employees involved, will be affected by the introduction of new technology.

- The design of the new technology and its impact on the way tasks will be performed in the future.

- The various ways future tasks can be organised and their scope for complementing the skills of the operator. Among the key issues here are the opportunities for challenge and variety, the utilisation of existing skills, new skills required, and appropriate learning and feedback mechanisms.

- The importance of ensuring that employees are encouraged to contribute their ideas and experience to the decision-making process.

- The approach to training. This should be imaginative, and the involvement of knowledgeable users in the design and implementation of training programmes may prove particularly effective.

The influence of organisational technology, then, puts a particular onus on training and development, as its thrust represents a challenge to individual employees and the organisation at large. The threat of skill, knowledge and attitudinal obsolescence is ever present. To counteract this, a continuous emphasis must be placed on employee development, to ensure that the entire workforce is kept up-to-date with changing and expanding technologies (Gunnigle and Flood, 1990). Furthermore, the capability of new technologies must be fully exploited to support increased productivity, while the fit between technology and employees must be maximised. Effective training and development can lead the way in reducing the debilitating gap that often exists between the acquisition of new technology and an organisation's ability to maximise its utilisation.

THE INFLUENCE OF ORGANISATION STRUCTURE

The organisation's structure can both influence the configuration of the training and development function and the skill requirements of the organisation. Paauwe (1991) has examined the impact of different structural configurations on training and development activities. The most relevant findings to emerge from this study are the following:

- *Simple Structures*: These are characterised by a small group of employees who do the basic work and a senior manager. Power is centralised and there is little formalisation and planning. Changes in policies on training and development are top-down, and it is unlikely that the organisation will have a specialist training function.

- *Professional Bureaucracy*: This structure is peopled by professionals who carry out standardised tasks using a given set of skills. Paauwe (1987) found that, in this structure, training and development activities are formalised and carefully planned, and although training and development policies are initiated at the top, the scope of the function is significant.

- *Machine Bureaucracies*: These are characterised by elaborate work systems with a heavy emphasis on standardised rules and procedures. The training and development activity is likely to be highly centralised and espouse a maintenance or status quo philosophy.

It is possible to identify a number of relationships between organisation structure and training and development. An organisation which is highly complex, differentiated and centralised, will provide few opportunities for the training and development function to become involved at a high level in the organisation. A high level of horizontal differentiation provides few opportunities for skill development and few promotional opportunities outside of the individual's narrow functional specialisation. Similarly, where high vertical differentiation exists, the training and development function is less likely to be involved in strategic issues, which are typically addressed at the top of the organisation.

An organisation characterised by high formalisation provides few development opportunities for employees and where jobs are typically governed by stringent rules and procedures, individuals have little room for discretionary activities. Scott and Meyer (1991) suggest that training can be viewed as a component of bureaucratic control.

ORGANISATIONAL CHANGE AS A CONTEXTUAL FACTOR

It is appropriate at this point to briefly outline the contextual impact of change on training and development. We can begin by referring to "change" as the overthrowing of tradition and the laying aside of patterned ways of living and working together in an organisation (Darcy and Kleiner, 1991).

Varying Organisational Perspectives

Depending on the perspective taken of the organisation, it is possible to visualise the influence on training and development in relation to the change process. Three different perspectives serve to illustrate this point.

1. A traditional perspective views the organisation as a political entity that can only be changed by the exercise of power or by bargaining among powerful groups. In this situation, unless the training and development function is acknowledged as occupying a position of power within the organisation, it cannot expect to exert significant influence or control over the change process. (The power and political context of training and development is comprehensively examined in the last section of this chapter.)

2. Taking a rational-economic perspective of the organisation implies that change strategies are based on empiricism and self-interest. There is a focus on acquiring useful knowledge, and on applying that knowledge in a way which is conducive to the effective performance of organisational tasks. Here, training and development can be expected to play a significant role in ensuring that this knowledge is successfully internalised.

3. Organisations can also be seen in terms of cultural systems, based on values, with shared symbols and shared cognitive schemes linking individuals together. Change strategies are therefore focused on altering the norms and values positions of organisational members, and we have already discussed the implications for training and development in such situations.

The predominant organisational perspective, therefore, impacts directly on training and development, in terms of the nature and extent of its involvement in the change process.

Principles of Change

Another aspect of the way training and development may be influenced arises from the three fundamental principles of organisational change identified by Bowers and Franklin (1977). These are:

1. *Congruence* — the intervention designed to implement the change must be adapted and tailored to fit the structure and function of the particular organisation. By implication, training and development activities must be carefully designed and structured to complement the process of change being undertaken.

2. *Predisposition* — there are certain points in the organisation where change is most likely to succeed. To facilitate the change process, training and development activities should be initially concentrated on these areas.

3. *Succession* — some changes can only be successfully implemented following the removal of pertinent barriers or obstacles. A primary aim of training and development, therefore, should be to assist the organisation to identify and overcome these barriers.

This demonstrates the shifting points of emphasis associated with training and development, even within one particular change programme.

Revolutionary/Non-programmed Change

Implementing a change process has always been a special management challenge. However, the nature of the change not only impinges on the general approach being adopted, but also on the approach to training and development. It is common to make a distinction between what could be described as routine or programmed change, and more revolutionary or major non-programmed change. Routine change is defined as referring to new circumstances which are deemed to be well within the scope of existing management approaches. Such change is usually dealt with on a daily basis, and encompasses issues as diverse as pricing alternations, handling disgruntled customers, replacing people, and shifting strategic properties.

On the other hand, major change requires individuals throughout the company to acquire behaviours and skills with which they may be totally unfamiliar. In such situations, an overriding emphasis is placed on the identification and learning of new skills and behaviour, and working to institutionalise these in order to sustain high performance. Indeed, it is on major, non-programmed change that more and more organisations are being forced to concentrate their efforts in the current environment, and it is this type of change process which is becoming increasingly widespread and familiar. This re-shaping process dictates that the training and development spotlight be aimed primarily at values and effecting value changes.

THE POWER AND POLITICAL CONTEXT OF TRAINING AND DEVELOPMENT

The power and influence of particular functions or departments in the organisation can greatly impinge on the way they are perceived and, by implication, on their effectiveness. The training function is far from being excluded from this proviso, and indeed the training and development profession has not traditionally viewed itself as occupying a powerful or influential position. Furthermore, "power" has often been seen as a dirty word, requiring efforts to demystify and de-satanise the topic. Beckhard (1969) describes power as the organisation's last dirty word while Machiavelli in his classic work, *The Prince*, challenges the negative connotations of power. He points out that power can be related to efficiency and capacity, rather than being associated with the more distasteful concepts of control, domination and oppression. Thus, when power is "on", a department can be productive, while a department can become bogged down if the power is "off".

Defining and Understanding Power

What exactly does power mean in organisational terms? Many definitions of power include an element which indicates that power is the capability of one individual/department to overcome resistance in achieving a desired objective (see Dahl, 1957; Emerson, 1962; Salancik and Pfeffer, 1977). Furthermore, it is generally agreed that power characterises relationships among social actors. Therefore, power is context- or relationship-specific. This is an important notion as it implies that the power of the training and development function is not an isolated feature, but one that can only be gauged with respect to other functions in a specific organisational setting.

Organisational power can be exercised in upward/downward (vertical) and/or horizontal directions in organisations. Vertical power is allocated according to the position held in the organisational structure. This type of power is not usually of help to the training and development function, because the ability of training specialists to get things done depends more on the number of networks in which they are involved, rather than their formal position in the hierarchy. However, horizontal power is important in any discussion concerning the power position of training, as it pertains to relationships across departments. Horizontal power relationships are thus not defined by the formal hierarchy, and power differences are not defined in any formal sense.

Power must also be distinguished from organisational politics. The latter has been defined as intentional acts of influence to enhance or protect the self-interest of individuals or groups (Allen et al, 1977). This definition makes it clear that political activity is that which is undertaken to overcome some resistance or opposition. It is furthermore focused around the acquisition and use of power, and can be distinguished from activity which involves decision-making based on rational or bureaucratic procedures. Nonetheless, in practice, the terms power and politics have shared meanings in many organisations. Essentially, this means that for the training and development function to have influence, it requires some power source or power base, coupled with the expenditure of energy in a politically skilful way when necessary.

Power and Authority

Hierarchical authority presents another means of getting things done in organisations. While there are many who think power is merely the exercise of authority, it is important to make a distinction between the two. The distribution of power can become legitimate over time, to the extent that individuals within the organisation expect and value a certain pattern of influence. Such legitimised power is denoted as authority. This transformation of power into authority has significant implications for the way influence is exerted. In relation to the training and development function, the exercise of power involves costs; in terms of resource expenditure, a certain level of effort, and the making of certain commitments.

In contrast, the exercise of authority is expected and desired in an organisational setting. In this way, the exercise of authority may actually serve to enhance the amount of authority subsequently enjoyed by the function. Therefore, the transformation of power into hierarchical authority is very important, because once transformed it is not resisted and the function no longer depends on the resources that generated power in the first instance. Within the context of training and development, several problems may be associated with the use of authority as a way of getting things done:

- The work of the training and development function requires considerable co-operation with many people who do not fall within its direct chain of command. As a result, it is largely dependent on those outside its purview of authority, whom it cannot reward or punish even if it desired to do so.

- Authority is based on the notion that whoever gives the orders is correct. However, when authority is vested in a single individual/department, mistakes can be made. This possibility has major ramifications for training and development, which must interact constructively with other functions if it is to be perceived as effective and useful.

- The use of authority is an outdated notion. Training and development espouses democracy and participation as part of its decision-making processes, and such elements conflict sharply with the concept of authority.

The training and development function, then, is rather restricted in the area of "pulling rank" through positional authority.

Another way of getting things done is by developing a strongly shared vision or organisation culture. If the training and development function could get people to share a common set of values about training and development, a common perspective on approach and methodology, and a common vocabulary, then it would not have to rely on authority or power. However, this is a difficult task in terms of the organisation as a whole, and particular complications arise when we focus on the functional level. This method has two specific problems — firstly, how a shared perception of training and development can be built upon, and secondly, how, in a strong training and development culture, new ideas which are inconsistent with that culture can penetrate. This latter point, especially, may present problems for a function which advocates continuous change.

The Power of the Training and Development Function

We can therefore see how the training and development function has difficulties with the formal authority and the shared vision options. Of even greater significance, however, is the fact that the training function has traditionally held an ambivalent attitude towards power, and has not been successful in its use. This is underlined by recent research on training and development specialists in Irish companies, which focused on assessing the power positions of the training and development function (Heraty, 1992). Before analysing the results, let us first outline the dimensions of a strategic contingencies model on which the research was based.

Strategic contingencies are defined as those events and activities, both inside and outside the organisations, which are essential for attaining organisational goals. Departments which are involved with strategic contingencies tend to have greater power, because those departments most able to cope with the organisation's critical problems or uncertainties acquire power in the process. Five dimensions are suggested in this regard by Salancik and Pfeffer (1977), which may be summarised as follows:

1. *Dependency*: what is the degree of interdepartmental dependency, and to what extent do other departments need what the training and development function can provide?

2. *Financial Resources*: the greater the resources of the training and development function, the more it can lean on other departments in the organisation.

3. *Centrality*: this dimension reflects the training and development function's role in the primary activities of the organisation. It is associated with power because it can be equated with the significance of the function's contribution.

4. *Substitutability*: can the training and development function's activities be easily performed by other departments and/or individuals, or by using external resources? The greater the range of substitutability, the lower the potential power.

5. *Coping with uncertainty*: departments that are involved in managing the environment, or in dealing with major problems, have power conferred on them.

Kanter (1979) extended the range of contingencies to include three further dimensions:

1. *Relevance*: does the training and development function carry out activities which are significantly related to achieving high priority organisational goals?

2. *Criticality*: departments that carry out critical tasks have greater power than those involved in less critical areas.

3. *Autonomy*: this refers to the scope of the training and development function in setting priorities for the rest of the organisation.

Drawing on this framework, let us now examine the research as illustrated in Table 8.2.

Control of Resources

The indication here is that the training and development function does control some important resources. It commands a certain level of investment, and has some ability to ensure that line managers carry out training and development activities. While some 31 per cent of respondents perceived that the resources controlled by the function were required by others in the organisation, over 50 per cent felt that the resources in the function's possession were not fundamental to organisational operations.

Centrality

The responses clearly highlight the fact that the training and development function lacks centrality, despite some 50 per cent of respondents indicating that training specialists had regular contact with managers in the organisation. Over 50 per cent felt that training and development was not a "part of the business" and that there was a low level of integration between the training function and organisational goals. In addition, it appears that the training specialist is less likely to be involved on broad level decision-making, and that resource allocation to the function is in line with strategic organisational goals.

Table 8.2: The Power Position of the Training and Development Function

Sample of Irish Training and Development Specialists (n=120)

	Agree Strongly %	Agree %	Not Sure %	Disagree %	Strongly Disagree %
Control of Resources — Strategic Response Type					
The T&D function has the ability to ensure line managers carry out their T&D requirements.	15	25	5	45	10
T&D policies are supported by a specific training budget.	22	26	10	25	10
An annual budget is set aside for the T&D function.	26	24	10	30	10
T&D function is a source of important information to the organisation.	12	27	11	37	23
T&D function controls resources which are required by others in the organisation.	10	21	11	35	17
Centrality of Function					
Head of T&D has regular contact with other key managers in the organisation.	28	22	12	28	20
T&D is perceived as "part of the business".	22	14	13	27	24
There is a low level of integration between the T&D function and organisation goals.	10	47	22	11	10
The training specialist is not highly involved in senior level decision making.	37	19	10	23	11
T&D function operates at all levels and parts of the business.	10	28	5	20	37
Resources allocated to the training and development function are based on the strategic goals of the organisation.	5	22	6	22	45
Substitutability					
Line managers are mainly responsible for implementing T&D policies.	23	22	5	24	26
T&D activities are mainly confined to external activities.	10	26	6	33	25

	Agree Strongly %	Agree %	Not Sure %	Disagree %	Strongly Disagree %
T&D function can be dropped in times of economic downturn.	15	23	21	20	21
The organisation relies mainly on external and development resources.	15	24	1	26	24
Line managers rely totally on the training specialist to undertake T&D activities.	13	18	3	30	35
Coping with Uncertainty					
The T&D function can reform a boundary spanning role.	8	19	3	22	48
Well-trained and developed human resources are viewed by top management as a means of attaining competitive advantage.	25	28	7	10	30
T&D function has the capacity to enable the organisation to manage its external environment.	5	15	17	22	41
Expertise					
T&D function has the ability to diagnose problems and anticipate needs.	22	33	5	28	12
T&D function has the expertise to determine and implement appropriate solutions once problems are diagnosed.	19	34	8	28	12
T&D specialist has fewer qualifications than their peers in other departments.	26	29	4	31	10
Members of the T&D function are perceived as experts by their peers.	17	28	5	24	26
The training specialist has change management skills.	17	13	5	36	29

Substitutability

There are strong signals that the training and development function suffers from substitutability problems. Line managers often carry out training and development activities, and there is also considerable reliance on external resources. Furthermore, 38 per cent of respondents indicated that the training and development function was likely to be "dropped" in times of economic downturn, exposing its positional fragility.

Uncertainty

Highly trained human resources are seen by a large number of respondents (53 per cent) as an important means of achieving competitive advantage. Nonetheless, over 60 per cent did not see the training and development function as having the capacity to enable the organisation to manage its external environment, while more than 70 per cent suggested that the function could not perform an external environment management role adequately or effectively.

Expertise

There is general perception is that the training and development function has the ability to diagnose problems and anticipate needs within the organisation. Additionally, 53 per cent of respondents felt that the function has the ability to complement appropriate solutions once problems have been diagnosed. However, over 50 per cent perceived that training and development specialists were not as well qualified as some of their peers in other departments. Similarly, 50 per cent did not see the specialist as an expert practitioner, and 65 per cent indicated that the specialist did not possess appropriate change management skills.

Heraty (1992) suggests that while the training and development function does control certain important resources, and has some problem-solving capabilities, it suffers with regard to high substitutability and its inability to differentiate its services. It also scores poorly on the issue of centrality, and would not have a major role to play in helping the organisation to cope with uncertainty. In summary, she indicates that the training and development function encounters significant barriers in its efforts to acquire and utilise power.

SUMMARY

In this chapter we have considered the range of environmental and organisational factors which influence the shape of the training and development function and the type of activities it engages in. We focused on eight sets of contextual factors: the external environment, the organisation's stakeholders, the organisation's culture, technology, structure, change, size and power. These variables operate in an integrated fashion to influence the way the training and development function is perceived, how it manages and evaluates activities and its place within the wider organisation. No one variable will have a prominent influence and the relative influence of each variable will vary over time. Consideration of these contextual variables now allows us to consider a range of models of training and development practice which may be adopted by an organisation.

Figure 8.1:   Values, Expectations and Evaluation Criteria of Training and Development Stakeholders

Key Stakeholder	Key Values / Expectations	No.	Key Evaluation Criteria	No.
Top Management N=16	• A maximum return on the training & development investment.	7	• Increased worker flexibility.	13
	• Training and development function should provide advice and consultancy support to line specialists.	10	• Training and development activities provided within budget.	12
	• Training and development should meet the strategic needs of the organisation.	9	• Increases in worker productivity.	14
	• Training and development has a significant contribution to make to organisation success.	6	• Optimum usage of training and development resources.	9
	• Training and development should help create values of change and innovativeness.	13	• Improves retention rate of employees.	7
	• Individual employees are responsible for their own development.	10	• Maximum exploitation of state grant aid for training and development.	12
	• Training and development function should have a customer focus.	8	• Performance speeds after training.	10
	• Training should help managers think strategically.	8	• Sales performance after training.	4
	• Training and development should promote teamwork and quality values.	12	• Facilitated major change within organisation.	11

Key Stakeholder	Key Values / Expectations	No.	Key Evaluation Criteria	No
Line Managers / Specialists N=16	• Training and development should facilitate achievement of departmental needs.	7	• Facilitation of change within department.	5
	• Training and development should eliminate skill gaps.	14	• Level of line involvement in training and development activities.	9
	• Line specialist should have involvement in the training and development process.	9	• Skilled performance reached in shortest possible time.	14
	• Training and development should have a job focus.	15	• Department training and development needs met within agreed time period.	12
	• Identification of training and development needs is a line activity.	12	• Contribution towards cost savings within department.	10
	• Training and development can promote worker harmony and adherence to rules and procedures.	12	• Improved communications within department.	8
	• Training and development strategies should fit in with the work requirements of the department.	12	• Training and development should have an immediate pay back.	10
	• Training and development facilitates team building.	5	• Responsiveness of training and development specialist to line managers requirements.	13
	• Training and development can eliminate demarcation and increase flexibility.	9	• Elimination of need to recruit trained staff.	6

Key Stakeholder	Key Values / Expectations	No.	Key Evaluation Criteria	No.
Training and Development Specialist N = 16	• To provide a service to line specialists.	9	• Number of days training undertaken.	12
	• To act as consultants and change agents.	7	• Number of training programmes undertaken.	11
	• To make a contribution towards the achievement of strategic goals.	13	• Number of employees trained.	14
	• To operate in a professional manner.	10	• Number of training course days.	15
	• To have credibility and status in the eyes of key organisation members.	13	• Categories of employees trained.	14
	• To increase power and influence in organisations.	10	• Meeting the objectives set out in the training and development plan.	15
	• To adopt a proactive approach to managing activities.	8	• Exam pass rates.	8
	• To achieve a balance between organisational and individual needs.	10	• The quality and relevance of training and development provision.	14
	• To encourage change in values and attitudes.	12	• Improve individual performance.	12
	• To involve participants and line specialists in the training and development process.	8	• Improve individual promotability.	9
	• To maintain and reinforce existing values and systems of the organisation.	7	• Training and development needs met within time specified.	11
	• To ensure consistency in training and development practices throughout the organisation.	12	• Integration of training development with HR activities.	13
	• To provide training and development that meets actually identified needs.	14		

Key Stakeholder	Key Values / Expectations	No.	Key Evaluation Criteria	No.
Personnel Managers N=16	• Training and development activities should integrate with other personnel activities.	10	• Level of skilled performance reached.	13
	• Encourage equal opportunity in the provision of training and development.	9	• Number of employees trained.	8
	• Training and development should be driven by the needs of customer.	13	• Types of training and development activities provided.	11
	• Training and development should facilitate major change within the organisation.	12	• Level of support for strategic activities of organisations.	11
	• Line managers should be involved in delivering training and development.	10	• Budgetary allocation to training and development.	15
	• Training and development should complement but not compete with other personnel policies.	14	• Effectiveness of training and development specialist role.	8
	• The personnel function should have overall responsibility for training and development within the organisation.	11	• Cost / benefit of training and development activities.	0
	• Training and development should be a continuous process within the organisation.	7	• Level of cooperation between training and development specialist and line managers.	13
	• Employees should carry the main responsibility for their own development.	11	• allocation of grant aid received from FÁS.	16
	• Training and development activities should be viewed as a long term investment.	8		
	• Training and development should be strategically linked.	11		

Key Stakeholder	Key Values / Expectations	No.	Key Evaluation Criteria	No.
Individual Employees N=32	• Involvement in identifying their needs. • Training and development should advance labour mobility and promotability. • Training and development should enhance job security. • Training and development activities should meet the personal needs of the individual. • Training and development should lead to status and recognition. • Training and development should be provided on a fair and equal basis. • Training and development should have a broader focus than the job itself. • The organisation should support financially an individuals development efforts. • Training and development can help toward obsolescence. • Training and development activities should result in certification.	13 18 11	• Did the training and development intervention meet individual needs. • Ability to earn maximum bonus. • Exam pass rate. • Achievement of certification • Increases individual promobility. • Level of involvement in decisions about training and development. • Increases in motivation and job satisfaction. • Facilitated the identification of career paths. • Level of financial support given by the organisation. • Amount of feedback received on performance. • Level of self-development encouraged.	14 10 6 17

Key Stakeholder	Key Values / Expectations	No.	Key Evaluation Criteria	No.
National Training Advisors FÁS N=10	• Training and development should facilitate full employment.	4	• Extent to which it has eliminated skill shortages.	8
	• Training and development should promote equality of opportunity and increased access.	10	• Increases in labour mobility.	5
	• Training and development should meet the needs of special groups.	9	• Level of private sector expenditure on training and development.	10
	• Training and development should meet social as well as economic objectives.	7	• A balance between technical and management elements.	7
	• Training and development is the primary responsibility of individual firms.	9	• Levels of expenditure on general training.	8
	• Special assistance should be given to small firms.	8	• Extent to which it has reduced unemployment.	7
	• To promote the image of Irish industry abroad.	6	• Extent to which future skill needs are met.	6
	• Training and development should help regulate performance standards within industry.	8	• Development of a technically competent workforce.	7
	• Training and development should lead to certification.	4	• Number of training certifications.	4
	• Training and development should enhance Irish competitiveness in the international context.	6	• Optimising FÁS resources.	8
	• Training and development should adopt a proactive long term perspective.	8	• Maximum return on state training and development expenditure.	7

Key Stakeholder	Key Values / Expectations	No.	Key Evaluation Criteria	No.
External Training Providers N=19	• To provide a professional service to clients.	12	• Extent to which needs of clients are met.	11
	• To avoid conflicts of interest.	10	• Level of client satisfaction with services provided.	14
	• To provide services based on a sound knowledge and expertise base.	11	• The attraction of high profile clients.	10
	• To use innovative learning designs.	10	• Extent knowledge base is updated.	7
	• To address the specific needs of clients.	14	• A good return for the client organisation on their investment.	9
	• To ensure repeat business and a long-term relationship.	9	• Focus on long-term benefits of training and development intervention.	8
	• To uphold confidentiality of information received as part of consulting process.	7	• Avoidance of conflicts of interest/breach of confidentiality.	12
	• Not to get involved in the client's political processes.	10		
	• To keep up with trends in training and development.	8		
Educational Establishments N=7	• To provide educational activities that meet the needs of industry.	3	• Number of business education programmes provided.	6
	• To provide ease of access to education and management development activities.	3	• Balance of technical and managerial provision.	4
	• To enhance the skill base of key decision makers within industry.	6	• Number of industry participants.	6
	• To help develop positive attitudes towards minorities, the environment, etc.	6	• Number of training course days.	5
	• To provide quality management education activities.	5	• Number and level of certification.	7
	• To foster good relationships between industry and education.	5	• Breadth of management education programmes.	7
			• Contribution towards employment and labour mobility.	5
			• Enhancement of image of education as a partner in industry.	4
			• The amount of attitude change.	6

Key Stakeholder	Key Values / Expectations	No.	Key Evaluation Criteria	No.
Trade Unions N=13	• To ensure that employees have knowledge and skill to perform key tasks.	8	• Amount of company resources spent on training and development.	12
	• To ensure that employee-initiated training and development efforts are recognised by organisation.	13	• Extent to which employees receive bonuses / extra payments for acquiring extra skills.	11
	• To encourage equality of opportunity and equal access in organisation's training and development provision.	13	• Extent to which the organisation has met its legal training requirements.	13
	• To secure basic training and development rights for employees.	12	• Level of concession given by management for increased flexibility.	10
	• To have organisations commit sufficient financial resources to training and development.	12	• Contribution of training to employment and increased labour mobility.	10
	• To ensure that multi-skilling initiatives take account of employee rights.	10	• Participation rates of employees in skills training.	9
	• To involve employees in decisions about their training and development.	12	• Level of craft training supported by government and employers.	8
	• To protect traditional craft skills.	11		
	• To retrain employees whose skills have become absolent.	12		
	• Training policies should be in line with existing agreements.	13		
	• Organisations should meet their statutory training and development responsibilities.	10		
	• Training and development should be matched by increased promotion opportunities.	11		

Figure 8.2: Human Resource Development Links to Organisation Strategy and Structure

Strategy	Structure	HRD Systems	HRD Management Development	HRD Professional / Personal Development	Job Related Training
Single Product	Functional	• HRD perceived in maintenance terms • HRD specialist limited status/power • Lack of strategic orientation in activities • Limited perspective of business needs	• Focus on single function • Largely unsystematic and lack of clarity with respect to needs • Management development needs subjectively determined	• Personal development not perceived as priority • Personal development costs borne by individual • Perceived by top managers as a luxury	• Unsystematic, largely on-the-job • Responsibility of supervisor, however unclear guidelines • No evaluation of results • Lack of clear standards
Single product (vertically-integrated)	Functional	• Functions of HRD more clearly defined • Problem-centred orientation toward activities • More conscious of business needs	• Emphasis on job rotation • Greater emphasis on performance and productivity (measures still subjective)	• Organisation more aware of services of outside training and educational agencies • Organisation may bear some of the costs of personal development	• More systematic with greater involvement by supervisors • Some attempt at cross training/multi-skilling • Experienced worker standard established

Strategy	Structure	HRD Systems	HRD Management Development	HRD Professional / Personal Development	Job Related Training
Growth by acquisition	Strategic Business Unit (SBU)	• Greater strategic focus • Emphasis on measurement of results • HRD specialist significant status/power • Production of HRD policies and plans • Usually medium term focus in plans/policies	• Emphasis on developing management teams • Greater awareness of cross functional expertise • Production of developmental sequences • Greater use of structural management development approaches	• Considerable investment in executive development • Managers encouraged to broaden knowledge/skills basis • Existence of financial assistance systems • Personal development seen as good in itself	• Cross-functional training; systematic multi-skilling • Exact measurement of skill levels attained • Recognition of motivational aspect • On-the-job training activities may utilise advanced training technology
Concentric (related) diversify internally	Multi-divisional matrix	• Corporate perspective • Explicit HRD mission, policies and plans • Clear criteria for evaluating success • Specific mechanisms for achieving strategy/HRD link	• Formal systems of development • A cross-functional/divisional or corporate focus • Emphasis on conflict-handling, political and interpersonal skills development	• Considerable investment in post-experience education • Perceived as an investment in employee • Greater use of MBA, etc. to develop potential managers who may now have a technical background	• Multi-skilling • Considerable specialist technical training • Emphasis on productivity and return on investment • Specific evaluation of learning

Strategy	Structure	HRD Systems	HRD Management Development	HRD Professional / Personal Development	Job Related Training
Conglomerate diversification (multiple products/ multiple consumers)	Global organisation	• Corporate HRD function • Standardisation of policies and planning mechanisms • Involved at strategy formulation and implementation stages • Corporate and divisional HRD staff • Strategy/structure/ HRD integration	• Functional / generalist orientation required of managers • Systems for goal setting, usually multiple goals • Interdepartmental / team relationships important	• Focus on cross-divisional, subsidiary, corporate executive development • Considerable financial investment • Professional development viewed as an upgrading and conversion mechanism	• Systems for on-the-job training very advanced; CBT, IV tech. used • Advanced systems of cross-training / multi-skilling • Technical training specialists • Systematic evaluation of standards

Source: Garavan, T. N. "Strategic Human Resource Development", *Journal of European Industrial Training,* Vol. 15, No. 1, 1991.

Figure 8.3: Life Cycle Stage, Culture/Strategy and Implications for HRD Activities

Life Cycle Stage	Key Culture / Strategic Features	Implications for Strategic HRD
1. Embryonic	• High level of cohesion • Dominant role of founder • Outside help not valued • Lack of procedures and planning systems • Politics play an important role	• Owner may not perceive need for HRD • Limited management expertise and succession problems • Changes may be unplanned / ad hoc • HRD may have to market its services aggressively
2. Growth	• Large variety of culture changes • Levels of cohesion decline • Emergence of middle management • Tensions/conflict may arise in organisations • Trying to get people to accept new ways of thinking • Diversification of business activities • Line/staff differences	• Initiation of career development activities • Inducting new recruits • Management development activities • Development of high performing teams • Involvement in the management of change • Reinforcement and maintenance of cultural values and briefs • Dealing with ambiguity and uncertainty
3. Maturity	• Institutionalisation of values and beliefs • Evolutionary rather than revolutionary changes • Inertia may emerge in organisation • Strategic logic may be rejected	• HRD function should be well-established • Maintenance HRD activities may be more appropriate • Lack of career opportunities may require novel HRD approaches
4. Decline	• Culture may act as a defence against a hostile environment • Major decisions may have to be taken • Readjustment necessary	• Management of change • Focus on changing the culture • Reassure employees that problems are being tackled • Organising problem centred/project/task activities

Source: Garavan, T.N. "Strategic Human Resource Development", *Journal of European Industrial Training,* Vol. 15, No. 1, 1991.

9

MODELS OF TRAINING AND DEVELOPMENT PRACTICE

INTRODUCTION AND LEARNING OBJECTIVES

This chapter aims to introduce the reader to alternative models of training and development that may be applied in an organisational setting. After reading this chapter you will understand:

♦ the range of models that are found in the training and development literature;

♦ the characteristics of each model;

♦ the strengths and weaknesses of each model and the situations where each is most appropriate;

♦ the comparative features of each model.

THE RANGE OF MODELS

One of the key features which has characterised the field of training and development over the last number of years is the continuing and, some would argue, growing gap between theory and practice. Donnelly (1987) suggests that we tend to operate in a pragmatic environment in which theory, where it exists, is often deduced from successful practice, and where practice is based on a judicious mixture of intuition and experience. One particular outcome of this has been the proliferation of "state of the art" development models, which, he suggests:

> can quickly become outdated, oversimplifications in an area that is becoming increasingly diverse and complicated. . . . It is essential that we continually analyse, question and, where necessary, modify what may be viewed as received truths within the area of training: time can have a halo effect on the individual.

He further suggests that training practices prior to the early 1960s were characterised largely by ad hoc approaches, where training was seen as an activity suitable only for a minority of skilled employees (apprentices), and there was no concept of training being central to corporate planning or strategy. However, from the mid-1960s onwards, faced with heightened international competition, it was increasingly recognised that one of the reasons for reduced competitiveness was many organisations' poor record of training. Levels of sophistication of training and development initiatives must be related accurately to projected technical and organisational changes, which should flow from corporate and manpower plans. Policies have traditionally been devised by practitioners. This approach may have an inherent weakness in that it facilitates the abdication by senior management of their legitimate training responsibilities, and may actually widen the gap between training activities and actual organisational requirements.

This chapter sets out the range of training and development models, from the traditional approaches taken to training, to the more strategic models of training and development advocated today.

AN UNSYSTEMATIC FRAGMENTED MODEL

The organisation that adopts an unsystematic approach to training views the training activity and the training function generally as a cost to be minimised at all times. Training, when carried out, is completed in an ad hoc manner and is reactive in nature — only undertaken as a result of external pressure. Training is not perceived as a cost-effective contributor to the achievement of organisation objectives, but rather as an expense to be incurred. Training practices are introduced in an unplanned fashion, with no clearly defined policies in place for their utilisation. Reid et al (1992) indicate that employees are largely responsible for their own training, with no facilitator or counselling back-up. Management development is practically non-existent and, should the organisation employ a training specialist, they are afforded negligible power, authority or influence in the organisation.

Barham, Fraser and Heath (1988) identify the following characteristics of an unsystematic/fragmented model:

- Training is not linked to organisational goals.
- Training is perceived as a luxury.
- Training, if undertaken, is directive.
- Training takes place in the training department.
- There is an emphasis on knowledge-based courses.
- Training is viewed as a discontinuous process.

Figure 9.1: Continuum of Training and Development Models

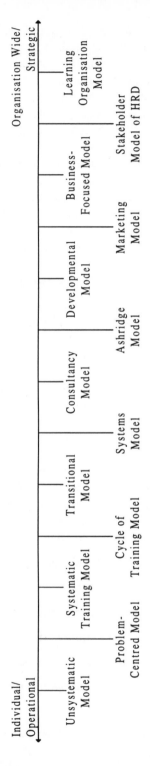

Where training and development is provided it is based on a common skills approach. Markwell and Roberts (1969) suggest that this approach is based on the assumption that the training and development requirements of employees in a given category are similar and can be met by a common programme. It lacks any sophistication since the learning intervention is not derived from systematic analysis and is usually limited to participation on a formal programme. Within the unsystematic model more attention is focused on the presentation of documentation and formal programmes with a view to securing grant support.

"Sitting by Nellie" is the norm in organisations which adopt an unsystematic model. This involves learning from an experienced co-worker. Such an approach ignores the fact that if Nellie is to be successful then she must:

- have an up-to-date knowledge of the work methods and standards required;

- have an ability to help trainees to learn new skills;

- have the time to instruct employees without losing a bonus or meeting their own job targets;

- have sufficient interpersonal skills to deal with trainee learning problems.

The unsystematic model is particularly prevalent in small companies and those where owner/managers perceive that training and development is of little value. Here the "self-made" manager who has experienced little formal training and development will often hold a genuine conviction that activities of this nature are superfluous for business success. This conviction is invariably supported by a belief in the natural law of leadership, where "cream always rises to the top".

Unfortunately, as indicated in the previous section, too many organisations in Ireland today are witness to the thriving existence of this model.

Bratton and Gold (1994) suggest that much learning did occur as a result of the "sitting by Nellie" approach, but as a learning system it is haphazard, lengthy and capable of passing on bad habits as well as good ones. In some cases, reinforced by employers' tendencies to de-skill work, workers are often unwilling to give away their "secrets" for fear of losing their jobs. Most significant, however, is that, given today's competitive environment, organisations cannot afford to practice unsystematic training. It is increasingly recognised that the organisation that fails to adopt a proactive, planned approach to employee development will not achieve optimum utilisation of its resources and will fail to maximise its potential in a given industry. Coupled with this, the growing trend of employees taking control of their own development, and the expectation that employer organisations will facilitate this development through systematic, proactive training and development opportunities, highlights that unplanned, ad hoc training is neither desirable nor acceptable.

A PROBLEM-CENTRED OR PLANNED MAINTENANCE MODEL

Buckley and Caple (1992) suggest that this approach to training is based upon urgent needs requiring "quick, accurate problem identification before taking remedial action". It is a highly reactive process which involves the identification and prioritising of performance problems, coupled with the generation and evaluation of results. Reid et al (1992) indicate that this approach is useful in situations where:

- the need for training is urgent, but resources are not available for a more extensive analysis;

- a further more expensive analysis is unnecessary, i.e. where an employee's work is unsatisfactory, in a specific area;

- the firm operates in a highly dynamic industry or in very uncertain markets.

Essentially this approach advocates the identification, by the training specialist, of the most pressing problem or training need, and taking action to deal with it. It is seen to produce immediate, cost-effective results, but can also have detrimental consequences where the specialist exercises poor priority choice in problem analysis. While this approach has merited considerable attention in the past, one must recognise that organisations cannot hope to be successful in the future through a constant reliance on the expertise of one certain individual. Attention has already been drawn to the potential problem of inaccurate problem analysis and priority scheduling. Organisations can no longer afford to view training and development as a peripheral activity, to be engaged as problems arise. There are numerous other organisations in any given industry that adopt a proactive stance and are seen to be extremely effective in achieving their corporate objectives.

There are two variants of the problem-centred model. In the less formal situation its application will usually involve the supervisor/manager identifying a problem, selecting a training or development activity which they see as relevant to satisfying that need and requesting the training specialist to provide or arrange the learning intervention. Such an informal approach suffers from a number of limitations. It may result in an incorrect identification of the problem. Further analysis may show that the problem did not have a training solution. It may result in a waste of resources and does not enhance the status of the training specialist who may be best described as a "provider".

In its more formal application the problem is identified as a result of training needs analysis by the training specialist. The specialist will be viewed as a professional who has the skills to carry out a rigorous analysis of the problem, thus ensuring that the correct solution is chosen. Ashton and Easterby-Smith (1980) suggest that this model will result in a higher degree of interest and commitment amongst stakeholders and result in a greater deal of visible activity particularly in terms of in-company and external formal training programmes. The problem-centred model is a pragmatic one in which the training specialist concentrates on a specific problem. Indeed it may be an appropriate strategy for a specialist who wants to quickly establish a power base and credibility.

Fonda and Hayes (1986) argue that a problem-centred/planned maintenance model does not see training and development making a significant contribution to the organisation. Furthermore, it assumes stable and predictable product markets and unchanging skill requirements.

Marsick and Watkins (1986) argue that a Taylorist-Fordist approach to control, through job design and de-skilling of jobs, continues to hold in organisations and reinforces an unsystematic or problem oriented model of training and development. Marsick and Watkins suggest that the machine ideal causes jobs to be seen as parts co-ordinated by a national control system, where performance can be measured in terms of the observable, behavioural and quantifiable while criterion-related attitudes are important only in so far as they can be manipulated to reinforce desired performance. Learning is then based on a deficit model which assesses the gap between the behaviour of employees and the set standard. Training simply attempts to close the gap by bringing employees to the desired standard or competence, but not beyond. This leaves little room for the consideration of attitudes, feelings and personal development.

A further implication of a maintenance or problem-centred approach may be the subservience of learning and training to accounting procedures which measure the cause and effect relationships between training programmes and output and profit in the short term. If no significant relationship can be found then there will be pressure to provide proof or cut the cost of the training.

All of this contrasts significantly with Japan and other countries in the Far East, and the more competitive European nations. Taylorist-Fordist models have long been rejected in favour of employees being viewed as assets to train and develop.

The problem-centred/planned maintenance model outlined here should not be confused with a problem-centred analysis of training needs (see Buckley and Caple, 1992; Harrison, 1992), which is discussed in Chapter 15. Neither should this model be associated with a proactive training strategy focused on identifying and providing timely solutions for organisational problems (Stuart and Long, 1985; Buckley and Caple, 1992).

A SYSTEMATIC TRAINING OR FORMALISED MODEL

The emergence of systems thinking and operational research typified the approach to management and organisational problems from the 1960s onwards (Taylor, 1991). Boydell (1976), the pioneer of the systematic training model, developed it in an attempt to professionalise the activity of training and thereby establish the credibility of trainers and the training function. A systematic model helps to ensure that randomness is reduced and that learning or behaviour change occurs in a structured format. Within a systematic model it is possible to identify a hierarchy of training outcomes:

1. Simple motor skills which demand little knowledge or application of knowledge, e.g. stamping documents.

2. More complex skills that require some knowledge base, e.g. starting up procedures for a particular machine.

3. Even more complex skills which require a non-procedurised application of knowledge, e.g. developing a training programme.

4. The ability to merge skills and knowledge in highly abstract or conceptual contexts, e.g. designing a new bridge.

5. The fusing of skills, knowledge and attitudes to give enhanced social and interpersonal skills as well as greater self-awareness.

The original systematic model included 10 sequential steps to effective training — from the identification of training needs to evaluation and follow-up. This original process has subsequently been modified and adapted by numerous theorists to the extent that modern systematic models typically comprise four main steps:

• assessment and identification of organisation training needs (macro level);

• assessment of job training requirements (micro level);

• programme design;

• evaluation and feedback.

This model is best viewed as a rational means of directing the organisation's resources. Based on an examination of organisational problems, threats and opportunities, top management sets the overall objectives, which are then broken down into manageable functional targets to be pursued by functional specialists working through their own sequence of stages.

The Industrial Training Act 1967 encouraged a systematic training model. The approach was widely adopted by Irish organisations and became ingrained into the thinking of many training specialists. The model certainly matched the perception of what most organisations would regard as rationality and efficiency. There is also an emphasis on cost-effectiveness throughout the model. There is also a preference for off-the-job learning partly because of the weaknesses inherent in the unsystematic model and partly in order to formalise training so that it is standardised, measurable and undertaken by training specialists. It is also tidy in that the training specialist can focus on the provision of separate training activities that reduce the complexity of day-to-day work activities and make evaluation a relatively easy task.

Taylor (1991) has argued that systematic models may not match organisational reality. He suggests two explanations.

- *The Rehabilitative Critique*: This argues that systematic models concepts are sound and can be used as a heuristic device and an approximation of reality. The model serves to highlight the problems to be overcome at each stage by refining techniques. For example, in identifying training needs, the training specialist may not perceive the real learning needs due to lack of access to information and low credibility with senior managers. The refinement would be for the training specialist to raise the profile of training.

- *The Radical Critique*: This argues that the systematic model is based on flawed assumptions and is mainly a legitimising myth to establish the role of the training specialist and to allow for management's right to define skill within the employment relationship.

Taylor concludes that while the systematic model may have helped to professionalise the training activity and to provide a simple and easily understood explanation of training procedures, it is an incomplete model and really only suitable for organisations operating in stable environments where goals can be clearly set. Taylor warns that continued adherence to the model will ultimately prevent the training specialist from tapping into the more complex but powerful organisational forces such as mission, culture, values, etc. We will return to Taylor's arguments when we consider his transitional model.

Thus, the increasing complexity of training and development activities creates a need for the extension of the model. Reid et al (1994) indicate that the traditional four-stage format is too simple to cover the complexity of current training activities, and that evaluation must be an inherent feature of every training and development cycle.

Other practical difficulties with the model include the following:

- The initial step of analysing training needs places a heavy emphasis on breaking things down into component parts in a mechanistic fashion which, in reality, can only be done with a limited number of jobs. Such an approach can ignore the important inter-relationships, networks, power relationships and cultural values, which influence learning in the organisation.

- A key presumption of the model is that the trainer, trainee, line manager and other interested parties will be able to agree on, and be equally committed to, the learning objectives formulated for the training initiative. This formulation of objectives tends to imply a desire to control learning with the outcome that any valuable learning that takes place which does not conform to these objectives, will be curtailed.

- A further presumption is that, once objectives and plans are drawn up, the resources are then acted upon. It fails to recognise that individuals differ in the ways in which they learn, the speed at which they learn, and the degree to which they are motivated to learn.

The systematic model is clearly an advance on the models already considered. Application of this model should ensure a greater commitment to training and development within the organisation. However, if a specialist were to stick rigidly to the various stages of the model, it could lead to problems in the long term. The model viewed at a macro level is quite attractive and would lend credibility to a newly established training and development function, but when considered at a micro level, its application to areas such as management development and more organic learning strategies is problematic.

It is suggested, therefore, that the use of the systematic model can no longer be justified, as it fails to meet the basic requirements of training and development, and is no longer relevant to current training and development interventions. The traditional model was typically income- and results-oriented, and focused on the learning of discrete skills that transfer readily to the workplace, producing immediate results. However, it neglects the multiplicity of factors that must be considered in today's HRD efforts, and, gives an oversimplified, if easily understood view of the HRD function.

A CYCLE OF TRAINING MODEL

Over the years the basic elements of the systematic training model have remained and most organisations that claim to have a systematic and planned approach to training would have some representation of it. A number of refinements have been suggested by advocates of a more realistic and more sophisticated model. Donnelly (1987) argues that, in reality, senior management may abdicate responsibility for training policy to training departments, with the consequent potential for widening the gap between training and organisation requirements. Essential prerequisites for any effort to implement a training model are a consideration of budgets, attitudes, abilities and the organisation's culture.

Donnelly (1987) identifies two particular weaknesses of the systematic model in advocating his cycle:

- One weakness of the model lies in its assumption that it is feasible to enter into an organisation-wide assessment of training and development without due consideration of the availability of budgets, managerial attitudes, the professionalism of trainers, and the potential capacity of the organisation to undertake changes within the cultural constraints of the present organisation philosophy. These factors will largely determine the extent, content and variability of subsequent assessments, and the acceptability and potential for success of future training and development activities.

- Furthermore, the model fails to consider the pre-entry requirements for moving from one stage to another. Mumford (1989) underlines the importance of such pre-entry requirements when arguing the need to determine ways in which individuals learn, and the importance of attitudes in the job environment.

Donnelly has therefore devised the cycle of training model as an alternative to the traditional four-stage model. It comprises four main sections, with a series of sub-sections, illustrating the pre-entry requirements which are used to help ensure the relevance of further activities. The model is based on the assumptions that:

- one must account for the plurality of interests of the various stakeholders in the organisation, and their interactions with each other;

- one must recognise the different types of learning required within organisations at different levels, at different times, varying at one end of the spectrum from highly specific and programmed skill learning to a highly unstructured, attitudinal "learning to learn" kind of learning at the other end;

- one should recognise learning as a total organisational process and not merely a functional specialism.

The model depicts four main blocks in the cycle:

- *Resource availability*. This initial block lists the main pre-assessment factors which must be checked before initiating the assessment.

- *Assessment of training needs: The Organisation*. This block comprises the major areas of concern in an organisation-wide assessment, and includes factors external to the organisation, likely to have implications for future training activities.

- *Assessment of training needs: The Job*. The focus in this section is on the learning problems associated with the job, and the activities concerned with job training analysis.

- *Programme design*. The final block is concerned with the design of training interventions, from the initial definition of behavioural objectives, to the implementation of HRD.

Donnelly (1987) suggests that this model underlines the importance of factors such as the availability of capital, cultural values, policies, allocation of responsibilities, and includes evaluation as an activity integral to the model itself, thus obviating the central limitations of the traditional systematic training model (see Figure 9.2).

Bramley (1989) also argues that an inevitable consequence of utilising a systematic model is that the training sub-system may become independent of the organisation context. He advocates a cycle that is open to the context by involving managers in analysing work situations to identify desirable changes and designing and delivering the training to bring the changes about. Evaluation occurs throughout the process with an emphasis on managers taking responsibility for encouraging the transfer into workplace performance of learning that occurs during training. Figure 9.3 represents Bramley's effectiveness model.

Figure 9.2: Cycle of Training: Modified Model

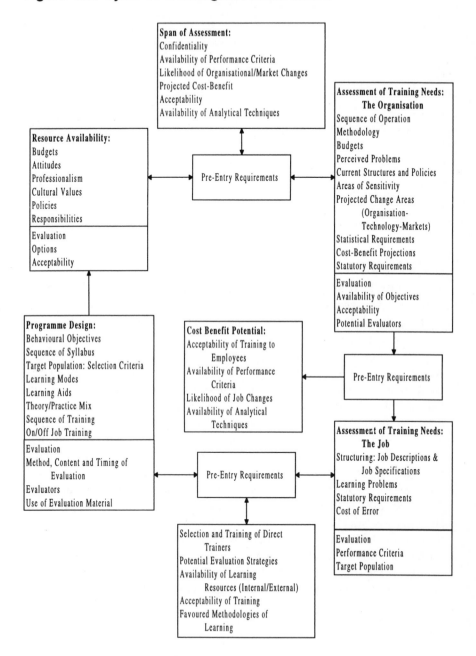

Span of Assessment:
Confidentiality
Availability of Performance Criteria
Likelihood of Organisational/Market Changes
Projected Cost-Benefit
Acceptability
Availability of Analytical Techniques

Assessment of Training Needs:
The Organisation
Sequence of Operation
Methodology
Budgets
Perceived Problems
Current Structures and Policies
Areas of Sensitivity
Projected Change Areas
(Organisation-
Technology-Markets)
Statistical Requirements
Cost-Benefit Projections
Statutory Requirements

Evaluation
Availability of Objectives
Acceptability
Potential Evaluators

Resource Availability:
Budgets
Attitudes
Professionalism
Cultural Values
Policies
Responsibilities

Evaluation
Options
Acceptability

Pre-Entry Requirements

Programme Design:
Behavioural Objectives
Sequence of Syllabus
Target Population: Selection Criteria
Learning Modes
Learning Aids
Theory/Practice Mix
Sequence of Training
On/Off Job Training

Evaluation
Method, Content and Timing of
Evaluation
Evaluators
Use of Evaluation Material

Cost Benefit Potential:
Acceptability of Training to
Employees
Availability of Performance
Criteria
Likelihood of Job Changes
Availability of Analytical
Techniques

Pre-Entry Requirements

Assessment of Training Needs:
The Job
Structuring: Job Descriptions &
Job Specifications
Learning Problems
Statutory Requirements
Cost of Error

Evaluation
Performance Criteria
Target Population

Pre-Entry Requirements

Selection and Training of Direct
Trainers
Potential Evaluation Strategies
Availability of Learning
Resources (Internal/External)
Acceptability of Training
Favoured Methodologies of
Learning

Figure 9.3: Bramley's Effectiveness Model

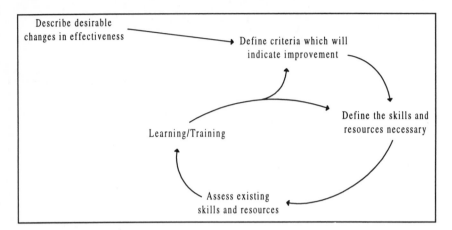

A TRANSITIONAL MODEL

Taylor (1991) has argued that the systematic training model could be improved if it were embedded in a map of the wider corporate strategic context. Figure 9.4 presents the model which describes as a double loop of corporate strategy and learning.

The inner loop is the systematic training model; the outer loop he describes as "crafted strategy" and learning. He argues that vision (a desired scenario), mission (a statement of why the organisation exists) and values must all come before attention is paid to objectives. Taylor is, however, tentative in offering such a model. Sloman (1994) suggests that Taylor's model retains the route-map feature of the systematic model, while at the same time embedding training and development in the wider strategic context. It also recognises that the organisation as a whole may be tentative in its approach to strategy formulation and development. This contrasts with the systematic model which is firmly based on a strategic management paradigm, i.e. a formal strategic planning process. Sloman does however point to two weaknesses. The model does not offer much potential guidance to practitioners, and the two loops differ in quality — the inner systematic loop is clear whereas the outer one varies in its visibility and tangibility. Few organisations may be able to define its existence.

Figure 9.4: Taylor's Transitional Model

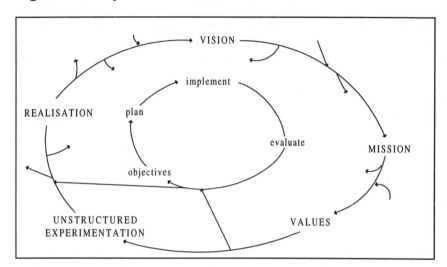

A SYSTEMS MODEL

The refinements to the basics of the systematic model advocate taking account of reality or the organisational context. A refined model must take account of inherent limitations of organisation reality that may prevent the models from operating or maintain training activity at a low level. This reality may have little consideration for training if organisation strategy and a culture which emphasise the short term. The Bramley model could, for instance, fall subject to a limitation in the form of a refusal by managers to become involved in training and development issues by neither facilitating the identification of training and development needs nor supporting learning transfer.

The use of the terms "systematic" and "system" in the training and development context has led to much confusion (see Atkins, 1983; Buckley and Caple, 1992; and Anderson, 1992). However, the term "systems" has a specialised meaning. A system is a set of interacting elements that acquire inputs from the environment, transform them and discharge outputs. Daft (1995) makes a distinction between a closed and open system. A closed system would not depend on its environment; it would be autonomous, enclosed and sealed off from the outside world. It would have all the energy it requires and could function effectively without the consumption of external resources. A true closed system does not exist; therefore the training and development function cannot be characterised as a closed system. The management of a closed system would be unproblematic, the organisation would be stable and predictable and the primary management issue would be to run things efficiently.

An open system must interact with its environment to survive. It both consumes resources and exports resources to the environment. It must continuously change and adapt to the environment. The training and development function can be characterised as an open system. This presents a major management task. Internal efficiency is just one issue: the major task is to find needed resources, interpret and act on environmental changes, dispose of outputs and control and co-ordinate internal activities.

Using the systems framework, the training and development function can be viewed as a system in itself or a vital subsystem of the larger system. There are basic activities and functions that must be carried out within the training and development subsystem:

- *Boundary Spanning Functions*: This activity is responsible for exchanges with the environment. On the input side it will secure financial and physical resources for the training and development function. On the output side it will market the activities of the function. This activity involves working directly with the external environment.

- *Production Functions*: This function produces the product and service outputs of the training and development department. This is where the primary transformation takes place. Examples of outputs include training and development policy statements, training and development plans, training programmes, open learning material, and trained/developed employees.

- *Maintenance*: This activity is responsible for the smooth running of the training and development function. It includes the preparation of training and development materials, maintenance of training resources etc.

- *Adaptation*: This function is responsible for ensuring that the training and development function adapts to the needs of its environment. It would include activities like training and development, needs identification, research on specific training and development initiatives and evaluation of training and development activities.

- *Management*: This activity is responsible for ensuring the direction and co-ordination of the training and development function. It will include activities like setting goals and policies for the function, devising an appropriate structure within the function and directing tasks.

These five functions/activities are interconnected and often overlap. Figure 9.5 presents a systems model of training and development.

Figure 9.5: A Systems Model of Training and Development

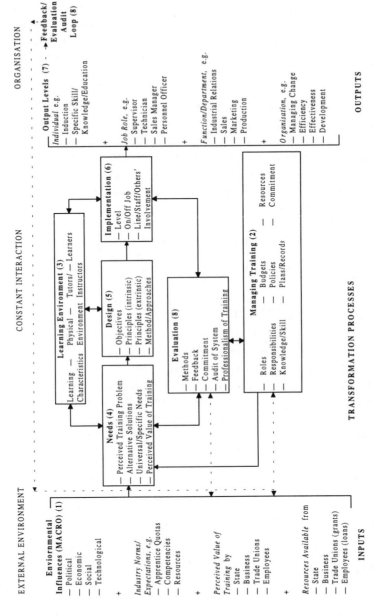

Source: Anderson, C. (1992), *Effective Training Practice*, London: Basil Blackwell.

Basically this model sees training and development as a vital sub-system, receiving inputs (people, information, finance, etc.) and transforming these into outputs (knowledge, skills, attitudes, growth and development, information, etc.), in line with organisational goals and objectives. The training and development transformation process is made up of a number of sub-systems which seek to adapt and maintain the process, ensuring some form of steady state or equilibrium. The outputs of the training and development option allow the creation of more energy. Adopting a proactive stance, and constantly interacting with other sub-systems, the training and development function plays a central role in the overall operating system. It is thus well-placed to respond quickly and effectively, providing solutions at organisational, departmental, group or individual levels.

The systems approach also places training and development in a strategic position, because of its awareness of changes in the internal and external environment, and the facilitation of feedback from other sub-systems (Buckley and Caple, 1992; Reid et al, 1992).

A CONSULTANCY MODEL

Saunders and Holdaway (1992) advocate a consultancy model which can facilitate greater control over what the training specialist does, and how, where and when they do it. They argue that the organisation would benefit because internal consultants offer more focused solutions, and the knowledge and expertise normally gained by hiring external consultants remains within the organisation (Figure 9.6).

Saunders and Holdaway make two important points in relation to their concept of a consultant:

- It is important to distinguish between consultancy skills which are required by all training and development specialists, and an internal consultancy role. The latter requires a particular perspective and a different relationship with stakeholders.

- The consultant is an employee of the organisation in contrast with external training professionals who offer their services to the organisation

Sloman (1994) argues that the adoption of a consultancy model can help the training and development specialist clarify their route through the management of training activities. The consultancy relationship will generally proceed through a number of stages: gaining entry, research and analysis, implementation and disengagement. The latter stage, however, is perhaps not appropriate to the training specialist context. In-house trainers do not disengage. They are continuously networking with stakeholders and their role must be ongoing within the organisation. To operate effectively, the training and development specialist must work effectively with line managers, and be seen as an equal partner with line management in running the business. This is perhaps the most significant limitation of the model. Its most significant contribution is that it offers a useful perspective on the skills required of an effective training and development specialist in the 1990s.

Sloman concludes, however, that overall it is not an appropriate model for the management of training and development within the organisation.

Figure 9.6 A Model of Training Consultancy

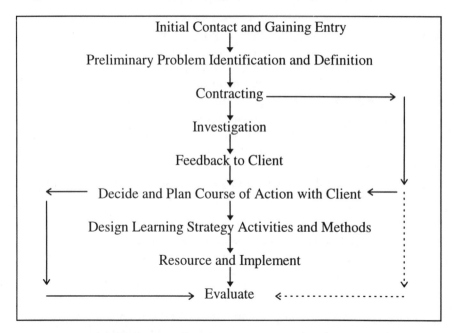

A DEVELOPMENTAL MODEL

There is a more developmental perspective towards training. The traditional view is that learning or behaviour change should continue until the experienced worker standard (EWS) is reached. Implicit in some of the previous models is the notion that "over-learning" could be costly, unnecessary and possibly damaging as trainee frustration may enter the scenario. A more developmental perspective tries to get employees to think for themselves to adapt. This humanistic self-learning perspective contrasts significantly with the traditional scientific management task training perspective which underpins the systematic model. The systematic model tends to reinforce the task specialisation of Taylorites and Post-Taylorites.

The British Institute of Personnel and Development (IPD) has tried to advocate a wider vision of development in the form of continuous learning. Continuous development (CD) is not a body of theory, nor a collection of techniques; it is an approach to the management of learning. Continuous development means (a) learning from real experiences at work; and (b) learning through working life, that is, not confined to useful but occasional injections of "training".

For the individual, CD means lifelong learning with a strong element of self-direction and self management. For the organisation, CD means the management of learning on a continuous basis through the promotion of learning as an integral part of work itself.

Therefore, an emphasis on management development, continuous learning and education rather than training alone is the essence of the developmental model. It is a more sophisticated model in that it sees development as part of a wider set of strategies initiated by management, to help the organisation adopt to change. Reid, Barrington and Kenney (1992) suggest that a developmental model seeks to achieve a high degree of fit between the development requirements of managers and the organisation's strategic objectives. The model recognises that an organisation operates in a dynamic environment and for it to succeed it must constantly adapt.

Bristow and Scarth (1980) enumerate a number of principles which underpin this model.

1. Learning objectives come from real problems and issues: The aim of developmental activities is to provide the situations and conditions for employees to achieve their potential. The model emphasises the use of current problems and issues as a vehicle or opportunity for learning.

2. A collaborative contract is created between the trainer, manager and participant setting out goals, methods and responsibilities: As the objectives of development emerge from the current work situation, it is better to set them collaboratively. The mutual recognition of development needs and the identification of goals is itself part of the learning process and should engender stronger commitment and ownership on the part of the learner.

3. Learning takes place within ongoing work relationships or groups: The model aims to bring changes in roles, norms and structures into the process of learning by developing individuals, together with those with whom they actually work.

4. Learning is seen as a total process involving all aspects of human experience; training tends to be work-related rather than life-based. However, the developmental model views learning in the context of the total person in all the areas of life rather than a particular skill or role that is being performed.

5. The learner directs their own learning: In the conventional systematic model the learner tends to become passive or dependent. Formal programme selling tends to further reinforce this dependence. The essence of the developmental model is to enhance learning and encourage the learner to take ownership and direct the learning.

6. The learning activity is integrated within the organisation: The developmental model views the learning activity as a total organisation process. Line managers and employees have defined roles.

7. Development takes place in the work setting: Burgoyne (1981) classifies the methods used in a developmental model under two headings:

   • Developmental: These are formal methods used to foster learning and include coaching, counselling and development programmes. They can take place within or outside of the organisation.

   • Structural: These are carried out with the intention of shaping effective careers and include mentoring, peer learning, performance management and succession planning. Structural activities are carried out within the organisation.

The model has a number of inherent weaknesses which may limit its application. Developmental and structural activities tend to emerge individualistically in response to specific problems or opportunities. This has the consequence of managers perceiving the training and development function as a series of disconnected sets of activities which may not support each other. Furthermore they may be perceived as a series of tactics without any strategy to integrate them. This fragmentation and lack of strategy may lend very little credibility to the training and development activity.

However, a development model that is well-established and implemented can be successful. It visualises the training process, as consisting of ongoing, strategically, work linked activities. Here are some characteristics of the developmental model:

• organisations should focus on the development of potential;

• development is essentially an on-the-job activity;

- structured activities increase developmental effectiveness;

- the embracing of a personal learning contract enhances the development process;

- emphasis should be given to personal development needs as well as organisational ones;

- development should consist of formal structured and informal interventions that are optimally integrated;

- development should be perceived as a continuous rather than a sporadic process;

- development should be a shared responsibility based on some form of learning contract;

- individuals should take steps to facilitate their own development where the organisation is not willing to do so.

A MARKETING MODEL OF TRAINING AND DEVELOPMENT

There is widespread acceptance of the notion that the training and development function does not market its activities very effectively. The marketing model is perhaps a response to this deficiency. There are two main proponents of this model, namely Stuart and Long (1985) and Gilley and Eggland (1992).

Gilley and Eggland suggest a number of reasons why a marketing model should be adopted. They include the following:

- *Client satisfaction*: to address employees' performance problems and satisfy their developmental needs.

- *Adjustment*: to enable the activities of the training and development function to adopt to changing environmental conditions.

- *Mission*: to help the training and development function to identify a mission for its activities.

- *Promotion*: to help training and development practitioners to develop promotional activities that communicate the values of training and development to organisational decision makers.

- *Programmes*: to help training and development practitioners to design, develop and deliver training and development programmes that are performance-based and needs-focused.

- *Visibility*: to enhance the visibility of training and development practitioners through communications.

- *Preparation*: to help training and development practitioners prepare themselves by considering the environment and culture of the organisations before they implement training and development strategies.

- *Self-appraisal*: to encourage the practice of self-appraisal by learning to identify the strengths and weaknesses of training and development activities.

- *Goals*: to set appropriate goals for the training and development function by identifying both its opportunities and constraints.

- *Resources*: to make effective use of resources by creating training and development strategies. This is especially necessary for training and development specialists in Ireland.

The basic argument of both Stuart and Long and Gilley and Eggland is that training and development functions are too narrow in their focus, and inclined to adopt one of the following orientations:

- *Production orientation*: Many training and development functions focus their efforts on producing as many programmes and activities as possible. The primary concern lies with activity without much attention being given to the real needs of the organisation. It is generally considered a reactive response to problems because there is often little attempt to analyse the training need or assess the relative importance of problems. A production orientation emphasises quantity over quality using measures of success such as number of participants, number of programmes, number of programme days, and so forth.

- *Product orientation*: In this case there is a focus on the product over everything else. The training and development function offers predetermined programmes which may have effective learning features which may not meet the needs of the trainee population. The training and development specialist considers himself/herself an expert over a larger population lacking the skills, abilities and academic qualities to design the learning intervention. A product orientation often causes the training and development department to resist any effort to modify current training and development strategies regardless of the reactions of stakeholder groups.

- *Sales orientation*: Research in the Irish context illustrates that a considerable proportion of training and development specialists believe that their primary purpose is to stimulate interest in training and development activities. As a result, they often fail to invest time in designing appropriate strategies to meet the needs of their stakeholders.

- *Financial orientation*: The essence of this orientation is a concern with costs over all other factors. Whether training and development is undertaken depends on whether it is catered for within the budget. This results in low-priority needs being met because they cost less. Such an orientation may result in a conservative orientation to the function.

The central premise of this model is the adoption of a marketing orientation. Kotler (1986) characterises a marketing orientation as "customer centralised". This means that the training and development function concentrates on increasing stakeholder satisfaction. This requires a client-oriented approach — a genuine interest in improving performance and satisfying the needs of stakeholders. It requires the effective management of the 4 P's: product, price, place and promotion.

Product

The considerations under the product banner relate to the quality of the training itself and the manner in which it is provided (the service). Attention to detail is a priority in relation to a number of issues, including: the level of professional training expertise; relevance and diversity of activities offered; branding associated with external courses; and packaging of training materials.

The overriding emphasis here is on the provision of training which is attuned to the needs of the trainee, and these should be the uppermost consideration in design and delivery of training.

Place

Place relates not only to where training activities are held, but also to distribution factors. The choice of physical location should take trainee logistical details into account, as well as the obvious availability of facilities and suitability of surroundings. Communication and information channels (normally involving provider/participant/manager relationship) must be carefully developed. Optimum participant levels for existing training events, and the speed of response to requests for new events, must also be decided.

Promotion

The active promotion of a product or service is perhaps the most obvious marketing tool. As with most promotional efforts, a useful strategy in a training situation is to draw attention to the benefits of activities provided. For instance, cost benefits (for the organisation) or enhanced career prospects (for the individual) may be highlighted and attention drawn to previous successful examples in this regard. The promotional drive can also be supported by focusing on specific requirements (at organisational, departmental or individual levels) arising out of systematic training needs analysis.

A further useful selling point may reside in the attractiveness of training resources and available technological innovations. Marketing activities should incorporate not just the training content, but also the support services at the trainers' disposal. In marketing, the importance of establishing and maintaining personal contact with clients is widely recognised, ant this personal touch is no less important for trainers.

Finally, to maximise eventual success, any promotional effort must concentrate on gaining the commitment and support of senior and line management for the activities being marketed.

Price

Unlike other marketing variables, which are associated with outgoing expenses, price is the only decision variable with income-generating connotations, and introduces several issues which must be given careful consideration.

The complex relationship between price, quality and trainee perceptions must be seen in subjective terms. In relation to training provision, for instance, "cheap" or "free" events are sometimes perceived as lacking in quality, purely on the basis of their being cheap or free, with the reverse often true of more expensive activities. In price-setting therefore, decision-making should take into account such factors as: the nature of the training need; the type of training being provided; status of the provider; and location (in-house/external).

Market research is also encouraged in this approach, and can incorporate many techniques familiar to trainers (needs analysis, performance appraisal, evaluation of previous events, etc.) supplemented by occasional surveys, questionnaires and interviews. The information gathered during this process can be analysed from a customer perspective, identifying areas where fruitful remedial action can be effected.

In overall terms, this model sets marketing guidelines which assists trainers to become more effective in marketing the training function and ultimately improving their ability to convince top management of the need for ongoing investment in training and development.

The marketing model is not without its weaknesses. It can lead to resource wastage in that it may encourage training and development activities that are not required because a sufficiently high level of competence has already been reached. Simply increasing the number of employees who engage in training and development will not necessarily have an effect on productivity, efficiency or profitability. Implications of a marketing model may lead the training and development specialist to claiming results or improvements that really do not exist. A marketing perspective may lead to a situation where it may create unnecessary needs and wants for training and development programmes. This could seriously hurt the credibility of training and development and its future effectiveness.

In the Irish context there are several major obstacles to implementing a marketing model. Studies by Heraty (1992), Garavan (1995) and other government-sponsored studies highlight a number of difficulties:

- Many training and development specialists lack a long-term commitment to the training and development function.

- Training and development specialists may not maintain or have access to the type of information required for decision-making and planning. Strategic marketing requires adequate and accurate information. It also requires accurate forecasts of future events and actions. Many Irish training and development specialists lack a long-term perspective.

- Some training and development specialists lack the skills to engage in effective marketing, particularly the skills to draw up strategic marketing plans for the function and have them communicated to stakeholders.

- Many training and development practitioners in Ireland rely on the past to determine future action and strategies. Such a narrow-minded focus may lead to an unwillingness to recognise change.

THE ASHRIDGE MODEL

Ashridge Management Research Group (Barham et al, 1988) studied training practices in leading-edge companies in the UK. They identified three levels of sophistication in terms of training and development, and advocate a focused approach which has the following characteristics:

- Training and development and continuous learning by individuals is perceived as necessary for organisational survival.

- Training is considered a competitive weapon.

- Learning is linked both to organisation strategy and to individual goals.

- Learning is viewed as totally continuous through an emphasis on the job development.

- Specialist training is available across the knowledge/skill/value spectrum.

- Self-selection for training is encouraged.

- Training is generally non-directive, unless knowledge-based.

- Many training interventions are utilised.

- There is an emphasis on measuring the effectiveness of training and development.

- The main responsibility for training rests with line management.

- Trainees adopt a wider role.

- There is an emphasis on learning as a process.

- There is a tolerance of failure as part of the learning process.

The Ashridge study suggests that the full potential of training and development is realised in those organisations that adopt a focused approach. The model puts more emphasis on personal development rather than formal training, driven both by the goals of the organisation and the needs of the individual. The model is strong on description rather than presumption. Sloman (1994) suggests that it describes an ideal state for training and development in an organisation and offers some useful benchmarks which can be used to assess progress. It does, however, give little advice to a training specialist who may be operating in an organisation where there is hostility to any training and development activity.

A BUSINESS-FOCUSED MODEL

A business-led model of training and development is associated with the work of Pettigrew et al (1988) and is an advance on the work of the Ashridge group. This model advocates that the propensity of an organisation to train and develop its employees is enhanced when a sufficient combination of proactive forces are in operation. The research undertaken by Pettigrew et al does demonstrate that training and development tends to get a higher profile when the organisation, reacting to a variety of business-related pressures and opportunities, is forced to take a more strategic approach to the management of its human resources. A number of significant triggers come into play. These include:

- business strategy: renewal of competitive edge, changes in product design, changes in manufacturing processes, changes in management systems, and improving quality of existing services and products;

- external labour market strategies;

- internal labour market needs: reduced numbers, high attraction rates, the need to attract and keep high quality recruits;

- internal values and systems: commitment to training and development systems and roles;

- external support for training and development: legislative requirements, funding opportunities, supplier and customer demands.

Figure 9.7 presents the model.

The forces that "trigger" training in an organisation will affect the
development of people in ways specific both to the organisation and to
its internal and external environment. The underlying principle of the
model is that simply investing in people's learning and development
cannot guarantee an effective contribution to the achievement of business goals. The development of people must operate as an integral human resource process falling within the umbrella of a general human
resource strategy that is aligned to corporate strategy.

As with most change initiatives, environmental forces represent the
catalyst for driving some form of employee development, particularly
where significant technological developments signal emerging skill
gaps. To this end, the model stresses the importance of strategic monitoring of the external environment to anticipate changing needs, and the
adoption of some form of strategic planning to cope with these changes.

The extent to which external pressures will facilitate training and development in the organisation is largely dependent on the availability of
the requisite skills in the external labour market. Where these skills exist
externally, the organisation may decide to recruit rather than develop its
internal labour market. However, with the pervasive spread of new technologies, and, concomitantly, the increased competitiveness of product
markets, more and more organisations are recognising the value of enskilling their own employees, and preparing for the day when the requisite skills will no longer be available externally. To this end the quality
of the internal labour market is upgraded and maintained through high
quality recruitment, selection, promotion, multi-skilling and flexibility.

Pettigrew et al (1988) suggests that several elements of the internal
labour market are critical to the effectiveness of training and development initiatives. They explicate a number of these critical factors, i.e.
not only should the function have the support of top management, but
the organisation should promote a training philosophy and foster a
learning culture that promotes continuous development. The authors
recognise the important role that line managers play in the development
of employees, but argue that many such managers are constrained by
time and budgetary concerns which often limit their involvement —
hence the necessity for strategic planning and co-ordinating of activities
to release the pressures placed upon line management, and allow for
their input into the training and development function.

Figure 9.7: Business-Focused Strategic Model

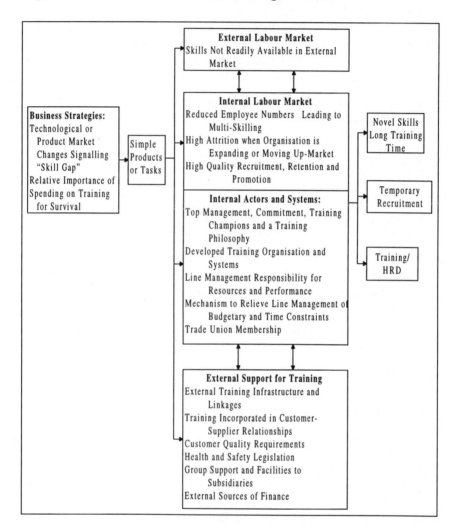

Source: Pettigrew, A., Hendry, C. and Sparrow, P. "The forces that Trigger Training", *Personnel Management*, December 1988.

The model further examines the external training infrastructure, in terms of the extent to which it facilitates organisational training and development, i.e. external sources of finance to offset training costs, training levies, legislation, suppliers and customers. Similarly, they indicate that opportunities for development may be severely curtailed where the organisation makes use of only a few people with a particular skill, or where training requires a long training period or heavy investment, resulting in a preference for temporary forms of recruitment such as the use of contract labour.

Research by Harrison (1992) and Garavan (1992), among others, identifies the types of people policies, which organisations implementing a business-focused model adopt. People policies in such companies tend to be characterised by:

- an emphasis on recruiting and processing those who demonstrate the competencies and behaviours that are needed to achieve organisational objectives;

- an emphasis on skilled leadership and management of people at all levels;

- high investment in training and development at all levels, covering job-related training and retraining, team building, job development and related systems of career planning and development;

- an increasing attempt to provide for an internalised career system characterised by continuous employment for employees who perform well, demonstrate a desire to learn and have positive attitudes towards change;

- incentives and rewards related to specific targets of performance and of behaviour;

- an emphasis on communication.

A STAKEHOLDER MODEL OF TRAINING AND DEVELOPMENT

The models which we have discussed previously in this chapter underplay, or do not significantly account for, the role of stakeholders in the formation and implementation of human resource development strategies. Nor is attention given to the manner in which stakeholder claims relate to contextual variables and the historical development of the training and development function. A stakeholder model of HRD treats stakeholders as a distinct but interrelated element of the HRD process. Figure 9.8 sets out the model.

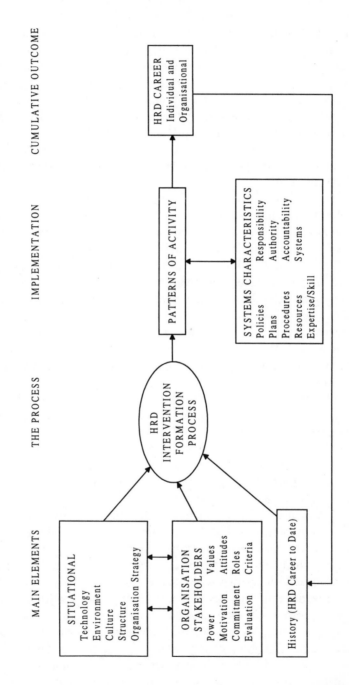

Figure 9.8: A Stakeholder Model of Strategic Human Resource Development

There is also a tendency in the literature to view strategy as a two-stage process of formulation and implementation — the first understood as a cognitive and analytical stage and the second as an administrative one. The stakeholder model uses the term "formation" rather than "formulation". The model basically argues that the formation of HRD strategies is determined by stakeholders, context and history and how these change over time. Any training and development strategy which emerges is influenced by the previous history of the training and development function. The strategic options open to the HRD function are a product of previous constraints and opportunities fashioned by earlier decisions and earlier stakeholder interests. Existing stakeholders will influence the process, but are bounded by the historical pattern of the HRD function's development.

The model identifies five important contextual forces: environment, technology, culture, structure and organisation strategy. The contextual factors are complex in that they account for wider environmental concerns as well as aspects of the organisational context.

The stakeholder influence is analysed in terms of seven characteristics: the power; values; motivations; attitudes; levels of commitment to training and development; perceived roles within training and development; and the evaluation criteria used to assess training and development effectiveness. No one stakeholder will influence the type of strategies adopted. It is the totality of stakeholder influences within the contextual factors and the historical development of the training and development function that is significant.

The phrase "patterns of activities" is used in favour of implementation. There is neither linearity nor inevitability to the pattern of developments of the training and development function within an organisation. The term "training and development career" is used to represent the cumulative effort of the training and development function, suggesting a less determinable perspective of the way in which strategy is implemented. This pattern of activities is influenced by "systems characteristics", which are defined in terms of policies, plans, procedures, rules, systems, expertise and skills that are part of the training and development function's internal workings. Such systems activities will significantly influence the pattern of activities and the cumulative training and development career that will emerge. This cumulative career feeds back into the training and development history and modifies the historical content for future training and development strategy formation.

Consideration of training and development from a stakeholder perspective has a number of important implications for the management of the training and development function, in particular the way in which conflicting priorities are managed, the recognition of power differences and the level of networking which takes place within the organisation.

THE LEARNING ORGANISATION MODEL

The term "learning organisation" has achieved considerable provenance in the training and development literature and amongst practitioners. It is often expressed as a desired or ideal state for training and development in an organisation. There is a diversity of views on the nature of the learning organisation model. Argyris and Schön (1978) argued that organisational learning involves the deletion of errors and their subsequent correction. Though their research focused on organisational learning, they helped develop the concept of the learning organisation. Kolb (1984) advocated the notion of a learning cycle by which individuals learn. Later contributors suggested that an individual's experience of the learning cycle can also be paralleled in the organisation. Sloman (1994) argued that a conceptual leap from individual to corporate learning is central to the notion of the learning organisation. Peters and Waterman (1987) accept this when they advocated that a learning organisation is a truly adaptive organisation trying lots of things, experimenting, making the right sort of mistakes.

Senge (1990) has perhaps made the most significant contribution to our understanding of the learning organisation model. He differentiates learning organisations from traditional authoritarian organisations. He argues that five elements exist in a learning organisation:

1. *Personal mastery*: the capacity to clarify what is important to the individual.

2. *Team learning*: in which assumptions are suspended so that a genuine thinking together occurs.

3. *Mental models*: the capacity to reflect on internal pictures of the world to see how they shape action.

4. *Shared vision*: the ability to build a sense of commitment in a group based on what people would really like to create.

5. *Systems thinking*: the capacity for putting things together and seeking holistic solutions.

He describes systems thinking as the fifth descriptive because it integrates the others.

Hammond and Wille (1991) argue that the learning organisation is of value when deliberate attempts are made to create conditions fundamental to its growth. They use the phrase "to man" to describe bringing together of people to achieve objectives in conditions where they are seeking ways of doing things in a better way. They envisage the learning organisation to be continuously looking at the detail of their actions in the light of the whole and informed by a shared vision.

Pedlar, Burgoyne and Boydell (1991) use the term learning "company" rather than organisation. They visualise the organisation as a "jigsaw" made up of eleven components, as shown below:

1. A learning approach to strategy formulation

2. Participative policy-making

3. Using information for learning

4. Formative accounting and control

5. Internal exchange of information

6. Flexibility in reward systems

7. Structures which facilitate learning

8. Inter-company learning

9. Continuous monitoring of the external environment

10. The creation of a learning climate

11. Self-development opportunities for all

Pearn and Kandola (1993) have examined the steps necessary to make the learning organisation a reality. These actions include the necessity to examine the concept at top management level, analyse the state of learning in the organisation, examine the role of training and trainers, upgrade the learning skills of employees, develop team learning and analyse jobs in terms of learning needs.

There is, however, a general recognition that the learning organisation model is not very precise. It describes utopian conditions. Honey (1991) offers a pragmatic perspective when he states that the conditions are impossible to create across the total organisation. He advocates that the training specialist should strive to create a mini-learning organisation in the parts they can influence. Incremental changes of this nature may eventually become transformational.

WHICH MODEL IS APPROPRIATE?

We have discussed 13 models of training and development in this chapter. They represent a progression in terms of sophistication and strategic approach. The factors that determine the choice of model were discussed in Chapter 8 and include technology, strategy, structure and culture of the organisation. The power and expertise of the training and development specialist will also be a significant factor.

SUMMARY

This chapter has sought to highlight some of the alternative models of training and development practice which exist. It will be apparent that the development of these models represents a fundamental shift in emphasis from one that is operational to one that is strategic. Many of the early models of training and development practice had their roots in education theory. They advocated individual, planned and systematic approaches which put an emphasis on operational problems. They also favoured off-the-job learning events. The more contemporary models have shifted the emphasis away from the individual to the organisation. They place training and development within the context of the organisation's environment, strategy and culture. They also extend the arena of learning to include both on and off-the-job learning, formal and informal, individual and organisationally focused. The essential features of the alternative models are presented in Figure 9.9. Consideration of the models has prepared us to consider training roles, responsibilities and philosophies in the next chapter.

Figure 9.9: A Comparative Summary of Alternative Training and Development/HRD Models

Model	Characteristics	Focus	Limitations
Unsystematic/ Fragmented Model	• Unplanned approach to training and development • No training policies • Individuals largely responsible for their own training	Operational	• Ad hoc, reactive • Training viewed as a cost rather than an asset
Problem-Centred/Planned Maintenance Model	• Involves the identification and prioritising of performance problems coupled with generation and evaluation of results	Operational	• Very reactive • High risk of inaccurate identification of priority problems • May lead to wasted resources
Systematic/ Formalised Model	• Grounded in systems theory • Highly structured • Rational means of directing organisation resources • A chain of events, from identification of needs to evaluation of outcomes	Operational	• Too simplistic • Low applicability in times of uncertainty • Does not recognise individual differences • Fails to consider the context within which training occurs
Cycle of Training Model	• Adopts a stakeholder approach • Considers learning a total organisational process • Consider wider organisational implications	Semi-strategic	• No incorporation of human resource considerations into strategic business planning • No facilitation of line management involvement

Model	Characteristics	Focus	Limitations
Transitional Model	• A double-loop of corporate strategy and learning • Recognises that strategies are not necessarily planned • Training is embedded in a wider organisational context	Strategic	• The strategy loop may be difficult to recognise within an organisation • It does not offer any practical advice to practitioners • Requires an experienced practitioner to operate effectively
Systems Model	• Views organisation as an open system with many training subsystems in interaction with one another.	Semi-strategic	• May result in too much of an internal focus. • Lack of integration between sub-systems.
Consultancy Model	• Advocates that the training specialist operate in a consultant mode • Provides training specialist with control over activities • Requires training specialist to develop consultancy skills	Strategic/ Operational	• Training specialist cannot disengage from the organisation once the assignment is completed • Does not fully recognise that training specialist is a continuing relationship

Model	Characteristics	Focus	Limitations
Ashridge Model	• Advocates a focused approach to training and development • Sees training as a competitive weapon • Training and development is intrinsic to the organisation and operates continuously	Strategic	• It is a descriptive rather than a prescriptive model • It does not indicate how training and development may become more focused • Training specialist will have difficulty with this model in an unreceptive environment
Developmental Model	• Structured O-J-T • Emphasises the learning contract • Joint responsibility for training and development	Operational	• Too much emphasis on development • May be viewed as impractical and not cost effective
Marketing Model	• Customer orientation to training and development practices • Identifies marketing guidelines to promote the training function	Strategic	• Training specialist has to have a customer focus. • Puts emphasis on identifying needs but may require a lot of expertise
Business-Focused Model	• Relates training needs to business requirements • Identifies external triggers for change • Stipulates the necessity for top management and line management support	Strategic	• Inadequate consideration of the stakeholder influences internally • Fails to consider the needs of individual employees

Model	Characteristics	Focus	Limitations
Stakeholder Model	• Looks at total context including stakeholders • Classifies other interacting variables	Strategic	• May have problems of applicability if organisation is not advanced in training terms
Learning Organisation Model	• Advocates that learning takes place at all levels within the organisation • Organisation has built-in learning capacities • Learning is continuous and transformational • Requires systems thinking on the part of the training and development specialist	Strategic	• A lack of precision in model • A Utopian view of how training should operate • Difficulty in applying it across the organisation • Requires a versatile training specialist

Source: Adapted from Heraty, N: (1992) "Training and Development: A Study of Practices in Irish-Based Companies", unpublished MBS thesis, University of Limerick.

10

TRAINING ROLES, RESPONSIBILITIES, TASKS AND PHILOSOPHIES

INTRODUCTION AND LEARNING OBJECTIVES

This chapter focuses on the training and development specialist. In particular we focus on types of trainer roles, responsibilities and philosophies. Having read this chapter you will understand:

♦ the key influences on trainer roles;

♦ the allocation of responsibilities for training and development within the organisation;

♦ the range of roles that training and development specialists may perform in an organisation;

♦ the relationship between training role type and power;

♦ alternative strategies to attain and hold on to power;

♦ the range of philosophies that the training and development specialist may have about training and development.

INFLUENCES ON TRAINER ROLES AND RESPONSIBILITIES

As we have outlined in Chapter Eight, there are numerous characteristics of the organisation itself which impact on training and development. These include the strategies and policies pursued by the organisation, its culture, structure and technology, its size and growth stage, as well as forces in its external environment. These factors interact to establish the climate of the organisation at any given time, and have a direct impact on the organisational approach to the "people" side of the business — in other words, on what has traditionally been called personnel management.

Personnel Management and Human Resource Management

We can readily associate a wide range of areas and activities with the human resource management function — planning, recruitment and selection, training and development, remuneration systems, performance appraisal, industrial relations, communications, health and safety, personnel records, etc., etc. A list such as this, of course, represents no more than a set of building blocks for which an architectural design is as yet unspecified, but it is important to note the inclusion of training and development as an activity within the general sphere of personnel management or human resource management. Armstrong (1988) provides the necessary blueprint, in stating that HRM is concerned with:

- obtaining, developing and motivating the human resources required by the organisation to achieve its objectives;

- developing an organisation structure and climate, and evolving a management style which will promote co-operation and commitment throughout the organisation;

- making the best use of the skills and capacities of all those employed in the organisation;

- ensuring that the organisation meets its social and legal responsibilities towards its employees, with particular regard to the conditions of employment and quality of working life provided for them.

Again, it is not difficult to perceive the integral role of training and development inherent in these concerns. However, while these points offer considerable help in illuminating what personnel management means in organisational terms, they must be interpreted flexibly. As Armstrong (1988) himself outlines, the specific shape and thrust of human resource management is dependent on the context of the organisation itself. Furthermore, recent years have witnessed considerable discussions about the changing nature of personnel management and the concept of human resource management (HRM). Detailed examination of this issue is outside the scope of this book (aspects of this debate are discussed in Guest, 1987; Storey, 1991; Gunnigle, 1991; Blyton and Turnbull, 1992; among others) but is important to understand the potential impact of the chosen human resource management policy on the role of training and development in the organisation. This has been outlined in some detail by Gunnigle (1991), and we can use this work as a basis for summarising this relationship.

The Range and Dimensions of Human Resource Management Policy Choice

In terms of human resource management policy choice, the range of approaches which may be adopted by any particular organisation is very broad. It is perhaps best to visualise this range by contrasting two positional extremes, one represented by traditional personnel management and the other by strategic HRM. In the traditional sense, considerations surrounding the management of human resources rarely encroach on decision-making at strategic level, being cast more in the reactive realm of dealing with short-term issues and problems. Strategic HRM, on the other hand, is specifically concerned with incorporating human resource considerations into strategic decision-making, being focused on maximising the utilisation of human resources in the pursuit of organisational objectives and goals. Human resource management policy choice can therefore be reflected in either of these positions, or in the various positions or states which lie in between.

There are several core dimensions which help to provide further understanding of these human resource management policy positions.

Strategic Integration

Low strategic integration means that human resource issues do not feature in strategic planning and are essentially a peripheral management concern. As we have already seen, this may be related to traditional personnel management approaches, prevalent in organisations where the primary business considerations are seen, for example, in operational, marketing or financial terms. Meanwhile, the realm of HRM supports greater levels of strategic integration. Here, however, it is necessary to differentiate between strategic HRM and business-led HRM (see Wood and Peccei, 1990). Briefly, business-led HRM reflects a situation where personnel policies and practices are linked to the strategic objectives of the organisation, but are themselves seen to constitute a lower-order strategic activity. On the other hand, the concept of strategic HRM espouses the integration of personnel policies and practices with the strategic planning of the organisation. Thus, the highest level of strategic integration is associated with strategic HRM.

In this context, the extent of strategic integration has an obvious impact on training and development within the organisation. It can be strongly suggested that, where a high level of strategic integration is evidenced, training and development will be seen as a long-term investment in the development of human resources and in the process of organisational learning. Consequently, the training and development function is more likely to enjoy the support of top management; have a pervasive influence; be involved in the development of strategic plans; and focus its activities on the achievement of strategic objectives. In stark contrast, a low level of strategic integration suggests that training and development will have a short-term perspective and will be regarded primarily as a (sometimes necessary) cost. The training and development function is likely to operate at the boundaries of the organisation, with its activities concentrated almost exclusively on reacting to problems.

Individualism

Another element of personnel policy choice may be highlighted through the extent to which the management of human resources reflects an individual perspective. High individualism is characterised by efforts aimed at developing human resources to their maximum potential.

A range of sophisticated personnel policies are pursued, incorporating comprehensive employee development as a central feature. In organisations where a low individualistic line is followed, management tend to view human resources in commodity terms and as a cost to be controlled. In line with such a philosophy, some narrowly-focused training activity may be deemed a necessity but there is a distinct lack of emphasis on broader-based employee development. If these two positions represent extremes, "paternalism" may be said to occupy much of the middle ground in between (Purcell, 1987). Here, a benevolent and caring approach is taken, and personnel policies reflect these considerations. However, while management see employees as a resource whose welfare must be catered for, they do not embrace the notion of employees as a resource to be developed, and therefore place little emphasis on the issue of training and development.

Collectivism

The final dimension, collectivism, is manifested in the extent of employee influence over decisions on employment-related issues, and the degree to which the right of involvement in this context is accepted and legislated for. High collectivism means that employee involvement is actively encouraged, with specific arrangements and mechanisms in place to ensure that management decision-making is actively influenced in the process. The resulting increase in autonomy can impact on training and development in a variety of ways, including:

- facilitating the acquisition of new knowledge and skills required through the adoption of changes to work organisation or operational procedures;

- supporting enhanced opportunities for self-development;

- training needs arising from greater employee responsibility for quality;

- supporting the implementation of team-working initiatives.

Low collectivism is associated with policies which repress employee involvement and effectively deny employees any influence over decision-making. The middle ground in this dimension has been defined as adversarial collectivism, where employee involvement may be grudgingly or reluctantly conceded, usually in insignificant terms. In either of these latter forms, the direct impact on training and development is seen as minimal. Indeed, by their very nature, the associated personnel policies are unlikely to encompass the notion of employee development to any great extent.

These dimensions illustrate the significant impact of personnel policy choice on training and development. They also highlight the fact that, in general terms, personnel policy choice revolves around two extreme positions on how human resources should be managed. One emphasises control over employees, while the other invokes employee involvement and commitment. An ever-increasing number of organisations are employing a commitment strategy, in response to the need for greater flexibility and an improved capability for coping with change. This has led to a growing focus on strategic HRM, as the most potent representation of such an approach. The thrust of strategic HRM is directed through the full spectrum of "personnel" activities, to maximise the contribution of human resources to organisational goals. This implies an integral role for the personnel function, and consequently for training and development.

RESPONSIBILITY FOR TRAINING AND DEVELOPMENT

The responsibility for training and development in organisations is often perceived as the exclusive preserve of the training specialist. However, it is important that communal responsibility is accepted for the training and development process, with different elements especially pertinent to various internal individuals and groups.

Top Management

There is strong consensus that the effectiveness of training and development in the organisation can be related to the degree of commitment shown by top management to the process. This must be seen as a logical deduction; after all, it is top management who hold the ultimate responsibility not only for setting strategic objectives, but also for devising the policies and plans through which these are expected to be achieved. Furthermore, it is top management who set the tone of organisational culture and values, and, in the practical reality of organisational life, this is transmitted mainly by virtue of their actions. It is the actions of top management which reflect the value placed by the organisation on its human resources, and which demonstrate their perception of the role of training and development in this context. The criticality of a company philosophy supportive of training, expressed through top management commitment. is emphasised by Pettigrew et al (1988). In addition, Harrison (1992) states that the cultural environment of the organisation is primarily created and perpetuated by top management, and consequently the overriding responsibility for training and development must be borne at this level.

The reality, however, is that in many cases top management is not committed to training and development activities. A number of reasons can be cited for this lack of top management support.

- Previous and present generations of top managers were not always systematically trained or developed as managers. They tend to devalue training and development and, in fact, may perceive it as either irrelevant or indeed as a threat to their position.

- Top managers are often too busy to consider the benefits of training and development or identify what resources and facilities are available.

- When organisational survival is the priority, the long-term fruits of investment in training and development are seen as something of a luxury.

- King (1989) points out that, in many organisations, expenditure on training is not treated as an investment in a financial sense but is instead perceived as a cost. This manifests itself in the lack of budgets, secrecy about the amount spent on training and development and the total reliance on external grant assistance. The Challenge to Complacency report (Coopers & Lybrand, 1985) supports this view on expenditure on training and development and concludes that the implicit link between training and profitability is often not recognised, or indeed understood.

- The training profession itself must also accept some of the responsibility for the lack of support from top management. Training specialists have not invested sufficiently in the marketing and quality of their services. This hinders their ability to convince top managers of the need to invest in training and development and of its contribution to improved organisational performance.

- Brown et al (1989) found that management training is primarily aimed at those at the bottom end of the management hierarchy. Senior level managers were often not included in training strategies. Reasons cited for this lack of training included senior management reluctance, the difficulty of providing the right sort of developmental activities, and doubts about the costs and benefits of such training. Senior managers are often not very concerned about their own development which may inhibit their ability to act as role models in a management development context.

Specific responsibilities pertaining to top management are put forward by the Training Technology Programme (1987) and Reid et al (1992). These are incorporated into the following summary, suggesting that top management should:

- Bear the primary responsibility for creating and sustaining a positive attitude to training and development in all its manifestations.

- Ensure that an integral role for training and development is interwoven with the strategic planning and implementation process. This will send a clear signal to the organisation at large about the importance of training and development.

- Determine training and development objectives and policies, in consultation with the training specialist.

- Provide the range of resources needed to enable the training and development function to operate effectively. This range includes budgetary allocation, people, facilities, time, etc.

- Periodically review the effectiveness of the training and development process in relation to the objectives set, and update policies and objectives in line with changing organisational circumstances (in consultation with the training specialist).

- Be personally associated with, and involved in, formal training and development events. A great boost to the importance of such events can be added by way of an introduction by a member of the top management team, as well as through subsequent enquiries to individuals about the learning benefits accrued.

- Consider their own personal and self-development needs, and initiate appropriate interventions. This is a significant way to lead by example, and provides an influential role model for subordinates. However, it is widely acknowledged that these measures are commonly neglected by top managers, even those who are apparently committed to training and development for all other members of the organisation.

Top management commitment to training and development is not a matter for delegation — it must be transmitted downwards, permeating the entire organisation. By accepting and carrying out the preceding responsibilities, top managers portray their commitment in an action oriented fashion, and show vital leadership in the area of training and development.

Line Management

There is widespread agreement that the line manager carries certain responsibility in relation to continuous employee development. A number of reasons can be put forward to justify this responsibility, including (a) adequate training must be provided to enable employees to perform their work to specific standards, and (b) employees should be afforded ongoing learning opportunities to develop their abilities and potential.

Line managers are ideally placed to:

- implement the organisation's training policy within their sphere of influence (Reid et al, 1992);
- continually assess employee training needs;
- facilitate in identifying appropriate wider development opportunities;
- provide advice, guidance, and counselling to employees on training and development issues.

Zenger (1988) points out that strategically-focused training and development functions have generated an enthusiastic involvement of line managers. Such involvement can manifest itself in a number of ways, not least among them the following:

- line managers conducting training sessions;
- consultation with line managers on changes they wish to witness in their subordinate's performance;
- line managers becoming involved in the coaching and counselling of subordinates;
- line managers learning skills being updated;
- active involvement in the training and development policy and planning processes;
- line managers being made responsible for the identification of training and development needs within their department.

Gunnigle and Flood (1990) see responsibility for continuous employee development resting with the immediate manager or supervisor. In their view the line manager is (a) best placed to assess, on an ongoing basis, the training and development needs of subordinates; (b) able to identify development routes for subordinates; and (c) ideally placed to provide advice, direction and counselling to subordinates. Mumford lends further support for this viewpoint in classifying the line manager as a key helper in the management development process. Garavan (1987) identifies the types of skills that line managers require to be effective participants in the training and development process, including the ability to facilitate learning, specific coaching and counselling skills, and the ability to adopt a participate and shared learning methodology.

Figure 10.1: Arguments Supportive of Line Involvement in Training

- Line involvement makes for a more responsive training capability.

- Line involvement lends credibility to the training function.

- Line involvement is more efficient.

- Performance problems are better identified.

- Performance standards are more accurately set.

- The content of training programme is more focused.

- Future training needs are better addressed.

- Transfer of learning back to the job is better.

- Line managers know the business — they are the ones charged with making it a success.

- Line involvement provides opportunity for practice and experimentation.

Research undertaken with line managers identifies several dimensions associated with the training and development aspect of their role. The following summaries highlight the basic elements linked to each dimensions.

1. Facilitator of learning — the line manager concentrates on developing the learning capabilities of employees by:

    - creating a suitable climate for learning

    - clarifying learning goals

- ensuring learning "comfort levels" are not exceeded

- relating past learning experiences to present activities

- providing useful learning concepts

- explaining the nature of the learning process (learning to learn).

2. Coaching/Counselling — the line manager focuses on providing assistance and encouragement to employees on an individual basis, through activities such as:

- identifying performance problems

- adopting a problem-solving approach

- providing regular and pertinent feedback on performance

- providing appropriate development opportunities through the work process

- attempting to enhance employees future job/career prospects.

3. Joint decision-making — the line manager seeks to involve employees in the decision-making process, through:

- shared responsibility for training and development

- establishing joint agreement on learning objectives

- using participative training methods

- encouraging self-development initiatives.

4. No involvement — here, the line manager envisages no direct personal role in the training and development process. This is typified in perceptions such as:

- training is of little value to the organisation

- the training function is entirely responsible for employee development

- training and development needs are best fulfilled through external events.

The first three dimensions — facilitator of learning, coaching/counselling, and joint decision-making — can be linked, separately and in combination, with positive learning outcomes. However, the remaining dimension, where no involvement in the training and development process is envisaged for the line manager, has a seriously undermining impact. For this reason, role clarification may represent a useful means of outlining the expected involvement of line managers and of allocating responsibilities in relation to training and development. Furthermore, it is vitally important that line managers are given the resources and training necessary to enable them to carry out these responsibilities, in tandem with measures to motivate them to do so. Harrison (1992) suggests four requirements in this regard and these may be summarised as follows:

1. Line managers' own job descriptions must focus on employee development, as a crucial element of their task.

2. Competence and motivation concerning such tasks must be seen as a prerequisite for selection to line management positions.

3. Training and development must be provided in the appropriate skills. These include performance appraisal, counselling and coaching, assessing training needs, and communicating effectively.

4. Reward systems must reflect the importance of employee development in line managers' performance.

This approach both enables and encourages the line manager to play an integral role in employee development, in conjunction with maximising employee effectiveness. While the nature and extent of involvement in the training and development process will undoubtedly vary from organisation to organisation, key elements of the line manager's role, in this regard, should include:

- promoting a learning environment and enhancing opportunities for employee development;

- accurately assessing individual and departmental training needs;

- securing employee agreement on, and commitment to fulfilling training needs;

- providing personal support and facilitating employees' learning;

- appropriately timing training and development activities to circumvent the possibility of irrelevant and/or non-transferrable learning;

- ensuring that the learning process is ongoing and systematic.

The relationship between line managers and the training and development function can somehow be a problematic one. Research and commentary by Ashton (1986), Mumford (1989) and Garavan (1987) identify a number of issues which need to be considered by a strategically-oriented training and development function:

- A key issue identified by many commentators is that of ownership of training and development activities. Key questions cited include: who are the key parties in the training and development system? Is there a need for an explicit learning contract? How are training and development activities to be shared? What is the policy/operations boundary?

- The competence of the line manager is vital to the successful implementation of strategic training and development and is cited by many commentators as a particularly difficult issue. Competency difficulties most often cited include: inability to appraise performance, lack of counselling skills, inability to identify skill gaps, poor listening skills, inability to emphasise with subordinates. Allied to these competency deficiencies may be a motivational one. Many areas of training and development are long-term in focus thus leading to the perception among some line managers that little impact on current performance may accrue from their involvement in the development of subordinates. Many line managers are also slow to acknowledge their deficient learning skills.

- Another critical issue is that of role definition. Ashton (1986) argues persuasively that different training and development activities require different degrees of involvement from line managers. Performance appraisal for example requires high line managers' involvement as does coaching, counselling, etc. Formal training programmes and self-development activities require considerably less involvement. This suggests that some form of role clarification is necessary as a basis for developing a strategically-oriented training and development function.

The Individual

At the outset, it is interesting to note that there is far more written about the responsibilities of management, in relation to employee development, and of the trainer, in relation to learners, than there is about the responsibilities of the employee "to be developed" or of those in "learning" situations. Indeed, this statement in itself provides a useful way of categorising individual responsibilities.

Harrison (1992) addresses individual responsibility for training and development, and advocates that:

- individuals should think about their own learning needs, in relation to their work, forthcoming changes, and their career aspirations;

- individuals should articulate their needs in this regard, and become involved in the decision-making process surrounding the fulfilment of training needs;

- self-directed learning and self-development are increasingly important for everyone, whether in or out of employment.

Figure 10.2: Suggested Processes for Advancing Line Involvement

- The training department must cultivate line involvement by being more responsive; having a professional approach; a good track record; and working in partnership with the line.

- It must prove its capability in areas such as problem diagnosis, support for business objectives, strategic planning and corporate change, and its ability to network within the company.

- The line should be encouraged to become involved in training for "developmental" reasons.

- Involve the line in designing training, delivering training programmes, reinforcing learning back on the job.

- Involve the line in performance issues — setting performance targets, linking training to performance problems.

- Speak the same "language" as the line manager.

- The training function can encourage the line by adopting a strong customer service ethos, by really listening to the needs of the line manager, and by responding to their needs.

- Position training as a strategic resource.

- Win over the line supervisors.

- Give the line the skills needed to be fully involved in training — at identification, design and delivery stages.

There are indeed meritorious proposals, and may be related to the aspirations of the individual stakeholder group (see Chapter 8) which includes financial support for individual development, increased promotion opportunities, improved labour mobility, and the avoidance of skill obsolescence. However, it is important to bear in mind the potential impact of the personnel policy choice of the organisation on this entire agenda. A strategy of commitment and involvement is likely to reflect the espousal of these responsibilities by individuals being actively promoted, while a control strategy is unlikely to witness any movement in this direction being tolerated, let alone encouraged.

Another aspect of responsibility in relation to training and development concerns the individual in a formal learning situation. Individuals participating in formal training and development activities should ensure that the benefits from learning outcomes are maximised, for themselves and for the organisation. In attempting to outline the components of this responsibility, a useful list of suggestions is provided in the Training Technology Programme (1987). These are incorporated into the following list, set out in a time frame format.

Before the Event

Individuals should gain an understanding of:

- why the training is being provided
- the learning objectives
- the proposed training methods.

They should ensure that the training is relevant to their:

- own specific needs
- experience and background
- abilities and capabilities
- personal development.

During the Activity

They should:

- participate and contribute as necessary and appropriate
- show and maintain interest
- raise queries if a point is not fully understood (remembering that in a learning context there is no such thing as a silly question!)
- ask the trainer to repeat a statement or procedure if necessary
- inform the trainer if, and how or where, the training need is not being satisfied
- provide occasional feedback to the trainer.

In the Immediate Future

They should:

- reflect on the learning process experienced

- consolidate learning with practice

- perhaps do some self-training as a follow-up

- give appropriate feedback to supervisor/front line manager.

At a Later Stage

They should:

- evaluate the training activity and assessing its relevance and suitability

- give feedback as appropriate to indicate where training might be modified to produce better results.

Embracing these elements of responsibility can lead to individuals enhancing their own learning processes, the transferability to the work situation of training received, their motivation to participate in future training activities and their desire to seek self-development opportunities. In this way also, individuals can contribute to improving the effectiveness of training and development within the organisation itself.

ROLES OF THE TRAINING AND DEVELOPMENT SPECIALIST

Using the plural term "roles" in the heading of this section is quite deliberate. It serves to highlight at the outset the incongruity of suggesting that there is one definitive version of the training specialist's role. To do so would be tantamount to ignoring the impact of the many variables lurking in the organisational context of training and development, as outlined in the previous chapter. Furthermore, even in situations where the responsibilities of the training specialist may be fairly well defined, it is quite probable that these will involve the adoption of a range of roles in attempting to maximise the effectiveness of training and development. Another important factor to consider is the evolving nature of the training specialist's role, bearing in mind the constantly changing environment of organisations themselves. This change is endemic, and likely to become even more so, and therefore the success of the training and development function is inextricably linked to the success of the training specialist in adapting to such change.

All of this, of course, does not exclude the fact that there are many elements of "best practice" which may have universal application in relation to the training specialist's role; neither is it to suggest that certain approaches, within a particular role, may or may not prove more effective and beneficial. These will indeed come into our considerations.

However, it is important to gain a full understanding of the inconstancy surrounding this issue. In appreciating the fluidity of their "role", training specialists may be enabled to adopt the mode or modes best suited to their circumstances, and hence, to enhance the process of training and development in organisational terms.

Variations on a Similar Theme

There is no shortage of literature on the role and functions of the training specialist, and many models and frameworks have been put forward in this respect. Let us now look briefly at some of these.

A combination of three roles, which encompass the work of the training specialist, is set out by Nadler (1969) as follows:

1. *Administrator* — essentially performing a "minder" role, including activities such as supervising ongoing programmes and arranging facilities and finance.

2. *Learning specialist* — functioning as an instructor, a curriculum builder, and a methods and materials developer.

3. *Problem-solver* — acting variously as an advocate, an expert, an alternative identifier, a catalyst and a process specialist.

All these functions are viewed as equally important, being performed in parallel to fulfil the training specialist role.

Four varying types of trainer role were identified by Bennett and Leduchowicz (1983):

1. *Caretaker* — here the need for training is associated with maintaining the smooth running of the organisation.

2. *Educator* — who uses training as a vehicle for changing systems and procedures within the organisation and adopt traditional approaches to achieve this.

3. *Evangelist* — with a similar thrust as educators, but adopting more radical approaches.

4. *Innovator* — also mainly concerned with bringing about change, but pursuing this by acting in a largely advisory capacity.

These are seen as separate and distinct roles which are adopted by training specialists. They are therefore seen to coincide with particular contextual factors in the organisation or with the personal perception of the training specialist.

From a study of various classifications, Bennett (1988) suggests that there are five key trainer roles (Buckley and Caple, 1992):

1. *Trainer* — the actual carrying out of training activities is seen as the primary concern and responsibility of the training specialist.

2. *Provider* — may be described as an expansion of the "trainer" role, whereby the training specialist is involved in the identification of needs, and in designing and delivering training programmes.

3. *Consultant* — as the term might suggest, the training specialist is mainly concerned with analysing organisational problems and suggesting appropriate training solutions.

4. *Innovator* — similar to the previous "innovator" role, with the primary focus on bringing about change and performing an advisory role to that end.

5. Manager — carrying out managerial tasks such as overseeing the development and implementation of training plans, and controlling and organising the operational details of the training department.

Buckley and Caple (1992) argue that the work of many training specialists is likely to incorporate certain elements from each of these roles.

These examples, and others (see, for example, Mumford, 1971; Phillips and Shaw, 1989) may essentially be seen as variations on a similar theme, whereby the role of the training specialist is perceived in terms of a range of possibilities. Furthermore, these may be broadly divided into three core roles of (a) maintaining the function; (b) managing/developing the function; (c) organisational change.

Different Perspectives on the Training Specialist's Role

We have noted the multiplicity of suggested models of the training specialist role. Johnson (1990) presents an interesting review of these models, relating their methodology and design to the resulting portrayal of the trainer. Three major perspectives on the role of the training specialist emerge, summarised below.

The Empirical Approach

This approach focuses on the nature of the work performed by the training specialist, based on factual and observational data. Johnson (1990) reports on a survey conducted with 28 training managers (all of whom were pursuing a Masters in Training and Development), using Morgan and Costello's (1989) "Trainer Task Inventory" model as a framework. This model categorises the tasks of the training specialist under three core dimensions, graded in accordance with their perceived centrality to the training role. These dimensions, as plotted in a decreasing order of centrality, are seen as (a) helping people to learn and develop; (b) helping people to solve performance problems; and (c) helping people to anticipate needs and problems, and to formulate policies. The model also incorporates four core elements of the training specialist's role, namely administrating, managing, knowing the organisation and employer's business, and self-development, which are depicted as cutting across all role dimensions. It highlighted a number of key trends.

Helping People to Learn and Develop. The perceived centrality and importance of this dimension was borne out by the responses received. The highest rate of involvement was recorded here, with 58 per cent of the associated tasks being performed. Another interesting feature was the extent of involvement in tasks related to specific areas of activity. Designing training events (81 per cent of identified tasks performed) and delivering training (67 per cent of tasks) where the most common activities with evaluation (only 51 per cent of tasks) receiving the least attention. Johnson (1990) interprets these figures to indicate a trend towards supply-led rather than demand-led training.

A further aspect of the results worth noting is the relatively balanced average distribution of responses.

Helping to Solve Performance Problems. The survey group undertook some 48 per cent of the tasks categorised within this dimension. However, a far greater dispersal of task involvement was evidenced, with some respondents showing almost total involvement, some recording very little or none at all, while others were ranged across all points in between. This suggests to Johnson (1990) that performing tasks related to solving performance problems is seen as a discretionary area for the training specialist.

Helping to Anticipate Future Needs. Only 24 per cent of the tasks identified with anticipating future needs, and generally facilitating the change process, were performed. Furthermore, a very skewed response distribution may be gleaned from the results. Most respondents declared minimal or no involvement in this area, a minority performed many of the relevant tasks. Very few occupied the ground in between these extremes. It was also revealed that those with the greatest involvement were all associated with large organisations. According to Johnson (1990), these results suggest that involvement at the strategic level is not within the discretion of the training specialist, but is more related to the size of the organisation.

Core Elements of Role. The performance of tasks identified with the proposed four core elements of the training specialist's role was returned at the following levels:

- self-development — 81 per cent (all respondents were Masters students)

- knowing the organisation/employer's business — 69 per cent

- administrating — 60 per cent

- managing — 47 per cent.

A normal distribution was evidenced for the first three elements, but a wide dispersal of responses was indicated for involvement in managing the training function. Johnson (1990) again suggests that the extent of involvement in this role element is largely a discretionary one.

The results of the Johnson study, conducted with training managers pursuing a Training and Development Masters, provides a useful opportunity to highlight some significant points.

1. The tasks identified with helping people to learn — perceived by this study as the most central to the training specialist's role — can be linked to a systematic approach to training. Many of the respondent specialists placed higher emphasis on designing and delivering training events than on assessment and evaluation activities. This may be due to the relatively active orientation of the former activities and their proximity to "training" itself, compared perhaps to the tediousness and detachment of the latter. However, the systematic approach to training (in its most basic form) visualises four activities — assessing training needs, designing training, delivering training, and evaluation — as a cyclical and continuous sequence of events. With each activity exerting critical influence on the nature of the "next" activity, the whole is seen as very much greater than the sum of its parts. Therefore, the rationale underlying the effectiveness of systematic training is undermined by lack of attention to any of its core activities. The notion that the tasks surrounding the systematic approach to training are those most central to the training specialist's role, suggests a rather narrow perspective of training and development within the organisation.

2. Some training specialists may indeed feel that helping to solve performance problems is a discretionary area of activity, as the survey results seem to imply. However, training specialists who opt out of this sphere of involvement weaken not only their own credibility and

influence, but also the relevance of training and development within the organisation. As Johnson (1990) points out, training directed at solving productivity and performance problems raises the overall credibility of training across the organisation. In addition, this area provides a real opportunity for the training specialist to relate, in quantitative terms, the benefits which can be accrued from this type of intervention. In so doing, the potentially positive influence on stakeholders such as top management, line management, and individual employees, cannot be overestimated.

3. The results may be interpreted to suggest that involvement in anticipating future needs and in the change process is more dependent on the organisational environment than on training specialists themselves. While this may be true to a certain extent, the discretion of the training specialist in elevating training and development issues to the strategic level may not be quite so restricted. It can revolve around the "twin peaks" of power and influence, and how these are acquired and utilised by the training specialist (this issue is dealt with in greater detail later in this section).

4. The comparatively low priority attached to managing the training function, and the suggestion that the degree of involvement in this area is perceived as being at the discretion of the training specialist, also merit some comment. Managing, in this context, can be reasonably proposed to mean planning, controlling and co-ordinating the activities and responsibilities of the training function. The consequences of the training specialist opting out of this role may be felt in someone else taking over this role, or in the role being neglected. In either case the status of the training specialist and function is adversely affected, and the cohesiveness of the training and development process within the organisation is likely to suffer.

The Theoretical Approach

This approach is based on conceptualising the imperative duties of the training specialist, and Johnson (1990) takes the model of Bennett (1986) as an example. The model envisages a series of stages in the life cycle of the training specialist's career and sets out basic precepts associated with each stage, which may be described in the following terms:

Stage 1   New to the position — focus on learning on the job, listening, following role models, and learning about the organisation.

Stage 2   Seeking opportunities to put own ideas into practice,
                 gaining credibility, and networking within the
                 organisation

Stage 3   Working with senior people within the company,
                 developing training for future needs, and participating
                 in strategic level decision-making.

Johnson (1990) integrates this life-cycle perspective with Bennett's
(1986) model of general trainer roles. The findings of her empirical
study, allowing for some overlap, suggests that:

- at Stage 1, "trainer"/"provider" roles predominate, and activities are
  centred around helping others to learn;

- at Stage 2, the role evolves towards "consultant", and problem-
  solving activities become the primary focus;

- at Stage 3, "innovator"/"manager" roles emerge, consistent with
  strategic involvement in facilitating growth and change.

This may indeed portray the progression of some training specialists, but
reservations must be expressed about the extent to which it represents an
ideal model. In the first instance, many training specialists (especially
experienced professionals) might be expected to undertake duties attach-
ing to all three stages immediate to becoming the training incumbent in
an organisation. Secondly, many of the imperatives associated with
Stages 1 and 2 can also be strongly identified with Stage 3 (for example,
learning about the organisation, learning on the job, putting own ideas
into practice, and networking, are all part of an ongoing process). Finally, it seems incongruous to place the "manager" role at the final stage
of progression — this may be better placed outside the sequence as a co-
ordinating factor applicable to all of the stages.

The sequential view might be more appropriate in illustrating the
changing nature of the training profession over time, with the initial
stages reminiscent of the traditional direct trainer/maintenance mode of
operating. The need for training specialists to advance and broaden their
role, In the current environment, is endorsed by Buckley and Caple
(1992), in suggesting that they change from:

- being passive, to becoming active in communicating the benefits of
  training (greater attention to effective evaluation may be implied
  here);

- reacting to problems, to adopting a proactive stance in identifying
  and dealing with performance problems;

- operating at the peripheral boundaries, to perceiving themselves and their function as having key influence in assisting the organisation to achieve its objectives;

- being merely technologists, to developing a strategic focus and formulating policies which add impetus to the notion of learning as a route to organisational success.

These are put forward as pertinent imperatives if the training specialist's role is to retain or indeed enhance its relevance within the organisation of today and the future.

The Perceptual Approach

This approach represents an attempt to build a "picture" of the training specialist's role, based on perceptions of trainers themselves and significant others. Johnson (1990), Harrison (1992) and Reid et al (1992) report on the work of the Training and Development Lead Body (TDLB) in Britain. The TDLB was set up to establish occupational standards for those in training and development roles. It provides a perception of the training specialist's role which is useful for inclusion here. They began by defining the key purpose of training and development in the following terms — to develop human potential to assist organisations and individuals to achieve their objectives. Aligned with this purpose are four typical training and development roles, identified as follows:

- to manage human resource development strategy

- to manage training operations

- to meet training needs in general

- to meet specialised training needs.

From this base, the TDLB have identified functional areas of competence and have developed national standards for training and development. However, this work is focused on role-holders, and we will have cause to examine it in greater detail in Chapter 11 which is entirely concerned with the training and development specialist.

These perspectives on the training specialist's role have incorporated reviews of what managers actually do, what training management should be about, and how the role is broadly seen. We will now look at the role in the broader organisational context, in examining the impact of power and influence and how this may be developed and used effectively.

Figure 10.3 presents a range of trainer role perspectives.

Figure 10.3 Alternative Trainer Role Typologies

Study	Ontario Society for T&D (1976)	Pinto & Walker (1978)	Training of Trainers Ctee (1978)	McLagan (1983)	Nadler (1984)
No. of roles identified and title given	*4 role categories*	*14 roles or activity areas*	*4 role elements*	*15 roles in 4 role clusters*	*3 roles and 12 sub roles*
Roles	• Manager • Consultant • Designer • Instructor	• Needs analysis and diagnosis • Determine training approach • Program design/devt • Dev. material resources (make) • Manage internal resources (make) • Manage internal resources (borrow) • Manage external resources (buy) • Indiv. devt. planning/counselling • Job performance related training • Classroom training • Group and org devt. • Training research • Manage working r'ship with managers/clients • Manage T&D function • Prof. self-devt	• Direct training instructor/tutor • Organising • Administration • Determining/ Managing • Consultancy/ Advisory	• Interface Cluster • Marketer • Transfer agent • Group facilitator • Instructor • Concept. Dev. Cluster • Programme designer • Instructional writer • Theoretician • Research cluster • Evaluator • Task analyst • Needs analyst • Leadership cluster • Strategies • Manager (unclustered roles) • Media specialist • Individual devt. counsellor • Programme administrator	• Learning Specialist • Facilitator of learning • Designer of learning programmes • Developer of strategies • Manager of HRD • Developer of HRD policy • Supervisor of programs • Maintainer of relations • Developer of HRD personnel • Arranger of facilities and finance • Consultant • Expert • Advocate • Stimulator • Change agent

Study	Hayton (1989)	Varlaam & Pole (1988)	Bennett (1988)	McLagan (1989)	Phillips & Shaw (1989)
No. of roles identified and title given	*5 role profiles 6 role types*	*4 trainer roles*	*5 trainer roles*	*11 roles*	*4 roles*
Roles	(role profiles) • Preparation • Teaching • Research • Management • Self-devt (job types) • Staff devt • Instructor • SD programme officer • SD officer • SD programme manager • SD research manager • SD manager	• Basic dedicated trainer • Advanced dedicated trainer • Training manager • Integrated training role	• Trainer • Provider • Innovator • Consultant • Manager	• Administrator • Evaluator • HRD manager • HRD developer • Indiv. career devt advisor • Instructor of facilitator • marketer • Needs analyst • Org change agent • Programme designer • Researcher	• Trainer • Training consultant • Learning consultant • Organisation change consultant

RELATIONSHIP BETWEEN TRAINER ROLE TYPE AND POWER POSITION

One of the most commonly referenced set of role definitions emanates from the work of Pettigrew et al (1982) — see, for instance, Harrison (1992) and Reid et al (1992). It provides a particularly useful means of looking at the relationship between the various roles outlined and the power position of the training specialist. Using case study research, this work identifies two key themes which impact on the influence and effectiveness of the training specialist. The first factor — congruence — focuses on the fit between the personality and style of the training specialist, the particular role occupied, and the culture of the organisation. The impact of the second factor — influence/survival — arises from the manner in which the training specialist, on an ongoing basis, manages the boundary between the activities engaged in and the rest of the organisation. The maintenance, development and change elements attributable to the various roles are easily identifiable, and the relatively low level of power and influence associated with the passive provider and provider (maintenance) roles is highlighted.

The study also suggested that change agents, managers, and role-in-transition trainers are more aware of the issues of boundary management. Furthermore, training specialists in these role types are most likely to formulate strategy and objectives, and to systematically attempt to broaden the range of their activities, than either the provider or passive provider. Thus, a relationship is seen to exist between the particular role definition applied to the training specialist and the relative power and influence enjoyed. However, the role adopted by the training specialist in any given situation does not always proceed simply from choice. Many circumstantial factors come into play; some of these exist in the organisation itself, while others may indeed be more attributable to the personal traits of the training specialist. In either case, they can represent barriers facing the training and development function in acquiring and using power.

Difficulties in Acquiring and Using Power

There is considerable consensus that training and development specialists are reluctant to acquire power (see Leduchowicz, 1984; King, 1989; Coopers and Lybrands Associates, 1985). Some of the reasons given may be summarised as follows:

- There is evidence to suggest that many training specialists do not view their activities as being at the cutting edge. This is promoting a situation where the training and development department has a relatively low status in the organisation, and furthermore there is little perceived need to be productive in what they do. The Challenge to Complacency report suggests that this lack of internal status has led many training and development professionals into networking and contact with fellow professionals in other companies.

- Bennett (1986) rightly observes that the training and development role is burdened with many role conflicts. Three types of conflict in particular are highlighted, namely (a) the trainer's internal conflicts, (b) the conflicting priorities between the training and development function and the wider organisation, and (c) the conflicts between line departments. These conflicts place high demand on the skills and credibility of the training and development specialist and the probability of failure in the role is high. Failure to manage this excess of role conflict weakens credibility and blocks access to power

- There is some evidence to suggest that training and development specialists are poor at marketing their services. King (1989), Spitzer (1984) and Galvin (1988), among others, argue that an effective training and development specialist must be able to educate top management and line specialists on the potential contribution of training and development. Trainers have some difficulties in doing this. A number of reasons can be cited: lack of clarity concerning the training and development specialist's role; lack of skills and knowledge; the organisation does not make its expectations clear; the trainer perceives the role as one of maintaining the status quo.

- There is considerable evidence to suggest that training and development specialists have limited perceptions of their roles. Handy (1985) and Leduchowicz (1984), for example, comment on training and development specialists' tendency to confine their duties to classroom and other administrative activities. Such a role perception would not be very effective from a strategic training and development perspective. This maintenance role perception manifests itself in other ways also. King (1989) argues that there is a reluctance on the part of training and development specialists to implement new ideas or keep themselves up-to-date on new developments. They may also perceive the role as a temporary one in their career path and as a consequence do not wish to make errors or upset the status quo. There is considerable evidence available to substantiate the "stepping stone" perception of the "training job" and while such a situation exists training and development specialists will find themselves in a vicious circle unable to command support from organisational leaders and unable to exert their influence over the organisation's training and development activities.

Complexity of Political Environment

Within many organisations, training and development specialists are faced with a two-dimensional problem. The first relates to their survival as staff employees, and the second concerns their efforts in building the training and development function. In the process of strengthening the function, the role holder encounters political obstacles ranging from in-ter-departmental power-plays to strategic manipulations, to back-stabbing between rival managers.

Top Management Bias Against Training

Gaining top management support for training and development is a significant challenge confronting many training specialists. Studies show that top management in many organisations display relatively little interest in the training activity. This complacency is often manifested in the level of training expenditure, the role and status of training specialists, and in the types of expectations held about the training and development function. Training specialists themselves are in some way to blame for this state of affairs, because:

- their use of training jargon is often perceived as a barrier to effective communication, contributing to an inability to coherently define the training and development role, and inhibiting the recognition of their professional status;

- low levels of self-esteem cause paralysis in many practitioners, and too few have traits commensurate with being an excellent trainer;

- they tend to exhibit poor marketing skills, often failing to adopt a customer focus or to convince top management of their worth.

The Ambiguity of the Training and Development Role

The training and development function often adopts a closed-system mode of thinking and/or defines its activities in a classroom and/or administrative mode. Furthermore, the role is generally shadowed with ambiguity, because the function serves many groups who frequently have conflicting expectations. This was highlighted in our previous examination of stakeholders in the training and development process. Thus, top management, line management, personnel specialists, and individual employees may have different perceptions and expectations of the training and development role. Such situations often lead training specialists to adopt a "safe" role and conform to desires and requirements which will satisfy organisational members.

However, a predicament arises when training specialists try to avoid being locked into a particular role, and at the same time, continue as providers in terms of organisational needs. Leduchowicz (1984) cites a typical example of a role lock, where members of the organisation with a limited concept of the training specialist's function see this as confined to scheduling classroom/workshop activities, securing training materials, and circularising course announcements. To further complicate matters, there is some evidence that training and development specialists do not enjoy the total trust of personnel specialists. Personnel specialists are generally protective of their empire. The research suggests they tend to view the training specialist as a junior rather than an equal.

Line Manager Involvement and Resistance

We have already identified the line manager as a key stakeholder in the training and development process, yet the relationship between this group and the training specialist can frequently be anything but positive. This relationship is often strained, because, as Grace and Straub (1991) point out, line managers may be excluded from the process by the training specialist. The root of this exclusion may be found in issues of ownership and the threat of substitution, and its manifestations include:

- an unwillingness to perceive line managers as experts in the progression of course development;

- a reluctance to use line managers as instructors for short-term skill-based training; and

- the exclusion of line managers from the training needs assessment process.

This tendency to inhibit the involvement of line managers in the training process limits the possibility of training and development specialists building up alliances and networks of influence within the organisation.

Of course, line managers may also resist the efforts of the training and development specialist. Such resistance is often founded on suspicion and lack of trust, which results in the refusal to co-operate with training specialists who try to offer advice which might improve work operations. A common reason for this non-co-operation lies in the perception of training specialists as occupying a staff role, and thereby being expected to provide a service in accordance with line managers' requirements.

Attempts to change this role are frequently interpreted as a threat and a move towards thwarting line authority through the generation of better ideas. Pettigrew (1985) suggests that these ideas are often seen to be in competition with line manager's notions and values. A perceived challenge to the values and competence of line management, inevitably attracts inflexibility and negative responses aimed at demolishing the strengths and foundations of the training specialist.

Difficulty in Meeting the Needs of Internal Customers

The training and development specialist is faced with certain difficulties in attempting to meet the needs of internal customers. These can manifest themselves in a number of ways:

- Suggested training activities may be rejected by managers/employers who view the training experience as inhibitive, and their participation as an admission of some deficiency in their work or themselves. This response is often the consequence of ignorance about the scope and value of training and development as an empowerment tool.

- The training and development function is frequently starved of the resources necessary to meet the demands of employees/managers, plus any extraordinary or unforeseen needs which might arise. Adequate resources are defined by the internal customer (manager/ employee). They may or may not prove sufficient.

- Internal customers assume comparative value. They expect the amount of energy and time expended in the training effort to weigh proportionately less than the extent of increased productivity and/or effectiveness they achieve as a result. However, in the context of training and development, analysing costs and benefits may not be quite so straightforward.

- As an internal supplier, the training and development function often experiences difficulty in accepting responsibility for all commitments made to internal customers. This problem stems from the high substitution factor previously outlined.

Failure to recognise, acknowledge, and tackle these difficulties in acquiring power and influence can significantly impede the effectiveness of the training specialist. This, in turn, can dramatically reduce the potential contribution of training and development within the organisation.

It must be borne in mind, that, while all organisational members have important roles to play, the training specialist bears primary responsibility and accountability for the training and development process (Wills, 1993). We have seen how factors relevant to its organisational context can affect the power of the training and development function. Let us now look at ways in which the training specialist can develop and use power effectively.

STRATEGIES TO DEVELOP POWER AND USE IT EFFECTIVELY

Strategic contingencies theory, as proposed by Salancik and Pfeffer (1977) and Daft (1995), provides a helpful outline on how the training and development specialist may acquire power and use it effectively. We will focus on five key contingencies.

Dependency

The training and development specialist should endeavour to cultivate dependency from top management and other departments in the organisation. On this point, as democratic values reach into the organisation, expert power grows in prestige, creating significant dependency and a lasting power base (Handy, 1990). The training and development specialist is the only one who can destroy or fail to renew this. Expert power is least often opposed or resisted. Furthermore, it is an effective source; if clients agree with the expert advice of the training and development specialist, they will endorse it without further control checks or negative attachments. The role of the training and development specialist should therefore encompass the use of expert power, combined with other power bases which may be built around the function.

Centrality

Centrality reflects the training and development function's role in the primary activity of the organisation, and this may present some difficulties for the specialist. However, a significant area on which the specialist can focus is that of strategic change. Training and development can make vital contributions in areas such as venture formation, increased customer focus, emphasis on quality, fewer organisational layers, etc. Indeed, an effective training and development function can identify the key strategic initiatives to which the organisation is committed and build its activities around these, as suggested by Noel and Dennehy (1991). They cite the example of a delayed responsive organisation. Here, the training and development function can facilitate the change process by developing managers in the art of delegation, eliminating unnecessary procedures, and creating an environment of risk-taking.

Coping with Uncertainty

The training specialist can play a significant role in assisting the organisation to cope with uncertainty. Three specific strategies may be pursued to this effect:

- obtaining prior information, such as forecasting skill shortages and identifying sources of needed skills, and providing expertise which enables the initiation of major organisational change;

- prevention by prediction, and forecasting negative events; and

- absorption, by taking judicious action after a specific event to reduce negative consequences.

Substitutability

This issue represents something of a dilemma for the training and development specialist. The very concept of substitutability is promoted by encouraging line managers to become actively involved in the training and development process. While this approach helps to build up alliances and networks, it also projects the message that training and development can be carried out by others in the organisation. To counteract the negative side of this balance, the specialist must be able to develop unique skills which cannot be performed by other readily available sources. Hunt (1986) states that knowledge is expertise until it is shared, and a remedy for the training and development specialist can be proposed in the guise of constant self-development and updating. In addition, a clarification of role boundaries should help to minimise the inherent difficulty posed by substitutability.

Control of Resources

Departments which are "revenue collectors" tend to accumulate power. However, this is largely a barren path for the training and development function, unless it adopts the somewhat uncommon approach of competitive tendering for training assignments. Nonetheless, the training and development specialist may be able to direct the function towards activities which make the organisation more cost-effective and safe. The exact nature of such savings are very much dependent on the organisational context.

These issues surrounding the role of the training and development specialist offer gateways to building a power base. However, the utilisation of political skills must also be incorporated into the specialist's role if the bases of power are to be employed effectively. This involves convincing those to whom the training and development function has access of its contribution. It further means using its resources, information, and technical skills to their maximum in "exploiting the art of the possible", in bargaining, in knowing where to concentrate its energies, and organising the fostering alliances. Training and development specialists often fail to exhibit these vital skills. Using Daft's (1995) framework, it is possible to identify specific political tactics which can form an integral part of the training specialists role in order to develop power. A typology of these tactics is presented in Figure 10.4.

PHILOSOPHIES OF TRAINING AND DEVELOPMENT

Various philosophical positions underpin attitudes towards training, development and education at organisational and national levels. To begin with, we will define philosophy as a position that an organisation or individual holds, relating to some activity or issue. It is a composite of values and beliefs, and it is developed through one's socialisation and present position. In the context of an organisation or social system, a number of factors determine philosophical values towards the training and development activity. Among these factors are:

- education and experience of trainers

- type of environment the organisation operates in

- the organisation's location

- composition of the workforce

- attitudes of top management

- nature of ownership

- number of stakeholders and their values and beliefs

- legal framework in which the training and development activity operates.

Philosophies on the Provison of Training and Development

Voluntarism
The philosophy of voluntarism advocates minimum state intervention in the provision of training and development. In this situation, the responsibility for training rests with the organisation or with individuals themselves. Additionally, with state support at a minimum, the full cost of training and development is borne by the organisation or the individual.

Figure 10.4: Political Tactics for Training and Development Specialists

Building coalitions	Expand networks	Control decision premises	Enhance legitimacy and expertise	Make preferences explicit and keep power implicit
• Take time to talk to other managers and persuade them to see your point of view • Huddle to resolve key issues • Motivate rather than exploit good interpersonal relationships • Concentrate on building credibility and trust	• Reach out and establish contact with top management and employees • Co-opt dissenters by getting them to see your point of view by involving them in training programme design and giving them credit in evaluations, etc. • Set up training and development committees to identify organisational training and development needs	• Present favourable information on training department activities • Selectively use this information to influence key decisions favourable to the training and development function • Evaluate the training and development function on a regular basis • Speak the language of the organisation	• Trainers can exert greatest influence if they have recognised legitimacy and expertise - external consultants and others • Recognised experts can be of great help to add kudos to evaluators • Choose external training and development resources wisely • Design training and development programmes with learners in mind	• Bargain assertively and persuasively • Use power quietly Don't throw your weight around and ensure your training and development is perceived to be beneficial to the organisation. • Demonstrate a willingness to take perks • Be clear on priorities and communicate them effectively

Source: Garavan, T.N. Barnacle, B. and Heraty, N. "The Training and Development Function: Its Search for Power and Influence in Organisations", *Journal of European Industrial Training*, Vol. 17, No. 7, 1993.

Voluntarism has been described by Reid et al (1992) as a laissez-faire philosophy, under which training and development requirements and activities are identified and initiated by individuals and/or their managers, as and when they seem appropriate. This philosophy can contribute to an overemphasis on specific job requirements in training, particularly in the realm of manual skills. This being the case, a likely result is the acquisition of skills and knowledge which have restricted application and transferability.

A voluntaristic philosophy presents a number of problems. Most notable are the following:

- It may lead to considerable inconsistency between the efforts that are taken by individual companies. Some organisations will accept responsibility for training and developing staff whereas others will not. The available research in Ireland suggests that these non-training companies are most likely to be small owner-managed firms.

- Many individuals will not make systematic investments in their own training and development. Where they do invest in this development it may have little value to the organisation or the wider economy.

- A voluntaristic philosophy has the potential to lead to skill gaps emerging in the labour market. Research (Roche and Tansey, 1992) on Irish companies reveals under-investment in training for many types of skill. Furthermore, individuals are often unwilling to bear the total cost of skills training. Individuals who do invest in training and development initiatives may find this investment goes unrecognised by the organisation they work for. This means that their investment produces little payback in terms of career mobility and advancement within the organisation.

- There is an in-built discriminatory element in a voluntaristic philosophy. Only those who can afford the cost will invest in training and development activities. Other groups and individuals who may be motivated to develop themselves will not have the resources to do so.

- The implementation of this philosophy by an organisation would significantly inhibit the achievement of other HR strategies such as TQM, flexibility and change.

- It may lead to leakages from the organisation and the economy in general because employees will seek out job opportunities which have a training and development commitment attached to them. At national level it could lead to a brain drain to high-training labour markets, within the EU for example.

- It may reinforce labour market segregation. Some categories such as female employees, the travelling community and ethnic groups tend to be located in the secondary labour market where low wages, poor conditions and limited training opportunities are available. Investment in training and development may be the only way to get out of this sector. In effect, a voluntaristic philosophy may sustain a vicious circle, because low wages do not provide sufficient resources for the individual to invest in his/her own training and development.

- The philosophy may contribute to a situation where there is little company-specific training. Specific training can be defined as training directly relevant to the production processes and systems of the organisation. A minimum level of such training is necessary for productivity and profitability of the organisation.

Interventionism

In direct contrast to voluntarism, interventionism sees the state and/or the organisation as having an inherent responsibility for training, expressed through legislation to achieve control of the state's training systems and a well managed training and development function at organisation level. These systems may incorporate support and funding, in conjunction with training grant/levy schemes, and organisations are expected to bear some/all of the costs involved in training and developing employees.

The underlying motive behind this philosophy is that, without active support and funding from the state, many organisations simply will not pursue training and development activities. Nonetheless, a major criticism of interventionism is the potential fostering of a dependency relationship between organisations and the state, in the area of training and development.

In the Irish context, the Industrial Training Act (1967) represented a key mechanism in an interventionist approach. However, the Labour Services Act (1987) signalled a change of direction for the state, effectively marking a return to a more voluntaristic philosophy at the level of the organisation.

An interventionist philosophy advocates the elimination of skill gaps, the enhancement of economic growth, and the encouragement of mobility within the organisation and the economy in general. At the level of the state, it involves a two-pronged effort; the provision of training facilities for the unemployed and the provision of financial resources for companies to train and develop staff. Those resources would be provided on the basis of agreed criteria. At the state level interventionism would involve the provision of financial and physical resources for training and development initiatives designed to cater for disadvantaged groups, such as the long-term unemployed, people with disabilities, the travelling community and small organisations. The second type of interventionism involves aid to companies. FÁS provides small companies with a larger percentage grant support than it does to larger companies. Furthermore it gives a higher level of grant aid to specific training activities such as technology training, business strategy development and the management of change.

At the level of the organisation, an interventionist philosophy will be reflected by the existence of a training and development function, a specific commitment of financial and physical resources for the function and the production of training plans.

An interventionist philosophy has a number of inherent weaknesses. It may lead to the creation of a dependency relationship. Companies may not invest in training and development unless they are given grant support for it. Likewise individuals will not invest in their training and development unless it is supported by the state and/or organisation. When the state or organisation makes systematic investments in the training and development of human resources they are creating expectations, particularly in respect of greater mobility, increased employment or promotion opportunities. An interventionist philosophy at state or organisation level works well if it has an explicit policy and plans to support it. At national level in Ireland, such a plan or strategy has not existed to any great extent. We have a multiplicity of training and development schemes for the unemployed, for example, yet at the organisational level there is a general absence of yearly training plans or a lack of procedures to identify training and development needs.

Traditionalism

Traditionalism (sometimes labelled "elitism") follows the convention that training and development is reserved for certain skills, crafts and professions. Its origins may be traced to craft apprenticeships, where front-end training and on-the-job experience, over a set period, was commonly referred to as "serving one's time" toward becoming a qualified craftsperson. A similar analogy may also be drawn with the traditional path to many professional qualifications. Thus, as Reid et al (1992) outline, this philosophy has its roots in long-established patterns of provision and application of training, which are deemed to have satisfactorily fulfilled the requirements of a country or an organisation, and which have remained unaltered over many years.

Essentially, traditionalism implies a restrictive approach, promoting access to training only for "high status" fields of employment. Trainees are typically expected to make some payment in time and financial resources for the privilege of being trained. It further embraces the notion that training is necessary only at the beginning of a career, i.e. since work and skill requirements are unchanging, retraining or updating of skills and knowledge are irrelevant.

Many criticisms have been levelled at this philosophy, in particular:

- It makes the assumption that skills, once acquired, will not become obsolete. It fails to appreciate that technological advances may deskill and/or create the need for new skills.

- It mitigates against the development of a flexible, multi-skilled work-force because it puts an emphasis on status differences and demarcation. Its basic premise is that certain categories should have access to training and there should be a limit on the numbers who are trained.

- It specifies a very limited role for the training and development function. Its main focus of activity would be on skills training delivered on a sporadic basis rather than an ongoing development.

Several of the weaknesses inherent in this approach have been acknowledged by the Irish government and are addressed in its proposed reform of the Irish apprenticeship system.

Continuous Development

The Institute of Personnel and Development (IPD) produced a code of practice on continuous development in 1984. Therein, continuous development is defined as self-directed, life-long learning, driven by policies which initially allow and subsequently facilitate such learning at work, through an individual's work experience.

Continuous development according to Wood, Barrington and Johnson (1990) means "learning from real work experiences at work; learning through working life, compared with useful but occasional injections of training". They identify five key facts of this philosophy:

- the integration of learning with work

- self-directed learning

- an emphasis on process rather than technique

- continuous development as an attitude

- simultaneous improvement in the performance of employees and organisations.

It is argued that an ethos of continuous development should be promoted in light of the current economic environment where such rapid technological changes are being evidenced and high rates of unemployment persist, as in the Irish context. Indeed, employers, trade unions, and governments alike are increasingly of the opinion that people of working age, whether currently employed or not, should be given constant encouragement, in tandem with ample opportunities, to update existing skills and/or acquire new skills and work capabilities.

Specific principles which underpin the continuous development philosophy include the following:

- Learning is a continuous process within the organisation which should be supported and reinforced by the organisation's culture.

- The role of the training and development function is to formulate policies and develop structures which encourage continuous development and to network with key stakeholders in the organisation to ensure that they understand their role and responsibilities within the continuous development process.

- The individual must accept ownership for his/her own development.

The IPD code points to a number of advantages of pursuing this type of philosophy, including:

- increased likelihood that strategic plans will be achieved;

- expectation that ideas will be generated in a form which dovetails with operational needs;

- the need for individual learning effort will be more readily acknowledged and acted upon;

- in an era of sharp competitiveness and ongoing threats to job security, the contribution of a learning ethos to organisational effectiveness will gain more widespread recognition.

Continuous development can therefore lead to improved operational performance and the joint development of both people and work. A continuous development philosophy does, however, have some limitations. It may involve a major initial cost element for the organisation depending on how the organisation seeks to implement such a philosophy. It focuses on more formal learning events or structured on-the-job activities. Furthermore, it assumes that line managers and individual employees are willing to accept ownership of continuous development activities. Garavan (1995) found that line managers and individual employees are often unwilling to accept and perform a role within a continuous development philosophy.

There is a presupposition of unitarism and commitment, whereby employees are assumed automatically to be willing to link their personal development to that of their employing organisation. Goss (1993) argues that the asserted link between individual learning and organisational performance is difficult to verify. This is particularly so with self-development, where improvements may take considerable time to accrue.

It is also argued that where self-development is lightly coupled to job demands, the result can be a narrow utilitarian conception of learning and knowledge. This is most unlikely to occur where self-development follows a strongly individual pattern and where the learner has few colleagues to discuss progress with.

An implied assumption underpinning the continuous development philosophy is that organisations are in a continuous state of flux and therefore they need to develop human resources continuously to match this situation. However, some organisations experience long periods of stability and so do not require such continuous development processes. Continuous development has the potential to create employee expectations of flexibility, mobility, challenge, empowerment and advancement. It may result in what could be termed an "over-trained" workforce which may present difficulties in the area of employee retention.

Humanism

The central premise of a humanist philosophy is that individuals should be the central focus of any training and development initiative. In some respects it suggests that individuals should have a bill of learning rights. Rights which this bill might contain include the following:

- opportunities to participate in decisions about the individual's training and development within the organisation, i.e. training and development activities should not be imposed;

- individual needs and the opportunity to increase potential should take precedence over organisation needs;

- any individual development which takes place should be valued by the organisation;

- there should be a guarantee of a minimum level of training and development for the individual within any one year.

This philosophy, it is suggested, does not sit well within a strategic HRD model. It advocates a much softer perspective in terms of training and development provision. Many organisations may have difficulties with a pure humanist philosophy. They would perceive the payback as occurring only in the long term and would have doubts about its ability to enable an organisation to achieve and sustain competitive advantage through its human resources. It may, however, be successfully implemented in voluntary and nonprofit-oriented organisations which may be more inclined to emphasise self-development. Humanism reinforces a person-type culture which advocates that the organisation exists to meet the needs of the individual rather than vice versa.

Utilitarianism

This philosophy of training and development provision is based on the imperative that training and development interventions provide the greatest return for the organisation and/or the economy in general. It also advocates that training and development activities are undertaken only if the benefits outweigh the costs. Therefore, the organisation will only invest in training and development initiatives that meet organisational needs. It requires a training and development function that is aware of what its organisational needs are and has completed cost/benefit analysis on the investment required to meet them. This philosophy is much in line with some of the principles of strategic-led human resource development which we will consider later. This philosophy is not without its limitations, however:

- There is an implicit assumption of unitarism underpinning the philosophy. The philosophy assumes common shared values, objectives and needs; in effect, a team-based approach within the organisation.

- It is output- or organisation-centred and may be perceived as a manipulative-type philosophy. Individual needs are important and may have a significant impact on creativity and flexibility levels within the organisation, yet this philosophy de-emphasises them. Furthermore, it may not sufficiently focus on the process of learning.

- The philosophy would tend to emphasise skill-oriented training which has a short payback period to the organisation, This could be at the expense of management and career development initiatives.

- Application of a utilitarian philosophy has the potential to become power/politics-driven. Departments or sectors of the economy who are better able to demonstrate the need and the benefits of training and development are more likely to get the resources to provide it.

- The philosophy is based on the assumption that costs and benefits of training and development are amenable to quantification. However, the qualitative benefits may be equally important but not measurable within the framework advocated.

Centralisation/Decentralisation

This set of philosophies are best viewed along a continuum. Centralisation, at one end of the continuum, advocates that the training and development function should be centralised within the organisation and/or that decisions at state level should be made by a central authority such as FÁS. The training and development function should have a recognised structural boundary and should be staffed by a specialist or subject matter expert. Decisions relating to participation in training and development should, according to this philosophy, be made by senior members of the organisation and/or the national authority. In the organisational context it advocates that individuals should be nominated to attend training and development activities rather that the initiative coming from individuals themselves. Centralisation basically advocates the bureaucratic management of training and development. In the national context it sees no role, or at most a limited role, for the regional organisations or the recipients of the training and development.

A number of limitations can be identified for this philosophy:

- The reasons for nominating individuals for training and development activities may not be explicit or relevant to the individual nominated. This may have significant implications for the motivation of the individual learner.

- It tends to reinforce the notion that training and development activities consist of contrived learning events, usually courses. It gives less emphasis to more natural learning activities within the organisation.

- It may reinforce the notion that individuals and line specialists are not responsible for their own development. Furthermore, individual development initiatives may be low on the list of priorities of the training and development function.

- This philosophy has the potential to lead to a discriminatory or elitist provision. Particular groups may not be nominated for training and development simply because they are not perceived as important by the central decision-makers.

- It has the potential to reinforce the oft-quoted perception of the training and development function as an "ivory tower" that is not in touch with the priorities of individuals and line specialists.

Decentralisation, at the other end of the continuum, advocates that training and development should be located at the level of the target groups who need the training and development. Transported to the organisational context, decentralisation advocates that training responsibility should rest with the individual learner and his/her superior. Training and development is seen as a line rather than a staff activity, with the line specialist playing a fundamental role in terms of accepting ownership. It seeks to move the emphasis away from formalised learning events towards work-integrated natural learning-type activities. A wholly decentralised philosophy has a number of limitations:

- It may result in the haphazard provision of training and development at both the organisation and state level. There is little overall co-ordination or control.

- Line specialists may not be sufficiently committed to the training and development process and may therefore give it a low priority. Even where they do demonstrate commitment they may have a limited perception of the role and scope of training and development, and they may perceive it in terms of formal learning events.

- Too much emphasis may be given to job-related training at the expense of wider management development and career-driven interventions.

- At the national level it could result in considerable disparities and gaps, whereby training provision is dependent on the commitment of local groups and organisations.

Figure 10.5 at the end of the chapter presents some of the implications arising from the pursuit of each of the training provision philosophies discussed.

Philosophies on the Purpose of Training and Development

Organisations tend to utilise training and development interventions for either of two broad purposes. One is to help maintain the status quo and thus follow a "maintenance philosophy", while the other is to enable organisational change take place through adopting a "change philosophy". We will now look more closely at these two philosophies.

Training and Development as a Maintenance Intervention

This philosophy is associated with organisations where training activities play a supportive, rather than a strategic, role. In this type of situation, the provision of training is mainly concerned with the acquisition of specific knowledge and skills. Binsted (1982) identifies a number of training types pertinent to this philosophy, including:

- *remedial* — aiming to rectify existing training deficiencies;

- *promotional* — preparing employees for promotion into a more senior role;

- *induction* — smoothing a new employee's entry into the organisation and attempting to ensure that initial work is performed to required standards;

- *role expansion* — aiming to further employee motivation through a process of job enrichment, which allows greater autonomy and decision-making over work planning.

Adoption of this philosophy indicates a conservative approach to training, and several attendant limitations have been identified. Where this philosophy is adopted, training:

- is too formal, embracing only conformance to existing situations

- reduces an organisation's ability to adapt to a change environment

- restricts full appreciation of external influencing factors

- precipitates the use of didactic, rather than participative, training methods.

Training and Development as a Change Intervention
In contrast to maintenance intervention, this philosophy argues that the role of training and development is to bring about change in the way the organisation operates. Training and development facilities change at a number of levels:

- change in the values and ethos of the organisation

- change in the organisation's systems and structures

- changes in employees' attitudes to meet cultural change initiatives

- changes in employee knowledge and skill levels to meet new job requirements.

This philosophy argues that by its very nature, training involves change and should be viewed in that light.

Training Delivery Philosophies
There are two schools of thought concerning how training and development should be delivered, namely, Instrumentalist and Existentialism. It must be stated at the outset, however, that few trainers are completely purist in their approach — a point best illustrated by way of a continuum of training philosophies, as follows:

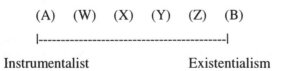

```
    (A)   (W)   (X)   (Y)   (Z)   (B)

    |-----------------------------------|

Instrumentalist                Existentialism
```

Research shows very few trainers invariably adopt an approach entirely consistent with either point A or point B. Indeed, taking the multiplicity of variables comprising the circumstances in which trainers operate, the vast majority will adopt an approach somewhere between A and B, contiguous with positions W, X, Y, or Z. Therefore, the philosophy governing the delivery of training and development is most appropriately viewed as a continuum. The characteristics of instrumental and existentialist trainers are as follows:

Instrumentalism

- Tends to be subject-based.

- Assumes that practice should be deduced from theory.

- Upholds a belief in the definite correlation between hours of study and amount of learning.

- Views the trainer as very important and highly valued contributor to learning process.

- Views the trainer as a subject-matter expert, thus: (a) allowing large attendance at training sessions, (b) having distant learner-participant relationships, and (c) using formalised learning mechanisms

- Espouses belief that it is possible to specify learning objectives in precise terms.

- Trainee participation is curtailed to minimum levels.

- Emphasis is on training content rather than learning process.

- Evaluation pursued through tests and questionnaires.

Existentialism

- Primary focus is on the individual learner.

- Views the trainer as a manager of learning and a process specialist.

- Trainer acts as coach/tutor/facilitator, who assists learners to formulate their own theories and develop their own skills and talents.

- Trainer perceives own role in terms of being a learning resource and a guide to other resources.

- Trainer promotes close, productive relationships with learners, and between individuals in learning groups.

- Emphasis on individual responsibility for monitoring progress of own development.

- Trainer feedback focuses on progress of individual, not on evaluation of performance or achievement.

- The context of learning is framed within the job and work environment of the individual.

- Training programmes are likely to feature (a) flexibility of approach, (b) frequent utilisation of group work, (c) a liability to constant change, and (d) little emphasis on objectives.

SUMMARY

In this chapter we considered the roles and philosophies of training and development. While the literature advocates a wide range of roles, a number of consistent theories are evident. Training specialists can perceive their roles as (a) providers, (b) administrators, (c) managers and (d) facilitators of learning. Similar diversity is evident in the area of trainer philosophies. Philosophies exist about the function of training and development, the way it should be delivered and more specifically the way in which it should be utilised in the organisation. Responsibility for training and development is a shared one including both the training and development specialist, top management, line specialists and the individual.

Figure 10.5: Application of Training and Development Philosophies — A Macro and Micro Perspective

	Macro Perspective (National)	Micro Perspective (Organisation/Individual)
Voluntarism	• Considerable sectoral inconsistencies become apparent in the amount of training provided. • Sectoral inconsistencies threaten labour market mobility. • Potential conflict with other governmental objectives, such as reducing unemployment. • Specific skill shortages and surpluses may arise, leading to conflict and disparity between levels of demand and supply.	• Individuals bearing the cost of their own development may be harder to retain. • Investment in personal development will most likely result in the pursuit of qualification-type programmes, not necessarily in line with organisational needs. • If individuals perceive a lack of organisational interest in their development, attitudes towards work itself may be adversely affected. • Potential ramifications for organisational effectiveness include; manpower disharmony; skill deficiencies; and poor management practice. • It may prove difficult to implement a change process. • These conditions present fundamental obstacles to organising a training function and establishing support for training.

	Macro Perspective (National)	**Micro Perspective (Organisation/Individual)**
Interventionism	• State involvement is likely to reduce sectoral training inconsistencies. • Labour market mobility should be considerably improved. • State-led training offers greater potential for alignment with wider government objectives and it could complement the drive towards unemployment reduction. • Its success will depend on the focus of related schemes and, if training is too highly subsidised, abuse of the system may result. • Community and enterprise type initiatives may be oriented towards general all-round development, rather than towards specific skills. • Interventionism facilitates a more integrated approach to manpower.	• Greater opportunity should be created for increasing the power and influence of the training function. • Organisations bearing the cost of training are more likely to adopt on-the-job training activities, rather than off-the-job training activities, in pursuit of greater learning transfer. • It allows organisations to increase their training budgets as grant assistance is available from the state. • It stimulates greater commitment to training and development at individual and organisational levels.

	Macro Perspective (National)	**Micro Perspective (Organisation/Individual)**
Traditionalism	• Strong possibility of specific skill shortages in labour market. • Possible over-supply of traditional craft skills. • Does not take account of ongoing changes in skills and training needs on a national scale. • Skill shortages make investment in new industry less attractive. • Not aligned with labour market demands.	• Unlikely to fulfil the skill requirements of a dynamic and constantly changing organisation. • Ignores the training needs of those outside craft/specialist areas. • Individuals bearing the cost of their own training will have a strong motivation to learn. • Front-loaded orientation overlooks skills obsolescence due to technological and other changes.
Continuous Development	• The availability of appropriate learning facilities and resources must be ensured. • All people of working age, whether employed or not, must be given frequent opportunities and ongoing encouragement to update their existing skills. • Poses a challenge to traditional thinking and practice in relation to training. • Government intervention needed by way of supportive legislation and provision of resources. • Promotes learning as a prerequisite for economic prosperity.	• Self-development is the responsibility of every in-dividual within the organisation. • Organisational goals must be understood and shared, and attained through continuous development of all employees. • Learning occurs through the experience of work. • Organisation members use each other as learning resources. • Individual developmental goals may not be compatible with organisational needs. • Possible confusion over specific responsibilities for learning objectives and promotion of learning activities. • Employee involvement in decision-making is promoted.

	Macro Perspective (National)	**Micro Perspective (Organisation/Individual)**
Humanism	• State should support the right of individuals to receive training and development. • Individual needs should guide the design and delivery of state sponsored training and development initiatives. • Individuals should have to participate in decisions about training and development provision at national level. • State should initiate legislation giving individuals a legal right to training and development.	• Individual needs should drive organisation training and development provision. • Individuals have a right to participate in training and development provision. • Organisations should guarantee employees a minimum level of training per year. • Individuals' rights to equality should be respected in training and development provision.
Utilitarianism	• National training and development provision should focus on the cost/benefit of policy initiatives. • Training and development provision should be directed at meeting the needs of employers. • The state training and development schemes should promote the greatest good for the economy as a whole.	• Organisation needs should direct the shape of training and development precision. • Organisations should only invest in training and development initiatives that produce more benefits than costs. • Training and development provision should be based on systematically-identified needs.

	Macro Perspective (National)	**Micro Perspective (Organisation/Individual)**
Centralisation	• State provision of training and development is decided at central level. • State organisations are in the best position to decide the training needs of employers and community groups. • State resources are managed by a single organisation. • Training and development is managed in a bureaucratic manner.	• Decisions about training and development are made centrally. • Employees are nominated to attend training and development programmes. • Employees do not have rights to be consulted about training and development activities. • Centralism leads to greater efficiency in terms of training provision.
Decentralisation	• State training provision is best directed at regional/local level. • Target groups are in the best position to decide on their training needs. • Training and development stakeholders are fully involved in all decisions on national training and development policy.	• Training and development is a line rather than a staff function within organisations. • Line managers and employees are the prime decision makers in training and development provision. • Training and development provision is dictated by the concerns of individual learners and line specialists.

11

ESTABLISHING A TRAINING AND DEVELOPMENT FUNCTION

INTRODUCTION AND LEARNING OBJECTIVES

This chapter focuses on the issues involved in establishing a training function within an organisation. Having read this chapter you will understand:

- the range of reporting arrangements and structures;

- the budgetary aspects of training and development;

- the importance of marketing and positioning the training function within the organisation;

- the range of training and development resources available;

- the issues involved in formulating and implementing training and development policies and plans;

- the scope and status of training in Irish organisations.

The question of where exactly the training and development function should be positioned within the "jigsaw" of the organisation's structure has been the focus of some debate, especially in more recent years. We have related the strong arguments that, if the training and development process is to contribute fully to the organisation's effectiveness, it should be linked integrally to strategic objectives and goals. In tandem with this notion, there is some recent evidence that the training and development function is being directly represented at ever more senior levels in organisations, sometimes indeed at Board level itself. Nevertheless, the traditional positioning of training and development, as a function within the personnel (or human resources) department, still pervades. The answer to this conundrum, therefore, lies primarily in the particular circumstances of the organisation itself, although the approach of training specialists themselves must also come into consideration in this context.

REPORTING RELATIONSHIPS AND STRUCTURES

Three main alternatives may be suggested in examining reporting relationships pertinent to the training specialist and function. It is important to relate these alternatives to the specific circumstances, environment, and cultural aspects of the organisation.

The most usual reporting arrangements for the training specialist (head of the training function) are:

1. *To the Chief Executive/Board.* Where the chief executive has a strong personal interest in training and development, it may transpire that the training specialist will have a direct reporting relationship to this level. This is more likely to occur in large organisations, and in situations where an integral role in achieving strategic objectives is mapped out for the training and development function.

2. *To the Personnel (HR) Manager.* This can be suggested as the predominant reporting relationship, certainly in the typical hierarchical structures which are a regular feature in traditional terms, and are indeed still quite common. Here, training and development is seen as one of a "package" of functions which together constitute the "personnel" department. In such situations, it is likely that the role envisaged for the training function, and its stature within the organisation, will largely reflect the perception of the personnel manager.

3. *To the Line Manager.* Having the training specialist report to line management must be seen as the least satisfactory arrangement of the three alternatives. It implies that a narrow, departmental focus is given to the training and development function, and that its activities are primarily concerned with day-to-day operational matters. However, this can represent the priority, short-term needs in some small or medium-sized organisations.

A number of advantages and disadvantages may be associated with each of these alternatives and these are set out in Figures 11.1 and 11.2.

Positioning and Structure — Recent Irish Research

Recent research by Heraty (1992), embracing a cross-section of 58 Irish companies, indicated that most training specialists operate at senior management level and report either to the general manager (or equivalent) or to the head of personnel/human resources. These results suggest that many training specialists are well positioned to become involved at the strategic level in their organisations.

Figure 11.1: Advantages of Alternative Reporting Relationships

Chief Executive/Board	Personnel (HR) Manager	Line Manager(s)
• It relates a strong message about the priority attached to training and development by the chief executive. • The training specialist has a "direct line" to the foremost authority in the organisation, and can use this facility to positively accentuate the importance of training and development. • The informal authority and overall credibility of the training specialist is increased, strengthening the power base of the training function. • Political difficulties and obstacles are more easily faced down or circumvented by the training specialist. • Greater resources may be allocated to the training function, and its access to resources is considerably eased. • The training specialist is appropriately placed to gain an understanding of the strategic priorities of the organisation. • An integral linkage between training and development activities and corporate objectives is more likely to be created and sustained.	• The personnel manager is more likely to have a good understanding of the training and development process, and of its potential contribution to overall organisational effectiveness. • The probability that the personnel manager will promote and support the training function is enhanced. • Where the personnel department holds a strong and influential position within the organisation, this will invariably be transmitted to its assembly of functions, including training and development. • A closer link is established between training and development activities and those performed by other functions within the department, facilitating synergy and reciprocation. • Ease of access to the same "personnel" data-base; preventing duplication of effort and creating and maintaining a standardised information network. • Criteria for assessing the effectiveness of training and development may be more qualitative than that assigned by top management.	• If the range of training needs is limited to one area/department, this relationship ensures a clear focus on specific operational problems. • Training activities are directly relevant to the needs of the area/department. • The line manager is more supportive of, and committed to, training activities.

Figure 11.2: Disadvantages of Alternative Reporting Relationships

Chief Executive	Personnel (HR) Manager	Line manager(s)
• Chief executives are usually very busy people, hence the training and development function may not receive adequately detailed attention. • The chief executive may not have an in-depth understanding of the training and development process. • Resentment may be generated among managers of other functions who do not report at this level. • Co-ordination and integration with other personnel functions may be diluted. • The chief executive's criteria for success are likely to have a quantitative orientation; long term and less tangible benefits such as reduced turnover and improved morale may not be taken fully into account. • There may be a tendency for the training specialist to report only "good news stories" in relation to training and development. • The training function may be seen as less accessible on an organisation-wide scale. • The training specialist may become more involved in power and politics than in the training and development process itself. • There may be an emphasis on training for training's sake, in response to pressure to demonstrate "activity".	• The training function may be perceived and reacted to as a subsidiary of the personnel department. • The personnel manager might under-represent training and development needs at higher levels. • There may be conflicting priorities among various personnel functions and tasks, especially in relation to the allocation of resources. • It increases the tendency to allocate the training role to someone with limited qualifications and expertise. • The power and influence of the training specialist may be deliberately restricted by the personnel manager. • The training specialist and function may be categorised by employees as another "personnel" function, thereby associating it with a "management" orientation and purpose. • Line managers' involvement in the training and development process might not be fully endorsed or encouraged.	• Training and development operates from a very narrow base. • It is very restrictive in terms of developing an organisation-wide focus for training and development. • Line managers' understanding and appreciation of the training and development process might prove a limiting factor. • Line managers' evaluation criteria are likely to be almost exclusively focused on quantitative data. • Bias might be evidenced in decisions concerning priorities for training. • The training function is divorced from other personnel activities. • Opportunities for developing the power and influence of the training functions are minimised, if not eliminated.

The average span of control of training specialists was examined, in an effort to gauge the typical size of the training and development function. Respondents were asked to indicate how many employees reported to them directly, or indirectly through subordinates, and the results are outlined in Table 11.1.

Table 11.1: Number of Employees Reporting to Training Specialists (n=58)

	< 5	5-9	10-14	15-19	20+
Directly	50	6	1	0	1
Indirectly	42	7	4	2	3

Source: Heraty, N. (1992) "Training and Development: A Study of Practices in Irish-Based Companies", mimeo, University of Limerick.

It emerged that the vast majority of training specialists have less than five people reporting to them, either directly or indirectly, which suggests that the training function, in most of the organisations featured, exercises direct control over few people. Indeed the typical responses was that one or two people reported to the training specialist. This may be reflective of the situation in many Irish organisations, where the training specialist (usually training manager or officer) has directly responsibility for one or two staff (commonly a training co-ordinator and/or a training administrator). It often transpires, however, that there are a number of training instructors in such organisations who report directly to line management but have a "dotted line" relationship with the training specialist.

BUDGETARY ASPECTS OF TRAINING AND DEVELOPMENT

A budget may be defined as a plan for systematic spending, and the process of developing an annual forecast in these terms falls within remit of almost all departmental managers. In this context, the training specialist is normally charged with projecting the expenditure on training and development (although in some cases training costs may be incorporated into other departmental budgets) as well as subsequent management of resources and activities in line with these financial guidelines. This is a very important aspect of the training specialist's job, and it is concerned with ensuring maximum return on the funding invested in training and development. While most training specialists intuitively perceive the potential benefits of training and development, its cost effectiveness must be demonstrated to those within the organisation who may not attach similar intrinsic value to the process. Not least of the considerations in this regard is the fact that the allocation of resources in subsequent years is often dependent on such factors.

Approaches to Budgetary Control

Three different approaches to budgetary control have been identified (see Nadler and Wiggs, 1986; Gilley and Eggland, 1989) which may be summarised as follows:

Budget Item Centre

This is a commonly utilised approach, whereby the training function is allocated an annual budgetary expenditure allowance based on its anticipated operational costs. It has several advantages in that the training function has a clear indication of the financial resources at its disposal, while it also encourages the participation of other departments which do not incur direct costs in training and development activities. However, funds which are allocated and controlled by a central source, rather than "earned" by the training function, may limit the motivation to initiate interventions in line with the real learning needs of the organisation and its employees.

Cost Centre

Under this approach, the training function charges other departments within the organisation for the training and development services it provides. At the end of the accounting year, the training function's budgetary performance is gauged in break-even, loss-making or profit-making terms. A number of advantages may be suggested for adopting this approach, including the following:

- organisational departments/units are made accountable for the training services they receive;

- the design and delivery of training programmes is founded on specific organisational and employee needs;

- the true costs of training and development are more clearly identifiable;

- there is a distinct onus on the training function to develop cost effective training services.

The major disadvantage identified concerns the need for line managers to plan their training in advance. Many face difficulties in this situation, as they may lack training in the identification of training needs and in the assessment of related costs and benefits.

Profit Centre

This is similar to the cost centre approach, except that there is a definite profit orientation allowing training services to be sold externally as well as internally. The advantages and disadvantages of the cost centre approach may also be applied here, with one notable addition. A further disadvantage relates to the possibility that training functions may concentrate on solely providing services which offer an immediate or short-term payback. The provision of training and development may therefore become unbalanced in the organisation as a whole, diluting the overall relevance and effectiveness of training. (For a detailed discussion on the question of whether or not the training function should operate as a profit centre, see Wills, 1993).

Preparing Budgetary Data

The specific approach to preparing and presenting budgetary data will inevitably vary between organisations. Nevertheless some broad guidelines may be put forward, concentrating at this point on the more general aspects of budget preparation (methods to identify the costs associated with specific training interventions are discussed in more detail in Chapter 13). Harrison (1992), Wills (1993) and Reid et al (1992) offer useful contributions in this area, and these form the basis of the following discussion.

Initial Budgetary Considerations

Several initial considerations should be taken into account in preparing training budgets. The proposed size of the budget must be realistically assessed, and factors influencing the level of training investment must be taken into account. These include the current financial position of the organisation, how training and development is perceived and marketed, the status and power of the training specialist and function, former levels of training and development activity undertaken, former budgetary allocation, and the availability of external funding (from government agencies, EU, etc.).

Undertaking a benchmarking exercise may prove useful, where comparisons with similar size organisations, especially competitors, can provide an indication of the level of investment required to improve competitiveness.

Finally, the format and detail of information being presented for financial purposes should comply with the normal conventions applicable within the organisation.

What Items Should Be Included in the Budget?

While it may seem an obvious point, it is important to include all items that contribute to the cost of training and development. Two types of training cost are commonly referred to: fixed costs, which are incurred irrespective of the level of training activity (e.g. salaries, overheads, etc.) and variable costs, which are directly related to the nature and extent of training provision (e.g. hire of rooms, materials usage, etc.). Examples of training costs as categorised by Reid et al (1992) include:

People Costs

- wages/salaries/fees of trainers (internal and external)
- travel, accommodation and subsistence expenses of trainers and trainees
- salaries of managers/supervisors engaged in training/coaching
- external assessors/auditors fees
- overhead costs pertinent to all internal trainers and trainees.

Administration Costs

- wages/salaries of training administration staff
- telephone/postage
- office consumables
- hire of training venues
- sundry documentation
- overhead costs.

Equipment Costs

- training equipment and aids
- depreciation on training buildings/fixtures/fittings/equipment
- overhead costs.

Cost of Materials

- purchase and/or hire of video/audio taped learning materials
- distance/programmed learning packages
- protective clothing
- books and journals

- sundry materials (folders, etc.).

Such categorisation offers assistance in identifying the various costs associated with training and development. This may also be approached by way of direct and indirect costs on the basis of on-the-job activities, off-the-job activities, and training administration.

Calculating Training Costs

Determining the cost of many of the items listed is easily achieved, while information leading to the identification of other costs (e.g. depreciation, overheads, etc.) should be readily accessible within the organisation. The total annual running cost of the training function can therefore be calculated in a relatively straightforward manner. (See Harrison, 1992; and Wills, 1993, for different approaches to calculating trainer-day costs and the cost of a day's training).

These must be seen as broad guidelines to budget preparation. The method of calculating annual training costs, the items included or excluded, specific information requirements, and many other budgetary aspects, are all subject to interpretation and circumstance.

A budget offers a means of measuring costs/expenditure against the amounts "set aside" for training and development, on a regular (usually monthly) basis. However, it may act as a constraint on the effectiveness of training and development activities. If underestimated, the training budget may be consumed before the end of the accounting year, leaving a period of time within which it may prove difficult to initiate much-needed interventions. On the other hand, overestimation often leads to a proliferation of end-of-year training activities aimed at ensuring that the budgetary allocation is "used up" rather than at achieving organisational training and development objectives. While the budgetary allocation for previous years may provide some guidance, it is important that each annual training budget is carefully considered against specific training plans and that contingency factors are taken fully into account.

MARKETING AND POSITIONING THE TRAINING AND DEVELOPMENT FUNCTION

The notion that the training function needs to "market" its services within the organisation is an alien one to many training practitioners. Being themselves imbued with the inherent perception that training and development is a prerequisite for success, it is often taken for granted that this understanding is shared on an organisation-wide basis. This may be reinforced when the organisation is enjoying substantial turnover and profits, and investment in training and development goes largely unquestioned. However, when the trough of depression follows the peak of success (as has become an all too often occurrence in recent times, affecting even market leaders), and financial belt-tightening results, the training and development budget invariably comes under the closest scrutiny. This reflects the notion that training and development is "nice to have" rather than a core and essential process in the organisation. Clearly, training and development practitioners need to adopt a radical approach in order to overturn this notion. In order to change the way training and development is positioned within the organisation, the services provided under its banner must not only be linked to the strategic objectives of the organisation, but they must also be effectively marketed.

Gilley and Eggland (1989) and Donnelly (1991) have highlighted the need to market training and development. We will draw extensively from these sources in examining how this might be best achieved.

Elements of Training and Development Marketing

With many definitions in existence for the term "marketing", we will confine ourselves to its broad implication of promoting the image of goods and/or services, and providing these (for sale) in response to consumer demand. Let us now look at some important elements in the marketing process and their application in training and development terms.

Alignment with Customer Needs

A basic premise in marketing is that the goods or services being offered should be aligned with the express needs of the customer. As a function with a service orientation, training and development must therefore be focused on specific needs of the organisation and the client (within the organisation). This means that a customer orientation should be adopted — services provided should be appropriate, timely and cost-effective — to demonstrate the ability of the training and development function to meet requirements. This ability must further extend to what might be called the "pre-sales" and "after-sales" service stage of the training and development process.

Demand

In basic economic terms, consumer demand creates the need for supply, and marketing strategies are devised to fulfil this demand (although it may be suggested that the aggressive marketing techniques employed in more recent times have been aimed at creating a demand for specific goods and/or services). The marketing of training and development must address the demand within the organisation. Such demand can arise as a result of changes in legislation, the introduction of new technology, changing work practice, etc. Within these areas specific client needs can be targeted, and by satisfying such needs training and development will be perceived as a vital contributor to organisational effectiveness.

Ideally, training and development should be linked to the demands inherent in the corporate objectives of the organisation. This has two major implications for the marketing of training. Firstly, it is imperative that training and development marketing strategies are not manipulative (based on the needs of the training function rather than on client/ organisational needs). Secondly, the suggestion that training and development should respond to specific demands for its services, should not be read as advocating a reactive approach — indeed a marketing strategy is enhanced by proactively identifying anticipated demand based on real future needs.

Exchange for Value

A primary aspect of marketing is the notion that the value of goods and/or services is exchanged for another value (usually money). This notion must be fully embraced by the training and development function, whether it operates as a service funded from central sources or as one drawing from departmental budgets. This means that the provision of services must take into account the financial investment involved as well as the reciprocal time, energy and commitment expended by clients and trainees. If the payback is perceived in relative terms, as equal to or exceeding the resources expended, a satisfactory exchange will be recorded. As with any marketing situation, the perceived value of an exchange transaction is a major determinant of customer satisfaction. By providing customer satisfaction in this way, training and development becomes identified as a "value for money" service and acquires an enhanced image within the organisation.

We have illustrated some of the core considerations pertinent to marketing training and development. This process may be broadly defined as the analysis, planning, implementation and control of training and development activities and events, aimed at achieving satisfactory exchanges of values with target markets, with the overall purpose of realising organisational objectives (Gilley and Eggland, 1992).

Steps in the Marketing Process

A number of specific steps have been identified through which the marketing of training and development can be effectively pursued. We will outline a summarised version of Gilley and Eggland's (1992) guide which sets out seven steps for training and development specialists to follow in devising strategic marketing plans.

Establish the "Mission" of Training and Development

The initial step in developing a marketing strategy is to establish the "mission" of training and development. This raises several questions such as:

- What is the overall purpose of the training function?

- Who (groups/individuals) can be said to constitute the customer base?

- What is of relative value to these customers?

- How relevant is the stated purpose of the training function in the light of the current context of the organisation?

- What will the future purpose of the training function be?

It is important that the mission statement answering these questions is agreed with and supported by not only those involved in the training function, but also by all organisational stakeholders in the training and development process. This suggests that an organisation-wide consultative approach should be adopted for the purpose of devising a stakeholder-friendly mission. To frame the scope of training and development within the mission statement, it may be useful to envisage dimensions such as: the sources of demand for training services; the nature and extent of the needs associated with this demand; and the way in which these needs can best be satisfied. Finally, while the mission statement should be distinctive and ambitious, it should also be grounded in practical reality.

Analysing the Internal and External Environment

Internal and external environmental analysis helps to establish the contextual factors which can impinge on the marketing strategy. Internally, these are seen as potential strengths or weaknesses, including:

- the financial and competitive positions of the organisation

- culture, values and attitudes

- managerial abilities

- present facilities and resources

- internal labour market profile

- centralised / decentralised operational strategy

- techno-structural influences.

The opportunities or threats in the external environment may result from:

- economic climate and forecasts

- socio-political conditions

- technological advances

- external labour market conditions

- legislation.

Having established the relevance of these contextual factors, it may be necessary to refine the training and development mission, prior to concentrating on its objectives and goals.

Setting Objectives and Goals

The objectives of training and development should flow from the thrust of the mission statement and should be focused on realising its aims. Goals are then set, to provide a quantifiable measurement against which the progress towards achieving these objectives can be gauged. In tandem with outlining specific achievement targets, goal-setting helps to determine the feasibility of objectives and to establish clear responsibility for their attainment. Clear goals also provide a framework for the training specialist in preparing training plans.

Target Marketing and Market Segmentation

This step is concerned with establishing parameters for the training and development marketing strategy within the organisation. In deciding target market areas the issue of segmentation must be addressed. In effect, market segmentation means that the overall market (the organisation) comprises a number of different segments (departments/groups of individuals) which may have varying training and development needs and demands. Identifying the characteristics of these segments helps to clarify whether an attempt should be made to provide services for all of the segments (mass marketing) or if certain sections should be specifically concentrated on (target marketing). The provision of training and development services can be related to five basic patterns of market coverage:

1. *Product/market concentration* — i.e. provision of particular type of training and development "product" (e.g. keyboard skills) is concentrated on a single market segment (e.g. data entry clerical personnel).

2. *Product specialisation* — i.e. provision of a particular type of product to all segments (e.g. company-wide total quality training).

3. *Market specialisation* — i.e. the full range of products is offered to a specific market segment.

4. *Selective specialisation* — i.e. the full range of products provided is tailored to meet the specialised needs of each segment.

5. *Full coverage* — i.e. a full range of products is offered to all segments.

In examining the various alternatives, the training specialist must bear in mind the overall mission and objectives of training and development. Selection is not confined to a single choice of market coverage, and a combination of marketing alternatives may be decided upon.

The Marketing Mix
The marketing mix refers to the controllable variables which form core activities in the pursuit of an effective marketing strategy. These are commonly identified as the "Four P's" — Product, Price, Promotion and Place. Let us look briefly at these in the context of a training and development marketing strategy.

Product. The focus of a product strategy is on the provision of relevant training and development programmes and learning activities. Their relevance is inextricably linked with the needs of the target market and with the overall needs of the organisation. In this sphere, it is useful to take account of the "Concept Live Cycle", whereby it is suggested that every training programme and learning activity proceeds through a cycle of stages from its invention to its disposal. These are presented as:

1. *Exposure Stage* — which refers to newly-developed programmes or activities which are only marginally utilised initially. Because the development outlay is front-loaded, the early costs of such programmes are likely to be high, and the promotion of their benefits and advantages is a marketing essential.

2. *Growth/Acceptance Stage* — this is reached when the adoption of a programme becomes more widespread, and, in this period of growth and greater participation, the development outlay is minimised. The resulting reduction in cost, combined with increased awareness, has a "multiplier" effect on its acceptance and utilisation. This situation is likely to breed similar programmes from competing providers. At this stage, marketing strategies tend to emphasise differences between versions of a programme.

3. *Maturity Stage* — this is reflected in a levelling-off of acceptance for a programme. It is likely to correspond with severe competition be-

tween the various providers who have entered the market, warranting an emphasis on programme innovations. As interest in a programme begins to wane, it may be necessary for providers to seek new markets and fresh marketing approaches.

4. *Declining Stage* — when interest in a programme goes into a downward spiral, its decline stage is at hand. New programmes may have superseded its perceived usefulness and providers must seriously consider its removal from the market arena.

Giving consideration to the life-cycle concept can prove useful for the training specialist. Identifying the positioning of particular programmes helps to establish their relevance in current and future terms, and harbours a constant awareness of change.

Place. The "place" variable is primarily centred around the need to provide the right product, to the right market, at the right time. Here, the training specialist is concerned with: training location, environment and facilities; timeliness; method of instruction; channels of distribution; service levels; etc.

Promotion. Creating an awareness of the availability of a product and/or service, and communicating its benefits and advantages to the target market, are the key areas associated with the promotional element of the marketing mix. There are a number of methods which the training function can employ in this regard, including personal selling, public relations and sales promotion.

Price. As a marketing feature, the price of a product and/or service is usually related to its cost and the perceived tolerance of the target market. The training function which operates on a self-financing basis must juggle both of these factors to achieve the correct pricing balance. On the other hand, the centrally-funded training function must overcome the frequent perception that "free" training programmes lack professionalism, status, quality, etc.

The training specialist should attach equal importance to these four main variables of the marketing mix, although the circumstances of each organisation will dictate shifts and adjustments in emphasis.

Overall Marketing Strategy
The choice of an overall marketing strategy for training and development within the organisation rests between four options. The alternative approaches may be summarised as follows:

1. *Product development* — centralising the financial and human resources of the training function on developing new programmes or revitalising those already in existence.

2. *Market penetration* — here the primary focus of the training function is placed on aggressive marketing, aimed at increasing the acceptance and utilisation of its training programmes in existing market areas within the organisation.

3. *Market development* — this represents an effort at creating a greater awareness and wider acceptance of training programmes in new market areas within the organisation.

4. *Diversification* — this strategy is centred around the development of new training programmes for new markets within the organisation. It can be used to particular advantage in situations where the growth of training and development is envisaged.

The choice of overall marketing strategy should dovetail with the mission and objectives of training and development.

Marketing Plans for Training and Development

Having proceeded through the previous six steps the marketing plan is essentially completed. It is an holistic process, involving a fundamental examination of the training and development role, as well as the purpose of the organisation itself. Implementing a marketing plan can improve the image and credibility of training and development. It helps to increase the training specialist's awareness of the fundamental nature of the exchange process, and also provides the foundation for devising training and development policies and plans.

TRAINING AND DEVELOPMENT RESOURCES

Appropriate and adequate internal resources must be allocated to the training and development function, and it may become necessary to seek and acquire external resources. In addition, all of these resources must be competently managed and properly utilised, to ensure that the contribution of training and development to the organisation is maximised.

Having said this, what exactly do we mean when we say "appropriate and adequate" internal resources? Here, it is important to remember the organisational context of training and development, and the fact that the nature of the resources needed will vary accordingly to circumstances. For instance, some (mainly large) organisations have their own purpose-built training rooms, complete with state-of-the-art equipment and learning aids. On the other hand, such facilities are way beyond the means, and often indeed the needs, of many smaller organisations. In a similar vein, some organisations employ large numbers of training staff, with ample administrative support, whereas a single individual may be expedited to carry the total workload associated with the training role elsewhere. The term appropriate and adequate, therefore, may be used to describe those resources which match specific organisational needs, and which enable the full implementation of training and development policies and plans.

Let us now look at the nature of training and development resources, under the following headings:

Personnel

There are a number of categorisations which may be applied to the "people" resource of the training function, and we will now summarise the relevance of each of these in turn.

Training Specialists

The value of an effective training specialist hardly needs emphasising at this point, except to say that such individuals can be expected to apply their skills, knowledge and abilities to the enhancement of organisational learning. Their contribution is pivotal: it is they who embody the image and vision of the training and development process, and who judiciously mould its shape and direction by harnessing the synergy of all training resources.

Trainers/Instructors

There are various people, both within and outside the organisation, who may perform a direct training role, including the training specialist (whom we have already mentioned) and line managers (who comprise our next category). An internal training resource can also be built up through the involvement of trainers and/or instructors. Trainers are commonly involved on a full-time basis, while instructors are often selected and trained to perform this role on a part-time basis, mainly to assist the initial engagement of employees in specific operational processes. In either case, they not only assist with on-the-job training, but are often the first regular point of contact for new employees and can therefore help to shape attitudes and create a positive approach to learning. The expertise of external trainers can also be called upon. This may be necessary to alleviate a heavy demand on internal trainer resources, or to provide specialist training (appropriate perhaps with the introduction of new technology).

Line Managers

The role of line managers in the training and development process has been discussed in Chapter 9. It is widely recognised that this group potentially represents a substantial training resource, and their fruitful involvement can extend across a wide range of training activities. In an overall sense, line managers enjoy a unique position in which to act as facilitators of learning, encouraging and motivating employees to become "knowledge" workers by applying the learning process in their day-to-day activities. They are ideally placed to identify individual and departmental training and development needs, and to contribute to the design and development of appropriate training activities. Line managers may also perform a direct training role, especially in induction and on-the-job training. Employees benefit from their advice and guidance prior to involvement in off-the-job training, while the training specialist similarly benefits in receiving feedback on the extent to which learning has been successfully transferred to the workplace. Line managers can help employees to identify and pursue career development opportunities, and their knowledge and advice is of major assistance in the selection of potential training instructors. However, their greatest contribution as a training resource may emanate from the example shown through their own personal commitment to training and development.

Trainees

Trainees themselves can also represent a valuable training resource. As a source of immediate feedback they can indicate areas requiring reinforcement, determine the requisite pace of learning, and identify inappropriate or unsuitable content areas or training methods. This provides useful information which can be fed into the design of future training activities. In group situations especially, the active participation of trainees and the sharing of experiences can enhance individual and group learning. Reid et al (1992) suggest that former trainees who are "satisfied customers" are useful ambassadors through their support for training and development.

External Advisors/Consultants

Further external resources can be utilised in the shape of National Agency training advisors. They offer assistance and guidance on many aspects of training and development, and can direct the organisation towards sources of available funding. External consultants offer professional training and development services and are often engaged on the basis of their specialist knowledge and expertise in a given area, or because of their perceived "political neutrality".

Top Management

The commitment of top management must also be seen as a vital resource. This can be demonstrated by their personal example, their support of and commitment to training and development, in addition to the allocation of appropriate financial resources to the training and development function.

Physical Resources

There are many types of physical resources which may be required by the training function. These include facilities, materials, equipment, etc., and they are available internally or externally to the organisation. The physical resource requirements of training and development are fairly obvious — appropriate training rooms, learning aids (overhead projector, flipcharts, audio-visual equipment, etc.), documentation/folders etc., machinery or equipment for demonstration/practice purposes, and so forth. On this point, Wills (1993), provides a useful checklist for site surveys relevant to selecting external training locations.

External training courses and programmes can also be classed as training and development facilities. Reid et al (1992) group such provision under several headings, including: private sector courses; industry group training schemes; professional associations; public sector education and training services; and courses run by trade unions. It is worth reiterating that developing linkages with local third-level institutions can provide a substantial training resource for organisations.

Time

The notion of time as a resource must not be overlooked, and it can broadly affect the training and development function in two ways. The length of time spent by individuals on any aspect of training and development constitutes one factor, while the time spent by individuals away from their normal work, in order to participate in training and development activities, is another. To fully utilise time as a resource, planning and scheduling of events and activities is of crucial importance. Adequate time scales must be allotted prior to training and development events in order to undertake appropriate activities (e.g. assessing training needs, setting training objectives, designing learning events, etc.). At the design stage itself, identifying the suitable length of time which must be devoted to specific interventions is a critical input. When scheduling training and development events, on-the-job, off-the-job, and off-site activities will all involve different time factors for consideration — these depend on training/instructors, trainees, and the availability of internal or external facilities. Balancing the need for training and development with the practical demands of production and/or service patterns must be seen as a primary concern during the scheduling process. Finally, appropriate time must be allocated for evaluation, and the timing of evaluation stages for specific events should be carefully planned.

Finance

We have examined the budgetary aspects of training and development earlier, and these encompass many of the issues relating to the allocation of financial resources in this regard. Suffice it to say, therefore, that the extent of financial investment has profound implications for each training and development resource category discussed.

Inadequate finances can seriously impact on the manner in which people, physical resources, and time can be applied to the training and development process. Thus, in the vast majority of cases, potential benefits and payback on training and development can be directly related to the financial resources apportioned to the training function.

Managing Training Resources

Having examined the nature of training and development resources, let us now look at an approach to managing these effectively. Harrison (1992) provides a useful guideline in this regard which may be summarised as follows:

1. Observe, and reflect on, the current situation, focusing on the availability, utilisation, and cost effectiveness of present resources.

2. Analyse the resulting information in the context of the organisation — significant factors in its operating environment (internal and external) and its strategies, plans, policies, and priorities — and of approaches to training and development which might be appropriate in the circumstances.

3. Think creatively of alternative ways in which available or potential resources may be employed.

4. Decide on a feasible course of action, concentrating on cost efficiency and effectiveness.

5. Monitor progress and evaluate results.

These are put forward as a cyclical set of procedures, indicating how the judicious management of training and development resources may be approached on an ongoing basis.

TRAINING AND DEVELOPMENT POLICIES AND PLANS

We are all probably familiar with the notion that the overall policies and plans of the organisation represent a formal framework through which it is proposed to pursue its goals and objectives. Policies and plans may be described as statement of intent: policies form the broad basis from which plans are devised; plans constitute a more detailed version of a proposed course of action. To maintain the equilibrium of the organisation, the basic tenets of this framework must be adopted by all the organisation's sub-systems in devising their own policies and plans. So it is, indeed, with the training and development function.

Training and Development Policies

As Reid et al (1992) comment, all organisations have a training and development policy, albeit one that is explicit or implicit, formal or informal. Therefore, the nature and emphasis of its expression may be essentially viewed as being organisation-specific, and as reflecting the overall philosophy of the organisation in relation to employee development.

In a general sense, a formal training policy provides guidelines through which the training and development activities within the organisation will be pursued. It defines the rights, roles and responsibilities of everyone in the organisation in this regard, and encompasses information concerning:

- the resources to be allocated to training and development;

- the nature and extent of training and development activities;

- how, and by whom, the assessment of training needs will be undertaken;

- the manner in which requests for training and development will be processed.

A formal training and development policy serves a number of useful purposes, including that it:

- clarifies the relationship between the overall goals and objectives of the organisation and the purpose of the training and development function;

- establishes a framework for the development and implementation of training plans;

- assists management in identifying training and development activities for resolving problems and exploiting business opportunities.

- sets out operational guidelines, by clearly stating the reasons why management is investing in training and development and the resources being allocated to this purpose;

- helps to ensure that all levels of management and supervision are aware of their responsibilities in relation to training and development, and of their expected levels of participation in associated activities;

- makes employees aware of the organisation's commitment to their training and development;

- may enhance the profile of the organisation in terms of the benefits perceived by potential recruits;

- acts not only as a source of information for all managers, but also clearly sets out for employees the type of education, learning, and/or development activities that they can undertake;

- can complement career development within the organisation and facilitate the establishment of related opportunities for employees;

- defines the context of the training and development function vis-à-vis other organisational activities.

As this list indicates, significant benefits and advantages can be envisaged as a result of the organisation adopting a formal training and development policy. However, much will depend on the approach to its formulation and implementation.

Formulation of Training and Development Policies

Training and development policies are not formulated in isolation or in a vacuum, and Reid et al (1992) identify numerous variables which impact on deliberations and developments in this respect. These include:

- the organisation's overall mission, goals and strategic objectives

- size, growth-stage, traditions and culture of the organisation

- nature and priorities of training needs identified

- the organisation's products and/or services

- top management's commitment to training and development

- past and current training and development policies, and how they were formulated, and implemented

- internal and external labour markets, and recruitment policy

- professionalism of training specialist and staff, and training experience of managers
- budgetary considerations and resources of training function
- statutory requirements
- economic, social, local, political and environmental factors
- involvement with national training agencies.

These variables influence not only the way training and development policies are formulated, but also the manner in which these are perceived and reacted to within the organisation.

Where a planned and systematic approach to training and development is evident, the above variables will usually be taken into consideration at the policy formulation stage. In addition, the policy will be seen as a living entity, subject to ongoing change as the organisation itself responds to influences in its environment. It will be widely communicated, as will alterations to its substance or direction, and there will be a well developed awareness of its contents and thrust throughout the organisation. In these circumstances the policy is likely to be drawn up by the training specialist and approved by top management (who may in fact contribute to its formulation). The policy is published and usually promulgated through policy manuals. The Department of Enterprise and Employment Survey (1993) indicates that many high technology companies in Ireland have written and published training and development policy statements, with the accruing advantages being seen as:

- the content is explicit and known to all employees;
- it forms a reference point for managers in the performance of their training and development activities;
- it provides a common focus for the purpose of training and development;
- it leads to consistency, equality of treatment, and greater understanding;
- utter dependence on the training function and specialist is lessened;
- it reduces the reliance on precedent, which may often be vague;
- it facilitates the planning process in the sphere of human resources.

If the planned approach to policy is thus seen to advantage, it can be contrasted with the ad hoc approach. This is usually typified by training and development policies being not so much formulated as evolving in an unco-ordinated and unsystematic fashion. They are also likely to be informal, implicit, lacking visibility, and subject to individual interpretation (or misinterpretation). They further tend to be distorted in their emphasis and application, and can be expected to embrace an operational, rather than strategic, focus. Consequently, numerous problems can be linked to the ad hoc approach, specifically the following:

- critical difficulties hinder attempts to adequately communicate the policy, leading to misunderstanding and inconsistency;

- without involvement in the formulation and approval of a formal policy, top management commitment to training and development is considerably weakened;

- lack of clarity and ambiguity lead to over-reliance on the training specialist and other key individuals;

- the coherence of the training and development planning process is seriously impaired;

- the credibility and influence of the training specialist and function are adversely affected.

Overall, then, there is much to recommend the planned approach to policy formulation. Nevertheless, this stage must not be seen as an end in itself. If the policy statement is to become more than just a list of admirable intentions, the policies themselves must be put into practice.

Implementing Training and Development Policies

The implementation of training and development policies must also be approached in a planned and co-ordinated fashion, and three main issues may be put forward for consideration in this respect.

Publicity

It is important that the policies are known, understood, and accepted by all those involved in their implementation. On this point, we have already advocated their publication in employee handbooks and their reinforcement during induction. Further useful opportunities to communicate policies arise during briefing sessions for line managers and employees, and departmental and company-wide meetings.

Procedures

Procedures are a critical element in the implementation process, acting as a vital conduit through which the substance of policies is transferred to the operational level of the organisation. As a regulatory factor, procedures ensure that policies are implemented fairly and consistently throughout the organisation. Their effectiveness is enhanced when they are written and published, and their use extends particularly to areas such as:

- induction/re-induction

- assessing training and development needs

- dealing with requests for attending specific training courses

- budgetary approval for training programmes

- evaluation of training activities.

Monitoring/Modification

It is essential that policies, and indeed procedures, are regularly reviewed to assess their relevance in the light of current organisational objectives. Indeed, this is a crucial factor, if policies are not to become outdated as the organisation undergoes change. Collecting information on the manner in which policies are being implemented helps to uncover problem areas and to facilitate appropriate modification. Monitoring can be carried out in a number of ways: through discussions with line managers, by informal walkabouts, through conversations with employees, etc. It is also important that a proactive approach to modifications is adopted, by developing an awareness of the potential impact of changes in the external environment. Of course the key mechanism for progressing training policies is the development and implementation of training and development plans.

Training and Development Plans

Training and development plans take their substance from the policy statement, and represent a firm and comprehensively detailed statement concerning how it is proposed to realise policy in a practical way. They can be expected to cover all activities encompassed by the training and development function, and may be broken down into sub-plans for specific areas of the organisation. While training and development plans are normally formulated on an annual basis, some organisations may further seek to establish plans covering a longer period. In general terms, training and development plans should project:

- the priorities of the training needs identified and the anticipated performance improvements;

- the nature, extent, and sequence of training and development activities;

- a clarification of roles and responsibilities;

- cost/benefit analysis;

- training locations and methods;

- the nature, extent, and sequence of evaluation methods.

Reid et al (1992) highlight the need to maintain a balance between available resources and the activities proposed, and see a typical plan containing elements such as the following:

- for each department — details on a regular basis (monthly, half-yearly) of training requirements by job classification, including the number of employees involved;

- similar details for those outside of normal departmental structures;

- for each time of training — targeted standard, classification of responsibilities, training strategy (on-the-job, external, mentoring, etc.), training costs, and start/duration/completion schedule;

- for categories of training — a summary of the budgetary allocation, by organisation and department.

Overall responsibility for training and development plans and their implementation may vary from organisation to organisation. However, it must be suggested that the credibility of the training function will be seriously eroded if the primary responsibility does not fall within its remit.

Within this proviso, it is imperative that training and development plans are formulated with the full involvement and commitment of senior and line management. A flexible approach in relation to training and development plans must also be adopted. The volatility of the external environment can trigger sudden and dramatic changes in the organisation's priorities, and an appropriate training and development response is often a necessity in order to maintain a business focus. A rapid response capability must therefore be developed by the training function, demonstrating its facility (and willingness) to shift the emphasis and priority of planned activities.

Much of the prescriptive commentary on policies and plans focuses almost entirely on the "tangible" aspects of training and development (e.g. assessing training needs, types of training being provided, individuals and groups covered, evaluation methods, resources, budgetary considerations, etc.). However, intangible elements, such as developing an ethos of organisational learning and promoting natural learning processes within the organisation, would also command attention at this stage. Intentions along these lines should be included in policy statements, while plans would include practical details of how it is proposed to create and sustain a learning environment within the organisation.

SCOPE AND STATUS OF THE TRAINING FUNCTION IN IRISH ORGANISATIONS

We will conclude this chapter by looking at the scope and status of the training function in an Irish context. Recent research by Heraty (1992), conducted with 58 training specialists from a cross-section of Irish organisations, highlights the outstanding issues in this regard. We will concentrate on two specific aspects of the research: (a) the nature and extent of training and development activities undertaken; and (b) the allocation of responsibility for training and development.

Training and Development Activities Undertaken

The focus of the research survey in this area was to determine the extent of strategic orientation be applied to the activities undertaken by training specialists in their daily work routine. Respondents were provided with a list of training and development activities, and asked to indicate those which they undertake on a regular basis. Tabulated results are presented in Table 11.2, showing the total percentage of respondents who indicated their involvement in the various activities, as well as a breakdown of organisation size and ownership.
Let us initially extract some of the significant findings:

- It emerges that some 85 per cent of respondents are actively involved in the identification of training and development needs, and this is evidenced across all organisational sizes and ownership groups.

- The next two priority areas are providing advice and guidance to line management on training and development (83 per cent) and evaluating programmes (83 per cent). However, a major discrepancy emerges in the extent of involvement across organisation size and ownership categories. Small organisations and those which are Irish-owned bear a distinctly unfavourable comparison to both medium/large organisations on the one hand, and those which are US/Japanese/European-owned on the other. This may be partly explained by the fact that most of the small organisations relevant to the survey also happened to be Irish.

- While the formulation of training and development policies (74 per cent) is ranked fourth overall on the list, the results in both the small (14 per cent) and Irish-owned (37 per cent) categories show a very low level of involvement. Indeed, the contrast with all other categories is even more unfavourable in this area.

Table 11.2 Training activities undertaken by Irish Training and Development Specialists and Relationship with Size and Ownership

ACTIVITY	Used	Organisation Size			Ownership		
	%	<100	101-500	501+	Irish	US/ Jap.	Eur.
Identification of T&D needs	85	75	80	99	72	97	83
Advice and guidance to line managers	83	22	79	89	57	91	79
Evaluation of T&D programmes	83	27	79	96	65	93	90
Formulation of T&D policies	74	14	68	87	37	85	78
Advice to individual employees on T&D issues	72	65	69	70	63	80	68
Securing physical resources for T&D	69	66	54	58	66	71	60
Undertaking direct training activities	67	11	49	45	62	78	77
Informing top management of T&D achievements	66	9	40	87	20	91	86
Formulation of yearly T&D plans	64	12	52	77	54	97	82
Liaison with Personnel function for integration purposes	62	53	41	67	62h	61	55
Formulation and monitoring of budgets	53	14	49	77	33	97	64
Implementing innovative and change activities in the organisation	52	8	34	87	23	87	71
Undertaking manpower planning-related activities	46	26	41	69	32	87	65

ACTIVITY	Used	Organisation Size			Ownership		
Advising top management of implications for T&D of corporate strategy	46	11	32	55	27	79	54
Conducting annual T&D audits	46	15	43	60	22	93	72
Undertaking personnel activities	43	57	39	32	41	41	47
Monitoring of external environment to assess implications for T&D	39	5	23	56	19	64	51

In seeking to determine the extent to which the training and development practices of the training specialists reflect a strategic orientation, it is necessary to focus on the key activities which reveal such an orientation. The following points are set out from this perspective:

- Environmental scanning is a critical determinant of a strategic orientation — it involves the training function in general, and the specialist specifically, taking cognisance of the environment within which the organisation operates, in order to accurately assess the necessity for changes in terms of both the present skill levels and the overriding corporate strategy. However, the results indicate that less than 40 per cent of respondents, in total, monitor their external environment, while 46 per cent advise top management of the implications of the corporate strategy for training and development, and only 52 per cent are actively involved in implementing change in their organisations. Furthermore, the levels of involvement in these activities in small organisations is minimal at best, while those in Irish-owned organisations are very low. Indeed, it is only in US/Japanese-owned organisations, that levels of involvement in these areas are consistently higher than 60 per cent.

- Other activities which can suggest involvement at the strategic level include formulation of training and development policies, formulation of yearly plans, formulation and monitoring of budgets, and manpower planning activities. With the exception of policy formulation (which we have already highlighted), the overall levels of involvement are again on the low side. This fact can be vividly illustrated by the indication that some 36 per cent of respondents are not involved in formulating yearly plans, and by the corresponding figures for budgetary activities (47 per cent) and manpower planning related activities (54 per cent). Once again the lesser involvement in small, and in Irish-owned organisations, is in evidence.

- While evaluation shows up prominently, formal audits of such activities, which could provide measurable results of the effectiveness of these programmes from a strategic viewpoint, are undertaken by just 46 per cent of specialists (it is possible of course that external audits are conducted in some cases).

The results suggest that training specialists are less involved at the strategic level than is necessary if the training function is to adopt a strategic focus. Given the importance of anticipating future changes and of planning accordingly, and considering the unique position of training specialists to facilitate organisational change, it is disappointing to note that so few of the respondents undertake such activities. In general, the results may be viewed in a somewhat positive light, since they indicate that training and development is largely a systematic, planned activity. However, they also suggest that training specialists reflect a greater concern for the activities themselves, than for becoming involved in the more strategic aspects of training and development.

This was further borne out by another aspect of the research, where respondents were asked to rank activities undertaken in order of perceived importance (limited to five activities). The identification of training and development needs was ranked as the most important activity, and the point must be made, that while this constitutes a necessary part of the training specialist's role, it is also an area that is increasingly being recognised as having line management involvement and responsibility. A strong case can be made for training specialists to reduce their pronounced concentration in this area, and to broaden their vision by conceptualising training and development, and the role of the training specialist and function, in more holistic terms. The formulation of policies was ranked as the second most important activity, while providing advice to line managers came in third, and evaluation was placed fourth. This means that the top four in order of perceived importance, correspond (although not in the same sequence) with the top four activities undertaken. Interestingly, the area which jumps into the fifth place in order of importance is informing top management of training and development achievements. Perhaps the significance of this lies in efforts to "legitimise" and justify the existence of the training function? It can be reasonably suggested that it is not a reflection of perceived strategic involvement, which in itself implies top management support for training.

Responsibility for Training and Development Activities

In this section of the research training specialists were presented with a list of activities and asked to indicate whether responsibility in these areas rested with themselves, with line managers, or extended to both. The results are presented in Table 11.3.

Table 11.3: Responsibility for Training and Development Activities

	Training Specialist		Line Manager		Both	
	N	%	N	%	N	%
Identification of T&D needs	16	26	10	18	32	56
Formulation of T&D policies	35	76	3	7	8	17
Translation of T&D policies into plans	28	68	4	10	9	32
Selection of T&D methods to be used	30	52	7	12	21	36
Deciding who in the organisation is to be trained	10	17	17	29	31	53
Undertaking direct training	8	16	12	24	31	60
Evaluation of T&D activities	28	56	2	4	20	40
Succession planning	15	43	6	17	14	40
Advising top management of implications of corporate strategy for T&D	29	87	0	0	4	13

The responses show that line managers generally have an active role to play in training and development in their respective organisations. Nevertheless, following closer examination it unfolds that line managers' participation and responsibility is largely confined to the operational aspects of the training and development process. The responsibility for policy formulation, translating policies into plans, and advising top management of the implications of corporate strategy for training and development, are clearly seen as the preserve of the training specialist (with little indication of even a share in this responsibility for line managers). On the other hand, the line manager's domain (shared to some extent with the training specialist) is seen to include the identification of training needs, deciding who is to be trained, and undertaking direct training. On this basis, while line managers may have wider responsibility for, and greater involvement in, training and development than was traditionally the case, they remain noticeably absent from participation in more strategically-oriented activities. Two significant factors can be suggested as a result. Firstly, the confinement of line management involvement may be said to contradict the notion of adopting a strategic orientation for training and development (certainly in its fullest sense). Secondly, line managers' exclusion from strategic activities may well result in their alienation, demotivation, or even in disputes concerning ownership and control of the training and development process.

Overall, the trends relating to the scope and status of training and development in Irish organisations reflect a reasonably healthy situation. However, it must be said that there is a strong preoccupation with the operational aspects of training and development, in tandem with the considerable measure of neglect attributable to more strategic activities. That the signs of this neglect are more glaringly obvious in small-sized (by implication Irish-owned), and in Irish-owned (as a specific category) organisations, must also be a matter of some concern.

SUMMARY

This chapter addressed the important issue of establishing a training function within the organisation. It is a complicated process and involves key decisions about reporting arrangements, the nature and size of training budgets, the identification of training and development resources, the marketing and positioning of the training department function and the formulation of training and development plans. We concluded the chapter by outlining the scope of training practices in Irish organisations. The basic message to emerge from this research is that indigenous Irish companies lag behind their rivals in the application of good training practice.

12

THE IRISH TRAINING AND DEVELOPMENT SPECIALIST: POSITION, SELECTION, CAREER ANCHORS AND ETHICS

INTRODUCTION AND LEARNING OBJECTIVES

In this chapter we consider a number of characteristics of training and development specialists, in particular their biographical characteristics, their position within the organisation, their selection to the position of training and development specialist, their direction as specialists, their career anchors and finally their credibility and ethics. Having read this chapter you will understand:

♦ the profile of Irish training and development specialists in terms of age, sex, education qualifications, career choices and anchors;

♦ the training and development specialist;

♦ the factors that influence the credibility of the training and development specialist;

♦ the ethical dimensions of the trainer's role and how Irish training and development specialists perceive their ethical position.

CHARACTERISTICS OF IRISH TRAINING AND DEVELOPMENT SPECIALISTS

Recent research by Heraty (1992) and Drea (1994), provides useful insight into characteristics of Irish training and development specialists. This research examines a number of important dimensions which we will consider here.

Biographical Characteristics

Training and development has traditionally been perceived as a male-dominated discipline, and indeed this notion has been largely supported by previous Irish studies. For instance, the IDA (1982) found that 93 per cent of respondents in a similar survey were male, while Shivanath's

(1988) research indicated that a substantially higher number of men than women were employed in the area of Personnel Management (inclusive of the training function). However, the findings reflect some movement away from this trend. Heraty (1992) found a ratio closer to 2:1, showing welcome broadening of female participation at this level of training and development, while Drea's (1994) sample was 70 per cent male and 30 per cent female.

Although there was considerable variance in the age group of the training specialists involved, both studies show that the greatest proportion was recorded in the 25-29 age bracket, representing just over 25 per cent. Furthermore, almost 50 per cent of those surveyed in both cases were aged less than 35 years. These results show a marked similarity to those found in the 1982 study, in which 47 per cent of respondents were under the age of 35 years.

All but three individuals (two British, one Swiss) were Irish nationals. This tends to suggest that the vast majority of companies operating in Ireland, both indigenous and multinational, tend to employ Irish training specialists. This is not an altogether surprising phenomenon.

Regarding membership of professional bodies/associations, 70 per cent reported membership of the IITD, 50 per cent were members of the IPM (now IPD) and 41 per cent held IMI membership.

Education Qualifications

Heraty (1992) found that only a small proportion of specialists had not completed some form of formal post-secondary education. Those who did not were in the upper age group and had gained considerable experience in other functional areas before becoming a training and development specialist. Approximately 20 had completed a diploma, 18 had attained a primary degree, 6 had post-graduate degrees, and 11 had acquired a professional qualification. For the most part, these qualifications were business-oriented (i.e. BBS, B.Comm., MBA).

Heraty (1992) compared the educational qualifications of male and females. The results showed that 32 per cent of female respondents had completed a diploma, whereas 35 per cent of male respondents had done so. Forty-two per cent of females held a primary degree, with the equivalent figure for males standing at 27 per cent. In the post-graduate category, 16 per cent of females and 8 per cent of male respondents had post-graduate diplomas or degrees, while in the professional qualification category, the figures recorded were males 22 per cent and females 11 per cent. These results tend to indicate that the comparatively low representation of females in the training and development specialist's role cannot be attributed to their lack of formal qualifications. Interestingly, more male than female respondents had opted for professional qualifications, which are generally pursued in the post-employment stage, reflecting perhaps higher levels of career advancement among males, the reasons for which are beyond the scope of this book.

In overall terms, the results indicate that Irish training and development specialists are highly educated individuals, lending credibility and prestige to the overall functioning of the training and development process in Irish organisations.

Position of the Training Specialist in the Organisation

Certain basic difficulties confront any effort at positioning the "level" at which the training specialist operates. Job titles vary across organisations, and this is particularly true in relation to training and development. In an effort to attempt a reasonable analysis, Heraty's study classified job titles according to generally recognised hierarchical positions: directorate (training/human resources development director), senior management (training and development manager), and junior management (training officer) levels. The results of a classification on this basis are presented in Table 12.1.

Table 12.1: Training Specialist's Position in Hierarchy

	Male	Female	Total
Director	2	3	5
Senior Management	22	9	31
Junior Management	11	6	17
Other	3	2	5

Source: Heraty:, N. (1992): "Training and Development: A Study of Practices in Irish-Based Companies", mimeo, University of Limerick.

The table indicates that many training specialists operate at senior management level in organisations. In addition, the low figure shown for those who have reached top management level is indicative of the current status of training. The analysis points to some 29 per cent of those surveyed as holding junior management positions. The classification "other" refers to those who operate primarily in a line management function, but also carry the responsibility for training and development.

Some interesting differences from a male/female perspective showed through in the analysis. While 15 per cent of the female specialists reside at directorate level, the comparable figure for males is just 5 per cent. We have seen that a greater proportion of female respondents have completed degree programmes. However, if this is a reason for the difference, how can the 60 per cent of males operating at senior levels be explained against the 45 per cent of females holding a similar position?

Apparently, no fundamental discrepancy existed in relation to service length in the training and development area. The 60 per cent – 45 per cent imbalance is most likely a result of the past and present gender discrimination affecting all occupations.

In conjunction with the positioning of training specialists, Heraty also examined their reporting relationships. As might be expected, most of the individuals reported either directly to the general manager or equivalent level, or to the head of human resources (equating in most cases to director level). Overall, this would seem to suggest that many training specialists are well-positioned to develop a strategic orientation for the training and development process in their organisations. Nonetheless, it might be put forward as a counter-argument that the proportionate number operating at junior management levels indicates a poor positioning for this purpose.

Training and Development Career Spans and Choices

In an effort to gauge career spans within the training and development function, respondents were asked to indicate the length of time they had been employed in this capacity. The results showed that over 50 per cent of the training specialists have been employed in the training and development area for less than three years, and that some 75 per cent have been thus employed for less than ten years. In the first place, this seems to suggest that the training and development function is a relatively young one in the organisations surveyed. However, it may also point to considerable turnover of those holding responsibility for training and development.

Respondents were further asked if working in the training and development area was their first career choice, and, if not, what has prompted them to become involved in this function. It is interesting to note that only 18 (32 per cent) of the training specialists affirmed that training and development was their first career choice. Of these, proportionately less females (25 per cent) than males (34 per cent) enter this area of employment as a priority choice. For the remaining individuals, two reasons were put forward as motivating their involvement in the training and development function. Either a position in this area became vacant which represented a step upwards in the organisation concerned, or a choice was made on the basis of a perceived opportunity for personal development. Overall, only 4 individuals (all male) nominated training and development as a career choice on the strength of its status within the organisation. This set of results could be interpreted to suggest that the training and development function, in terms of power and status, is seen as a somewhat limiting career option.

This is further borne out, to a certain extent at least, by another area of investigation. To find the attraction of individuals of working in the training and development area, Heraty presented respondents with a number of statements in this regard and asked to indicate the extent to which each was agreed or disagreed with. The results are presented in Table 12.2 where the percentage figures represent the proportion of re-spondents who either agreed or agreed strongly with the various state-ments.

Table 12.2: Attraction of Training and Development Area for Specialists

Attraction	%
Opportunity to utilise interpersonal skills	97
Opportunity to carry out good professional practices	90
Opportunity to work with organisational problems	88
Opportunity to act as facilitator of change	83
Opportunity to enhance personal development	74
Interesting subject matter involved	69
Opportunity to facilitate the development of others	67
Opportunity to act as a direct trainer	66
Opportunity to gain experience for promotion to general management	53
Hierarchical position in the organisation	17
Job security attached to position	17

Source: Heraty, N. (1992), "Training and Development: An Study of Practices in Irish-Based Companies", mimeo, University of Limerick.

The data illustrate that the primary attraction of training and develop-ment to Irish training and development specialists is centred around the opportunity to develop their own skills, to utilise these in a professional manner, to facilitate the development of others and to act as an agent of change within the organisation. An image is thus conveyed of training and development specialists being drawn towards training and develop-ment because of the content and orientation of the work, more so than on the basis of the job's career advancement prospect. It also suggests that training specialists are concerned with fulfilling their own intrinsic work needs. It may be implied, however, by the low "attractiveness" of hierarchical position, that power and influence are largely unimportant in the realm of training and development, indicating a misunderstanding or underestimation of their true significance.

Career Anchors of Training Specialists

Schein (1978) sees the career anchor as a component of a self-concept which builds on whatever self-insight an individual has acquired from the experiences of growth and education. It cannot become a mature self-concept until a career occupant has had enough real occupational experiences to know his/her talents, motives and values. Using Schein's typology Drea (1994) examined the career anchors of Irish training and development specialists.

Technical Functional Competence
This individual likes the opportunity to apply technical/functional skills and has a strong talent or motivation for a particular area of work. Drea (1994) found that Irish training and development specialists rated this as their most important anchor, where a considerable proportion of Irish training and development specialists surveyed have a strong sense of identity with their work and are proud of their functional expertise, their self-esteem hinges on exercising their particular talents.

General Management Competence
Individuals with this anchor have a range of competencies that are necessary for management and have the ambition to rise to a level where they can make organisational decisions. This was the second highest reported anchor. This suggests that Irish training and development specialists wish to contribute to the success of the business and to think cross-functionally and integratively. It also suggests that they have good interpersonal skills as well as understanding of the technical dimensions of different functions.

Authority/Independence
Individuals with this anchor want to have jobs that allow them flexibility regarding when to work and who to work with. They dislike organisational rules and restrictions. This anchor was ranked fourth by Irish specialists. This may help explain why many training and development specialists are steered towards consulting. This role allows them authority and variety.

Service/Dedication to a Cause

Individuals who hold this anchor like the opportunity to pursue work that achieves something of value to their profession. It suggests that they will pursue opportunities even if it means changing the organisation. Irish training and development specialists ranked this third in terms of their anchors. This is consistent with the helping nature of the training and development role. Characteristics associated with this anchor include the decision to work with people and serve humanity.

Life Style

Individuals who hold this anchor want a career situation that allows them to integrate personal and family needs with the requirements of the career. This individual needs flexibility above all else. This was ranked fifth by Irish training and development specialists.

Security/Stability

Individuals who have this anchor tend to be concerned with financial security and are less concerned with the content of their work and status within the organisation. Irish training and development specialists ranked this sixth. This is a trend because such individuals are less likely to champion change and like to be reactive rather than proactive.

Pure Challenge

For this individual the only meaningful reason for pursuing a job/career is that it permits the job holder to win out over the impossible. They like intellectual work with novelty and variety. These individuals like to exercise their competitive skills. Irish training and development specialists ranked this seventh.

Entrepreneurial/Creativity

These individuals like an opportunity to create an organisation of their own. They also want financial success. Only a very small proportion of Irish training and development specialist would have this as a dominant career anchor. Table 12.3 presents the main results.

Commitment to Training and Development

On the basis of the results outlined in the previous table, it would appear that an overriding commitment to remaining in the training and development function could be applied to many of the training specialists. However, a degree of conflict with this notion arose when it was put to a direct test. In this instance, respondents were asked whether, if offered a promotion within their present function, or into another managerial function, with all other things being equal (salary, status, etc.), they would choose to continue a career in training and development.

Table 12.3: Career Anchors of Irish Trainers

Career Anchor	First Preference	Second Preference	Third Preference	Overall Rank
	%	%	%	
Technical/Functional	14	16	32	1
General Management	25	21	10	2
Service/Dedication to a Cause	14	16	14	3
Authority/Independence	21	12	9	4
Life Style	14	9	16	5
Security/Stability	5	16	11	6
Pure Challenge	5	5	11	7
Entrepreneurial Creativity	5	7	0	8
N=85				

Source: Drea, V. (1994), "An analysis of the career and career anchors of people in the training profession", unpublished thesis, University of Limerick.

In such a situation 62 per cent of training and development specialists indicated that they would remain within the training and development area, but 34 per cent signalled otherwise. Respondents were further asked how they viewed their career direction in future terms, and the results are presented in Table 12.4.

Although 62 per cent of training and development specialists (when faced with the immediate choice) professed their interest to remain within the training and development function, these results show that only 19 per cent of specialists directly see this as their long-term goal. It may be put forward that those who envisage progressing to the personnel/HRM sphere of operations, as well as those intent on becoming self-employed consultants, see themselves as still involved in the general area of training and development. However, the general thrust suggests that while many of these individuals see themselves as committed to the training and development function within the organisation in the short-term at least, their long term ambitions are removed from direct responsibility in this context.

Table 12.4: Perceived Career Direction of Training Specialists

	%
General Management	31
Personnel / HRM	31
Training and Development	19
Self-employed Consultant	14
Owning own Business	5

Source: Heraty, N. (1992), "Training and Development: A Study of Practices in Irish-Based Companies", mimeo, University of Limerick.

The fact that 31 per cent of respondents aspire to general management positions is an interesting feature. Furthermore, when the training specialists were asked if they perceived their role as an appropriate lead into a general management position, more than two-thirds of those responding did so in the affirmative.

Irish Training Specialists — A Typical Profile?

The research provides some interesting details about those who hold primary responsibility for training and development in Irish organisations. By taking the main characteristics identified, it facilitates the drawing of a broad profile of Irish training specialists, which reads as follows.

The typical Irish training specialist is male, in his late twenties, and of Irish nationality. He holds either a diploma or a degree in a business related subject, and is likely to be a member of the IITD. He operates at management level in his organisation, reports to the general manager, and has two employees reporting to him. He has been employed in the training and development function for approximately four years, joining the training function as a result of a promotion rather than as a first career choice. The value he places on his job is weighed more on the basis of involvement in various organisational activities, than on extrinsic attachments of the position itself. While he is fully committed to the training and development function, this commitment is essentially of a short- to medium-term nature — his future ambitions are focused on a move into the broader area of HRM, or indeed into general management.

These characteristics provide a snapshot of the typical profile of Irish training and development specialists. It is important to remember, of course, that this should not be interpreted as anything other than a broad generalisation, and that there are many training specialists who might be classed as "unrecognisable" on the basis of such a photo-fit.

SELECTING THE TRAINING AND DEVELOPMENT SPECIALIST

It hardly needs emphasising that selecting the training and development specialist is a process which must be given careful consideration. The appropriateness of the resulting selection decision will undoubtedly leave an indelible imprint on training and development within the organisation. Despite the obvious implications in this regard, many organisations approach selection of the individual, in whom the primary responsibly for training and development will be vested, in an off-hand or casual manner. This may arise from a less professional method of recruitment in general, or it may be a symptom of the way training and development itself is perceived in the organisation. Such instances may explain, in part at least, why "training" is sometimes allocated to an individual who possesses neither the requisite experience or qualifications, but who may be seen to possess a "safe pair of hands". Therefore, notwithstanding the odd occasion when such a haphazard selection process unearths a suitable incumbent, the importance of adopting an appropriate selection process cannot be overestimated.

The general recruitment and selection process will not be outlined in detail here. It is recommended that best practice in this area should be followed, and this is comprehensively detailed by numerous contributors — see for example Armstrong (1988) and Torrington et al (1991). However, many of the attendant core elements will arise as we examine the central issues involved in selecting the training specialist.

The "Fit" between the Individual and the Organisation

A primary consideration in selecting the training and development specialist is ensuring an appropriate fit between the individual and the organisation concerned. This means that the current environment of the organisation must be taken fully into account, particularly in terms of its training and development philosophy, and raises questions such as:

- What are the current and likely future strategic goals and objectives of the organisation?

- How can training and development best contribute to their realisation?

- Does the role of training and development currently exist within the organisation?

- If so, is this role seen as appropriate in the light of current/future needs?

- If not, what type of role is envisaged as appropriate in the light of current/future needs?

The answers to these questions help to specify the type of individual best suited to the role of training specialist in the context of the organisation. For example, if the organisation is undergoing or planning change, it is likely that the training specialist will be expected to perform a change agent type role. Therefore, taking the operating environment into consideration helps in the analysis of the type of role(s) visualised for the training specialist and the associated job requirements.

Defining Requirements

The most common approach to defining the requirements of a particular job combines two main elements under the heading of job analysis — a job description (basically setting out the overall purpose of the job and the main tasks involved), and a personnel specification (basically identifying the skills, knowledge and attitudes required to perform the job successfully). This means that four main questions should be addressed (Gilley and Eggland, 1992):

- What are the job requirements?

- How is the job currently being performed?

- What are the future job requirements?

- What knowledge and skills are needed for the job, in current and future terms?

There is a universal method for defining job requirements, in relation to the training and development specialist, that makes use of competence-based standards for trainers. These have been developed around particular models which encompass the various roles and tasks involved in the work of the training specialist, and definitions of associated areas of competence. Competence-based standards can prove a useful tool in the selection process, as they focus on the requirements of the training specialist's job (what needs to be done) as well as on the competencies of the individual employed (how what needs to be done, should be done).

It should also be remembered that there may be occasions when it is more appropriate for the role incumbent to dictate job requirements (Harrison, 1992). For instance, the nature of the work undertaken may be decided on the basis of agreed recommendations suggested by an incoming training specialist. In the lead-up to such situations, the organisation may have decided that their requirement is for a particular strategy and direction for training and development. We move now to consider criteria for selecting training and development specialists which have a more general orientation.

Criteria for Selecting Training and Development Specialists

Irrespective of the organisational context, and of the exact type of role(s) envisaged, the training and development specialist is the person ultimately responsible for the training and development process within the organisation. This means that this individual is also charged with facilitating learning and behaviour change in an enthusiastic and interesting manner, thereby enabling learners to increase their own level of knowledge and skills, and to modify their behaviour, in the pursuit of improved performance (Gilley and Eggland, 1992). In accordance with this perspective, Suessmuth (1978) has identified ten criteria, with a specific order of importance, as a basis for selection. These have been elaborated on by Gilley and Eggland (1992), and may be summarised as follows (in their ranked order):

1. Has the desire to be a trainer — wants to lead others in the learning process.

2. Relates well to others — has good interpersonal skills (this is designed as a highly subjective criterion, but is seen as essential because the facilitation of learning means working closely with people).

3. Intelligence — has the ability to quickly adapt and adjust to learners' answers and the context of the learning objectives.

4. Intrinsic motivation — primarily focused on job satisfaction through self-actualisation, rather than monetary/security conditions.

5. Adaptable to change — as the chief purpose of training and development is to promote change in others, the training specialist must also display a willingness to change and to seek opportunities for personal growth.

6. Outgoing and enthusiastic — having the flair and ability to make the learning process interesting, exciting and enjoyable.

7. Analytical — capable of analysing one's approach to the facilitation of learning, in terms of trainees/learners, learning content, learning methods and so on.

8. Self-awareness — this is seen as related to criterion number 5, as it reveals an individual's self-knowledge. Awareness is the obvious first step in the change process.

9. Secure within self — being satisfied with oneself, thereby demonstrating internal congruence (this is also put forward as an attribute needed in more managers and employees in a general sense).

10. Experience — being well-versed in specific subject matter (expertise in the facilitation of learning is taken for granted as an expectation).

The first four criteria are seen to represent essential attributes for a training specialist, and therefore as decisive "musts" for a suitable candidate. The remaining six are classified in the "nice to have" category, and their absence is not suggested as a basis for automatic rejection of a candidate. While each of these criteria may be used in the selection of training specialists, their significance is likely to vary considerably between organisations. It is important to remember, therefore, that each organisation must identify the most appropriate criteria in relation to its particular circumstances and needs, and emphasise these accordingly during the selection process (Gilley and Eggland, 1992).

TRAINING AND DEVELOPING THE TRAINING SPECIALIST

The overall role of the training and development specialist is integral to the training and development process within the organisation. It embraces primary responsibility for training and development, in conjunction with the facilitation of learning. It is underwritten by appropriate training and development for the training specialist. On this point, specific training and development needs are very much linked to the type of role undertaken and the context of the organisation itself. Nevertheless, there has been considerable movement towards the establishment of widely applicable standards of competence for training specialists, and it is on this area that we will initially focus.

Competence-based Standards for Training and Development

There is a growing emphasis on competence-based standards for occupational categories in general, both from a national and international perspective. The training and development profession has also come under this microscope and, in this context, a number of models for competence-based standards have been drawn up. Garrick and McDonald (1992) have examined several of these models and identify a number of common features. They all:

• define the training roles to which they apply;

- cluster areas of competence in some way;
- define the required competencies;
- set performance criteria; and
- define the context — either for their utilisation or for forming the basis of trainer assessment.

Let us now look briefly at the models examined:

UK Model

The Training and Development Lead Body (TDLB) have developed occupational standards for all those with training and development roles (Harrison, 1992). The competencies thus defined encompass the key purpose of training and development, the key roles involved, units of competence, and elements of competence associated with each unit. These standards are seen to represent best practice, and are built around five functional areas of competence pertinent to the training specialist. The areas are largely based on the systematic training cycle and embrace (a) identification of needs; (b) design and planning; (c) delivery of interventions; and (d) evaluation.

Canadian Model

In Canada, a standards-based model has been developed by the Ontario Society for Training and Development (OSTD). The model is built around 15 areas of competence encompassing knowledge, understanding and demonstrable skills. With an emphasis on values and attitudes, it is seen to have a more developmental focus than the UK model. It incorporates four types of training role — instructor, designer, manager and consultant.

US Model

The American Society for Training and Development (ASTD) Model identifies 11 training roles and some 35 competencies. This model differs from the others in that its competencies are related to three levels of expertise — basic, intermediate, and advanced. This allows for progression from one level to the next, and thus offers the ingredients for an established career path for training professionals.

Australian Model

The National Training Board (NTB) is the driving force behind developments in Australia. The NTB Model, like that in the UK, identifies units (seven in all) and elements of competence, with specified performance criteria.

Garrick and McDonald (1992) suggest that the main differences between the models concerns the purposes underlying their definition, the wishes of the particular stakeholders who were the catalyst for their development, and the specific context within which these developments took place.

There has been some debate over the entire notion of competence-based standards and this is discussed in detail in Chapter 15. However, in general terms, the introduction of competence-based standards can prove particularly useful in determining the training and development needs of training specialists. Such standards can also form the foundation for qualifications which are based on demonstrated abilities, catering for the accreditation of prior learning experiences.

General Competencies for the Training and Development Specialist

Another focus for the training and development needs of training specialist comes from the ASTD Model for Excellence (McLagan and Bedrick, 1983), whereby the following list of competencies are put forward in order that training specialists can perform effectively (Gilley and Eggland, 1992):

- organisation-behaviour understanding

- delegation skill

- cost/benefit analysis skill

- intellectual versatility

- feedback skill

- data-reduction skill

- presentation skill

- relationship versatility

- industry understanding

- organisation understanding

- furthering skill

- group-process skill

- negotiation skill

- adult-learning understanding

- computer literacy

- career-development knowledge
- personnel/HR field understanding.

This may appear a daunting list and it is important to reiterate that specific training and development needs of the training specialists may vary considerably, depending on the context of the organisation. However, a list such as this provides a useful basis for identifying strengths and weaknesses and for appropriately prioritising training and development needs.

So far we have concentrated on the nature of the training and development needs of training specialists. Let us now consider some ways through which these needs may be satisfied.

Professional Development of Specialist

In many countries, training and development qualifications may be pursued through formal programmes and much of this provision is overseen by national training organisations (bodies, institutes, associations, etc.). We will concentrate on the programmes provided by the Irish Institute of Training and Development (IITD), which have become an increasingly popular medium for the attainment of formal qualifications in this country.

IITD Certificate in Training and Development

The overall aim of the Certificate programme is to enable participants to develop the necessary knowledge, skills, and confidence to undertake training activities. It specifically caters for:

- individuals who have an interest in training and development and may wish to pursue it as a career;
- individuals who have recently taken up a position in the training function at a relatively junior level;
- technical trainers with considerable involvement in operator training;
- supervisors or front-line managers who are interested in acquiring a knowledge and understanding of systematic training.

The Certificate programme has a strong "train the trainer" focus, and its structure, learning methods, and assessment procedure are framed accordingly. The programme comprises a minimum of 75 contact hours, and its content is broken down into three integrated modules as follows:

Module 1   Systematic Training

Module 2   Interpersonal Skills Development
                 Delivering Training

Module 3   Training Strategies
                 Training Administration

A range of learning methods are used which are designed to combine sufficient theory and practice. Assessment is on-going throughout the programme, through a combination of module assignments, classroom activity and a comprehensive programme project and presentation. The Certificate programme is also a foundation course for the IITD Diploma in Training and Development.

IITD Diploma in Training and Development

The Diploma programme gives intensive coverage of the management of human resources within the organisation. In particular, it concentrates on the main issues involved in employee development and how this activity relates to the wider context of personnel and organisational behaviour. The aims of the Diploma are:

- to provide a detailed knowledge of the issues involved in the development of employees;

- to provide a detailed understanding of the context within which the training function must operate;

- to create an understanding of the relationship between training and development and other human resource functions with the organisation;

- to develop skills in the area of training, policy formulation, planning, course design, training evaluation, and training needs analysis;

- to provide an understanding of the national framework within which training and education operates;

- to impart an understanding of specialist areas such as management development, organisation development, and team building.

The programme is commonly pursued on a two-year, part-time (evening) basis, comprising more than 200 contact hours. The courses taken include: Management Systems Application, Organisation Theory and Behaviour, Training and Development, Human Resource Management, National Training Policy and Management Development.

The first year focuses on the core aspects of the programme content, while the second year concentrates on specialist areas. There is an emphasis on experiential (individual and group) assignments as well as written examinations, culminating in the completion of a major project. Within the project, it is expected to undertake a major area of research within the training and development field, to demonstrate the use of survey methodology, and to demonstrate the ability to organise, write and present a set of reasoned arguments.

Training and Development for Role Categories

A comprehensive outline of various ways through which training specialists can develop specific competencies for the roles they may be expected to perform is provided by Bennett (1988). We will summarise these under the following role categories:

Trainer Role

The formal opportunities for training and development pertinent to the trainer role include "train the trainer" programmes, such as the IITD Certificate programme previously outlined. However, a number of informal activities are also facilitated in this context, including:

- observing effective practitioners (e.g. at conferences, seminars, workshops, training sessions, etc.), subsequently practising what has been learned, and evaluating success;

- working through and with others by seeking advice and feedback;

- confidential practice (e.g. in front of a mirror, or using a tape recorder, video camera, microphone, etc.);

- reading current journals and books to keep abreast of latest approaches and developments;

- reflecting on an event and working out methods of improving effectiveness.

Provider Role

Again, formal activities such as the Certificate and Diploma programmes previously outlined are deemed relevant here. On an informal basis, it is also useful to seek opportunities to work with and learn from experienced practitioners. This has special relevance in the areas of pilot-testing and evaluation procedures.

Consultant Role

To perform this role effectively it is important that a sound knowledge and experience of the training and development process is interwoven with consulting skills. While the previous two role categories incorporate the former aspect, participation in a relevant formal programme can help to provide consulting and influencing skills, as well as improving analysis, problem-solving, and advisory capabilities. Informal activities which can prove of considerable assistance in a consultant role include:

- setting up action-development groups with fellow training specialists;

- seeking co-consulting opportunities with an experienced practitioner;

- keeping abreast of latest trends and developments by reading current material, conferring with management consultants, and attending pertinent conferences and workshops;

- working with, and learning from, action researchers;

- establishing a network of key senior managers within the organisation, with whom current business issues may be discussed.

Innovator/Change Agent Role

This is seen as the most difficult role to develop, overlapping as it does with the consultant role, but being primarily concerned with linking training and development with business strategy and the change process. However, the training specialist may develop broader insights into this role by:

- conferring regularly with fellow training specialists from other organisations;

- keeping abreast of developments in the external environment by reading current material, and attending relevant conferences and events;

- visiting other organisations/study tours of overseas countries;

- acquiring external expertise (academic or consultant).

Manager Role

The IITD Diploma course, which combines employee development, the management of the training function, and the management of human resources in general, is a very appropriate formal programme for developing the knowledge and skills required in the manager role. Participating in formal general management programmes can also prove very beneficial in this regard. The manager role can also be developed through less formal activities, such as:

- working and conferring with effective line managers;

- having a senior line manager as a mentor;

- involvement in management development groups with fellow training specialists from other organisations;

- talking over problems with line managers;

- arranging to spend some time in a line management role;

- keeping abreast of developments in the managerial field by reading current material, and attending relevant conferences and events.

This summary provides a flavour of the very useful framework of development opportunities offered by Bennett (1988). The emphasis on "networking" with managerial colleagues inside the organisation and with fellow training specialists in other organisations, is especially noteworthy.

THE CREDIBILITY OF TRAINING AND DEVELOPMENT SPECIALISTS AND THEIR EFFECTIVENESS

The credibility and standing of the training and development specialist within the organisation is of vital importance. These factors can greatly affect the way training and development itself is perceived and pursued, thereby directly impinging on the nature and extent of its potential contribution to the success of the organisation. There are various means by which the credibility rating of the training specialist within the organisation can be gauged. These include the extent to which the specialist is (a) viewed and utilised as a critical resource; (b) acts as an internal consultant to management; and (c) is valued as a significant organisational asset. The level at which the training specialist operates, the measure of trust and respect commanded, and the resources allocated to the training function itself, can also prove revealing indicators in the same regard. In essence, these signals serve to highlight the effect of the training specialist's credibility — we still need to know what factors trigger the rating enjoyed. A primary determinant must be the overall effectiveness of the training specialist, the element of which we will now consider.

Evaluating Training Specialist Effectiveness

In a situation where training specialists' credibility is linked firmly to their effectiveness, it is of obvious importance that they should be concerned with the factors and issues surrounding this notion. To this end, Bennett (1988) outlines an "effective trainer checklist", derived from research conducted by the Manpower Services Commission (UK) with the involvement of hundreds of trainers and managers. This checklist is not put forward as a definitive listing, but is suggested as a framework which can be developed by individual training specialists, and adapted to individual situations and circumstances. It sets out a series of questions, under a range of headings, which can assist trainers to assess their effectiveness, while taking the context of the organisation into account. The areas which come in consideration in this exercise include:

- trainer competencies

- trainer characteristics

- trainer role-orientation and roles adopted

- trainer style (of delivery)

- organisation culture

- organisation training and development needs/purpose

- overall effectiveness (outcomes from training and development process)

- skills needed to survive the constant threat to investment in training and development (i.e. technical, personal, political, innovating skills)

- attitudes to training and development within the organisation.

Bennett (1988) stresses one overall important conclusion from the research — the effectiveness of the training specialist hinges on the extent of congruence between the role adopted and the context of the organisation itself. The checklist is therefore seen as a useful tool in assisting the training specialist to achieve this fit.

Characteristics of Effective Training Specialists

A number of characteristics associated with effective training specialists have been identified by Nadler and Wiggs (1986) and elaborated on by Gilley and Eggland (1992). These can be used as a basis for suggesting that effective training specialists must have the ability to:

- plan and implement activities that promote and foster training and development, in line with the needs of the organisation, its managers, its employees, and indeed its customers;

- take a futuristic perspective, in establishing and prioritising the goals and objectives of training and development activities (over a one-to five-year time span);

- identify and establish an appropriate structure for the training function and recognise the implications arising from the positioning of the training function within the organisation;

- demonstrate effective communication skills in dealings with training staff, line managers, and most importantly, with top management;

- understand, develop and maximise the utilisation of appropriate training and development information systems, which expedite the collection and dissemination of pertinent internal and external data;

- align their personal approach and operational mode with the training and development philosophies they promote (essentially, practising what they themselves preach);

- demonstrate technical competence, appropriately reconciled with a practical orientation and application;

- build the confidence of crucial stakeholder groups (i.e. top management, line management, training staff, and employees) in the training and development process, by gaining their involvement and participation in relevant levels of decision-making.

These characteristics can be essential competencies, which lead to the enhancement of the training specialist's credibility in overall organisational terms. To a large extent they are focused on the training specialist in a "training manager" role.

ETHICAL DIMENSIONS OF THE TRAINING SPECIALIST'S ROLE

While ethical issues are an important concern in all facets of business life, they merit particular consideration in relation to the training and development specialist's role. In the first place, training and development can be related to extrinsic factors such as pay, career development, promotion prospects, status, working conditions, health and safety, the allocation of which often differs between employees, etc. Training and development is also integrally linked to intrinsic factors such as sense of achievement, personal growth and advancement, self-actualisation, recognition, etc., the allocation of which differs also. In addition, training and development is essentially aimed at bringing about change and this has obvious repercussions in the area of people's attitudes and behaviours. A further aspect that cannot be overlooked is the confidence and trust implied by the bond between trainer and trainee in a learning situation.

This accumulation of ethically-oriented issues means that the training specialist's role carries with it a high degree of sensitivity. As a result, training specialists must aspire to high ethical standards, and must conscientiously adhere to the precepts of honesty and confidentiality in performing their work. Furthermore, to maintain the integrity and standing of the training and development profession itself, training specialists must be seen to take cognisance of a personal moral responsibility. This means applying a set of socially ethical principles to training and development practices and decisions.

While some ambiguity may arise from individual interpretations of ethics in general, specific issues have been raised for the attention of training specialists. Let us now examine some of these.

Application of Ethical Issues to the Systematic Training Cycle

Ethical questions for the training specialist, set within the stages of the systematic training cycle, have been highlighted by Newby (1982), and include:

Identification of Training Needs

The major ethical question arising from the identification of training needs relates to whose interests are best served by the training intervention, and concern the emphasis placed on the terms of reference within which problems will be identified and training goals and objectives set.

Setting Objectives

At issue here is the assumption that training goals and objectives are rightfully imposed on the basis of serving the interests of the organisation. This can prove a particularly sensitive point in the case of training which is aimed at changing values, beliefs, and/or attitudes. An ethical dilemma can arise if individuals are seen to be forced into a training situation which they consider to be akin to brainwashing.

Training Methods/Media

Ethical dimensions can also be associated with the training methods/media employed. For example, some forms of sensitivity training, participation in role-play situations, or "performing" before a video camera, may provide emotional or highly stressful experiences for some individuals and may infringe on an individual's privacy.

Conducting Training

Several issues come into consideration at the training delivery stage. Expertise may be used to manipulate trainees in a negative way, perhaps by attempting to achieve conformity. Trainer perceptions are also an issue needing attention; where for instance, first impressions, a previously expressed opinion about an individual (or group of) trainee(s), or prejudicial baggage, come into play.

Evaluation

Some key ethical questions are seen to surround evaluation, particularly concerning the methods employed, the "for whom and by whom" aspects, and the potential consequences of the process for all those involved. By way of example, evaluation may be covertly linked to assessment, or may be manipulated to show misleading results.

In overall terms, Newby (1982) poses the central question of whether or not training specialists have the moral right to choose whatever means they deem necessary to achieve their ends, in relation to the training and development process.

Categories of Unethical Behaviour

Specific guidelines have been put forward for training specialists in order to identify categories of unethical behaviour (Cadwell, 1991; Snell, 1986, 1989, 1991). These may be summarised to include:

Dishonesty/Deceit

- giving misleading information or concealing significantly relevant information, about the nature, purpose, or potential consequences of a training decision and/or intervention;

- withholding, manipulating, or falsifying the results of a training decision and/or intervention.

Violation of Confidentiality

- exposing or revealing private/confidential data concerning individuals, groups and/or organisations, other than that explicitly related for disclosure beforehand.

Exaggeration/Concealment of Competence

- marketing services under the misleading pretence of competence and/or accomplishment in a particular area

- foraging into areas where competence is not assured / failing to clarify areas of questionable competence

- cloaking questionable competence and/or accomplishment behind specific labels or titles attached to one's remit.

Professional Misconduct

- setting up/conducting training events which lead to embarrassment, anguish, guilt, etc.

- setting up/conducting training events which are aimed at achieving own objectives and do not help in the development of individuals concerned;

- use of profanity, making sexist, racist or abusive remarks, or engaging in sexual innuendo;

- acting in a superior manner, or belittling the input or efforts of others;

- providing critical feedback out of a desire to punish or gain retribution;

- giving preferential treatment, taking sides, or being overly biased on the basis of one's own allegiance or vested interests;

- plagiarising the work of others or not giving due credit to others' contributions.

Professional Laxity

- failing to keep abreast of latest developments in training and development field;

- falling below acceptable standards of work and/or behaviour (merely going through the motions);

- acting as an "entertainer", rather than as a facilitator of learning;

- advocating/providing training solutions which may achieve short-term gains at the expense of long-term erosion (creating dependency but leaving unfinished business).

This list of unethical standards and practices is by no means exhaustive, but does serve to illustrate that such manifestations cover a wide range of issues. It also highlights the fact that, in terms of ethics, the professional training specialist's most serious responsibility resides in the welfare of trainees.

Professional Code of Practice

Codes of practice for training and development professions have been drawn up by training institutions and bodies in many countries. Recent research (Hogan, 1994) has served to identify a number of positive aspects, as well as various disadvantages, of such codes of practice. Let us now look at these in turn.

Positive Aspects of Codes of Practice

Codes of Practice can:

- serve as a communication mechanism to inform training specialists of their obligations to their profession;

- help to ensure consistency of standards and practice across the professional body;

- guide training specialists in their work practices and help them to resolve ethical dilemmas;

- communicate a positive message about the training and development profession and can therefore enhance long-term levels of professionalism and status.

Disadvantages of Codes of Practice

- Their effectiveness largely depends on the willingness and good faith of training specialists to observe the espoused code. They operate within a voluntaristic framework and do not carry any legal implications, relying instead on the willingness of the relevant body to enforce them.

- They may be limiting, as their reach may not be sufficient — the training specialist may be inclined to follow the code but in so doing may contravene or fail to fulfil the client's directions and wishes. Such situations represent a dilemma for the training specialist, but if a serious ethical issue is at stake, it should be publicised.

- They are static, and need continuous and vigilant updating to maintain their pertinence.

The prestige and status of the training and development profession is dictated by the ethical standards of its practitioners. Therefore, professional bodies and institutes need to ensure that codes of practice are widely promulgated and implemented. This process might be assisted, and ethical dilemmas made easier for training specialists to resolve, through the nomination of individuals from whom guidance may be sought.

Ethical Principles of Irish Trainers

Hogan (1994) has investigated the ethical issues and dilemmas experienced by Irish training consultants. She interviewed eight consultants in depth and identified the following principles:

- *Competence*: Each consultant felt that they had to possess the required competence and skill to carry out the job professionally and competently.

- *Expertise*: Each consultant felt that they needed to work within their area of expertise and in general would not go outside their specialist expertise even if the financial inducement was considerable.

- *Time Scale*: All the consultants held strong views about the time frame agreed to do the work. It was felt that this time frame should be adhered to where possible.

- *Illegal Activities*: The consultants indicated that they would not engage in illegal activities that would break the law, no matter what the financial inducement was.

- *Confidentiality of Information*: All of the consultants agreed that the individual had rights and that if information gathered during a training needs identification process was required to be kept confidential, then this should occur. The name of the employee giving this information should remain confidential particularly if it could prove detrimental to the employee within or outside the organisation.

- *Information from Client Organisations*: The consultants generally agreed that they would not use information uncovered in organisation A for the benefit of organisation B, without the former's consent.

- *Nature of the Individuals*: The consultants interviewed believed that human nature should be accommodated. Individuals have emotions, attitudinal preferences and personalities that have to be respected in the training situation. Trainees have to be respected and accepted for what they are and trust must be built up between the consultant and the trainee. Some of the consultants believed that this trust will facilitate an open training relationship and facilitate the full development of human potential. There was a strong belief that trainees should not be misguided or misled and should not be put on the spot unless there were very exceptional circumstances.

- *Non-Discriminatory Practices*: All of the consultants expressed the need to promote non-discriminatory practices in their work. Areas where non-discriminatory practices were advocated included gender disabilities, ageism, sexuality and statutory rights to training.

- *Involvement in the Learning Process*: There was a general consensus that the learner should be involved in the learning process, where this was possible. It was felt that this involvement should be encouraged at the outset and the learner should be made aware of it.

- *Objectivity in Areas of Conflict and Controversy*: Almost all of the consultants felt that it was possible to remain objective in areas of conflict and controversy. It was anticipated that the training consultant should have the interpersonal and judgmental skills to rise above individual differences and see the wider picture. He/she should have the skill to discuss individual disputes and solve them using objective principles. Where possible the differences should be resolved between the two parties.

The research in general illustrates that ethical problems within the training field are complex and contentious. The consultant has to strive to reconcile training activity with the ethical expectations of the key stakeholders. Hogan poses the notion of trainers as ethical investors. If the specialist shows ethical care and commitment in their work, then they earn the respect of clients, and trainees will work more effectively with them.

SUMMARY

This chapter considered the Irish training and development specialist. From the limited research available we can state that the typical specialist is male, in his late twenties, holds a diploma or degree in a business related area, operates at management level in the organisation and joined the function as a result of promotion, rather than as a first career choice. Irish specialists tend to have technical, managerial and service career anchors.

This chapter also emphasised the importance of systematically selecting and developing the training and development specialist. Effective trainers tend to engage in planning activities, have a futuristic perspective, have an appropriate structure of training function in place and demonstrate effective communication skills.

Training and development specialists encounter many ethical dilemmas in the performance of their tasks. The research available on Irish specialists suggest that they are aware of these dilemmas.

13

TYPES OF TRAINING AND DEVELOPMENT INTERVENTIONS

INTRODUCTION AND LEARNING OBJECTIVES

This chapter considers the range of training and development interventions that are available to the training and development specialist. Having read this chapter you will understand:

♦ the range of contextual variables that influences the choice of intervention;

♦ the range of planned training and development interventions available;

♦ the costs and benefits of alternative strategies;

♦ the criteria for selecting the most appropriate intervention;

♦ the issues involved in selecting external consultants.

CONTEXTUAL FACTORS INFLUENCING THE CHOICE OF INTERVENTION

The implementation of training and development policies and plans is facilitated through the use of training and development interventions. This process will vary considerably between organisations, and it is obviously a critical matter that the choice of intervention is appropriate to the pertaining organisational circumstances. In this vein, contextual factors weigh heavily as an influencing factor on the choice of intervention. Let us now summarise some of these factors, as outlined by Tracey (1992).

Organisational Strategies

The strategies adopted by the organisation indicate its intended current and future direction. These strategies emanate from a thorough assessment of the internal strengths and weaknesses of the organisation, and of the opportunities and threats which are seen to exist in its external environment. They form the basis for strategic plans, which are aimed at achieving the objectives and goals of the organisation. In the current, and predicted future environment, this process is usually concerned with maintaining or improving competitiveness, cost effectiveness, existing service levels, and return on investment.

As we have consistently stated, if training and development is to contribute fully to the ongoing success of the organisation, or indeed to putting the organisation back on a successful track, it must be integrated with overall strategies, goals, objectives and plans. This means that the choice (and the priorities) of training and development interventions must have their genesis in, and flow from, this integrative mechanism.

Technological and Scientific Advances

The sweeping and highly pervasive advances in technological and scientific fields are continuously impacting on organisations. In their slipstream, organisations bear witness to ongoing changes in human resource requirements, operational methods and approaches, and product and service innovations, as well as increasing investment in research and development.

Their effect on training and development continues to be no less revolutionary and the choice of training interventions is constantly under their influence. This has an obvious direct impact in terms of operator training and the updating craftpersons maintenance skills. However, the reach of technological and scientific advances is increasingly extending beyond this narrow horizon, to trigger the demand for flexible workforces, changes in supervisory and managerial roles, a greater need for computer literacy, and wider appreciation of information technology systems. Advances are also being made to provide for the changing nature of health and safety hazards and restrictions.

Composition of the Workforce

The composition of the workforce embraces a number of factors which affect the choice of training and development intervention. Workforce profiles, which incorporate age, sex, education and qualification levels, work experience, previous training and development, etc., are one consideration. Another is the extent and orientation of trade union membership as this can be linked to particular trade union attitudes to employee training and development. The transferability of prevailing workforce skills affects their mobility, and is thus an important factor.

Organisational Policies

The policies pursued by the organisation in relation to the management and development of human resources exerts significant influence on the choice of training and development intervention. We have already discussed the impact of personnel policy choice on the training and development process itself (see Chapter 9) and this carries over to the choice of intervention. An additional factor is the influence of recruitment, promotion and career management policies.

Reid et al (1992) outline two aspects of the organisation's learning policy and approach which impinge on intervention choice. The first relates to whether learning is essentially seen in purely individual terms (personal development) or if it is viewed as a process linking individual learning with the organisation's learning needs. The second is concerned with whether learning within the organisation follows a largely evolutionary path (ad hoc), or if it is riveted to planned learning mechanisms (systematic).

Factors relevant to the organisation's training and development policies, which inherently affect the choice of intervention, include:

- position in the organisation hierarchy of, and the extent of power and influence enjoyed by, the training function;

- resources allocated, in terms of the numbers and expertise of training staff, and the facilities which may be accessed;

- budgetary allocation (approved expenditure) and training costs; and

- the orientation of the training and development process (long or short term, extent of integration with corporate strategy, etc.).

It is evident that there are numerous variables which feed into the decision-making process surrounding the appropriate choice of training and development intervention. In determining this choice, it is important to see specific interventions in operational and political terms — rather than theoretical or philosophical terms (Reid et al, 1992).

INFLUENCE OF TRAINING MODEL ON TRAINING INTERVENTION

Though it is improbable that a single methodology applies to all training and development carried out in the organisation, certain uniformities emerge in the approach taken, and these identify the organisation's chosen training model. We discussed an array of training models in Chapter 8. Our concern here is identifying their impact on training and development intervention selection.

Unplanned

A lack of any perceptible approach is signified by situations in which the training and development process is largely unplanned, uncoordinated and unregulated. Such circumstances do not of course preclude the occurrence of training and development, nor indeed of learning, in so far as these are a natural by-product of ongoing work experiences. For instance, we are all probably familiar with the so-called "sitting-by-Nellie" form of training, as well, however, as being aware of its limitations.

In organisations which fit into this category, training and development interventions may be described as being "uncontrolled". They do not emanate from policies and/or plans, have no budgetary allocation, are not subject to any priority, and their effect is not deliberately measured or scrutinised (although it may well be adversely reflected across a wide range of performance criteria). As a consequence, the overall benefits derived are likely to be haphazard in nature, short-term in focus, and the potential benefits of training and development will be severely restricted in their scope and effect. Lost opportunities for coherent individual and organisation-wide performance improvements are the most probable outcome.

Even where a non-approach to training and development intervention is manifested, some individuals are likely to pursue personal development activities. However, without a formal structure, positive learning outcomes are seldom channelled towards organisational goals and objectives, and such individual efforts often go unrecognised and without reward. As a result, a particularly damaging pattern emerges: those who are interested in personal development and improvement seek out better opportunities in pastures new.

Educational Approach

In organisations leaning towards this approach, training and development interventions are planned around formal education programmes. This means that specific individuals or groups are targeted, encouraged, and facilitated to pursue programmes which are of a relatively long-term nature and usually lead to the attainment of a formal qualification.

Management and employee development may be incorporated into this type of approach. The management standards developed under the Management Charter Initiative (MCI) in the UK promotes a qualifications framework in this regard, although such a competence-based approach has been the subject of some criticism (see Harrison, 1992). In Ireland, formal management qualifications are increasingly becoming linked to MBA-type qualifications — Waterford Crystal, for example, have adopted this approach with a group of their managerial staff, using a distance learning format. Again, in the UK the National Council for Vocational Qualifications (NCVQ) have developed a framework through which employee development can be linked to the attainment of formal, nationally recognised qualifications. In Ireland, a framework to provide a similar facility is being developed by the National Council for Vocational Awards (NCVA).

In the overall Irish context, the availability and accessibility of various types of formal educational programmes is growing — through ACE provision, a greater range of distance and open learning provision, and a growing focus on the establishment of partnership-type arrangements between organisations and educational institutions. The educational approach can be a relatively inexpensive intervention strategy, as much of this provision is geared towards formal off-the-job activities outside normal working hours. However, it is also important to bear in mind possible drawbacks in the shape of lack of integration with the actual work situation and possible problems with the transfer of learning. For instance, in Japan, formal education is essentially considered part of the pre-employment stage, and formal qualifications are seen only as a foundation upon which continuous on-the-job learning is added (especially in relation to the development of effective managers).

Problem-centred Approach

Where a problem-centred approach is prevalent, training and development is likely to follow a reactive pattern, with interventions being focused on specific performance problems as they arise. Buckley and Caple (1992) suggest that this approach often reflects a "pressurised" situation, leading to inadequate analysis and potentially inappropriate training solutions.

They see this type of approach as often accompanied by the perception that an instant training solution is necessary to deal with a specific problem, and that such problems emanate from the people operating within the system rather than from other factors within the system itself. It generally reflects a situation where occasional financial investment in training and development is targeted at a particular area and the intervention pursued can provide quick and effective results albeit, without any long-term payback.

Systems Approach

We have previously outlined the notion of the organisation as an "open system". In this approach, training and development is perceived as one of the linked "sub-systems" within the organisation, and is therefore affected by ongoing changes in other sub-systems. In effect, such changes trigger training and development needs, and interventions are built around satisfying these requirements. This can be visualised, for instance, by changes in technology which may be a catalyst for a range of interventions targeting operators, craftspersons, supervisors, and line managers. It is also important to bear in mind that as a sub-system itself, changes of training and development policies and plans affect other sub-systems, and this situation can also create wider training and development needs.

Competency-based Approach

Increasing number of organisations are adopting competency-based approaches to human resource management and development. Such approaches are concerned with the identification of agreed and demonstrated competency standards (in the shape of knowledge, skills, and behaviour) which reflect effective performance in a given role or job. Boam and Sparrow (1992) attribute the rising popularity of competency-based approaches to two factors — the failure of major change programmes to deliver the intended results, and the growing link between business performance and appropriate employee skills. They see the attendant benefits to an organisation in terms of:

- a common language system which spells out the nature of effective performance;

- clearly defined selection criteria;

- improved performance review process and assessment of career potential;

- an enhanced facility for self-assessment and development;

- a critical tool for the developing the desired business culture;

- a useful element in the building of successful teams;

- a method for identifying potential implications in relation to job and organisational design; and

- a basis for coaching and training.

This list highlights the broad nature and scope of the training and development interventions which might accompany competency-based approaches.

These are some of the generalised approaches which may be adopted by the organisation. Combinations of these may appear in some organisations, for instance, an "educational" approach to management development might conceivably be accompanied by a "problem-centred" or an "analytical" approach to training and development in general. It may be noted that a "systematic" approach has not been included here — the reason for this will become evident as we look at planned training and development interventions.

PLANNED TRAINING AND DEVELOPMENT INTERVENTIONS

With the exception of those situations where training and development is entirely an informal and unplanned activity, interventions are deliberately pursued which are aimed at improving effectiveness through the process of learning. Training and development interventions can be regarded as planned activities.

Planned training and development interventions can be broadly segregated into two main categories, on-the-job and off-the-job. Let us now look at the various types of interventions pertinent to each category.

On-the-Job Interventions

Orientation Training
This usually takes place on the job and is the joint responsibility of the training and development specialist and the supervisor. Orientation training usually covers the following areas: introduction to the company, important policies and practices within the company, benefits and services, a review of employee expectations, introduction to fellow employees, introduction to the facilities and the job.

New employees go through a process of organisational socialisation. Nelson (1987) states that this involves learning attitudes, standards and patterns of behaviour that are expected by the organisation. This learning process is both continuous and intense. The function of the training given is to convey to new employees the expected standards of behaviour and to deal with any anxieties the employee may have. New employees often have unrealistically high expectations about the amount of challenge and responsibility they will have. Systematic orientation training can help clarify how realistic these expectations are.

The supervisor is an extremely important component of the socialisation process. The greater the skill level of the supervisor in this area, the greater the new employee's confidence and the quicker their adaptation to the organisation. Once orientation is completed the employee is usually ready for on-the-job training.

Training on-the-Job
Activities under this heading are normally associated with initial training and cross-training of an organisation's employees. It commonly follows

a routine of demonstration and instruction, interspersed with practice. The training may be given by the proverbial "Nellie" or more effectively by those trained in instruction methods. In some cases, initial demonstration, instruction and practice takes place in an internal off-the-job location, through simulated on-the-job activities.

Wexley and Latham (1991) make ten useful suggestions for the implementation of successful on-the-job training programmes.

1. Employees functioning as trainers must be convinced that training new employees does not jeopardise their own job, status, security, etc.

2. Individuals serving as trainers should realise that their additional responsibilities are instrumental in obtaining rewards for them.

3. Trainers and trainees should be carefully paired in order to minimise differences in background, personality and attitudes. These differences may inhibit communication and understanding and the training itself.

4. The choice of trainers should be based on their ability to train and their desire to take on this additional responsibility.

5. Skilled employees chosen as trainers should be systematically trained in the methods of instruction.

6. It should be made clear to employees serving as trainers that their additional responsibilities are not a basis for exploiting others.

7. Trainers should be rotated to compensate weaker instruction by some trainers and to expose the trainee to the specific know-how of various workers.

8. Organisations should realise that there is a possibility that production may slow down, equipment may be damaged and poor quality products may be made, as a result of training.

9. Trainers must be conscious of the need for close supervision in order to avoid trainee mistakes and the learning of incorrect procedures.

10. On-the-job training should be used in conjunction with other training approaches such as job aids and programmed instruction.

Coaching

Coaching normally takes the shape of one-to-one guidance by a manager, aimed at developing the appropriate knowledge, skills and attitudes in a fellow manager or supervisor. However, particular employees may also receive such individual guidance from a supervisor or manager.

Wexley and Latham (1991) identify four important functions of coaching:

1. It lets employees know what the supervisor thinks about their job performance.

2. It enables supervisors and employees to work together on ways in which employees can improve their performance.

3. It improves communication and collaboration between supervisors and employees.

4. It provides a framework for establishing short- and long-term personal goals.

Many supervisors and managers find coaching a difficult process. They often resist communicating negative information to employees because they feel uncomfortable when put in the position of "playing God". They may lack the skills needed to handle the coaching intervention. Managers are required to fulfil two conflicting roles — judge and helper. The supervisor/manager is a judge. When they are observing an employee's performance as a helper the role entails working closely with employees in order to improve job performance. The characteristics of an effective coaching system include the following:

- Employees should have substantial participation in the coaching process.

- Specific goals should be established as part of the coaching process.

- Specific improvement goals should be mutually set by the supervisor and employee.

- The supervisor should have a helpful and constructive attitude.

- Criticism should be avoided.

- Feedback should be provided to the trainee on both behaviour and performance.

- Coaching is highly effective when the supervisor models the correct behaviour expected.

- Effective coaches are alert to situational constraints that might interfere with the subordinate's performance.

- Coaching should be carried out on a continuous basis.

Apprenticeship Training

Organisations that employ skilled craftpersons usually do so by means of apprenticeship programmes. This on-the-job programme typically last four years. The intervention involves the organisation delegating the responsibility for socialisation and training of new employees to a master crafts person. It may also involve elements of classroom instruction. During these classroom sessions, each apprentice is typically given a workbook with materials to be read, problems to be solved and reading assignments. The craftspersons often use the classroom sessions for lectures, giving demonstrations and providing practice.

A major objection to apprenticeship training is that many trade unions control apprenticeship training entry. In doing so they create not only labour shortages and high wage rates but may also discriminate against women and other groups. This has occurred more so in the United States and the United Kingdom than in Ireland. In Ireland the amount of apprenticeship training has varied considerably in the last five years.

Job Aids/Instruction Manuals

Pursell and Russell (1990) describe a job aid as instructional material that is located on the job to assist an employee in recalling information that was presented during training. A study undertaken by Duncan (1986) demonstrates that job aids are capable of facilitating the learning process as well as reducing training time. They are best at teaching job skills and are particularly valuable when integrated into a training programme. They help employees to recall training after they return to their jobs.

Planned Experience/Job Rotation

Interventions in this category are designed to broaden the individual's experience within the organisation and are usually pertinent to management and supervisory development. A common approach is that called the "Cook's tour" where an individual spends a certain amount of time working in various departments. Managers may also be encouraged to gain experience and further their learning through action learning activities, being assigned special responsibilities or to specific projects or problem-solving groups.

With planned experience/job rotation, trainees get an overall perspective of the organisation and an understanding of the interrelationships among its key parts. It facilitates trainees becoming clearer about their career aspirations and their commitment to the organisation, and it increases their self-awareness, problem-solving and decision-making skills.

In order to be effective as an intervention, the planned experience must be tailored to the needs and capabilities of the individual trainee. The trainee's aptitudes, education levels, previous experience and interest patterns should determine their particular range of assignments. The length of time in each department should be determined by how fast they are learning, and they should be placed in locations where they will receive feedback, reinforcement and monitoring of their performance by experienced and committed managers/supervisors.

Mentoring

The term "mentoring" dates back to Greek mythology where Odysseus asked his friend Mentor to teach his son Telemachus what could be learned from books as well as the ways of the world. In the modern context (Murray, 1991), mentors are usually people typically two or three levels higher in the organisation than the trainee, who are motivated to help less-experienced employees understand the way the organisation works and to acquire specific job skills.

Kram (1985) suggests that the ideal mentor is a manager who is experienced, productive, and has good interpersonal skills. They will typically be 8-15 years older than the protégé and will facilitate the personal development of the employee. The mentoring relationship can be initiated by both parties and it may have varying degrees of formality. However, in the Irish context, the research illustrates that most mentorships are informal (Sweeney, 1993). There is evidence to suggest that some Irish organisations are attempting to establish formal mentoring programmes.

Training and development specialists have a major role to play in this mentoring process. They can define clearly the purpose and goals of the mentoring programme and select mentors based on their interpersonal skills and interest in developing employees. It may also be necessary to provide mentor training programmes so that mentors know how to apply the principles of learning, share information openly and demonstrate good interpersonal competencies. The list below highlights mentor-protégé relationships.

- Mentors, in identifying relationships with male protégés, tend to report quicker satisfaction from the mentor relationship.

- Mentoring relationships tend to serve more psychological functions when women are involved. The affective emotional aspects of the relationship are more important for female protégées.

- Age and number of subordinates appear to affect the quality of the mentoring relationship.

- Most mentoring relationships tend to be developed informally.

- For maximum effectiveness mentoring should occur on a weekly basis.

- The most effective mentors are usually two or three levels higher in the organisation than the protégé.

- Most mentors are men because most senior positions in organisations are occupied by men.

Learning Contracts

A learning contract is a written agreement between a manager, his or her trainee, and the trainer setting out what the trainee is going to learn, how they are going to learn it, and, where applicable, how they are going to apply their learning in the workplace. It is a means of helping learners structure learning activities systematically.

Prideaux and Ford (1988) suggest that the learning contract is developmental both for the trainee in that it challenges the learner's ability to be self-directed and to set appropriate work objectives. Garavan and Sweeney (1994) identify a number of underpinning principles:

- Trainees will become more effective because learner-centred involvement makes them more committed and motivated to learn.

- Trainees are provided with an opportunity to work towards satisfying their own development needs within the organisation context.

- The learner contract requires the trainee to take responsibility for their own learning and its application in the workplace.

- In order to create a climate where the trainee takes on those responsibilities, it is necessary for the trainer to become more facilitative and act as a resource to both the trainee and their manager.

- Learning contracts require a review by the trainee of the process, as well as the content, of the learning.

- Learning contracts are based on real organisational problems in a specific workplace context.

- They allow the trainee to see positive results from their efforts. This sense of achievement tends to be a further motivator for learning and improvement.

- Qualitative as well as quantitative objectives can be catered for in a learning contract.

Learning contracts, if properly implemented, can address a number of specific training problems. Particularly they address the "OK in theory but will it work in-practice" attitude. Trainees often view theory as the hobby of academics who do not operate in the real world. Sometimes middle and senior management categories feel that they do not need training and development. They are not open to learning. They may also encounter difficulties in applying the learning because of poor support from superiors. The learning contract is an effective way of overcoming these difficulties.

Learning Logs

Learning logs often play an important role in the learning contract, particularly those which address behavioural issues (Else, 1992). The contracts are structured around the learning cycle and the logs are used to enable the learner to consciously develop skills of reflection, and to keep a record of learning and achievement. Learning logs particularly facilitate reflective learning. Altman (1982) suggests that reflective thought is a basic thought structure which emerges when adults learn and allows for the development of more advanced forms of thinking. Merizow (1992) suggests three types of reflective learning:

1. *Affective Reflectivity*: becoming aware of how we feel about the way we are observing, understanding, thinking or acting.

2. *Discriminant Reflectivity*: where we assess the effectiveness of perceptions, thoughts, actions and habits of doing things.

3. *Judgmental Reflectivity*: where we become aware and make value judgements about our perceptions, thoughts, actions and habits.

Through these three stages the learner is personalising what is learned by applying insights to their work situation. Dixon (1990) suggests that the reason adult learners do not transfer their learning and development to the workplace is because the new skills conflict with the assumptions they have previously made about themselves, others and the organisation. She proposes that critical reflection is necessary for adult learners to bring to conscious awareness the assumptions that underlie current skills and to test these assumptions to find out whether they are achieving their desired goals.

Learning logs are a useful way of encouraging this learning process. The discipline of keeping the log on a regular basis, following an agreed format, should improve the reflective learning process. Figure 13.1 presents some of the difficulties involved in undertaking reflective learning processes.

Figure 13.1: Problems in Undertaking Reflective Learning

- It requires high levels of self-discipline.
- It is easy to skip, to conclude "that will do", particularly when feeling demotivated or passive.
- It requires high levels of self-confidence to analyse your own behaviour.
- You sometimes just do not know what you are looking for, what you are reflecting on.
- It can make you feel unhappy and uncomfortable about the situation you have just been in, and subsequently discourage you from reflecting the next time.
- It is hard to reflect when you are being criticised, you are too busy defending yourself.
- It is easy to lapse when something more important turns up.
- It is hard to complete when things are going well.
- It will stop if you cannot see the benefits.
- It is boring when nothing exciting or momentous has happened.
- It is hard when you have no support, or are feeling alone, threatened.
- It can't just be thought about, it must be written down.
- It is hard to pick up once put down.
- It is difficult to distinguish between facts and assumptions.
- It can be difficult to identify how your feelings and thoughts relate to your actions and vice versa.

Computer-based Training

Computer-based training (CBT) facilitates learning using a PC and/or interactive video software and discs. The instructional principles underlying CBT are designed to reinforce learning. CBT is primarily used to improve job skills.

In a CBT training situation the material is presented in easy stages and the trainee moves from one stage to another by answering questions and understanding. The answers are given immediately afterwards and some provision may be made for remedial work and further practice if the trainee "gets it wrong".

CBT is now being used to develop many different types of job skills to employees. However, it requires particular skills and competencies of the trainer. On this point Bhugra (1986) suggests that creative teams may be useful. He found that the skill profile of CBT teams in a number of organisations was based in the belief that the only skills which fell outside the trainer/programmer's skill base were technical and occasionally consultancy skills. The creative team relies on the training and development specialist to correctly carry out the needs identification process, and to write the appropriate learning objectives. The creative team can then design the training. This creative team may consist of writers, graphic artists and programmers.

The research results on CBT are encouraging. Hassett and Dukes (1986), for example, demonstrate that CBT can result in a 30 per cent reduction in training time and an 80 per cent increase in retention of training content. They also argued that the computer is sensitive to individual differences in learning rates among trainees. The computer terminal cannot become impatient or irritated with a slow learner, likewise it does not slow down the fast learner.

Off-the-Job Training Strategies

In-House Training Programmes/Corporate Classrooms
In-house training programmes are a familiar feature in many Irish organisations. Their provision can be focused on particular groups (e.g. supervisors, training instructors, etc.), can be aimed at particular areas of need (e.g. health and safety, computer literacy, etc.) or may involve all organisation members (e.g. total quality, customer service, etc.). Internal and/or external expertise may be utilised when running such programmes.

An extension of in-house training programmes is the notion of corporate classrooms. The objectives of such classroom reunions is to teach employees job skills. They have features similar to traditional colleges and they incorporate up-to-date instructional technology. The ambience is different, however, in that the participants are older and hold full-time jobs in the company. The courses are company-oriented and practical, with the length varying considerably. Besides skills, the trainees learn about the company's espoused values, and the systems and procedures that operate within the organisation. The best known example of a corporate classroom is Hamburger University in the USA.

External Training Programmes
External training programmes may have a similar focus to that outlined for the internal variety, the only difference being that their provision takes place outside the organisation. Again, internal and/or external expertise may be drawn on in their delivery. There is also an ever-increasing range of options in terms of external courses (short full-time, part-time evening/weekend, part-time on a "staggered days" basis, etc.) with providers including educational institutions, professional bodies

and institutions, private training companies, etc. Many of these courses lead to qualifications at certificate, diploma or degree level.

Workshops

Workshops involve problem/solution learning through peer exchange. The basic idea behind workshops is that learning occurs through the sharing of particular experiences. For this to be possible, workshops must involve people who are already competent in a particular area and who are both capable and willing to switch from the role of learner to trainer and back again during the workshops. The interactions should also be monitored by a facilitator.

Workshops place emphasis on free discussion, the exchange of ideas, the decentralisation of effort and the practical implementation of skill. Ideally participants should initiate workshops themselves, but in practice they are initiated by trainers. Recently there has been a tendency to categorise workshops as action learning programmes. Revans (1983), for example, defines action learning as a means of development that requires the learner, through responsible involvement in some real and complex problems, to achieve intended change sufficient to improve their behaviour in this area. Workshops, however, may not be as active a learning process. They may include some formal inputs and therefore more passive learning.

Open and Distance Learning

There is a significant increase in the availability and accessibility of open and distance learning programmes. Apart from encouraging individual participation in this type of provision, many organisations are setting up links with educational institutions with the aim of establishing qualification-based programmes for management groups.

Although these two categories of intervention are often grouped together, they have distinct characteristics. In the open learning situation, the learner can choose their own goals, they can choose the sequence and depth of learning, there is unrestricted access from an educational point of view and a variety of learning processes can be chosen (Snell and Binsted, 1982). Distance learning is characterised by geographical separation of learner and trainer, use of a least one formal medium such as print, video or computer, a self-learning process and a specific delivery. In practice, most training programmes of this type contain elements of openness and distance.

The provision of this type of intervention has major implications for the trainer's role. Clarke (1986) describes the trainer's role as that of facilitator and identifier. The personal qualities which trainers require are patience, tolerance and an ability to cope with frustration, perceptive ability, understanding of the trainee's situation, as well as a friendly approachable and trustworthy disposition. They also must be prepared to tolerate disruption in private life and possess a flexible approach.

Externally-based Planned Experience Programmes

There are various ways to further broaden the knowledge and learning base of managers through externally-based planned experience. Secondment to another organisation for a period of time is one option, albeit one that is not particularly prevalent in the Irish context.

More frequently utilised interventions include attendance at seminars, workshops, conferences, etc., and "fact-finding" visits to organisations which have a reputation for best practice in a particular area (TQM, WCM, ISO, etc.). With the growing focus on quality and service, information gathering (and sharing) visits to customers and suppliers are becoming a more prominent feature.

As we can see, therefore, the range and variety of possible interventions is quite extensive. A number of advantages and disadvantages associated with each type of intervention is presented in Figure 13.2 at the end of the chapter.

COSTS AND BENEFITS OF ALTERNATIVE INTERVENTIONS

There is some justification for the common perception that training specialists in many organisations fail to present a strong financially-balanced argument in favour of investment in training and development. Several reasons can be put forward to explain this state of affairs, including:

- Training specialists tend to view the process of training and development in intrinsic terms (e.g. they have an innate sense of the value of learning, personal growth and advancement of the learner, enhanced job satisfaction, etc.).

- Training specialists inherently see training and development as a "good" thing and as something which should "automatically" be pursued in organisations.

- In a general sense, the training function might be said to operate at one end of a "consideration for human resources" spectrum, while the finance department is often perceived as operating at the opposite end. The financial / accounting area is therefore not usually one of intense interest to training specialists.

- It is probably fair to say that training specialists would tend to avoid, rather than court, the attentions of the finance department. This may stem from a lack of confidence in discussing financial costs/benefits of training and development.

- Many training specialists focus their process of evaluation on qualitative rather than quantitative criteria. This in itself may reflect perceived difficulties with quantifying the benefits of training and development in monetary terms.

While all of these shortcomings might be categorised as "understandable", it is becoming increasingly important for training specialists to embrace techniques and approaches which examine training and development from a financial viewpoint (Buckley and Caple, 1992). In a cost-competitive environment, training specialists must broaden their expertise in working with financial data and demonstrate not only relevance, but also value for money and achievement of cost-effective results (Darling, 1993).

Analysing Costs and Benefits

To ascertain if training and development interventions are providing value for money, it is necessary to set out their costs and benefits in financial terms. The ongoing costs of training and development have been outlined under its budgetary aspects and these apply across the full range of interventions pursued by a particular organisation.

However, we will confine ourselves here to the specific costs and benefits associated with the various types of interventions.

Training on-the-Job/Coaching/Mentoring

The costs incurred from training, on-the-job coaching and mentoring depend largely on how it is approached. The costs associated with the traditional "Nellie" approach, for instance, may be seen as confined to the production time lost by "Nellie" while instructing the trainee. However, hidden costs can be related to problems such as longer lead-time for the trainee to reach expected levels of performance, as well as more serious long-term effects. If training instructors are used, the cost of their own training as well as their wages must be taken into account. These wage costs are minimised in many organisations by using operator/instructors who perform their normal tasks when not engaged in training.

The benefits of training on-the-job, coaching and mentoring are probably the easiest of all to quantify in financial terms. These include cost factors directly related to:

- higher production or service levels

- quicker turn-around times on orders

- better product and service quality

- less rejects and re-work

- reduced customer returns / complaints

- higher levels of job satisfaction.

These factors have a direct impact on the organisation's turnover, profit margins and consequently on profit levels, and therefore the benefits of such training can be measured in bottom-line financial terms.

Planned Experience/Job Rotation

Interventions in this category normally incur little direct cost. The salary of an individual on internal secondment might even be directly offset by the contribution made during this period, while assignments or projects are largely integrated with an individual's ongoing work.

The inexpensive nature of interventions here may be used to balance the difficulty in quantifying the benefits in financial terms. While the overriding targeted benefit is by nature long-term and qualitative, it may be possible to relate financial savings to results of assignments and/or projects undertaken.

In-house Training Programmes and Workshops

There are several cost factors associated with the provision of in-house training programmes. These mainly include wages/salary paid of time spent off-the-job, loss of productive work input (production itself, supervision, mental capacity, etc.). Other contributory factors can concern the replacement of participants, the need for overtime working, etc. In-house programmes may also bear costs related to the identification of training needs and the development of training content and materials. Furthermore, costs may be attributable to the utilisation of external expertise at particular stages in the development and/or delivery of programmes.

The quantification of financial benefits is very much dependent on the nature of the training programme or course. Some examples may serve to highlight this point, as follows:

- Health, safety and welfare training programmes can contribute to substantial savings due to a resulting reduction in accidents and costly claims.

- Employee relations training can help to circumvent industrial action, etc.

- Specific training courses can lead to significant reduction in the "cost of quality".

- Substantial savings can accrue from improved managerial decision-making, time management, problem-solving capacity, etc.

It is relatively easy to suggest a strong link between training programmes and general financial benefits such as these, but establishing a definite, quantifiable link requires the application of focused evaluation techniques, sometimes over a lengthy period.

External Training Programmes and Courses

Many of the costs and benefits associated with in-house programmes are also relevant here. However, in addition to the "off-the-job" costs, the price of the programme itself, as well as attendant expenses (which may include travel, subsistence, accommodation, etc.), must be taken into account. The loss of specialised expertise during problem situations, etc., represents a further possible cost.

A benefit which might be added to those outlined for in-house programmes might arise from the acquisition of specialised knowledge precluding the latter need to hire external expertise. The previous comments concerning evaluation are also applicable to external programmes or courses.

Open and Distance Learning

The basic cost of open and distance learning programmes is usually quite high, and further costs can be incurred from the requirement to periodically participate in residential elements (these may include travel, accommodation, etc.). While residential elements are commonly organised around weekends, some programmes specify longer periods and the costs related to time spent off-the-job must therefore be taken into account.

It is particularly difficult to quantify the benefits from this type of development in monetary terms, and the payback must certainly be seen as evolving over a long period of time. However, adopting a focused evaluation approach may help to identify specific financial benefits.

Externally-based Planned Experience

Several cost factors can be readily associated with this category. Secondment to another firm (especially one in another country) can mean considerable expense in respect of travel, accommodation, and subsistence, as well as obvious "off-the-job" costs. While the same types of expense and costs arise in connection with site-visits, these are considerably lessened by the shorter time period involved (generally a day or

two at the most). Similar expense and costs can be allocated to attendance at seminars, conferences, workshops, etc., not forgetting the actual
fee for the event itself.

Externally-based secondment is aimed at long-term development, and
it is again difficult to align the results with direct monetary benefits.
More tangible financial benefits may be identified from site visits, or
from attendance at conferences, seminars, workshops, etc. These could,
for instance, bring a quantifiable payback through acquisition and application of specific knowledge which helps to clarify customer or supplier
requirements, assists with the implementation of a new procedure or
system, or casts fresh insight on a problematic operational area.

The preceding examples highlight the difficulty encountered when attempting to attach a financial value to the potential benefits of some interventions. This is especially relevant to development-focused interventions where the benefits are essentially intangible in immediate cost
terms. However, even when benefits cannot be specifically costed, they
should be predicted or reported in cost-related fashion.

CRITERIA FOR SELECTING THE MOST APPROPRIATE INTERVENTION

We have already seen that there are advantages and disadvantages, as
well as costs and benefits, which may be applied to the various types of
interventions. Making an appropriate selection, therefore, is obviously a
matter for critical consideration. A wayward decision at this stage in the
training and development process can negate the most expertly designed
and delivered intervention, and seriously impair its eventual effectiveness. It can also mean that the training and development provided does
not bring a value-for-money return to the organisation.

Criteria relevant to the decision-making in this area are discussed by
Reid et al (1992) and Buckley and Caple (1992), and these form the basis for the following summaries.

Compatibility with Objectives

In an overall sense, the choice of intervention should be consistent with
the strategic goals and objectives of the organisation, and of course with
the objectives of training and development itself. Within this proviso,
selection should take into account the desired outcome of specific interventions. Considering the following range of questions, which focus on
a number of important considerations, may prove useful for this purpose:

- Can the planned intervention be linked to a clear training and development need in terms of the strategic objectives of the organisation?

- Does it sit comfortably with the organisation's culture and wider human resource policies, plans and procedures?

- Is it compatible with the organisation's training and development mission and policies?

- Is it primarily concerned with short-term training and development needs, or has it a longer-term career development focus?

- Is it mainly aimed at the enhancement of knowledge or practical skills?

- If enhancement of knowledge is the priority, is this requirement centred around a theoretical dimension or a practical understanding of procedures, rules, etc.?

- To what extent does attitudinal change form part of the objective?

- Does the objective have a common problem-solving orientation?

- Does the objective encompass elements of creativity and innovation?

- Is the objective linked to the need for reinforcement, reward, status or prestige?

Constraints

At the outset, it is important to acknowledge that training and development interventions are invariably subject to constraints. These are usually associated with the availability of resources, but other factors often come into play also. In taking cognisance of this fact, a crucial element in selecting an intervention is to identify and take into consideration the nature and extent of such constraints. The issues arising in this regard commonly include:

1. Time

   - the overall time-frame for the intervention

   - length of time available for design and preparation

   - time needed for the actual delivery in order that objectives will be met

   - length of total delivery time required to accommodate trainee numbers and availability

   - time schedules of trainers (internal and external).

2. Resources

- budgetary allocation and finances currently available

- internal training staff expertise (schedules, range and depth of knowledge and skills)

- range, availability and cost of external programmes and courses

- internal training facilities (environment, size, equipment, etc.)

- availability of accommodation, travel schedules, etc. (relevant to externally-based interventions)

- availability of external funding (government agencies, EU, etc.)

- schedules and cost of external trainers / consultants

- administrative support capability

- availability of trainees.

3. Political Factors

- the power and influence enjoyed by the training function

- maintaining a political balance in respect of organisational and departmental priorities, trainee representation, and management involvement in decision-making.

- the culture of the organisation (extent of freedom in relation to design, content, and methods).

Target Population

The profile of proposed participants is another significant area for consideration in the selection process. General information may be gleaned from administrative records, which helps to provide a broad overview of participant profiles. However, it must also be ensured that special needs are identified, and it may be advisable to confer with relevant managers or the personnel department as appropriate. The following issues may be of concern in securing a profile of the target population:

- trainee numbers and location within the organisation

- age

- experience within current work situation

- previous experience (within and outside the organisation)

- levels of expertise, and abilities/aptitudes

- education and previous planned learning experiences
- special needs (e.g. specific individual disability or disadvantage)
- family circumstances (e.g. in the case of external secondment)
- motivational forces (how intervention is perceived by trainees).

Likelihood of Learning Transfer

This criteria is concerned with helping to overcome the barriers that block the transfer of learning to the work context. These barriers take many forms, including:

- employee relations affecting management and/or trade union attitudes
- work overload
- crisis management
- personal fears and insecurities
- perceived inequity of reward systems
- perceived value of the intervention to the individual's work setting
- bureaucratic procedures
- line-managers with negative perceptions of training and development
- lack of top management commitment to training and development
- restricted opportunity to practice what has been learned.

It goes without saying, of course, that many of these barriers represent fundamental obstacles to an effective training and development process and must be overcome in order for learning to thrive within the organisation. However, if a learning transfer barrier does exist, it places an extra emphasis on the appropriateness of the choice of intervention.

These criteria should be referenced assiduously when selecting the most appropriate training and development intervention. The foregoing may be used as a form of checklist to assist with this process.

THE USE OF EXTERNAL CONSULTANTS

In relation to planned training and development interventions, various situations and circumstances exist within many organisations which trigger the need for external expertise. This requirement may be directed towards services which embrace analysis and advice, development of materials, and/or direct training provision, and the blanket term "consultant" is often applied to those who provide any of these services. Much has been written about the common perception of consultants and it is undeniable that the very mention of the term tends to evoke widely contrasting images, perspectives, opinions, and attitudes. This fact in itself may be related to the contrasting levels of expertise, professionalism, and effectiveness of those who call themselves consultants. Indeed, there is little to prevent anybody (certainly in an Irish context) from pronouncing themselves a consultant, in whatever field they choose (including that of training and development). It is against this background that the use of external consultants by the organisation is viewed.

Why use an External Consultant?

There are several main reasons why the organisation may decide to utilise the services of an external training and development consultant, including (Johnson, 1990):

- the need for specific expertise or experience which does not exist internally (this can apply to any aspect of the training and development process);

- to supplement existing internal resources (perhaps to cope with high demand);

- to undertake a discrete project or piece of work (perhaps with a research element);

- the periodic use of consultants may be advocated by company policy (this may be seen as a way of preventing the development of insular viewpoints or approaches);

- specific external funding may be available for such services.

While each of these reasons can justify the use of an external consultant, it is important to validate this choice before any firm commitment or contract is completed. A rigorous decision-making process should be pursued, and a real need to use external resources identified, before this approach is finally settled on.

This is not to suggest that professional training and development consultants are anything other than an excellent resource, which, if appropriately utilised, can prove a significant factor in the overall success of an intervention.

A number of general advantages and disadvantages associated with using external training and development consultants is presented in Figure 13.3 at the end of the chapter.

Choosing an External Consultant

Having established and validated the need for using an external consultant, the next step is to ensure an appropriate choice. Usually the problem in this area is more to do with quality rather than quantity — there is a growing tendency for individuals to enter this field. It is important, therefore, that careful consideration is given to the background, qualifications, expertise and experience of external consultants. One approach is to opt for a well-established and reputable consultancy group, although this may prove rather expensive. Networks are also a useful way to seek out consultants who have successfully undertaken comparable work, and earn a recommendation or referral on that basis. In Ireland, the IITD produce a useful membership directory which separately lists its members who are engaged in consultancy.

Whatever selection method is adopted, preliminary discussions are usually held on a provisional basis. This may be followed by the submission of a written proposal or it may be appropriate for the consultant to make a formal presentation of a proposed approach. The stages leading to the actual selection may follow an order such as (Johnson, 1990):

- Assessment criteria are drawn up by the training specialist, which may incorporate (Holtz, 1983):

  - the provider's understanding of the training need;

  - qualifications, experience, and specific expertise of those expected to perform the work;

  - qualifications of the proposing organisation (as an organisation).

- Prospective providers are invited by the training specialist to participate in outline discussions.

- A short list is compiled and detailed proposals are invited.

- Having examined proposals it may be necessary to invite prospective providers for further discussion/clarification.

- A decision is made, based on which provider best meets the needs of the organisation in respect of the intervention in question.

These stages are followed in turn by the "contracting" stage.

Contracts

When engaging the services of an external consultant it is considered good practice to draw up a contract which sets out the obligations of both parties. Cockman et al (1992) and Connor and Davidson (1985) see the purpose of a contract in terms of:

- helping to further define the assignment;

- clarifying in both the client's and the consultant's minds the work to be performed;

- setting agreed parameters and boundaries for the assignment;

- setting mutual expectations, goals, and objectives;

- establishing agreed ground rules for procedures and behaviour between the client and the consultant.

It is advisable to build appropriate flexibility into contracts to cater for possible changes in the nature and scope of the assignment being undertaken (Johnson, 1990).

SUMMARY

In this chapter we considered a range of training and development interventions. There is very little formal evaluation of the effectiveness of these strategies. Most of the evaluation is based on logical analysis and common sense. Many factors determine the effectiveness of these interventions. The considerable potential of on-the-job interventions that not been exploited by organisations. Therefore such interventions are an excellent means of developing job-related skills because they allow for active practice, immediate feedback, positive and transfer of learning. Off-site interventions are considered less effective on these criteria.

Figure 13.2: Advantages and Disadvantages of Different Training and Development Interventions

Type	Advantages	Disadvantages
Orientation Training	• gives employee an understanding of specific expectations • can set a good example for further training • lays the foundation for job skill training • helps reduce unrealistic expectations	• often carried out unsystematically • trainee may get bad impression of organisation • length of time allocated may be too short • supervisor may lack the skills and knowledge necessary
Training on-the-job	• trainee performs the job during training • opportunity to introduce "learning to learn" concept to trainee • potentially high in learning transfer • can be seen as a natural learning process • particularly appropriate and useful for skills training • it is an inexpensive approach • quick and highly relevant feedback and results • one-to-one coaching useful for developing appropriate management style	• trainee may pick up "bad habits" from "Nellie" • training needs may be narrowly focused • learning environment and conditions may not be favourable (e.g. noise levels, etc.) • trainee may feel pressurised to reach set performance standards • feedback and results may be given in an open forum

Type	Advantages	Disadvantages
Apprenticeship Training	• suitable intervention for developing special skills to craftperson level • utilises the skills of master craftspersons within the company • employee gets a certificate on completion • can be used in many areas of company • can be evaluated easily	• takes a long time to complete • it may restrict entry to training for certain categories • may be poorly planned and supervised • master crafts person may have poor training skills • possible lack of integration between classroom elements and work elements
Job Aids/ Instruction	• assists employees in remembering precise and complex procedures and rules • helps ensures that employees avoid committing critical errors • guides employees during a time when operating procedures are in a process of change • may be easy to produce and copy • may reduce training time	• may be ignored by the trainee • may be poorly designed • may be too complicated for the employee • may be used in isolation rather than integrated with other strategies • difficult to evaluate their effectiveness • may be at variance with operational practices
Planned Experience/ Job Rotation	• high probability of positive transfer of learning • relatively inexpensive approach • can help to build a team spirit and reduce inter-departmental competition • broadens the organisation's managerial knowledge base	• may have an unsettling effect on trainee • trainee may develop into the proverbial "jack-of-all-trades and master of none" • trainee may be made to feel "an unwelcome outsider" in host department • trainee's duties/activities may not be properly planned or defined

Type	Advantages	Disadvantages
Mentoring	• can be used in conjunction with coaching and computer-based training • makes use of experienced managers as learning resource • can be used to teach job skills and communicate organisation values • can be formal or informal • it is a flexible method	• mentoring may contribute to perpetuation of an inappropriate culture • mentor may not be sufficiently skilled at identifying development needs • may feature poor mentoring skills • may not occur with frequency • lack of commitment on the part of mentors • poor supply of mentors • may be culturally constrained • may not have the openness required to be effective
Computer-based Training	• individual tutoring • trainees may begin training at any time • learning is self-paced • performance of trainee can be monitored • consistent presentation using attractive design features • large numbers can be trained at the same time • comparatively easy to update material • high retention rates and reduced learning time	• costly to design • need special equipment • not suitable for skills training • trainees may fear working through computer technology • administration of large number of trainees may be difficult • not a very visible form of training

Type	Advantages	Disadvantages
In-House Training Programmes/ Corporate Class Rooms	• potentially higher transfer of learning than from external programmes • programme content can be tailored to meet specific organisational needs • exercises/discussions may be aimed at solving real problems • increases flexibility in arranging training schedules • useful when providing similar training for large numbers • training provided on-site may induce greater feeling of relevance • pace of delivery and learning may be more flexible	• schedules may be more prone to disruption • time "off-the-job" cost considerations • may be relatively expensive to provide • organising and scheduling can be time consuming • participation may be seen in terms of reward by trainee • participation may be based on functional/departmental quotas • tendency to fulfil "blanket" training needs
Learning Contract	• gets the involvement of key individuals in the development process • helps to ensure that training and development needs are correctly identified • makes the evaluation process clearer • gives training and development greater perceived relevance • reflects real organisational problems and situations • helps to facilitate communication between line manager and subordinates	• requires an effective management process on the part of the training specialist • requires considerable commitment from the line specialist and the individual learner • may be costly to implement and manage • supervisors may perceive it as time wasting and an extra burden • may lead to disillusionment if the results anticipated in the contract do not accrue

Type	Advantages	Disadvantages
External Training Programmes and Courses	• participants can benefit from broader range of experiences and viewpoints • may provide access to purpose-built learning environment • useful for developing specialised knowledge and/or skills • promotes networking outside the organisation • some provision does not necessitate time spent off-the-job	• potential difficulties with transfer of learning • can involve considerable time spent off-the-job • generally very expensive • participation may be seen in terms of reward • participation may be based on functional/departmental quotas • may create false or unrealistic expectations and/or trigger restlessness
Workshops	• learning occurs through realistic situations • the learning process is more attractive to participants • learning transfer problems are minimised • group members support one another • it is a particularly suitable format for senior managers who do not like being "taught"	• participants need to have prior knowledge of inter-active learning processes • participants need to have similar levels of knowledge and experience to benefit from the learning • there may be a mismatch of expectations if participants expect passive learning • the task of making generalisations from concrete situations is left to individual participants

Type	Advantages	Disadvantages
Open and Distance Learning	• study takes place in individual's own time • programme assignments/ projects may be directed at organisation's needs • can facilitate career planning process • can broaden the individual's and the organisation's learning horizons and capability • useful for attaining specialised knowledge linked to a qualification • all learning resources are inclusive • facilitates the creation of learning groups within the organisation	• heavy front-loaded expenses • requires adapting to a particular learning style • participants must have strong self-motivation • participants may require extensive support systems • relatively high drop-out rate • may adversely affect some individuals' work programme
Externally-based Planned Experience	• provides an external perspective of the organi-sation • appropriate for inducing attitude change • provides an insight into external best practice • helps to build external networks • can be used as a tangible reward for superior performance • can help to clarify customer/supplier perspective and needs • may provide opportunity to learn from leading edge theorists and practitioners	• transfer of learning may be limited • can involve heavy expense • may give the impression of providing "junkets" or pleasure trips • may be difficult to match development needs with specific activities • on return, recommenda-tions may be made which fail to embrace external cultural, social, economic or political factors

Figure 13.3: Advantages and Disadvantages of Using External Training and Development Consultants

Advantages	Disadvantages
• offers professional expertise in designated areas • offers a broader range of approaches and techniques • may be attuned to state-of-the-art approaches and techniques • can evoke a certain credibility within the organisation • may be seen as a comparatively neutral figure • can provide a broad range of practical examples from previous experience • can circumvent bureaucratic procedures or political intrigue • subject to availability, can be used on a "when required" basis • can be used for "delicate" subject-matter areas • brings a fresh perspective to problem identification.	• can be very expensive • approach and methods may not fit with organisation climate/culture • may not live up to "advance publicity" • may cause resentment among internal training staff • element of suspicion may restrict co-operation or adversely affect learning environment • may need time to become familiarised with organisational context • tend to be stronger on analysis/implementation than on evaluation • may suffer from perception that their commitment is transitory (are only passing through the organisation).

14

LEARNING: THE INDIVIDUAL AND THE ORGANISATION

INTRODUCTION AND LEARNING OBJECTIVES

This chapter focuses on learning processes at the level of the individual and the organisation. Having read this chapter you will understand:

♦ the alternative theories of learning;

♦ important learning conditions and principles;

♦ the significance of individual differences in the learning process;

♦ the learning transfer process and the factors which facilitate/inhibit this process;

♦ the issues involved in managing the organisation as a continuous learning system

THEORIES OF LEARNING

Before examining theories of learning, it is necessary to define what we mean by the term "learning" itself. Finding a conclusive definition of learning is difficult, as quite a number have been put forward over time. From a training and development perspective learning may be summarily defined as "a complex process of acquiring knowledge, understanding, skills, and values in order to be able to adapt to the environment in which we live". Such adaptation, generally, involves some recognisable change in our behaviour, though this is not always the case.

A fundamental feature of learning, therefore, is that it is acquired. How this may occur is dependent on three main factors:

• the innate qualities of the learner (i.e. intelligence);

• the skills of the teacher (i.e. as applied in tuition, instruction, etc.);

• the conditions in which learning takes place (i.e. the learning environment).

Of these, the development of innate qualities is considered outside our control and not normally subject to change by external influences, it being identified more with the process of biological maturation. This in itself brings to light an important aspect of learning: there are certain capabilities which individual learners cannot attain, despite tuition or instruction, practice of experience. However, both of the other factors represent externally controlled influences which can be said to temper the effectiveness of learning.

Let us now look at some of the learning theories which have evolved over time.

Philosophical Theories

Our current understanding of learning has been influenced by a variety of past scholars and researchers. Indeed, the roots of learning theory may be traced back to Plato and Aristotle, and the notion of the "trained mind", whereby training is seen to require extensive self-discipline and control. They proposed that the exercise of mental faculties (e.g. reason, memory, will-power, etc.) was crucial to the development of the individual and ultimately of the community at large. Some of the practical effects of this approach have filtered down to our education systems, to the extent that:

- learning is structured;

- teaching methods are didactic (i.e. telling/directing)

- the subject-matter is taken as important in its own right (e.g. maths, geography, etc.)

- memorising and rule-learning are crucial.

In a major reaction to the mental discipline approach, the French philosopher Rousseau (1712-1778) adopted a more humanistic view of learning. He saw people as basically good and active beings, who are free and self-directing. This led to his emphasis on instincts and feelings in the educational sphere. From these foundations, Rousseau's followers introduced the idea of "learners" needs as an important factor to consider. These early ponderings have much in common with the notion of self-actualisation expounded by several eminent psychologists since the 1950s.

Behaviourist Theories

The greatest stimulus to modern thought on learning has undoubtedly stemmed from results of scientific experiments carried out at the turn of the last century by "Behaviourists". Scientists such as Pavlov (1848-1936) and Thorndike (1874-1949) based their theories on the observed behaviour of their subjects (mostly animals). Making no assumptions about the thinking or feeling processes that might be implied in their experiments, they merely described or predicted overt behaviour, and were especially concerned with connections between stimuli and responses in learning. Following in the behaviourist tradition, Skinner (1938) mainly focused on the concept of reinforcement of behaviour. The work of these scientists is significant, not only for its direct contribution to training practice, but also because the reaction to their ideas in theoretical circles provoked the emergence of other learning theories. Some of the key concepts arising from this work include:

- The law of readiness — the circumstances under which a learner tends to be satisfied or annoyed, to welcome or reject.

- The law of exercise — the strengthening of a particular response through repeated practice.

- The law of effect — strengthening or weakening a particular response on the basis of subsequent reward or punishment.

While adding considerably to our understanding of how people learn, the work of these behaviourists did not prove acceptable to other researchers in the field of learning as related to human behaviour. The main criticisms concern the fact that no allowance is made for factors such as "insight" or "imagination", and the consequent notion that learning and behaviour are not necessarily synonymous. In other words, even though learning has taken place (e.g. the individual knows that driving fast in foggy conditions can be extremely hazardous) a person may choose not to apply this learning (e.g. may still be unwilling to drive slowly). The argument is thus advanced that while learning and behaviour are undoubtedly interrelated, this does not mean that they are one and the same thing.

Cognitive Theories

The cognitive school of thought essentially sets out to describe the person as a knowing being rather than a simple or complex mechanism. The early advocates of cognitivism, such as Wertheimer (1889-1943) and Koehler (1887-1967), were known as "Gestaltists". These psychologists were particularly interested in the subject of perception, i.e. in how human beings and animals "see" their world, and from their experiments they demonstrated that learning is a matter of assembling one's world into meaningful patterns, rather than just making connections between separate elements. This view of perception was encapsulated in the statement that "the whole is greater than the sum of its parts".

Key aspects of learning associated with cognitive thought, include:

- a person develops a map of the world and extends this map through experience;

- new facts may be taken in which call for extending (assimilation) or revising (accommodation) this map;

- reflective or accumulated data can lead to insights about patterns and relationships (a holistic view of learning).

Gestaltist theories thus saw learning as a complex process, involving the exercise of problem-solving capacity, mental mapping, intuition, imagination, perception and purpose. They also held that learning could be latent (i.e. stored away until required for use). Figure 14.1 presents the key differences between Behaviourist and Gestaltist theories.

Figure 14.1: Key Differences between Behaviourists and Gestaltists

Behaviourists	Gestaltists
Learning is basically about making connections between a Stimulus and a Response.	Learning is primarily a question of how the environment is perceived.
Desired responses can be elicited by the use of rewards, which can also reinforce behaviour.	External rewards are less important than internal "mapping".
Learning is synonymous with behaviour.	Learning can be latent and can manifest itself in behaviour.
Evidence for learning is objective.	Evidence for learning is subjective.

The notion of "insight learning", which is particularly related to understanding, can also be included in the cognitivist domain. Lunzer (1968) has described insight in terms of the following characteristics:

- suddenness of solution;

- immediacy and smoothness of behaviour;

- ability to repeat solutions without error on successive presentations of original problem;

- ability to transpose the solution to situations exhibiting the same re-lational or structural features, but in a different context.

Insight thus represents the dawning of understanding, whereby a person grasp the essentials of a problem, can formulate a solution, and then apply the learning from this experience on a future occasion, while acknowledging the learning situation. For instance, when a person is engaged in basic information gathering, or learning basic skills routines, the application of insight is not required. Its principal relevance is to situations of a complex, problem-solving nature.

Experiential Theories

Experiential theories are associated with a "humanistic" view of how learning takes place. Our understanding of the learning process has been significantly advanced by the outstanding work of a number of contributors in the humanistic field.

Carl Rogers

Rogers (1969) presents a theory of learning which emphasises the learner's own involvement. It encapsulates the view that, in a training situation, the focus of learning is best directed at the experiences of the learner, rather than at the actions of the trainer. Thus the aim of educators and trainers should be to facilitate, rather than direct, the learning of others. He enunciated a number of principles which may be summarised as follows:

- People have a natural tendency and potential for learning.

- Significant learning takes place when the subject-matter is perceived as relevant by the learner.

- Learning which involves change in oneself is threatening and may be resisted.

- Learning which appears threatening can be acquired, and exploited, when external threats are minimised.

- Much significant learning is acquired by "doing".

- Learning is facilitated when the learner participates responsibly in the learning process.

- Self-initiated learning, involving the whole person (emotionally and intellectually), is the most lasting and pervasive form of learning.

- Independence, creativity, and self-reliance are all facilitated when self-criticism and self-evaluation are encouraged (rather than external forms of evaluation).

- Learning about the process of learning is essential to enable individuals to cope with change.

- The task of the facilitator is to provide an environment in which individuals can set their own learning goals.

These points reflect a liberal and humanistic viewpoint, whereby the emphasis of education and training is learner-centred. For many managers and trainers this approach may be difficult to follow, in lieu of the measures dictated by the collective needs of the organisation. Nevertheless there is a growing body of evidence to suggest that a trainee-centred approach to employee development contributes more to the achievement of corporate goals than one which is based on predetermined outcomes and the needs of the organisation.

David Kolb

The theme of self-initiated and self directed learning is also taken up by Kolb (1984), whose work has been particularly influential in management development. He sees classroom learning as a special activity, one which is cut off from the real world and which fails to satisfactorily integrate learning and doing. This idea leads to the importance of distinguishing class-room learning from problem-solving. The former is viewed as a process in which the teacher or trainer directs learning on behalf of the learner. The latter, by contrast, involves the learner in an active role, one in which the responsibility for achieving a solution rests with the individual and not with the teacher or trainer. Kolb (1984) set out a model of experiential learning which combines the characteristics of both classroom and problem-solving types of learning. Figure 14.2 presents an adaptation of Kolb's model by Anderson (1987) which suggests a four stage process model, charting the progress of learning through the stages of concepts, techniques, application and transfer.

Figure 14.2: The Experiential Learning Cycle

concrete experience

APPLICATION LEARNING METHODS	TRANSFER LEARNING METHODS
Syndicate exercise (new material) case-study individual or group	Situation role play
Simulation role play with video-trigger or case-study trigger with feedback from group	Open discussion
Rolling role-play	Free discussion, structured discussion
Presentation of group/individual work	Drawing/free discussion
Design exercises of group/individual work	Action planning self/shared
	Problem-solving techniques to explore and share issues of transfer
	Personal letters to self
	Follow-up projects
	Learning log

APPLICATION FACILITATION SKILLS	TRANSFER FACILITATION SKILLS
Briefing and debriefing skills	Handling role-play
Giving group and individual feedback	Dealing with stress
Problem-solving	Counselling skills
Role playing	Briefing and debriefing skills
Using video or case-study triggers	Giving feedback
Balancing feedback using BOOST	Managing group feedback
Preparing and using written briefs	Running free/open discussion
	Running structured discussion
	Problem-solving methods/interventions

active experimentation — application | transfer — reflective observation

techniques | concepts

TECHNIQUE FACILITATION SKILLS	CONCEPT FACILITATION SKILLS
Practical lesson-delivery skills	Formal presentation
Model presentation	Instructional techniques
Giving feedback individual or group	Feedback individual or group
Selection of example video	Experiential methods
Working with video clips	Briefing and debriefing skills
In-tray exercise	
Assignment briefing and debriefing	
Assignment preparation and use	

TECHNIQUE LEARNING METHODS	CONCEPT LEARNING METHODS
Practical technique/model demo	15- to 20-minute tutor input (lecturette)
Checklist with jointly completed examples	Structured training session IDC with visuals
Practical exercise used to give first hands-on using a new technique/model	Directed reading and feedback pres/discussion
Video of role-play to show technique/model in action	Commercial training video for analysis and feedback - individual/group
In-tray exercise (graded)	Use of a game to induce experiential learning
Training assignment	

abstract conceptualisation

The starting point of the model is a concrete experience of some kind (e.g. using a computer keyboard for the first time). Following this, the trainee makes observations and reflects on these (e.g. about the layout of the keys), and begins to formulate abstract concepts (e.g. begins to make sense of the keyboard). These concepts are then tested in a new situation (e.g. by practising on the keys), which provides a fresh experience and thus the cycle beings again. As Boydell (1976) emphasises, experience of itself is not the same as learning. Learning (the acquisition and application of knowledge and skills) occurs subsequent to the experience being reflected on and assessed by the learner.

Important aspects of the learning cycle include:

- It encompasses inductive and deductive learning. Inductive learning is the process in which the learner experiences an event or stimulus and draws a conclusion from it (e.g. a rule or guiding principle). On the other hand, deductive learning commences with the rule or principle, which is subsequently applied by the learner.

- It stresses the continuous (cyclical) nature of the learning process.

- It emphasises the central position of the individual's needs in governing the direction of learning. The experiences we seek, the way we interpret them, and how we test out our ideas, are all strongly influenced by felt needs and goals.

- The four stages of the cycle encompass feeling, observing, thinking and doing. By implication, effective learning requires the involvement of three different levels — feeling, thinking and doing.

A further significant contribution from Kolb is the Learning Cycle Inventory (LSI), which he describes as a "simple self-description test, based on experiential learning theory, that is designed to measure the strength and weaknesses of learners in relation to the four stages of the learning cycle". The aim of the test is to help individuals to identify their "learning style" (their approach to solving problems). In essence the four stages of the cycle can be combined to form two major dimensions of learning — a concrete/abstract dimension, and a reflective/action dimension — and the results indicate an individual's dominant learning style as allocated to each quadrant.

As indicated, the dominant styles are set out as:

- *Converger* — favours the practical application of ideas, and tends to prefer working with "things" rather than with people. This style is usually characteristic of those with an engineering orientation.

- *Diverger* — greatest strength is imagination and the ability to see situations from a variety of perspectives. Shows a strong interest in people issues, a fact reflected in the predominance of this style amongst personnel managers.

- *Assimilator* — this style represents a penchant for abstract thinking and a concern for ideas in themselves. Tends to be manifested in those engaged primarily in research and planning activities.

- *Accommodator* — reminiscent of the action approach to problem-solving, with an emphasis on personal involvement and risk-taking. This style is often found in marketing and sales staff.

Honey and Mumford on Learning Styles

A separate instrument for assessing learning styles has been developed by Honey and Mumford (1989). This consists of a questionnaire which allows individual to agree or disagree with specific statements. The resulting scores are plotted on a two-dimensional chart to provide a learning profile. The learner's style is thus mapped in relation to the following learning styles:

- *Activists* — people whose days are filled with activity and new experiences. They thrive on challenge, but generally become bored with implementation and consolidation.

- *Reflectors* — thoughtful and cautious people. They usually have a fairly low profile in organisations.

- *Theorists* — logical thinkers, who like a good theory and tend to be detached, analytical and rational.

- *Pragmatists* — action-oriented people who prefer putting ideas into practice.

The identification of learning styles can be beneficial in a number of ways:

- Learners themselves can gain a better understanding of their preferred approach to learning. They are also facilitated in identifying those styles which may need to be improved in order to achieve a better learning balance.

- Training methods can be designed to cater for learners' preferred approaches to learning (remembering, of course, that it is usual to have a mix of learning styles in learning groups).

- It can assist managers, by sharpening their awareness of how individuals are likely to react in particular problem situations.

The preceding outlines comprise a mere summary of the many variations on learning theory which have been put forward. Understandably, all theories have their supporters and critics. In addition, new complexions are being added to existing theories, while new thinking emerges on an ongoing basis. Clearly, where a complex process such as learning is concerned, it would be unwise to suggest one approach as being the "best" or the "most appropriate" in a universally applicable sense. Furthermore, where learning in organisations becomes the focus of attention, there are many variable contextual factors which increase the uncertainty regarding which is the most suitable learning approach. It follows, therefore, that training specialists should have a sound understanding, not only of learning theory itself, but also of how it may best be applied in a given situation. On this point, Kramlinger and Huberty (1990) offer a useful illustration, in the form of a continuum, of each of the main theories and their associated learning methods. They also set out the advantages of each main theory group.

Which Theory is the Best?

> Behaviourism might be all right for teaching pigeons to bowl, but what is best for achieving real performance — behaviourism or humanism (or perhaps cognitivism)?

The above quote by Kramlinger and Huberty (1990) illustrates the amount of debate surrounding learning theories. They proceed to illustrate the range of existing theories along a continuum, as shown in Figures 14.3 and 14.4.

Kramlinger and Huberty (1990) outline the advantages of each perspective, and show the techniques of achieving the learning objectives of the three methods, shown in Figure 14.5.

Figure 14. 3: Alternative Theories of Learning — Learning Objectives and Different Perspectives

Learning Objective	Techniques		
	Humanist	Cognitivist	Behaviourist
Knowledge			
Transmit information	Inductive discussion Inductive game Debrief experience Relevance discussion Active elaboration	Lecture/film Graphic illustration Panel/interview SMI Class presentation Reading Question and answer Review	Multiple choice Memorisation Association
Verify information	Confirmatory discussion	Test	Question with answer
Skill			
Induce response	Discussion action Visualise action Inductive case study	List steps Demonstration Success stories	Behavioural model Behavioural samples Prompting/cueing
Strengthen response (practice)	Mental rehearsal Project	Case study	Work sheets Skill drill (game) Simulation Role play
Apply the skill	Action plan Planning guide Elaboration (skit) Contract	Coaching/feedback	Realistic practice Job aid prompts On-job reinforcement

Figure 14.4: Alternative Theories of Learning — What's Mainstream and What's Not

Left   Mainstream   Right

Levels Types	*Extreme humanism*	*Radical humanism*	*Moderate humanism*	*Classical cognitivism*	*Moderate behaviourism*	*Radical behaviourism*	*Extreme behaviourism*
Methods	Hot tubs Massages Self-directed therapy	Open-ended exploration Skits Meditation Visualisation Ropes courses	Expectations Experiences Discussions Games Action plans	Logical outline Reading Lecture Demonstration	Terminal objectives Prompting Modelling Cueing	Intermediate objectives Programmed instruction Consequence management	Brainwashing, punishment Behaviour modification

Least structure   Most structure

Source: Kramlinger, T and Huberty, T. (1990) "Behaviourism vs. Humanism", *Training and Development Journal*, December

Figure 14.5: Advantages of Particular Learning Perspectives

Humanism	Behaviourism	Cognitivism
1. Draws on peoples experience 2. Treats people as adults 3. Adapts to diverse needs and expectations of learners 4. Develops critical thinking, judgement and creativity	1. Clear objectives 2. Ensures behavioural practice 3. Best for acquiring behavioural skills 4. Highly specific 5. Observable and quantifiable	1. Fast 2. Treats people as adults 3. Provides rationale upon which action is based 4. Builds up a base of information, concepts, rules.

LEARNING PRINCIPLES AND CONDITIONS

A distinction can be drawn between learning (the internal process) and performance (the external results). Performance is the effective learning observed in behaviour. Interest in organisational training and development derives from two sources — the needs of organisations (which are predominantly centred on performance), and the concern of trainers (on methods of learning). It is the emphasis on learning and what the trainee does or undergoes, as opposed to what the trainer does, which most marks the changes in training and development in recent years. Performance is a demonstration of the fact that learning has taken place; it is the measurable behaviour from which underlying learning can be inferred. The aim of a technology of training is to expedite the process by arranging conditions so that learning is much more rapid and effective.

Factors which facilitate learning are a critical consideration, and these learning principles and conditions are summarised below.

- It is important to recognise that individuals have diverse traits and capabilities.

- Learning is best achieved at the trainee's own pace.

- Self-motivated trainees learn quicker.

- Stress-based motivation creates emotional distraction and is less effective than no motivation at all.

- Learning under a positive incentive (reward) is more effective than negatively-influenced learning (threat of punishment).

- Learning is facilitated by meaningful material — an integration of learning experiences which the trainee can transfer to the job.

- Active participation is better than passive reception.

- Knowledge of results (feedback) is vital.

- Learning must be reinforced frequently and immediately.

- Presentation and practice must be spaced and distributed as appropriate.

- Ample opportunity for appropriate practice must be provided.

- The rate of learning may be influenced by personality interactions of trainer and trainee.

- The role of the trainer is to assist the trainee in his/her willingness to change.

- There may be some transfer of learning.

- A systematic approach to the identification of training needs and to the planning of training programmes should be adopted.

- Validation (comparison of criterion test and pre-entry tests) should be undertaken).

- As far as possible, evaluation should be couched in cost-benefit terms.

- Alternative ways of learning should be considered.

- Training/development is not a solution to every problem.

There is a variety of learning principles arising from this list which merit elaboration.

Motivation to Learn

For effective learning to take place trainees must want to learn, in other words, they must perceive the learning process as the means of achieving certain desired goals. However, motivation is a complex area, and there are considerable variations in the way individuals might be motivated in a training and development context. In this vein, Otto and Glaser (1970) suggest a classification of motivation factors based on the kind of rewards which may be associated with learning:

- Achievement: Reward is based on a feeling of attainment and success.

- Anxiety: Here, reward is seen more in terms of the avoidance of failure or punishment.

- Approval: Reward is centred around recognition / praise (from peers, the trainer, manager or supervisor, family, etc.).

- Curiosity: Reward is represented by an increased opportunity to explore the environment.

- Acquisitiveness: Reward is reflected in tangible benefits (pay, promotion, etc.).

This classification highlights that both intrinsic and extrinsic motivational factors may be relevant in the learning process. Intrinsic motivation is inspired by the need to fulfil personal, deeply-felt needs, i.e. achievement/curiosity classification). While organisational training programmes may not always appear to the trainee as pertinent to "innermost needs", there are some helpful ways of utilising intrinsic motivators, including:

- stressing the future of the learning activity (using examples/problems which are likely to be encountered at a future work stage);

- providing feedback during the learning experience (showing the extent of progress towards final objectives);

- relating the learning activity to interesting and meaningful material;

- maintaining a certain amount of "suspense" during the learning activity.

It is not usually feasible to rely entirely on intrinsic motivators, and use must also be made of extrinsic factors (i.e. as identified in the acquisitiveness/approval classification) which may be artificially related to the learning activity and therefore helping to reinforce it. The trainer will usually find it useful to emphasise long-term benefits in this regard. In any case, it is generally much more effective to reward, and to maximise the probability that the learner will experience success, than it is to punish errors (i.e. anxiety classification) or criticise mistakes and failures. Punishment is considered a poor motivational technique, because its consequences are less predictable. The problems associated with punishment in this context are seen to include:

- although it may deter wrongdoing, it gives no indication of the correct response;

- it may be counter-productive in that it tends to fixate behaviour (rather than eliminate it) and focus the attention of the trainee on incorrect responses;

- it may prove emotionally disturbing and create negative attitudes towards the trainer and/or the learning activity itself;

- its effects on behaviour are relatively less permanent than those driven by reward.

Reid et al (1992) argue that curiosity is among the most powerful motivators, and link this to the common success of discovery methods of learning. In general, intrinsic motivators may be related to cognitive and experiential theories of learning; while the extrinsic variety have their roots more in behaviourist theories.

Involvement of the Learner

Learning should be seen as an active, rather than a passive, process. It is usually more successful when it incorporates the active involvement of the learner. Roscoe (1995) suggests that all development activities basically embrace self-development; even when learning opportunities and facilities are provided, individuals must accept responsibility for their own development. The trainer should therefore be seen as a facilitator, rather than a teacher in the pedagogic sense. Adopting a learner-centred orientation in this context is discussed by Pont (1991) and consequent implications for the trainer may be summarised as follows:

- The role of the trainer is essentially to create an environment conducive to learning. An informal environment is considered most appropriate, as strict formality can trigger tension and stress which may seriously impede learning.

- Individuals involved in self-directed development occasionally need appropriate support and guidance. This need should be recognised and catered for by the trainer.

- The trainer should ensure that each individual's store of experience is tapped into and utilised as a common learning resource.

- Participative measures should be widely engaged during training programme, as they:

  – are consistent with, and supportive of, a cyclical learning approach;

  – increase and broaden learning attention spans;

- encourage the development of self-insights and insight into others;

- deepen the levels of learning experience, especially in relation to inducing attitude change.

- Learners should have some involvement in deciding the content of training programmes. This increases their ownership and control of the learning process and helps to overcome resistance factors.

- In situations where the main focus of learning is on the acquisition of knowledge, a variety of learning methods should be employed. These should be commensurate with subject-matter and individual learning styles, to trigger greater receptivity.

Active involvement and participation is inherent in discovery learning. In training programmes which are focused on the acquisition of complex skills, learners should be provided with the opportunity to discover common elements, principles, and relationships for themselves. This method has been used successfully in "conversion training" for older workers who have to learn new skills, and also in the initial training of young people with a background of little formal education. Active participation in the quest for understanding tends to result in more effective learning and greater levels of retention (Belbin and Belbin, 1972).

The concept of involvement is primarily rooted in the humanist school of learning theory.

Knowledge of Results/Feedback/Guidance

Providing the learner with feedback on the extent of their progress is a good motivation strategy. Learners who know when a response is correct or not, whether they are improving or not, and the extent of any improvement, can engage in a process of goal setting. This not only makes the learning more interesting, but self-development (itself an powerful motivator) implies the involvement of learners in setting their own objectives and targets.

Good feedback is seen as that which is specific, well-timed (immediate) and checked to ensure effective communication (Kolb, Rubin and McIntyre, 1974). The specificity or amount of feedback provided must be appropriate to the particular capabilities and stage of development of the learner. It appears that for each stage and for each trainee, there is an optimum level of feedback which should be given. Blum and Naylor (1968) illustrate the hypothesised relationship between the specificity of feedback and the amount of learning (see figure 14.4).

Figure 14.6: The Relationship between Feedback and Learning

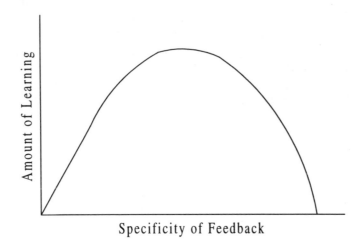

Source: Blum, M. C. and Naylor, J. C. (1968), *Industrial Psychology: Its Theoretical and Social Foundations*, New York: Harper and Row.

Feedback can be classified as direct (e.g. personal observation of a process, direct comments of trainer, etc.) or indirect (e.g. check by quality inspector). On the other hand, Buckley and Caple (1992) refer to extrinsic and intrinsic feedback. Extrinsic comes from sources external to the process or activity (e.g. the trainer, other trainees, or mechanical devices), while intrinsic is associated with cues or stimuli within the task or job itself (e.g. a distinctive sound, a visual clue, a particular "feel", etc.). In this sense, they see effective training partially in terms of using extrinsic feedback to direct the trainee's attention to the intrinsic cues. This can serve to encourage trainees to monitor their own performance and to focus on intrinsic feedback when initial training is completed (and extrinsic feedback from the trainer is largely withdrawn).

Trainer guidance can be said to include the giving of feedback, but it also incorporates directing or re-directing the trainee in the correct and most effective way to approach what is being learned. Proper guidance is critical in enabling trainees to unlearn inappropriate or unsuitable practices and in preventing the incorrect behaviours becoming patternised. Proper guidance can be seen as a balance between two extremes — maximum or minimum guidance. Maximum (or too much) guidance can hinder a trainee's adjustment in the post-training phase. However, with minimum (or zero) guidance, a learner is forced to proceed on a trial-and-error basis, uninformed of correct responses and not prevented from making errors. This lack of guidance prolongs the learning period and may lead to the formation of "bad habits" which become difficult to eradicate. Both extremes are thus undesirable, and effective guidance is a question of striking a balance dictated by the context of the learning.

Knowledge of results, feedback, and guidance can be directly related to the learning principles evoked in Kolb's Learning Cycle — the trainee has an experience (in this instance feedback) which leads to observation and reflection on the learning activity. This is followed by generalising or theorising about possible future ways of performing the activity, and by testing through subsequent practice.

Standards

Learners should have clearly defined targets and standards which are challenging but realisable. As already outlined, learners should have an input into determining these standards. It is also important that the trainer accepts that such standards can be the subject of review and change. Roscoe (1995) argues that, while standards must contain an element of challenge or stretch to motivate the learner, this should be structured and paced to form a gradual process. If the standards are too tight or overly challenging, the learner is likely to experience high levels of stress. If this is prolonged, it may eventually lead to burnout, failure to absorb learning effectively, and possibly to fear of future learning activities. On the other hand, if the standards are less than challenging, the learner is prone to boredom and over-confidence. This can lead to stunted development and the adoption of a dismissive attitude towards future learning activities. It is crucial, therefore, that targets and standards are set at appropriate levels, are monitored and reviewed on an ongoing basis, and that individual differences are taken into account.

Retaining/Forgetting Learning

Because that which has been learned can so easily be forgotten, practice is necessary for the maintenance of a skill or the retention of knowledge. Unless practice is continued, forgetting can take place very rapidly. However, the rate of forgetting varies significantly between individuals and according to the subject or skills learned. There is evidence, for example, to suggest that perceptual-motor skills can be retained for a considerable period of time, although this is not the case with many forms of learning which fall into passive decay through disuse. In general terms, learning which needs to be retained for a long period of time should be the focus of "overlearning". Forgetting can occur for a number of reasons:

- Retroactive inhibitions — where the learning of new material interferes with past learning.

- Proactive inhibition — where past learning may inhibit or interfere with new learning

- Repression — motivation to forget learning which has some distasteful connotation.

One consolation for the learner who forgets is that relearning something usually takes less time than the original learning process.

Conditions of Practice

There are four issues of importance here: active practice, overlearning, massed versus distributed practice sessions, and the size of the unit to be learned.

1. Active Practice: When the trainee is learning a new skill they should be given an opportunity to practise what is being taught. During the early stages, the trainer should be available to guide the trainee's practice. Repeating the essential movements of the skill allows the trainee to be provided with the internal or precipitate cues that regulate motor performance. As practice continues, internal cues leading to errors are progressively disbanded and internal cues associated with smooth and precise performance are retained.

2. Overlearning: This concept is defined as providing trainees with continued practice far beyond the point when the task has been performed correctly several times. Overlearning is important for a number of reasons. It increases the length of time that training material will be retained and it makes the learner more reflective (i.e. the trainee will have to concentrate less strongly on the task as it becomes more automatic). Trainees will also be more likely to maintain the quality of their performance on the job during periods of emergency and, most significantly perhaps, overlearning helps trainees transfer what has been learned to the work situation.

3. Massed versus Distributed Practice: A significant problem in designing a training programme is the problem of whether to divide the practice into segments or to plan one continuous session. The answer to this question depends on the nature of the task. Generally, distributed practice sessions interspersed with reasonable periods of rest allow greater learning of skills than continuous practice. The rule is not as clear-cut when it comes to learning factual information. Generally, the less meaningful the material to be learned and the greater

its length or difficulty, the better distributed practice becomes relative to massed practice. It also appears that the less brain ability the trainee possesses the more that person will benefit from distributed practice.

4. Size of Unit to be Learned: Figure 14.7 identifies three basic strategies for unit size.

Figure 14.7: Size of Unit to be Learned — Basic Strategies

Strategy	Phase 1	Phase 2	Phase 3	Phase 4
Whole training	A+B+C	A+B+C	A+B+C	A+B+C
Pure part-training	A	B	C	A+B+C
Progressive part-training	A	A+B	A+B+C	A+B+C

Whole learning consists of practising all sub-tasks during all phases of learning. Using a pure part-strategy, successive sub-tasks are produced separately in successive phases of training. Progressive part-training adopts an extra element at each phase.

There is much discussion on the effectiveness of each strategy. Strauch (1984) advocates using a so-called holistic approach to employee training, which should focus on the total task at all times during the training. However, the suitability of each strategy depends on the characteristics of the task itself — e.g. task complexity and task organisation. Task complexity refers to the difficulty of each of the sub-tasks whereas task organisation refers to the degree of interrelationships among the set of sub-tasks. For highly organised tasks the whole method appears to be more effective whereas both part-strategies are better when task organisation is low.

Meaningfulness of the Material

This concept refers to training material that is rich in association for the trainee and is thus easily understood by them. Wexley and Latham (1991) suggest four strategies to increase meaningfulness.

1. Trainees should be provided with an overview of the material to be learned. Seeing the overall picture facilitates the trainee in understanding how each unit of the training programme fits together.

2. The material should be presented using examples, concepts and terms familiar to the learner.

3. Meaningfulness is facilitated when material is sequenced in a logical manner.

4. Complex intellectual skills are composed of simpler skills and the attainment of these subordinated skills is essential before the complex skills can be acquired.

CHARACTERISTICS OF THE LEARNER

An important feature of learning is the impact that individual characteristics of the learner may have on the effectiveness of the process. "Learners" cannot be classified into a homogenous grouping. There are a number of factors underlying the difference between individuals in a learning context.

Let us look initially at some general themes about adult learners. Lindeman (1926) set out the following principles which have retained their relevance to the present day:

- Adults are motivated to learn as they experience needs and interests that learning will satisfy. Therefore, these are appropriate starting points for organising adult learning activities.

- Adults' orientation to learning is life-centred, and the appropriate units for organising adult learning are life situations as opposed to subjects.

- Adults have a deep need for self-direction. The role of the teacher is to engage in a process of mutual enquiry with them, rather than to transmit knowledge and evaluate learner's conformity to it.

- Individual differences among people increase with age. Adult education must make optimal provision for differences in style, time and pace of learning (we will return to the topic of individual differences later).

Knowles (1974) takes up the notion of self-direction in adult learning and argues that with growth and maturity, a person's self-concept moves from one of total dependency to one of increasing self-direction.

Adult learners are seen to bring considerable "baggage" to the learning situation, including:

- unique motives for wanting to learn

- previous learning history (including good and bad learning experiences)

- self-confidence, self-esteem, and self-image

- learning style

- preferred pace of learning

- physical state

- personality

- view of the world

- fears and anxieties

While this pattern may reflect the mindset of adult learners as a whole, a multiplicity of shades are represented within each individual mindset and these differences may be coloured by a number of factors. Several significant factors determining the individual differences have been identified by Buckley and Caple (1992), and these may be summarised as follows:

Age

Age levels can contribute to differences between learners in a variety of ways, triggering the need for particular consideration from the trainer. Levels of ability to retain knowledge and skills are affected by increasing age. Age can also impinge on attitudes, motivation and enthusiasm, while levels of confidence and intelligence also tend to vary in this respect. Trainers can help to overcome potential difficulties caused by such differences by:

- building confidence through reassurance, feedback, and involvement;

- taking account of disparity within learning groups — using smaller groups and varying the pace of learning appropriately;

- providing participative learning methods for older learners;

- breaking complex material down into suitable learning "parts";

- being aware of the possibility of high degrees of unlearning needed by older learners.

A more detailed summary of difficulties which increase with age, as well as suggestions as to how training should be adapted accordingly, has been presented by Newsham (1969).

Levels of Intelligence and Ability

Level of intelligence and ability is another differentiating feature among learners which must be catered for. This feature can affect the trainer's approach in several significant ways, for example:

- Learners with comparatively low levels of ability prefer to work from concrete examples, which they can subsequently relate to general principles. However, the reverse is usually true of those with higher levels of ability.

- Learners with lower intelligence levels generally find it easier to manage learning and practising a complex task if it is divided into "parts" which are tackled on a cumulative basis. However, those of higher intelligence may find it easier to contemplate the task as a "whole".

- Trainees with lower intelligence levels tend to experience greater difficulty with unstructured learning situations.

Background and Emotional Disposition

It is important for the trainer to take account of the background and emotional disposition of learners. There are a range of factors encompassed by this consideration, including:

- Some individuals approach training activities with a degree of apprehension. This may stem from anxiety about being "put on the spot" or having perceived limitations exposed in some way. These individuals need a great deal of reassurance at the outset and may be helped by their involvement in setting their own learning goals.

- Some learners assume a teacher/pupil relationship as exists between trainer and learner (a likely carry-over from school days). This can result in a reluctance to challenge propositions or to enter fully into discussion. The trainer should encourage contributions from such individuals, and reinforce the validity of their participation in this way.

- Previous experiences may provoke sceptical tendencies in some learners. It may prove difficult to overturn these, but trainers can elicit co-operation through focusing on the importance of the activity and relating learning closely to the actual work situation.

Factors like these need special attention because they may take some time to come to light.

Learning Styles

We have discussed learning styles in our preceding overview of learning theories, and their relevance can be especially related to individual differences. Arment (1990) outlines three important facts about learning styles:

1. By the time we reach adulthood, each of us has developed our own method of learning, reflected in a unique and well-established learning style.

2. Trainers also have well-established learning styles and preferences.

3. The more compatible the style of learning with the approach to training adopted, the more likely it is that a positive training/learning experience will occur.

Mumford (1986) argues that little consideration is generally given to the existence of different learning styles in the design and implementation of training and development activities, and believes this to have seriously negative implications.

Learner characteristics play a significant role in the learning process. Learning is a very personal experience, and each individual has a set of experiences unique to them. An individual's eventual store of knowledge and skills is dependent on the variety, breadth and quality of these experiences and the ability to identify the learning points embraced.

Trainability

Trainability is a function of the individual's ability and motivation. Ability in this context refers to the extent to which the individual possesses the aptitudes or skills to perform the tasks in question. Motivation is concerned with those variables which influence the trainee's effort, persistence and choices. Trainees' involvement in their jobs and careers are significant antecedents of learning during training and behaviour change after learning. Another important variable is the individual's expectations that participation in training will lead to desired outcomes such as feelings of accomplishment, greater responsibility, etc. Anxiety also appears to be a significant factor in trainability. Anxiety has been shown to facilitate performance in relatively simple types of learning but to interfere with the learning of complex tasks.

The concern with trainability has led to the development of trainability tests. Trainability tests are used to improve the selection process of untrained applicants for training programmes. These tests generally take the following form:

- Using a standardised form of instruction and demonstration, the trainer teaches the applicant the task.

- The applicant is asked to perform the task unaided.

- The trainer records the applicant's performance by noting errors on a standardised check list and by making a rating of the applicant's likely performance in training.

Downs (1985) concludes that trainability tests produce significant levels of validity and are quite useful in predicting an untrained applicant's subsequent success in training and job performance.

TRANSFER OF TRAINING

The term "transfer of training" refers to the carry-over effects of learning — the extent to which proficiencies and abilities acquired during a training session may be applied to the actual work situation or to the learning of a new, but related, skill. In some circumstances negative transfer occurs because the learning experience may create inhibitions which impede the acquisition of new skills. Occasionally there may be no observable effect. However, positive transfer refers to cases where learning in one situation actually enhances learning in another (Gagne, 1977). Positive transfer can arise in various ways:

- Transfer-through-principles theory — once a general principle has been learned, all of the problems of a given class may be solved as soon as they are presented. In these instances, however, it is still necessary for the learner to recognise common properties in the two "stimulus" situations (e.g. the learning situation and the job situation). This principle underlies much off-the-job training, especially in the realm of transferable skills.

- Identical-elements theory — this theory draws attention to the relationship in one situation (e.g. learning) and another (e.g. job performance). A problem here is the potential difficulty of measuring the degree of similarity between stimuli and responses. The technique is nonetheless applicable to situations where specific stimuli and corresponding responses can be clearly identified (e.g. learning to drive a car).

In more complex tasks, learners progress from making simple stimulus-response connections, through trains of thought and verbal associations, to the ability to discriminate between situations and to develop rules and concepts, so that they finally acquire the ability to solve problems for themselves. The overall implication suggests that there is a hierarchy of learning, and that training should proceed from lower to higher levels.

The research identifies two sets of factors which affect learning transfer: organisational and social factors. Latham and Crandall (1991) identify pay and promotion policies and environmental constraints as two organisational factors. These variables influence the level of training transfer because they affect training outcome expectations. Bandura (1986) suggests that trainees may believe that they are capable of performing a specific behaviour but may choose not to do so because they believe it will have little or no effect on their status in the organisation. Therefore, high-outcome expectations are fundamental to the transfer of training in the job setting. Latham and Huber (1992) demonstrate that systems of pay for performance are effective strategies for bringing about training transfer.

Environmental constraints have a negative effect on a trainee's outcome expectations. Peters et al (1985) identify eleven constraints, namely: the lack of job-related information, tools and equipment, materials and supplies, budgetary support, required services and help from others, task preparation, time availability, physical aspects of the work, environment, scheduling of activities, transportation and job-relevant authority.

Two significant social variables which affect transfer are peer-group influences and supervisory support. Peer interaction can provide support and reinforcement not only for the learning but for the application of learning to the job. Failure to achieve this support can result in alienation during and after training. Supervisory support is a critical factor. Good supervisory support increases trainee outcome expectations that the learning skills will be valued by the organisation.

Figure 14.8 outlines some principles of learning transfer.

MANAGING THE ORGANISATION AS A CONTINUOUS LEARNING SYSTEM

The concept of the "learning organisation" continues to grow in importance and popularity. Many commentators endorse the view that future success is becoming ever more dependent on the capacity of the organisation to learn faster than its competitors. The organisation is increasingly seen as an organism which must learn faster than the rate of change to ensure its survival. Senge (1990) believes that the impulse to learn lies at the heart of an impulse to become generative and therefore learning organisations are focused on generative learning. According to Jaccardi (1989), success in the face of changing environment depends on wisdom and learning. Understanding the relationship between creativity, productivity, and learning leads to recognition of the need to adopt a learning culture. The notion of a learning culture means that the process of learning permeates through all of the organisation's systems, and that a systems view and the learning organisation are interlinked. Thus, learning helps to facilitate organisational change and improvement, as well as creating a greater appreciation of systems dynamics.

Figure 14.8: Maximising Retention and Transfer of Learning

Before
- Conduct a needs analysis among multiple stakeholders.
- Seek out supervisory support for training.
- Inform the trainees regarding the nature of the training.
- Assign tasks prior to the training.

During
- Maximise the similarity between the training situation and the job situation.
- Provide as much experience as possible related to the task being taught.
- Have the trainees practise their newly-learned skills in actual situations that they will encounter back on the job.
- Provide for a variety of examples when teaching concepts or skills.
- Label or identify important features of a task.
- Make sure the general principles are understood before expecting much transfer.
- Provide trainees with the knowledge, skills and feelings of self-efficacy to self-regulate their own behaviours back on the job.
- Design the training content so that the trainees can see its applicability.

After
- Make certain that the trained behaviours and ideas are rewarded in the job situation.
- Get trainees to rank the learning points in terms of relevance to their particular work setting.
- Get trainee to generate specific activities that will help to apply the goal to the workplace.

Characteristics of a Learning Organisation

Pedler et al (1991) have identified a number of characteristics pertinent to a learning organisation, and these can be briefly summarised as follows:

A Learning Approach to Strategy

This means that the organisation's strategies, objectives, and policies, are formulated against the background of a consciously structured learning process, allowing business plans to be developed and revised on a continuous basis. Business plans are thus an instrument of strategic thinking which is influenced by a learning ethos.

Participative Policy-making

The process of strategy formulation and policy-making is shared widely among organisation members and decisions are likely to reflect shared commitment and support.

Informating

Information technology is utilised as a source of empowerment; improving access to relevant information and thereby decision-making at all organisational levels, and promoting a learning focus.

Formative Accounting and Control

The organisation's financial systems are structured to promote the "small business unit" concept, and financial decision-making is integrally linked to the learning process.

Internal Exchange

The vision of internal units as valued "customers" and "suppliers" predominate product, service and information exchange mechanisms.

Reward Flexibility

Reward systems are openly reviewed and reconstructed to reflect needs, on the basis of commonly-agreed principles and the redistribution of power as well as reward.

Enabling Structures

Roles and boundaries are loosely defined and structured, in order to enhance the organisation's response flexibility and encourage individual and business growth and development. This is based on the premise that too much similarity in a job environment reduces the ability to adapt and learn.

Boundary Workers as Environmental Scanners

The importance of learning from the external environment is emphasised and all members who communicate with customers, suppliers and clients engage in this activity. Feedback information gathered through this process becomes the source of learning opportunities.

Inter-company Learning

Learning is not confined to the organisation itself, but is extended to embrace mutually advantageous alliances with customers, suppliers and even competitors. Information is shared, and there is joint investment in areas such as training, research and development, and market development.

Learning Climate

The nub of the learning organisation is the establishment of a learning culture. Managers see their roles in terms of facilitating others' learning, encouraging experimentation, and advancing continuous improvement through lived and shared experiences.

Self-development for All

There is an inherent attachment to the concept of self-development, which is reflected in the encouragement of personal responsibility for learning and the availability of resources and facilities to support this purpose.

These characteristics represent a blueprint for the learning organisation, but building the model can be a complex process. Commitment, energy and time are thus essential ingredients for success.

Towards a Learning Organisation

The organisation cannot become a continuous learning system surreptitiously; neither can it do so overnight. The driving force for managing the movement towards a learning organisation must reside at the top of the organisation. However, by its very nature, a learning organisation cannot be constructed by a management directive. Instead, it must be pursued by effectively influencing, persuading and communicating across all organisational levels. It means:

- attending to the requirements of all members and groups, and building a sense of cohesion and group purpose and support;

- identifying and satisfying individual motivational and developmental needs;

- harnessing the efforts of all members to meet the desired goal.

It therefore requires the establishment of a clear vision of what needs to be achieved and the adoption of appropriate strategies to enable this. These strategies may be devised by examining various aspects of training and development in the current organisation in terms of the "vision", for example:

- *Positioning*: How congruent is the training function with the current goals of the organisation? How is it perceived by organisational stakeholders? How should it be perceived in order to ensure the success of the vision?

- *Power*: What is the power base of the training function? What influences and resources does it have? What status issues may arise and how can these be best managed?

- *Processes*: What are the internal systems which co-ordinate training and development activity? What are its current communication flows (internal/external)? How are these likely to support or hinder the vision?

- *People*: What is the current store of organisational knowledge, skills and expertise? How do they relate to the vision? What are the attitudinal motivational factors which shape the culture of the organisation? What are the likely sources of resistance? What is the best approach to motivating and encouraging the acceptance of the vision?

- *Product*: What are the current training and development products/services? What are the delivery mechanisms employed? How effectively does the training function contribute to business goals and objectives? How will it need to change in order to resource, support and encourage the vision? What will the training and development function "look like" in the learning organisation?

- *Plans*: What are the strategies which will encourage learning and transformation? What is the most appropriate and effective starting point? What are the support structures which must be put into place? At what speed should progress be paced? What will the role of the training function be?

Key Activities for the Training Specialist

It is clear that the training specialist must adapt and change in order that the new vision of learning is managed effectively. Key activities for the training specialist are put forward as:

- communicating and consulting on an organisation-wide basis;

- encouraging active commitment and participation, and enabling growth and development;

- promoting an atmosphere of mutual trust;

- encouraging challenges to existing methods and processes;

- facilitating self-direction and the acceptance of responsibility for individual actions and learning;

- promoting and utilising feedback systems, which enable continuous improvement through the sharing of experiences and learning.

In order to develop a learning culture, the training specialist must adopt an holistic view of training and development, as generative learning cannot exist without a holistic perception and a clear focus on the systems that control events. The training specialist must exploit the possibility of using the tools of systems thinking to gather the learning ideas from all parts of the organisation into a coherent, functional whole.

LEARNING TO LEARN AND SELF-DEVELOPMENT

There is a growing focus in organisations on the importance of the individual's contribution to success. In "empowerment" and "total quality" cultures, individuals are expected to accept greater responsibility at their level of operations and to follow a path of continuous improvement. At the core of this movement is the recognition that employees have far more to offer than just performing work in a functional manner; their contribution can also encompass creativity and innovation. Indeed, the term "knowledge employees" has been coined to describe the requirements of future workforces. Increasing individual's capacity to learn, and their involvement in a process of self-development, can significantly enhance participation along these lines. Learning to learn and self-development must therefore be fostered and facilitated in organisations, if the contribution of the workforce is to be maximised.

Skills of Learning

Learning to learn is essentially concerned with improving the ability to learn. According to Law (1986), learning skills can be described as ways of organising and co-ordinating learning activities, so that changes in behaviour or disposition are retained. She outlines research into this area undertaken by Downs and Perry (1984), who identify a list of internalised learning skills (those most likely to be present in most people to some extent). They include:

- self-questioning;
- imagining;
- clarifying, ordering, grouping, summarising, relating, comparing, contrasting, associating, structuring;
- reviewing, monitoring, checking;
- predicting;
- evaluating and assessing;
- formulating hypotheses;
- deciding;
- selecting.

Many of these skills can be linked to the "observation and reflection" and "conceptualisation" stages of Kolb's (1984) learning cycle.

This list of learning skills highlights the type of activities which facilitate learning to learn. However, the learner must be made conscious of these activities, and their capacity to utilise these skills must be effectively developed.

Overcoming Learning Blockages

Barriers to effective learning are also discussed by Law (1986) and some common blockages are seen to emanate from learners':

- fears about being perceived as silly or stupid;
- anxieties over the possibility of failure;
- lack of knowledge and direction concerning what to learn;
- anxieties over feeling too old to learn;
- visualisation of difficulty with memorising and remembering things;
- lack of confidence;
- memories of not being successful at school.

Many of these effects result from deep-seated causes, identified by Law (1986) as:

- a basic lack of learning skills;

- never having learned to learn (in terms of adult learning);

- previous learning experiences (where they had been discouraged from challenging or questioning, had been expected to learn too much too quickly, or had not been encouraged to fully understand what was being "taught");

- the perception of learning purely in terms of memorising or repeating a behaviour;

- the belief that the quality of their own learning is outside their control;

- inappropriate training methods or training approaches.

In encouraging individuals to develop their own learning abilities, the training specialist must be aware of the potentially deep-rooted nature of learning blockages.

Promoting Learning to Learn and Self-development

Harrison (1992) provides a useful list of six major activities which can help to promote learning to learn and self-development, and these may be summarised as follows:

1. *Self-development of those who have responsibility for others' learning*. In order to effectively facilitate others' learning, it is critical that those charged with this task understand the nature of learning skills. It is also important that they have a sound appreciation of their own learning skills and styles — both Kolb's (1984) and Honey and Mumford's (1989) learning styles exercises are useful for this purpose.

2. *Promote self-directed learning*. The process of self-development and self-directed learning should be encouraged, facilitated and adequately resourced within the organisation. Responsibility for self-development cannot be forced, but its acceptance by individuals should be actively encouraged and this can be approached in several ways, including:
   - the performance appraisal mechanism;
   - career counselling;
   - personal learning/development plans as outcomes of specifically facilitated workshops;
   - guidance and coaching.

3. *Promote awareness of opportunities for continuous learning*. This means creating an environment where the natural process of learning

can thrive and prosper. Every opportunity for promoting and encouraging the integration of learning with everyday working life should be exploited.

4. *Design training events to develop learning styles and skills.* Two elements come into play here. Firstly, training events should be designed with the accommodation of the full range of learning styles in mind. Secondly, specific training and development interventions could be aimed at developing those learning styles and skills which may be latent in individuals.

5. *Seek to reduce organisational barriers to the development of appropriate learning styles and skills.* A diversity of learning approaches should be adopted in planned training interventions. This is particularly relevant where a "preferred" approach to training and development has been singularly operated in the organisation. Such a situation can lead to an over-reliance on "trusted" methods and the stifling of experimentation which could lead to improving the effectiveness of training and operating processes.

6. *Promote the consideration of learning styles in the appraisal process.* Learning styles and skills should be promoted as an influential factor in performance appraisal, as well as being extended to the selection process. In this context appropriate criteria should be developed to assist and guide those involved in these areas.

These pointers can provide a useful focus for the training specialist, in assuming a facilitative role and assisting the spread of a learning-to-learn and self-development ethos in the organisation.

SUMMARY

The underlying theme of this chapter is how to make the learning process an effective one. The learning process will be affected by the organisation's culture, strategy, systems and structure. Within this context there is a variety of explanations on how learning takes place and the types of conditions that facilitate the learning one. The learning transfer process is a complicated process, influenced by a range of organisational and environmental factors. The research illustrates that there is a move away from considering learning as an individual process to a focus on developing a continuous learning environment within the organisation.

15

ASSESSING TRAINING AND DEVELOPMENT NEEDS: THE ORGANISATION

INTRODUCTION AND LEARNING OBJECTIVES

Both this chapter and the next consider the issue of training and development needs analysis. When designing learning events it is necessary to identify the type and level of skills, knowledge and attitudes needed for effective job performance. This information can be obtained through a process of training needs analysis. After reading this chapter you will understand:

♦ the nature of training needs and the benefits and difficulties involved in the needs identification process;

♦ the types of training needs that can exist within an organisation;

♦ the important data sources for identifying needs;

♦ the main steps involved in carrying out an organisational analysis;

♦ key decision points that need to be undertaken when conducting a needs analysis;

♦ the nature of competencies.

TRAINING NEEDS

In an organisational context, a need is a discrepancy or "gap" between "what is" and "what ought to be", i.e. desired performance as against actual performance (Figure 15.1).

Figure 15.1: Performance Gap

| The Need | = | Desired Performance "What Ought to Be" | − | Current Performance "What Is" | = | Performance Gap |

If the organisation is not set to meet its objectives there is a gap, or "need" — perhaps for new machinery, better raw materials, or for a new skill, knowledge or attitude — a training and development solution.

Needs can be more than just "wants" (something people would like to do). In fact very often, individuals will not even be aware of them, particularly if they are not familiar with organisational goals.

Needs can be current or future, immediate or developmental, they can concern tasks, knowledge or attitude and occur at individual, job and even organisational level. With so many possible manifestations it becomes clear that a systematic and comprehensive way of identifying needs is required.

Training and development needs differ from other needs because they have a training solution. Training needs form the goals for training and also the criteria for before-and-after training assessment. As such, they are crucial and it is a golden rule that no training should be undertaken unless it is designed to meet a clearly defined need. Gunnigle and Flood (1990) remind us that "the ability to accurately identify and prioritise training needs to the maximum benefit of the organisation's goals is the cornerstone of organisational training and development".

WHAT IS NEEDS ANALYSIS?

Needs Analysis (NA) is the systematic process of determining and ordering goals, measuring needs and deciding on priorities for action. There are three important elements to this definition.

- *Systematic* — haphazard and ad hoc procedure, run the risk of overlooking some areas and over-emphasising others.

- *Goals* — because each need forms a training and development priority, the organisation needs to establish the desired standards, the actual standards, and thus the gaps.

- *Priorities* — the satisfaction of the "need to know" is always subject to resource allocation, it will never be possible to meet every need. Thus, there will always have to be an element of conflict resolution between different priorities depending on the resources available. Davies et al (1987) indicate that such issues should be resolved by referring to the corporate and human resource plans, to establish which needs will make the greatest contribution to these goals.

Figure 15.2 outlines the stages in Needs Analysis. It is important to remember that a training needs analysis should be carried out not just at individual level, but at occupational level and organisational level also.

Figure 15.2: The Stages of a Training Needs Analysis

1. Determine Scope and Purpose
   - the objectives — why data is needed, constraints, scope, authority

2. Identify Data Need
   - data to identify goals (performance standards)
   - data to prioritise them, data to identify needs — the gaps, data to prioritise needs, identify solutions.

3. Design the Data Gathering Approach

4. Gather Data
   - identifying desired performance standards, identifying actual performance standards measuring the gaps and
   - measuring the needs at organisational, job and individual level

5. Analyse and Verify the Data
   - aim to uncover trends, verify outcomes with those involved, identify real reasons for performance gaps, identify needs
   - prioritise

6. Generate Alternative Solutions
   - training
   - non-training
   - refer to relevant people

7. Consider All Other Influences
   - The organisation — culture, objectives, systems
   - The external environment — legal, competitive, economic and technical pressures and trends
   - The training policy — implications for scope and resources
   - The people — current standards, ability, understanding, motivation.
   - The dividends of training — atmosphere, learning, attitude.

8. Set Training Priorities

There are many benefits and difficulties involved in carrying out a training needs analysis. Some of them are outlined in Figure 15.3.

Figure 15.3: The Benefits/Difficulties of Training Needs Analysis

The Benefits of Needs Analysis	The Difficulties in Needs Analysis
• Attention is focused on the most important needs, and this ensures best use of resources	• Time-consuming
• Provides information on required content, facilitating training course design.	• May generate excessive expectations.
• The involvement of many people helps generate consensus and commitment.	• May have difficulty obtaining co-operation and thus not identify real needs.
• NA provides a logical, documented "case" to justify subsequent action.	• Dependent on level of managerial support.
• Ensures non-training needs are isolated so that training is not used as a "cure-all" solution.	• May be perceived as an exercise in paperwork only.
• Raises the profile of the training department.	• Managers may feel that training is the obvious solution and that analysis is pointless.
• Systematic and comprehensive.	• Emotional barriers — people may close up if they feel their inadequacies are being highlighted.

The success of NA depends on the skill of the analyst — if skills are poor, the results will be unreliable and perceived badly, possibly jeopardising future training.

Despite the potential difficulties, needs analysis is a vital preliminary activity for any training and development intervention and a skilled analyst should be able to convince management of this and generate the support and co-operation that is necessary to make it possible.

Needs analysis is crucial to the whole context of training because it ensures that training and development occurs only where there is a valid need for it, and thus that it is not automatically used as a "cure-all" solution. It is a systematic way of ensuring all training and development needs — future and developmental as well as immediate needs — are uncovered and prioritised so that the most important of them can be met first, thus ensuring the most efficient use of the available resources.

By carrying out a systematic analysis, the training and development specialist is able to have their finger on the pulse, with a broad up-to-date view of all that is happening in the organisation, enabling contact with all personnel as opposed to isolation (Smith, Delahaye and Gates, 1986). This gives them the necessary macro and micro perspectives to best diagnose training and development needs, and thus, to help deal with the organisation's problems and prepare it for future opportunities.

In this chapter, we focus on organisational training needs — but it is crucial to remember that not every performance problem has a training solution. Pearn and Kandola (1988) argue that the use of the term needs analysis is preferable to the traditional training needs analysis, as the latter, they logically argue, pre-diagnoses a solution. In this way the training and development can assume a more "consultative role", bringing a variety of possible needs and solutions to light.

Type of Training Needs

As already mentioned, needs manifest themselves in a number of ways. Although there is much focus on individual needs, in fact, they occur at three levels. Figure 15.4 outlines the three levels.

Figure 15.4: Level of Training Needs Analysis

Level	Concern
Organisational	What does the organisation need to achieve its goals? Does it have the capability? Are there any strategic long-term objectives to consider?
Job or Occupational	Special skills, knowledge or attitude training needs for particular jobs
Individual	Where individual skills fall short of those required

Source: Boydell, T. H. (1976), *A Guide to Job Analysis*, BACIE, London

Each of these need groups influence each other — organisational needs highlight needs for particular groups and thus carry implications for individual needs. Armstrong (1988) suggests that "super-ordinate" needs may also result. These he describes as strategic development needs.

Latham (1988) makes a similar distinction to Boydell (1976) when he talks about microtraining and macrotraining needs. This distinction he believes is important for three reasons. First, it positions the training and development specialist in a role akin to an air traffic controller who monitors the radar screen, sweeping the environment. Changes occurring inside and outside of the organisation appear as blips, some of which require action. Second, not all blips are the same size or are configured the same way. The nature of the corrective action depends on the scope of the problem. Finally, some changes are predictable, even cyclical. They recur.

Current and Future Needs

Boydell (1976) suggests that current needs arise from faults in the present situation. Any attempt to solve these needs involves change. The most usual response is by reactive needs analysis, which involves investigation of performance problems using a problem-solving approach (Buckley and Caple, 1992). It is important to realise that training and development will not always be a suitable solution. Needs analysis or front end analysis is important so that the problem is clearly and objectively understood before any training is suggested.

Future needs, on the other hand, arise from organisational changes and are usually diagnosed by proactive needs identification. They are prompted by internal and external factors such as:

- corporate strategy changes

- human resource plans

- skills inventories, matched against future requirements

- technology, organisational, product or legislative changes

- employee surveys and organisational reviews

- customer surveys

- personnel procedures such as appraisal, exit interviews, etc.

Such needs are usually more developmental in nature, and there can be a temptation to dismiss them and deal only with immediate needs. In such a situation there can be little development and the organisation will find it difficult to progress and achieve its goals. It is a very short-sighted option to take.

Knowledge, Skills and Attitude Needs

Training and development needs can be categorised in other ways as well.

- *Knowledge Needs*: occurring in situations where, for example, the learner needs to learn more about the process, or a briefing on the company (e.g. induction), new legislation, new systems etc.

- *Skill Needs*: where the task requires the learning (or re-learning) of particular skills

- *Attitude Needs*: e.g. interpersonal skill needs or corporate identity type needs

Differing Perceptions

Another issue to bear in mind is that highlighted by Smith and Delahaye (1988) in their discussion of the marketing approach to training. They suggest that there are four parties to a training decision:

- The User (learner)

- The Decider (manager)

- The Influencer (supervisor)

- The Initiator (person who suggested training)

These roles may all be held by one person, or individually performed, but in either case each role-holder will have a different perception of the training and development need which they will wish to see satisfied. They also suggest that every need has three facets:

- The tangible needs — physical manifestation (e.g. a course)

- The core concept — e.g. increased efficiency

- The intangible need — the icing on the cake as it were, e.g. timing, location, etc.

This is an important consideration for the trainer who must try and facilitate the needs identified by each stakeholder.

IDENTIFYING TRAINING NEEDS

Pepper (1984) divides needs identification into two categories:

- Primary — perceiving the existence of a situation or problem which merits further analysis.

- Secondary — the subsequent examination of a situation to define the exact needs.

Most trainers act at the secondary stage, relying on a line manager or supervisor to bring needs to their attention, but it is very important that the training and development specialist be able to carry out primary identification also, or broader needs may go unrecognised. Pepper reminds us of a number of situations which trainers should watch out for, which he describes as training opportunity generators, such as:

- new recruits

- promotions

- introduction of new technology and systems

- maintenance of standards

- maintenance of adaptability etc.

This means that the training and development specialist needs to be pro-active in identifying training opportunities and needs and therefore should conduct ongoing systematic needs analysis. Figure 15.5 provides a list of the indicators and the sources the specialist should monitor as part of this process.

Levels of Analysis

Analysis should be undertaken in layers from macro to micro — the appropriate depth depending on the scope and objectives of the needs identification process. Influencing factors include:

- money and time available

- managerial support and co-operation

- intended use of data (course design)

- degree of reliability/validity necessary

- quality of information emerging

- cost of analysis versus value of information.

Olivas (1988) identifies four data categories:

- Data to define the need. Performance Analysis — desired performance against actual, thus identifying the gaps.

- Data to identify the solution. Potential training and development sources, internal and external.

- Data about those needing training. Defining the training population individually (career profile and aspirations) and organisationally — leading to a training population profile.

- Data to plan delivery. Who, what, when, where, how much?

Figure 15.5: Data Sources for Training Needs Identification

Level	Source	Training Need Implications
Strategic/ Organisational	• Corporate objectives • Manpower plans • Skills inventories • Organisational statistics (absenteeism, etc.) • System changes • Management requests • Exit interviews	• Emphasis/direction training must take • Current capability versus future needs • Areas needing development • Identifies trends and problem areas • New equipment/systems call for training • May apply in other areas as well • May identify problems like poor supervision, etc.
Operational Job Level	• Operational man-power plans • Job analysis/job description • Task analysis • Person specifications • Training surveys • Performing the job • Observe output • Review literature • Ask questions • Working groups • Analyse operating problems	• Profiles future requirements, indications, etc. • Indicates exact requirements of each job • Very detailed job analysis • Profiles skills/characteristics job holders need • Up-to-date information on needs • Shows trainer the needs of a new recruit • This may be delegated to line manager • Journals, guidelines, approaches of other companies • Of the job holder, the supervisor, the manager • Combine several viewpoints • Differentiate environmental problems etc.

Level	Source	Training Need Implications
Individual Job	• Appraisal, career development, etc. • Interview • Questionnaire • Individual job analysis • Tests • Attitude surveys • Training progress charts • Assessment centres • Manager's recommendation	• Identifies weaknesses and development needs • Self-analysis involves the worker, increasing motivation • Gives employee time to consider his needs • Compared with job description • Of knowledge, skill, achievement • Determining morale and motivation • Up-to-date records • Intensive assessment • The manager can identify individual needs

Source: Adapted from Smith, Delahaye and Gates (1986); and Gunnigle and Flood (1990).

Thus, the job of the training and development specialist is to decide how much analysis is required to satisfy these four requirements and meet the company's objectives, bearing in mind that the more extensive the analysis, the surer the conclusions. Excessive analysis (paralysis) is wasteful, costly and ultimately redundant. Figure 15.6 identifies different levels of analysis within the process.

A TRAINING NEEDS ANALYSIS ONGOING MODEL

In their discussion of training needs analysis, Smith, Delahaye and Gates (1986) propose a model which acts as a guide to the long term process of needs analysis within the organisation. They identify three specific stages:

• *Surveillance*: Continuous review of the state of the organisation by monitoring data of the type outlined in Figure 15.6. This ensures a broad and up-to-date picture of the organisation at all times with a constant eye to training needs and opportunities.

- *Investigation*: If a gap or future need is suspected, a detailed investigation is undertaken using TNA techniques as outlined later in this chapter and the next chapter.

- *Analysis of Investigation*: i.e. using prescribed analytical techniques to determine the needs and the alternative solutions and integrating these into the training and development plan.

This model outlines the type of approach training and development specialists should adopt on an ongoing basis to best perform their role. Before reaching this stage, however, a full organisation needs analysis and review is necessary, so that the required performance standards and objectives are defined. The remainder of this chapter will outline the steps involved in carrying out an organisational review.

ORGANISATIONAL REVIEWS

What is an Organisational Review?

An organisational review is a macro-level needs assessment usually undertaken when major training and development initiatives are planned. Guided by the strategic goals of the organisation, an organisation review looks at:

- the organisation's current capabilities in terms of desired performance;

- the current training systems, standards, trainers — their strengths, weaknesses and scope for improvement;

- the extent and cost of training for present and future employees;

- the attitudes of line managers including their knowledge of, and commitment to training policy;

- training and development priorities and necessary actions.

An organisation review is undertaken to systematically uncover and analyse long term training and development needs across the whole organisation, which are specifically geared towards the organisation plans and objectives.

Figure 15.6: Levels of Analysis in Training Needs Analysis

External Environment Analysis	• Trends in technology, competition, economy and the legal situation — all push factors influencing training needs
General Organisational Analysis	• Corporate objectives, manpower plans, strengths, weaknesses • Current performance statistics • General survey of managers regarding their department's needs

Occupational/Job Training Analysis	• Four basic approaches to analysis: Comprehensive, Key Task, Problem Centred (reactive), Core. The trainer must choose the appropriate approach for their objectives and select the techniques most suitable from the following:
	  – Job analysis (including job description and specification)
	  – Stage and keypoint analysis, task analysis, faults analysis
	  – Social/Interpersonal, hierarchical, DIF, procedural, knowledge/topic — each of these techniques is explained later in the chapter and provides progressive levels of analysis.

Individual Analysis	• Performance Analysis against desired performance identified from above techniques • Individual job analysis • Individual needs analysis via assessment/appraisal
Target Population Analysis	• Individual personnel records, age, past training, length of service etc.

Wexley and Latham (1991) point out that organisational analysis involves an examination of how the organisation interfaces with the external environment. The environment in which an organisation operates can be a critical factor in determining whether training and development should be conducted. Specifically:

- If the training and development function is to survive it must be supported financially by the organisation. The level of this support is determined by the overall profitability of the organisation.

- The environment in which an organisation operates can impact upon training and development needs. It can influence the way managers do their jobs, how decisions are made and the types of skills and levels of flexibility required.

As already mentioned, an organisation review is usually undertaken when a major training initiative is planned. However, Reid, Barrington and Kenny (1992) suggest five other situations that require a review:

- when setting up a training department for the first time

- in response to corporate planning

- in order to develop a training budget/plan

- when there is a major change in the organisation's activities

- in response to a training audit.

Figure 15.7 outlines the main elements of an organisation review of training and development needs.

Reid, Barrington and Kenney (1992) suggest two approaches which can be used in carrying out an organisational review. They are:

1. *The Global Approach* — where each job category in the organisation is analysed for skill, knowledge and attitude content and the resulting specifications used as assessment criteria against which all shortcomings represent training requirements.

2. *Critical Incident/Priority Problem Approach* — rather than seeking out every single training need, this approach aims to identify particular problem areas which have training solutions.

An important consideration in the context of an organisational review is the skill of the analyst. At an organisational level, an analyst must have excellent diagnostic ability and strategic vision if they are to propose solutions which will best advance the needs of the organisation. This is a major responsibility especially as the analyst will be party to the organisations' strategic objectives. If they are not suitably skilled then the effectiveness of the review and indeed of the whole training and development process could be severely jeopardised.

Figure 15.7: Stages in Organisation Review

Prepare for Review	• Ensure you have a clear brief • Inform everyone involved and enlist their support

Collect the Data	• Using methods already outlined
	• Taking account of external influences/trends
	• Using key informants:
	  – Top Management — organisation objectives
	  – Personnel Department — policies, profiles, statistics, etc.
	  – Finance Department — past training expenditure
	  – Department Managers/Supervisors — for insight on their needs and expectations (self-rating)

Analyse Data	• Disregard irrelevant information • Identify clear gaps • Weigh their relative importance
Generate Recommendations	• Must clearly support organisation objectives • Must be justified, costed, feasible and specific • May recommend further analysis

Source: Reid, M., Barrington, H. and Kenney, J. (1992), *Training Interventions*, IPM, London.

KEY DECISION POINTS IN THE ORGANISATIONAL NEEDS IDENTIFICATION PROCESS

Who Should Undertake It?

Needs identification is an excellent development experience which can be delegated. If the tasks are shared, there is an opportunity to check whether responses are influenced by the individual identifying the needs. In the case of organisations with a strong central training and development function and a lower profile training presence at local or departmental level, delegating the job to departmental or local training officers can have a beneficial effect on their role, i.e. representing a move towards an internal consultant role. Senior managers could carry out this work via staff development or appraisal interviews, but somehow these rarely work, perhaps due to a fear that in hierarchical organisations, or those with strong power politics, exposure of needs rather than a front of invincibility may put paid to promotion prospects or even one's job. A symptom of good management development is co-operation between managers on the diagnosis of their respective needs. It is unlikely that management development alone, without the support of other interventions, will achieve this.

Who to Interview?

It has been wryly stated that those who are most in need of being interviewed are least likely to subject themselves to such an experience. The decision concerning which group of managers, or which type, is likely in a large organisation to be wrong (in terms of some ultimate objective criterion) simply because there are so many other managers who could be interviewed. Given a decision to interview managers within a given "band", a number of approaches to sampling may be chosen from, depending on criteria such as the following:

- How well respected is the training and development function in the organisation?

- How quickly does any training and/or development activity need to happen?

- How special do individual departments, or particular groups, believe they are?

- Where is the role of the training and development function best understood?

- Who hasn't been talked to for a long time whose support may be useful?

- What would make most sense in an ideal situation, where time and money are plentiful and job security is assured?

- How rigorously do the training and development staff need to justify what they do?

How to Sample?

There are six alternative approaches to sampling which may be adopted.

Catch-as-Catch-Can

Whoever happens to be available becomes the sample in this instance. This makes sense if there are budgetary conditions. A dozen quick interviews might give at the very least an impression of diversity, and if further clues were felt to be necessary, they could be asked to compare their needs with those of colleagues whom they know. The important thing here is to make sure people keep the appointments, and that your itinerary is a sensible one in terms of travel time. Go for some diversity on a crude basis, such as location, age or gender.

Stratified Sampling

This is the approach often used in public opinion polls. Criteria such as type of department, gender, age range, number of subordinates, proximity of boss, contact pattern (e.g. contacts inside the organisation or outside; sits on committees with other specialists or does not; meets clients or does not; location; background profession; educational background, etc.) can be used. Ideally, a few people fitting each of the configurations of the criteria would be interviewed, to check whether certain criteria were more powerful than the uniqueness of each individual in influencing the needs which were identified. In practice, one could very quickly discover that everyone within the organisation would need to be interviewed to fill each cell in the matrix. The training and development specialist may have to rely on personal judgement to identify which criteria are likely to matter, and the ability to judge will depend on a knowledge of the organisation, which if not possessed could be gleaned from key informants.

Grounded Theory

This is very much stratified sampling on an as-you-go-along basis. After a few interviews, the training and development specialist thinks that certain differences in responses are due to certain sampling criteria, they choose the next few respondents from those categories which they suspect may account for the differences (e.g. if one suspects that older people are more likely to fear computerisation and need some "desensitisation", the next few respondents should be chosen with the "age factor" in mind to see if preliminary suspicions are borne out).

Starting with Friends

A useful approach, if the training and development specialist envisages other people doing the interviewing, is to encourage them to begin interviewing in parts of the organisation where they feel they are most accepted. As confidence builds up, they may feel more comfortable to venture elsewhere, and they may get some useful feedback on their approach to interviewing from their "friends" too.

Random Sample

The one drawback with this approach is the temptation to believe that 12 random interviews are better at indicating the overall spread of needs than 12 catch-as-catch-can. Random sampling, in this context, means that individual names are selected by lot or on an arbitrary basis, and then pursued for an interview. Randomness, even with a large sample, is no guarantee that the findings offer a good prediction of the popularity of certain programmes, unless people who decide which programmes are attended are interviewed.

Everyone

Everyone should be involved in the training needs appraisal process. This does not happen.

Selection or Consultation?

The development activity may well already be designed in fine detail, in which case the prime aim of the survey will be to discover who needs it. Selection of participants may also be the aim, where task forces, self-development groups, action-learning sets, autonomy labs, etc., are envisaged. A certain amount of screening is necessary in any event. Where there is any doubt about what will be provided, or where development is planned to be geared to individual needs rather than the wishes of the majority, the prime focus will be on consultation, or better still, going in with an open mind and finding out the training needs.

What Questions to Ask?

The argument against using a fixed schedule of questions is that it is better to ask a poor question once than to ask it 20 times. Schedule interviewing also assumes a certain model of interview. Some people advocate asking no questions at all. If the survey has been set up to investigate needs within a particular area of management development, it is still possible to conduct interviews with no prepared questions, or to make up questions on the spur of the moment, as one does in everyday conversation. One approach is to use a schedule of questions posed to the interviewer; it is then up to the interviewer to find the information to answer the questions set. With a fixed schedule of questions, addressed to the respondent, it is probably more cost-effective to do the bulk of research via questionnaire.

Analysing the Results

With large-scale surveys, a pragmatic approach involves a straight-forward content analysis, based on the topic headings, subdivided according to the aspects which receive most emphasis (e.g. "time management" can be subdivided into "attitude toward delegation", "prioritising tasks", "dealing with interruptions", "living with stress", "general self-discipline", etc.). The main value of the results in that they provide the training and development specialist with real-life examples on the programmes. The results draw attention to the more subtle aspects of the topics. It is in the analysis that much subjective judgement comes into play, for example, in deciding whether because certain areas of potential need are hardly mentioned they are largely unnecessary, or whether a non-mention indicates a blindness to vital needs requiring an awareness and therefore extra special emphasis is required on such an area in the programme.

Translating Needs into Objectives

How tightly objectives are defined depends on the degree to which the training and development specialist can live with flexibility on a training programme.

COMPETENCY APPROACH TO NEEDS ANALYSIS

The notion of "competence-based standards" is steadily gathering momentum, and in recent years there have been significant developments in this area. These are apparent from a national and international perspective, and they encompass both educational and occupational processes.

We need to clarify the meaning of the terms competence and competency. In general terms, the result of an individual's capability (skills and knowledge) may reflect competence or competency (demonstrated ability to perform work to a certain standard). To avoid ambiguity, both competence and competency are taken here as interchangeable terms. A succinct definition of a job competency has been put forward by Boyatzis (1982) as:

> an underlying characteristic of a person, in that it may be a motive, trait, skill, aspect of one's self-image or social role, or a body of knowledge which he or she uses.

Background to the Competency Approach

The competency approach was devised in the 1970s, when the American Management Association (AMA) commissioned McBer and Company (a behavioural research firm) to address the question — what are the characteristics that distinguish superior performance by working managers? Following research on a sample of some 2,000 working managers (incorporating 41 different job types, across 12 organisations in both private and public sectors) a set of managerial behaviours was identified, in order to characterise superior performance. The behaviours were grouped into 18 competencies, contained within four main clusters of a generic model (see Figure 15.8). The major significance of this development was that the identification and description of competencies was arrived at by studying managers who were outstanding performers, as opposed to approaches based on theory, expert opinion, or job analysis.

Some widely accepted notions concerning the competency concept may be summarised as follows (Boyatzis, 1982):

- The organisation has goals, policies, procedures and subcultures which must be maintained while the manager is performing the job effectively.

- Effectiveness can be taken to mean the attainment of specific results through specific actions.

- Job-specific results must contribute to the results from others so as to yield a composite contribution to the organisation's output (whether this is goods or services).

- Certain characteristics or abilities of the manager enable demonstration of the appropriate actions, and these may be called managerial competencies.

- Competency is context-oriented; where there is a good fit between the individual's competencies, the job demands, and the organisational environment, effective action or performance will occur.

- The organisation has an implicit responsibility to allow competence to flourish.

The competency model has been adapted in the UK by the Management Charter Institute (MCI) (for managerial competencies) and the Training Agency (for national vocational qualifications — NVQs). Organisations are becoming increasingly aware of the utility of the competency model, and the number of companies introducing competency frameworks is rising steadily.

FIGURE 15.8: GENERIC COMPETENCY MODEL

Goal and Action Management Cluster

- Efficiency orientation — concern with doing something better (in comparison with previous personal performance, others' performance, or a standard of excellence)

- Proactivity — disposition towards taking action to accomplish something

- Concern with impact — concern with the symbols and implements of power in order to have impact on others

- Diagnostic use of concepts — use of a person's previously-held concepts to explain and interpret situations.

Directing Subordinates Cluster

- Use of unilateral power — using forms of influence to obtain compliance

- Developing others — ability to provide performance feedback and other help needed to improve performance

- Spontaneity — ability to express oneself freely and easily.

Human Resources Management Cluster

- Accurate self-assessment — realistic and grounded view of oneself

- Self-control — ability to inhibit personal needs in the service of organisational goals

- Stamina and adaptability — energy to sustain long hours of work and flexibility orientation to adapt to changes in life and the environment

- Perpetual objectivity — ability to be relatively objective rather than limited by excessive subjectivity or personal biases

- Positive regard — ability to express a positive belief in others

- Managing group process — ability to stimulate others to work effectively in a group setting. Use of socialised power — use of influences to build alliances, networks or coalitions.

Leadership cluster

- Self-confidence — consistent ability to display decisiveness or presence

- Conceptualisation — use of fresh concepts to identify a pattern in an assortment of information

- Logical thought — a thought process in which a person orders events in a causal sequence

- Use of oral presentations — ability to make effective oral presentations to others.

Source: Boyatzis, R. (1982) *The Competent Manager: A Guide for Effective Performance*, New York: Wiley.

The Competency Debate

There has been some debate surrounding the topic of competency. This has centred on the advantages, on the one hand, and the limitations, on the other, which may be applied to the utilisation of such an approach. These may be briefly summarised as follows:

General Advantages/Benefits

In an overall sense, adopting a competency approach offers a coherent and uniform way of improving organisational performance. It is seen as a means of establishing a fundamental relationship between effective management practices, successful performance, and the achievement of organisational strategies, objectives and goals.

In more specific terms, the espoused advantages of a competency approach are the following:

- Clear and unequivocal benchmarks of effective role performance are established.

- An organisation-wide structure is put in place which helps to integrate and prioritise individual and organisational development needs.

- Training and development is undertaken in the context of a planned and structured approach to change and improvement.

- The effectiveness of current performance may be appraised, and development needs identified, against commonly agreed parameters.

- Self-management of training and development is encouraged and facilitated.

- A useful reference framework is provided for the selection process, which helps to achieve the proper fit between candidates and the organisation.

- A database of information, with multi-purpose application, may be accessed, reviewed, and updated as appropriate, on an ongoing basis.

- Competencies are focused on effectiveness, and are seen as a unique linking mechanism between individual performance and that of the organisation itself.

General Limitations/Disadvantages

The competency approach has been the focus of some critical comment. This is mainly centred around its "management as a science" orientation and the perception that it is largely a mechanistic approach. Competency-based approaches to training and development have been related to the fundamental philosophical belief that it is within the realms of possibility to determine the outcome of an event prior to its happening. Edmonstone (1988) identifies further trends of the competency-based approach:

- a firm belief in science and objectivity

- a dedication to efficiency

- a determination to measure outcomes

- an emphasis on measurable performance

- an ultimate concern with precision at all stages.

It has also been argued that the complexity and diversity of managerial work places a restriction on the potential accuracy and appropriateness of competency listings against which training and development needs can be assessed. Further limitations in this context have been related to the difficulty of defining managerial tasks except at a generalised level, the "power and political" environment in which managers must operate, and taking no account of the changing nature of managerial roles. On this basis, managerial competence is viewed as a matter of wide-ranging, fragmented, and ever-changing activity, dependent on others' behaviour as well as their own (Harrison, 1992).

In overall terms, many of the commentators on this topic are supportive of the competence approach. While there is critical comment, for the most part it represents concerns and reservations about the manner in which competency-based approaches are utilised, rather than outright rejection of the notion itself. These concerns should be considered by organisations adopting the competency approach, including issues such as the following (Burgoyne, 1988):

- the measurability of competencies and the appropriateness of methods used;

- accommodating different styles and strategies of managing;

- how managerial competencies may be related to the whole person;

- how generalised competency listings may be applied to different role categories;

- the ethical and moral content of professional management and how it may be represented in competency listings;

- how individual competence contributes to and integrates with collective or organisational competence.

The thrust of these issues is not to criticise the competency approach per se, but to draw attention to the possibility that their capability may be misrepresented, and to the importance of realising that they can be subject to inappropriate application.

The debate surrounding competencies is likely to continue, fuelled no doubt by research studies and the ongoing emergence of detailed evidence from organisations themselves. However, a credible indication of their accepted potential is evidenced in the work currently being undertaken to develop competence standards for training and development specialists. Leading training and development bodies and institutes across Europe are involved in this work, and this is seen as a significant seal of approval for the competency notion in general. Indeed, many training specialists are currently facilitating the introduction of competency-based approaches.

The Empirical Evidence

A major survey conducted in 1994 (HR-BC/IRS, UK), in which 91 organisations participated, provides an interesting insight into various aspects of the competency approach, a brief analysis of which is presented here.

Organisation Size/Degree of Implementation

Of the participating organisations, some 70 per cent were large (in excess of 500 employees), while only 12 per cent employed less than 200 people. Many had fully implemented a competency framework, while others were at the piloting stage.

Key Reasons for Introducing a Competency Framework

The primary reason for introducing a competency framework is the desire to "improve performance through people". Specific priorities in the managerial area, in recorded order of importance, are:

1. Performance improvement (28 per cent)

2. Training and development needs (21 per cent)

3. Culture change (19 per cent)

4. Better recruitment (13 per cent)

5. Qualifications/standards (8 per cent).

Methodology Employed

The majority of the organisations favour a framework developed by identifying the traits or behaviours of high achievers and the qualities desired for business success. The MCI standards are also recorded as being used by some public sector areas and in organisations with a high customer interface. Hybrid combinations are being developed by others, integrating MCI standards with their own behavioural analysis. The most successful frameworks are those high in participation; they begin with the identification of competencies through focus groups and critical incident (or behavioural event) interviews, and are usually piloted with smaller groups prior to full implementation. Almost two-thirds of the organisations have engaged external consultants to assist with the definition of their competencies, to conduct interviews, and/or to work with focus groups.

Effective communication is seen as vitally important — nearly two-thirds of those surveyed have used briefing groups, while some 37 per cent have backed this up with special booklets. Interestingly, some 27 per cent have introduced the competency framework to the workforce as part of their performance appraisal process.

Core Competencies Identified

Those using behavioural methods often identify a number of core competencies, which are seen to contribute to organisational objectives, regardless of an individual's function or level. Frequently occurring core competencies are communication, business awareness, organising and planning, change orientation/flexibility, and customer focus.

Time/Cost

Developing competency frameworks is seen as a lengthy process. Most commonly, implementation is taking between 12 and 24 months. A small minority have taken less than six months or more than 24 months.

Costs obviously vary a great deal, but, in some organisations, these have been related to the number of employees to give an estimated "cost per head". On this basis, half of those responding estimated a cost of £10 per employee and 25 per cent incurred costs of £30, while some 20 per cent estimated costs at £100 per employee.

Benefits of the Framework

For many organisations, who were still at the early development or piloting stage, it was too early to declare benefits. However, there were a number of organisations what were able to specify beneficial outcomes through utilising competency frameworks. Corporate benefits are derived from the ability of competency frameworks to link the management of people with business goals, and from the way that they act as an integrating agent across all human resource practices. Another key theme is improved managerial performance, following on from a clearer understanding of what constitutes effective performance. Line managers have become better equipped to perform their people management functions more effectively. They have also gained a greater understanding of the performance levels expected of those reporting to them, how these can be measured, and what training and development needs are required to remedy any shortfall. Individual staff members stressed the ability of competency framework to provide role clarity, so that they are more clear about the demands of the job, and of the greater objectivity offered in assessing their own performance.

Competency Frameworks — The Present Position

Various advantages, benefits, and limitations associated with the adoption of a competency-based approach have thus been outlined. An overall perspective suggests that a competency-based approach offers considerable potential benefits in the form of improved organisational performance.

In examining how this potential can be realised, it might be useful to begin by taking a "front-to-back" view, and stating that a desire for improved overall performance is a logical objective of organisations in general. It is also relatively straightforward to agree with the idea that effective and/or superior individual performance in collective managerial terms, will fundamentally contribute to this objective. Taking a further step backwards, the notion of competency is derived from "underlying characteristics of effective and/or superior performance". This means that the causal link between the development of individual competencies and improved organisational performance is strongly established. The main issue at stake for organisations, therefore, is suggested as finding the most appropriate way to define, introduce, and subsequently utilise competency profiles and frameworks. The measure of success in this process will essentially determine the extent to which potential benefits are actually realised.

In summary, the critical test of competencies may lie in the capacity of organisations to develop and apply them in ways appropriate to their contextual environment.

SUMMARY

This chapter outlines the issues involved in carrying out an organisational training needs analysis. The decision to conduct an analysis of organisational training needs will provide a firm basis for deploying training and development resources. It provides the training and development specialist with a review of what is going on, and a basis for building networks and credibility, as well as justifying investments in training and eliciting support from senior management. From an organisational perspective it can clarify the role that training and development can play and serve as a basis for building training into the business. The traditional philosophy of training in Ireland as a front-loaded model, meant that training and development needs were often only identified as a once-off episode. However, a philosophy of continuous learning requires the ongoing identification of needs. The training and development specialist must pay greater attention to this process.

16

ASSESSING TRAINING AND DEVELOPMENT NEEDS: THE JOB AND THE INDIVIDUAL

INTRODUCTION AND LEARNING OBJECTIVES

In this second chapter on the needs identification process, we consider analysis at the level of the job and the individual. After reading this chapter you will understand:

♦ the differences between job analysis, job synthesis and task analysis;

♦ the key questions to be considered when making training decisions from task analysis data;

♦ the range of analytical techniques that can be used to analyse jobs;

♦ the issues involved in assessing employee performance.

OBJECTIVES OF OCCUPATIONAL/JOB ANALYSIS

Occupational/job analysis is a process in which the performance requirements of an occupational field or job are defined and analysed. The objectives of occupational job analysis are to:

• define a functional occupational field or job;

• document the planned utilisation of people in that occupational area;

• see the actual work sites and observe workers on the job;

• interview workers and document details of their job performance;

• validate workers' comments by observation and follow-up interviews with supervisors;

• establish the accuracy of performance conditions, restraints or supports, i.e. what the performer is actually given or denied in the work performance;

• verify the existence and accuracy of criterion-referenced standards;

• document all data relevant to an occupational area or job.

JOB ANALYSIS, JOB SYNTHESIS AND TASK ANALYSIS

Job Analysis

The *Glossary of Training Terms* (Department of Employment, 1978) describes job analysis as "the process of examining a job in detail in order to identify its component tasks". The detail and approach may vary according to the purpose for which the job is being analysed, e.g. training, equipment, design, work layout. In designing a training course/ programme, the specific job must initially be analysed. The job analysis will identify the necessary knowledge and skills required by the job holder, and describe the tasks involved in the position. Because the job analysis is the basis for effective training and development programme design, unreliable and incomplete findings will result in an inadequate training programme producing poorly qualified employees.

In order to design and implement effective performance-based training, an in-depth understanding of the job content is essential. Answering several relevant questions about the job may provide the adequate information. These questions can include:

- What tasks are involved in the job?

- How is each task achieved?

- Why is the task relevant?

- Is there a sequence in which these tasks are performed? If so, what is it?

- What materials are used to perform the task?

Job Analysis Techniques

A variety of techniques have been designed to conduct a job analysis. Due to context variations, not every technique will be appropriate for every situation. The choice of technique will also invariably affect the cost, quality and quantity of the findings. At the end of the day, the technique chosen must complement certain organisational factors, such as time limits, the number of jobholders, job type, existing task lists, and the availability of specialists.

When individual techniques or a combination of techniques seem appropriate, the choice may be further focused by considering the advantages and disadvantages of each. The advantages and disadvantages of five different job analysis techniques are presented in Figure 16.1.

Figure 16.1: Advantages and Disadvantages of Alternative Job Analysis Techniques

Job Analysis Technique	Advantage	Disadvantages
Observation of job holders at work	• Illustrates what the holder accurately does, not what they say they do. • Few people are needed to conduct the analysis, the research and recording are done by the observer. • Minimal (if any) disturbance caused to the operations process. • Helpful when analysing tasks which the job-holder has difficulty in describing.	• Expensive and time-consuming to observe activities and prepare the job analysis schedule. • Employees, when conscious of being observed, can produce a biased performance. • Inappropriate for jobs consisting of intellectual rather than manual tasks.
In-person interview of jobholders and supervisors	• People prefer to talk rather than complete a questionnaire, so the response rate is usually high. • Any misinterpreted questions can be immediately classified. • Recording of interview responses can be kept on tape or in note-form. • Most suitable for jobs requiring mental application or personal judgement.	• Performing interviews and compiling results can be expensive and time-consuming. • Over-dependence on the interviewer's contribution, and ability to mention all tasks. • Interview scheduling may conflict with operational activities or individuals' timetables.

Job Analysis Technique	Advantage	Disadvantages
Telephone interview of jobholders and supervisors	• Inexpensive in relation to other techniques. • Relevant data can be gathered in a short time period, on the job, or at home. • People prefer to talk rather than complete a questionnaire, so the response rate is usually high. • Any misinterpreted questions can be classified immediately. • More suitable for jobs requiring mental application or personal judgement.	• An "in-person" interview tends to be more personal than a telephone interview. • Over-dependence on the interviewer's co-operation and ability to recall all job tasks. • Contacting busy individuals, or receiving a return call from them, may be extremely difficult. • Being confused with telemarketing and the negative response it can incur, many individuals refuse to take the call.
Jobholders and supervisors completing questionnaires	• Suitable for jobs involving intellectual tasks. • An economical way of surveying many people. • A lot of data can be received in a short time period. • The individuals can complete the question-naire at their own pace. • All respondents are asked the same question in the same format. • Material gathered can be easily manipulated and analysed.	• Knowledge, time, and hard work are necessary to compile a clear, understandable questionnaire. • Heavy dependence placed on recall, and questions may be misun-derstood or answered dishonestly. • Low response rate, especially when there is no incentive incorporated. • Those that are returned, may be inadequately completed or not filled in by the intended respondent.

Job Analysis Technique	Advantage	Disadvantages
Consensus Group, i.e. jury/panel of jobholders and supervisors	• The number of people participating is kept low. • An individual's input can help others to recall more relevant material. • Results are gathered and verified in a short time period. • Misunderstanding can be classified immediately, and consensus can be reached on differing viewpoints. • This technique is suitable for tasks involving personal decision-making and mental application.	• Can be costly in terms of requiring a recorder, and an interviewer with interpersonal skills, are needed for the procedure. • The panel has to be made up of co-operative individuals with beneficial communication skills. • Supervisors may consciously/unconsciously inhibit their subordinates contribution. • Can be time-consuming, and requires full-time commitment.

Combination of Observation and Interview

The combination of the on-site observation and the individual interview is strongly recommended as an information-collection technique suitable for many different jobs. The analyst can observe the employee's performance directly through the use of a video camera, or utilising simulation methods. The individual interviews can be performed over the telephone, but are more effective if done at the workplace. The interviewing procedure can be beneficial in classifying observation notes and receiving data on unobserved tasks. While there are costs in terms of time and the human resources involved (i.e. the skilled job analyst and co-operative job holders), there is the benefit of valid information as a result of first hand observation and individual interviews.

Job Analysis is a "process of examining a job". Thus it is not a particular document, but rather gives rise to certain documents, the products of an analytical examination of the job (Boydell 1976). A job description, or the more in-depth job specification, are the tangible results of a job analysis.

Job Synthesis

According to Reid, Barrington and Kenney (1992), "A job synthesis is the technique by which a new job or task can be examined in order to produce a job specification and subsequently, appropriate training". The trainer can be assisted in an analysis of a new/revised job, by a number of people. These include:

- employees within the organisation who previously held jobs related to the new position;

- employees of other organisations experienced in this new area;

- new recruits with relevant knowledge/experience;

- those conducting trial and error work within the firm's organisation and methods department;

- managers and supervisors who are involved with job holders.

Any training activity designed through job synthesis needs to be closely monitored and reviewed frequently, as it is quite doubtful that the job specification will be completely accurate at the first attempt.

Task Analysis

When designing systematic training and development programmes, task analysis is regarded as a significant element of the procedure. As a result of task analysis, a training design is constructed, outlining not only the course content but also the performance to be achieved, and the method(s) of training used to do this. Training design is discussed in detail in Chapter 17.

Different Methods of Task Analysis

The methods of task analysis differ from the rough-and-ready job break-down to the skills analysis resulting from work study methods and recording activities. However, logical trees and algorithms are now used regularly for analysing complex activities. A number of forms of task analysis are examined in Figure 16.2.

Hierarchical Task Analysis

The most important characteristic of this technique developed by Annett and Duncan (1967) is the division of a job and the design of its duties, tasks and subtasks into a family-tree format (Figures 16.3 and 16.4). This technique can be used to analyse a complete job or one of its main operations, and can be applied to a variety of tasks. The hierarchical

analysis clearly highlights the different levels of duties, and when necessary can sort them in order of priority.

Figure 16.2: Analysis of Interpersonal Skills

Stage	Cues	Responses (voice, eye, gesture)	Attention Points
1. Manageress (M) becomes aware of customer (C).	M sees/hears C enter shop.	M (busy writing) puts pen down, makes eye contact with C and smiles. M also tries to assess C. M decides course of action.	M is prepared because she is facing shop entrance while working — stops working to impress C and to prepare for her. M smiles to make initial welcoming contact, M makes judgement about type/mood of C and looks for signals.
2. Manageress contacts and greets customer.	Notes C's continuing stiffness and hostility.	M comes around counter to C — gestures to further her into the shop. M smiles warmly with direct eye contact, greets C questioningly by name.	M removes barrier of counter to reduce anxiety — encourages C away from other customers. M's greeting designed to get C to talk, to relax and feel important.

Source: Buckley, R. and Caple, J. (1992)

When conducting hierarchical job analysis, it is suggested to explain
each operation using an active verb, rather than a general heading in order to avoid any misinterpretation; for example, "change engine oil" is
more effective than "engine oil". Another practical note of advice is to
avoid filling the diagram in with extra information, and to use a form of
coding to indicate references. Extra data may be found in accompanying
manuals, job aids, or pieces of legislation. The training specialist uses
this technique so that:

- a detailed design of the complete job is produced;

- the varying levels of difficulty/simplicity involved are illustrated;

- the overlapping of tasks is highlighted;

- the learning process is assisted by presenting the tasks in a sequence.

However, the trainer may face the difficulty of not knowing when to stop analysing, and not realising how in-depth the analysis should be. Naturally, in some cases the degree of analysis may be very obvious, however other tasks may demand more detail. Annett and Duncan (1967) developed a principle of analysing each operation in terms of:

- the probability of inadequate performance without training, and

- the costs of inadequate performance to the system.

Figure 16.3: Family Tree or Hierarchy of Tasks

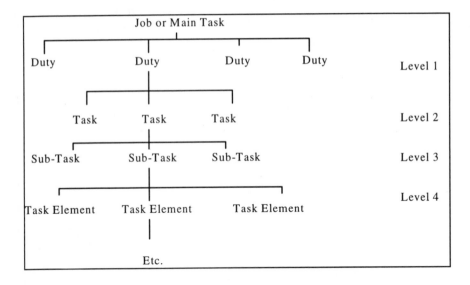

Source: Annett and Duncan (1967) "Task Analysis and Training Design", *Occupational Psychology*, Vol. 41, pp. 211-221.

DIF (Difficulty, Importance, Frequency) Analysis

Usually the question of whether training is necessary or not is quite obvious, however the DIF analysis can be useful in situations where the decision is unclear.

Taking DIF analysis at its most simplistic level, it can be useful in determining the depth of analysis to be made in the hierarchical task technique. However, its significance lies in its provision of criteria by which the decision to train is made. These criteria are (a) the level of difficulty integrated into the job, (b) the importance of the task to the complete process, and (c) how frequently this duty occurs. Figure 16.5 illustrates how tasks can be analysed in a "difficulty, importance and frequency" order. For example, when a task is difficult, important and frequently performed, training is necessary. However, the process may become more complex when, for example, a duty is difficult, important but not frequently performed. The figure clearly illustrates that trainee should be over-trained i.e. the job holder is fully trained for the rare oc-casions this duty occurs.

Figure 16.4: Example of Hierarchical Task Analysis for Service Engineer

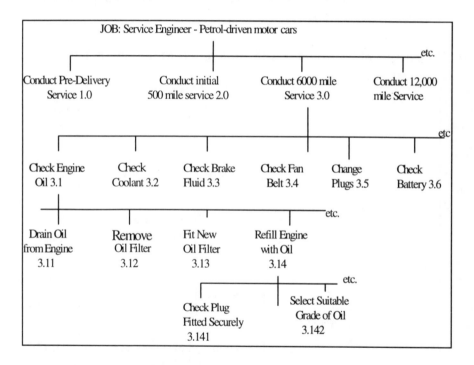

Source: Annett, J. and Duncan, K. D. (1967) "Task Analysis and Training Design", *Occupational Psychology*, Vol. 41, pp. 211-221.

The DIF analysis can be further developed by introducing varying degrees of difficulty, importance and frequency, and consequently devising different levels, which hold varying training priorities and standards.

Level 1   Gives training a high priority, and results in an "over-trained" standard.

Level 2   Attempts to achieve a standard where, once training guarantees competency, it will no longer be required.

Level 3   Sets the training priority midway on the scale, and ensures a standard where the task will be completed adequately.

Level 4   Suggests on-the-job training and relevant practice will be adequate for the specific job

Level 5   Recommends that the duties involved should be learned whilst doing the job, and that formal training is unnecessary.

Figure 16.5: Example of DIF Analysis and Levels of Training

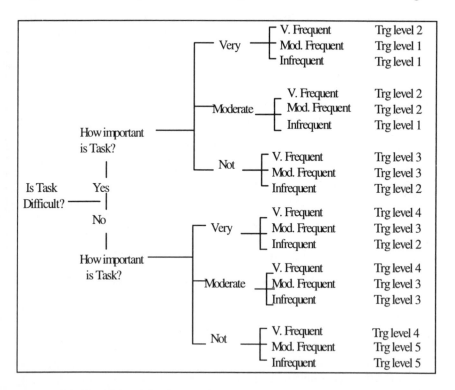

Source: Buckley, R. and Caple, J. (1992), *The Theory and Practice of Training*, Third Edition, Kogan Page, London.

The trainer has the unenviable task of trying to assess the degree of difficulty involved in a task and its relative importance. Through the use of questionnaires and interviews, s/he can obtain the relevant data from job holders, recent trainees and supervisors. However, trainers must be conscious of certain underlying factors:

- Job holders and their supervisors can hold differing interpretations of the same job.

- The job holder may have difficulty in assessing their own job objectively.

- The experienced operator may give an inadequate difficulty assessment, due to their over-familiarity with the task

- Some job holders may misinterpret the assessment's objectives, and withhold any negative input, because they feel their personal performance is being measured.

With these findings, the trainer is better equipped to prioritise the allocation of resources, and define necessary training standards.

Procedural Analysis

This technique is used in two cases:

1. When the tasks cannot be arranged into a sequential order, and the completion of duties may involve a number of options, an algorithm or decision tree may illustrate this data effectively.

2. When more than one employee is involved in completing a procedure (e.g. operators on an assembly line, or the transferring of documents). Any difficulties preventing an effective operation may be highlighted by devising a decision tree, which links the work of the relevant employees, e.g. a decision tree may illustrate that the problems are not due to poor employee performance, but the existence of too many links in the chain. (See Figure 16.6)

Knowledge and Topic Analysis

Knowledge analysis provides further detail on the knowledge items included in the job specification. Any relevant diagrams, notes, procedures or samples will count as additional data.

Topic analysis is a more in-depth form of knowledge analysis. This involves dividing a topic into more detailed elements and then presenting them in a hierarchical format. Davies (1971) suggests that to identify the elements/rules, the analyst should ask certain questions:

- At what level of knowledge does the analyst expect the trainee to perform specific tasks or procedures?

- To what standard does the analyst expect the trainee to perform specified tasks or procedures?

- How will the analyst study and quantify expected behavioural changes?

Figure 16.6: Example of Algorithm/Decision Tree Procedural Analysis

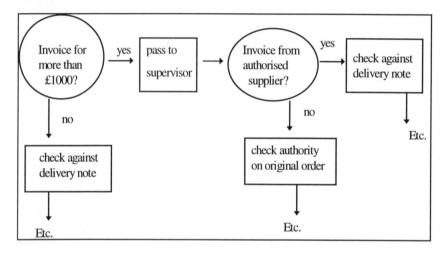

Source: Buckley, R and Caple, J. (1992), *The Theory and Practice of Training*, Third Edition, Kogan Page, London.

Davies stresses the relevance of carefully-written rules, which are arranged in a logical and natural sequence.

Gagne (1977) suggests that topic analysis, because it is so time-consuming, should be utilised in conjunction with target population analysis. When the topic analysis is used to further define the results of target population analysis, the elements that do not need to be taught are eliminated from training needs and content.

Target Population Analysis

This technique determines the target population, i.e. selects trainees from inside and outside the organisation and identifies particular characteristics of the target population before their introduction to the training programme, e.g. level of knowledge, attitudes, etc.

After some form of job analysis/synthesis has been implemented, the first phase of deciding the target population is introduced. The target population selection criteria are compiled with the help of person specifications, and/or additional personnel data (e.g. existing personnel and training records, in-house research, or inter-organisational training research). Where new training schemes are being implemented, detailed person specifications are used.

The next step involves assessing the potential trainees against the criteria previously established. Through the use of performance appraisals and psychometric tests, an applicant's potential for successful training can be assessed. For jobs where manual and hand-eye coordination skills are essential, a trainability test may be introduced. Downs (1985) emphasised that the test must incorporate the critical aspects of the job and elements which the trainee will find difficult during the training.

By comparing the details of the job specifications with performance/skill levels of the target population, the level of the deficiency can be diagnosed (i.e. the training gap). The target population's existing abilities will probably be known already by an alert trainer, and, if not, additional information can be obtained. In the case of external candidates, previous training and personnel records can be examined, or immediate supervisors or managers can be consulted. For external applicants, a sample of the target population can provide extra information through the completion of questionnaires, surveys or interview.

Having completed this element of the target population analysis, the general content of any subsequent training has been identified. A DIF analysis may highlight that only some of the tasks or task elements will require training. These training needs can be further subjected to a topic or skills analysis, which should provide additional information about the potential trainees, and consequently provide the basis for designing entry tests. The trainer and the client can further review the training content analysis, by considering any organisational constraints such as the availability of resources, social or political influences, and organisational priorities.

Protocol Analysis

Protocol analysis involves working out cognitive problems through analysis of recorded discussion of these problems. When it is combined with other techniques, such as structured observation, it can provide a powerful means of analysing tasks with a strong cognitive component.

Truelove (1995) identifies two broad approaches to the use of this technique:

- The use of initial, on site recordings of the spoken reasoning as the problem is being worked or a sequence of events is being followed.

- The recording of thoughts retrospectively as soon after the event as possible.

Doing instant recording can possibly interfere with the job at hand and possibly distort the outcome, whereas retrospective recording can lead people to changing their mind, especially if the outcome is unfavourable.

Within the context of training and development needs analysis, protocol analysis has three main uses:

- to identify the thought processes which are used by effective operators who follow a complex sequence of operations;

- to identify the problem-solving skills of a manager who is deemed effective;

- to identify the diagnostic skills of a trouble-shooter on a complex task.

INDIVIDUAL/PERSON ANALYSIS

Person analysis focuses on the individual employee. It addresses the questions, "who needs training?" and "what type of training should it be?" Wexley and Latham (1991) identify two key steps in carrying out person analysis:

- analysing how the particular employee is performing his or her job;

- determining the specific skills and knowledge that an employee needs to acquire in order to perform the job accurately.

Assessment of Performance

There are three basic approaches that can be used to ascertain whether an employee is performing his/her job to the level required. These are behavioural measures, economic measures and proficiency tests.

Behavioural Measures

Behavioural measures involve ratings based on observations of an employee's on-the-job behaviour by managers, peers, subordinates, etc. These measures are dependent for effectiveness on human observation and accuracy in reporting these observations. These observations are subject to four errors of perception:

- *data law effect* — the tendency to award the same ratings to an employee on a range of performance criteria, prompted by a bias toward uniformity in rating;

- *simultaneity effect* — the tendency of the rater to judge more favourably individuals perceived as similar to himself;

- *first impression* — the tendency to evaluate another person after an initial meeting; and

- *contrast effect* — the tendency to evaluate subordinates in comparison to one another rather than against predetermined criteria).

Economic Measures

This simply involves the organisation recording things like sales volume, waste rates, number of accidents and so on. Economic measures are of two types: those dealing with production such as units produced, number of rejects, and those dealing with personnel information, such as attendance, lateness, grievances etc. Economic measures are however problematic in the context of assessing individual employee performance. They cannot be meaningfully applied to many jobs, e.g. managerial work. Behavioural measures are more appropriate where the outcomes are qualitative in nature.

Proficiency Tests

These consist of a number of possible alternatives. One alternative is to take a work sample where the employee is asked to perform the duties required in a job. Another alternative involves the use of written job knowledge tests to assess employees. Proficiency tests possess a number of advantages: They allow an employee's skills to be compared to known standards, they are relatively easy to administer and have been properly validated. The major limitation is that the employee's performance during testing may not reflect daily performance on the job.

The training and development specialist is advised to use a combination of behavioural, economic and proficiency measures in order to get as accurate an assessment as possible.

Determining Specific Skills and Needs

This step involves systematic diagnosis of each employee's strengths and weaknesses, using the information collected during the performance appraisal process. An alternative method may involve some form of self-assessment. Research by Ford and Noe (1984), among others, shows that many organisations use self-report data as an important source of information about training needs.

Such self-rating systems have strengths and limitations. On the positive side, they prevent the situation arising of forcing employees to "need" training and development programmes. Recent research by Noe and Schmitt (1986) and Hicks and Klimoski (1984) demonstrates that such individuals become dissatisfied with the training and suffer from motivation problems. They are also less likely to transfer their skills back to the job. On the negative side, what employees perceive as their needs may be more an expression of preference. Latham (1988) points out that employees' perceptions of training needs are influenced by their attitudes towards training in general. Specifically, employees who have negative attitudes towards training and development are less likely to identify a need for training and development. Research by Garavan (1995) and McEnery and McEnery (1987) also demonstrates that employee and supervisor need assessments do not correlate highly with one another.

OBTAINING THE REQUIRED INFORMATION

It would be unusual if all the information required were available on demand. This means that the training and development specialist will have to select a range of data collection methods. These range from the simple to the sophisticated, and have major implications for the ability to analyse data.

Questionnaires

Questionnaires are often used to identify training and development needs. However, the training and development specialist who considers using a survey needs to be aware that design, piloting, implementation and analysis are highly skilled activities. Questionnaires fall into three categories:

- *Structured Questionnaires*: These require the respondent to give a specific answer to each question. The format is usually one of multiple choice. This format requires extensive piloting to be effective. The major weakness of this type of questionnaire is that the survey designer largely determines the outcome of the survey. Piloting can eliminate the resulting bias.

- *Semi-Structured Questionnaires*: These allow the respondent to provide some spontaneous comment, and responses are more qualitative in nature. Piloting of this type of questionnaire is also essential because it helps eliminate any vagueness in the questions.

- *Open Questionnaires*: These use only key reference points or areas to be investigated in the training needs survey. This question requires a skilled interviewer to administer and is a very difficult format to analyse.

Interviewing

Interviews are a common method for analysing jobs and identifying training and development needs. The training and development specialist should conduct a probing interview with at least one job holder before conducting the needs analysis. The interview method should provide the specialist with a detailed description of the job. The major advantage of the method is that it allows the trainer to probe when descriptions are unclear, inconsistent etc. Interviews require the specialist to have sufficient knowledge about the job and good interviewing techniques.

Observation

There are many times when training and development specialists need to observe the use of a skill or a process. This can be done through structured observation which can only be conducted by a specialist with acute observational skills. A useful method of behavioural observation is outlined in the Rackham, Honey and Morgan (1976) behavioural analysis model. They use a logging system to record verbal contributions under different categories: seeking information, giving information, asking, understanding, agreeing, suggesting, action, blacking etc. Observation is subjective. Every individual has a particular way of interpreting what they see. Two individuals may interpret the same visual cue differently. It may be necessary to build in a double checking procedure to ensure that the data collected is valuable. Every detail needs to be noted in order to be effective and the training and development specialist must have an open receptive mind.

Good observation requires that performance or productivity measures are unobtrusive. Employees are unaware that their work is being scrutinised. Training and development practitioners compare actual work group outputs to (a) work standards, minimally acceptable levels of scrap, downtime, or product rejects; (b) objectives, pre-established targets for producing quality or quantity; or (c) exemplars, individuals or groups producing far more or making far fewer errors than other individuals or groups.

Performance or productivity measures help training and development practitioners identify proficient or deficient performance, but do not reveal the cause(s). While differences in group performance are attributable to various causes, one being the lack of an appropriate mix of skills within the group. Training and development practitioners need only compare the prior training, education and experience of high-performing to low-performing groups. Differences may reveal employee development needs in low-performing groups and unique competencies in high-performing groups.

Brainstorming

This is a well-known technique of obtaining many possible contributions on a topic, usually from a group of employees. It can be used in a training needs identification context, to get as many possible views about the job from different job holders. There are two important principles which underpin the use of brainstorming: judgement is suspended, and that quantity breeds quality. For the technique to be successful, a number of issues need to be considered:

- The setting or general criteria are important.

- Sufficient time must be given with no interruption.

- Members must be briefed well before the event in order to ensure that they know the problems to be addressed.

- The composition of the group is important. Cohesive groups are better than non-cohesive groups in brainstorming sessions.

The brainstorming approach is valuable for revealing aspects which might otherwise not be mentioned, because the triggering action of an individual's contribution may jog someone else's memory.

Diaries

This method involves the maintenance of diaries by a series of job holders over an agreed period of time. The entries in the diary will relate to all the activities performed at work during the review period. The diary can take a traditional open format or employees can be trained to perform some analysis. At the end of the agreed period the entries can be examined and analysed to identify the range of tasks involved and to draw up a job specification. The diary method is a form of self-analysis replacing simple personnel self-analysis which is often incomplete, and it can be followed up by the training and development specialist's classification as necessary.

Group Discussion

Group discussions are general enough to be used for almost any purpose. They range from group interviews, in which training and development practitioners question job incumbents about work tasks, to open forums, in which supervisors openly explore employee development needs with members of a work group. They can also be useful in developing a general training plan by job class and in identifying employee educational needs or employee development needs.

Critical Incident Techniques

This technique was developed by Hanagan, an American psychologist, during the Second World War. The aim of the technique is to gather information from job holders about job behaviours which have a significant influence on the success or failure of an outcome. The technique forces the job holder to be quite specific when discussing skills, performance standards or attitudes.

The technique can be used in three ways: by one-to-one critical incident interview, by questioning groups with up to six participants, or by a critical incident questionnaire. Some researchers would debate whether the quality of information is improved or disimproved by using group participation instead of one-to-one interviews. The technique tries to achieve a balance between the structured interview and the open unstructured interview.

Delphi Technique

The Delphi technique, named after the ancient Greek oracle of Apollo, was developed by the Rand Corporation and has been widely applied to research problems. Typically, Delphi participants are chosen for their special expertise. Participants remain anonymous and never assemble as a group. Instead, information is solicited from them by written survey. The results are compiled by researchers, and fed back to participants with more questions, and this process continues until participants agree on key issues.

To apply this approach to instructional needs assessment, training and development practitioners begin by clarifying purpose. They decide (for example) to assess recurring training needs of job incumbents, career or educational interests of people facing different central life concerns, career-routes through an organisation, developmental needs of a work group, or non-employee development needs. Whatever the purpose, training and development practitioners begin by developing a questionnaire. They can do so by themselves (without the help of others) or they can interview people and use the interview results as the basis for survey questions. The participants should be chosen with care and should be knowledgeable about the subject. Training and development practitioners then contact participants, secure their co-operation, explain the Delphi procedure to them, finalise questions on the Delphi survey, send the survey to participants, receive completed surveys, compile the results, send the results back to participants for comment and critique, and continue this process until participants agree on key issues.

The Delphi procedure's chief advantage is that participants are not pressured — as they sometimes are in meetings — to conform to the ideas expressed by articulate or respected group members. Chief disadvantages include the cost and time needed to carry out a Delphi. Moreover, separate Delphi studies must be carried out to identify job training needs, career educational needs, and work group development needs.

Nominal Group Technique

The nominal group technique (NGT) takes its name from the way the process itself works. People are assembled in a small group. However, the group exists in name only — that is, nominally. In many ways similar to the Delphi, NGT has been applied to strategic business planning, HR planning, training needs assessment and futures research.

NGT may help assess training, education or development needs — depending on what issues are examined. Training and development practitioners (a) select one or more panels of knowledgeable people; (b) assemble group members in one place; (c) explain NGT to participants; (d) ask participants to generate ideas, identify performance problems, assess needs or prioritise instruction, and record their ideas on slips of paper, one idea to each slip; (e) have participants hand in their slips to the group facilitator (the training and development practitioner); (f) record each idea on a blackboard, flip chart, or overhead transparency so that all group members can see it; (g) encourage discussion following the generation of ideas; and (h) rank ideas by majority vote.

NGT is advantageous for two reasons. First, the silent generation of ideas prevents group pressures for conformity from affecting individuals. Second, ideas stem from participants rather than training and development practitioners or others. NGT is disadvantageous for three reasons. First, voting on ideas forces individuals to set priorities even when they see no need for action. Second, individuals may be subtly pressured to conform to group opinions during discussion or voting. Third, it is difficult to follow up on the many ideas that can be generated in NGT, with the result that good ideas are lost and participants are sometimes frustrated.

Co-Counselling

In the context of training needs identification, this technique involves two job holders coming together and being encouraged to interview each other about their jobs. If the atmosphere is relaxed a considerable amount of information can emerge. A record must be made of the discussion so that a job analysis can be done using the information collected. Various methods can be used to record the information but from the training and development specialists point of view, a video or audio recording is the most effective.

SELECTING DATA COLLECTION METHODS

What specific data collection method should be used in a training needs analysis? There is much discussion on this in the training and development literature. Ulschak (1983), Steadham (1980) and Rothwell and Kazanas (1991) identify nine issues that should be considered:

1. *Employee Involvement*: Should the training needs assessment process build learner commitment to meeting needs once they are identified and how important is learning involvement for the organisation?

2. *Time Available*: How much time is available to carry out the assessment process? When does management require the results?

3. *Costs*: What are the costs of alternative data collection methods and are there financial constraints imposed by the organisation?

4. *Relevance*: Will particular methods produce data which will be usable and actionable by the training and development specialist?

5. *Skills Required by Specialist*: Is the training and development specialist capable of using alternative data collection methods? Does s/he have the skills to design questionnaires, carry out interviews and analyse survey data?

6. *Respondent Skills*: Does the job holder possess the necessary skills to provide useful information?

7. *Relationships*: What is the relationship between the training and development specialist and the potential trainee? It may, for example, be difficult to schedule interviews or carry out surveys if the employees distrust the motives of the training and development specialist. They may be reluctant to speak their minds, and reveal their true work problems.

8. *Level of Awareness*: What importance do prospective learners attach to a specific need area? When their awareness level is high, data

collection efforts are easier because employees see benefits in responding.

9. *Management Preferences*: Do managers or supervisors prefer one data collection method over another? Obtaining needs assessment information from attitude survey results, for example, may be difficult if supervisors fear that poor morale in their work group will reflect on their competence.

Figure 16.7 presents the strengths and weaknesses of alternative data collection methods.

PRIORITISING TRAINING NEEDS

A training needs identification process will identify many training needs. It will not be possible, given resource constraints, to meet all of these needs, so some form of ranking system is necessary. In order to do this, specific criteria need to be set and each need identified and analysed against these criteria. The key criteria may include the following:

- What needs to be achieved? The overall objectives which the training must meet should be made clear.

- What is the justification? In terms of operational activities how urgent are the needs?

- What type of needs are they? The needs identified may be once-off, recurring or continuous. They may require small amounts of training or more substantial longer-term learning, or they may be complete areas of knowledge, skill or qualification.

- What kinds of learning are required? The learning may consist of theory or knowledge, the development of existing expertise, or it may involve exposure to new ideas, or sources of information, or attitudinal change.

- Where do the needs exist? Are the needs at the operational level or at more senior levels in the organisation. What is the motivation of these groups to learn, their availability for training, and the characteristics of the work environment from which they come.

- What is the resource availability? The nature of the financial resources available will determine the extent to which needs are met. Other resource constraints include time and the availability of expertise, internal or external to the organisation, to carry out the training.

- What are the policies of the organisation? The existing policies of the organisation will help to shape priorities and there may also be political considerations.

Figure 16.7: Strengths and Weaknesses of Selected Data Collection Methods

Methods	Criteria				
	Incumbent Involvement	*Management Involvement*	*Time Requirement*	*Cost*	*Relevant Quantifiable Data*
Attitude Surveys	Moderate	Low	High	High	High
Employee Interviews (by trainer)	High	Low	High	High	Moderate
Questionnaire Surveys and Inventories	High	High	Moderate	Moderate	High
Observation	Low	High	High	High	Low
Brainstorming	High	High	Moderate	Moderate	Low
Diaries	High	Low	High	Low	Low
Critical Incident Technique	High	Low	High	Low	Moderate
Normal Group Technique	High	High	High	Moderate	Moderate
Co-Counselling	High	Low	Moderate	Low	Low
Delphi Technique	High	High	High	Low	High

The end result of the training needs identification process is the production of a training and development plan. This plan should be produced by the training and development specialist and is used to strategically plan what kind of training will be conducted in the near future.

SUMMARY

Training needs identification is a resource-intensive process involving the collection and confirmation of information that will elicit agreement from management. Some training and development specialists view the process as too wide-ranging and one that should be undertaken by management consultants. However, it is important that specialists concern themselves with making training and development part of the business. In order to do this effectively, they must have a wide view of the organisation. The training needs identification process can provide this information. We have presented several approaches that organisations can use to determine training needs at job and individual level. Not all organisations will be able to afford the time and money required for these techniques. A reduced application of these approaches is better than not using them at all.

17

THE DESIGN OF TRAINING AND DEVELOPMENT INTERVENTIONS

INTRODUCTION AND LEARNING OBJECTIVES

In this chapter we consider the training design process. The starting point for any design of a training and development intervention should be the needs identification process we considered in Chapters Fifteen and Sixteen. The design of a training and development intervention is a complex process with many variables and prerequisites. Having read this chapter you will:

♦ understand how characteristics of the training population will influence the training design process;

♦ understand how elements of the organisational context will influence the training design process;

♦ understand the main issues involved in writing learning objectives;

♦ appreciate the range of learning structures that are available to the training and development specialist;

♦ be able to evaluate the range of learning methods and tactics available to the specialist;

♦ understand the dynamics of training delivery and the importance of an appropriate learning environment.

A MODEL OF TRAINING DESIGN

Figure 17.1 presents a model of training design which forms the structure of this chapter. The model clearly demonstrates that there is a range of factors which influence the choices made by the training and development specialist. These include learning principles, characteristics of the target population and a number of organisational constraints. We have dealt with a number of these issues in previous chapters.

Figure 17.1: Model of Training Design

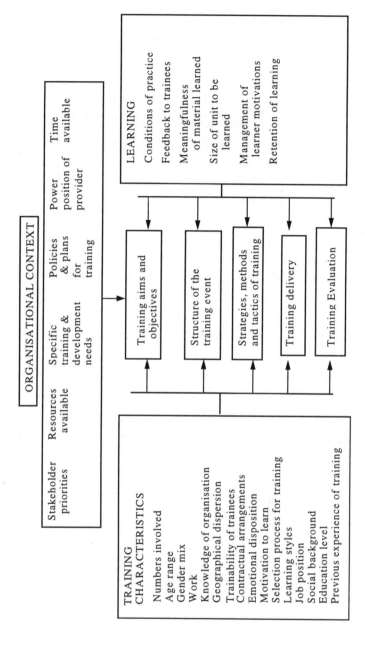

Organisational Constraints

There will always be a number of organisational constraints that will influence decisions about the design of training and development interventions. Some of these constraints derive from organisational policies, the priorities of the key stakeholders and the power position of the training and development specialist. Others will have been negotiated or agreed by the training and development specialist when identifying the specific needs. Specific elements of the organisational context are worth mentioning.

Policy and Planning Context

This refers to the existence of policies and plans relating to the provision of training and development. These policy constraints may be externally or internally imposed. They may be well formulated and written or they may be unwritten and unplanned. These policies may set limits on the types of training and development activities that are acceptable. Training and development plans set out specific commitments to training and development activities within a given time period. Any training intervention which is undertaken will usually have to fit within the plan. It is accepted, however, that there may be no written plan as such, so that all training activity is reactive.

Training and Development Needs Context

Any training and development intervention undertaken should be in response to specifically identified training needs. These needs may have been identified as part of an organisational review or they may have been identified at occupational, job or individual level. The nature of the needs identified will shape the structure, learning methods and delivery of the training and development.

Resource Content

There are three resource bases which may place constraints on the training and development specialist. First, a certain level of financial resources may be allocated towards training and development within the organisation. All training provided must fit within this budget. Physical resource limitations relate to the availability of training facilities, programme materials and accommodation. Irish organisations vary considerably in their allocation of dedicated space to training and development. Some organisations have staff, colleges and training centres, whereas others find it more cost-effective to use conference centres and hotels as the venues for their training and development. In other cases, on-the-job training may be more appropriate; other physical resource limitations may include the availability of computer terminals and special learning packages. A third resource limitation relates to specialist training expertise. This may be available internally or it may have to be bought in.

Stakeholder Context

The priorities and expectations of the different stakeholders involved may significantly shape the type and nature of the training intervention provided. These stakeholder expectations may be explicit or implicit and an effective trainer will be aware of them when designing the intervention.

Power/Political Context

The training and development department is not immune to power and political considerations. The introduction of a training and development programme, as well as its content and methods, may be subject to political scrutiny within and outside of the organisation. Buckley and Caple (1992), for example, suggest that senior managers can become suspicious of discussion periods included in the design of training programmes. They may view these as an opportunity on the part of the trainees to criticise the style of management, organisation, etc. We have already discussed the significance of power in earlier chapters. In the present context it has five major implications:

- It may determine the amount of co-operation the training and development specialist gets from line managers.

- It may influence the extent to which participants will actually attend training programmes provided by the training department.

- It will determine the amount of resources that the function can secure.

- It will determine the amount of commitment given by senior management within the organisation.

- It may determine the innovativeness of the interventions adapted by the training and development function.

Time Context

Some commentators would contend that time is one of the greatest constraints. Buckley and Caple (1992) suggest that training and development specialists are usually expected to read "quality" to mean the needs of the organisation. Time constraints make themselves evident in three ways:

- There is a consideration of time in terms of how soon the programme can be delivered.

- There is a major issue of how much time there is available to design the training programme and select the appropriate materials.

- There is also a balance to be achieved between the length of time people can be away from the workplace to attend training and development programmes and the length of time required to achieve the learning objectives.

TRAINING POPULATION CHARACTERISTICS

The term training population refers to all those to whom the training and development will be given. There is a whole range of factors to be considered here, and at best training and development specialists will only have a broad picture of the training population when planning the training and development intervention. There will, however, be a need to know some specific characteristics of the training population when the specialist starts delivering the training intervention. It may be possible to establish specific procedures and mechanisms to collect this information. We will comment on a number of training population characteristics here, identifying their implications for the training intervention.

Age

There is some research on the relevance of age to training design. It is well-established that physical and mental abilities deteriorate with age. Numerical aptitude and intelligence decline from the early twenties. Age also influences short-term memory, the capacity to process information and to eliminate mistakes made early in the training. Older learners are more likely to be apprehensive in the training situation and have a greater need for participation and involvement in the training situation. Newsham (1969) suggests a range of learning issues in relation to the adult learner. These are presented in Figure 17.2.

Intelligence and Abilities

The intelligence and ability range of trainees has a major bearing on the methods to be employed as part of the training and development intervention. Stammers and Patrick (1975) suggest three propositions:

- Trainees in the lower ability range usually prefer to progress from concrete examples to general principles. The reverse is the case for trainees with high intelligence levels.

- Depending on task complexity, higher-intelligence groups can cope with training a task as a whole, whereas lower-intelligence groups learn better through a part-method.

- Lower-level ability trainees have difficulties in coping with unstructured training situations.

Figure 17.2: Problems of Learning for the Adult

Difficulties increase with age	Suggestions for adapting training for the older learner
When tasks involve the need for short-term memory	• Avoid verbal learning and the need for conscious memorising. This may often be accomplished by making use of "cues" which guide the trainee. • When possible, use a method which involves learning a task as a whole. If it has to be learned in part, these parts should be learned in cumulative stages (a, a+b, a+b+c, and so on). • Ensure consolidation of learning before passing on to the next task or to the next part of the same task (importance of self-testing and checking).
When there is "interference" from other activities or from other learning	• Restrict the range of activities covered in the course. • Employ longer learning sessions than is customary for younger trainees (i.e. not necessarily a longer overall time, but longer periods without interruption. • To provide variety, change the method of teaching rather than the content of the course. A change of subject matter may lead to confusion between the subjects.
When there is need to translate information from one medium to another	• Avoid the use of visual aids which necessitates a change of logic or a change in the plan of presentation • If simulators or training devices are to be used, then they must be designed to enable learning to be directly related to practice.
When learning is abstract or unrelated to realities	• Present new knowledge only as a solution to a problem which is already appreciated.
When there is need to "unlearn" something for which the older learner has a predilection	• Ensure "correct" learning in the first place. This can be accomplished by designing the training around tasks of graduated difficulty.
As tasks become more complex	• Allow for learning by easy stages of increasing complexity

Difficulties increase with age	Suggestions for adapting training for the older learner
When the trainee lacks confidence	• Use written instructions • Avoid the use of production material too soon in the course. • Provide longer induction periods. Introduce the trainee very gradually both to new machinery and to new jobs. • Stagger the intake of trainees. • If possible, recruit groups of workmates. • Avoid formal tests. • Don't give formal time limits for the completion of the course.
When learning becomes mentally passive	• Use an open situation which admits discovery learning • Employ meaningful material and tasks which are sufficiently challenging to an adult • Avoid a blackboard and classroom situation or conditions in which trainees may in earlier years have experienced a sense of failure.

Source: Newsham (1969) *The Challenge of Change to the Adult Trainee*; reprinted with permission of the Controller of Her Majesty's Stationery Office.

Background and Emotional Disposition

An individual's emotional state or disposition can influence the learning process. Factors such as anxiety, level of self-esteem, fear of failure, self-efficiency, and lack of confidence, are factors that will influence motivation and willingness to learn. The composition of these elements may require the trainer to modify the pace and style of delivery, the nature of the goals set and the extent to which the intervention will contain individual learning elements. The reverse situation may also be evident with trainees who are over-confident, arrogant or unwilling to recognise that they have learning difficulties.

Gender

This is a controversial area. There is some research available which demonstrates gender differences that arise in the training and development process. In relation to training needs, Berryman-Fink (1985) focused on male and female managers' views of the communication needs and training needs of men and women in management. Both male and

female managers identified four skill areas for women managers; assertiveness, confidence building, public speaking and dealing with males,
whereas male managers needed training in listening, verbal skills, non-
verbal communication, sympathy and sensitivity. Tucker (1985), however, found no significant difference between women's and men's ex-
pressions of training needs. Streker-Seeborg et al (1984) have investigated whether training economically-disadvantaged women for male-
dominated occupations increases the probability of their achieving employment. The results showed that despite training they were much less
likely than their male counterparts to become employed in male dominated occupation. Schuler (1986) found that training could develop job-
relevant activities for women, but could not diminish the initial difference that existed between males and females prior to training.

There is some research to show that women are better at learning in
group training situations than men, and that they may have more reflective learning styles than males. Males are more theoretical and action-
oriented in their styles.

Educational Background

The educational level of participants has implications for several dimensions of the training design process. Education levels can determine
the levels of confidence that they bring to the learning situation. It can
result in particularly well-developed attitudes about the learning process
itself (some of which may be negative), and it will determine the extent
to which the training and development specialist can use different training methods. It may also determine the type of objectives that may be set
and the starting point of deciding the training content.

Job Position

Job position first of all determines the nature of the training and development needs. Berwick et al (1984) found that supervisors rated technical factors, such as written communications as their highest need, middle
level managers rated human resource issues such as leadership skills,
appraisal skills as most important; and upper level management rated
conceptual needs goal setting and planning skills highest. Gordon et al
(1986) found that trainees with greater seniority tended to require more
time than standard to complete training than people with less seniority.

Job position also has implications for the learning methods and the
time frame for the evaluation process.

Motivation of the Trainee

There is much evidence to support the view that learning is inhibited if the trainee has no desire or is not motivated to learn. Trainees may also differ as to whether they are likely to be intrinsically or extrinsically motivated. Furthermore, if rewards are related to the task being learned, the trainees will see the task as interesting and meaningful and will gain intrinsic satisfaction for acquiring the skill. Many trainees will, however, be extrinsically motivated, which means that the trainer will need to evoke both intrinsic and extrinsic motivation in order to stimulate trainee interest and effort. Wexley and Nemeroff (1975) have demonstrated that goal setting can be usefully applied in a management training context to increase motivation. Figure 17.3 demonstrates the relationships between learning performance, motivational level and task difficulty.

Figure 17.3: The Relationship Between Learning Performance, Motivational Level and Task Difficulty

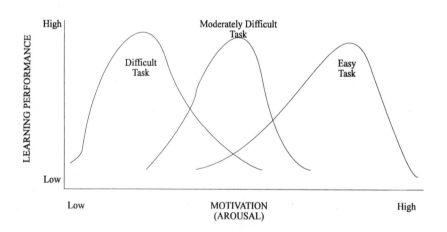

The maintenance of motivation during training events is also important. This requires the training and development specialist to vary the process by using techniques such as visual aids, varying the pitch, pace and tone of voice; introducing humour and varying the activity of the group. Folkard (1987) questions the conventional wisdom that new material should be covered in the morning and early afternoon periods and then consolidated in the evening. Immediate retention generally appears to be better in the morning. However, for some tasks retention may be higher following presentation in the afternoon and evening. He suggests three reasons for this:

- Trainers recognise the onset of the mental dip and make greater efforts to stimulate trainees.

- Trainees may perceive a decline in their attentiveness and therefore put greater effort into concentrating on the training material.

- Particular trainees are predisposed towards more effective performance later in the day.

The research also illustrated that there are "morning" and "evening" types. The former wake earlier and become fully operational mentally fairly quickly but get tired early in the evening. The evening types demonstrate the converse.

Physical Characteristics

Physical features of the individual trainee may be significant. Factors such as ill-health, physical injury and fatigue are important, but of even greater significance is the body clock of the trainees. This refers to the ongoing changes in body processes and the effect this may have on receptivity and learning performance. This is of particular significance when the trainees have been doing shift work prior to a training programme which is organised around normal day attendance. Folkard (1987) points out that they may require time and some advice on how to adjust and stabilise their circadian rhythms before the training begins.

Selection Process

The way in which a trainee is selected for the training has implications for the motivation of the trainee and their willingness to learn. There are various scenarios.

- The participant may be nominated by a higher authority in the organisation. They may not know why they were nominated or they may perhaps view it as a reward.

- The participation may have come from a systematic training needs identification process requiring formal agreement by the trainee and their superior. In this case the trainee should understand the precise reasons for selection.

- The participant may decide to do the training on their own initiative. In this case it is to be expected that the trainee will be highly motivated to attend.

- The trainee may be selected because it is a reward for service rather than in response to a specific learning deficiency.

- Participation in the programme may arise from a learning contract process. In this case it is likely that the trainee may see positive reasons for attending.

Work Experience/Knowledge of the Organisation

The amount of work experience which the trainee has will both influence both the content of learning methods included in the training intervention. The individual's knowledge of the organisation may be significant in that part of the programme for new employees may focus on the ethos and values of the organisation.

Contractual Arrangements

There is research evidence to suggest that the trainee's contractual arrangement with the organisation influences both access to training and the type of training. Employees who are part time/temporary or on fixed-term contract have fewer opportunities for training within the organisation. They are also less likely to receive training and development in areas such as management and supervision.

Previous Experience of the Training Situation

This variable may be particularly significant for older employees. Trainees may have high levels of anxiety about the training situation which may diminish their feelings of self-efficacy, i.e. their conviction that they can master the training material. The trainer needs to be aware of this possible anxiety and design activities that help reduce it.

Learning Styles

The context of learning styles has emerged in the training and development literature in recent years. The contributions of Kolb (1974, 1984) and Mumford (1986) are particularly relevant here. The idea of a learning style refers to the fact that individuals differ in their propensity or indication to learn from different activities or approaches. Some people prefer practical exercises at the early stage of training while others like demonstrations and explanations before reflecting on the content and assessing its relevance. Others are inclined towards theoretical abstract discussion to establish a thought process and method of action, whereas other individuals prefer to be given information or to be taught skills that they believe can be used in their work environment. Figure 17.4 presents Mumford's typology of learning styles.

Figure 17.4: A Typology of Learning Styles

Learning Style	Activists	Reflectors	Theorists	Pragmatists
Characteristics	• Enjoy the here-and-now • Dominated by immediate experiences • Thrive on the challenge of new experiences • Bored with implementation	• Like to stand back and ponder • Observe from different perspectives • Enjoy observing other people in action • Collect lots of data	• Keen on assumptions, principles, theories, models and systems thinking • Like rationability and logic • Are detached and analytical • Like to hear things and fit them into rational schemes.	• Search out new ideas and experiments • They see problems and opportunities as a challenge • They like to try everything out in practice • They have a practical mind set.
Learn Best When:	• They can involve themselves in the short, here-and-now activities • Training activities are new and novel • Excitement and drama are included in training activities • Thrown in at the deep end in training	• Allowed to watch and or think • Given an opportunity to review what has happened • They can exchange views with other trainees in a risk-free environment.	• Ideas offered as part of a system or model • They are intellectually structured • Learning situations are structured and purposeful • Required to participate in complex situations.	• They can see obvious links between concept and job • Introduced to new ideas or techniques for doing things • They have a chance to try things out • They can concentrate on practical issues.
Learn Least When:	• Asked to be passive • Required to observe and assimilate • They are given theoretical explanations • They have precise instructions to follow.	• They are forced into the limelight • They are given cut-and-dried instructions • Moved on rapidly from one task to another • Required to make short cuts	• The activity has no apparent purpose • The situation involves emotions and feelings • Involved in situations which are ambiguous • Subject matter is shallow or superficial.	• The learning content is not perceived as relating to a particular need • There is no practice or clear guidelines on how to do it • The content is divorced from reality • No apparent rewards to be gained from the content.

Source: Mumford, A. (1986) "Learning to Learn for Managers", *Journal of European Industrial Training*, Vol. 10, No. 2, pp. 1-28.

Kolb's (1984) ideas differ in some respects from those of Mumford (1986). Kolb argues that the organisation of new knowledge, skills and attitudes is a process of confronting four modes of experiential learning. These are concrete experiences, reflective observation, abstract conceptualisation and active experimentation. Learning consists of moving in varying degrees between these models. Kolb does not conceive learning styles as fixed personality traits, but rather as adaptive orientations influenced by a range of factors such as psychological make-up, educational experiences, career, present job and career. Buckley and Caple (1992) suggest that the analysis of Kolb and Mumford's work has three important implications for the training and development specialist:

- The trainee's level of intelligence will influence their learning style.

- Individual's will have varying degrees of flexibility in terms of learning styles.

Learning style differences suggest that individuals gather and process information differently and may have particular attitudes towards activities.

Reid, Barrington and Kenney (1992) point out that it is important for the trainer to realise that they have a natural learning and teaching style and when devising learning methods they should consider the trainee's preferences or try to balance both sets.

So far we have considered two elements of the model, namely organisational content and training population characteristics. We have already dealt with a number of learning principles in Chapter 14, so we will focus on the design process in this chapter.

LEARNING AIMS AND OBJECTIVES

The purpose of setting learning aims and objectives is to state as clearly as possible what trainees are expected to be able to do at the end of the training and development intervention. Sanderson (1995) suggests five reasons for having objectives:

1. They are the starting point for training design, giving a rationale for the selection of content and training methods.

2. They provide the learners with greater ownership of the learning process and can facilitate them in organising and directing their activities accordingly.

3. They provide the basis for the evaluation of the training intervention on completion.

4. An objective communicates the goals of the training intervention to key stakeholders within the organisation. It provides an organisational justification and helps to assure that the training and development is perceived as relevant.

5. They prevent too much or too little training. Too much training is costly and if irrelevant, it can lead to confusion on the trainee's part. Too little training results in further performance problems.

Mager (1975) provides advice on how to write objectives. He was concerned with clarity and communication and defined useful objectives as ones which enable all involved to be in agreement about the behaviour required. He identifies three components:

1. *The Behavioural Component*: This describes in clear terms what a learner has to do to demonstrate successful learning. Mager referred to this as a terminal behaviour. He suggested that trainers should use words that are open to few interpretations.

2. *The Conditions Component*: The trainer needs to state the conditions or limitations under which the trainees will perform. The objective must specify any tools or equipment available to aid the task or the range of problems to be solved or equipment to be mastered.

3. *The Criterion Component*: This provides the standard of performance. It tells us how well the learner has to do to be considered successful. The standard may be concerned with quality, speed or accuracy.

Mager (1975) suggests the following as a test of an objective: "Can another competent person select successful learners in terms of the objectives so that you, the objective writer, agree with the selection?" If the answer is yes, then the objective is sufficiently defined.

Dissenting Views on Objectives

There is some controversy about the value of objectives in training design. Sanderson (1995) points out that most jobs are complex and the time and effort spent in reducing skilled performance to a set of specific objectives can be daunting. In order to deal with this, the 80/20 rule has been invoked. This suggests that 80 per cent of the effort should go into the crucial 20 per cent of the programme. A related problem is posed by complex, open-ended jobs such as management, where it is extremely difficult to formulate precise standards or statements of desired behaviour.

There is also some doubt about the value of objectives themselves. Davies (1976) suggests that objectives are effective in promoting learning, but specific behavioural objectives are no more effective than general ones. Process skills such as selling and customer interaction, cannot easily be reduced to a simple statement of the activity without losing the key feature of effective performance. The solution suggested to this problem involves a specification of the objective of the behaviour rather than specifying the precise behaviour of the learner. This approach has been described as behaviour modelling (Bandura, 1986) and is based on eliciting the key behaviours and the sequence of behaviours shown by particularly competent employees. Buckley and Caple (1992) suggest a number of problems:

- Learning objectives may, in their rigid specification of desired training outcomes, (in terms of performance conditions and standards), create a cold, clinical approach to training, which ignores the human element.

- Writing objectives assumes that the performance that a trainee has to demonstrate must be observable and measurable. This leads to the suggestion that parts of the programme which provide general interest, enrichment of material, or an educational slant, should be cut out. It may also mean that creative approaches and innovation may be sacrificed for standard delivery mechanisms.

- There is considerable debate about how objectives should be expressed. The writing of objectives may become an end in itself. Furthermore writing objectives for knowledge-based training is tedious and pointless. It is suggested that the best that can be done in this case is to repeatedly describe performance using repeatedly words such as "state" or "list". It may be futile to do this where no attempts are made to evaluate whether trainees can actually state or list the knowledge that they have been exposed to.

- The area of attitudinal training poses particular problems. It is relatively easy to write performance statements describing attitudinal behaviour, but there are significant problems in measuring whether such changes have taken place. In the case of psychomotor and procedural skills the task is significantly easier.

- The mechanical or engineering model of training, implied by the adoption of a behavioural objective approach, is considered manipulative and contrary to the notion that the individual should have control and choice during the learning process. Other educational commentators suggest that behavioural objectives are relevant to role training but not to the acquisition of interpretative skills and the ability to apply knowledge and skills to new situations.

STRUCTURE AND CONTENT OF THE LEARNING EVENT

There are a number of issues to be considered when deciding on the structure and content of the learning intervention. These include questions about the timing of the training, the place, the delivery structure, the content and its sequence.

Time Required for the Learning Event

This may appear to be a simple issue but it becomes complicated when a group of learners is involved, the objectives vary in nature, and there is a requirement for group learning situations. The time frame for group learning events is often based on individual judgement, but may however be forced on the training and development specialist by various organisational constraints. Roscoe (1995) suggests that inputs of knowledge should be limited to a maximum of around an hour at a time. Skill objectives which require time for practice, on the other hand, should exceed the time for knowledge input by a factor of two or three. He also suggests that practice and feedback should follow the input immediately and review of practice and feedback should come as soon after practice sessions as possible. Learners may also benefit from a period of reflection in their learning. It is generally accepted that the more time that is available the greater the amount of practice there should be. When time is inadequate for the proposed learning event, the objectives and methods need to be reviewed.

Place of Learning

The venue for the learning event has to accommodate the number of learners using the methods outlined in the programme. The location must also meet the expectations and status of the learners if appropriate outcomes are to be achieved. In the case of one-to-one training, the venue must allow freedom to concentrate without workplace interruptions. For group learning situations, the training room must be large enough to accommodate the group and must allow for the use of the proposed methods. This requirement includes the physical arrangement of the furniture which may facilitate or inhibit discussion between participants and small group work. Some media and methods require power supplies, room blackouts, technical support and writing materials. Residential accommodation may be considered more appropriate when the trainees need to be away from day-to-day work pressures or if the training requires intensive work and concentration.

The Delivery Structure

The training and development specialist is faced with a number of options when deciding on the delivery structure: a compressed structure, a modular type programme, a part time evening structure and a workshop. On-the-job training is of course an option but we have already considered it in Chapter 12.

A Compressed Structure

This is also known as concentrated training and normally requires the training to be carried out over a concentrated period of time, ranging from one day to one week depending on the objectives and content of programme. A compressed programme structure has the following characteristics:

- the programme is self-contained

- it normally involves the use of a variety of methods

- objectives are achievable within the time period

- the course will follow a predetermined sequence

- it exists as an entity only during the hours of its presentation.

This is a commonly used structure in Irish organisations.

A Modular Structure

Modular structures involve the delivery of the programme in distinct modules with varying degrees of time between each module. This structure can be designed to deliver independent modules or they may be integrated. Each module will cover a self-contained cluster of concepts which are presented to the learner using a range of methods appropriate to the objectives. With modular structures, the dominant variable that defines the methods, strategies, allocation of time and other resources is the content. Modular structures are often used by Irish companies to deliver qualification-type programmes.

Workshops/Seminars

This is a commonly used structure and has application to a wide range of topics and training needs. In-house workshops and seminars are preferred by organisations that have large enough training departments and a large enough trainee population. Workshops have the following characteristics:

- they usually focus on a specific topic or issue;

- they involve considerable sharing of ideas and discussion of issues;

- they may involve the generation of new ideas and problem-solving;

- they involve small group work and some form of facilitation;

- they may be used to share new research findings or concepts.

The effectiveness of this structure depends on the particular workshop facilitator, the organisational relevance of the content, and the backgrounds of the workshop participants. Wexley and Latham (1991) suggest that many workshops are enjoyed by participants but result in little or no positive transfer of learning. Hollenbach (1989) has examined the effectiveness of the workshops structure and found that it produced lasting behaviour changes in managers, such as a broader perspective, strategic thinking, self-confidence, ability to make executive decisions and interpersonal skills.

A Part-time/Evening Structure

This structure requires trainees to attend training in the evening on a part-time basis, or continuously over a specified period. It is usually organised on a part-time basis. It allows a busy organisation to deliver its training but require considerable commitment from trainees to attend regularly. Many in-company professional programmes are delivered in this way. Figure 17.5 presents advantages and disadvantages of different structures.

Figure 17.5: Advantages/Disadvantages of Alternative Programme Structures

Programme Structure	Advantages	Disadvantages
A Compressed Programme	• Gives participants an opportunity to get immersed in training • Saves costs when travelling is involved • Lots of material can be covered • May increase effectiveness of learning because trainees know that this is all they are going to get • Allows for use of many different methods.	• Trainees may have difficulties being away from work for so long • There may be difficulties in concentration • Costly in terms of lost production time • May have variable levels of learning • If trainer is poor, there is little possibility of changing them for a new trainer.

Programme Structure	Advantages	Disadvantages
Workshops/ Seminars	• Allow for participation of trainees • Can be organised to meet work requirements • Good for problem-solving and creative decision-making • Can be applied to many areas of training • Relatively cost-effective to operate.	• Require an experienced facilitator • Only suitable for a small number of trainees • May not be suitable for certain types of learning objectives • May be perceived by management as useless because of their abstract nature.
Part-time/ Evening Structure	• Does not require the trainees' total absence from work during the training • Suitable for trainees who are not used to prolonged concentration • Trainees may be highly motivated because participation may be seen as a reward • Can build in a range of projects and work-based activities • Gives employee opportunity to manage their own learning.	• Cuts into leisure time of employees • Course attendance may place pressure on family life • Transport costs may be a negative factor • In case of qualification-type programme, long term commitment is required • High drop-out rates during training.

Content and Its Sequence

The objectives of the programme will determine the content of the training programme. The training and development specialist can often identify content which is related to the objective but not essential to it. This content should be assessed in terms of what must be learned to achieve the objectives, (i.e. what should be included and what could be included).

Once the content is decided, the next issue is its sequencing. There are a number of options. The most straightforward method is to base it on the training needs analysis and organise it on a logical order. However there are some other issues. These have been usefully summarised by Roscoe (1995) and Tracey (1992) and are outlined in Figure 17.6.

Once the content sequence has been identified, it is then possible to select the training methods. We will consider this issue in the next section.

Figure 17.6: Sequencing Training Content

- Start from existing knowledge, skill and attitude.
- Place easily learned tasks early in the sequence.
- Offer more than one practice session to develop skills and use feedback.
- Give spaced practice to allow development of performance standards.
- Give trainees a context or framework to use in organising what they are to learn.
- Follow advice with practice.
- Practice subsidiary skills throughout the learning event.
- Place the whole learning in context, then introduce the parts.
- Continuity of subject matter is superior to a series of unconnected activities.
- Introduce broad concepts and technical terms that have application through the training early in the programme.
- Use links between learning.
- Sequence should follow from content
- Introduce a concept of skill in the task in which it is most frequently used.
- Sequence can be organised around content that is known-unknown, concrete-abstract, general-particular, observation-reasoning/theory, simple-complex, overview-detail.
- Do not overload any task with elements that are difficult to learn.

Source: Tracey, W. R. (1992) *Designing Training and Development Systems*, Third Edition, New York: AMACOM.

LEARNING STRATEGIES, METHODS AND TACTICS

The training and development specialist is faced with a wide variety of learning strategies, methods and tactics when designing a training intervention. We will now focus on the options under the three areas: strategies, methods and tactics.

Learning Strategies

A number of classifications have been used to distinguish between different strategies. They have been categorised as centralised and decentralised, as trainer-centred and learner-centred. Trainer-centred strategies are best described in terms of formal programmes. They are structured by the trainer who leads the trainees through a series of lessons, exercises, activities and experiences towards the achievement of a specific set of objectives. The pace, sequence, style and tactics of the training programme is controlled by the trainer. Learner-centred strategies put the onus of responsibility for learning upon the trainee. The trainee is actively involved in the pace, sequencing, choice of material and the management of the learning process. The trainer is viewed as a resource or a manager of resources. Both strategies correspond with the instrumental and existential philosophies that we discussed in Chapter 12.

Figure 17.7 presents the main advantages and disadvantages of both strategies. The strategy chosen will depend on what the training and development specialist knows about the training population, and the organisational constraints.

Another categorisation of learning strategy is that provided by Davies (1983). He divides learning strategies into didactic, skill-building and inductive strategies.

- *Didactic Strategy*: This strategy places an emphasis on providing the nuts-and-bolts information to learners (i.e. providing them with the theoretical basis). The rationale behind this strategy is that trainees acquire information through hearing, seeing, and being shown the interconnections between the contents of the information provided. Didactic strategies are located in the academic domain and are developed through deductive thinking. They are therefore more appropriate to instruction than facilitation.

- *Skill-Building Strategy*: This strategy is designed to generate increased effectiveness in the behaviour of learners (i.e. the development of skills). The theoretical basis of this strategy stresses the improvement of behaviour through practice and problem solving. This strategy uses a range of methods such as case studies, business games, demonstrations and role plays.

- *Inductive Strategy*: This strategy stresses learning through discovering. Its main assumption is that learning occurs through shared experiences leading to generalisations. It involves not only doing things but also talking about them in order to abstract the key learning points. This strategy relates to the learner's social domain. It puts an emphasis on the active involvement of the participants, using methods such as exercises, projects, brainstorming and workshop-type activities. The approach used in executing this strategy is one of facilitation, since brainstorming of information by the trainer has already taken place.

Figure 17.7: Advantages and Disadvantages of Trainer and Learner Centred Strategies

Strategy	Advantages	Disadvantages
Trainer-centred	• Line managers may be able to relate to this strategy • Trainers find it easier to plan, administer and control • Trainees often like a well-structured programme • It provides an opportunity for trainees to mix with their peers	• The learner is moved along with a pace which is dictated by the timetable • It could result in great variations between participants in terms of learning • The trainer may not be technically skilled to make the necessary decisions • It requires a trainer who is highly skilled in presentation and instruction
Learner-centred	• The emphasis is on the learner • It allows the trainee to take ownership of activities • The trainer can adopt a more management role and be a facilitator • It may lead to deeper learning	• It demands unique skills of the trainer. • Its success depends on the disposition, motivation and skills of the learner • The learner may not like situations that are instructional and unfamiliar. • Not everyone is able to pace their own learning • There is a substantial effort involved in setting up and managing the learning process

Figure 17.8 outlines the advantages and disadvantages of the three strategies outlined.

Learning Methods

Organisations undertaking training interventions can choose from a wide and varied range of learning methods. Huczynski (1983) found 303 methods being used by different organisations and educational institutions. The methods selected must enable the performance stated in the learning objectives to be developed. If knowledge is to be acquired, then lectures, reading and computer-based training may be appropriate. Different training methods will require resources in terms of training skills, technical support, material, accommodation and other factors. These factors must be considered when selecting the appropriate methods. We will now review a number of methods.

Figure 17.8: Advantages/Disadvantages of Didactic, Skill-Building and Inductive Strategies

Strategy	Advantages	Disadvantages
Didactic Strategy	• Quick strategy for imparting lots of information in a short period of time • The thread of the topic is not lost because of interruptions • Can be adopted to large groups • Content can be fixed and timing determined	• Perceived as dull and boring • Continued use counterproductive in a training context • A passive strategy for the learner • There may be a lack of understanding by learners of which the trainer may be unaware
Skill-Building Strategy	• Trainees are considered participants rather than students • It is an active learning strategy • Participants are encouraged to correct misunderstanding • Feedback is given at regular intervals	• There may be frequent interruptions • Requires a lot of time to implement • Not suitable for large groups • May not be suitable for certain types of skills
Inductive Strategy	• Encourages group learning • Leads to high-level learning outcomes • Learners take ownership of the process • Can produce creative outcomes	• Requires specialist skills from the trainer • It assumes that the learners have the knowledge base • Participants may not be willing to participate

DIDACTIC LEARNING METHODS

Lecture

The lecture is defined as a method of learning which involves the trainer in transmitting information orally, usually supported by visual aids. Its object is to transfer information and achieve the comprehension of knowledge. There is little or no participation by the trainees until they are invited to ask questions, usually at the end. The lecture method has been frequently criticised as a training and development technique. There is a one-way flow of communication from trainer to trainee. The learner is a passive agent. It is a deficient method for training job-related skills and its focus on verbal and symbolic understanding is not always appropriate for training individuals of low ability. The lecture method ignores differences among trainees' abilities, interests, backgrounds and personalities, and since it proceeds at a single rate the slow learner is forced to keep pace or fall behind, while the fast learner is being held back. It also prevents individualised feedback and reinforcement to trainees.

Instructional Talk/Demonstration

The objective of this method is to assist the acquisition, comprehension and assimilation of knowledge related to a specific skill. It is a tutor-controlled method that requires the trainer to make use of a variety of aids and techniques, leading eventually to a demonstration that illustrates the skill. Usually part of a follow-up to a lesson or training session, it is used to provide a model for trainers before they are called to practice themselves. It is generally considered an effective method for reinforcing correct procedures and attracting the interest of trainees. It is a time consuming process that requires careful preparation by the trainer. It is a very adaptable method in that it can be used in many training situations. It does however run the risk of turning into a lecture.

Audio-Visual Methods

Audio-visual methods can be used in almost any training and development situation. The format used can vary between films, videotapes and slides, and TV. There is substantial evidence to suggest that the amount of knowledge gained through audio-visual methods is no less than that acquired through conventional lectures. Schramm (1954) found that audio-visual methods were as good, if not better, than the lecture. They offer unique advantages over the lecture method, and are particularly useful in the following situations:

- when there is a need to illustrate how certain procedures should be followed over time;

- where there is a need to expose trainees to events not easily demonstrated in lectures;

- when the training is going to be used organisation-wide and is far too costly to ask the trainees to travel to a central location;

- when audio-visual methods are supplemented with lectures in discussion before and after the training session.

Audio-visual methods attract trainees' attention by using their unique features, like instant replay, slow motion, close ups, etc. Miller (1957) argued for the necessity of following audio-visual activities with methods such as group discussion, skill-building exercises and role play methods.

Case Study

This method involves presenting a trainee with a written description of an organisational problem. Each trainee is given an opportunity to read the case study in private, analyse the issues and then meet other trainees in a small group to discuss the various problems and proposed courses of action. It is a non-directive method and can be used to highlight specific principles and concepts. The trainer's role is primarily that of catalyst providing information sources when appropriate, maintaining the direction of the discussion, posing specific questions and encouraging the participation of trainees. No attempt is made to lecture the trainees.

The method aims to teach trainees how to identify and analyse complex problems and to formulate decisions. It exposes trainees to a wide variety of approaches and perspectives and it also allows managers to derive principles and later apply them on the job. Campbell et al (1970) argue that the method is not very useful for the learning of general principles and there is a lack of control over the inferences that trainees may draw from the case scenario. Argyris (1980) identifies four limitations of the case study method:

- Most trainers dominate the classroom interactions by advocating positions, asking questions and making connections in order to maintain control of the learning process.

- Trainers often act to save face for the participants as well as for themselves.

- Participants often observe that the trainer's behaviour is often incongruent with what they espouse.

- Very few trainers attempt to relate the participant's behaviour in the training session to their behaviour on the job.

It is generally accepted that, for this method to be beneficial, it must simulate as closely as possible the work situation of the trainee. Pigors and Pigors (1987) point out that as soon as trainees find themselves in the situation of having to investigate facts they will lose confidence in the trainer's credibility and integrity.

Role Play Method

This method requires trainees to actually respond to specific problems that they encounter in the workplace. The technique asks trainees to enact situations and this enables them to learn by doing, rather than by merely talking about the problem. Shaw (1967) argues that the role play method incorporates four theoretical approaches to learning:

- active participation, allowing the opportunity for practice, experimentation and trial and error learning;

- modelling, where trainees can observe how others handle problems and imitate appropriate behaviours;

- knowledge of results, where participants can learn about their personal strengths and weaknesses and receive feedback from other trainees;

- practice, through repeated experience with a series of role play problems.

Typically not all members of a training group are involved in role play at the same time — some act as observers, and some form of discussion follows immediately after each role play.

The appropriateness of the role play method depends on the nature of the training objectives. However, it may give participants a greater insight into their own behaviour and that of others. Videotape playback may also be used to analyse the role plays and can be used to demonstrate effective behaviour to the trainees. The role play is not often used in isolation. It is usually used in conjunction with other methods such as lectures, case studies, and the incident method. Burke and Day (1986) have examined its effectiveness in management training. They found that it is effective in terms of reaction learning and job behaviour outcomes. It does, however, sometimes meet with resistance from trainees and can be perceived as a "bit of a lark" rather than a serious learning opportunity. It is also a time-consuming method and requires expert facilitation by the training specialist if it is to be effective.

The Incident Method

This is a variation of the case study method. Unlike the case study, this method provides the trainees with only a brief statement of the problem. Trainees must gather additional information by means of questions and answers with the team leader, who supplies only the information that is specifically requested. Pigors and Pigors (1987) describe the method as a five-step procedure:

1. Start with an incident. Trainees begin the case by reading a page that depicts some point. They are asked to imagine that the incident has just occurred and take on the role of a manager responsible for coping with it.

2. Collect and organise factual information on a case as a whole. The trainees now question the trainer for about 20-30 minutes. Then they eliminate irrelevant facts to end up with a manageable store of information.

3. Visualise key facts as interrelated factors and formulate an action issue. The group break up into sub-groups and each sub-group highlights the key elements of the case and creates diagrams that attempt to portray the interrelationships between the elements of the case.

4. Make presentations and test reasoned opinions. The sub-groups make presentations and after the full range of opinions have been presented and analysed, final solutions are formatted.

5. Reflect on the case as a whole. The trainees are invited to promote themselves to the role of senior executive and engage in long-term high-level thinking. They are thus given the time to see opportunities that were overlooked.

The incident method may be supplemented by role playing and workshops and has been widely adopted as part of management training programmes.

Management Games

Unlike the role play method, management games require participants to play themselves. This method is commonly used on management and supervisory training programmes. The games can be classified as simple or complex, computer-based or manually operated, media- or player-dependent or rigidly programmed or flexible. Coppard (1976) points out that they can also be categorised on the basis of their functional purposes. Management games require careful selection and must be in line with the needs of the organisation. Several advantages of this method have been proposed. Managers can gain considerable experience in a short period of time; the games are intrinsically interesting for trainees; they are realistic, competitive and there is immediate and objective feedback. It is a useful method for understanding complex interactions among organisational units. However, some limitations have been identified. Sometimes participants may become too involved in beating the system and they fail to grasp the principles involved. It may stifle creative approaches to problem-solving and it is time-consuming and expensive to implement. The existing research demonstrates that games increase trainees' enthusiasm and enjoyment of the learning process. (Ernest, 1986). There is limited research available on this method's impact on subsequent job performance.

Inductive Methods

Discussion Method

This method consists basically of a small group meeting in which a facilitator (a) helps a group to identify and define a problem; (b) guides the discussion so that it is directed toward the problem; and (c) summarises the principles or explanations that reflect the consensus of the group. The objectives of the discussion method are to present new and complicated conceptual and cognitive information to trainees in order to develop decision-making skills, and to change/modify employee behaviour. Discussion group facilitators have a number of important roles. They:

- must state the problem in such a way that the group does not become defensive;

- must supply essential facts and clarify questions;

- draw out trainees' contributions so that everyone participates;

- relate the ideas and feelings expressed in a clear form;

- ask questions that will stimulate problem-solving behaviour;

- summarise as the need arises.

Despite its demands, there is evidence to suggest that this method improves understanding of complex information, as well as problem-solving and decision-making skills. Some research (Butler, 1967; Bond, 1956) does show that the discussion method more effective than lectures in changing employee behaviour, but it is also seen to have limited application. In particular, this method is not suitable for large groups and can be time-consuming to implement.

Project Method

This method has an action learning basis. Trainees are asked to focus on a major organisational problem and to devise solutions. Action learning projects are based on three essential characteristics: (a) challenging objectives; (b) evaluation of alternatives; and (c) full participation of members in the group/learning set. They ensure that the learner takes a full part in a small intimate group of fellow learners (a learning set). The set must be small enough to allow high trust and detailed knowledge of one's colleagues, yet large enough to provide opportunities for challenge and support for each member during the learning process. Revans (1983) states that learning can be viewed as two distinctive activities; one is the conscious questioning of one's experience and a continual reorganising of that experience in the light of the results of the questioning process. This is P. learning. Action learning requires careful monitoring of, and reflection on, whatever is being done so that the learning process is deliberate, responsible and accountable.

Action learning projects have a number of advantages. In particular, trainees have an opportunity to take responsibility for their own learning — i.e. they also encourage teamwork and give the trainees opportunities for in-depth analysis. The operation of action learning project groups requires considerable discipline and dedication by the set members. They are only successful if used on a small group, usually involving between 4-7 trainees. There may also be problems with hypersensitive trainees and group dynamics issues which undermine the effectiveness of the project as a learning mechanism.

Games, Simulations and Exercises

We will group these three methods together, although they have distinct features. Games are competitive, have rules, involve scoring and have participants who are players. Simulations attempt to represent reality — and require participants to behave as they would in real life. Exercises do not have rules, they often involve the analysis of situations and require trainees to remain objective. However, they are usually shorter than case studies.

Games are introduced into training programmes for a variety of reasons: to inject some fun into the training process; to produce competition and generate energy; to provide opportunities for team work and to allow some generalisation of learning. Simulations may involve the adoption of particular roles, and require trainees to make decisions about doing or not doing something. They involve trial and error where the errors provide the basis for learning.

In exercises, the participants are expected to discuss various situations and devise a variety of solutions. Exercises may consist of task completion, brainstorming activity and problem-solving situations. They again allow the opportunity for generalisation of learning.

Figure 17.13 at the end of the chapter categorises and analyses each method.

REINFORCEMENT AND TRANSFER TACTICS

Reinforcement and transfer tactics are used to ensure that trainees retain the knowledge and skills that they have acquired and apply that knowledge and skill in the workplace. Training interventions, by their very nature, are usually short, intensive and artificial. It is therefore important to build reinforcement and transfer tactics into the training design. We will consider a number of the more useful ones here.

Briefing and Debriefing

Briefing consists of informing trainees and line managers about the objectives, methods and structure of the programme. The debriefing process confirms the use that will be made of the training and it may make provision for additional or remedial training. The briefing and debriefing process helps to ensure that trainees are motivated and prepared to begin the training and apply it later in the workplace.

Tests, Exercises and Practices

These may include a range of activities (including written and oral tests of knowledge, knowledge questionnaires, exercises and case studies) which test (a) intellectual skills; (b) trainee familiarity with new procedures; or (c) trainee competency in the practice of manual skills. The aim is two-fold: to check that trainees have learned something and to reinforce the learning so that there is a possibility of it being applied back in the workplace. Wexley and Latham (1991) demonstrate that the reinforcement of correct answering responses and performance increases the probability of recall of information and the retention of skills.

Handouts

These are summaries of the main learning points concerned during the training programme. While trainees should be encouraged to take their own notes they will not always do so. The handout can overcome this problem. Buckley and Caple (1992) claim that handouts which are well constructed and well-presented are read, and when appropriate they are used as job aids.

Refresher Courses

These may be necessary if job changes occur and not all skills acquired are exercised frequently, or if job holders do not get the kind of feedback they need to maintain or develop their skill levels. A refresher course can serve to remind trainees of the main content of their training. Further courses are very useful for attitudinal development.

DELIVERING THE TRAINING EVENT

Having decided on objectives, structure, methods and tactics, the next phase of training design concentrates on delivery of the training event. This stage involves consideration of (a) how people learn, (b) the instructional style and the approach of the training specialist, (c) the learning environment, (d) training room techniques and (e) the selection of trainers.

The Nature of Individual Learning

In designing a learning event, it is helpful for the training and development specialist to have some knowledge of how people learn. The following paragraphs combine the commentaries of experts in this area.

The Thinking Brain

Sperry and Ornstein (1977) have demonstrated that the brain is divided into left and right halves, with each performing specialist functions. Although the two halves are connected, they do perform somewhat different tasks, as shown in Figure 17.9.

Sperry and Ornstein also attributed to the right brain the ability to deal with certain kinds of conceptual thought. The right brain responds to the challenge of making sense out of complex data. Diamond (1988) has demonstrated that when people are exposed to material with a positive emotional content, certain chemicals are produced in the brain which make them feel good. Diamond's work also indicates that positive, nurturing, stimulating and learning-oriented environments produce individuals of greater intelligence.

Imitation/Modelling

This is a very powerful mode of learning. It plays a significant part in many training situations. Bandura (1986) is a proponent of social learning theory. He argues that most human behaviour is learned observationally through modelling. Through the process of observing others, an individual forms an idea of how behaviours are performed and the effects they produce. This coded information serves as a guide for action. Because people can learn from example, before actually performing the behaviour themselves, they are spared trial and error. The theory holds that people do not merely react to external influences but actually select, organise and transform stimuli that impinge upon them. Modelling processes can be used in the training context to train supervisors and managers in interpersonal skills; however, it relies on having the required underpinning knowledge and skills which will support performance. Some learning objectives may not be appropriate for the imitation approach because there is nothing to observe.

Figure 17.9: Right and Left Brain Functions

The Right Brain handles:	The Left Brain handles:
• language	• forms and patterns
• mathematical	• spatial manipulation
• formulae	• rhythm
• logic	• musical appreciation
• numbers	• images/pictures
• sequence	• imagination
• linearity	• tune of a song
• analysis	
• words of a song	

Being Told

This is often the first and only approach considered by the training specialist. "Being told" can take many forms in the training situation, including the use of a lecture, a video, an audio tape, a handout, a book or some job aid. The essence of "being told" is that the required knowledge is communicated to the learner. It is a suitable method if the objective relates to knowledge, but if it requires the trainee to do something, then being told will have to be supplemented by trial and error.

Thinking

This can be considered as an independent way of learning even though it underpins the previous approaches. If a trainee knows the desired learning objective, then they can learn through thinking about how it should be achieved. There is some research to show that learning increases significantly for trainees who have a clear learning objective to work to before the learning event, compared with trainees who start a learning event without knowledge of objectives.

Using Learning Curves and Plateaux

In order for a training event to be effective, the trainer must monitor the progress of individual trainees over the duration of the programme. Learning curves can play a significant role here, and serve three very important functions:

- They provide diagnostic information that allows the trainer to assess the effectiveness of different methods and tactics.

- They can be used to give feedback to the trainee.

- They can alert the trainer to difficulties being experienced by trainees.

Bass and Vaughan (1966) identify three typical shapes that represent trainees' learning experiences. Each one requires a different set of responses from the trainer. Figure 17.10 presents the three different curves.

Figure 17.10a: Positively Accelerated Learning Curve

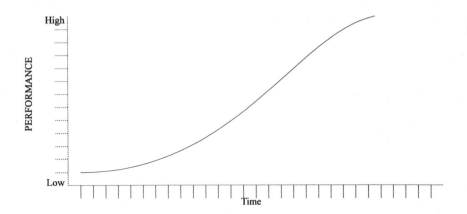

Positively-Accelerated Learning Curves
This type of curve is usually associated with difficult and complex training material or may exist where the trainee does not have the educational or knowledge background, or the special aptitudes, to pick up the task quickly. The trainee's motivation may be similarly very low and this significantly affects initial learning. In order for learning to take place the trainee needs considerable guidance and encouragement.

Figure 17.10b: Negatively Accelerated Learning Curve

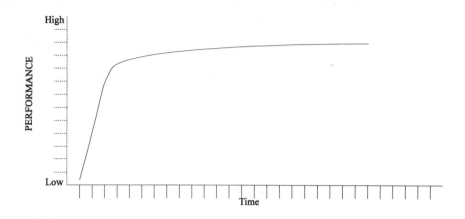

Negatively-Accelerated Learning Curves

These curves indicate that the trainee experiences rapid early progress followed by marginal or minor improvements in learning. This may occur for a variety of reasons. The task to be learned may be reasonably easy allowing dramatic initial progress. The trainee's previous experience may allow them to organise the material in a meaningful manner. Further explanations may relate to the motivations of the trainee at the start of the training period.

Figure 17.10c : S-Shaped Learning Curve

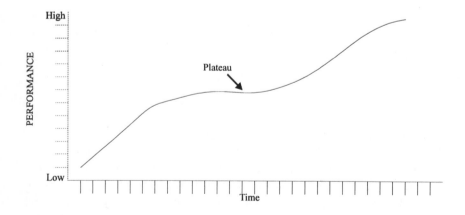

S-Shaped Learning Curves

This illustrates a period of learning when no progress is in evidence. This is referred to as a learning plateau and may only be a temporary feature. Bass and Vaughan (1966) provide four explanations for this shape.

1. They suggest the "hierarchy-of-habit" hypothesis which puts forward the notion that certain skills are made up of a series of habits that form a hierarchy. The habits at the top of the hierarchy are more complex. The learning of these is dependent on having mastered less complex habits. The plateau occurs when the transition is being made to higher level habits.

2. A complex task consists of several simple tasks or parts. As the learner tackles each part of the task, they meet and eventually overcome new problems. This gives way to accentuated learning.

3. Boredom, fatigue and motivation characteristics may also lead to the plateau.

4. Incorrect responses or bad habits may have to be eliminated and while this is happening no new learning is taking place.

Reid and Barrington (1994) suggest that specific abilities may vary in their degree of importance as competence in a skill increases. Initial progress in learning may be dependent on one particular ability; however, in order to improve, the trainee has to use another ability not yet developed. Being familiar with learning plateaux allows the trainer to take constructive steps. These may involve some practice, changes, the introduction of incentives, and/or detailed feedback.

Instructional Style and Approach

New trainers often pattern their training technique and style on past educational experiences, or else model their behaviour on someone else's. The trainer approach is generally based on pedagogy (the art of teaching) instead of andragogy (the art of adult learning). Knowles (1980) argues that trainers must be aware of five things about adult learners:

1. Adults are self-directed. This requires the trainer to engage in a process of inquiry, analysis and decision-making with trainees.

2. Adults need to know why they should be learning material and how they can use the new skills and knowledge the trainer wants them to acquire.

3. Adult learners have diverse backgrounds, education levels, abilities and learning styles which have to be accounted for in the style and approach of the trainer.

4. Adults are motivated to learn as they develop needs and interests that learning will satisfy.

5. Adults learn through experience. The training must provide opportunities for active participation and experimental exercises.

Reiss (1994) suggests that within the training situation the trainer wears three hats: expert, facilitator and ego ideal. As an expert, the trainer goal is to transmit information and the concepts relevant to the area of training. It is up to the trainees, however, to determine whether the information will be incorporated into their work. As a facilitator, the trainer's goal is to promote creativity and growth, on the learner's own terms, and to help the trainee overcome obstacles to learning. The trainer is also the ego ideal. They play an essentially heroic or charismatic role in the training situation and in doing so may be serving up an ego ideal or role model for the trainees. The training specialist can accomplish this by showing enthusiasm, commitment, devotion, and standards of excellence.

Creating a psychological climate conducive to learning is a major responsibility of the trainer. A learning climate does not simply consist of the physical set-up but also includes psychological support. McKeachie (1974) suggests that there are three essential characteristics that the trainer should exhibit in this respect:

- Displaying a caring attitude towards the learners and valuing their experiences.

- Displaying enthusiasm, which is revealed through words and actions which emphasise the message.

- Being an active listener. This encourages an open environment for communications and it lets the trainee know that the trainer cares about their responses, comments or questions.

In creating the correct psychological climate the trainer may be faced with difficult training-room situations, particularly the resistant, negative or disruptive trainee, the "show-off", the tardy trainee or an unresponsive audience.

- *Resistant/Negative Learner*: This trainee feels some resentment towards the programme. Clues to resistance include excessive questioning which challenges the relevance of what is being done, questions about the competence of the trainer, or disruptive behaviour.

- *A Show-off*: This trainee needs to participate and may attempt to dominate proceedings. The challenge for the trainer is to channel that enthusiasm in a constructive way. Show-offs can often be utilised effectively in training role plays and exercises.

- *A Tardy Trainee*: This trainee demonstrates a lack of concern for the training and shows a complete lack of interest. The general rule is to not draw attention to this trainee.

- *An Unresponsive Audience*: Audiences are sometimes unresponsive because they are confused or unsure about the programme. This problem can be overcome by having appropriate briefing processes and some discussion of expectations at the beginning of the training. Unresponsiveness may also occur because the trainees are introverted by nature.

Physical Environment Conductive to Learning

A key ingredient of successful training is the creation of an appropriate physical environment in which the learning will take place. The seating arrangement is an important element of this physical environment. This arrangement may be learner-centred or trainer-centred. Reiss (1994) identifies four different seating arrangements:

1. *Chevron Seating*: The Chevron arrangement is a variation of the traditional classroom arrangement in which the tables are arranged at a slight diagonal so that the trainees can see one another as well as the trainer. With Chevron seating it is possible to seat a large number of trainees in a small area. However, it is generally very trainer-centred. If the goal is one of knowledge acquisition reinforced with audio-visual methods, then this is an effective arrangement. Chevron seating is not conducive to activities with small groups or to active training-room discussion.

2. *Fan-Type Seating*: This gives each participant a good view of the trainer and any audio-visual methods that are used. It also facilitates good communication between participants and trainers. It is most suitable for small group activity and participants can easily alternate between lecture, group activity and group discussion.

3. *U-Shaped Seating*: If the training programme requires both presentation and group discussion/activity, the U-shaped arrangement may be most effective. It does, however, limit the use of the front of the room, and participants along each side of the U cannot see the others

on that row. The number of participants will determine the size of the U and a large room is required to make this arrangement effective.

4. *Conference-Style Seating*: If total group discussion is the main training requirement, with limited presentation and no small-group interaction, a conference style table arrangement is generally considered effective. Emphasis in this arrangement is placed on the proximity of the learners to each other rather than to the trainer.

The four seating arrangements are illustrated in Figure 17.11.

Effective Training Room Techniques

A final test of the trainer relates to their ability to utilise appropriate training room techniques. We have already discussed a range of training methods earlier in this chapter — however, there are additional elements which characterise the effective trainer.

- *Setting Expectations*: What the trainer states at the beginning of the training session sets the tone for the rest of the programme. It is useful to start the training by clarifying expectations of the trainees. This may involve asking participants to introduce themselves and outline their objectives or expectations for the training programme. This process allows participants to get acquainted with one another. These expectations may be listed on a flipchart for future reference. It is equally important that the trainer discusses their expectations. These will cover the degree of learner involvement and the level of work required. The trainer should also assure trainees of confidentiality in the training room.

- *Use of Questioning*: Questions are perhaps one of the trainers' most important techniques. Asking the right questions at the right time can determine the success of the overall programme. Questions can be categorised as either general or information-specific questions. General questions explore the learners' opinions, feelings or attitudes and are used to uncover participants' feelings, to stimulate group discussion, and to test participants' reasoning processes. Information-specific questions deal with the subject matter of the training. They relate to specific concepts and information and are excellent tools to (a) test for understanding, (b) reinforce specific concepts, and (c) discover participants' existing knowledge base. The technique of asking questions is applicable at any stage of the training programme.

Figure 17.11: Alternative Training Room Seating Arrangements

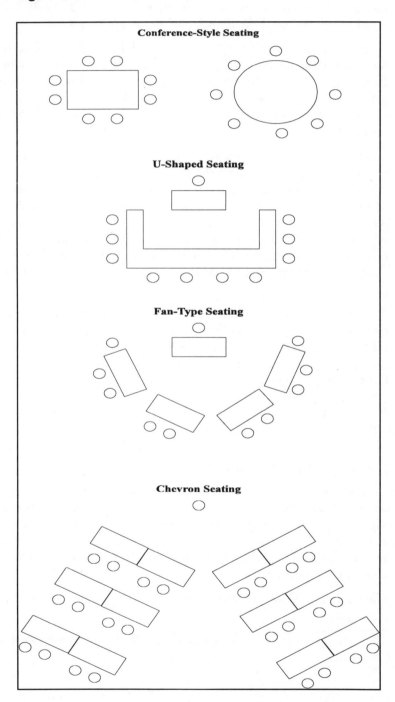

The trainer will also be expected to answer questions from participants. There are two ways to deal with these questions. It may be referred to the group as a whole or the trainer can answer it. The latter should only be done if the participants are unable to answer

- *Constructive Feedback*: Feedback is essential for effective learning. Such feedback should be descriptive rather than evaluative, it should focus on specific behaviours, and it must be wanted by the learner. The trainer should avoid acting like an evaluator or judge. He/she should strive to act like a coach by giving detailed and descriptive feedback.

- *Managing Time*: A significant challenge for the trainer concerns pacing the programme within the given time constraints. It is important that the trainer is never rigid in relation to time. They should adjust the programme if necessary. The key criterion should be whether the learners understand the concepts rather than the amount of time it will take to explain it. The trainer should be attentive to the body language of trainees. This will help to determine when a break is necessary. Some form of break should occur every 60 to 75 minutes.

- *Making Presentations*: Most training programmes include a presentation of some sort. Presentations require a specific set of skills from the trainer. A good training presentation requires consideration of six issues: the purpose, the audience, the circumstances, the plan, rehearsal and practice, and the use of visual aids.

Figure 17.12 presents a check list of questions the trainer may ask after the delivery of a training event

Selection of Direct Trainers

The trainers involved in the delivery of training require a variety of skills. They may need to act as coaches, facilitators, counsellors and managers of group-learning situations. The mistaken assumption is often made that trainers who are experts are also able to train others. This assumption is incorrect. Buckley and Caple (1992) suggest several characteristics of poor trainers:

- They adopt a highly directive style of training which allows little participation.

- They make unrealistic assumptions about the trainees' level of knowledge.

- They display impatience or intolerance when trainees fail to understand concepts.

- They lack commitment to the subject being taught.

- They lack verbal/oral skills.

- They refuse to accept criticism and lack sociability and interest in trainees.

- They try to teach too much too quickly.

It is therefore important to select trainers who do not have these weaknesses

Figure 17.12: Self-Assessment of Training Presentation

- Was the material appropriate to the group?

- Were the main points clear?

- Was there too much or too little material?

- Did the trainer use the communication aids effectively?

- Did the trainer encourage participation?

- Was the trainer heard and understood?

- How well was the time used?

- Were the aids appropriate for the session?

- Did the trainer use jargon which may not be understood
  by the trainees?

- Were the training objectives achieved?

The trainer may also be required to do one-to-one training. Megginson and Boydell (1979) state that the interpersonal skills required by the trainer are similar to those of a skilful counsellor. These include attending, observing, remaining silent, drawing out, giving and receiving feedback, and suspending judgement. These are also useful in group situations combined with skills in listening, analysing, correcting, guiding, prompting, controlling and summarising. In exercising the latter set of skills, the trainer is acting as a facilitator. This is significantly different to the role that many direct trainers adopt.

SUMMARY

This chapter has attempted to detail the complex nature of the training design process. Training design is often approached as the simple task of filling in the blanks on a timetable. There are, however, many variables which determine the shape of the final design. These variables are furthermore highly interconnected and demand the ability to continually reassess previous decisions and to change the design if necessary. The bottom line test of any training design is whether the trainees actually achieved the learning objectives set for the learning event and if the performance problem is solved. A training intervention that is well-designed, well-implemented, and capable of achieving tangible results, considerably enhances the credibility of the training and development specialist.

Figure 17.13: Alternative Training Methods

Learning Method	Learning Strategy Implemented	Advantages	Disadvantages
Lecture	Didactic Strategy	• Fast method of imparting knowledge • Thread of topic not interrupted by trainees • Suitable for large groups • Cost-effective • Many trainees feel comfortable with it • Everyone gets the same thing.	• Limited participation of, and feedback to trainees • Difficult to check understanding • Recall of material may be poor • Not suitable for skills development • May result in boredom if trainer skills are poor.
Instructional Talk/ Demonstration	Didactic/Skill-Building Strategy	• Suitable to introduce a job procedure or skill • Can be adapted to many training situations • Allows participants to model behaviour • Can use visual aids to heighten attention.	• Risk of turning into a lecture • Demonstration may be poorly done • May have to be repeated if trainees are weak • Training aids need to be effective • Only effective with small audience.
Audio-Visual Method	Didactic Strategy	• Suitable for large audiences • Can be placed in any part of training programme • Can provide a multi-scenario experience • Can be used as a basis for group work • Useful to summarise concepts.	• Participants may find case study too difficult • Difficult to design • Takes up a lot of programme time • Requires expert facilitation • Trainees may not make links with work content • No one right answer.

Learning Method	Learning Strategy Implemented	Advantages	Disadvantages
Case Study	Induction Strategy	• It exposes trainers to a wide variety of problems and situation • It allows trainers to devise principles that can later be applied • It encourages maximum participation • It allows trainer to act as a catalyst • It allows greater learning transfer where trainees discover principles for themselves • It encourages the development of alternatives.	• It takes up a lot of training time • The trainer may dominate the process • The trainees may be unable to identify with the case used • The trainees may depend on the trainer for the answers as opposed to working through the case • If the case has to be augmented in some fashion the trainees may lose confidence in the process.
Role Play	Skill-Building Strategy	• It provides opportunities for practice and experimentation • Trainees can observe others and imitate successful behaviour • It provides participants with an opportunity to assess their strengths and weaknesses • Trainees can observe the extent of their learning through successive role plays • It is ideal for interpersonal skills development.	• It requires expert facilitation about the trainer • Trainees are generally wary and nervous of feedback • The role play situation may be incongruent with the normal practice of trainees, hence learning transfer may be limited • It is a time-consuming process • Role plays can rarely be used in isolation.

fig 17.13

Learning Method	Learning Strategy Implemented	Advantages	Disadvantages
Incident Method	Skill-Building Strategy	• More closely based on organisation reality • Less material to read and comprehend • Develops participants' questioning skills • Not as time-consuming as role play • Can be used with other techniques • Elicits favourable reactions from trainees.	• Trainees may be embarrassed or uncomfortable with method • Could be regarded as "a bit of a lark" • Outcomes may not be predictable • It requires expert facilitation and debriefing • Uses a lot of training time • Trainees need a knowledge base and understanding of context • Not suitable at the beginning of a programme.
Management Games	Skill-Building Strategy	• Valuable way of assessing performance of trainees • A wide variety of games available • Active involvement from participants • On-going feedback from game itself • Can be used to develop global thinking • Facilitates team building • Can achieve higher order skill development.	• Absorbs a lot of training time • Needs an experienced facilitator • Participants must have high level of contextual knowledge • Not applicable to certain training objectives • Can oversimplify complex real-life situations • Difficult to timetable • May not get the commitment required of participants.

Learning Method	Learning Strategy Implemented	Advantages	Disadvantages
Group Discussion	Inductive Strategy	• Participants encouraged to play a major role • Facilitates the exchange of ideas • Critical thinking can be stimulated • Social and interpersonal skills are exercised • Trainees can generalise from the discussion.	• Not suitable for large groups of trainees • Requires competent and knowledgeable trainees • Needs to be well-facilitated, otherwise trainees may stray from the point • Trainees can become entrenched in their attitudes • Time-consuming • May be over-dominated by particular trainees.
Project Method (Action Learning)	Skill-Building/ Inductive Strategies	• Trainees given a chance to take responsibility for their own learning • Helps to develop initiative and creativity • May be used to assess trainee performance • Can be used to develop teamwork • Trainees can generalise learning.	• Projects require high commitment from trainees • Can generate anxiety and stress • May lead to conflict • Trainees may be sensitive to feedback on their project work • Not suitable for lower-level/unskilled employees.
Games	Inductive	• Introduce an element of competition into learning • Can be used to develop teamwork • Allow important lessons to be drawn by trainees and trainer • Can be purchased off the shelf • Have wide applications in training situations.	• May be perceived as childish • Participants may get upset about losing • The lesson to be learned may be lost • Some games are so widely used participants may know the answer • Need careful discussion, briefing and debriefing.

Learning Method	Learning Strategy Implemented	Advantages	Disadvantages
Simulations	Inductive Strategy	• Can be used as an icebreaker • Can be physical or psychological in orientation • Can be paper- or computer-based • Can illustrate certain principles effectively • May vary in length • Provide learning variety.	• They may not be carefully constructed • All possible decisions need to be anticipated in advance • They may be time-consuming • Can be rejected by trainees as irrelevant • May be seen in fun terms alone.
Exercises	Inductive/Skill-Building Strategies	• Can be used with individuals or groups • Encourage the active involvement of trainees • Trainees take responsibility for learning process • Learning points of exercise can be generalised • Lots of exercises available • May be geared to needs of organisation.	• Trainees need careful briefing on purpose of exercise • Exercise may not be demanding enough or may prove too complicated • May require trainees to be too frank/open • May require advance participation and may be seen as extra work rather than learning.

18

EVALUATING, AUDITING AND BENCHMARKING THE TRAINING AND DEVELOPMENT FUNCTION

INTRODUCTION AND LEARNING OBJECTIVES

In this chapter we will consider training evaluation and the auditing of the training and development function. When organisations evaluate their training and development activities they usually want to know whether such activities are efficient or not. However, a more rigorous test, requiring more detailed analysis, attempts to answer the question "was the training effective?" It involves not only finding out whether the training was well done but also whether it was worthwhile for the organisation. Having completed this chapter you will understand:

♦ the terminology used in training evaluation;

♦ the many purposes for which evaluation may be undertaken in a training and development context;

♦ the many perspectives on evaluation;

♦ the differences between training evaluations and training audits;

♦ the key issues involved in auditing and benchmarking the training and development function.

NATURE OF EVALUATION

The penultimate stage in the training and development process is the evaluation and monitoring of the training and development intervention. It is an important but often neglected process. The level of complexity involved can vary, depending on the commitment given to it. In simplistic terms it can consist of an information-gathering process from trainees which results in some amendments being made to the training and development intervention. A more complex variation involves data collection from all of the key stakeholders in the process. Easterby-Smith and Mackness (1992) point out that each stakeholder has their own principles, aims and objectives and these have to be clearly identified before the process can proceed. Before we discuss the issues involved, it is first of all necessary to define a number of terms used in evaluation methodology.

Evaluation versus Validation

Goldstein (1986) defines evaluation as "the systematic collection of descriptive and judgmental information necessary to make effective decisions related to the selection, adoption, value and modification of various instrumental activities". This definition implies that evaluation is about the use of data gathering techniques designed to examine a particular aspects of the learning process. Evaluation should not be confused with validation, the two types of which are now outlined:

- *Internal validation*, which is defined as the use of a series of tests and assessments designed to ascertain whether a training programme has achieved the behavioural objectives specified.

- *External validation*, which is defined as a series of tests and assessments designed to ascertain whether the behavioural objectives of an internally valid training and development programme were based on an accurate initial identification of the training and development needs.

Validation is considered to be too narrow in scope in that it does not reflect the perceptions of participants and fails to take account of unanticipated effects of the training and development intervention.

The notion of validation is therefore not very useful in the training and development context. It is perhaps better to adopt a broad view of evaluation which covers the effects of training and development interventions in overall terms and specifically concentrates on the evaluation of the training programme and the training process.

Context, Input and Output Evaluation

If we accept this broad view then it is possible to identify three specific areas of evaluation.

- *Context Evaluation*: This refers to the situation within which the learning event has taken place. Specific questions which will be addressed here include the accuracy of the needs identified, the way in which the learning event was conducted and the appropriateness of the learning objectives set. Issues such as organisational culture and structure are also of relevance here.

- *Input Evaluation*: This refers to the resources used to meet the learning needs, the content and the methods used and the specific costs of all these inputs.

- *Output Evaluation*: This involves consideration of the immediate, intermediate and ultimate outcomes.

Immediate outcomes relate to changes in knowledge, skill or behaviour after the training intervention. It attempts to assess whether or not the training has been effective in communicating its message. *Intermediate outcomes* relate to evidence that knowledge, skill and behaviour which have been learned are being put into use on the job. The basic question is whether the various stakeholders can identify changes in behaviour, skills and attitudes. *Ultimate or long-term* outcomes refer to the long-term effectiveness of the individual team and/or organisation as a result of the training intervention. This level of outcome is difficult to undertake and is only feasible if the training and development intervention has some relationship with corporate, strategic and business needs.

Figure 18.1 outlines a number of content issues for evaluation.

WHY EVALUATE TRAINING AND DEVELOPMENT INTERVENTIONS

Easterby-Smith (1986) offer three general purposes of evaluation: proving, improving and learning.

Proving/Summative Evaluation

Summative evaluation is concerned with testing whether or not the training and development programme has achieved the stated objectives. It is a judgmental activity, the purpose of which is to prove or disprove the effectiveness of the training and development .

Improving/Formative Evaluation

Formative evaluation is concerned with refinement of the training and development programme while it is still running. Evaluation information is collected and fed back into the training and development system to help guide design changes. As far back as 1963, Cronbach stated that "the greatest service evaluation can perform is to identify aspects of the course where revision is desirable".

Figure 18.1: Content Issues for Evaluation

Issue	Brief Description of Issue	Key Questions
Purpose of Training	The reason for offering the training	• What performance problem is to be solved by training? • What career objectives are to be met by employee education? • What organisational objectives are to be supported by developmental activities?
Linkage to Needs	The relationship between training, education, or development and the needs to be met by them	• Are training objectives clearly linked to identified needs? • Are objectives for training linked to job performance problems? • Are objectives for education linked to staffing plans? Individual career plans? • Are objectives for development linked to long-term organisational strategy?
Marketing	The way the training is promoted/communicated to stakeholders	• Are stakeholders clearly identified? • Are their interests clear? • Is training promoted to them based on their interests and needs?
Objectives/ Goals	• The general outcomes to be met by training • The specific outcomes to be met by a training course, educational experience, or developmental intervention	• Are the training goals for each programme stated? • Are training objectives for each programme, lesson, and unit clearly stated?

Issue	Brief Description of Issue	Key Questions
Desirable Outcomes	The desired impact of training on the job; the desired impact of education on career mobility; the desired impact of development on a part of the organisation; the culture, or a stakeholder group	• Are the desired on-the-job effects of training clarified? • Is someone held accountable for transfer of learning from the training setting to the work setting?
Assessment of Outcomes	The way the outcomes of training, education or development will be measured	• Is it clear how participant reactions to training will be measured? • Is it clear how behaviour will be measured? • Is it clear how on-the-job effects will be measured?
The Setting	• Where training will be carried out • Where evaluation will be carried out	• What is special about the training setting? • What is special about the evaluation setting?
The Learners	The people for whom the training is intended	• What assumptions are made about the learners? • What prerequisite skills are needed?
Training	The subject matter to be delivered	• Does the subject matter match objectives? • Is the subject matter selected/prepared appropriately?
Provision for Differences	Planning for differences between learners	• How are differences between learners recognised? • How are differences between learners dealt with during training?
Logistics	Planning for delivering the training	• Are the resources available for carrying out training? Planned for?
Testing of Training	How learning will be measured at the end of training.	• Are test items clearly linked to training objectives? • Have tests been tested?

Issue	Brief Description of Issue	Key Questions
Implementation of training	How the training will be carried out	• Do representation methods match objectives?
Application	How training will be applied on the job	• What on-the-job application is desired? • How will on-the-job application be measured?
Effects	The results of training in improved productivity, cost savings, improved quality of work life, improved morale.	• What effects are possible? • What effects are desired? • What effects are being achieved?
Use of Information about Effects	How information about the effects of training will be used.	• Who wants to know about training? Education? Development? • What decisions will be based on the information?

Learning

This purpose recognises that evaluation cannot be divorced from the process on which it concentrates i.e. learning. This requires an evaluation of the level of learning achieved in terms of knowledge, skill and attitude changes.

Figure 18.2 suggests questions under each of these general headings. Bramley (1991) suggests three more specific purposes of evaluation:

1. *Feedback*: This is similar to Easterby-Smith's "improving" category and is concerned with providing quality control over the design and delivery of training and development activities. The information which needs to be collected for feedback evaluation includes:

   • the extent to which programme objectives are being or have been met.

   • before and after measures of knowledge, skills, attitudes and behaviour.

   • evidence of learning transfer to the workplace.

   • perceived benefits of the programme to the individual.

2. *Control*: Control evaluation relates training and development policy and practice to organisational strategies. It may also involve consid-

eration of the costs and benefits of the training and development function. Specific information required to fulfil this purpose includes:

- measures of the worth of the output of the training and development function to the organisation;

- measures of cost and benefits;

- an analysis of the contributions of different training interventions.

3. *Research*: Research evaluation aims to add to existing knowledge of training and development principles and practice. A key issue here is "validity" of which there are two types: internal and external. Internal validity may be defined as the extent to which particular conclusions may justly be drawn from the data. External validity refers to the extent to which conclusions drawn from the experimental situation may be applicable generally to other situations.

KEY STAKEHOLDERS IN THE EVALUATION PROCESS

Who are the main clients of the training and development evaluation process? It is possible to identify different stakeholder groups. Easterby-Smith and Mackness (1992) examined the role which organisational stakeholders and their different interests may play in the evaluation process in a major computer training initiative in a government department. The sponsors (the senior managers responsible for the overall success of the computerisation project) had a major interest in meeting project deadlines. They viewed the role of evaluation as proving that the training initiative was enabling effective implementation. The interests of the trainers on the other hand were to identify and record weak areas of the training programme, and therefore the dominant purpose of the evaluation was improving the quality of the training and their own performance. For the trainees, their primary interest was in learning what was needed. This study recognises the political dimension of evaluation and that the ultimate success of an evaluation exercise depends upon the ability to clarify the principal, the purpose of the evaluation and the interests that are being served. McEvoy and Butler (1990) suggest that all too often the purpose of training evaluation is not sufficiently thought through. They argue that before an organisation embarks upon a training evaluation exercise, it should carefully determine exactly what objectives it is trying to achieve. We will next examine individual stakeholder perceptions of training evaluation.

Figure 18.2: Reasons for Evaluation of Training and Development

Proving	Learning	Improving
• Did we select the right candidates? • Is there a need for a follow-on programme? • Was there learning transfer? • Will the investment in training yield results over a long period of time or will results be immediate.	• Did the participants perceive learning to be relevant to their current job? • Did the participants have sufficient knowledge to make necessary changes and to implement the learning? • Did the participants have the necessary capacity to learn and perform? • Did the trainer provide skilled guidance? • Does the organisation provide adequate opportunities and facilities for the trainees to use new skills and knowledge? • Have we taken into account that the trainees have different starting points and will therefore have different finishing points?	• Were the participants' perceptions and expectations of the programme equal to what it turned out to be? • Did we design a proper training course and use proper work-based programmes? • How can the present programme be improved? • Was the training environment such that it fostered a good relationship between trainer and trainee? • Are the correct mechanisms used to evaluate training? • Does the evaluation deal with sub-text as well as the obvious?

Sponsor (Senior Management)

According to Rye (1988) organisations invest in training and development as an act of faith and little evaluation of either the training and development intervention or the people involved in it is carried out. Newby (1992) suggests that top management will carry out both formal and informal evaluations of training programme participants. At the formal level, he identified the use of performance and productivity appraisal, attitude surveys and costs/benefit analysis studies as key indicators while informal evaluation involved assessment of particular participants.

Garavan (1994) illustrates that top managers use a wide range of quantitative and qualitative evaluation measures. Increased productivity and flexibility are seen as key criteria, as are the extent to which training and development facilitates change, increased performance and the extent to which good use is made of resources allocated.

Providers (Trainers)

It is generally accepted that there is a need for the provider to evaluate themselves, the product and the systems utilised in order to build on/enhance their reputation and ensure a continued commitment to training and development by their organisation. The provider is often not satisfactorily positioned to carry out evaluation of their activities. Therefore, it is important to call on an independent agent to undertake it. Garavan (1995) has researched the evaluation criteria of training and development specialists. They are primarily concerned with the quality and relevance of training and development interventions to others in the organisation and the meeting of the objectives set out in the training programme. Irish training and development specialists tend to under-emphasise qualitative measures however. They are less concerned about performance improvement and the enhancement of the career planning/promotion process.

The Participants

Participants evaluate themselves in a personal and private way and compare themselves with other trainees. They can also be formally directed to do so in a structured manner as part of the training and development intervention. Formal evaluation usually requires the participant to assess the trainer. Participant perceptions of the provider and the product will usually be subject to differing individual viewpoints and the group dynamics within the training situation. In many situations however the participant has a limited involvement in the evaluation process. Research by Garavan (1995) suggests that participants use a wide range of criteria and those most often cited included; the level of involvement in decisions about training and development and the level of financial support given for training and development initiatives of a personal development nature. The achievement of certification and the elimination of performance gaps is also significant to participants. Participants are also concerned with process-type criteria such as the amount of feedback received from the trainer and the enjoyment of the programme.

Line Managers/Supervisors

Line managers have a central role to play in the training and development process, particularly on the route towards continuous employee development. However, while many organisations may espouse such a philosophy, there is limited evidence of widespread practice and acceptance of these responsibilities by line managers. Leicester (1989) found that there was little implementation of continuous development policy at line manager level. However, in organisations where line managers were trained in interpersonal skills and had an explicit responsibility for managing people, employees were more likely to be trained.

Garavan (1995) found that line managers give considerable emphasis to the attainment of skilled performance in the shortest possible time and the contribution of training and development activities to cost savings within the department. They are also concerned with their level of involvement in the training and development process and tend to have a short-term perspective on the payback from training and development.

The Agent

The aim of the agent is to provide a "warts and all" assessment. Elliott and Knibbs (1981) recommend that the agent carry out an evaluation of the expectations of all the stakeholders in order to pinpoint areas of agreement and disagreement. This will require the agent to explore alternative evaluation methodologies and data collection methods.

HISTORICAL AND THEORETICAL DEVELOPMENT OF TRAINING EVALUATION

Theories on evaluation are not new. The first formal evaluation was carried out in the US in 1943 as part of the Training Within Industry Scheme (TWIS) implemented in response to the expansion of production during the Second World War. The TWIS is a ten-hour training package for supervisors. Over one million supervisors received such training. Results from the scheme indicated that in two-thirds of the companies, production increases of more than 25 per cent had been recorded. Although it is probable that production increases were caused by factors other than training, the evidence was impressive enough to retain the scheme in existence. The concept of evaluation did not materialise until quite a number of supervisory groups had been trained and evidence was needed to justify further expenditure on the training programme. From this tenuous base training evaluation spread to other countries. However, there have been significant developments in the field of training evaluation since the TWIS.

Scientific/Experimental Approaches and Goal-based Evaluation

Training evaluation has an educational antecedent. Measurement and assessment of people became popular at about the same time as scientific management was influential. Tyler (1950) was one of the most influential people in this area. He proposed an approach which has a number of phases as follows:

1. Collect, from as wide a constituency as possible, a pool of objectives which might be related to the curriculum.

2. Screen the objectives carefully to select a subset which covers the desirable changes.

3. Express these objectives in terms of the student behaviours which are expected.

4. Develop instruments for testing each objective. These must meet acceptable standards of objectivity, reliability and validity.

5. Apply the instruments before and after learning experiences.

6. Examine the results to discover strengths and weaknesses in the curriculum.

7. Develop hypotheses about reasons for weaknesses and attempt to rectify these.

8. Modify the curriculum and recycle the process.

His model was a significant advance over existing evaluation systems which were based on judgement. Using the scientific approach it was hoped that a direct link between training and changes in work performance could be drawn. Partlett and Hamilton (1977) argue, however, that this approach fails to account for the dynamic nature of the training and development process, i.e. unexpected and unintended consequences. Furthermore, it does not deal with the sophisticated and complex nature of trainees. The following quotation by Davies et al (1987) highlights the clinical nature of the approach.

> Students — rather like plants — are given pre-tests (the seedlings are weighed and measured) and then submitted to different experiences (treatment conditions). Subsequently, after a period of time, their attainment (growth or yield) is measured to indicate the relative efficiency of the methods (fertilisers) used.

A Systems Evaluation Approach

This approach advocates analysis of the total system and the relationship between sub-systems. The purpose of the evaluation is to improve the interface between the sub-systems in such a way as to increase the effectiveness of the total training and development system. Ross, Freeman and Wright (1979) identify four questions which would be asked within a systems approach.

- Is the programme reaching the target population?

- Is the learning intervention effective?

- How much did the learning intervention cost?

- Is the learning intervention cost-effective?

Bramley (1991) is highly critical of this approach. He suggests that the questions are posed by policy-makers who are interested in the facts and not the opinions. There are also difficulties relating to the representation of data collected. The findings may not be representative of all the stakeholders.

A Naturalistic Approach

This approach was introduced in direct response to scientific approaches. The most potent criticism of experimental/scientific approaches was made by Cronbach (1963). He put forward three criticisms:

- If evaluation is to be of use to training and development specialists it needs to focus attention on how decisions are made. This requires an identification of the stakeholders, their priorities and the evaluation criteria they will use.

- Evaluation should focus on "improving" purposes rather than summative purposes.

- Evaluation used for developing a particular programme would be more useful if focused on performance characteristics of that programme rather than on making comparisons between programmes.

There have been a number of contributions which fit within the naturalistic approach: Scriven (1972) proposed that the evaluator should not set out to discover what the designer's objectives are. Objectives- or goal-based evaluation will yield a measure of intent that may reflect all that has been achieved. The evaluator looks for the expected and tends not to recognise unanticipated changes. The goal-free method would overcome this problem as the evaluator is deliberately unaware of the objectives of the learning intervention and thus able to pick up unintended effects. The general consensus is that this model has remained at a conceptual level with little attempt to apply it to practice. Bramley (1991), among others, suggests that goal-free methods were overstated as a reaction to goal-based evaluation.

Another contributor, Stake (1978), used the term "responsive evaluation" to describe a strategy in which the evaluator is less concerned with the objectives of the programme than with its effects in relation to the key stakeholders. Responsive evaluation requires identification of stakeholders and their different positions. The evaluator then makes personal observations of the programme in order to get a direct sense of what it is about. These observations will allow the conceptualisation of issues and problems which the evaluation should address.

The third contribution is by Partlett and Hamilton (1977). They describe a form of evaluation which they label "illuminative evaluation". Its primary concern is with description and interpretation rather than with measurement and prediction. They reject the classical evaluator's stance of seeking an objective truth and instead acknowledge the diversity of questions posed by different stakeholders. Legge (1989) largely supports this view. She suggests that research on the evaluation of organisational change interventions is often of little use to the practitioner, because it is too rigorous and many factors of interest are left out. Secondly, most of the research is so badly designed it is not possible to draw conclusions. She suggests that a contingent approach be adopted which addresses four major questions to stakeholders: Should the programme be evaluated? What functions should the evaluation serve? What approach best matches the functional requirements? What constraints will be placed on the intervention because of the evaluation approach?

Figure 18.3 outlines three different models of evaluation.

STEPS IN THE TRAINING AND DEVELOPMENT EVALUATION PROCESS

Let us further examine the process of evaluation in terms of a logical sequence of events.

Identifying Evaluation Goals

This is a very important stage of the process because it determines the overall structure of the evaluation effort and defines the parameters that influence later stages of the evaluation. Some evaluation goals are qualitatively different from others. For example, some goals may relate simply to measuring trainee reactions subjectively, while others may be concerned with measuring changes in trainee performance back on the job.

Figure 18.3: Models of Evaluation

	Scientific	**Systems**	**Naturalistic**
Period	1950s	1970s	1980s
Expected outcome	Scientific proof	Improvement	Understanding processes
Typical methods	Measures, controls, statistics	Focus on events objectives, feedback and control	Qualitative, grounded, progressive, focusing
Features	• Rigorous • Distanced	• Pragmatic • Semi-involved	• Rigorous • Highly involved
Problems	• Results ambiguous • Does not explain cause and effect.	• Not practical • Limited view of training and development • Informal feedback often more useful.	• Hard to generalise • May lose independence • Labour intensive • Not so convincing.

Source: Easterby-Smith, M. (1986), *Evaluation of Management Education Training and Development*, Aldershot: Gower.

Hamblin (1974) suggests five levels of evaluation. He argues that they are linked in a causal chain. Training leads to reactions which in turn leads to learning. Learning has an effect on job behaviour, on the organisation and on the achievement of ultimate goals. The level at which evaluation is required must first be selected, and then the objectives which the training is to achieve at that level must be specified. The evaluation task is to assess whether or not the objectives have been achieved. The levels are as follows:

1. *Reactions*: The reactions of trainees to the training experience itself. Trainees are asked how useful or even how enjoyable they feel the training is, what they think of the individual sessions and speakers, what they would like included or taken out and so forth.

2. *Learning*: Evaluation at the learning level requires the measurement of what trainees have learned as a result of their training — the new knowledge, skills, and attitudes they have acquired.

3. *Job Behaviour*: At this level evaluation attempts to measure the extent to which trainees have applied their learning on the job. This constitutes an assessment of the amount of transfer of learning that has taken place from the training to the job itself.

4. *Organisation*: Evaluation at this level attempts to measure the effect of changes in the job behaviour of trainees on the functioning of the organisation in which they are employed.

5. *Ultimate Value*: This measure of how the organisation as a whole has benefited from the training in terms of greater profitability, survival or growth.

Developing an Evaluation Strategy

Harrison (1992) suggests five different kinds of evaluation strategy:

1. *The Value-for-Money Strategy*: Hall (1984) suggests that this strategy is appropriate to use when top management's view of training and development is that if it cannot prove its financial worth then it should not be done. A value-for-money approach will address the following issues: the identifiable costs of training both direct and indirect; identifiable benefits to the firm in financial terms; comparison of costs and benefits to give a cost-benefit ratio; determining whether other types of learning events, or other media would be more cost-beneficial.

2. *Investment-Value Strategy*: This strategy puts an emphasis on assessing not only the immediate cost-benefit of learning events, but also whether the end results are of real value to the organisation. A learning event may be highly cost-beneficial but it may not have been the most appropriate one to use.

3. *Objectives-Centred Strategy*: Here the client and the training and development specialist work together to set objectives for the learning intervention. The strategy utilises the concept of a learning contract, where both parties agree jointly on the kinds of outcomes to measure, how these are to be measured and undertake to accept the final evaluation.

4. *Auditing Strategy*: This strategy involves a comprehensive assessment of the learning event and the training and development function. We will consider it later in this chapter when we discuss audits.

5. *Business-Led Strategy*: The essential considerations here relate to where the organisation is going in terms of workforce characteristics and the role that training and development can play. This strategy

would fit in to the business-led model of training and development that we discussed in Chapter 8. Hendry et al (1991) comment that overall business performance does not of itself provide a evaluative feedback for training and development. However, it does highlight the costs of not training/developing employees.

Selecting and Constructing Measurement Tools

Having decided on a particular evaluation strategy, the evaluator must select or construct the measurement tools that best fit the data requirements. It is necessary for the evaluator to judge in advance the tool's reliability and validity in order to establish a match between the data and the tool.

Reliability answers the question: "Does the tool provide a consistent and accurate measure of the behaviour being assessed?" Validity is a more complex concept and is therefore a lot more difficult to establish. A measurement tool is valid if it meets certain criteria, which include face validity, content validity, and start validity. The following are some of the tools commonly used: questionnaires; performance assessments; tests; observation checklists; problem assimilations; structured interviews; performance records.

The type of measurement tool an evaluator selects will vary according to the level of evaluation that needs to be carried out. If the evaluator is concerned with the measurement of individual cognitive abilities, then data collection and analysis techniques need to go beyond the traditional types. For example, detailed measures of recall, error, and reaction time, can be built into the training as it is being undertaken.

Analysing Evaluation Data

This stage of the process involves the ability to tie the results of the data-gathering effort to the original goals of the evaluation. The following questions are asked:

- Is the information collected relevant?

- Is the evaluation strategy gathering enough information to answer the key questions raised?

- Is the measurement procedure disruptive to the training and development activities?

- Are the analytical procedures appropriate for answering the questions raised?

Timing of Evaluation

Figure 18.4 outlines three key time periods for carrying out evaluation. Each of these time periods have specific considerations associated with them. Planning and consultation are vital requirements if the evaluation of training is to be a productive activity.

METHODS OF EVALUATION

There are many methods of evaluation available to the training and development specialist. Some of these are discussed below.

Post-Programme Assessments

These are commonly referred to as "happiness sheets" because trainers are usually ask that they be completed immediately after the training intervention has finished. The research (Dawson, 1995) illustrates that they are the most frequently used method of evaluation. They provide the training and development department with a useful means of assessing how trainees have received the training. This data can provide useful insights into the design components of the programme. It can be particularly useful in assisting the training specialist in evaluating the effectiveness of different learning methods. This is perhaps where the method can make its most significant contribution.

Pre- and Post-Programme Tests

This is a useful and scientific way of assessing the level of learning which has taken place. It can take the form of a knowledge questionnaire, a practical orientation test, or some form of work demonstration which is assessed by the trainer. These provide objective information and, if administered before the programme, can demonstrate the actual level of learning which took place, forming the basis of useful feedback for the individual participants.

Job Behaviour Questionnaires

A systematic approach to evaluation can involve an examination of how the training-influenced job behaviour in the long term. This requires evaluation to be carried out at various intervals following the programme. These questionnaires may be distributed to line managers and supervisors or they may be used in conjunction with interviews. Specific questions which may be included are:

- What benefits have trainees gained and what opportunities have they had to apply the learning?

- What barriers to learning transfer were encountered?

- What specific job behaviour change took place since the training?

- How has the line manager facilitated the implementation of the learning?

Figure 18.4: Key Time Periods for Evaluations of Training

Pre-Training	• The reason for training should be established. Trainees should be aware of the purpose of the training, as it applies both to them personally and to the company. • Needs assessment evaluation should include more than skills measurement. Information on company and trainee expectations provides useful information for the training agency and important feedback for both the company and the trainee which may not otherwise occur. • It may be appropriate to carry out a self-evaluation exercise with trainees.
During Training	• It is important to respond to the views and needs of trainees throughout the programme. Trainers need to be vigilant throughout the course and sufficiently flexible and accommodating. • Informal contact with trainees throughout the programme or through the use of "happiness sheets". • "Happiness sheets" should be used as long as the trainer is aware of their limitations. Non-responses must be followed up.

Post-Training	• Management should be encouraged to provide feedback about trainees. This should assist implementation of training and facilitate re-entry to the work situation. Feedback to trainers helps improve future programmes.
	• Where possible, encouraging trainees to remain in contact with each other on a formal or informal basis can be supportive.
	• Long-term follow-up evaluation of trainees
	    – provides a more comprehensive assessment for both training agency and sponsor.
	    – reinforces the message of the training programme for the trainee.

The key criteria for success when using questionnaires are timing, involvement, and question design. Timing is important. Trainees should receive the questionnaire at a time when they are ready to complete it. Involving the trainee in the evaluation process can improve the response rate. The questionnaire should be pilot-tested to get feedback from line managers and trainees. All of these lend credibility to the training evaluation process.

Trainee Interviews

It is often useful to interview former trainers to assess in detail the effectiveness of the training. Interviews are most effective if they follow a structured pattern and allow for comparison of responses. The interview method is time-consuming and demands the commitment of resources. It does, however, allow the training and development specialist to gain a significant amount of information covering knowledge, skill and attitude assessment. If such a method is combined with another evaluation technique, it can provide the training and development specialist with a good understanding of the effectiveness of the training programme.

Group interviews have been used increasingly in recent years. These elicit the views of a trainee group and are capable of yielding a wealth of feedback to the training and development specialist.

Records of Performance

Many organisations may hold performance records in the form of detailed appraisals or production related data. They can provide the training and development specialist with a clear indication of the effectiveness of the training programme. Furthermore, it should be possible to identify those employees with low performance who have not received training. This can provide evidence of a training need as well as justification for an increased training investment in the future.

Repertory Grids

Grid analysis helps trainers assess performance on two dimensions simultaneously. It enables the training and development specialist to assess the skill level attained as well as the motivational level involved. Both factors can be plotted on a grid. This method enables the trainer to assess real training requirements and to follow up the delivery of training once it is completed. Truelove (1995) suggests five uses of the repertory grid technique in the field of training and development:

- to gather information from employees about issues in preparation for the design of a questionnaire;

- to gather constructs that employees use to describe the role of the training and development function;

- to tailor the provision of training to yield the actual needs of employees by gathering information about what is important to them;

- as a counselling method to elicit information relevant to the development of staff;

- to evaluate a method of training by gathering and comparing information from trainees.

Assessment/Development Centres

Many companies now run centres designed to assess potential and to determine the development needs of employees. Each type of centre provides the training and development specialist with information which will be of use for evaluation purposes. Within the assessment centre process, the potential identified may be directly related to previous training and development interventions and may provide useful insights into its value. Development centres provide the trainer with an opportunity to check that the identified training needs of individuals are being met. Wynne and Clutterbuck (1994) suggest that information provided by development centres provides an ideal base on which to build evaluation programmes which test the effectiveness of training delivery against a set of specifically designed training needs.

Figure 18.7 at the end of the chapter lists the advantages and disadvantages of alternative evaluation tools.

SUBJECTIVITY AND THE EVALUATION PROCESS

The training evaluation process is a subjective one. The following scenarios are not uncommon where trainees are asked to evaluate an intervention:

- If trainees had a good time, if they feel they have worked hard but also had something of a holiday, they will be positive.

- In many instances, returning the sheet is a condition of leaving the centre.

- If the trainees have become cohesive as a group, it is likely they will be mostly positive and will say the same thing. Individuals who have different views will either suppress them or will not return the form.

- Because the form is filled in at the training centre, taken from participants and delivered to an interested party, the trainees still remain under the ethos of the centre and are therefore unlikely to be extremely negative unless they have been very badly treated in some area.

- Cunning trainers arrange the "best bits" at the beginning and the end. For similar reasons evaluators advise administering questionnaires when things are "on the up".

An evaluation is only as good as the instruments it uses, the means of application and the seriousness of approach. High-quality training requires high-quality evaluation which deals the sub-text issues such as the following.

The Individual Perception of Utility

Course questionnaire do not assess usefulness in a real sense — that is in a work climate, but the trainees' perception of usefulness which may be coloured by enjoyment, how much they have been entertained by the tutor etc. They may feel differently after a weekend at home or a week at work. Their opportunity, or lack thereof, to use the course content will also affect their perception. The nature of the training group and their place in it will also affect their response. Being back at work and away from the supportive nature of the group dynamic and shared experience, may result in a change of view.

Transfer of Learning

Trainees may be strongly critical of a training programme because they have not been able to transfer the learning to the workplace. It is important to recognise that the effects of training vary between individuals and departments in an organisation. In an evaluation process, subjective factors which cause this must be taken into account. Trainees have different starting points, therefore they will have different finishing points. Support and interest of their colleagues, superiors and subordinates will also vary. A mechanism for accommodating these irregularities in the evaluation process must be developed.

The Informal Evaluator

Informal evaluation of the trainees and the course is carried out by people who are close to trainees. According to Cunningham (1986), a trainee's wife, who found her husband more pleasant on his return from each part of a series of courses, encouraged him to attend regularly. Another wife resented the closeness her husband felt to a group she did not know at all, which put a strain on his continued attendance. Support or lack of it from individuals some way "related" to the trainees may affect their views, which in turn will affect their input on future courses and general behaviour.

Pre-Course Evaluation

Little work has been done on pre-course subjective issues. Individuals expectations are important, though it is usually participants' skills which are assessed and not their expectations. According to Gruenfield (1966) trainees' expectations of training influences the effect of that training upon them.

Self-evaluation

A participant will be prompted by training to engage in self-evaluation which will have a bearing on behaviour and learning. Trainees will have positive and negative feelings about being selected for, or choosing, training and will compare themselves with their colleagues. They may have to adapt to an environment which may be stressful (because of the need to adapt to a new situation) and exciting (because it offers the chance to break the rules for a few days). All of this has a bearing on their physical and mental well-being and on their views of themselves, the training programme, the trainer, the participants, the company, etc. This influences their behaviour, learning, performance and transfer and is an area largely untouched by research.

AUDITING AND BENCHMARKING THE TRAINING AND DEVELOPMENT FUNCTION

Auditing the Training Function

Murphy and Swanson (1988) describe auditing as a process that produces an official accounting and verification of the training and development function. It relies on samples of information that are critical to the organisation and key decision-makers. Auditing in the context of training and development refers to the totality of learning activities within an organisation. The aim is to get a snapshot of what is going on within the organisation in terms of learning.

Rothwell and Kazanas (1991) state that before a comprehensive review of the training and development function takes place, six preconditions must be met.

1. A training and development plan must exist. This means that the training and development specialist has succeeded in planning for long-term training needs across the organisation.

2. The purpose of each training intervention must be known.

3. There must be a clear statement of training goals. Results are sought from training for each job category and for all job categories taken together.

4. Each training and development intervention must be systematically planned and evaluated.

5. Each training and development intervention should simultaneously reflect the job requirements for its target learners, the organisational requirements and priorities, and the organisational strategy for training and development.

6. The evaluation results for each training and development intervention should be systematically collected and stored.

To carry out an audit effectively, Rothwell and Kazanas (1991) suggest that the training and development specialist should begin by setting a policy that such audits will be conducted at periodical intervals. A special committee composed of representatives of key stakeholder groups, should be formed. Regardless of who is involved, it is necessary to clarify the purpose, goals and objectives of the audit, select people who possess the skills necessary to carry it out, establish an audit plan and clarify precisely what will be done with the results once they are received.

Bramley and Hullah (1987) state that one of the key issues in auditing should be an examination of the extent to which the training and development function contributes to organisational goals. They suggest that a survey be carried out with a number of line managers to ascertain ways in which training and development could help improve the effectiveness of their department.

The survey may entail:

- a discussion of various aspects of organisational effectiveness with other members of the sample;

- asking managers or supervisors the priorities that are important in their section of the organisation;

- discussion as to what extent the present training and development provision helps with these key areas of effectiveness;

- discussion on whether some other forms of training activity might help.

Heraty (1992) found that Irish training and development specialists use a combination of what she describes as hard and soft criteria in their training audits. Hard criteria include quantitative measures, e.g. training undertaken, while soft criteria have a qualitative focus but are more difficult to measure. Table 18.1 presents the results. Hard criteria cited by respondents, include the number of days training undertaken, the contribution of training and development towards cost savings within the organisation, the numbers of training course days and exam pass rates.

Heraty suggests that these criteria may be used because of the need for the training and development function to be seen to contribute to the bottom line. Hard criteria cannot be seen as critical audit tools since they do not indicate the level of quality of training and development interventions, nor the degree to which training and development is effective.

The top seven criteria mentioned combine elements of both hard and soft criteria. The most significant soft criteria cited include meeting the needs of employees, and the provision of high-quality training and development interventions. When specialists were asked to rank the criteria in terms of their perceived importance, meeting the objectives set out in the training and development plan was seen as the most important, followed by the need to provide high-quality training, contributions towards major cost savings, providing training within allocated budgets and finally the number of employees trained. Heraty (1992) suggests that the criteria listed represent a move away from the traditional unsystematic model of training. However, the criteria used are, as yet, too short-term in orientation to fit within a strategic HRD or business-focused model of training and development.

Schendel and Hofer (1979) suggest that the outcomes of an auditing process can be used to address five key issues:

1. *Goal Consistency*: To what extent are the goals/objectives of existing training and development strategies internally consistent? Is there unified direction across training and development activities? Are they integrated with strategic business plans and human resource management policies?

2. *Design Process*: How well designed are the processes used to formulate training and development interventions?

3. *Strategy Implementation*: How well can training and development interventions be implemented? Will key stakeholders do their share and is the training and development function capable of doing its share?

4. *Indicators*: How well are training and development interventions working? Have indicators been established to provide feedback about the effectiveness of training and development interventions in the early stages of implementation?

Table 18.1: Relationship between Criteria Used to Assess Training and Development Activities, Organisation Size and Ownership

Criteria	Used	Size			Ownership		
	%	≤ 100	100-500	500 +	Irish	US/ Japan	Euro
Numbers of employees trained	72	95	78	45	89	63	62
Meeting objective in T&D plan	62	50	63	91	58	69	62
Types of T&D needs met	59	41	56	66	58	72	65
Meeting the needs of employees	58	51	58	67	52	71	60
Providing high-quality T&D activities	57	32	57	79	43	94	78
Categories of workers trained	55	65	53	41	88	56	65
Number of days training undertaken	53	88	53	51	86	57	66
T&D activities provided within allocated budget	52	46	57	63	74	64	69
Number of training programmes undertaken	47	25	48	54	49	52	43
Facilitating major changes in the organisation	47	8	45	48	32	84	42
Performance speeds after training	45	65	57	31	35	39	51
Ability to meet customer quality standards	40	24	36	45	36	45	42
Contribution towards specific cost savings	40	67	54	43	78	37	33
Improved communications	34	7	24	57	43	69	57
Number of training course days	31	45	33	43	41	33	38
Time saved by a particular method	29	57	31	27	54	22	29
Sales performance after training	28	10	32	22	35	66	47
Ability to meet demands of line department for trained staff	25	8	24	35	11	57	32
Elimination of need to recruit or employ trained staff	24	23	18	24	24	45	24
Increased individual promotability	24	9	14	43	26	43	22
Exam pass rates	19	23	18	22	46	14	18
Improved ability to recruit	14	13	17	21	17	44	20
Improved graduate retention rates	10	0	7	19	7	13	10
Ability to earn maximum bonuses	7	0	17	11	4	12	6

5. *Training and Development Intervention Content*: How well do existing or proposed training and development interventions meet the needs and conform to the values of key stakeholders inside and outside the organisation?

By addressing these issues, the training and development specialist can choose training and development interventions that are appropriate to the organisation and its environment.

Benchmarking

Auditing can allow the organisation to benchmark its training and development function. Figure 18.5 outlines a range of benchmarking terms. Benchmarking is the process of comparing the organisation's training and development function against universally accepted measures of performance. Figure 18.6 summarises a range of training and development measures that Irish firms use to benchmark their training activity. These methods encompass three broad areas: (a) measures of training activity, (b) measures of training results, and (c) measures of training efficiency.

Measures of training activity focus on the amount spent on training and development, the number of hours training per employee, the percentage of employees trained in a given year and the number of training staff per 1,000 employees.

Measures of training results focus on the reaction of training participants to the training provided, the level of learning which participants achieve, the behavioural changes brought about in trainees as a result of participation on the training programme, the cost savings which accrue to the organisation as a result of the training and the revenues and profits generated by each trainee.

Measures of efficiency focus on the training costs per participant hour and the training staff time spent on billable or key tasks.

The development of these measures will allow the organisation to make comparisons across different industries. The data available in the Irish context demonstrate that many companies do not assess the percentage of payroll spent on training and development, the percentage of employees that receive training, the average improvement in on-the-job performance, or the productivity and effectiveness of training and development staff.

Figure 18.5: Benchmarking Terms used in Training and Development

Annual Internal Training Expenditure: The total gross expenditure made by internal training organisations for education and training staff salaries and benefits, occupancy, information-systems charges, depreciation, course material, classroom rentals, communications such as catalogues or advertisements, and hiring costs for external instructors and consultants. It does not include student salaries and benefits while in training, student travel and living expenses, costs of personnel other than education and training staff, seminars or consultations paid for outside the training programme, tuition reimbursement, or customer training.

Annual Training Expenditure: The sum of tuition reimbursement and refunds and the cost of outside education such as seminars, executive education and company-sponsored residential graduate study.

Annual Training Plan: Training requirements for employees in business units.

Application: A measure of the degree to which employees apply classroom learning in the actual job environment. It may include input from the trainee, team members, subordinates, or superiors.

Business Results: A measure of the degree to which "business performance" has changed as a result of the application of training. It may include a calculation of the return on investment or other qualitative "value" analysis.

Buyer/payer: One who pays for training design, development, or delivery.

Centralised Training Function: A part of the company identified in the organisation chart with responsibility to all businesses and employees in the organisation.

Contract: Non-employees who provide services or products, such as suppliers, college professors, and instructors from other companies.

Customer: One who establishes specifications in the design and development process, pays for participants or is a participant.

Delivery: An activity or event that transfers the content of training material to the employee.

Delivery Cost: The sum of instructor fees or costs; training materials, manuals, or classroom aids; distribution; classroom rental and overhead; rental and depreciation costs for technology, equipment or software, and registration. Excluded are marketing, advertising, participant sourcing and participant salaries.

Design: Activities including identifying customer requirements; stating training purposes; defining skill, knowledge, or proficiency requirements at the end of training; translating requirements into learning objectives; selecting delivery media and methods; placing learning in sequence; and determining measurement criteria.

Design and Development Time per Learning Hour: The number of person hours (by contractors or internal staff) required for the design and development (through the pilot run) of every hour of learning.

Development: Activities including determining the subject-matter source (which may overlap with design); creating but not publishing, instructor guides, student material, and teaching aids; validating development with customers and pilot sites; working with partners or publishers (which may begin in design); selecting and certifying instructors, if needed; and planning event marketing.

Education and Training Staff: A full-time employee who fills an education and training job indicated by code or by reporting to an education and training function.

Individual Development Plan: A specific programme for training or developmental experiences such as job rotation and task-force assignments.

Integrated Human-performance System: An approach to human resources in which selection, training, appraisal, reward, and career development are driven by common criteria or competencies.

Internal: Work completed by permanent employees of the organisation.

Learning: A measure of the facts, principles, techniques, and so forth that were understood or absorbed by the trainee. It may include pre-testing and post-testing or simulation of knowledge and skills learned in class and used on the job.

Line-on-loan: Company employees whose primary role is not training, but who support education and training products and services on a rotational, project, or ad hoc basis.

Managers and Supervisors: Employees who determine the training to be implemented and pay for it.

Programme: A training event or learning experience.

Reaction: A measure of how well trainees liked a training programme and how satisfied they were with such factors as course delivery, content, materials and environment.

Source: To purchase programmes from external providers.

Sponsor: One who identifies the training need and takes responsibility for reviewing and approving programme design.

Participant Day: The total hours employees spend on internal training courses, divided by eight.

Top Training Job: The highest-level position that has full-time training responsibility.

Total Annual Training Expenditure: The sum of the annual internal training expenditure and the annual external training expenditure.

Total Company Payroll: Total wages and fringe benefits of all permanent full-time and part-time employees.

Training: Synonymous with "education and training" and "training and development".

Training-effectiveness Strategy: A formally (documented or informal plan to measure the effect of training on individual trainees or teams and on the whole organisation).

Training Organisation: The company function responsible for designing, developing, delivery, or sponsoring courses, training events, or production of learning tools or materials. Training organisations are made up of at least one full-time designated training professional.

User: A participant in a training programme.

In its most general sense, benchmarking of the training and development function is worthwhile because it provides information which can be used by the specialist to improve the contribution of training and development to the organisation. Phillips (1984) observes that benchmarking is important because it makes good economic sense to assess the value of planned learning, it demonstrates results to top managers, provides the training and development function with an indication of its standing relative to training and development functions in other organisations, leads to greater satisfaction among training and development staff members because they receive feedback on results and promotes increased professionalism in training and development. Rothwell and Kazanas (1991) point out that benchmarking stimulates improvement generally, providing feedback which triggers additional plans and actions.

SUMMARY

In this chapter we considered the evaluation, auditing and benchmarking of training and development. Monitoring and evaluation are essential to the success of learning activities within the organisation. Evaluation is more often talked about than done. However, it is possible to draw a number of conclusions. Core learning events are concerned with soft skills rather than hard ones, the more difficult to evaluate. The higher up the organisation hierarchy the learning event occurs, the more difficult the evaluation task becomes. Furthermore, the longer the delay in measuring the learning event, the greater the difficulty. Successful evaluation requires before and after measurement using measures that are apt, systematic, objective and feasible. Our discussion reveals that measurement must be a collaborative process involving all of the stakeholders.

Auditing and benchmarking is a logical extension of evaluation. These activities help the training and development function to make an effective contribution to organisational goals and to adopt a strategic approach to its activities, values and focus.

Figure 18.6:   Training and Development Benchmarks Used by Irish Organisations

Metric Name	Metric Type	Model for Calculation
Percent of payroll spend on training	Training Activity	Total training expenditures ÷ total payroll
Training pounds spend per employee	Training Activity	Total training expenditure ÷ total employees served
Average training hours per employee	Training Activity	Total number of training hours (hours x participants) ÷ total employees served
Percent of employees trained per year	Training Activity	Total number of employees receiving training ÷ total employee population
Training staff per 1,000 employees	Training Activity	Number of HRD staff ÷ total employee population x 1000
Average percent of satisfied training customers	Training Results: Reactions	Total number of customers rating HRD services "good" or "effective" ÷ total number of customers who completed customer satisfaction surveys
Average percent gain in learning per course	Training Results: Learning	Average percent of learning gain (difference between pre- and post-test) for each training programme, averaged over all programmes examined.
Average percent of improvement in on-the-job performance after training per course	Training Results: Behaviour	Average job-performance gain (difference between pre- and post-training behaviour) for each class, averaged over all classes measured.
Cost savings as a ratio of training expenses	Training Results: Bottom Line	Total savings in scrap or waste ÷ pounds invested in training
Revenues per employee per year	Training Results: Bottom line	Total yearly revenues or sales ÷ total number of employees
Profits per employee per year	Training Results: Bottom Line	Total yearly gross profits ÷ total number of employees
Training costs per participant hour	Training Efficiency	Total costs of training ÷ total number of hours of training
Billable rate (time on task)	Training Efficiency	HRD staff time spent on billable or key tasks ÷ total HRD staff time

Figure 18.7: Advantages/Disadvantages of Alternative Evaluation Tools

Method	When Used	Advantages	Disadvantages
Personality Tests	Useful to assess post-course personality change	• Help to distinguish patterns in response to a number of questions answered by a large number of people. • They may help in selecting managers for particular forms of training and development. • They can be used in a pre- and post-situation.	• It is assumed that an individual's personality is a fixed trait and does not change over time. • Unless appropriate standards and norms have been developed in advance, it can be very difficult to interpret individual results. i.e. they can only be used by someone who is professionally trained in their use.
Attitude Scales	At any stage of training and development process	• Measures strength of attitudes, without individual's knowledge of what is being measured. • They are less technical than personality tests. • They allow for comparison of results. • They can be used in a pre- and post-training evaluation situation.	• Scales are tedious and large numbers of questions are necessary to get an accurate measurement of a single attitude. • Difficulties arise in interpretation unless a bank of data has been built up from previous occasions. • Attitude scales can be difficult to construct. • The quality of insights gathered may be poor.

Method	When Used	Advantages	Disadvantages
Rating Scales	At the end of a course	• Give trainees an opportunity to rate the course. • Are very straight forward as they only ask one question for each objective • They are extremely flexible • They allow the evaluator to identify the problem areas • They are easily constructed • They are a low technology way of getting quantitative data.	• Trainee may give negative report because they did not get on well on the programme. • They do not give much indication of what may be done to solve a problem • Problems arise when seeking to interpret rating scales • They should only be used as a supplement to more extensive evaluation • They may ignore important variables.
Attainment Tests	When training is completed	• Focus on outcomes derived from management training. • Can be used to make pre- and post-course comparisons.	• They are difficult to construct (i.e. to make the wrong answers look right). • They are difficult to evaluate if the participant has not understood what they are supposed to have learned. • Participants may focus on answering the questions asked and possibly not learn anything.

Method	When Used	Advantages	Disadvantages
Observation	At any time during the programme	• Excellent for immediate evaluation of the learning • Can provide a large amount of information • May be used in conjunction with other methods • May be possible to use some framework or workshop • A relatively cheap method • A useful mechanism for giving feedback.	• Not suitable for assessing long-term results. • Data gathered may be inconsistent • Need to have a trained observer • Can only observe a small sample of employees • Observer may be viewed with suspicion.
Assessment/ Development Centres	Can be used before or after the programme	• They use multiple methods and dimensions • They have relatively high validity • They provide a large amount of information to the training specialist • They can serve multiple purposes • Pre- and post-course comparisons are possible • Excellent for the assessment of skill changes and behaviour/attitudes.	• They are very costly to administer • They require specialist expertise to set up • Participants may perceive that there is a hidden agenda • They require time and high involvement from participants • Not useful for rapid or immediate feedback.

Method	When Used	Advantages	Disadvantages
Participant Reaction Questionnaires	At the end of course to assess trainees reaction to the programme	• Helps gain information which directs improvements in the programme • Facilitates the justification of training costs to management • They can be used to obtain data from large numbers of people without much cost • They are useful in conjunction with other methods • They are relatively easy to analyse • They provide a vehicle for expression without fear of embarrassment • Interviewer bias is avoided • Uniform data are gathered that allow for comparisons.	• There is an expectation that training should be entertaining • Participants may not have sufficient knowledge to answer questions • Learning is perceived as passive, not active • Questions may be in an area the participants do not see as important • They are more useful for gathering superficial data than "in depth" data • They can not adapt easily to changing circumstances and needs • The response rate to questionnaires can be very low • They are complex to design • The responses are subject to bias and group dynamic effects • The return of questionnaires is difficult to achieve • Questions may have different meanings to different people.

Method	When Used	Advantages	Disadvantages
Interviews	At any stage	• Allows the training to influence the process of evaluation • Can be deep and flexible and provide the opportunity to check out meanings in both directions • They are a natural way of gathering data when people are at hand • Interviews may be particularly suited to evaluations that are intended to serve the purposes of improving or learning • Feelings of the trainee are revealed • The interviewer can observe and calculate non-verbal behaviour • A high rate of participation is provided • The interviewer has an opportunity to follow up or probe for leads • Respondents are allowed maximum opportunity for free expression.	• They are time-consuming and expensive • Respondents may feel they are being put on the spot • Quantification of results may be difficult • Scheduling of interviews may be difficult • The overall reliability of responses can be limited • Interview responses are sometimes biased.

Method	When Used	Advantages	Disadvantages
Critical Incident Method	For specific measures. Before start. After completion.	• This information may have high credibility when convincing senior management or stakeholders about the value of the training • Contributes to the objectives of training • It has the ability to focus on identifiable issues and events and to evaluate in some depth • It produces anecdotes and examples which are very close to normal managerial language • Provides a very useful complement to a more comprehensive evaluation study.	• It focuses on a very small sample of the total range of incidents • The sampling depends on whatever the respondent decides is of significance • The high degree of control given to respondents over the content provided may be unacceptable to the evaluator • Participants may not record the critical incidents carefully • There may be differences of interpretation.

19

STRATEGIC HUMAN RESOURCE DEVELOPMENT

INTRODUCTION AND LEARNING OBJECTIVES

The final chapter of this book focuses on a theme we have touched on at various stages — strategy-driven training and development. This we label strategic human resource development. Having read this chapter you will understand:

♦ the factors that have led to the emergence of strategic human resource development;

♦ the nature of strategic human resource development and how it differs from traditional training and development;

♦ the extent to which companies adopt a strategic approach in their training and development;

♦ the elements necessary to have strategic human resource development operate within the organisation;

♦ the key trends in human resource development in the next five years;

♦ the characteristics of a training and development function that practices strategic human resource development.

THE EMERGENCE OF A STRATEGIC HUMAN RESOURCE DEVELOPMENT PERSPECTIVE

There are many critical factors which organisations must consider as they face into the future. Technology is advancing at a frenetic pace, especially in relation to the transfer and accessibility of information and the increasing ease of establishing communication networking facilities. The continuing removal of trade barriers and tariffs, the consequent globalisation of markets, the volatility of consumer demand within existing markets, currency fluctuations and political upheaval are by now familiar characteristics of an environment where "all is flux". The capability of people to cope and manage within such an environment is a vital element in the success of any business and ultimately a determinant in national economic performance. The new business context is prompting senior management to take a greater interest in the development of their organisations' human resources.

Some specific triggers can be identified which have helped to generate this interest:

- difficulties in recruiting skilled, competent managers;

- the need to develop a more flexible and adaptable skill base;

- a demand for leadership and team-building skills at all operational and administrative levels;

- a requirement for all organisational functions to adopt a strategic focus;

- the need to integrate the potential of all employees with business objectives;

- a greater emphasis on performance evaluation and management;

- the increasing necessity for human resource and succession planning.

These are among the significant forces which are underpinning the promotion of strategic human resource development (HRD) in more and more organisations. As an essential cog in the machinery of managing organisations, the HRD function is being looked at to provide effective solutions to many business problems. Figure 19.1 outlines important strategic pressures relevant to human resource development activities.

Within most formulations of HRM, training and employee development represents the vital if not the pivotal component. Keep (1989) argues that the case for a strategic approach to training and development is easily made if human resource management is to have significant meaning. Bratton and Gold (1994) argue that a move to strategic human resource management is a powerful signal of a subsequent emphasis on HRD. They identify three specific signals. First, the replacement of the words "training cost" with "investment" should allow people involved in HRD to take a long-term view of its outcomes. Second, HRD acts as a triggering mechanism for the progression of other HRM policies that are aimed at recruiting, retaining and rewarding employees (who are recognised as the qualitative difference between organisations). Third, HRD harbours the prospect of unleashing the potential of all employees.

Figure 19.1: Strategic Pressures Impacting on the Training and Development Function

New Technology
- Technical changes in products, processes and information systems
- Redesigned managerial work
- Decision support systems eroding the difference between technical and general managers
- More information, power and knowledge at lower levels
- Market need for more rapid product development

The Drive for Quality
- Business pressures for higher quality design of products and delivery of service
- Top-quality programmes requiring deeper understanding of internal customer-supplier workings
- Knowing how to deliver what the customer wants

New Competitive Arrangements
- Changes in regulatory contexts such as privatisation, deregulation, conversion to agency status
- Increase in strategic alliance and joint venture arrangements
- Increasing number of acquisitions, mergers, takeovers and diversifications

Internationalisation of Business
- "Globalisation" of business markets
- Redrawing of new economic groupings, e.g. Single European Market, Pacific Rim

More Flexible and Responsive Organisation
- Decentralisation in mature and declining industries
- Short-term performance improvement pressures
- An increased number of people operating at the boundary of the organisation
- Moving from bureaucracies to "adhocracies"
- Reduced rules and formalisation, product and national boundaries within the organisation
- Accelerated movement of small firms through start up, growth, maturity and decline stages.

Supply of Resources
- Demographic pressures reducing the supply of human resources
- Limited mobility of staff (e.g. north/south divide) creating a need to manage with what is available
- Educational provision unable to match organisational demand
- Long-term shift from a buyer's to a seller's labour market in specific regions of the country
- Growth of the "me" culture with demand for individual development

Bratton (1992) argues that the inspiration for western organisations to reap the benefits from HRD has come from the success of Japanese companies. Brown and Read (1984) highlight the conviction of Japanese management that business success based on high standards of performance was dependent on a highly trained and developed workforce. They found that training and development policies were always constructed in the same context as business plans and strongly related to them.

HRD cannot be integrated into strategy unless senior managers want that to happen. The "conversion" of senior managers presents difficulties, however. The literature suggests that many managers view strategy as deliberate and purposeful. Senior managers scan the environment, develop alternative strategies and formulate plans. This suggests that the extent to which HRD becomes a feature of strategy depends on the ability of top managers to see important environmental trends in HRD terms, i.e. learning opportunities. Pettigrew, Hendry and Sparrow (1988) recognise the importance of a positive culture for HRD and the existence of HRD champions among senior managers who contribute to a company philosophy that supports HRD in espoused terms at least. Such a top-down view of strategy is not shared by everyone. Mintzberg (1987) provides a view of strategy formulation which can foster learning within an organisation if senior managers allow it. He argues that strategies can emerge from the actions of employees. The process requires the reconciliation of emergent learning with deliberate control. Within this perspective integrating HRD into strategy requires the development of the senior management so that the dilemmas between control and emergent learning are resolved.

DEFINING STRATEGIC HUMAN RESOURCE DEVELOPMENT

Ever since the arrival of the term "human resource development", it has come to be used in many different contexts. This has led to considerable confusion with various individuals, organisations and professional bodies applying the label to widely differing activities. Nadler and Nadler (1989) define human resource development as organised learning experiences provided by the employer, in a specified period of time for the purpose of increasing job performance and providing growth for individuals.

ASTD (1990) contend that HRD includes training and development, organisation development and career development. However, there are some commentators who would exclude the latter two activities. Other definitions by Hall (1984) and Caccioppe, Warren-Langford and Bell (1990) emphasise the strategic dimensions. Harrison (1992) points out that the phase HRD is now used to the undoubted annoyance of many who prefer softer phrases such as "employee development" and "training and development." She defines it in a strategic context as developing people as part of an overall human resource strategy. It involves the provision of learning experiences in the workplace in order that business goals can be achieved. She argues that it involves the alignment of training and development activities with the organisation's mission and strategic goals so that, through enhancing the skills, knowledge, learning ability and motivation of employees at all levels, there will be continuous organisational and well as individual growth. Garavan (1992) defines it as the strategic management of training development and management/professional education interventions aimed at facilitating the achievement of organisational goals, while at the same time ensuring the full utilisation of the knowledge and skills of employees.

Guest's (19921 comments on strategic HRD would support this definition. He points out that human resources can be integrated into strategic plans. If human resource policies cohere, if line managers have internalised the importance of human resources and this is reflected in their behaviour and if employees identify with the company, then the company's strategic plans are likely to be more successfully implemented. The terms "strategy" and "strategic" have been frequently mentioned. Ogbanna and Wilkinson (1988) have defined corporate strategy as a firm's relationship with its environment, its main objectives and its means of accomplishing them. Therefore, strategic HRD must be seen as a proactive corporate activity as opposed to a reactive activity.

The view is supported by Beer and Spector (1989) who consider the differences between traditional training and development and strategic HRD as follows: Strategic HRD can be viewed as a proactive, system-wide intervention, with it linked to strategic planning and cultural change. This contrasts with the traditional view of training and development as consisting of reactive, piecemeal interventions in response to specific problems. HRD can only be strategic if it is incorporated into the overall corporate business strategy. It is in this way that the HRD function attains the status it needs to survive and to have a long-term impact on overall business performance and respond to significant competitive and technological pressures.

Rothwell and Kazanas (1991) further elaborate on the differences between traditional training and strategic human resource development.

- Strategic human resource development is more positive than traditional training. It advocates the involvement of many stakeholders rather than simply the training and development function acting as a provider.

- Strategic human resource development puts less emphasis on the role of experience. Traditional training activities provide individuals who are lacking in knowledge and skills with structured opportunities to receive the fruits of deskilled organisational experience. When viewed this way, training and development is a maintenance subsystem, intended to improve organisational efficiency by increasing routinisation and predictability of human behaviour. It is appropriate to rely on experience if future events and situations will be similar to the past. However, experience is not always appropriate in preparing for the future. Strategic human resource development advocates that individuals should anticipate knowledge and skills needed in the future rather than react after problems become apparent.

Megginson and Pedlar (1992) point out that HRD is not simply about training, although training activities are an important component. The tendency to equate one with the other is a fundamental misconception and therefore clouds people's expectations of what to expect from the training and development function. They point out that training departments suffer from structural and management limitations which mean that on their own they can never give the quality of service and contribution to individual and organisational performance that is expected of the function.

Acceptance of a definition of human resource development which has a strategic emphasis requires much of the training and development function. Megginson and Pedlar (1992) suggest nine questions which must be asked.

1. What changes in skills and competencies are required to support improved job performance in specific individuals?

2. What are the particular deficiencies in performance that need to be addressed?

3. What changes in technology, production processes and organisation culture are dependent on employees learning something new?

4. What current opportunities are provided to help staff acquire new skills?

5. Who has responsibility in the organisation for ensuring that the appropriate learning opportunities are provided?

6. How can managers and employees be persuaded to see that continuing training and development is the form rather than the exception?

7. What changes in the general behaviour of staff would improve their job performance or that of others?

8. What have we learned from our previous experiences with training and development?

9. What specific mistakes have we made and what are their implications for learning?

ASSUMPTIONS AND PHILOSOPHIES OF STRATEGIC HUMAN RESOURCE DEVELOPMENT

Harrison (1993) and Rothwell and Kazanas (1991) outline a range of values and assumptions which underpin strategic human resource development.

- Strategic human resource development assumes that there is an overall mission statement for the organisation and that the HRD effort should be related to it. It is important to link business mission to planned learning experiences so that people who question the value of HRD also question the value of the company.

- It assumes that every major plan of the organisation is weighed in terms of human skills available to implement it and alternative ways of obtaining those skills. Training and development is not the only way to obtain needed skills. There are alternative ways of finding these skills and the "where" and "how" of obtaining these skills should be explicitly considered.

- It assumes that people at all levels in the organisation share responsibility and accountability for training and development. Planned learning is an essential component of every employee's job. Strategic HRD advocates that managers, supervisors and employees should be evaluated on how well they develop themselves and contribute to the development of others. Pay decisions, promotions and transfers should depend to some extent on how well employees meet this criteria.

- It assumes that there is formal systematic and holistic planning processes within the organisation. Training and development will have difficulty in supporting organisational goals unless all plans are articulated clearly. Such planning processes will furnish opportunities for linkages and information-sharing.

Philosophy refers to the systems of beliefs and values which training and development practitioners possess. Zemke (1985) has surveyed the philosophies of HRD practitioners. Many practitioners believed the most appropriate philosophy for HRD was to prepare employees to develop specific skills necessary to perform effectively in their current jobs.

However, fewer than 40 per cent of practitioners indicated that this statement reflected their own values. Practitioners also indicated the least appropriate value, also one associated with long-term employee development, as "to help employees recognise and realise their full potential as human beings". Yet this was rated second highest statement reflecting their personal values. Zemke comments that this discrepancy between what HRD practitioners value and what they consider appropriate merely underscores the pressure they face to adapt to a short-term orientation. This however, contrasts significantly with strategic HRD which advocates proactive long-term perspectives.

RELATIONSHIPS BETWEEN BUSINESS PLANS, HR PLANS AND HRD

Rothwell and Kazanas (1989) identify a multitude of possible relationships between strategic plans, human resource plans and HRD:

1. *Top-Down Approach*: Here top managers envisage the organisation as it will exist in the future and embody this vision in a formal strategic plan. In a top-down approach, a comprehensive HR plan is necessary before strategy can be formulated to guide the HRD effort, because knowledge and skills are available from alternative sources. To use a top-down approach HRD practitioners have to link HRD plans to plans of the human resource department and the organisation. Organisation and HR plans must be decided first. This means that HRD efforts can only support these plans, if it is driven by them and has little impact on how they are formulated.

2. *Market-Driven Approach*: This perspective advocates that HRD practitioners must convince the organisation that their products and services should be utilised. Zemke (1985) argues that a major problem with this approach is the tendency of managers and employees to think about learning needs on the basis of past problems. Using a market oriented approach requires the HRD practitioner to classify employees into distinct groups, predict what knowledge or skills employees will probably need in the future, assess the knowledge/skills that are available in each group at present, decide how to close the gaps between the present and future knowledge/skills requirements, plan appropriate interventions and mount a marketing campaign to inform managers.

3. *Career-Planning Approach*: Schein (1978) argues that this is a third way of looking at the relationship between business plans, HR plans and HRD interventions. He argues that individual career plans must be taken into account if employees are to be committed to strategic

business plans. To use this approach, HRD practitioners must establish individual development programmes, identify learning experiences that will facilitate the achievement of career objectives while at the same time helping the organisation implement its business and HR plans and deliver these learning interventions.

4. *The Futuring Approach*: HRD efforts can be linked to strategic business plans through the strategy formulation process itself. Formulation can occur in formal or informal ways. The essence of training and development interventions is to analyse problems of implementation, define and clarify these problems and consider solutions. Some of these solutions may have a HRD element.

5. *Performance-Diagnosis Approach*: This approach advocates the use of training and development interventions to examine the organisation's internal strengths and weaknesses. The assessment of strengths and weaknesses provides clues about possible strategy. In analysing performance problems HRD practitioners frequently encounter information of value to strategy-making. This can be fed back to strategists for use in subsequent planning so that corrective action can be taken. This approach has the ability to project future trends and visualise possible future trends and their implications. The HRD practitioner can contribute in a number of ways: facilitate the effective interaction of strategists; facilitate strategy meetings, design structured exercises that aid decision-making; and design exercises to help management structure their thinking on strategic issues.

6. *Artificial-Experience Approach*: Rothwell and Kazanas (1991) argue that HRD practitioners can seek to link business HR plans and HRD efforts through simulations of future conditions. This can be done in planning processes using scenarios to plan what to do and how to do it under future conditions. The HRD practitioner can design learning interventions to produce artificial experience. Such interventions are designed to discover possible future learning needs. Managers create rather than receive information. In order to use this approach effectively HRD practitioners should use approaches to identify what the future may hold, prepare descriptions of future conditions, put managers through a range of exercises, discuss the results and guide managers to discover the future learning needs of the organisation.

7. *Pulse-Taking Approach*: Training and development interventions can be used effectively to collect information about how well strategic plans are being implemented. Small group activities can be used to take the pulse of the organisation.

8. *The Educational Approach*: The HRD effort can be linked to business and HRD plans by the HRD practitioner offering instruction on strategic-thinking skills. Rothwell (1985) has hypothesised that HRD departments which offer training on strategic planning are more likely to become involved in strategy formulation than those who do not. This training/education may take a number of forms:

   • education about the theory of strategic thinking;

   • education tied to training which involves theory on strategic thinking and the strategic plan of the organisation;

   • training where participants are taught specific skills they need to achieve specific objectives to use this educational approach. HRD practitioners must clarify their primary purpose (i.e. education or training) and then select appropriate interventions to meet this purpose.

9. *Interpersonal Approach*: This approach is based on the premise that a substantial percentage of corporate strategy is informal, existing only in the minds of top managers. For HRD practitioners to be aware of these informal plans, they must interact effectively with top managers. This requires practitioners who have sufficient status, credibility and interpersonal skills. It also requires an ability to pose the right questions and stimulate managers to articulate their plans.

10. *The Rifle Approach*: This approach advocates that HRD efforts should be restricted to fill a few strategic objectives of the organisation. This approach demands a highly directed, concentrated effort. To use the rifle approach, HRD practitioners should identify one or two problems lending themselves to solutions through a HRD intervention. These problems should be related to the organisation's strategic objectives. It is generally accepted that HRD practitioners should strive for as many linkages between HRD activities and business plans as possible. Rothwell (1985) argues that HRD practitioners have a responsibility to act in ways that help strategists realise their vision of the future.

THE EXISTENCE OF STRATEGIC HUMAN RESOURCE DEVELOPMENT

The Price Waterhouse Cranfield Survey (Gunnigle, 1992) clearly showed that in several European countries great interest was expressed in the increased use of training. Personnel managers in all of the countries studies listed training and development as one of the most important objectives of their function for the next three years. The results revealed that personnel managers were using training more as a recruitment strategy. Organisations in all countries had increased training expenditure over the previous three years for all categories of employees. However, the emphasis on the increase in training investment was towards the upper echelons or the organisation, particularly management. Holden (1992) reported that while expenditure on training had increased, particularly in management development, there were still many organisations where spending was below 2 per cent of salary/wages. This analysis was reinforced by survey results showing a relatively low number of days given over per annum to training. They further argued that training could not be seen as a true investment since many organisations did not know how much they spent. Table 19.1 presents the Price Waterhouse survey results on training expenditure in Ireland.

Table 19.1: Proportion of Annual Salaries and Wages Spent on Training in Ireland

% of Salaries & Wages	% of Companies N=267	% of Small Organisations N=129	% of Large Organisations N=138
0.01 - 0.5%	7%	8%	6%
0.51 - 1.00%	14%	13%	15%
1.01 - 2.00%	16%	19%	14%
2.01 - 4.00%	14%	15%	13%
4.01% +	10%	10%	10%
Don't Know	39%	35%	42%

Source: The Price Waterhouse Cranfield Project on International Strategic Human Resource Management (Gunnigle, University of Limerick, 1992)
Note: The Price Waterhouse Cranfield study used a 200-employee cut-off to distinguish between small and large organisations

The research undertaken by Felstead and Green (1993) and Dench (1993) raises the question of whether, and to what extent, increases in training amongst different occupational groups are due to employers thinking strategically about their long-term needs for human resource development and the lifetime development of employees or simply responding to immediate business needs.

There is evidence to suggest that managers are receiving special attention. Rolfe et al (1993) and Felstead and Green (1993) illustrate that managers are viewed as of central importance to the business and there is a need to meet their expectations of continuous development. Rolfe et al's study of the electronics sector in the United Kingdom reveals a mixture of practices:

- In the case of highly-qualified staff, employees appreciated that they must not only plan ahead but take account of their expectations because the consequence of little training is high staff turnover.

- In the case of staff with intermediate skills, they found evidence of employers discouraging staff from studying to degree-level because it was perceived that there might not be opportunities for them within the company and they might leave and be difficult to replace.

- In the case of production employees, they found evidence that companies were paying attention to the potential of this group but only a small number were actively training and promoting them.

Ross (1993) studied 243 small and medium manufacturing companies in England and found that training was still very much an ad hoc activity in terms of both the selection of training interventions and their evaluation. He found that the practice of evaluation was primarily about assessing the training intervention as an end in itself with an inappropriate focus on the individual. Pettigrew et al (1988) found in a sample of 20 firms that evaluation of training was mostly informal or non-existent. There were inadequate systems to support evaluation and most firms did not take a strategic approach.

A research study by the Department of Enterprise and Employment (1993) surveyed 210 Irish companies. Eighty per cent of participating employers responded positively that they provided training for their employees and 14 per cent indicated that they did not. A similar survey in 1992 found figures of 81 per cent and 19 per cent respectively. The 1993 study found that 27 per cent of micro-companies (1-9 employees) and 11 per cent of small companies (10-50 employees) did not provide training and in total 17 per cent of Irish companies responded that they did not provide any training. Table 19.2 presents the findings of the Price Waterhouse study on training activity levels. The types of training activities carried out do not suggest a focused strategic approach on the part of employees. Some training activities such as quality training, training for new technology and management development do suggest a strategic emphasis, however other categories were more operational in emphasis.

From the series of studies carried out in England and Ireland the conclusion must be drawn that no over-arching strategic view is being taken about the provision and organisation of human resource development. Indeed, Hallier, Glover and Lyon (1993) argue that the British employers' approach to human resource development is too short-term, too exclusively oriented to immediate business purposes and taking too little interest in the careers of managers. However, research by Garavan (1993) suggests that Irish organisations use a mixture of short-term and long-term considerations and are also prepared to invest in longer-term training and development strategies. Also evident is a strong emphasis on personal development.

Table 19.2: Number of Days Training per Year by Small and Large Companies for Different Categories of Employees

Category of Employee N=267		< 1 Day %	1-3 Days %	3-5 Days %	5-10 Days %	Don't Know %
Management	Total	5	33	25	6.5	35
	Large	1	31	23.5	10	34.5
	Small	-	35	26.5	3	35.5
Professional/ Technical	Total	-	34	20.5	7	38.5
	Large	-	29.5	19.5	9	42
	Small	-	38.5	21	5	35.5
Clerical	Total	1	42.5	14	4	39.5
	Large	1.5	43.5	13	2	40
	Small	.5	.5	15	6	36.5
Manual	Total	1	27.5	11	4	57.5
	Large	1.5	33.5	10	3.5	51.5
	Small	.5	22	12	5.5	60

Source: The Price Waterhouse Cranfield Project on International Strategic Human Resource Management (Gunnigle, University of Limerick, 1992)

CHARACTERISTICS OF STRATEGIC HRD

There is a growing amount of literature on the essentials of strategic HRD. We will focus on a number of the more important HRD characteristics identified in the literature.

Integration with Organisational Missions and Goals

A central feature of strategic HRD, according to the literature, is the integration of training and development into wider business planning. Human resources in this context are seen as a vital factor in business planning, and training and development are viewed as making an effective contribution to business goals. Barham et al (1988) point out that strategic HRD involves a move from activities that are fragmented to a situation where training and development is more systematically linked to such goals (referred to as the formalised approach). Burgoyne (1988), writing in the context of management development, proposes a six-level model, level six of which constitutes strategic development of the management of corporate policy. Burgoyne notes, however, that there is considerable progress to be made before many companies reach something akin to level six. Zenger and Blitzer (1981) and Zenger (1982) characterise the effective HRD function as one that keeps riveted to its organisation's goals. It is aware constantly of the mission, goals and the genuine needs of the organisation. This awareness can be achieved in both formal, highly structured and informal ways. Zenger perceives a strategically integrated function as systems-oriented, capable of seeing the macro picture and possessing the potential to develop a master plan of training and development that interlocks with the corporate master plan and overall tactical activities.

Top Management Support

Strategic HRD should command the support and participation of top management. The essential message emerging from the literature is that when management at board level treat HRD as an important contributor, the HRD function wields a higher profile.

The reality, however, is that in many cases top management are not committed to training and development activities and do not adopt the appropriate perspectives.

A relatively small proportion of Irish senior managers are educated to levels enjoyed by some of our EC partners and few have been the recipients of sustained development programmes. Consequently, training and development for their employees has not received a high priority. Like our British counterparts, there is a considerable attachment to informality in the way we conduct business. This mitigates against the adoption of a comprehensive training and development activity.

There is evidence to suggest that corporate objectives tend to be short-term in focus with business strategies defined by short-term profit and financial criteria (Kakabadese, 1990). This focus often conflicts with the long-term developmental aspirations held by training and development specialists for their employees. (Heywood, 1989; Hendry et al, 1991; Anderson and Harrison, 1993). Furthermore, the limited horizons adopted by organisations has led to the managerial ascendancy of financial specialists and a cost-control culture. Training and development specialists find themselves in a less than strategic position to push their priorities and the return on their activity is difficult to measure in financial terms.

The training and development profession itself must accept part of the blame. Research undertaken by Garavan (1992) shows that some Irish training and development specialists are apathetically acquiescent in their low-responsibility, low-status, reactive, restrictive roles and are lacking in professional qualifications and expertise. The research also highlights that where positive attitudes exist towards training and development it is often derived from a situation where a failure to train had an immediate impact on the business rather than the credibility of the training and development specialist. The study also revealed two other limiting factors: first, a considerable number of training and development specialists lack professional qualifications, for example membership of the Irish Institute of Training and Development; second, many designated training specialists did not give the highest priority to the training and development activity, spending less than 20 per cent of their time on the training. This is similar to the British situation in many respects (Hyman, 1992).

Environmental Scanning

The strategically-oriented HRD function must have continuous knowledge of its external environment. A strategic HRD function must, according to Higgs (1989), have the capacity to analyse the external environment in terms of the opportunities and threats which it presents for both the business and HRD strategy. The external environment can act as a double-edged sword for the HRD function. On the one hand, a competitive environment presents major opportunities since it highlights the role of human resources as a key component of business success. This in turn will present the opportunity to discuss HRD strategies at the highest level and ensure that the first characteristic discussed, that of integration, is achieved. On the other hand, the environment can also act as a threat to the HRD function. Stiff competition, if not tackled effectively, can reduce profit margins and consequently lead to a reduction in training budgets. This situation clearly points to the need for HRD strategy to be well positioned in the overall business context. Olson (1986) illustrates how the characteristics of the organisations' environment shape the type of HRD activities it engages in:

- Large companies spend heavily on training mainly because they have outgrown their ability to meet their skill needs. Workers are trained externally.

- High-technology companies, because of their short product life cycles, invest heavily in HRD because it is viewed as a necessary weapon in their capacity to develop new products and adapt to market trends.

- Firms operating in highly-competitive industries such as the automobile industry, the electronics industry and the financial services sector, view training as a strategic tool which allows them to deal effectively with skill shortages.

- Other service-intensive industries view HRD as a means of ensuring the success of their automated service and customer interaction systems. Invariably employees with the highest levels of environmental interaction tend to receive the most intensive training.

Pettigrew et al (1989) have modelled these and other factors and specified driving forces which help explain an organisation's inclination and capacity for general HRD activities. Two environmental factors, namely technological and product-market changes, were perceived as a major trigger for training. Their effect is greatest when they impact on the whole organisation and change the skill profile required. While these environmental forces may trigger training, the authors point out that a range of supporting factors and conditions are necessary if the HRD function is to respond accordingly.

Existence of Complementary HRM Activities

Keep (1989) argues that HRD can only be effective if there is a coherent package of complementary measures aimed at servicing various aspects of the employment relationship. Some of these measures are:

- improvements in the area of corporate manpower planning and forecasting;

- a focus on upgrading the quality of employees being recruited;

- the forging of closer links with educational institutions at all levels in the educational system

- a greater formalisation of performance appraisal and training needs procedures

- a range of career development systems both individually and organisationally focused.

Buckley and Caple (1992) rightly point out that in the past HRD has adopted a closed-system mode of thinking. This has had the consequence of making it unresponsive to organisational needs, unaware of how its activities link in with HRM activities and lacking of any significant evaluation programme. HRD must view itself as one strategy available to an organisation wishing to retain, develop and motivate its human resources. Indeed, Keep (1989) argues very persuasively that strategic training and development activities are central to the reality of anything that can meaningfully be described as human resource management. This will be considered in more detail later when discussing the possible contribution of strategic HRD.

One may conclude that not only does strategic HRD provide an impetus for a more integrated HRM approach, but it is also necessary to have a close integration between HRD and other HRM activities.

Expanded Trainer Role

There is much commentary on the present deficiencies that beset the role of the trainer in many organisations. Some of these deficiencies are worth considering:

- There is evidence to suggest that many training specialists do not view their activities as being at the cutting edge. Training specialists see that the HRD department has a relatively low status in the organisation, and therefore perceive little need to be productive in what they do. The Challenge to Complacency report (Coopers & Lybrand, 1985) suggests that this lack of internal status has led many HRD professionals into networking and contact with fellow professionals in other companies.

- Bennett (1986) rightly observed that the HRD role is burdened with many role conflicts. Three types of conflict in particular, namely the trainer's internal conflicts, conflicting priorities between the HRD function and the wider organisation, and conflicts between line departments, were highlighted. These conflicts place high demands on the skills and credibility of HRD specialists and the probability of failure in the role is high.

- There is some evidence to suggest that HRD specialists are poor at marketing their services. King (1989), Spitzer (1984) and Galvin (1990) among others, argue that an effective HRD specialist must be able to educate top management and line specialists on the potential contribution of HRD. Trainers have some difficulties in doing this. A number of reasons can be cited: lack of clarity concerning the HRD specialist's role; lack of skills and knowledge; the organisation does not make its expectations clear; the trainer perceives their role as one of maintaining the status quo.

- There is considerable evidence to suggest that the HRD specialists have limited perceptions of their roles. Handy (1990) and Leduchowicz (1984), for example, comment on the HRD specialist's tendency to confine duties to classroom and other administrative activities. Such a role perception would not be very effective within a

strategic HRD perspective. This maintenance role perception manifests itself in other ways also. King (1989) argues that there is a reluctance on the part of HRD specialists to implement new ideas or
keep themselves up-to-date on new developments. They may also
perceive the role as a temporary one in their career path and as a consequence do not wish to make errors or upset the status quo. There is
considerable evidence available to substantiate the "stepping stone"
perception of the "training job". While such a situation exists, HRD
specialists will find themselves in a vicious circle unable to command
support from organisational leaders and unable to exert their influence over the organisation's HRD activities.

Suffice it to say that a strategic focus requires considerable role-change
for the HRD specialist. Dimensions along which change is required include:

- from being passive and maintenance-oriented to being more active in
  marketing the benefits of training;

- from adopting a reactive response to taking on a more proactive role;

- from perceiving themselves as peripheral and powerless to perceiving
  the HRD function as central to the achievement of organisational
  objectives;

- from being simply learning specialists to developing a more strategic
  role. Such a role involves giving direction to the HRD function and
  ensuring appropriate policy and planning initiatives.

A strategic HRD function requires a specialist who can in Bennett's
(1986) terms be a combination of trainer, provider, consultant, innovator
and manager.

HRD Plans and Policies

An essential feature of the corporate planning process is the formulation
of business plans and policies. For HRD to be strategic in its focus, it
must undertake similar activities. Hales (1986) sets out a number of
propositions on the development of HRD plans:

- A strategic business plan must exist before a strategic HRD plan can
  be developed. An HRD plan developed separately from the business
  plan will remain short-term and operational in focus.

- Strategic HRD plans require top management sanction and involvement. A lack of involvement may result in HRD plans that are not in

line with the organisation's mission. Furthermore, this lack of involvement may result in reduced commitment at lower levels.

- If the organisation is dominated by short-term considerations in its planning the HRD plan will reflect similar characteristics.

- HRD plans are derived from both strategic business plans and an analysis of the internal and external environment. The internal and external analysis forms a critical base from which decisions are made concerning the HRD plan.

- The HRD plan provides the link between business activities and HRD activities.

Hendry and Pettigrew (1986) also recognise that HRD planning only becomes strategic when it includes monitoring of environmental trends and the modelling of alternative scenarios. When the implications of this kind of monitoring are fed into the business planning process on an ongoing and long-term basis, the opportunity may be presented for HRD planning to influence business planning rather than simply react to it. They also see the status of HRD planning improving, as it would no longer be perceived as a numbers exercise and a mere consideration of skill deficiencies.

Policies are an essential component of the implementation phase. Policy formulation has in the past been ignored in the training and development literature. However, in more recent times, there is a growing recognition of its importance within the HRD context.

Line Manager Commitment and Involvement

Zenger (1982) points out that strategically-focused HRD functions have generated an enthusiastic involvement of line managers. Such involvement can manifest itself in a number of ways, not least among them the following:

- line managers conducting training sessions;

- consultation with line managers on changes they wish to witness in their subordinate's performance;

- line managers becoming involved in the coaching and counselling of subordinates;

- line managers' learning skills being updated;

- active involvement in the HRD policy and planning processes;

- line managers being made responsible for the identification of HRD needs within their department.

Gunnigle and Flood (1990) see responsibility for continuous employee development resting with the immediate manager or supervisor. The reasons cited for this belief include the following: the line manager is best placed to assess, on an ongoing basis, the training and development needs of subordinates, and can facilitate in identifying development routes for subordinates and is ideally placed to provide advice, direction and counselling to subordinates. Mumford (1989) classifies the line manager as a key helper in the management development process, and Garavan (1987) has focused on the types of skills that line managers require to be effective participants in the HRD process. Three dimensions of the line manager's role, namely facilitating learning, specific coaching and counselling skills, and the ability to adopt a participative and shared-learning methodology, were identified.

One may conclude that strategically-oriented HRD functions must be precise/clear with line management about the support they desire and expect. They must have the ability to sell to line managers the need for their involvement. Issues of ownership and control must be clarified also.

FUTURE TRENDS IN HUMAN RESOURCE DEVELOPMENT

Addison and Haig (1994) identify eight possible trends that are likely to emerge within the HRD field, in the 1990s.

1. From operational training to the strategic development of human resources. Hilb argues that strategic human resource development has to be based on a holistic company mission which is developed by top management. Furthermore it must be linked on other human resource instruments such as selection, appraisal and reward systems.

2. From a one-dimensional to a three-dimensional approach of human resource development. Hilb argues that the definition of human resource development needs to be broadened. Training and development activities must no longer be modelled on the traditional career in promotion terms. Other career paths must come within the notion of HRD. These include, geographical, functional and divisional job rotation within the company or with outsiders and permanent job enrichment.

3. From the development of only a cadre of people to the development of all human resources. We have discussed research earlier in this chapter which illustrated that many companies still provide develop-

ment possibilities only to a cadre of employees and as a consequence do not utilise non-managerial talents. There is a considerable body of evidence which suggests that European companies will move away from this narrow view.

4. From an ethnocentric to a Eurocentric approach to human resource development. Herman and Perlmutter (1979) suggest that multinational companies have four options in terms of career development: (a) all key positions are filled by HQ country nationals, (b) all positions are filled by local nationals, (c) all key positions abroad are filled by third-country nationals and (d) a Eurocentric option where all key positions abroad are filled by the foremost talented individuals within the European operation, regardless of nationality. Hilb argues that a Eurocentric approach has many advantages including the development of transitional capabilities, the creation of greater career possibilities, and the potential to tap into rich European-wide human resources.

5. From a single man-oriented to a dual-career and family-oriented development of human resources. Schein (1982) argues that the dual-income household is well on its way to becoming the norm of the future, creating a need for new relations between home and work and thus demanding changes in both areas. Deutcheman (1990) points out that if companies want to motivate the new generations of young individual freedom-minded employees they will have to provide jobs which (a) empower managers who act as exemplary coaches and (b) incorporate permanent useful learning experiences.

6. From a past-oriented to a future-oriented approach to human resource development. Human resource development must support individual potential appraisal programmes in order to evaluate the future talents of employees. Hilb suggests that bottom-up reviews of human resource portfolios will include the establishment of action plans relating to changes in job assignments, the development of individual and dual-career plans for high potential individuals with outstanding performance, proactive out-placement activities for people with weak performance, complementary training programmes for reporting, counselling, coaching and innovative team building that meets both the needs of the individual and the organisation.

7. From mechanistic to organic learning settings. An important HRD trend in larger organisations will be the creation of a company-type university. This will be a university without walls providing a flexible structure for the training and development of employees. This trend will create immediate line involvement and ownership on the

development process. It will also operate HRD at a more sophisticated level, particularly when key managers and educational institutions are involved.

8. Greater awareness of the business cycle. As business cycles adjust to fluctuating markets and environments, the HRD manager will be called upon to run the HRD department as a business in itself. In some organisations such as the ESB, the HRD group is already expected to make a profit, or at least break even. However, unless a HRD group is selling its services to external clients for cash, it will be difficult for it to make a profit. The ability to operate a successful business is something the HRD manager will be expected to possess. They will involve the tracking of development and operating costs, assigning costs to services, getting competitive bids on work done outside the department and networking with vendors, etc.

CRITICAL ELEMENTS OF A STRATEGIC HUMAN RESOURCE DEVELOPMENT FUNCTION

Galbraith and Nathanson (1978) were among the first commentators to focus attention on the role of human resource management in strategy implementation. They emphasised the importance of various components of the human resource management process to the strategy and structure of the organisation. If, in the same manner, the human resource development function is to be strategic in orientation, then it must align itself to these important variables, i.e. strategy and structure.

For HRD to achieve a corporate perspective, it must ask itself a number of critical questions, the answers to which will determine its effectiveness within the organisation. Among these critical questions are the following:

• To what extent does the HRD specialist have regular contact with other key members of the organisation?

• Are there appropriate systems in place to allow the discussion of problems and the review of progress on specific projects?

• Does the HRD function have the expertise to diagnose organisational problems?

• Has the HRD function the appropriate expertise required to implement solutions once key problems are diagnosed?

• Does the organisation have a formal corporate HRD mission statement and/or corporate HRD policies?

- Is there a top management group or individual who gets involved in the policies and activities of the HRD function?

- Are there mechanisms in place which allow the HRD specialist to participate in corporate strategy sessions with other key managers?

- Is there a clear definition of the roles, responsibilities and policies of the HRD function?

- Are there systems in place which allow for the periodic review and/or revision of the organisation's HRD mission statement and/or corporate HRD policies?

- Are the resources of the HRD function allocated on the basis of organisational priorities?

- To what extent are HRD needs-identification processes future-oriented rather than crisis-oriented?

- What are the priorities when evaluating the results of the HRD function? What is the balance between behavioural issues and organisational results?

A strategically-oriented HRD function can make a significant contribution to the success of an organisation. This will manifest itself in the organisation's ability to innovate, the quality of its strategic decision making, individual performance and productivity, and how closely the skills of the organisation are aligned with its strategic mission and plans. Figure 19.2 suggests a number of relationships between strategic issues and training.

SUMMARY

This chapter has sought to outline some of the key features of strategic HRD as part of an integrated HRM approach. There is evidence of some progress in the way organisations view the learning process and the energy they devote to the development of a learning workforce. In a small number of organisations learning and development have become key features of the employment relationship. However, in many organisations, there are significant barriers to HRD, most significantly the attitudes of key stakeholders within the organisation. There is an emerging consensus on the elements of strategic HRD and the trends in learning that will emerge in the next five to ten years. However, there is some acceptance that negative attitudes to HRD remain the primary stumbling block.

Figure 19.2: Strategic Issues and the Link with Training and Development

Broad Issues

- The training specialist needs to understand the environment in which her or his organisation operates. Is the organisation's current industry evolving or stable? What do the growth trends in the industry look like? Who are the main domestic and foreign competitors and what is the organisation's competitive advantage over those competitors? How can or will the organisation capitalise on competitor's strategic vulnerabilities? (For example, is the organisation capable of widening the competitive gap in its favour?)

- Why has the organisation been successful in the past? What strategies has it successfully employed? What was learned during that time that can be applied under the new strategy? What forces have driven the organisation to select a new strategy?

- What technology does the organisation plan to use? If the organisation plans to use new technology, when will it come on line? Any new processes? When will they be instituted?

- Are innovations anticipated in the industry that could change the competitive playing field? Will these be radical breakthroughs or modifications to existing products or technologies? What effect would there be on the organisation's product and its competitive position?

- What new management philosophies or procedures such as constant quality pursuit (kaizen), working through teams, and participative management will be instituted by the organisation? When?

- Are there any regulatory issues — current, pending or anticipated — that could influence strategic considerations?

- What functional strategies will be employed by the various divisions or operating units to effect the overarching strategy? Why? How?

Human Resource Issues

- The training specialist needs to understand the workplace profile of the organisation. What are the current strengths and weaknesses of the workforce? In the aggregate, is the workforce technical? Is it skilled? What kind of education or training have most employees received to enter their positions? What do they need to stay current? Is it a flexible and adaptable workforce?

- What changes if any, must occur in the job(s), organisational culture, and skill level of the workforce?

- Is the organisation's decision to pursue an umbrella strategy likely to result in lay-offs or other turnover? How much is anticipated?

- How will union contract agreements be affected? What is the strategic role of the union?

- What human resource management policies should be reviewed or modified in the light of the organisation's strategic emphasis (such as selection, hiring, appraisal, rewards, or career development)?

- What are the training implications of the overarching strategy? Of each functional/operational strategy and its companion tactics? How could training help the organisation reach any or all of its strategic goals?

- What kind of specific training programs are needed? Are they needed in basic workplace, technical, product knowledge, managerial/supervisory, or motivational skills? Does the organisation have in-house capability to implement the necessary programmes? Are there outside experts who can assist? Who are they?

- How has training been regarded by the workforce in the past? By management? How credible are the programmes and the trainers? How will these views affect future training efforts?

- Does the organisation have an employee educational assistance plan (tuition reimbursement)? Do many employees take advantage of it? If so, how can it be used to enhance worker skills?

- What kind of training evaluation process is currently being used? Does it provide information on return on investment? If not, would such a process contribute to the strategic information flow?

- Is there a formal procedure to ascertain if current training is appropriate in the light of a new strategy or, alternatively, to identify training needs that will be dictated by the new strategy?

- Do human resource management functions other than training (such as selection, hiring, appraisal, rewards, or career development) need to be reviewed? Should they be modified?

Source: Adopted from (1990) Carnevale, A. P., Gainer, L. J. and Villet, J., *Training in America*, pp. 202-5, San Francisco: Jossey Bass.

REFERENCES

Addison, R. M. and Haig, C. (1994) "The HRD Manager" in W. R. Tracey (Ed) *Human Resource Management and Development Handbook*, 2nd edition, New York: AMACOM.

Adler, N. J. (1991) *International Dimensions of Organisational Behaviour*, Boston: Kent Publishing Co.

Advisory Committee on Management Training (1988) *Managers for Ireland: The Case for the Development of Irish Managers*, Dublin: Department of Labour.

Allen, R. W., Modinson, D. C., Porter, L. W., Renwick, P. A. and Mayers, B. T. (1977) "Organisational Politics: Tactics and Characteristics of its Actions", *California Management Review*, Vol. 22, pp. 77-83.

Allen, H. J., McCormick, B. and O'Brien, R. J. (1991) "Unemployment and the Demand for Retraining: An Econometric Analysis", *Economic Journal*, Vol. 101, pp. 190-201.

Altman, P. (1992) *Adult Learning and Education*, New York: Croom Helm.

American Society for Training and Development (ASTD) (1990) *Careers in Training and Development*, Alexandria: VA: ASTD Press.

American Society for Training and Development (ASTD) (1990) *Trainers' Tool Kit: Needs Assessment Instruments,* Alexandra, VA: ASTD Presss

AnCO Report (1987) *Training for the Employed*, Dublin: AnCO.

Anderson, C. (1992) *Effective Training Practice*, London: Basil Blackwell.

Anderson, G. and Harrison, R. (eds.) (1993) *Strategic Human Resource Management*, Maidenhead, UK: Addison Wesley.

Anderson, J. R. (1987) "Skill Acquisition — Compilation of Weak Method Problem Solution", *Psychological Review*, Vol. 94, pp. 192-210.

Annett, J. and Duncan, K. D. (1967) "Task Analysis and Training Design", *Occupational Psychology*, Vol. 41, pp. 211-221.

Aontas (1989) *For Adults Only: Adult and Continuing Education Provision in Ireland*, Dublin: Aontas.

Aontas (1994) Submission to the National Education Forum, Dublin Castle.

Argyris, C. (1980) "Some Limitations of the Case Method: Experiences on a Management Development Programme", *Academy of Management Review*, Vol. 5, pp. 291-298.

Argyris, C. and Schon, D.A. (1978) *Organisational Learning: A Theory of Action Perspective*, Wokingsham: Addison-Wesley.

Arment, L. (1990) "Learning and Training: A Matter of Style", *Industrial and Commercial Training*, Vol. 22, No. 3, pp. 16-21.

Armstrong, M. (1988) *Handbook of Personnel Management Practice*, London: Kogan Page, 3rd edition.

Arrow, K. J. (1962) "The Economic Implications of Learning by Doing", *Review of Economic Studies*, Vol. 29, pp. 155-173.

Ashton, D. (1986) "Current Issues in Line/Staff Relationships", *Management Education and Development*, Vol. 10, Part 2, pp. 105-118.

Ashton, D. and Easterby-Smith, M. (1980) *Auditing Management Development*, Aldershot: Gower.

Ashton, D., Maguire, M. and Spilsbury, M. (1990) *Restructuring the Labour Market*, Basingstoke: MacMillan.

Atkins, B. (1983) "To What Extent is a Systems Model Appropriate to the Diagnosis of Training Needs and the Conduct of Training in Organisations?", *Programmed Learning and Education Technology*, Vol. 20, pp. 243-252.

Atkinson, J. S. (1989) "Four Stages of Adjustment to the Demographic Downturn", *Personnel Management*, August, pp. 20-24.

Attley, B. (1994) "The New Organisation: The Trade Union Perspective", Paper presented at the IITD National Conference, Waterford.

Bandura, A. (1986) *Social Foundations of Thought and Action*, Englewood Cliffs, N.J: Prentice-Hall.

Barham, K. (1991) "Developing the International Manager", *Journal of European Industrial Training*, Vol. 15, No. 1, pp. 12-17.

Barham, K., Fraser, J. and Heath, C. (1988) "Management for the Future", Ashridge Management College.

Barro, R. J. (1991) "Economic Growth in a Cross-Section of Countries", *Quarterly Journal of Economics,* Vol. 100, pp. 407-43.

Bass, B. M. and Vaughan, J. A. (1966) *Training in Industry:The Management of Learning*, London: Tavistock Publishers.

Beardwell, I. and Holden, L. (1994) *Human Resource Management: A Contemporary Perspective*, London: Pitman.

Becker, G. S. (1962) *Human Capital: A Theoretical and Empirical Analysis,* New York: National Bureau of Economic Research.

Beckhard, R. (1969) *Organisation Development: Strategies and Models*, Reading, MA: Addison-Wesley.

Beer, M. and Spector, B. (1989) "Corporate Wide Transformations in Human Resource Management", in Walton, R. E. and Lawrence, P. R. (eds.) *Human Resource Management: Trends and Challenges,* Boston: Harvard Business School Press.

Belbin, E. and Belbin R. M. (1972) *Problems in Adult Retraining,* London: Heineman.

Bennett, R. (1986) Interveiw at Oxford Polytechnic, Oxford, 3 July.

Bennett, R. (1987) *Improving Training Effectiveness*, London: Gower.

Bennett, R. (1988) "The Nature and Context of Training for Success", *Journal of European Industrial Training,* Vol. 12, No. 2, pp. 26-31.

Bennett, R. and Leduchowicz, T. (1983) "What Makes for an Effective Trainer?", *Journal of European Industrial Training,* Monograph, Vol. 7, No. 2.

Bentley, T. (1991) *The Business of Training: Achieving Success in Changing World Markets*, London: McGraw-Hill.

Berryman-Fink, C. (1985) "Male and Female Managers", Views of the Commercial Skills and Training Needs of Women in Management; *Public Personnel Management*, Vol. 14, pp. 307-313.

Berwick, E. L., Kindley, R. and Pettit, K. K. (1984) "The Structure of Training Courses and the Effects of Hierarchy", *Public Personnel Management*, Vol. 13, pp. 109-119.

Bhugra, A. (1986) "Computer-Based Training: A Case for Creative Skills within Development Teams", *Programmed Learning and Educational Technology,* Vol. 23, No. 3, pp. 24-27.

Binsted, A. S. (1982) "The Design of Learning Events Parts 1 and 2", *Management Education and Development,* Autumn-Spring.

Binsted, D. S. and Snell, R. S. (1982) "The Tutor-Learner Interaction in Management Development — Part 3, Facilitator Learning via Input/Lecture", *Personnel Review,* Vol. 11, No. 1, pp. 3-13.

Blum, M. C. and Naylor, J. C. (1968) *Industrial Psychology: Its Theoretical and Social Foundations,* New York: Harper and Row.

Blyton, P. and Turnbull, P. (eds.) (1992) *Reassessing Human Resource Management,* London: Sage.

Boam, R. and Sparrow, P. R. (eds.) (1992) *Designing and Achieving Competency: A Competency-based Approach to Developing People and Organisations,* London: McGraw-Hill.

Bond, B. W. (1956) "The Group Discussion — Decision Approach: An Appraisal of its Use in Health Education", *Dissertation Abstracts,* Vol. 16, p. 903.

Borris, V. (1983) "The Social and Political Consequences of Over Education", *American Sociological Review,* Vol. 48, pp. 454-467.

Bowers, D. and Franklin, J. (1977) "Survey — Guided Development using Human Resource Management in Organisational Change", *Journal of Contemporary Business,* Vol. 1, pp. 43-55

Boyatzis, R. (1982) *The Competent Manager: A Guide for Effective Performance,* New York: Wiley.

Boydell, T. H. (1976) *A Guide to Job Analysis,* London: British Association for Commercial and Industrial Education.

Boydell, T. H. (1976) *A Guide to the Identification of Training Needs,* 2nd edition, London: British Association for Commercial and Industrial Education.

Bramham, J. (1988) *Practical Manpower Planning,* London: IPM.

Bramley, P. (1989) "Effective Training", *Journal of European Industrial Training,* Vol. 13, pp. 11-14.

Bramley, P. (1991) *Evaluating Training Effectiveness: Translating Theory into Practice,* London: McGraw-Hill.

Bramley, P. and Hullah, H. (1987) "Auditing Training", *Journal of European Industrial Training,* Vol. 11, No. 6.

Bratton, J. (1992) *Japanisation at Work,* London: MacMillan, p. 109.

Bratton, J. and Gold, T. (1994) *Human Resource Management: Theory and Practice,* London: MacMillan.

Braverman, H. (1974) *Labour and Monopoly Capital,* New York: Monthly Review Press.

Breen, R. (1991) *Employment, Education and Training in the Youth Labour Market,* Dublin: ESRI

Bristow, S. and Scarth, R. (1980) *Personnel in Change,* London: Institute of Personnel Management.

Brown, G. F. and Read, A. R. (1984) "Personnel and Training Policies — Some Lessons for Western Companies", *Long Range Planning,* Vol. 17, No. 2, pp. 48-57.

Brown, H., Peccei, R., Sandberg, J. and Welchman, R. (1989) "Management Training and Development: In Search of an Integrated Approach", *Journal of General Management,* Vol. 15, No. 1, Autumn, pp. 69-82.

Buchanan, D. and Boddy, D. (1982) "Advanced Technology and the Quality of Working Life: The Effects of Word Processing on Video Typists", *Journal of Occupational Psychology,* Vol. 55, pp. 1 - 11.

Buckley, R. and Caple, J. (1992) *The Theory and Practice of Training,* London: Kogan Page.

Burgess, P. (1993) *European Management Guides: Training and Development,* London: Institute of Personnel Management.

Burgoyne, J. (1988) "Management Development for the Individual and the Organisation", *Personnel Management,* June.

Burgoyne, J. (1981) "Organisational Policies for Management Development", paper presented at the Irish ATM Conference, Dublin, July.

Burgoyne, J., Stuart, R. and Pedlar, M. (1984) *A Manual of Self-Development,* London: Kogan Page.

Burke, M. J. and Day, P. R. (1986) "A Cumulative Study of the Effectiveness of Managerial Training", *Journal of Applied Psychology*, Vol. 71, pp. 232-245.

Butler, E. D. (1967) "An Experimental Study of the Case Methods in Teaching: The Social Foundations of Education", *Dissertation Abstracts*, Vol. 27, pp. 2912.

Caccioppe, R., Warren, Langford, P. and Bell, L. (1990) "Trends in Human Resource Development and Training", *Asia Pacific Human Resource Management*, May, pp. 55-67.

Cadwell, R. (1991) "Ethics of Training", *Arena: Journal of the Irish Institute of Training and Development*, Dublin.

Callender, C., Toye, J., Connor, H. and Spillbury, M. (1993) *National and Scottish Vocational Qualifications: Early Indications of Employers' Take-up and Use*, London: Institute of Manpower Studies.

Campbell, J. P., Dunnette, M.D., Lawlor, E. E. and Weick, K. E. (1970) *Managerial Behaviour: Performance and Effectiveness*, New York, McGraw-Hill.

Carnevale, A. P., Gainer, L. J. and Villet, J. (1990) *Training in America*, San Francisco: Jossey-Bass.

Casey, T. (1993) *Skill Acquisition and Changing Industrial Structure,* Report undertaken for European Commission's Task Force on Human Resources, January.

Chalofsky, N. and Reinhard, C. (1988) *Effective Human Resource Development,* San Francisco: Jossey-Bass.

Chandler, A. (1962) *Structure and Strategy*, Boston: Harvard University Press.

Chapman, P. (1993) *The Economics of Training,* London: Harvester-Wheatsheaf.

Clancy, O. (1994) "The New Apprenticeship Scheme", paper presented at Irish Institute of Training and Development Conference, Waterford.

Clancy, P. (1988) *Who Goes to College,* Dublin: Higher Education Authority.

Clarke, A. (1986) *Tutor Competencies for Open Learning,* London: Manpower Services Commission, UK.

Clement, R. W., Pinto, R. P. and Walker, J. W. (1978) "How do I Hurt Thee? Let me Count the Ways: Unethical and Improper Behaviour by Training and

Development Professionals", *Training and Development Journal,* Vol. 32, pp. 10-12.

Clutterbuck, D. (1989) "Training: A World of Change", *Training and Development,* February, pp.15-16.

Cockman, P., Evans, B. and Reynolds, P. (1992) *Client-Contract Consulting: A Practical Guide for Internal Advisers and Trainers,* London: McGraw-Hill.

Collard, R. (1989) *Total Quality: Success through People,* London: Institute of Personnel Management.

Collins, R. (1979) *Functional and Conflict Theories of Educational Stratification,* New York: Oxford University Press.

Connor, R. A. and Davidson, J. P. (1985) *Marketing your Consultancy and Professional Services,* New York: John Wiley and Sons.

Coopers and Lybrand Association (1985) *A Challenge to Complacency: Changing Attitudes to Training,* a report to the Manpower Services Commission, and the National Economic Development Office, Sheffield,: Manpower Services Commission.

Coppard, L. C. (1976) "Gaming, Simulation and the Training Process", in R. L. Grace (ed.) *Training and Development Handbook: A Guide to Human Resource Development,* New York: McGraw-Hill.

Costine, P. (1994) "Irish Trade Union Attitudes to Training and Development in Manufacturing Industry", Sheffield University Masters of Education and Training thesis.

Craig, L. (1991) "The Labour Process Debate: A Theoretical Review, 1974-1988", in D. Knights, and H. Willmot (eds.) *Labour Process Theory,* London: MacMillan.

Craig, L. (ed.) (1992) *Training and Development Handbook; A Guide to Human Resource Development,* New York: McGraw-Hill.

Cronback, T. (1957) "The Two Disciplines of Scientific Psychology", *American Psychologist,* Vol. 12, pp. 671-684.

Cronback, L. T. (1963) "Course Improvements through Evaluation", *Teachers College Record,* Vol. 64, pp. 672-683.

Culliton, J. (1992) *A Time for Change: Industrial Policy for the 1990s, Report of the Industrial Policy Review Group,* Dublin: Stationary Office.

Cunningham, I. (1986) "Developing Chief Executives and Evaluation", Ashridge Management College.

Curson, C. (1986) *Flexible Patterns of Work,* Wimbledon: Institute of Personnel Management.

Daft, R. L. (1995) *Organisation Theory and Design,* 5th edition, New York: West.

Dahl, R. A. (1957) "The Concept of Power", *Behavioural Science,* Vol. 2, pp. 201-215.

Darcy, C. and Kleiner, P. (1991) "Leadership for Change in a Turbulent Environment", *Leadership and Organisational Development Journal,* Vol. 12, No. 5.

Darling, P. (1993) *Training for Profit: A Guide to the Integration of Training in an Organisation's Success,* London: McGraw-Hill.

Davidow, W. and Malone, M. (1992) *The Virtual Corporation: Structuring and Revitalising the Corporation of the 21st Century,* New York: Harper Business.

Davies, A., Stock, J., Macleod, J., Williams, C., Hughes, A., Garbett, J. and Cross, M. (1987) *The Management of Training,* Vol. 7, London: Pantenon Publishing Group Ltd.

Davies, I. (1983) *Management Development: Concepts and Issues,* London: Gower.

Davies, K. (1971) *The Management of Learning,* New York: McGraw-Hill.

Davies, K. (1976) *Objectives in Curriculum Design,* Maidenhead: McGraw-Hill.

Dawson, R. (1995) "Fill This in Before You Go: Under-Utilised Evaluation", *Journal of European Industrial Training,* Vol. 19, No. 2, Sheets 3-8.

Deegan, J. (1994) "A Note on Tourism Training in Ireland", Limerick: University of Limerick.

Deegan, N. (1994) "Education for Enterprise", Sheffield University Masters in Education thesis.

DeGeus, P. (1988) "Planning as Learning", *Harvard Business Review,* March-April, pp.70-74.

Deming, W. (1989) *Profound Knowledge,* Salisbury: British Demographic Association.

De Meyer, A. and Ferdows, K. (1991) "Removing the Barriers in Manufacturing — A Report on the 1990 Manufacturing Survey", Fontainebleau: Insead.

Dench, S. (1993) The Employers' Manpower and Skills Practice Survey (EMSPS) Why Do Employers Train? Employment Department Social Science Research Branch Working Paper 5.

Denison, E. F. (1967) "The Training Trap — Why the Growth Rates Differ?" *Economist*, Brookings Institute, Washington DC, 21st April.

Department of Employment (1978) *Glossary of Training Terms,* London: Stationary Office.

Department of Employment and Enterprise (1993) "A Survey of Employers' Training Practices", Dublin, European Social Fund Programme Evaluation Unit.

Deutchman, A. (1990) "What 25 year olds want", *Fortune*, August, p. 48.

Deutcheman, M. (1990) "The Way Forward for Evaluation of Tailormade Training", *Journal of European Industrial Training,* Vol. 14, No. 8.

Devereux, E. and Ronayne, T. (1993) "Labour Market Provision for the Long Term Unemployed: The Social Employment Scheme", Limerick: PAUL Partnerships.

DeVries, M. and Warmerden, T. (1992) "Training: Just How Flexible is this Necessity?", *Journal of European Industrial Training,* Vol. 16, No. 9, pp. 16-22.

Diamond, A. M. (1988) *Enriching Heredity*, New York: MacMillan.

Dineen, D. A. and Lenihan, H. (1994) "Vocational Training and Labour Markets: Analyses of the Generation and Use of Information of Recruitment Policies and Forward Management of Human Resources in Ireland", Department of Economics, College of Business, University of Limerick.

Dixon, N. M. (1990) "Action Learning: Action Science and Learning New Skills", *Industrial and Commercial Training,* Vol. 22, No. 1.

Dobbs, J. (1993) "The Empowerment Environment", *Training and Development*, February, pp. 55-57.

Donnelly, E. (1987) "The Training Model, Time for a Change", *Industrial and Commercial Training,* Vol. 19, No. 3, pp. 6-14.

Donnelly, E. (1991) "The Need to Market Training", in Prior, J. (ed.) *Handbook of Training and Development,* 2nd edition, London: Gower.

Downs, S. (1983) "Industrial Training" in A.P.O. Williams (ed.) *Using Personnel Research*, Herts: Gower.

Downs, S. (1985) "Retraining for New Shifts", *Ergonomics*, Vol. 28, pp. 1205-1211.

Downs, S. and Perry, P. (1984) "Developing Learning Skills", *Journal of European Industrial Training,* Vol. 8, No. 1, pp. 21-26.

Drea, V. (1994) "An Analysis of the Careers and Career Anchors of Training Professionals" (degree thesis) University of Limerick.

Duffy, K. (1993) "Training: Why we lag behind our Euro Partners", *The Irish Independent, Business and Recruitment Supplement*, March 18, p. 3.

Duncan, C. S. (1986) "The Job Aid has a Future", in *Introduction to Performance Technology,* Washington DC: National Society for Performance Instruction, pp. 125-128.

Duncan, R. B. (1972) "Characteristics of Perceived Environments and Perceived Environmental Uncertainty", *Administrative Science Quarterly*, Vol. 17, No. 3.

Dwyer, C. (1988) "The Education Training and Employment of Travellers — 21 Years On", Dublin, Report of the National Co-ordination for the Education of Travellers.

Earley, F. (1993) An Analysis of Traveller Training Centres, Athlone: Regional Technical College.

Easterby-Smith, M. (1986) *Evaluation of Management Education, Training and Development,* Aldershot: Gower.

Easterby-Smith, M. and Mackness, R. (1992) "Completing the Cycle of Evaluation", *Personnel Management,* September, pp. 38-42.

Edmonstone, J. (1988) "A False God? How Relevant is Competency Based Education and Training to the NHS?", *Health Services Management*, Vol. 84, No. 6, pp. 156-160.

Edwards, R. (1975) "The Social Relations of Production in the Firm and Labour Market Structure", *Politics and Society*, Vol. 5, pp. 83-108.

Elias, P. and Healey, M. (1994) "The Provision and Impact of Job-Related Formal Training in a Local Labour Market", *Regional Studies,* Vol. 28, No. 6, pp. 577-590.

Elliott, C. K. and Knibbs, J. R. (1981) "Expectations of Training", *Journal of European Industrial Training,* Vol. 6, No. 1, pp. 13-17.

Else, J. (1992) "Learning Logs and Reflection Skills", *Training and Development,* March.

Emerson, R. M. (1962) "Power-Dependence Relations", *American Sociological Review,* Vol. 27, pp. 31-41.

Employment Department (1993) "Employee Development Programmes", *Employee Development Bulletin,* Vol. 37, January.

Ernest, P. (1986) "Games: A Rationale for their Use in the Teaching of Mathematics in School", *Mathematics in School,* Vol. 8, pp. 2-5.

European Centre for the Development of Vocational Training (1992) "Support Policies for Business Startups and the Role of Training", Dublin CEDEFOP.

Evan, W. M. and Freeman, R. E. (1993) "A Stakeholder Theory of the Modern Corporation: Kantian Capitalism", in Chyssedes, G. D. and Kolan J. H., *An Introduction to Business Ethics,* London: Chapman and Hall.

FÁS (1989) *Apprenticeship: A New Approach*, Discus, Dublin: FÁS.

FÁS (1991) Annual Report and Account, Dublin.

FÁS (1993) Commercial Report "Skills Strategies Get Upgrading", *The Sunday Business Post,* November 21, pp. 17-20.

Felstead, A. and Green, F. (1993) "Cycles of Training? Evidence from the British Recession of the Early 1990s", University of Leicester.

Finegold, D. (1991) "Institutional Incentives and Skill Creation: Preconditions for a High-Skill Equilibrium" in Ryan, P. (ed.) *International Comparisons of Vocational Education and Training for Intermediate Skills*, London: Falmer.

Finegold, D. and Soskice, D. (1988) "Prescription", *Oxford Review of Economic Policy,* Vol. 14, No. 3, pp. 21-53.

Fisher, J. (1986) "Forging a Link between Technology and Training", *Personnel,* April.

Folkard, S. (1987) "Circadian Rhythms and Hours of Work", in *Psychology at Work*, P. D. Warr (ed.), London: Penguin.

Fombrun, C., Tichy, N. M. and Devanna, M. A. (1984) *Strategic Human Resource Management*, New York: John Wiley.

Fonda, N. and Hayes, M. (1986) "Is More Training Really Necessary?" *Personnel Management*, November.

Fonda, N. and Hayes, M. (1986) "Management Development: The Missing Links in Sustained Business Performance", *Personnel Management*, December, pp. 50-3.

Ford, J. K. and Wroten, S. P. (1984) "Introducing New Methods for Conducting Training Evaluation and for Linking Training Evaluation to Programme Design", *Personnel Psychology,* vol. 37, pp. 651-656.

Ford, J. K. and Noe, R. A. (1984) Self-Assessed Training Needs: The Effects of Attitudes Towards Training Managerial Level and Function", *Personnel Psychology*, Vol. 40, pp. 39-53.

Fortune (1992) "Workforce: Looking Ahead", December, pp. 52-66.

Fortune (1993) "Managing in the Midst of Chaos", April, pp. 38-48.

Fox, A. (1966) "Royal Commission on Trade Union and Employers Association", Research Paper 3, Industries, Sociology and Industrial Relations. HMSO.

Fox, A. (1966) "Management Ideology and Labour Relations", *British Journal of Industrial Relations*, Vol. 4.

Freeman, E. and Reed S. (1983) "Stockholders and Stakeholders: A New Perspective on Corporate Governance", in U. K. Huvinga (ed.) *Corporate Governance: A Definitive Exploration of the Issues,* Los Angeles: UCLA Extension Press.

Gagne, R. M. (1977) *The Conditions of Learning*, 3rd edition, London: Holt, Rinehart and Winston.

Galbraith, J. and Nathanson, D. (1978) *Strategic Implementation: The Role of Structure and Process*, St. Paul, MN: West Publishing.

Gallie, D. and White, M. (1993) *Employment Commitment and the Skill Revolution*, London: PSI.

Galvin, D. (1988) *Managers for Ireland: The Case for Development of Irish Managers*, Advisory Committee on Management Training, Dublin: Department of Labour.

Garavan, T. N. (1987) "Promoting National Learning Activities within the Organisation", *Journal of European Industrial Training*, Vol. 11, No. 7, pp. 18-23.

Garavan, T. N. (1991) "Strategic Human Resource Development", *Journal of European Industrial Training*, Vol. 15, No. 1, pp. 17-31.

Garavan, T. N. (1992) *A Study of Training and Development Practices in Ireland*, Department of Management, University of Limerick.

Garavan, T. N. (1992) "The Reform of Training in Ireland: The Response of Training Professionals to the Culliton Report", paper presented to National Executive Council on Training and Development Implications, Wednesday, 21 October, Limerick.

Garavan, T. N. (1995) "Beware of Your Stakeholders: The Role of Stakeholders in the Training Management Process", *Journal of European Industrial Training*, Vol. 19, No. 7.

Garavan, T. N., Jankowicz, D. and Pattinson, B. (1984) "The Provision of Training and Development: A Regional Training Centre", Limerick: National Institute of Higher Education.

Garavan, T. N. and Sweeney, P. (1994) "Supervisory Training and Development, The Use of Learning Contracts", *Journal of European Industrial Training*, Vol. 18, No. 2, pp. 17-26.

Garavan, T. N., Barnacle, B. and Heraty, N. (1993) "The Training and Development Function: Its Search for Power and Influence in Organisations", *Journal of European Industrial Training*, Vol. 17, No. 7, pp. 22-32.

Garrick, J. and McDonnell, R. (1992) "Competency Standards for Industry Trainers: Alternative Models", *Journal of European Industrial Training*, Vol. No. 7, pp. 16-20.

Gibb, A. (1987) "Enterprise Culture — Its Meaning and Implictions for Education and Training", *Journal of European Industrial Training*, Vol. 11, No. 2.

Gibb, J. (1993) "Enterprise Culture Education: Understanding Enterprise Education and Its Links with Small Business, Entrepreneurship and Wider Education Goals", *International Small Business Journal*, Vol. 11, No. 3.

Gill, C. and Mullins, L. (1990) "The Effective Management of Training", _Industrial and Commercial Training_, March.

Gill, J. (1988) _Factors Affecting the Survival and Growth of the Smaller Company_, London: Gower.

Gilley, T. and Eggland, S. A. (1992) _Principles of Human Resource Development_, Maidenhead: Addison-Wesley.

Gold, M. (1993) _The Social Dimension: European Policy in the European Community_, London: MacMillan.

Goldstein, I. L. (1986) _Training in Organisations_, Monterey, CA: Brooks Cole.

Goldstein, I. L. and Associates (1989) _Training and Development in Organisations_, San Francisco: Jossey-Bass.

Gordon, M. E., Cofer, J. L. and McCullough, P. (1986) "Relationships Among Seniority, Past Performance, Inter job Sililarity and Trainability", _Journal of Applied Psychology_, Vol. 71, pp. 518-521.

Goss, D. (1993) _Principles of Human Resource Management_, London: Routledge.

Grace, P. and Straub, C. (1991) "Managers as Training Assets", _Training and Development Journal_, June, pp. 49-54.

Gruenfield, L. W. (1966) "Personality Needs and Expected Benefits from a Management Development Programme", _Occupational Psychology_, Vol. 40, pp. 75-81.

Guest, D. (1991) "Personnel Management: The End of Orthodoxy?", _British Journal of Industrial Relations_, Vol. 29, No. 4, pp. 149-176.

Gunn, J. (1982) "A Study of Training and Development Practitioners' Roles in Australia", _Training and Development in Australia_, Vol. 8, No. 3, pp. 8-10.

Gunnigle, P. (1991) "Personnel Policy, Choice; The Choice for HRD", _Journal of European Industrial Training_, Vol. 15, No. 3.

Gunnigle, P. (1992) "The Price Waterhouse Study, Ireland", Limerick: University of Limerick.

Gunnigle, P. and Flood, P. (1990) _Personnel Management in Ireland: Practice, Trends and Developments_, Dublin: Gill and MacMillan.

Hales, L. D. (1986) "Training: A Product of Business Planning"; *Training and Development Journal,* Vol. 4, July, pp. 65-66.

Hall, D. T. (1991) "Business Restructuring and Strategic Human Resource De-velopment*", in Business Restructuring; Turbulence in the American Workplace,* Oxford: Oxford University Press.

Hall, D. (1984) "Human Resource Development and Organisational Effective-ness" in Fombrum, C., Tichy, N. and Devanna, M. **(eds.)** *Strategic Human Resource Mangement,* New York: John Wiley and Sons.

Hallier, J., Glover, I. and Lyon, P. (1993) "The Ageism Taboo in Human Re-source Mangement Research", University of Stirling, School of Management.

Hamblin, A. C. (1974) *Evaluation and Control of Training,* Maidenhead: McGraw-Hill.

Hammett, J. (1994) "The Changing Work Environment: High Technology and the Baby Boomers Challenge Management to Adopt", *Employment Relations Today,* Vol. 11, No. 3, pp. 297-304.

Hammond, V. and Wille, B. (1991) "The Learning Organisation" in J. Prior (ed.) *Gower Handbook of Training and Development*, Aldershot: Gower.

Handy, C. (1985) *Understanding Organisations*: London: Penguin.

Handy, C. (1987) *The Making of Managers: A Report for the NEDO, the MSC and the BIM on Management Education, Training and Development in the US, Germany, France, Japan and the UK,* London: National Economic Develop-ment Office.

Handy, C. (1990) *Inside Organisations*, London: BBC Books.

Handy, C. (1990) "The Contrasting Philosophies of Management Education", Annual Conference of European Foundation for Management Development, London.

Harrison, R. (1992) *Employee Development*, London: Institute of Personnel Management.

Harrison, R. (1993) *Developing Human Resources for Productivity*, Geneva: International Labour Office.

Harrison, R. (1993) *Human Resource Management: Issues and Strategies,* Wolkingham: Addison-Wesley.

Harrison, R. (1993) "Developing People for Whose Bottom Line?" in R. Harrison (ed.) *Human Resource Management: Issues and Strategies,* Wolkingham: Addison-Wesley.

Hashimoto, M. (1981) "Firm Specific Capital as a Shared Investment", *American Economic Review,* Vol. 71, pp. 475-82.

Hassett, J. and Dukes, S. (1986) "The New Employee Trainer: A Floppy Disk", *Psychology Today,* September, pp. 30-36.

Hasting, C. (1993) *The New Organisation: Growing the Culture of Organisational Networking,* London: McGraw-Hill.

Hayton, G. (1984) "Job Profiles of Training and Development Personnel in Australia", Adelaide: TAFE Natural Centre for Research and Development Ltd.

Hendry, C. (1991) "International Comparisons of Human Resource Management: Putting the Firm in the Frame", *International Journal of Human Resource Management,* Vol. 2, No. 3, pp. 415-40.

Hendry, C., Jones, A., Arthur, P. and Pettigrew, A. (1991) "Human Resource Development in Small to Medium Sized Enterprises", Research Paper No. 88, Sheffield: Department of Employment.

Hendry, C. and Pettigrew, A. (1986) "The Practice of Strategic Human Resource Management" *Personnel Review,* Vol. 15, No. 3.

Heraty, N. (1992) "Training and Development, A Study of Practices in Irish-Based Companies", Masters thesis, University of Limerick.

Herman, D. S. and Perlmutter, H. V. (1979) *Multinational Organisational Development,* Reading, MA: Addison Wesley.

Heyes, J. and Stuart, M. (1994) "Placing Symbols before Reality: Re-evaluating the Low Skills Equilibrium", *Personnel Review,* Vol. 23, No. 5 pp. 34-50

Heywood, T. (1989) *Learning Adaptability and Change: The Challenge for Education and Industry,* London: Paul Chapman.

Hicks, W. D. and Klimoski, R. J. (1984) "The Process of Evaluating Training Programmes and its Effects on Training Outcomes", paper presented at 44th meeting of Academy of Management, Boston.

Higgs, M. (1989) "A Strategic Approach to Training and Development", *Training and Development,* November, pp. 11-14.

Hillery, B., Kelly, A. and Marsh, A. (1975) "Trade Union Organisation in Ireland", Dublin: Irish Productivity Centre.

Hillery, J. M. and Wexley, K. N. (1974) "Participation in Appraisal Interviews Conducted in a Training Situation", *Journal of Applied Psychology,* Vol. 59, pp. 168-171.

Hills, S. (1991) "Why Quality Circles Failed but TQM Might Succeed", *British Journal of Industrial Relations*, Vol. 29, No. 4, pp. 54-69.

Hinnings, C. R. (1990) "Structural Conditions of Intro-Organisational Power", *Administrative Science Quarterly,* Vol. 19, No. 10, pp. 22-44.

Hitchins, D. and Birnie, J. E. (1993) "Productivity and Economic Performance", in NESC Report No. 95. Education and Training Policies for Economic and Social Development, Dublin.

Hodgetts, R. and Luthans, F. (1991) *International Management,* New York: McGraw-Hill.

Hofstede, G. (1993) "Cultural Constraints in Management Theories", *Academy of Management Executive,* Vol. 7, No. 1, pp. 81-93.

Hogan, C. (1994) "Ethical Issues and Dilemmas Experienced by Training Consultants", MEd Thesis, University of Sheffield.

Holden, L. (1992) "Does Strategic Training Policy Exist? Some Evidence from Ten European Countries", *Personnel Review,* Vol. 21, No. 1.

Holden, L. and Livian, Y. (1993) "Does Strategic Training Policy Exist? Evidence from Ten European Countries in A. Hegewisch and C. Brewster, *European Developments in HRM*, The Cranfield Management Research Series, Aldershot: Kogan Page.

Hollenback, G. (1989) "What did you Learn in School?" Studies of the Advanced Management Program, unpublished manuscript, Harvard Business School.

Holtz, H. (1983) *How to Suceed as an Independent Consultant*, New York: John Wiley and Sons.

Honey, P. (1991) "The Learning Organisation Simplified", *Training and Development Journal,* Vol. 9, No. 7.

Honey, P. and Mumford, A. (1986) *Using Your Learning Styles,* 2nd Ed. London: Peter Honey.

Honey, P. and Mumford, A. (1989) *The Manual of Learning Opportunities*, London: Peter Honey.

Hopland, J. (1993) quoted in Sparrow, P and Hiltrop, J. M., *European Human Resource Management in Transition*, London: Prentice-Hall.

Huczynski, A. (1983) *The Handbook of Management Development Methods*, Altershot: Gower.

Hullier, J., Glover, I. and Lyon, P. (1993) "The Ageism Taboo in Human Resource Management Research", University of Stirling School of Management.

Hunt, J. W. (1986) *Managing People at Work, A Manager's Guide to Behaviour in Organisations*, 2nd edition, Maidenhead: McGraw-Hill.

Hussey, D. E. (1985) "Implementing Corporate Strategy Using Management Education and Training", *Long Range Planning*, Vol. 18, No. 5, pp. 18-37.

Hussey, D. (1988) *Management Training and Corporate Strategy — How to Improve Competitive Performance*, London: Pergamon.

Hussey, D. and Lowe, P. (1990) *Key Issues in Management Training*, London: Kogan Page.

Hyman, J. (1992) *Training at Work: A Critical Analysis of Policy and Practice*, London: Routledge.

Hyman, R. (1978) *Industrial Relations — A Marxist Introduction*, London: Macmillan.

Hyman, T. (1975) "Training and Development" in B. Travers (ed.) *The Handbook of Human Resource Management*, London: Blackwell Business.

IEF Research Limited (1989) *Training in Britain: Employers' Attitudes*, London: HMSO.

IEF Research Limited (1992) *Skill Needs in Britain*, London: HMSO.

Industrial Policy Review Group (1992) *A Time for Change: Industrial Policy for the 1990s*, Dublin: Stationery Office.

Jaccardi, A. (1989) "The Social Architecture of a Learning Organisation", *Training and Development Journal*, Vol. 43, No. 11, November, pp. 49-51.

Jenkins, D. (1983) *A Textbook of Techniques and Strategies in Personnel Management*, London: IPM.

Johansson, H. J., McHugh, P., Pendlebury, A. J. and Wheeler, W. A. (1993) *Business Process Re-engineering: Breakpoint Strategies for Market Dominance,* Chichester: John Wiley.

Johnson, G. (1990) "Managing Strategic Change: The Role of Symbolic Action", *British Journal of Management,* Vol. 1, No. 4.
Johnson, G. and Scholes, K. (1992) *Exploring Corporate Strategy,* London: Prentice Hall.

Johnson, K. (1990) "The Role of The Training Manager", MED Distant Learning Programme, Sheffield University.

Johnson, R. (1990) "The Role of the External Consultant" MED Distant Learning Programme, Sheffield University.

Juran, J. (1988) *Planning for Quality,* New York: Free Press.

Kadlor, M. and Mirlees, P. (1981), quoted in D. Hitchins and J. E. Birnie, (1993) "Productivity and Economic Performance", NESC Report No. 95, Education and Training Policies for Economic and Social Development, Dublin.

Kakabadese, A. (1990) "Top People, Top Teams", paper presented at IITD Conference, Changing People and Business, Limerick, April 21, 1991.

Kakabadese, A. (1991) *The Wealth Creators: Top People, Top Teams and Executive Best Practices,* London: Kogan Page.

Kanter, R. M. (1979) "Power failure in Management Circuits", *Harvard Business Review,* July - August

Keep, E. (1989) "Corporate Training Strategies: The Vital Component", in J. Storey (ed.) *New Perspectives on Human Resource Management,* London: Routledge.

Kenny Report (1984) "Life Long Learning", report of the Commission on Adult Education Dublin: Government Publications.

Kerins, A. (1993) *Learning Societies and Low Unemployment: Education and Training in Low Unemployment Countries,* Dublin: Irish Management Institute.

King, C. (1993) "The Future Training Requirements of the Tourism Industry", Athlone: Diploma in Training and Development.

King, W. (1989) "Advisory Power and Predicament in Organisational Training", *Journal of European Industrial Training,* Vol. 13, No. 3.

Kirconnell, P. (1988) "Practical Thinking about Going Abroad", *Business Quarterly*, Autumn.

Kirkpatrick, D. L. (1967) "Evaluation of Training", in Craig, R. L. and Bitten, L. R. (eds.) *Training and Development Handbook*, American Society for Training and Development, New York: McGraw-Hill.

Knowles, M. S. (1974) *The Adult Learner: A Neglected Species*, Houston: Gulf.

Knowles, M. S. (1980) *The Modern Practice of Adult Education: From Pedagogy to Andragogy*, Chicago: Follet.

Kolb, D. A. (1984) *Experiential Learning — Experience as a Source of Learning and Development*, New Jersey: Prentice Hall.

Kolb, D. A., Rubin, I. M. and McIntyre, F. M. (1974) *Organisation Psychology: An Experimental Approach*, New Jersey: Prentice-Hall.

Koontz, H. and Weihrick, H. (1988) *Management*, London: McGraw-Hill.

Kotler, P. (1986) *Marketing Management: Analysis, Planning and Control*, New York: MacMillan.

Kram, K. E. (1985) *Mentoring at Work: Developmental Relationships in Organisational Life*, Glenview, IL: Scott Foresman.

Kramlinger, T. and Huberty, T. (1990) "Behaviourism vs Humanism", *Training and Development Journal*, December.

Labour Force Survey (1985) *Survey of the Irish Labour Force*, Dublin: Government Publications Office.

Latham, G. (1988) "Human Resource Training and Development", *Annual Review of Psychology*, No. 39, pp. 545 - 582.

Latham, G. P. and Crandall, S. R. (1991) "Organisational and Social Influences Affecting Training Effectiveness", in J. E. Morrision (ed.) *Training for Performance*, Chichester: Wiley.

Latham, G. P. and Huber, B. L. (1992) "Problems Encountered in Pay Research", *Journal of Organisation Behaviour Management*. Vol 27, No. 1.

Law, C. (1986) *Helping People Learn*, Cambridge: Industrial Performance Unit.

Leduchowicz, J. (1984) *Guide to Trainer Effectiveness*, London: Manpower Services Commission

Legge, K. (1989) "Human Resource Management: A Critical Analysis", in Storey, J. (ed.) *New Developments in Human Resource Management*, London: Routledge.

Leicester, C. (1989) "The Key Role of the Line Manager in Employee Development", *Personnel Management*, March, pp. 53-7.

Lindeman, E. C. (1926) *The Meaning of Adult Education*, New York: New Public.

Long, R. (1992) "Protecting the Investment in Training", *Journal of European Industrial Training*, Vol. 14, No. 7, pp. 21-27.

Lucas, R. R. (1988) "On the Mechanics of Economic Development", *Journal of Monetary Economics*, Vol. 22, pp. 3-42.

Machiavelli, N. (1961) *The Prince*, London: Penguin Books.

Mager, R. F. (1975) *Preparing Instructional Objectives*, 2nd edition, Los Angeles: Fearon.

Mahnkopf, B. (1992) "The Skills Oriented Strategies of German Trade Unions: Their Impact on Efficiency and Equality objectives" *British Journal of Industrial Relations*, Vol. 30. No. 1 pp. 61-81.

Mangham, I. and Silver, M. (1986) *Management Training, Context and Practice*, London: Economic and Social Research Institute.

Manpower Services Commission and Institute of Training and Development (1984) *Trainer Task Inventory*, Buckingham: Institute of Training and Development.

Markwell, D. S. and Roberts, J. J. (1969) *Organisation of Management Development Programmes*, Aldershot: Gower.

Marsick, V. and Watkins, K. (1986) "Learning and Developing in the Workplace", paper presented to the American Society for Training and Development Professor Conference, St. Louis.

McCarthy B. (1994) "Work and Mind: Searching for our Celtic Legacy" *The Irish Journal of Psychology*, Vol. 15, No 2 and 3, pp. 372-390.

McCarthy, D. T. (1991) "Developing a Programme for Soviet Managers", *Journal of Management Development*, Vol. 10, No. 5, pp. 26 31.

McCarthy, E. J. and Perreualt, A. H. (1985) *Basic Marketing: A Managerial Approach,* Homewood, IL: Irwin.

McDonald, G. (1989) "Manager Attitudes to Training", *Asia Pacific Human Resource Management*, Vol. 27, No. 4, pp. 22.28.

McEnery, J. and McEnery, J. M. (1987) "Self Rating in Management Training Need Assessment: A Neglected Opportunity", *Journal of Occupational Psychology*, Vol. 60, pp. 44-60.

McEvoy, G. M. and Butler, P. (1990) "Five Uneasy Pieces in the Training Evaluation Puzzle", *Training and Development Journal*, August, pp. 34-42

McEwen, Y. and Young, W. (1988) "Flexible Working Arrangement in Continuous Shift Production", *Personnel Review*, Vol. 7, pp. 12-19

McKeachie, W. J. (1974) "Instructional Psychology", *Annual Review of Psychology*, Vol. 25, pp. 161-193

McIlroy, R. (1991) "The Permanent Revolution Conservative Law and Trade Unions", Nottingham, Routledge.

McIver, C. (1992) Skill Shortages in Ireland, Dublin FÁS.

McLagan, J. (1989) *Models of HRD Practice* Alexandria; ASTD.

McLagan, P. and Bedrick, R. (1983) *Model for Excellence*, Alexandria; VA: ASTD.

Megginson, D. and Boydell, T. (1979) *A Managers Guide to Coaching*, London: British Association for Commercial and Industrial Education,

Megginson, D. and Pedlar, M. (1992) *Self-Development: A Facilitators Guide*, Maidenhead: McGraw-Hill

Merizow, J. (1992) *A Critical Theory of Adult Learning and Education*, New York: Croom Helm.

Metcalf, H., Walling, A. and Fogarty M. (1994) *Individual Commitment to Learning: Employers Attitudes*, London: Employment Department Research Series No. 40., November.

Miller, N. E. (1957) "Scientific Principles of Maximum Learning from Motion Pictures", *AV Communications Review*, Vol. 5, pp. 3-7.

Millstein, I. and Katsch, S. (1981) *The Fruits of Corporate Power*, New York: MacMillan.

Mincer, J. (1974) "On the Job Training: Costs, Returns, and Some Implications", *Journal of Political Economy*, Vol. 70, No. 5, pp. 50-79.

Mintzberg, H. (1987) "The Strategic Concept, Parts 1 and 2", *California Management Review*, Vol. 24, No l. 3, pp. 1-22.

Mojset L. (1991) "The Irish Economy in a Competitive Institutional Perspective", NESC Report No. 93.

Mooney, P. (1989) "The Growth of the Non-Union Sector and Union Counter Strategies", Dublin: Trinity College, unpublished PhD thesis.

Morgan, R. and Costello, F. (1989) *Trainer Task Inventory*, London: MSC Publications

Morley, M. and Garavan, T. (1993) "The New Organisation — Its Implications for Training and Development", paper read to the Irish Institute for Training and Development, National Conference, Galway, April.

Moss, G. (1993) *The Trainees Desk Reference*, London: Pitman, 2nd edition.

Mullins L. (1989) *Management and Organisation Behaviour*, London: Pitman.

Mumford, A. (1971) "The Manager and Training", *London Times Management Library*.

Mumford, A. (1986) "Learning to Learn for Managers", *Journal of European Industrial Training*, Vol. 10, No. 2, pp. 1 - 22.

Mumford, A. (1986) "Learning to Learn for Managers", *Journal of European Training*, Vol. 10, No. 2, pp. 1-28.

Mumford, A. (1994) *Management Development: Strategies for Action*, London: Kogan Page, 2nd edition.

Murphy, B. P. and Swanson, R. A. (1988) "Auditing Training and Development", *Journal of European Industrial Training*, Vol. 12, No. 2.

Murphy, J. (1994) "The Training of People with Disabilities in Ireland", Limerick: University of Limerick.

Murphy, J. and Coldrick A. J. (1989) The Role of the Social Partners in Vocational Education and Training including Continuing Education, Training in Ireland, Berlin: CEDEFOP

Murphy Report (1973) "Adult Education in Ireland", a report of the commission appointed by the Minister for Education. Dublin, Government Publications Office.

Murray, M. (1991) *Beyond the Myths and Magic of Mentoring: How to facilitate an Effective Monitoring Programme*, San Francisco: Jossey-Bass.

Nadler, L. (1969) "The Variety of Training Roles", *Industrial and Commercial Training*, Vol. 1 No. 1.

Nadler, L. (ed.) (1984) The Handbook of Human Resource Development, New York: John Wiley and Sons.

Nadler, L. and Nadler, Z. (1989) *Developing Human Resources*, 3rd edition, London: Jossey Bass.

Nadler, L. and Wiggs, G. D. (1986) *Managing Human Resource Development — A Practical Guide*, San Francisco: Jossey Bass.

National Council for Vocational Award (NCVA) (1992), "The New Europe: A National Framework for Vocational Education" Dublin: NCVA

Nelson, D. L. (1987) "Organisational Socialisation: A Street Perspective", *Journal of Occupational Behaviour* Vol. 8, pp. 313-329.

NESC (1993) "Education and Training Policies for Economic and Social Development", No. 95, October, Dublin: NESC

Newby, A. C. (1982) "Ethical Issues for Training Practitioners" *Journal of European Industrial Training* , Vol. 6, No. 3, pp. 10-14

Newby, A. C. (1992) *Training Evaluation Handbook*, Aldershot: Gower.

Newsham, D. B. (1969) "The Challenge of Change to the Adult Trainee", Training Information, Paper 3, London: Stationary Office,

Noe, R. A. and Schmitt (1986) "The Influence of Trainer Attitudes on Training Effectiveness: Test of a Model", *Personnel Psychology*, Vol. 39, pp. 497-523.

Noel, J. L. and Dennehy, R. F. (1991) "Making HRD a Force in Strategic Organisational Change", *Industrial and Commercial Training*, Vol. 23, No 2, pp. 17-19.

Nordhaug, O. (1990) "The Role of Training and Development", *HRM Journal*, Vol. 1, No. 2, Winter.

Northcraft, G. and Chase, R. (1985) "Managing Service, Demand at the Point of Delivery", *Academy of Management Review*, Vol. 10, pp. 66-75.

Oakland, J. (1989) *Total Quality Management*, London: Heinemann.

O'Connell, J. (1992) Working with Irish Travellers, Dublin: DTED6 File Irish Travellers, New Analysis and Initiatives, Pavel Point Publications.

O'Connor, J. and Lyons, M. (1982) "Venture Initiation in Irish Society", Dublin: The Industrial Development Authority, Ireland.

O'Connor, J. and Lyons M. (1983) "Enterprise — The Irish Approach", Dublin: The Industrial Development Authority, Ireland.

O'Dalaigh, C. (1994) "New Developments in Education and Training", IITD National Conference, Waterford.

OECD (1989) *Education and the Economy in a Changing Society*, Paris: OECD.

OECD (1990) *Education in OECD Countries, 1987-88*, Paris: OECD.

Ogbanna, E. and Wilkinson, J. (1988) "Corporate Strategy and Corporate Culture: The Management of Change in the UK Supermarket Industry", *Personnel Review*, Vol. 17, No 6, pp. 10-13.

Ohmae, K. (1990) "Triads of Power". New York: McKinsey Consultancy.

Olson, L. (1986) "Training Trends: The Corporate View", *Training and Development Journal*, Vol. 8, No. 4, pp. 32-35.

O'Sullivan, D. (1989) "Adult and Continuing Education in the Irish Republic: A Research Guide", *International Journal of Life Long Learning*, Vol. 8, No. 3, pp. 211-234.

Otto, C. P. and Glaser, R. O. (1970) *Management of Training*, London: Addison-Wesley.

Paauwe, J. (1991) "Limitations to Freedom: Is there a Choice for Human Resource Management", *British Journal of Management*, Vol. 2, pp. 103-119.

Parlett, M. and Hamilton, D. (1977) "Evaluation as Illumination", in D. Tanney (ed.) *Curriculum Education Today*, New York: McMillan.

Pearn, M. and Kandola, R. (1988) *Job Analysis: A Practical Guide for Managers*, London: IPM

Pearn, M. and Kandola, R. (1993) *Becoming a Learning Organisation: A Toolkit,* Marlowe: Institute of Training and Development.

Pedlar, M. (ed.) (1991) *Action Learning in Practice*, 2nd edition, Aldershot: Gower.

Pedlar, M., Burgoyne., J. and Boydell T. (1991) *The Learning Company*, Maidenhead: McGraw-Hill.

Pedlar, M. and Boutall, J. (1992) Action learning for Change, Bristol: National Health Service Training Directorate.

Pepper, A. D. (1984) *Managing the Training and Development Function*, Aldershot: Gower.

Perrow, C. (1987) "A Framework for the Comparative Analyses of Organisations", *American Sociological Review*, Vol. 32, pp. 194-208.

Peters, T. J. and Waterman, R. H. (1987) *In Search of Excellence*: *Lessons from America's Best Run Companies*, New York: Harper and Row.

Peters, L. H., O'Connor, E. J. and Eulberg, J. R. (1985) "Situational Constraints, Sources, Consequences and Future Considerations", in J. Ferris and K. Rowland (eds.) *Research in Personnel and Human Resource Management*, Vol. 3, pp. 79-114.

Pettigrew, A. M. (1985) *The Awakening Giant — Continuity and Change at ICI,* Oxford: Basil Blackwell.

Pettigrew, A. M., Jones, E. R. and Reason, P. W. (1982) *Training and Development Roles in their Organisational Setting*, Sheffield: Training Division, MSC.

Pettigrew, A. M., Hendry, C. and Sparrow, P. (1988) "The Forces that Trigger Training", *Personnel Management*, Vol. 20, No. 12, pp. 28-32.

Pettigrew, A. M., Hendry, C. and Sparrow, P. (1988) "Linking Strategic Change, Competitive Performance and HRM: Results of a UK Empirical Study", paper presented at British Academy of Management, 2nd Annual Conference, Cardiff Business School, UMIST, September, pp. 1-57.

Pettigrew, A. M., Hendry C. and Sparrow, P. (1989) *Training in Britain: Employers perspectives on Human Resources*, London: HMSO.

Pfeffer, J. (1981) *Power in Organisations*, New York: Pitman.

Phillips, J. (1984) "Evaluation of HRD Programs" in L. Nadler (ed.) *The Handbook of Human Resource Development*, New York: Wiley-Interscience.

Phillips, K. and Shaw P. (1989) *A Consultancy Approach for Trainers*, Aldershot: Gower.

Pigors, P. and Pigors, F. (1987) "Case Method", in R. L. Craig (ed.) *Training and Development Handbook: A Guide to Human Resource Development*, New York: McGraw-Hill, pp. 414-429.

Pinto, R. P. and Walker, J. W. (1978) "What Do Training and Development Professionals Really Do?", *Training and Development Journal*, Vol. 32, No. 7, pp. 58-64.

Pont, T. (1991) *Developing Effective Training Skills*, Maidenhead: McGraw-Hill.

Porter, M. E. (1985) *Competitive Advantage*, New York: Free Press.

Porter, M. E. (1990) *The Competitive Advantage of Nations*, New York: Free Press.

Prais, S. J. (1991) "Vocational Qualifications in Britain and Europe: Theory and Practice", *National Institute Economic Review,* No. 105, pp. 26-34.

Prais, S. J. and NIESR, Research Team (1990) "Productivity, Education and Training: Britain and other Countries Compared", *National Institute Economic Review,* London, National Institute of Economic and Social Research.

Price Waterhouse/Cranfield (1990) The Price Waterhouse/Cranfield Project on International Strategic Human Resource Management: Report, London: Price Waterhouse.

Prideaux, G. and Ford J. (1988) "Management Development: Competencies, Contracts, Teams and Work-based Learning: Part I". *Journal of Management Development*, Vol. 7, No. 1, pp. 56-68

Purcell, J. (1987) "Mapping Management Styles in Employee Relations", *Journal of Management Studies*, Vol. 21, No. 5.

Pursell, E. D. and Russell, J.S. (1990) "Employee Development", in K. N. Wexley (ed.) *Developing Human Resources*, ASPA/BNA Series, Washington, DC: Bureau of National Affairs.

Quinn-Mills, D. (1985) "Planning with People in Mind", *Harvard Business Review*, July-August.

Rackham, N., Honey, P. and Morgan, G. (1976) *Behavioural Analysis in Training*, London: Kogan Page.

Rajan, H. (1992) *A Zero Sum Game — Business Know-How, and Training Challenges in an Integrated Europe*, London: Industrial Society Press

Rainbird, H. (1990) *Training Matters — Union Perspectives on Industrial Restructuring and Training*, Oxford: Basil Blackwell

Rainbird, H. (1993) "Continuing Training" in K. Sisson (ed.) *Personnel Management in Britain* (2nd edition) Oxford: Basil Blackwell.

Reid, M., Barrington, H. and Kenney, J. (1992) *Training Interventions*, 2nd edition, London: Institute of Personnel Management.

Reid, M. and Barrington, H. (1994) *Training Inventions*, 3rd edition, London: Institute of Personnel and Development.

Reid, P. (1991) "Introduction" in Reid, P. (ed.) *Global Management: Culture, Context, Competence*, Berkhamsted: Ashridge Management Research Group, pp. 1 - 2.

Reiss, C. (1994) "Conducting Classroom Training", in Tracey, W. (ed.) *Human Resource Management and Development Handbook*, 2nd edition, New York: Amacom.

Revans, R. W. (1983) *The ABC of Action Learning*, Bromley: Chartwell-Bratt.

Rhinesmith, S., Williamson, J., Ehlen, D. and Maxwell, D. (1989) "Developing Leaders for the Global Enterprise", *Training and Development Journal*, April.

Rhinesmith, S. (1991) "An Agenda for Globalisaiton", *Training and Development Journal*, November.

Robinson, K. (1988) *A Handbook of Training Management*, London: Kogan Page.

Roche, F. and Tansey, P. (1992) Industrial Training in Ireland, Report submitted to Industrial Policy Review Group, Dublin; Department of Industry and Trade.

Roche, W. K. and Larragy, J. (1987) "The Trend of Unionisation in the Republic" in *Industrial Relations in Ireland*, Dublin; Department of Industrial Relations, UCD.

Rogers, C. R. (1969) *Freedom to Learn*, Columbus: Free Press.

Rolfe, H., Christie, I,. Lakey, J. and White, M. (1993) *Developing Technical Skills in Electronics.* London: PSI.

Romer, P. (1986) "Increasing Returns and Long-run Economic Growth", *Journal of Political Economy*, Vol. 94, No. 5, pp. 1002-1037.

Romiszonski, A.J. (1981) *Designing Instructional Systems*, London: Kogan Page.

Roscoe, J. (1995) "Analysis of Organisational Training Needs", in S. Truelove (ed.) 2nd edition, *Handbook of Training and Development*, Oxford: Blackwell Publishing.

Roscoe, J. (1995) "Learning and Training Design" in S. Truelove (ed.) *The Handbook of Training and Development*, 2nd edition, London: Basil Blackwell.

Ross, K. (1993) "Training and Evaluation in SMEs: Manufacturing Enterprises in the West Midlands", *Local Economy*, Vol. 8, No. 2, August.

Ross, P. H., Freeman, H. and Wright, S. R. (1979) *Evaluation: A Systematic Approach.* Beverley Hills: Sage

Rothwell, W. and Kazanas, H. (1991) *Strategic Human Resource Planning and Management*, Englewood Cliffs, N.J: Prentice Hall.

Rothwell, W. (1983) "The Life Cycles of HRD Departments", *Training and Development Journal,* Vol. 37, pp. 74-76.

Rothwell, W. (1985) Management Training in Support of Organisational Strategic Planning in Twelve Illinois Organisations, unpublished doctoral thesis, Urbana, IL: University of Illinois.

Rumelt, R. (1974) *Strategy, Structure and Economic Performance*, Cambridge, MA: Harvard University Press.

Rye, A. (1988) "Management Training: Acts of Faith, Scenes of Competence" *Journal of General Management*, Vol. 13, No. 3, pp. 21-26.

Salancik, G. and Pfeffer, J. (1974) "The Bases and Use of Power in Organisational Decision Making: The Case of the University", *Administrative Science Quarterly*, Vol. 19, pp. 453-73.

Salancik, G. and Pfeffer, J. (1977) "Who Gets Power and How They Hold on to it: A Strategic Contingency Model of Power", *Organisation Dynamics*, Winter, pp. 3-21.

Sanderson, G. (1995) "Objectives and Evaluation; in S. Truelove (ed.) *The Handbook of Training and Development*, 2nd edition, Oxford: Basil Blackwell.

Saunders, M. and Holdaway, K. (1992) *The In-House Trainer as Consultant*, London: Kogan Page.

Schein E. (1978) *Career Dynamics*, Reading, MA: Addison Wesley.

Schein, E. (1982) Individuals and Careers, Technical Report 19, Office of Naval Research.

Schein, E. (1985) *Organisational Culture and Leadership*, San Francisco: Jossey-Bass.

Schein, E. (1986) "What you Need to Know about Organisational Change" *Training and Development Journal*, January.

Schein, E. (1992) "How can Organisation Learn Faster", address to World Economic Forum.

Schemer, R. (1996) "How Can Service Businesses Survive and Prosper?" *Sloan Management Review*, Vol. 27, Spring, pp. 21-32.

Schendel D. and Hofer, C. (1979) "Strategy Evaluation" in D Schendel and C. Hofer (eds.) *Strategic Management : A New view of Business Policy and Planning*, Boston: Little Brown and Co.

Schneider, B. and Schmitt, N. (1986) *Staffing Organisation*, 2nd edition, Glenview IL: Scott, Foresman.

Schneier, C., Shaw, D. and Beatty, R. (1993) "Companies' Attempts to Improve Performance while Containing Costs: Quick Fix versus Lasting Change", *Human Resource Planning*, Vol. 15, No. 3, pp. 1-26.

Schonberger, R. (1982) *Japanese Manufacturing Techniques: Nine Hidden Lessons in Simplicity*, London: Collier, MacMillan.

Schonberger, R. (1986) *World Class Manufacturing*, New York: Free Press.

Schramm, U. (1954) "How Communication Works", In Schramm W. (ed.) *The Process and Effects of Mass Communication*, Urbana, IL: University of Illinois Press.

Schuler, R. (1986) "Strategic Human Resource Management and Industrial Relations", *Human Relations*, Vol. 42, No. 2, pp. 157-184.

Schuler, H. (1986) "Females in Technical Apprenticeships: Development of Aptitudes, Performance and Self Concept", in S. E. Newstead, S. H. Irvine and P. L. Dann (eds.) *Human Assessment: Cognition and Motivation*, The Hague: Nijhoff.

Schuller, T. and Bostym, A. M. (1992) "Learning: Education, Training and Information in the Third Age", Carnegie UK Trust.

Schultz, T. W. (1963), from his Presidential Address to the American Economic Association.

Scott, W. and Meyer J. (1991) "The Rise of Training Programmes in Firms and Agencies: An Institutional Perspective" in L. Cummings and B. Slaw (eds.) *Research in Organisation Behaviour*; New York: JAI.

Scriven, M. (1972) "Pros and Cons about Goal Free Evaluation", *Evaluation Comment*, Vol. 3, No. 4, pp. 1-4.

Senge, J. M. (1990) *The Fifth Discipline: The Art and Practice of the Learning Organisation,* New York: Doubleday.

Sewell, G. and Wilkinson, B. (1992) "Employment or Emasculation? Shop Floor Surveillance in a Total Quality Organisation", in P. Blyton and P. Turnbull (eds.) *Reassessing Human Resource Management*, London: Sage, pp. 97-115.

Sharplin, A. (1985) *Strategic Management*, New York: McGraw-Hill.

Shaw, M. E. (1967) "Role Playing", in R. L. Craig and L. R. Bittel (eds.) *Training and Development Handbook*, New York: McGraw-Hill, pp. 206-224.

Shivanath, G. (1988) "Personnel Practices in Irish Companies", Masters thesis, University of Limerick.

Sinclair, T. and Collins, A. (1992) "Training and Development's Worst Enemies — You and Management", *Journal of European Industrial Training*, Vol. 16. No. 5. pp. 21-25.

Sisson, K. (1989) *Personnel Management in Britain*, Oxford: Basil Blackwell.

Skaliotis, M. (1988) "Recent Developments in the Labour Force and Work Patterns in Greece", in BIPE, S. J. Prais and N. Nadler (eds.), New Forms and New Areas of Employment Growth, Proceedings of International Conference held at

Paris, June 19, 20, 1987, Commission of the European Communities, Luxembourg, pp. 93-108.

Skinner, B. L. (1938) *The Behaviour of Organisations*, New York: Appleton-Century -Crosts Publishers.

Sloman, M. (1994) *A Handbook for Training Strategy*, Aldershot: Gower.

Smith, A. (1776) *The Wealth of Nations*, London: MacMillan, 1937 edition.

Smith, D. and Delahaye, S. (1988) TNA-A Marketing Viewpoint, *Journal of European Industrial Training*, Vol. 13, No. 2, pp. 8-12.

Smith, J., Delahaye, H. and Gates, P. (1986) "Some Observations on INA", *Training and Development Journal*, August, pp. 63-68.

Snell, R. (1986) "Questioning the Ethics of Management Development: A Critical Review of Management Education and Development, *Management Education and Development*, Vol. 17, No. 1, pp. 43-64.

Snell, R. (1989) "Applying Socialist Ethics to Management Development", *Management Education and Development*, Vol. 20, No. 3, pp. 153-167.

Snell, R. (1991) "Managers' Development of Ethical Awareness and Personal Morality", *Personnel Review*, Vol. 19, No. 1, pp. 13-20.

Snell, R. S. and Binsted, D. S. (1982) "The Tutor-Learner Interaction in Management Development — Part Four, The Facilitation of Learning by Discussion", *Personnel Review*, Vol. 11, No. 2, pp. 3 - 13.

Sparrow, D. and Hiltrop, J. M. (1993) *European Human Resource Management in Transition*, London: Prentice-Hall.

Sparrow, P. and Pettigrew, A. (1988) "How Halfords put its HRM into Top Gear", *Personnel Management*, Vol. 20, No. 6, pp. 30-34.

Spence, M. A. (1973) "Job Market Signalling", *Quarterly Journal of Economics*, Vol. 87, pp. 355-75.

Spence, M. A. (1974) *Market Signalling Information Transfer in Hiring and Related Screening Processes*, Cambridge, MA: Harvard University Press.

Sperry, D. and Ornstein, R. (1977) *The Education of the Initiative Mode: The Psychology of Consciousness*, London: Harcourt Brace.

Spitzer, D. (1984) "Why Training Fails", *Performance and Instructional Journal,* September, pp. 6-15.

Stammers, R. and Patrick, J. (1975) *The Psychology of Training*, London: Methuen.

Stake, R. (1978) "Responsive Evaluation" in D. Hamilton et al (eds.) *Beyond the Numbers Game*, Berkley, CA: McCutcheon.

Stainer, G. (1971) *Manpower Planning,* London: Pitman Publications.

Steadman, S. (1980) "Learning to Select a Needs Assessment Strategy", *Training and Development Journal*, Vol. 34, No. 1, pp. 56-61.

Steward, A. (1991) "Performance Appraisal", in Prior, J. (ed.) *Handbook of Training and Development,* 2nd edition, Aldershot: Gower.

Stokes, Kennedy, Crowley (1993) *The Performance of Irish Companies*, Dublin: Stokes, Kennedy, Crowley.

Storey, J. (1980) *The Challenge to Management Control*, London: Kogan Page.

Storey, J. (ed.) (1991) *New Perspectives on Human Resource Management*, London: Routledge.

Storey, J. (1992) *Developments in the Management of Human Resources,* Oxford: Basil Blackwell.

Strauch, R. (1984) "Training the Whole Person", *Training and Development Journal*, Vol. 38, pp. 82-86.

Streker-Seeborg, I., Seeborg, M. C. and Zegeye, A. (1984) "The Impact of Non Traditional Training on the Occupational Attainment of Women", *Journal of Human Resources*, Vol. 19, pp. 452-471.

Stuart, R. and Long, G. (1985) "Towards Marketing the Training Function, Part 1: Adopting a Marketing Perspective", *Personnel Review,* Vol. 14, No. 2, pp. 32-37.

Stuart, R. and Long, G. (1985) "Towards Marketing the Training Function, Part 11: Making Marketing Decisions", *Personnel Review,* Vol. 14, No. 3, pp. 29-32.

Suessmuth, P. (1978) *Ideas for Training Managers and Supervisors,* San Diego, CA: University Associates.

Sweeney, G. P. (1987) *Innovation, Entrepreneurs and Regional Development*, London: Francis Printer.

Sweeney, M. (1993) "The Use of Mentoring in Management Development", University of Limerick, degree thesis.

Tannehill, R. E. (1970) *Motivation and Management Development*, London: Butterworth.

Tansey, P. and Roche, F. (1992) *Industrial Training in Ireland*, report submitted to Industrial Policy Review Group, Dublin: Department of Industry and Trade.

Taylor, H. (1991) "The Systematic Training Model: Corn Circles in Search of a Spaceship", *Management Education and Development*, Vol. 22, Part 4, pp. 258-278.

Thurley, K. (1990) "Towards a European Approach to Personnel Management", *Personnel Management*, Vol. 3, No. 2, pp. 285-306.

Torrington, D. and Hall, L. (1991) *Personnel Management: A New Approach*, 2nd Edition, Hemel Hempstead: Prentice Hall.

Torrington, D., Hall, L., Haylor, L. and Myers, J. (1991) *Employee Resourcing*, London: IPM.

Tracey, W. (1992) *The Handbook of Training and Development Systems*, 2nd Edition, New York: American Management Association.

Training of Trainers Committee (1978*) Training of Trainers: First Draft of the Training of Trainers Committee*, London: Training Services Division, Manpower Services Commission.

Truelove, S. (1995) *The Handbook of Training and Development*, 2nd edition, Oxford: Basil Blackwell.

Tucker, F. D. (1985) "A Study of the Training Needs of Older Workers", Implications for Human Resource Development Planning", *Public Personnel Management*, Vol. 14, pp. 85-95.

Tyler, R. W. (1950) *Basic Principles of Curriculum and Instruction Design*, Chicago: University of Chicago Press.

Ulschak, F. (1983) *The Theory and Practice of Need Assessment*, VA: Panteon Publishing.

Van Naanen (1976) *Breaking in Socialisation to Work, Handbook of Work Organisation and Society,* Chicago: Rand McNally.

Varlaam, C. and Pole, C. (1988) *The Training Needs of Trainers in Industry and Commerce: A Feasibility Study,* Sheffield: The Training Agency.

Warr, P., Bird, M. and Rackham, N. (1974) *Evaluation of Management Training,* London: Gower.

Walsh, J. (1994) Report on the Implementation of the Third EU Poverty Programme by the Partnership, Limerick, April.

Walton, R. E. (1985) "From Control to Commitment in the Workplace", *Harvard Business Review,* March/April, Vol. 2, pp. 77-79.

Webb, T. (1989) "Negotiating for Training", *Industrial and Commercial Training*, Vol. 21, No. 5, pp. 18-22.

Webster, F. E. (1979) *Industrial Marketing Strategy,* New York: John Wiley.

Wellins, R. and George, J. (1991) "The Key to Self-Directed Teams", *Training and Development Journal,* Vol. 45, No. 4, pp. 26-32.

Wexley, K. M. and Nemeroff, W. F. (1975) "Effectiveness of Positive Reinforcement and Goal Setting as Methods of Management Development", *Journal of Applied Psychology*, Vol. 60, pp. 446-50.

Wexley, K. and Latham, G. (1991) *Developing and Training Human Resources in Organisations,* New York: Harper Collins.

Whipp, R. (1991) "Human Resource Management: Strategy, Change and Competition, the Role of Learning", *International Journal of Human Resource Management,* Vol. 2, No. 2, pp. 165-91.

Whitley, R. D. (ed.) (1992) *European Business Systems: Firms and Markets in their National Contexts*, London: Sage.

Wickens, P. (1987) *The Road to Nissan,* London: MacMillan.

Williamson, O.E. (1985) *The Economic Institution of Capitalism,* New York: New York University Press.

Willis, N. (1988) "Training: Joint Action by Management and Unions", Industrial and Commercial Training, Vol. 20, No. 6, pp. 3-6.

Wills, M. (1993) Managing the Training Process, Putting the Basics into Practice, London: The McGraw-Hill Training Series.

Wilson, B. (1987) "The Systematic Design of Training Courses", Training Technology Programme, Vol. 1, Open Tech, MSC.

Wood, S., Barrington, H. and Johnson, R. (1990) "An Introduction to Continuous Development", in Wood, S. (ed.) *Continuous Development,* London; Institute of Personnel Management.

Wood, S. and Peccei, R. (1990) "Preparing for 1992? Business Led Versus Strategic Human Resource Management", *Human Resource Management Journal,* Vol. 1, No. 1, pp. 63-89.

Wright, V., (1986) "Does Profit Sharing Improve Employee Performance?", *Personnel Management,* November, pp. 46-50.

Wright, V. (1991) "Performance-related Pay", in F. Neale (ed.) *Handbook of Performance Management,* Wimbledon: IPM.

Wynne, B. and Clutterbuck, D. (1994) "Using Evaluation Techniques", in J. Prior (ed.) Handbook of Training and Development. Aldershof Gower, 2nd edition.

Yeomans, W. (1989) "Building Competitiveness through Human Resource Development Renewal", *Training and Development Journal,* October, pp. 77-82.

Zemke, R. (1985) "In Search of a Training Philosophy", Training, Vol. 22, No. 10, pp. 93-98.

Zenger, J. H. and Blitzer, R. J. (1981) "How Training Managers Become Corporate Heroes/Heroines", *Training*, December.

Zenger, J. H. (1982) "Assessing Training Results: Its Time to take the Plunge", *Training and Development,* Vol. 20, January.

Zenger, J. H. (1988) "Training for Organisational Excellence", *Journal of European Industrial Training,* Vol. 9, No. 7.

INDEX